COMMITTED TO MEMORY

Committed to Memory

The Art of the Slave Ship Icon

CHERYL FINLEY

Princeton University Press

Princeton and Oxford

Copyright © 2018 by Princeton University Press
Published by Princeton University Press,
41 William Street, Princeton, New Jersey 08540
In the United Kingdom: Princeton University Press,
99 Banbury Road, Oxford, OX2 6JX

press.princeton.edu

FRONT COVER Malcolm Bailey, *Untitled*, 1969. Acrylic on composition board,
48 × 71 ¹⁵/₁₆ inches (121.9 × 182.7 cm). Whitney Museum of American Art, New York.

BACK COVER Ingrid Pollard, *Untitled*, from *Oceans Apart*, 1989. Printed
Xerox, acetate, printed text, 24 × 20 inches. Courtesy of the artist.

First paperback printing, 2022
Paper ISBN: 978-0-691-24106-7
Cloth ISBN: 978-0-691-13684-4

All Rights Reserved

Library of Congress has cataloged the cloth edition as follows:

Names: Finley, Cheryl, author.
Title: Committed to memory : the art of the slave ship icon / Cheryl Finley.
Description: Princeton : Princeton University Press, 2018. |
     Includes bibliographical references and index.
Identifiers: LCCN 2017028275 | ISBN 9780691136844 (hardcover : alk. paper)
Subjects: LCSH: Slave trade in art. | Brookes (Ship) — In art. |
     Metaphor in art. | History in art. | Art, Modern — Themes, motives.
Classification: LCC N8243.S576 F56 2018 | DDC 709.04 — dc23
LC record available at https://lccn.loc.gov/2017028275

British Library Cataloging-in-Publication Data is available

Design by Julie Fry

This book has been composed in Miller and Apex.

Printed in the United States of America

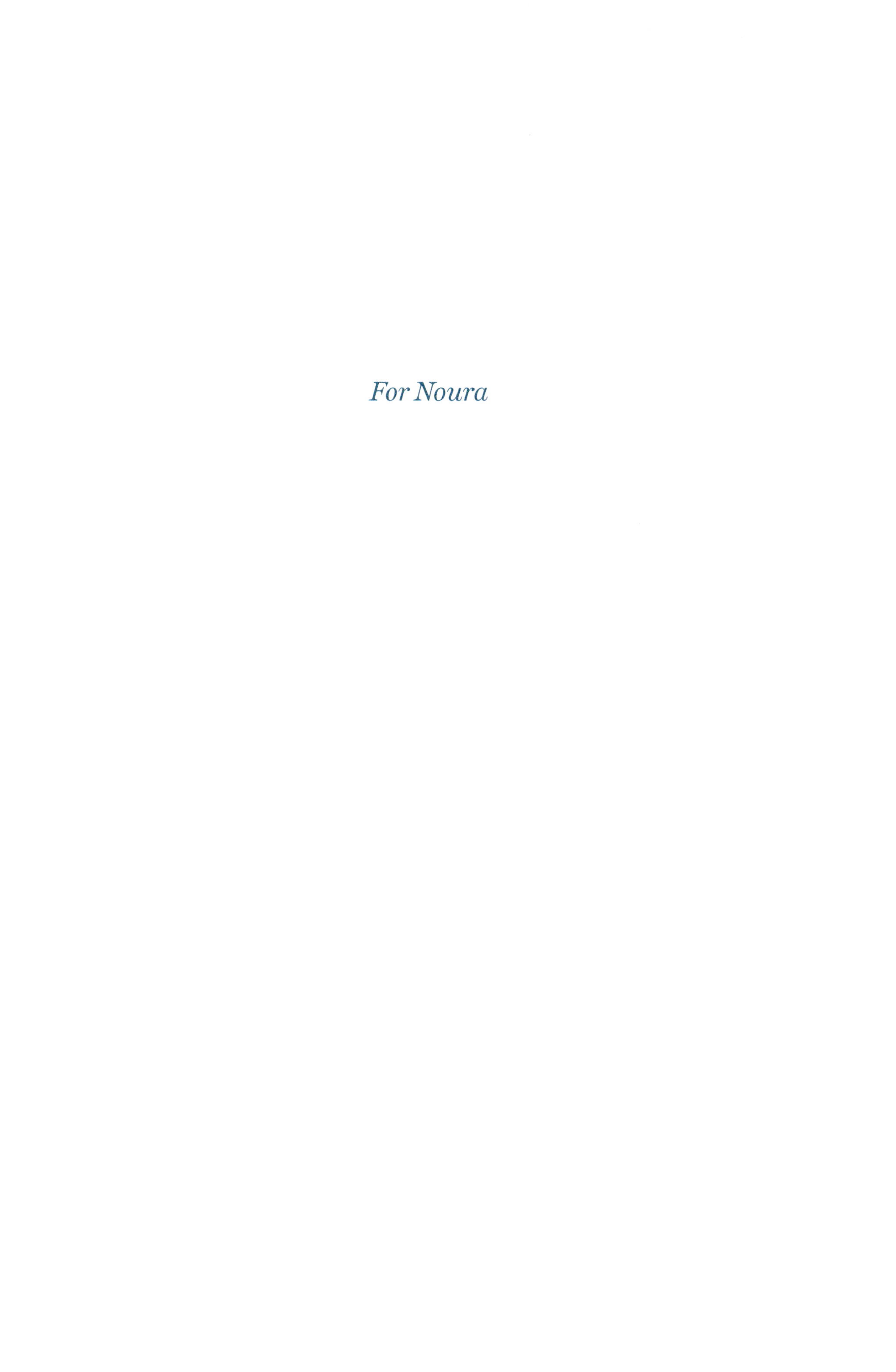

For Noura

CONTENTS

THE IDEA FOR THIS BOOK began in a graduate seminar at the Yale Center for British Art twenty years ago, when I came across an original engraving of the abolitionist print that is the subject of this study. Obsessed by the detail, history, and message of that eighteenth-century impression, it later became the focus of my dissertation, *Committed to Memory: The Slave Ship Icon in the Black Atlantic Imagination* (2002). I was fortunate to have generous mentors at Yale, who encouraged me to take risks. Hazel V. Carby, Robert Farris Thompson, Paul Gilroy, Kellie Jones, and Laura Wexler guided this project at its earliest stages, providing essential support, feedback, and advice. In many ways, this study is indebted to the foundational work of Robert Farris Thompson and Paul Gilroy on the Black Atlantic; the innovative approaches to memory studies introduced to me by Hazel V. Carby, Laura Wexler, Dolores Hayden, and Joseph Roach; and the exemplary art historical training of Judith Wilson and Kellie Jones.

A project of this magnitude would not have been possible without the support of many institutions, libraries, and foundations. Postdoctoral fellowships from the Ford Foundation and the American Academy of Arts and Sciences provided the time, resources, and intellectual community at a pivotal moment as I was reimaging the dissertation for publication as a book. Dissertation research and writing was supported by the Center for Advanced Study in the Visual Arts, National Gallery of Art; the Ford Foundation; the Whitney Humanities Center; the Center for Advanced Study of Religion at Yale; the Beinecke Rare Book and Manuscript Library; the British Art Center; the Center for the Study of Race, Inequality and Politics at Yale; the Pew Program in Religion and American History; the Paul Mellon Foundation; and the Gilder Lehrman Center for the Study of Slavery, Resistance and Abolition.

I am grateful for the many lunchtime meetings of the Sisters' Seminar (Diana Magloni-Kerpel, Stephanie Sears, and Zoe Simone Baker) in whose patient presence many of the theoretical considerations of memory and identity were first identified for this study. Over time, other friends and working groups heard presentations, read drafts, and offered valuable feedback at crucial stages of the project's development, including Deborah Willis, Julie Wolf, Alexandra Harris, and Mark Alexander Wright; the Photographic Memory Workshop at Yale, spearheaded by Laura Wexler, Leigh Raiford, and Robin Bernstein; the Mourning

Group at Harvard, with Robin Bernstein, Vincent Brown, Glenda Carpio, and Barbara Rodriguez; and the Slavery in the Artistic, Literary and Historical Imagination working group at the Gilder Lehrman Center at Yale, chaired by Deborah McDowell and John Stauffer.

I am indebted to Cornell University for providing a supportive and innovative scholarly home that champions interdisciplinary work. In the History of Art Department, I cherish collaborating with friends and colleagues, who have offered generous resources, close readings, and instrumental feedback: Annetta Alexandridis, Ben Anderson, Judith Bernstock, Ananda Cohen-Aponte, Iftikhar Dadi, Maria Fernandez, Salah Hassan, Kaja McGowan, Claudia Lazarro, Laura Meixner, Andrew Moisey, An-Yi Pan, Lisa Pincus, Verity Platt, Jolene Rickard, Cynthia Robinson, and Shirley Samuels. My students never cease to impress me and indeed their work has enhanced this project, too. I am especially grateful to Amanda Gilvin and Hannah Ryan, who provided valuable research assistance in securing images. I also wish to acknowledge the many librarians at Cornell who championed this project: Eric Kofi Acree, Sharon Powers, Saah Nue Quigee Jr., Marsha Taichman, Katherine Reagan. I thank the talented photographic specialists Rhea Garen, Kark Fitzke, and Simon Ingall of DCAPS, who assisted with digitizing several images that appear in this book.

This book has grown from conversations with other friends across campus in long car rides to New York, over dinner, in coffee shops, and walking the gorgeous Gorges: Brett DeBary, Petrine Archer-Straw, Carole Boyce-Davies, Kate McCullough, Samantha Sheppard, Amy Villarejo, and Sabine Haenni. I wish to recognize the special contribution of Mary Pat Brady, who read early drafts of the manuscript and arranged for me to meet Hanne Winarsky, who brought it to Princeton University Press. Now in the able hands of the editorial team headed by Michelle Komie, I am finally ready to let it go out in the world. I couldn't ask for a more patient, understanding, and forthright editor than Michelle Komie or a more professional and detailed production team than Sara Lerner, Steven Sears, and Hannah Zuckerman. Thank you for believing in my project and seeing it through to fruition after so many years.

I am humbled by the generosity of the artists and curators, who gave of their time to talk to me about their work, and whose wisdom and vision have contributed to this book in profound ways: Terry Adkins, Elizabeth Alexander, Amiri Baraka, Sanford Biggers, Maria Magdalena Campos-Pons, Willie Cole, Robert Croslin, Godfried Donkor, Dr. David C. Driskell, Mary Elliott, Mary Evans, Tom Feelings, Neville Garrick, Joy Gregory, Sunil Gupta, Reverend Marshall E. Hatch, Marshall E. Hatch Jr., Stephen Hayes, Romuald Hazoumé, Rita Keegan, Roshini Kempadoo, Eugene Lee, Horace Ove, Joe Overstreet, Keith Piper, Ingrid Pollard, Marianetta Porter, Betye Saar, Yinka Shonibare, Ike Udé, Nari Ward, Deborah Willis and Hank Willis Thomas. Your work is *the art of the slave ship icon* and much appreciation is owed to you for granting me permission to reproduce your work here. I also thank the archivists, studio managers, gallerists, and dealers who helped to provide images and permissions: Hank Willis Thomas Studio, Sanford Biggers Studio,

Halley K. Harrisburg and Michael Rosenfeld, Jack Shainman Gallery, October Gallery, Alexander and Bonin, Swann Galleries, Rodney Moore, Zak Ove, Corrine Jennings, Kenkeleba Gallery, Romare Bearden Foundation, Diedre Harris Kelly, Dianne Johnson-Feelings, Patricia Willis, Nancy Kuhl, the de Menil Collection, Lehmann Maupin Gallery, and James Cohan Gallery.

I am grateful to the friends and family around the world who opened their homes to me during the research and writing phase of this project: William and Betsy Sledge, Diana Magaloni-Kerpel and Michael Layton, Zelda Cheatle, Michael Birt, Joy Gregory, Bea Freeman, the family of Kofi Blankson (Paa Kwesi Ocancy and Mother Rosamond Arkonful); Pascale Vallet, Dr. Helen Holte-DaCosta, Penelope Dixon and Michael Ball, Jessica Allison, Rachel Schlass, Kirsty Allore and Angus Beasely, and the Gear Family.

Finally, I thank my family for sustaining me throughout the past several years with patience, generosity, and understanding. I thank my sister, Lisa, for her unwavering support of my endeavors; and my mother, Gail T. Finley, for always believing in me. The idea for this book took root at about the same time that the first of my nephews and nieces were born and they seemed to make its premise all the more relevant. When my daughter, Noura, was born, she began posing the difficult questions that only a child would know to ask and the book's message became all the more urgent. I am ever in awe of her quick wit and kind soul. She is the future.

Cheryl Finley
Ithaca, New York

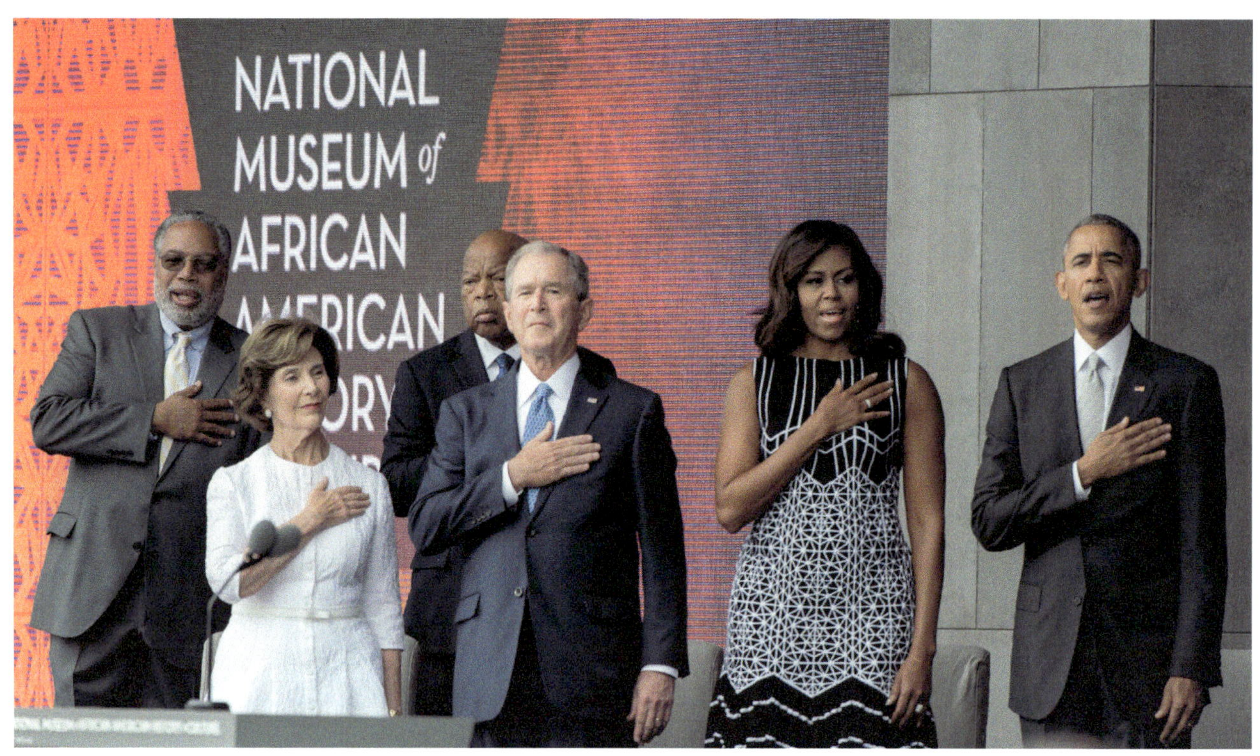

I.1

Gediyon Kifle, *Dedication Ceremony*, National
Museum of African American History and
Culture, Washington, DC, September 24, 2016
(LEFT TO RIGHT: Lonnie G. Bunch III, Congressman
John Lewis [D-GA], First Lady Laura Bush,
President George W. Bush, President Barack
Obama, First Lady Michelle Obama).

THE PRACTICE OF MNEMONIC AESTHETICS

I spent years looking around the world trying to find slave ship pieces…as almost like a religious relic. [They] are really the only tangible evidence that these people existed.
—Lonnie G. Bunch III, director, National Museum of African American History and Culture (fig. I.1)

The multimedia installation *La Bouche du Roi*, or the Mouth of the King, was created by Romuald Hazoumé of the Republic of Benin between 1997 and 2005 (see fig. I.3). It is named after a well-known site of memory on the coast of Benin from which African captives were transported during the transatlantic slave trade with the blessing, or rather the avarice, of the king, and the collusion of African, European, and American traders. The artwork comprises 304 plastic petroleum canisters made to resemble masks, with the spout serving as a mouth and the handle as the nose. These dark plastic, bulbous canisters are arranged in rows forming the shape of the now iconic, schematic engraving of a slave ship successfully deployed by British abolitionists in the late eighteenth century to shed light on the horrors of the slave trade in order to build parliamentary support for its cessation. In Hazoumé's installation, each mask represents a living person with a name, a voice, and individual beliefs while hidden microphones whisper their presence in the Yoruba language. Painted symbols and small objects affixed to the canisters, such as *ibeji*, carved wooden figures that represent the souls of deceased newborn twins, reiterate Yoruba religious and cultural beliefs and the *orishas* or deities to whom the enslaved might have prayed.[1] Strategically placed between the masks following the pattern of the schematic template are cowrie shells, rifles, tobacco, beads, spices, and liquor bottles, which reference the trade goods that would have been used to barter for human beings. In my interview with the artist in March 2007 at the October Gallery in London, Hazoumé told me that he had seen pictures of *Description of a Slave Ship* (1789), the abolitionist print after which his installation is modeled, in textbooks and tourism brochures (fig. I.2). It was a familiar image, he said, in certain parts of the Republic of Benin, including Porto-Novo, where he lives, owing to the burgeoning commerce in heritage tourism and the UNESCO-sponsored slave routes project, both commercial ventures that have increased awareness about the shores of the Republic of Benin as important sites of memory

The Atlantic Slave Trade

On Both Sides, Reason for Remorse

By HOWARD W. FRENCH

ABIDJAN, Ivory Coast

FROM the moment the White House announced that President Clinton would stop at Senegal's Gorée Island, one of this continent's most famous monuments to the Atlantic slave trade, a polemic was re-launched in the United States and in much of Africa over how and indeed whether Mr. Clinton should apologize for the centuries-long capture and sale into bondage of millions of Africans.

For some, the very idea of an apology was offensive. Weren't Africans engaging in slavery themselves well before the first Europeans came and carried off their first human cargoes? Didn't African chiefs themselves conduct razzias, or slaving raids, on neighboring tribes and march their harvest to the shores for sale?

For others, though, the Atlantic trade in Africans was one of the greatest crimes humanity has known, and remains one that has never been properly acknowledged. "The Holocaust was certainly a great tragedy, but it only lasted a few short years," said Joseph Ndiaye, the curator of the Maison des Esclaves, the featured stop on Mr. Clinton's trip to Gorée. "We never stop hearing about the Holocaust, but how often do we dwell on the tragedy that took place here over 350 years; a tragedy that consumed tens of millions of lives?"

In the end, an appropriately solemn Mr. Clinton stopped short of an outright apology for America's part in the slave trade, finding other ways to express his regret as he focused on the future. That Mr. Clinton so artfully chose to sidestep African slavery's long history should have come as no surprise to anyone familiar with its cruel and complicated details. Even today, few subjects are so prone to passionate disagreement. As ever, people from each leg of the triangular Atlantic trade — Europe, Africa and the Americas — still use the slave experience as a vacant screen upon which they project their own misperceptions and justifications.

The Colonial View

In the United States, the conservative columnist Patrick Buchanan recently echoed a sentiment heard often from whites who resent attempts to make them feel guilty for slavery: "When Europeans arrived in sub-Saharan Africa, the inhabitants had no machinery and no written language. When the Europeans departed, most of them by 1960, they left behind power stations, telephones, telegraphs, railroads, mines, plantations, schools, a civil service, a police force and a treasury."

Even disregarding the wildly benign view of Europe's colonial legacy, many historians say Mr. Buchanan's assumptions — of a savage continent being blessed with the gift of European civilization — are as erroneous as they are widespread. Early European travelers to West Africa, in fact, found societies that by many measures, from commonly available technology to general living standards, were not so different from home.

"The smelting of iron and steel in West Africa was similar to that in Europe in the 13th century, before the advent of power driven by the water wheel," wrote Hugh Thomas, the author of "The Slave Trade" (Simon & Schuster, 1997). "Senegambia had iron and copper industries, and the quality of African steel approached that of Toledo before the 15th century."

It would be dishonest to lay all of Africa's subsequent problems on the slave trade. But most experts do not doubt that the forces unleashed by Europe's demand for slaves, gold and other African goods radically destabilized societies that were embarking on their own path toward development, and laid waste to whole regions of this continent. "The discussion of how Africa became what it did subsequent to 1500 very quickly becomes an argument over what the slave trade did to the continent,"

Continued on Page 4

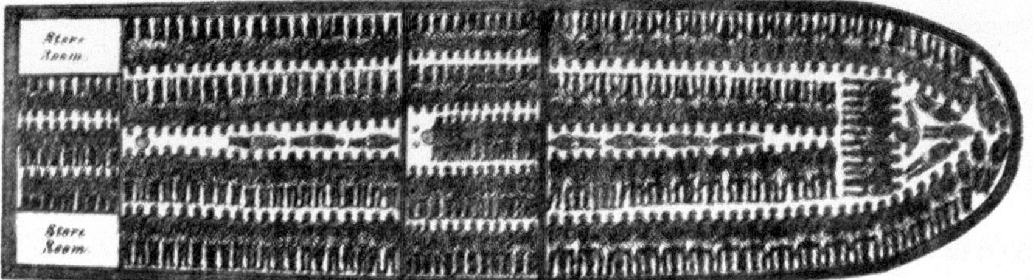

Corbis-Bettmann

The lower deck of a slave ship, in a 19th century lithograph; the slaves were packed so tightly they could breathe only with difficulty, according to a doctor of the time.

I.2

Howard W. French. "On Both Sides, Reason for Remorse," April 5, 1998, *New York Times.*

of the transatlantic slave trade. Providing a contemporary context for Hazoumé's slave ship is a video narrated by the artist discussing the treacherous, illegal gasoline trade from Nigeria to Benin. Still photographs from the video, contrasting individual motorcyclists weighed down by hazardous fuel canisters with gorgeous beaches of the mouth of the River Porto Novo, illustrate the devastating lingering effects of centuries of economic, social, and racial oppression (fig. I.3). The darkened exhibition space creates an ominous yet somber mood for the viewer, providing a place of reflection and commemoration.

La Bouche du Roi was acquired by the British Museum to mark the 2007 Bicentenary of the Parliamentary Abolition of the Transatlantic Slave Trade Act by the United Kingdom. The installation was on view at the British Museum in London from March 22 to May 13, 2007, prior to being sent on a carefully orchestrated tour to cities and institutions that were historically significant to the slave trade and its abolition: Hull, Liverpool, Bristol, Newcastle, and the Horniman Museum in London.[2] That large-scale installation used *Description of a Slave Ship* to enter into a conversation between the past of the slave trade and the present-day corruption and loss of life that takes place along the route of the illegal gasoline trade between Nigeria and Benin.

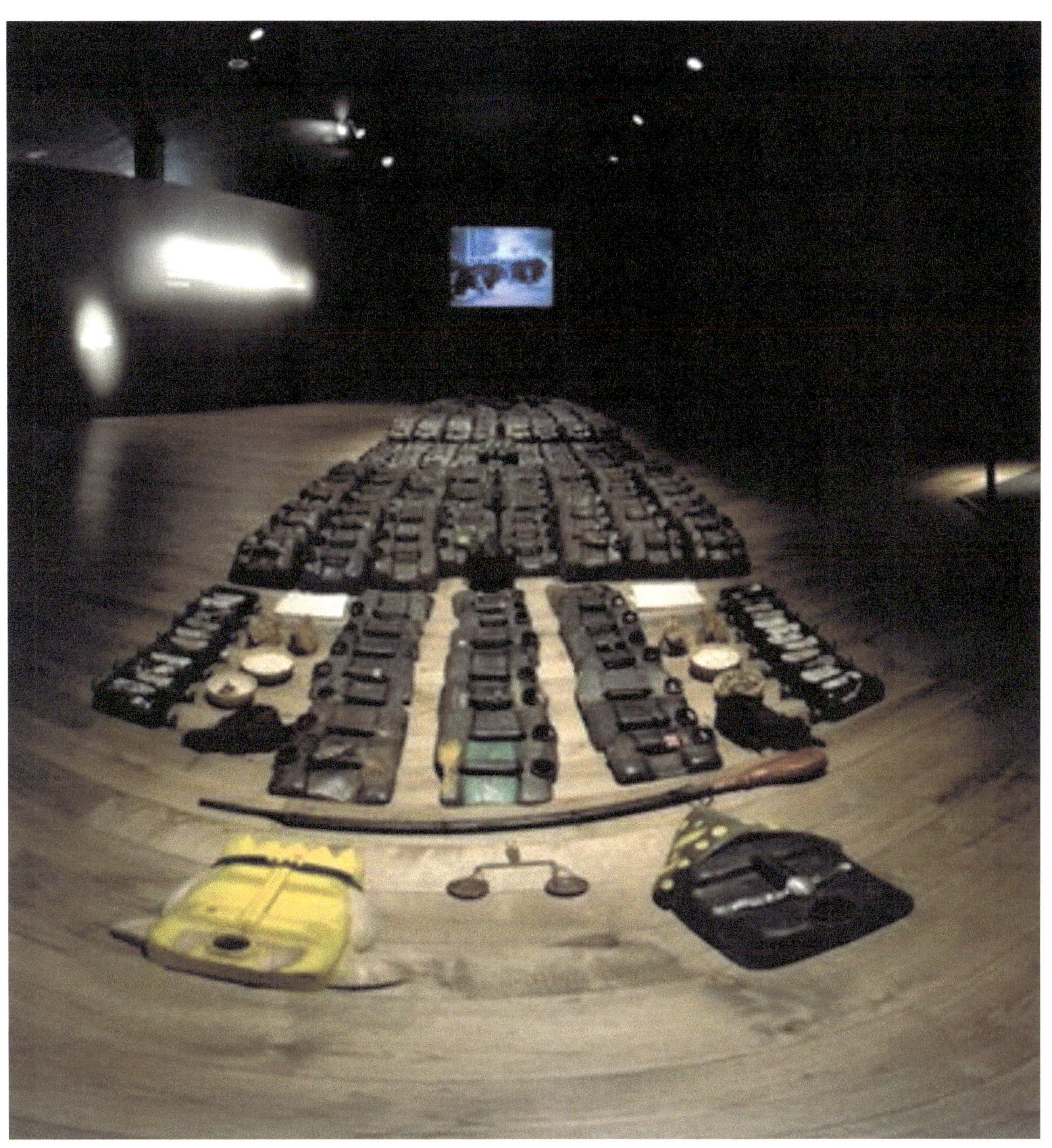

I.3
Romuald Hazoumé, *La Bouche du Roi*, 1997–2005,
mixed media (oil drums, plastic, glass, shells,
tobacco, fabrics, mirrors, metal) installation view
with video at the Horniman Museum, South London.

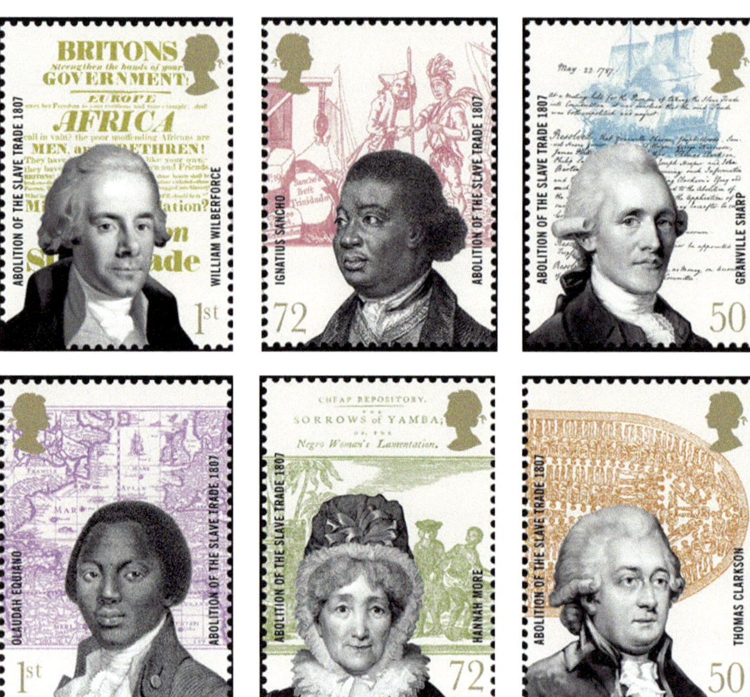

I.4

Postage stamps issued by the Royal Mail
commemorating the bicentenary of the
Abolition of the Slave Trade Act, 2007.

During the bicentenary commemoration of the Abolition of the Slave Trade Act by the United Kingdom, *Description of a Slave Ship* was at the center of several national and international commemorative events. It was featured in print form in numerous exhibitions around the country and even made part of the graphic imagery of postage stamps issued by the Royal Mail to mark the bicentenary (fig. I.4). The endeavors to enable this image to stand as a marker for the memory of the Middle Passage and the graphic violence of the transatlantic slave trade against black and white people vary in scale, scope, and intent. In recent years, several attempts have been made to revisit *Description of a Slave Ship*, to embody it, to reinvent it, to memorialize it. At Durham University in the United Kingdom, 274 school-age children commemorated the Bicentenary of the Abolition of the Slave Trade Act on July 13, 2007, by participating in a reenactment of *Description of a Slave Ship* on Palace Green in Durham City between the Castle and the Cathedral. Wearing black trousers and red T-shirts printed with rows of black figures, they laid themselves down on a full-size print-out of the most recognizable bullet-shaped section of *Description of a Slave Ship* to, in the words of Education Outreach Officer Sarah Price, "have a sense of what the stifling space was like in the hold, to know the sufferings of African captives in the confines of dank slave ships."[3] Aerial photographs taken of the scene recorded the life-size public performance of this unforgettable image while reinforcing the exacting technology of vision that has structured the visual empathy of *Description of a Slave Ship*, thereby reproducing the same way of seeing that the image has demanded for more than two hundred years. Not unlike the touring presentation of Hazoumé's *La Bouche de Roi*, this was one of many times the public performance of *Description of a Slave Ship* was reenacted in the United Kingdom that year, revealing a practice of *mnemonic aesthetics*, a process of ritualized remembering, underlying contemporary presentations of the art of slavery.

I BEGIN with a selection of works from the 2007 bicentenary that use *Description of a Slave Ship* to start a conversation about the practice of mnemonic aesthetics and its crucial relationship with what I call the *slave ship icon*, the most enduring image from the history of transatlantic slavery. In this book, I trace a visual genealogy of the slave ship icon in the minds, memories, and creative work of black artists and their allies in the twentieth century and today. Throughout history, poets, painters, orators, and later, photographers, installation artists, performance artists, and sound artists have employed mnemonic strategies that contribute to a sustained and recognizable practice of remembrance in African diaspora visual culture. Without a doubt, the slave ship stands as the most prominent visual metaphor for the historical memory of the Middle Passage. As Paul Gilroy writes, "The image of the ship—a living, micro-cultural, micro-political system in motion—is especially important for historical and theoretical reasons," serving as a lens through which we may, as he says, "focus attention on the Middle Passage, on the various projects for redemptive return to an African homeland, on the circulation of ideas and activists as well as the movement of key cultural and political artifacts."[4]

The image I call the *slave ship icon* began as the official British abolitionist plan of the slave ship *Brooks*—a schematic representation of the crowded lower deck of the slave ship's human cargo hold. When it was first created in England in 1788, the striking schematic engraving *Description of a Slave Ship* exposed the underbelly of a commercial vessel bearing human cargo, depicting the means of transporting enslaved Africans to the Americas via the Middle Passage, one of the formative experiences of the African diaspora. In studying this image, we find that it has had at least two lives. The British abolitionists who created it used it as a political print—a visual weapon—in their fight to end the transatlantic slave trade. The artists, engravers, and printers who modified and distributed it were white men working primarily in Europe and North America. The political and propagandistic activity surrounding the slave ship icon was particularly dynamic in the late eighteenth and early nineteenth centuries, up until the abolition of both the slave trade and slavery itself. What followed was a period of dormancy, perhaps of apparent death.

Then, beginning with the New Negro Arts Movement (a.k.a. the Harlem Renaissance), the slave ship icon underwent a process of rebirth. In this second life, the slave ship icon was (and continues to be) reappropriated, symbolically repossessed, by the descendants of those who were the subject of the image, by diasporic Africans, that is, by black Atlantic artists and their allies. It has since come to have a special place in the souls of those black folk who descend from that forced migration, and it has proven to be one of the most powerful images of the last 230 years. In looking for comparable images in Western culture, one must turn to such iconic subjects as the crucifixion. Undoubtedly, the crucifixion offers a compelling parallel, for both images have been repeatedly rendered and reworked over the centuries, but they simultaneously embody death and rebirth. The slave ship icon frequently has been likened to a coffin and to a womb. It is a site of death, of dying Africans, and of new life, of a people who would persevere in the face of slavery and unspeakable cruelty to become a free people who helped define the modern era.

Since the beginning of the New Negro Arts Movement, visual artists working in cosmopolitan metropoles around the black Atlantic rim—the coasts that circumscribe the passage from Africa to the Americas to western Europe—have reimagined the slave ship icon in their works. Miguel Covarrubias, Amiri Baraka, Betye Saar, Romare Bearden, Keith Piper, María Magdalena Campos-Pons, Godfried Donkor, Hank Willis Thomas, and Romuald Hazoumé have taken hold of the slave ship icon in their works of book illustration, painting, theater, performance, installation, printmaking, photography, and film. These artists have redeployed the slave ship icon as a symbolic marker, making it central to their works as they relate the Middle Passage to their historical origins as well as their present moment. Public historians and exhibition designers at museums and memorials alike also have called upon its architectural schematic as a kind of blueprint for designs of installations that seek to tell the story of transatlantic slavery, colonialism, and empire.

The slave ship icon has remained a persistent phenomenon in contemporary culture here in the United States and throughout the black Atlantic. It appears with remarkable frequency in fashion, film, and digital media as well as in works of fine art. It has been a favored design for T-shirts that recast the history of slavery in cataclysmic, unforgiving terms, with the slogans "African Holocaust" (fig. I.5) or "Never Forgive, Never Forget." Posters protesting the prison industrial complex and the rise of global capitalism have featured the plan of the slave ship as a visual reminder not only of the way things used to be but also as a portent of the future. The plan of the slave ship seems to have inexhaustible uses in digital space as well, inching across the opening page of the Keith Piper's *Relocating the Remains* CD-ROM and website (2000) and appearing on countless other websites and blogs about African American and African diaspora history and culture. Even as the disaster of Hurricane Katrina unfolded in late summer 2005, some political and cultural commentators noted how residents of New Orleans stranded on Interstate 10 brought to mind images of the slave ship icon. In a live interview with reporter Anderson Cooper of CNN, the Reverend Jesse Jackson remarked, "Today I saw five thousand African Americans on the I-10 causeway desperate, perishing, dehydrated, babies dying. It looked like Africans in the hull of a slave ship"[5] (fig. I.6). In a more recent and recurring tragedy at sea (fig. I.7), where thousands of African migrants attempt to reach the shores of Europe in makeshift boats, aerial photographs and installations by artists, such as Hazoumé, use the slave ship icon to position and/or to lend a certain urgency to their depictions. Even illustrated

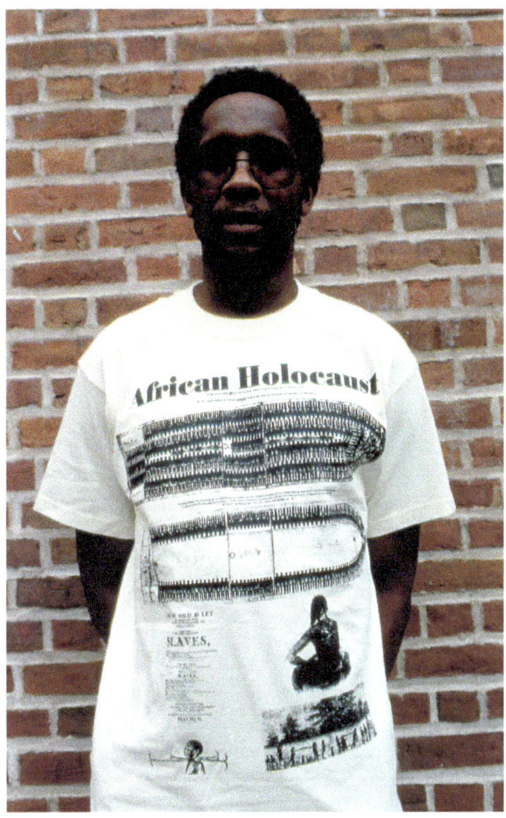

I.5
Bernie Staggers posing with the *African Holocaust* T-shirt designed by Daryl McRay, Nubian, New York, 1999, showing the slave ship icon and other popular images from the history of slavery, New Haven, Connecticut.

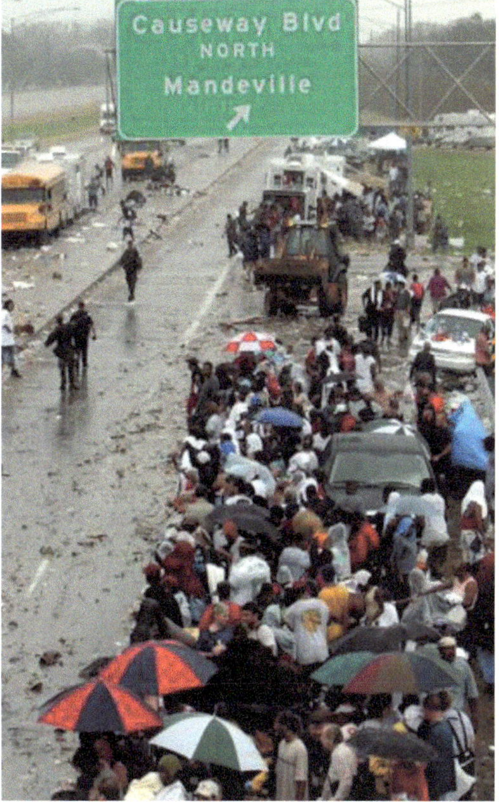

I.6
Thousands of residents wait in the rain on Interstate 10 outside of New Orleans to be moved to shelters, Thursday, September 1, 2005, in the aftermath of Hurricane Katrina.

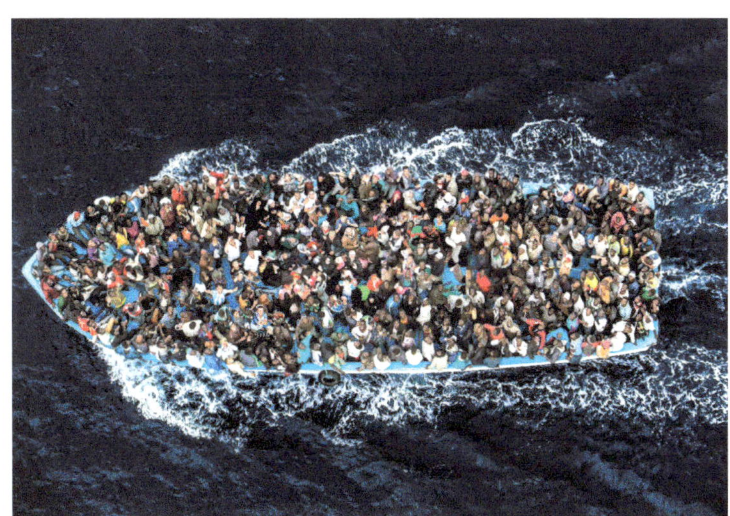

I.7
June 7, 2014—Mediterranean Sea: Italian navy rescues asylum seekers traveling by boat off the coast of Africa.

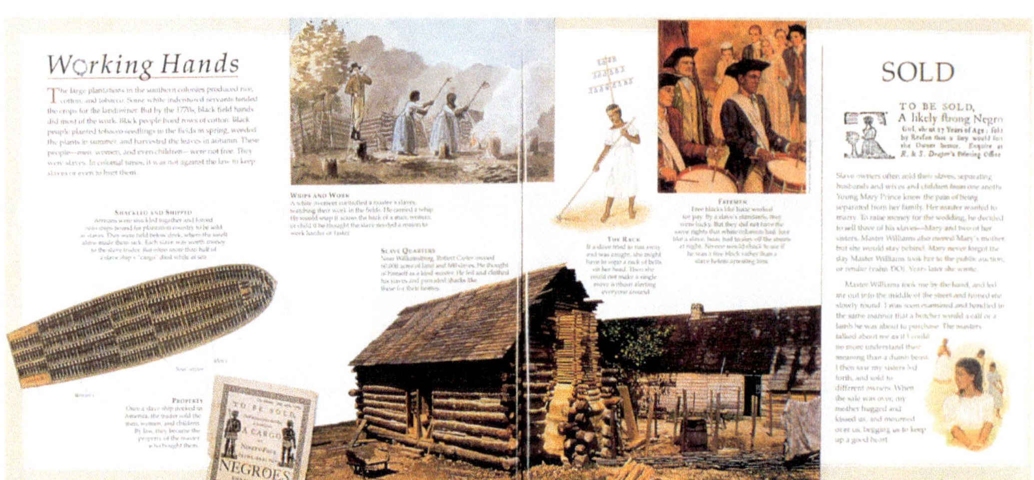

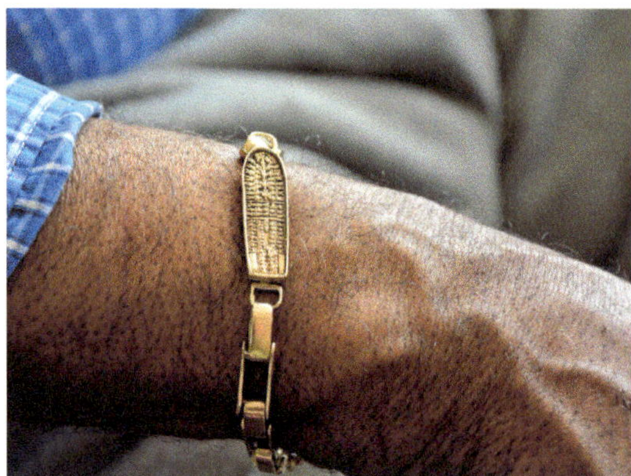

I.8 ABOVE

Two-page spread from *Felicity's World*, American Girl doll book.

I.9 LEFT

Robert Croslin, *Slave Ship Bracelet*, 24-carat gold, 10 inches, worn by Dr. David C. Driskell.

I.10 BELOW

Two-page spread from Swann Galleries' February 24, 2010, African Americana auction.

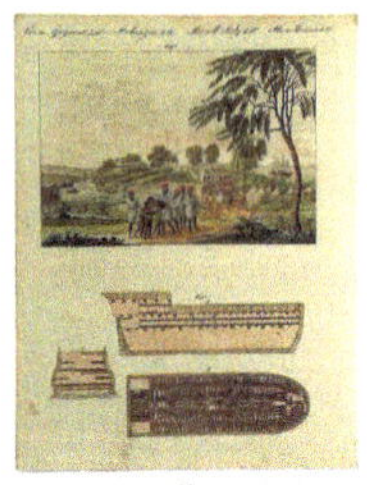

85 • SLAVE SHIP DIAGRAM. **Untitled engraving of Arab slavers herding Africans toward a waiting ship, and another engraving of the hold of a slave-ship.** 9-1/4x7-1/4 inches, hand-tinted with printed captions in French, German and Latin at the top of the page, "Miscellanea."
Np, circa late 18th century   [300/400]

86 • (SLAVERY AND ABOLITION) WOOD, SAMUEL, EDITOR. **The Mirror of Misery; or Tyranny Exposed.** Vignette title-page, double-page woodcut of the hold of a slave-ship, seven large woodcuts in the text. 12mo, original marbled paper-covered boards with later cloth spine; boards rubbed and worn; some pages loose, paper lightly, and for the most part evenly toned; one large plate with some stains; doggerel verse "Steal Not This Book my Friend" on front free end-paper, signed Phebe Gray, 1808.
New York: Samuel Wood, 1807   [1,500/2,500]

FIRST EDITION, RARE. One of the earliest appearances of the notorious slave-ship's hold printed in an American book. No copies are located by OCLC. Wood issued two more editions of this little tract. Shaw and Shoemaker, citing two locations, Nhi, and PPAmP; Sabin, 49427.

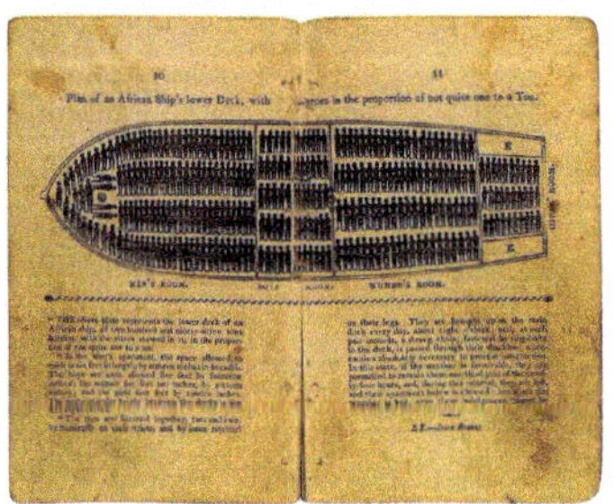

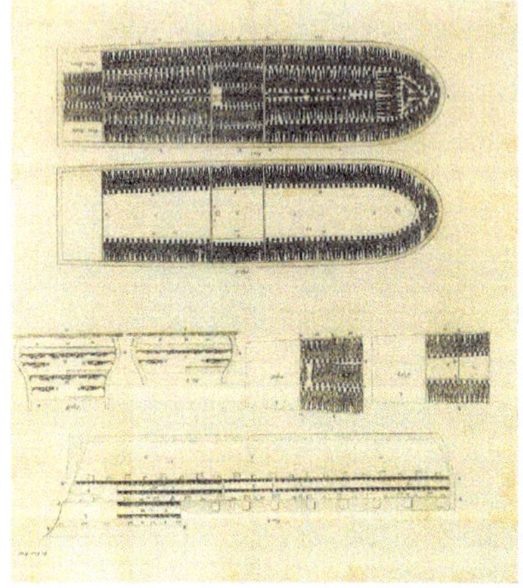

87 • SLAVE SHIP DIAGRAM. **Engraving of the hold of the slave-ship "Brooks."**
18x16 inches; creases where folded.   London: Helmsley, [1808]   [1,500/2,500]

The hold of the notorious slave-ship Brooks, as seen in a cutaway diagram from Thomas Clarkson's History of the Rise, Progress and Accomplishment of the Abolition of the Slave Trade, London, 1808. This image was originally used by William Wilberforce when presenting his evidence of the inhuman cruelty of the slave-trade before Parliament in 1791.

88 • STILL, WILLIAM. **The Underground Railroad, a Record of the Facts, Authentic Narratives, Letters, Etc.** Copious illustrations. 780, [12] pages. Thick royal 8vo, original deeply embossed covers, decoratively stamped in gilt; extremities lightly rubbed, small white spot on the spine; inner hinges started.
Philadelphia: People's Publishing Co, 1879   [400/600]

REVISED EDITION. In the Preface Still recounts how his mother twice fled to freedom with her four children, the second time having to leave two of the older ones behind. He tells how, after over forty years, one of them turned up in his office in Philadelphia, not realizing he had come to his brother. Still's history remains the single best account of the Underground Railroad ever written. Not simply because of its extraordinary size and scope, but because Still writes from firsthand experience, and a personal knowledge of most of the key figures.

children's books published for the American Girl doll franchise have illustrated an early version of the slave ship icon to discuss the life of Felicity, a young girl whose lifetime is set on a plantation during slavery (fig. I.8). Dr. David Driskell, the venerable historian of African American art, owns a gold bracelet designed by Robert Croslin of Hyattsville, Maryland, which he regularly wears (fig. I.9). At Swann Galleries in New York annual auctions of African Americana held since 1998 have sold examples of the slave ship icon taken from abolitionist tracts and books. In the February 2010 auction, three different versions were offered for sale with estimates ranging from $300 to $2,500 (fig. I.10). Regardless of commercialization, this image continues to inflict a psychic impact on the black and white people who wear it, view it, and in other ways consume it.

Despite the evident and ongoing generative power of this image, its visual and cultural history, told from the point of view of art history and African American studies, has remained largely untold until now.[6] What about the graphic quality of the slave ship icon enables it to continue to have resonance for us today? What has compelled artists and curators to use it as a visual memory aid and a teaching tool? Why is there an urgent need for ordinary people to attempt to embody it, to revisit the terror it represents, to reenact its profound silence and pain? How has the symbolic possession of the past through the use of the slave ship icon shaped an artistic practice of mnemonic aesthetics among an increasing number of African diaspora artists, architects, and cultural innovators? In this first-ever art-historical study to illustrate the significance of this image in the black Atlantic imagination, I have set out to answer these questions. By unpacking the contents of the hold, so to speak, we can begin to understand how the slave ship icon has stood as a template for the historical memory of the Middle Passage for visual artists around the black Atlantic.[7]

THE BLACK ATLANTIC

This enduring image served to galvanize the formation of African diaspora identity and aesthetic practice in the second half of the twentieth century and today in a process that hinges on a ritualized politics of remembering that I call mnemonic aesthetics. The parameters of this study are mapped out by the artistic, geographic, and philosophical definitions of the black Atlantic, a redemptive space in which the slave ship icon developed, traveled, and was eventually reclaimed by African diaspora artists and their allies. Art historian Robert Farris Thompson first charted this discursive space in his pioneering work on Afro-Atlantic artistic exchanges, circulations, and traditions, *Flash of the Spirit: African and Afro-American Art* (1983). In that work, he asserted, "since the Atlantic slave trade, ancient African organizing principles of song and dance have crossed the seas from the Old World to the New"[8] and went on to show how the same was true for art:

> Aspects of the art and philosophy of the Yoruba of Nigeria and the Republic of Bénin; the Bakongo of Bas-Zaire and neighboring Cabinda, Congo-Brazzaville, and Angola; the Fon and Ewe of the Republic of Bénin and Togo; the Mande of

Male and neighboring territory; and the Ejagham of the Cross River in southeastern Nigeria and southwestern Cameroon, have come from sub-Saharan Africa to the western hemisphere.[9]

Thompson's notion of the black Atlantic was expanded and reaffirmed in later works like *Face of the Gods: Art and Altars of Africa and the African Americas* (1993) and influential essays such as "The Song That Named the Land: The Visionary Presence of African-American Art" (1989).[10] These works and the exhibitions, artists, and musicians they have inspired remain pivotal for shaping the field of African diaspora art history and for the ways in which they discursively map the black Atlantic through a ritual return to Africa from the Americas and back again in the performance, percussive, musical, and visual traditions of black people, suggesting spiritual, aural, oral, and visual connections that are affirmed in works of art today and in years past.

Cultural theorist Paul Gilroy's assertion that the slave ship connected the points of the black Atlantic world is also an essential part of the framework in which this study operates:

> It should be emphasized that ships were the living means by which the points within the Atlantic world were joined. They were mobile elements that stood for the shifting spaces between the fixed places that they connected. Accordingly they need to be thought of as cultural and political units rather than abstract embodiments of the triangular trade. They were something more—a means to conduct political dissent and possibly a distinct mode of cultural production.[11]

Gilroy's formulation of the black Atlantic, charted in his seminal work the *Black Atlantic: Modernity and Double Consciousness*, has given shape to this book and its insistence on how mnemonic strategies influence cultural practices and their waves of resurgence, their ebbs and flows in and out of cosmopolitan centers around the Atlantic rim. His incisive claim that the slave ships were "a means to conduct political dissent and possibly a distinct mode of cultural production" is further affirmed in the works of art produced by contemporary black artists and their allies as they interrogate, redeploy, and imagine the eighteenth-century engraving that is the subject of this study.

THE PRACTICE OF MNEMONIC AESTHETICS

Naturally, art-historical inquiry into the visual culture of slavery is often chronologically bound to the eighteenth and nineteenth centuries, when most of the imagery of slavery and the slave trade was produced. By recognizing the vital role of memory in the works and working habits of contemporary artists, the conversation can be extended into the twentieth and twenty-first centuries. Contemporary artists employ a practice of remembering as a creative strategy—a mnemonic aesthetics. In a purposeful, artistic process that I have called *symbolic possession of the past*, contemporary African American and African diaspora artists have found it necessary to reach back in time to reclaim important emblems and icons of history as a way of understanding their relationship to the present. Practicing a form of mnemonic aesthetics, they reinterpret the symbols of the past to focus on the unfolding of black history, identity, and culture.

To be sure, the use of visual and literary metaphors to recreate the memory of the Middle Passage has been one of the defining characteristics of black Atlantic artistic practice. Beginning with the slave narrative, filtering through the autobiographical novel, and taking hold of the literature of migration, the memory of slavery has been used as a strategy for reclaiming the past, a tool of resistance, and a means of reinforcing personal and group identity. Contemporary visual artists recalling the historical memory of slavery rely on images, testimony, and archival records that evoke the pain, suffering, and gruesome details of the experience of slavery, but at the same time hint at the strength and perseverance necessary to survive, in Gilroy's words, its "ineffable sublime terror." These artists often work and rework, reimagine and reinterpret the material sources they use as a base. By making ritual sojourns to the past, visual artists exercise the same sense of responsibility for their history that Toni Morrison has identified in the work of African American writers. As she notes, "Black Americans were sustained and healed and nurtured by the translation of their experiences into art."[12]

The ritualized politics of remembering—which I call mnemonic aesthetics—is a key cultural practice of artists of the African diaspora today. This practice both rehearses and privileges the fragile and fleeting associations of memory and forgetting. Based on repetition and rhythm, with references to the mechanical reproduction of ephemera, the aural and visual shape of sonic communication, and the seriality of film and postmodernist practices of installation and performance, mnemonic aesthetics "adopt a variety of forms" according to film theorist Vivian Sobchack, such as "rote quotation, duplication, appropriation, cyclical recurrence or the repeated use of images, objects, and sounds; rhythmic and repetitious patterning of images, objects, sounds and music whose modes can be ritualistic, mantric, or spiritual."[13] These aesthetic strategies of repetition and rhythm are mobilized in a concentrated effort to keep hold of a memory that threatens to disappear. It is no wonder, perhaps, that mnemonic aesthetics was first born out of the age of mechanical reproduction and later reborn in the postmodernist practices of performance, installation, new media, and sound art.

The practice of mnemonic aesthetics further reveals how artists have found it important to insist on their connection to the history of slavery, so that present generations can understand its contemporary ramifications for the processes of identity formation. This strategy of making history tangible and present is vital to the practice of remembrance, identified by Walter Benjamin as key for the survival of oppressed peoples, as a safeguard against the recurrence of unspeakable crimes.[14] To be sure, as French historian Pierre Nora has pointed out, "The passage of memory to history has required every social group to redefine its identity through the revitalization of its own history."[15] Artists working in this tradition of remembrance mark the points of pain and suffering or strength and resistance as loci of collective memory and means of building group identity. For the artists of the African diaspora, this tradition of remembrance is constituted in such themes as the Middle Passage, lynching, rape, plantation slavery, racial violence, and slave revolts. Of these themes, the Middle Passage, marking the painful origins of the African diaspora in the transatlantic slave trade, is one to which artists have returned with passionate frequency.

WHAT MAKES AN ICON?

How does a cheaply made political print become an artifact, and then an icon? This process moved along two interrelated trajectories. First, artists and engravers subjected the image to a constant, if uneven process of refinement and transformation. They redrew it in response to changing circumstances and political strategies in the struggle to end the slave trade; those who created and subsequently reconceived the image often had strong ideas, more or less explicitly articulated, on how it should function politically and aesthetically. In many respects, the original plan of the slave ship was an "anti-art" image. Its creators recognized that it was a brutal, painful, and political image, a calculated outrage, even an obscenity. It certainly differed from many of the decorative, satirical, narrative, or sentimental prints and engravings based on well-known paintings that enlivened middle-class homes of the late eighteenth and early nineteenth centuries, such as works by William Hogarth, Isaac Cruikshank, or George Morland. And yet within little time, as the image achieved its reproductive and polemical zenith, this is exactly what happened: Quakers and other members of the abolitionist movement and their sympathizers began hanging the image in their homes.

We must consider the ways in which the slave ship icon affected people who saw it posted as a broadside or printed in a tract in the eighteenth and nineteenth centuries as well as those who experience it today. This image tore at the hearts of many who saw it, and this effect was greatly ramified by the revolution in printing technology occurring at roughly the same time. An image of such power inevitably exceeded the narrow purposes of illustration. It became a political weapon that was appropriated for a variety of causes. Eventually it was used not just to advocate for the end of the slave trade, its initial purpose, but the end of slavery itself. In a simultaneous, unlikely reversal, Swedish-born naturalist Carl Bernhard Wadström in his *Essay on Colonization* also used it to promote African colonization as an alternative to the slave trade in the late eighteenth century. The slave ship icon was conceived at a time of great change that shaped the modern era: from the age of enlightenment to the era of colonialism, from mercantilism to industrialization. None of these historical developments escaped its effect or failed to influence its reception.

Refer to "that image of the slave ship" in conversation with just about anyone, and they will know what you are talking about; he or she will surely conjure some vague facsimile of the image in their head. In this study, I refer to this almost universally known image as the *slave ship icon*. The word *icon* comes to us from the ancient Greek *eikon*, meaning image or picture, but it has a deeper significance in both the sacred and secular realms. In the history of Byzantine art, *icon* refers to a painting of a holy person or one of the traditional scenes from Orthodox

Christianity, the religion of the Byzantine Empire. Byzantine icon paintings were placed in the sacred space of the church in order for parishioners to develop a connection to the holy persons and events they depicted. The pictorial language of icon paintings provided the symbolic reinforcement of the liturgical teachings meant to create and sustain belief. In other words, icons provided a link between earthbound believers and the divine, and between the material and the spiritual worlds. The icon thus became integral to liminal space, between these two worlds, as well as a transportive vessel, moving between two continents.

The image of the slave ship functions in some ways as a religious icon. It becomes the de facto but unacknowledged icon of Quakers and radical Christians, who generally banned religious images from their practice of worship and from their homes. Rejecting traditional Christian icons, they created their own contemporary versions. The slave ship icon was, according to a leading figure in the fight to end the slave trade in Britain and member of the London Committee of the Society for Effecting the Abolition of the Slave Trade Thomas Clarkson, "designed to give the spectator an idea of the sufferings of the Africans in the Middle Passage."[16] The enslaved African, individually and collectively, experienced some of the same ordeals and tortures that were suffered by Christ. Just as the crucifix, as a powerful icon, serves as the focal point of Christian beliefs and represents Jesus's sacrifice to redeem humanity, the slave ship icon was made by abolitionists to convert nonbelievers to a cause that was deeply religious, humanitarian, and moral—of which the need to abolish the slave trade was but one immediate substantiation. Nor should we be surprised to find that the slave ship icon has continued religious resonance in the twentieth century and today. In 2000, a new and radically revised rose window was installed at the Chicago-based New Mount Pilgrim Missionary Baptist Church in which the torso of an Africanized Christ figure is emblazoned with the crowded lower deck of the slave ship icon.

An analysis of the formal elements of *Description of a Slave Ship* reveals the semiotic aspects of its iconicity and begins to answer the question of why this image, of the many images of slaves and the slave trade produced and circulated during slavery's long history, has been so lasting in our imagination. The repeating visual details—the shackles; the sexualized female bodies; the compacted bodies in discomfort; the uniform, silent, anonymous bodies; the keenly planned distribution of the bodies within the compartments—were purposefully and systematically employed to generate the icon's semiotic effectiveness and remain meaningful visual testimonies to the system of New World slavery.

Equally and perhaps more significant than the vivid presences in *Description of a Slave Ship* are the absences—the glaring omission of sailors and slave traders, and more subtle absences of affective detail. Of course, what remains completely invisible, perhaps too great to be seen at all, are the corporate and individual investors in the slave trade, the governments that supported the commerce, the African traders who supplied their countrymen and women, and the church that condoned the trade. These absences signal a historical amnesia that artists of the twentieth century and today find it necessary to restore.

The formal elements that are there have become buoys, beacons, and anchors for visual artists, writers, and cultural workers in the twentieth century and today as they lay claim to and assert control over their past. It is precisely this combination of visual presence and absence that has helped make the plan of the slave ship so generative in the black Atlantic imagination. As we shall see, these absences have left spaces for other narratives to be told. The slave ship icon becomes complete only with the added perspective of the viewer. It calls out to the viewer to make it whole.

THE ICON AND AFRICAN DIASPORA ART

In his seminal study, *African Art in Motion: Icon and Act,* art historian Robert Farris Thompson lays out a theory of icons in black Atlantic expressive culture, particularly that of the Yoruba in dance, ritual, and movement. This work has informed my own study in its insistence on the ways in which icons of the body convey meaning through the consolidation and refinement of expressive forms in rituals of repetition and renewal. Thompson notes, "The icons of African art are…frequently attitudes…of the body, arranged in groupings which suggest a grand equation of stability and reconciliation."[17] Thompson's relationship of the icon to the body also suggests the spiritual nature of icons when performed in the Yoruba sense or when worshiped or painted in the Byzantine sense. That icons in the Yoruba sense are "attitudes" further reinforces this point. As Thompson explains, "Thus, icons of elevated happening and command, standing, sitting, and riding on horseback, seem balanced by icons of service or submission: kneeling, supporting with the hands, and balancing loads on the head."[18] He points out that these icons of bodily motion or attitude appear and reappear in the carved arts of the Yoruba as well. Moreover, these icons of dance or performance and icons of religious images possess a hypnotizing power—a control over the imagination that can produce a transcendental state through ritual repetition, performance, and practice—linking the performer or painter to a higher state of consciousness. "The intensification of iconic resonance by simplification of expressive means," Thompson suggests, is a key mode in which icons convey meaning in African and African diaspora art.[19]

While *Description of a Slave Ship* was created in a late eighteenth-century Western tradition of printmaking deeply indebted to Enlightenment-era attitudes and ideas of scientific and economic measurement, in the hands of artists and cultural producers of the late twentieth century and today it has been revitalized and transformed through a series of mnemonic practices that reference Thompson's notion of "iconic resonance" as well as theories and practices in African American music, film, literature, and performance. Visual artist and cinematographer Arthur Jafa talks about African diaspora creative transformation as situated in the "space of treatment rather than the space of material." He offers the example of John Coltrane's repeated performance of Rogers and Hammerstein's *My Favorite Things*:

> What interests me is how Coltrane's improvisations never seek to entirely erase the original melodic material.…Coltrane keeps his transformations and the

original sources equally evident. That's because it's not primarily about the point
of departure or the point of arrival, but the spaces between these points.[20]

This transformation is related to what Huston Baker Jr. calls the deformation of mastery, which transforms an obscene situation into a "single self/cultural expression."[21] The artist Betye Saar, for instance, does this in her series of assemblage constructions that reclaim and empower the old stereotype of Aunt Jemima with a new sense of agency and purpose. Although the creators of *Description of a Slave Ship* were purposely revealing an obscene situation in order to destroy it, they could not transform it in the terms suggested by Jafa or Baker. They created the "material" but they could not turn the obscene into black self-expression. As Baker metaphorically describes this process, it is "the tunneling out of the black holes of possession and 'tight places' of old clothes, into, perhaps, a new universe."[22]

The focus on the "space of treatment" or the "deformation of mastery" is also closely aligned with literary historian Henry Louis Gates Jr.'s consideration of African American literary aesthetics, with his emphasis on reversal and repetition with a signal difference. In his seminal study, *The Signifying Monkey: A Theory of African-American Literary Criticism,* Gates declares, "The texts in the Afro-American canon can be said to configure into relationships based on the sorts of repetition and revision inherent in parody and pastiche."[23] In this influential work, Gates theorized a uniquely African American practice of "signifying" as a creative tradition of revision found in the slave narrative. As he elaborates, "Much of the Afro-American literary tradition can be read as successive attempts to create a new narrative space for representing the recurring referent of Afro-American literature, the so-called Black Experience."[24] This has obvious parallels in the visual arts and is particularly relevant when the question of the black experience turns to the Middle Passage. With the slave ship icon, the people whose ancestors were the object of the drawing take symbolic possession of the image in the twentieth century and make it their own.

The artists' works and exhibitions discussed in parts II and III of this book demonstrate the afterlife of the slave ship icon and what Marianne Hirsch has termed the *postmemory*—how "the memories of traumatic events live on to mark the lives of those who were not there to experience them."[25] Many of the artists I interviewed have alluded to a ritual need to refashion and reform this image. Frequently, the works they have produced are not singular; rather, they exist in series, installations, or successive works on the same theme completed over a period of time, revealing a practice of mnemonic aesthetics. For example, the installation and video artist María Magdalena Campos-Pons first reimagined the slave ship icon in the installation *Tra…*, short for the Spanish *travesía*, or crossing, exhibited at the Havana Biennale in 1991. The following year, she redeployed the slave ship icon in the installation and performance *The Seven Powers Come by the Sea* at the Institute of Contemporary Art in Boston. In both works, the artist marked life-size wooden planks resembling coffins with stick figures in the schematic layout of the slave ship icon. The act of using and then *reusing* or, in the words of Arthur Jafa, "shaping and reshaping" their own work might be likened to the kind of ritualized aesthetic practice that defines mnemonic aesthetics.[26] This is especially true of the artist Willie Cole, who uses the scorch of an iron to make prints that resemble the slave ship icon and refer to rituals of scarification, on the one hand, and branding, on the other.

The idea of ritual associated with mnemonic aesthetics refers back to the dimension of spiritual conversion of the icon. Underlying these practices is a strong sense of duty: the responsibility to create works that recall the history of the artists' African origins and to ensure that this history's significance is never forgotten. They use memory as an aesthetic tool and organizing principle to emphasize recurrent themes that have shaped the African diaspora: the Middle Passage, plantation slavery, the longing for Africa, and racial violence directed at black people, to name a few. In this way, individual works of art make visible and commemorate the stories of pain and suffering, strength and resistance, or triumph and celebration that reconnect these artists to their roots. The practice of mnemonic aesthetics takes a further cue from Paul Gilroy, who argues that the artistic urge to return to the memory of slavery is a way of "organizing the consciousness of the racial group socially and striking the important balance between inside and outside activity—the different practices, cognitive, habitual, and performative, that are required to invent, maintain and renew identity."[27] Thus, mnemonic aesthetics aid in identity formation through visual art production, dissemination, and display.[28] Their projects constantly relate a sense of communal diasporic history to their own personal experience and continually carry on a conversation between individual and group experience that is part of the process of shaping identity, affirming group belonging, and marking a sense of temporal and geographical place. This process of relating the present and personal to the historic and communal is a validating process, one that reasserts both the presence and existence of the artist and the African diaspora in time and space.

BRIEF OVERVIEW OF THE SECTIONS OF THE BOOK

Part I, "Sources/Roots," establishes the slave ship icon as the preeminent image of the abolitionist movement in late eighteenth- and early nineteenth-century England and America. It offers a brief history of the original image, including its political and historical context, conception, distribution, and initial use. It provides the reader with the analytical tools to understand the historical significance of the slave ship icon, its visual organizing principles, and the political and artistic movements that propelled its widespread circulation around the Atlantic rim. Part II, "Meanings/Routes," considers the postmemory of the slave ship icon in the context of three of the major artistic movements of the twentieth century: the New Negro Arts Movement (1919–29), the Black Arts Movement in the United States (1965–76), and the Black Arts Movement in the United Kingdom (1981–95). The third and final section of the book, "Rites/Reinventions," examines the continued presence of the slave ship icon in our daily lives: in the built environment of museums and monuments; in the popular culture of T-shirts, jewelry, film, and body adornment; and in performance, installation art, and art that informs and is informed by religious practice. Here I show how mnemonic aesthetics influence contemporary vernacular culture and political strategies of reparations as well as forms of religious worship. This section of the book discusses the urge to inhabit the psychic if not physical space that the slave ship icon suggests.

How has the slave ship icon come to so richly enfold and ignite the black diaspora's imagination about their shared history of transformation? In providing an art-historical timeline, a consideration of the ways the slave ship icon has been appropriated and reimagined, adopted for different artistic purposes, and ritually returned to again and again, my book reveals salient aspects of contemporary African American and African diaspora art practices and canon formation. The practice of mnemonic aesthetics is indeed an artistic practice of survival; like the Sankofa bird, these artists are engaged in a process of "go back and retrieve it," gathering up the lessons of history and refashioning, reimagining their emblems for their present moment, if not for the future.

THE 2007 BICENTENARY AND THE PRACTICE OF MNEMONIC AESTHETICS

The tour of Romuald Hazoumé's *La Bouche de Roi* to six carefully chosen venues around the United Kingdom from March 22, 2007, to March 1, 2009, charts an orchestrated program of national absolution, repentance, and perhaps admission of guilt, but it also demonstrates the practice of mnemonic aesthetics. All venues had ties to the history of the slave trade or its abolition. London was a principal port engaged in the slave trade in the late seventeenth and early eighteenth centuries. It also profited heavily from slave-grown sugar after the abolition of the slave trade. Liverpool was the leading slave trading port in all of the United Kingdom, especially in the last half of the eighteenth century. Bristol was an important slave trading port. Manchester manufactured trade goods that were used to barter for African captives. Hull was the home of Member of Parliament William Wilberforce, who first introduced legislation before Parliament calling for the abolition of the slave trade. *La Bouche de Roi*'s choreographed movements around the United Kingdom suggest a pilgrimage of reconciliation in spite of protests that the brutal history of Britain's involvement in the slave trade was overlooked in the framing and execution of bicentenary events. The repetition of bodies and sections that are illustrated in the slave ship icon are not only reworked in plastic petroleum canisters that compose *La Bouche de Roi*, but also in the very circulation of the installation to its various venues. Its tour emulates the vast dissemination of the original prints of *Description of a Slave Ship* to the countryside, city centers, and abroad during the busiest period of slave trade abolitionism in the United Kingdom from 1789 to 1807. Through this state-led effort, *La Bouche de Roi* (and the historical and contemporary references it makes) was promoted as a symbol of national memory and reconciliation during the bicentenary celebrations. By using the popular abolitionist's engraving to comment upon contemporary social, political, and economic ills—and by inserting images, narratives, and objects that were not visualized in the original engraving—Romuald Hazoumé breathes new life and new meaning into the slave ship icon.

SOURCES/ROOTS

1788–1900

IDEA: IMAGE AND TEXT

CREATING THE SLAVE SHIP ICON IN GREAT BRITAIN AND THE UNITED STATES, 1788

THE FIRST ABOLITIONIST ENGRAVING of a slave ship, titled *Plan of an African Ship's Lower Deck with Negroes in the Proportion of Only One to a Ton* (1788), was conceived by the Plymouth Committee of the Society for Effecting the Abolition of the Slave Trade in England (fig. 1.1). Viewed from above this schematic plan shows a cargo hold packed with hundreds of enslaved Africans—represented by tiny, uniform, darkly shaded figures—and so hints at the barbarity they were made to suffer during the Middle Passage, the transatlantic voyage from Africa to the New World slave markets. Among the first to publicly acknowledge the visual impact of this image, printed on paper 6¾ by 16 inches, was African-born Olaudah Equiano (1745?–1797), whose letter to the Plymouth Committee appeared in a London newspaper, the *Public Advertiser,* on February 14, 1789. In his own carefully chosen words, Equiano professed:

> Having seen a plate representing the form in which Negroes are stowed on board the Guinea ships, which you are pleased to send to the Rev. Mr. Clarkson, a worthy friend of mine, I was filled with love and gratitude towards you for your humane interference on behalf of my oppressed countrymen.[1]

An ex-slave and free man of color living in London, Equiano was an outspoken opponent of the slave trade, who regularly described his personal experience of slavery at public gatherings.[2] His public performances had gained Equiano such a reputation that by the time his letter appeared in the *Public Advertiser,* he was on the verge of publishing his enormously successful autobiography, *The Interesting Narrative of the Life of Olaudah Equiano or Gustavus Vassa, The African,* in March 1789 (fig. 1.2).[3]

It is not hard to imagine why Equiano immediately recognized the print's capacity to serve the goals of abolition. For him, it provided a shocking visual reminder of a place and an experience that he himself had known. Yet still it must have been difficult for him to conceive of how *anyone* could render such an image. Indeed, one wonders just exactly what he felt, what he remembered when Thomas Clarkson showed him the oblong engraving of the plan of the slave ship. As rudimentary as it was in its initial rendering, Equiano nevertheless was transfixed by its power, perhaps even in a state of utter disbelief at its ability to represent such a site of terror

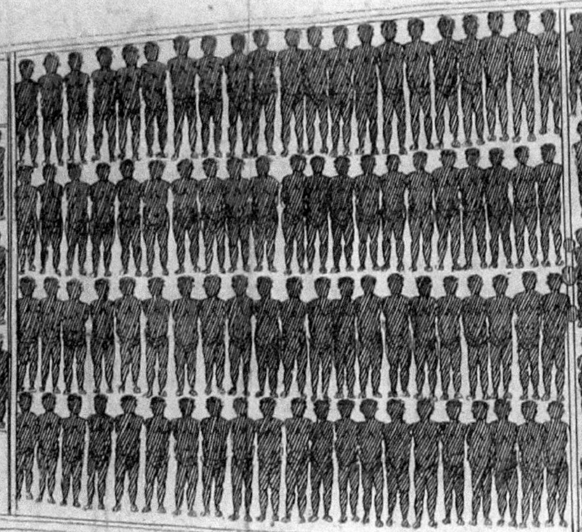
Plan of an African Ship's lower D
Store Room
Girls
Room
Store room
Womans room
Boys

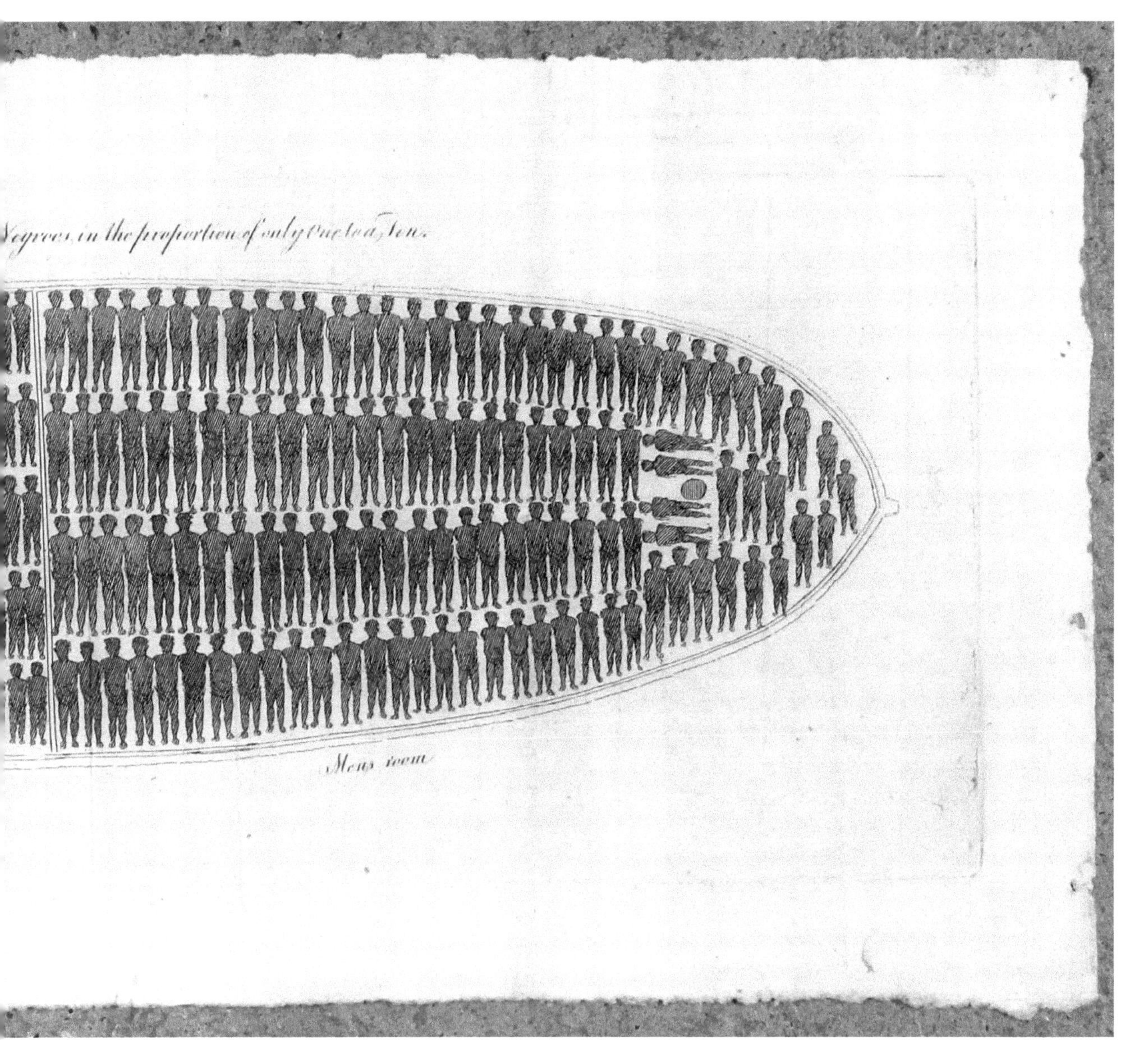

1.1

Plymouth Committee, *Plan of an African Ship's Lower Deck with Negroes in the Proportion of Only One to a Ton*, 1788, copper engraving 6³/₄ × 16 inches.

1.2 TOP
Frontispiece and title page of Samuel Wood's
American edition of the *Life and Adventures
of Olaudah Equiano or Gustavus Vassa,
The African*, 1829.

1.3 BOTTOM
Detail (showing Men's Room), Plymouth
Committee, *Plan of an African Ship's Lower
Deck with Negroes in the Proportion of
Only One to a Ton*, 1788, copper engraving.

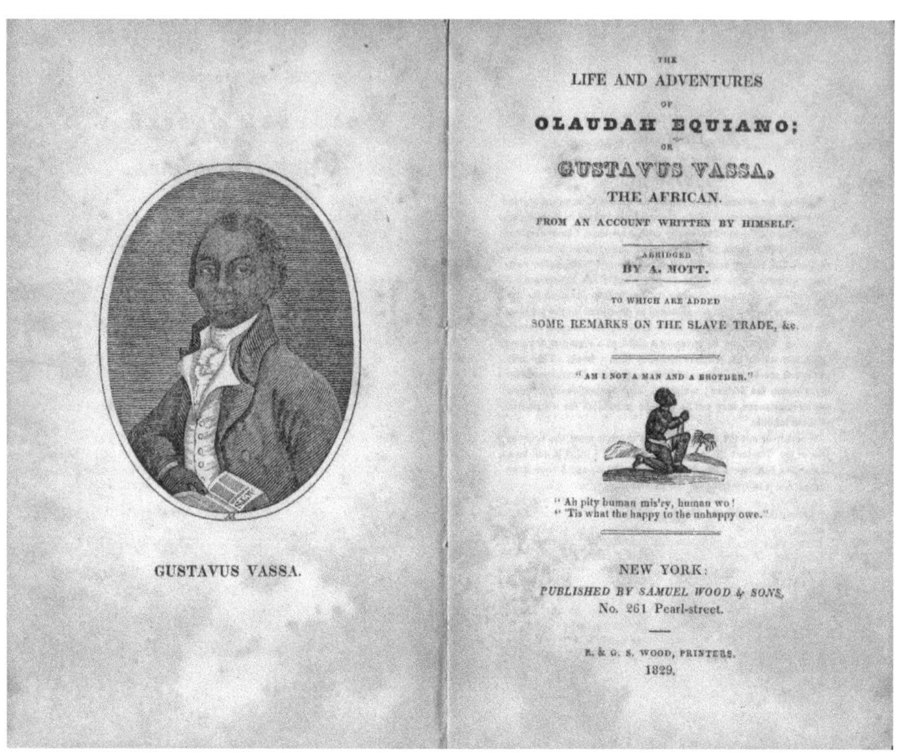

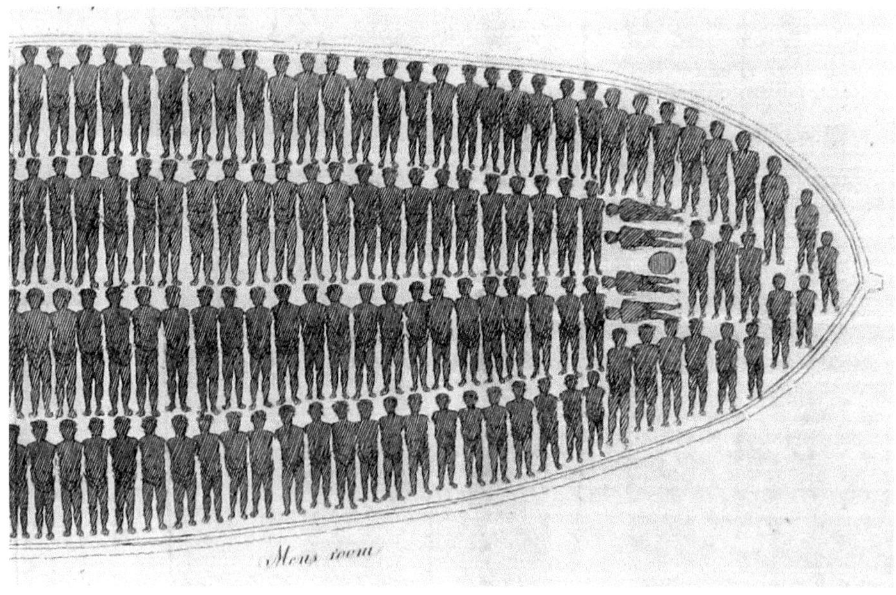
Mens room

and violence. In that moment of recognition, the wound from the initial trauma of being torn away from the land and people he knew and forcibly taken to some unknown people and place was slashed anew. One can picture how his eyes might have followed the contours of the darkly shaded figures, counting each one, possibly imagining the face of someone he once knew. Fine black lines representing the walls that divided groups of figures by age and sex might have caused him to pause and think about which space he had occupied or the people who had lived and died next to him. The combination of rows and rows of black figures separated and surrounded by fine black lines schematically mapped the space of the hold, marking a route to untold horror. The labels "boy's room," "girl's room," "men's room," "women's room" appeared as sign posts indicating the contents stored within (fig. 1.3).

The title above the bullet-shaped schematic, "Plan of an African Ship's Lower Deck with Negroes Stowed in the Proportion of Only One to a Ton," bluntly and succinctly described the purpose of the drawing while revealing a modern system of calculation, commerce, brutality, and human domination. So haunting in its graphic depiction, the plan of the slave ship must have seemed capable of psychically transporting Equiano back to that foundational moment in the swollen belly of the slave ship when he was born into an African diaspora. As he described in his autobiography:

> The closeness of the place, and the heat of the climate added to the number in the ship, which was so crowded that each had scarcely room to turn himself, almost suffocated us. This produced copious perspirations, so that the air soon became unfit for respiration, from a variety of loathsome smells, and brought on a sickness among the slaves, of which many died, thus falling victims to the improvident avarice, as I may call it, of their purchasers. This wretched situation was again aggravated by the galling of the chains, now become insupportable; and the filth of the necessary tubs, into which the children often fell, and were almost suffocated. The shrieks of the women, and the groans of the dying rendered the whole a scene of horror almost inconceivable.[4]

This scene in which Equiano recounts his chilling memory of psychological terror and physical captivity in the hold of a slave ship is one of the defining moments of his narrative and a passage that since has been recited frequently as an eyewitness account of the Middle Passage.[5]

As an eyewitness and a survivor then, Equiano was in a unique position to endorse the plan of the slave ship, the first graphic representation to provide a visual complement to his own unforgettable hell. By lending public support to this image, his letter situated it within a discourse of artistic production, political action, and popular representations of the black body. The fact that Equiano recognized the hundreds of roughly drawn, nude black figures lying neatly in the coffin-shaped hold as his "oppressed countrymen" breathed life into their corpse-like representations. Indeed, by calling them his "oppressed countrymen," Equiano immediately brought the issue of their humanity to the attention of his readers. Moreover, his reference to "worthy friend" and prominent London Committee member Thomas

Clarkson (1760–1846) located Equiano's position within abolitionist circles and his ability to stand as a spokesman for the movement.

This first engraving of a crowded slave ship interior was not an isolated print. Rather, it served as the illustration for a small, square, four-page pamphlet printed by the Plymouth Committee. Not only was Equiano profoundly affected by the image, he was deeply moved by the explanatory text of the abolitionist tract as well. The cataclysmic text of the pamphlet reads:

[1] The annexed Plate represents the lower deck of an African Ship of 297 tons burthen, with the Slaves stowed on it, in the proportion of not quite one to a ton.

[2] In the Men's apartment, the space allowed to each is six feet in length, by sixteen inches in breadth.—The boys are each allowed five feet by fourteen inches.—The Women, five feet ten inches, by sixteen inches; and the Girls, four feet by one foot each.—The perpendicular height between the Decks is five feet eight inches.

[3] The Men are fastened together, two and two, by hand cuffs on their wrists and by irons rivetted on their legs.—They are brought up on the main deck every day, about eight o'clock, and as each pair ascend, a strong chain is fastened by ring bolts to the deck, is passed through their Shackles; a precaution absolutely necessary to prevent Insurrections.—In this state, if the weather is favourable, they are permitted to remain about one-third part of the twenty-four hours, and during this interval they are fed, and their apartment below is cleaned; but when the weather is bad, even these indulgences cannot be granted them, and they are only permitted to come up in small companies, of about ten at a time, to be fed, where after remaining a quarter of an hour, each mess is obliged to give place to the next in rotation.

[4] It may perhaps be conceived, from the crouded state in which the Slaves appear in the Plate, that an unusual and exaggerated instance has been produced; this, however, is so far from being the case, that no ship, if her intended cargo can be procured, ever carries a less number than one to a Ton, and the usual practice has been to carry nearly double that number: The Bill which was passed during the last Session of Parliament, only restricts the carriage to five Slaves for three tons; and the Brooks, of Liverpool, a capital ship, from which the above sketch was proportioned, did, in one voyage actually carry 609 Slaves, which is more than double the number that appear in the Plate.—The mode of stowing them was a follows—Patforms, or wide shelves were erected, between the decks, extending so far from the sides towards the middle of the vessel, as to be capable of containing four additional rows of Slaves, by which means the perpendicular height between each tier, after allowing for the beams and the platforms, was reduced to two feet six inches; for they could not even fit in an erect posture; besides which, in the Men's apartment, instead of four rows; five were stowed by placing the heads of one between the thighs of another. —All the horrors of this situation are still multiplied in the smaller vessels. The Kitty, of 127 tons, had one foot ten inches and the Venus of 146 tons, only one foot nine inches perpendicular height above each layer.

[5] The above mode of carrying the Slaves, however, is only one, among a thousand other miseries, which those unhappy and devoted creatures suffer from this disgraceful Traffick of the Human Species; which in every part of its progress, exhibits scenes that strike us with horror and indignation.—If we regard the first stage of it on the Continent of Africa, we find that a hundred thousand Slaves are annually produced there for exportation, the greatest part of whom consist of innocent persons, torn from their dearest friends and connections, sometimes by force, and sometimes by treachery. Of these, experience has shewn, that five and forty thousand perish, either in the dreadful mode of conveyance before described, or within two years after their arrival at the plantations, before the are seasoned to the climate.—Those who unhappily survive these hardships, are destined, like their beasts of burden, to exhaust their lives in the unremitting labours of a Slavery, without recompence, and without hope.

[6] The inhumanity of this Trade, indeed, is so notorious, and so universally admitted, that even the advocates for the continuance of it, have rested all their arguments on the political inexpediency of its abolition; and in order to strengthen a weak cause, have either maliciously or ignorantly confounded together the emancipation of the Negroes already in Slavery, with the abolition of the Trade; and thus many well-meaning people have become enemies of the cause, by the apprehensions, that private property will be materially injured by the success of it.—To such, it becomes a necessary information, that liberating the Slaves forms no part of the present system; and so far will the prohibition of a future trade be from injuring private property, that the value of every Slave will be very considerably increased, from the moment that event takes place, and a more kind and tender treatment will immediately be insured to them by their Masters, from the necessity every planter will then be under to keep up his stock, by natural means; a practice which some humane inhabitants of the Islands have pursued with the greatest success, and upon whose estates no new Negroes have been purchased for a number of years, the death vacancies having been supplied by young ones, born and bred in their own plantations.—Thus then the value of private property will not only suffer no diminution, but will be very considerably inhanced by the abolition of the Trade.—It now only remains to see how the Public and the Slave Merchants will be affected by it.

[7] It is said by the well wishers to this Trade, that the suppression of it will destroy a great nursery for seamen, and annihilate a very considerable source of commercial profit.—In answer to these objects, Mr. Clarkson, in his admirable treatise on the impolicy of the Trade, lays down two positions, which he has proved from the most incontestible authority.—First, that so far from being a Nursery, it has been constantly and regularly a Grave for our Seamen; for that in this Traffick only, more Men perish in ONE Year, than in all the other Trades of Great-Britain in TWO Years: And, secondly, that the balance of the trade, from its extreme precariousness and uncertainty, is so notoriously against the Merchants, that if all the vessels employed in it were the property of one man, he would infallibly, at the end of their voyages, find himself a loser.

[8] As then the *Cruelty* and *Inhumanity* of this Trade must be universally admitted and lamented, and as the policy or impolicy of its abolition is a question which the wisdom of the Legislature must ultimately decide upon, and which it can only be enabled to form a just estimate of, by the most thorough investigation on all its relations and dependencies; it becomes the indispensible duty of every friend to humanity, however his speculations may have led him to conclude on the political tendency of the measure, to stand forward and to assist the Committees, either by producing such facts as he may himself be acquainted with, or by subscribing, to enable them to procure and transmit to the Legislature, such evidence as will tend to throw the necessary lights on the subject.—And people would do well to consider that it does not often fall to the lot of individuals, to have an opportunity of performing so important a moral and religious duty, as that of endeavouring to put an end to a practice, which may, without exaggeration, be stiled one of the greatest evils at this day existing upon the earth.

By the Plymouth Committee,
W. Elford, Chairman.

N.B. Subscriptions are received at the Plymouth, Naval, and Western Banks.[6]

A portion of Equiano's published letter to the Plymouth Committee commends the sentiments of the final paragraph by reiterating them, albeit in more concise and rhetorically effective language:

It is the duty of every man, every friend to religion and humanity, to assist the different Committees engaged in this pious work; reflecting that it does not often fall to the lot of individuals to contribute to so important a moral and religious duty as that of putting an end to a practise which may, without exaggeration, be stiled one of the greatest evils now existing on earth.[7]

Together, Equiano and the Plymouth Committee successfully linked the horrifying image of the hold of a slave ship with issues of "humanity" and "religious and moral duty." These themes dominated the political agenda of the abolitionist movement and resonated with other social and political struggles that cried out for public attention at the end of the eighteenth century.

Equiano's ties to Clarkson, the Plymouth Committee, and the larger British public reflect a complex series of exchanges that demand our closer scrutiny. Like the depths of the ocean, these transactions have multiple layers that may offer a still deeper understanding of the manner in which the plan of the slave ship circulated. Along our own voyage of discovery, we have to ask what it meant for Equiano to issue his public stamp of approval—in essence to sign off on the plan of the slave ship? Along with his advice and celebrity, did the Abolition Society seek the voice of an authentic victim/survivor? Both Clarkson and Equiano must have seen how the plan of the slave ship would resonate with his forthcoming autobiography, and vice versa. Their connection to each other and the abolition committees at London and Plymouth also hinted at an ongoing artistic and political debate over how to make the plan of the slave ship the best and most effective piece of visual propaganda. Discussions between the different abolitionist committees that participated in that debate were centered on questions of form, content, distribution, and use. Equiano was one of the first to recognize that the Plymouth Committee had developed a powerful visual tool for the abolitionist cause, and in doing so he put the idea of "the form in which Negroes are stowed on board the Guinea ships," in the public imagination. His enthusiasm was soon to be echoed by many others.

GENEALOGY OF THE SLAVE SHIP ICON

By 1790, British and American abolitionists had printed at least six different engravings representing the tightly packed hold of a slave ship, each one with a distinct format and varying degrees of descriptive text. These are the earliest examples of what I call the slave ship icon.[8] They involve a genealogy, a complex progression and transformation in which image and text change, but then relations between image and text are fundamentally altered. These versions of the abolitionist engraving testify to the flourishing print culture of the late eighteenth century and to the ways that religious and political groups employed this rapidly changing medium to develop one of the first grassroots political campaigns.[9] The Quaker-led system of abolitionist committees provided a ready vehicle for the dissemination of illustrated pamphlets, tracts, and broadsides.

The genealogy of these early prints of the plan of the slave ship has been the subject of some confusion among scholars. The result is a loss of historical specificity, which attenuates the relationship between this image and the different stages of the powerful social movement that it articulates. Perhaps not unexpectedly, both popular and scholarly attention has focused primarily on what became the most widely disseminated version of the slave ship icon, *Description of a Slave Ship* (and its later variations), a detailed broadside with expanded longitudinal and cross-section views developed by the London Committee in April 1789 (see fig. 2.2). While scholars agree that the concept for the detailed broadside originated with the Plymouth Committee, none have identified the original prototype praised by Equiano, the very first iteration of *Plan of an African Ship*…conceived by the Plymouth Committee.

Most scholars who study the history of the slave ship icon within the context of the abolitionist movement in England and America emphasize its instrumental role as visual propaganda: the image helped to stimulate grassroots support that put an end to the slave trade.[10] For sources, they often cite Thomas Clarkson's *The History of the Rise, Progress, and Accomplishment of the Abolition of the African Slave-Trade by British the Parliament*, published in England and the United States in 1808 (one year after both countries agreed to abolish the slave trade).[11] In his seminal history, Clarkson does two things that shape subsequent analyses of the slave ship icon. First, he includes a large folding copper engraving modified from the "famous print of the plan and section of a slave ship" redesigned by the London Committee in April 1789. It shows only the numbered, lettered schematic sections, cross sections, and longitudinal views, not the descriptive text, which is abstracted in the main body of the book. It is this image and its adaptations that became popular in the 1790s and early 1800s, and would remain so in the period leading up to the abolition of slavery in the United States. Second, in recounting how the slave ship icon came to be part of the abolition society's arsenal of provocative images, Clarkson asserts somewhat boastfully, "The committee at Plymouth had been the first to suggest the idea; but that in London had now improved it."[12]

Hardly an unbiased observer to these events, Thomas Clarkson was an active participant in the unfolding of history: a leading member of the London Committee and one of its five members assigned to redesign the image originally put forth by the Plymouth Committee. Scholars have discussed the slave ship icon as visual propaganda of the abolitionist movement, but they have never adequately examined the artistic processes by which it emerged to be the leading visual print of the movement or why it is still an indelible presence today.

In *Popular Politics and British Anti-Slavery: The Mobilisation of Public Opinion against the Slave Trade, 1787–1807*, J. R. Oldfield details the activities of the Plymouth Committee and acknowledges its instrumental role in creating the plan of the slave ship. He even suggests that Clarkson should have more graciously acknowledged the London Committee's indebtedness to the Plymouth Committee: "While distinctly an improvement, therefore, it is clear that the London print owed a great deal to the Plymouth committee, both in conception and in design."[13] Plainly responding to Clarkson, Oldfield notes, "Clarkson hints that the London Committee improved on the original design by giving it the form of an actual ship, that is the *Brooks* of Liverpool. Clearly, this was an exaggeration."[14] Providing visual evidence of his claim, Oldfield chose to reproduce in his book the second and final Plymouth Committee print realized as a broadside showing the Abolition Society seal with the kneeling slave (see fig. 1.8), *not* the more popular London Committee broadside.

In Marcus Wood's *Blind Memory: Visual Representations of Slavery in England and America, 1780–1865*, the author reproduces visual *excerpts* from broadsides drafted by both the Plymouth and London Committees. However, in choosing to print just the schematic images and not the texts that are an integral part of each broadside, Wood is able to show how the London *Description of a Slave Ship* relies on advancements in naval architecture to produce an image capable of being visualized in three dimensions. He contends that "the Plymouth *Plan* is simple," while the subsequent London *Description of a Slave Ship* displays a "graphic authority" wherein "the ship itself has now been drawn up according to a precise set of measurements. These measurements are of a completely different nature from the crude rule of thumb proportions upon which the single view of the Plymouth *Plan* was based."[15]

The meanings of these various early prints of the slave ship icon are derived from the specific historical moments in which they were made and different national or transnational contexts in which they circulated. In order to grasp the relevance and longevity of the slave ship icon—why it remains so powerful and popular an image today—this study examines the foundational prints, including those leading up to its most widely reproduced format as well as later, equally important variants. As with any iconic image or important work of art, early sketches help to explain how an image takes shape, conveys different meanings, and ultimately functions over time.

By undertaking a close reading of some of the earliest examples of the slave ship icon produced in Britain and the United States by mid-1789, this chapter aims to reconstruct how this image developed, both visually and textually, as the leading piece of abolitionist propaganda. Much of the prior critical analysis of the slave ship icon has focused largely on the schematic image and with little attention to the remarks that accompany the early broadsides, pamphlets, tracts, or books.[16] This tendency to isolate the visual without analyzing the textual has led to a understanding of this image as broadly "antislavery," when, in fact, it was used by abolitionists over time to address distinct political issues: the regulation of the slave trade, the abolition of the slave trade, African colonization, the suppression of the slave trade, and the abolition of chattel slavery. The image that forced Equiano to write his moving letter to the Plymouth Committee remains key to understanding the continued appearance of the slave ship icon in black Atlantic cultures to the present day.

THE STRATEGIC SIGNIFICANCE OF PLYMOUTH

It is both fitting and ironic that the slave ship icon originated in Plymouth, home to the legendary slave trader Sir John Hawkins (1532–1595), who made the first successful English slave-trading venture to the coast of Africa in 1562–63. In this pioneering exchange, Hawkins violently seized more than three hundred African slaves, ivory, and wax from a Portuguese ship off the coast of the Sierra Leone peninsula in West Africa. He then sailed across the Atlantic to the "Indies of Nova Hispania" where he traded these (twice) stolen goods for a sizeable profit. Returning to Plymouth with a cargo of "hides, ginger, sugars, and some quantities of pearles," Hawkins's maiden voyage spurred British interest in the triangular trade, particularly the lucrative business of bartering captive African bodies.[17] The following year in 1564, Hawkins gained the support of the British crown when Queen Elizabeth I loaned him a Royal Navy ship, the *Jesus of Lubeck*, for his next slaving venture.[18] The implications of the Queen's material investment in Hawkins's second expedition to the coast of Africa and New Spain cannot be understated. As artist Keith Piper explains, "The ship was the literal embodiment of the alliance between the rhetoric and symbolism of the Church and the economic and expansionist demands of the State."[19] In other words, this transaction was evidence enough that both the church and the state almost from the very start condoned the slave trade.

The material wealth amassed from Hawkins's first two voyages earned him the reputation of a wise and accomplished captain among his English counterparts. To honor his achievements, he was granted a coat of arms and crest by Queen Elizabeth I (fig. 1.4), which is depicted in a portrait of Sir John Hawkins, painted by Hieronymo Custodis in 1591, when Hawkins was fifty-eight.[20] Centered at the top of the ornate crest was "a demi-Moor, in his proper colour, bound and captive, with annulets on his arms and ears."[21] This figure of a black man is like the pistil of a golden flower and stands as a reminder to all who see it that African bodies were the source (and the crowning glory) of Hawkins's wealth and fame.

Hawkins's third and final voyage to the coast of Africa left Plymouth in 1567 with a convoy of six ships, including four supplied by the Queen.[22] By that time,

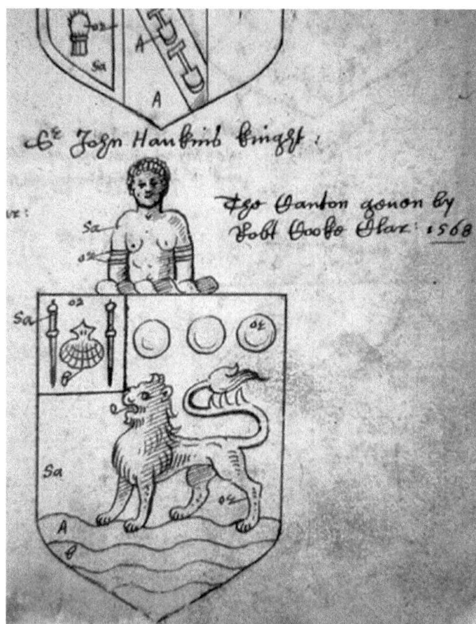

1.4
Artist unknown, shield and crest
of Sir John Hawkins, c. 1568.

Hawkins had won the confidence and respect of Queen Elizabeth and many noted English investors, but the Spanish and Portuguese held him in an entirely different light. With them, he had a reputation for being brash and violent in his business dealings, a real pirate plundering Portuguese ships and trading in forbidden areas along the African coast and in the Spanish West Indies. His brazen defiance of Spanish laws against unlicensed trading by other nations to the Spanish colonies precipitated the near total demise of his last African venture in the Spanish West Indies and added fodder to the brewing animosity between England and Spain, a rivalry of increasing commercial and religious dimensions.[23]

By 1585 England was at war with Spain, a battle fought at sea for the next twenty years in which Plymouth played a prominent role. It supplied the Royal Navy with many of the ships and men that defeated the Spanish Armada in the English Channel. Strategically situated on the southwest coast along the shores of Plymouth Sound, Plymouth was endowed with a naturally deep and protected harbor with direct access to the Atlantic Ocean via the English Channel. What is more, with a redeemed Hawkins as treasurer and later comptroller of the Royal Navy and a coterie of other famous naval heroes and explorers, Plymouth became an important naval stronghold, serving as a military staging area for the provisioning of manpower and supplies.[24] To add to Britain's defenses, a permanent naval base with an extensive dockyard system was built there in 1696 and expanded in the 1770s. From these docks, British naval invasions were led against other enemy nations throughout the particularly battle-scarred eighteenth century.[25] Yet despite the pioneering example of Sir John Hawkins, Plymouth had little direct involvement in the slave trade to Africa in subsequent years.[26] Instead, Plymouth's foreign trading interests rested in Newfoundland, France, and the colonies across the Atlantic, with exports of locally produced woolens, cloth, and herring. Another significant portion of Plymouth's merchant shipping trade involved the transportation of convicts to the colonies in the Americas in the seventeenth and eighteenth centuries.[27] By the end of the eighteenth century, Plymouth had grown to be the most prosperous town in Devon, a vital conduit for the surrounding regional network of commerce and communication.[28]

THE SOCIETY FOR EFFECTING THE ABOLITION OF THE SLAVE TRADE

In Plymouth, as elsewhere in England, the fight against the slave trade owed much to the organizing efforts of the Society for Effecting the Abolition of the Slave Trade, which was established in London on May 22, 1787 (hereafter referred to as either the London Committee or the Abolition Society). According to its mission statement, recorded in the minute book at the first meeting, the London Committee was organized "for procuring such Information and Evidence, and for distributing Clarkson's Essay [1785] and such other Publications, as may tend to foster the Abolition of the Slave trade, and for directing the application of such monies as are already, or may hereafter be collected, for the above purposes."[29] The chairman of the London Committee was the Anglican barrister Granville Sharp, who had developed a national reputation for defending the rights of black people in England, beginning with the case of James Somerset, decided in 1772 by Lord Mansfield.[30]

The Abolition Society gained its organizational structure through a vast web of committees, largely based on the long-standing networks of correspondents and committees previously instituted by its Quaker members.[31] Nine of its twelve charter members were Quakers, who relied upon their personal and religious ties to the Society of Friends to enlist subscribers and to set up committees in other towns and provinces around the nation.[32] As Judith Jennings explains, "The Quaker-dominated London Committee was providing organization and focus, while country abolitionists were providing a broad base of religious, socio-economic and geographic support."[33] The country committees focused on local agitation at the grassroots level, through collecting subscriptions, compiling petitions, and gathering evidence in support of abolition. Their work was essential to the success of the national petition drives of 1788 and 1790, wherein thousands of signatures were sent to Parliament from around the country calling for an end to the slave trade.

In addition to the established networks of Quaker Friends, the Abolition Society depended heavily on charter member Thomas Clarkson, its principal organizer. He was just twenty-five years old in 1785 when his dissertation, written in Latin, won first prize at Cambridge University.[34] It was translated into English the following year and published as *An Essay on the Slavery and Commerce of the Human Species, Particularly the African*.[35] This and his other publications fueled the propaganda machine of the London Committee and helped to shape the ideological and theoretical foundation of the abolitionist movement. According to his biographer, Clarkson conceived the abolition campaign "and mobilised the national voice behind it until, at the end, it was irresistible.... He was the architect and later the historian of the first national campaign for human rights that Britain had known."[36]

Clarkson was young, energetic, and determined. The poet Samuel Coleridge called him "the moral steam-engine, or the Giant with one idea."[37] That idea was abolition.

In the summer and fall of 1788, Clarkson traveled from London to establish country committees in the southwest, arriving at Plymouth in early November.[38] There he met William Elford (1749–1837), one of the leading figures of Plymouth and a true renaissance man—an artist, banker, politician, and scientist. As a friend of William Pitt the younger, the prime minister of England who would vigorously argue for the abolition of the slave trade in Parliament the 1790s, Elford was intimately tied to the political scene in London and attuned to the growing national interest in abolition. He would later serve as mayor of Plymouth (1797) and Member of Parliament for Plymouth (1796–1806).

At the first meeting of the Plymouth Committee, held on November 3, 1788, William Elford assumed the leadership role of chairman, while John Tingcombe—his business partner at the banking firm Elford, Tingcombe and Clerk—agreed to serve as treasurer.[39] Their sons, Jonathan Elford, Esq., and Jonathan Tingcombe; five ministers, and a doctor were among the twenty charter members. As with many of the other country committees and the London Committee in particular, the Plymouth Committee was made up of a middle- to upper-class membership. Elford and his fellow Plymouth Committee members took to the Abolition Society's purpose with passion, zeal, and ingenuity. Within two weeks of the committee's formation, they had obtained crucial evidence concerning the operation of the slave trade from James Bowen and Thomas Bell, masters in the Royal Navy.[40] They also took in subscriptions—donations—from thirty-five people including all the members of the committee and five women. In addition to gathering sensitive naval intelligence and raising funds, the Plymouth Committee assisted with the local circulation of abolitionist literature acquired through the London Committee.

By mid-1788 the London Committee had printed and distributed approximately 85,000 copies of at least twenty different books and tracts.[41] Their focus on information dissemination not only reflected the role of propaganda in driving the formation of a grassroots political campaign, it also pointed to the simultaneous development and revolution of print culture in England. By the beginning of the eighteenth century, weekly and then daily newspapers were places for posting information and notices, a form of mass media that abolitionists in the late eighteenth century were quick to use. The various country committee printed notices, articles, and advertisements announced and documented their activities, such as the formation of new committees, treasurer's reports, parliamentary updates, and new publications. Advances in printing technology and consumer marketing in the last half of the eighteenth century made it possible to print large quantities of written and illustrated materials for the growing number of people who were both literate and able to purchase books, pamphlets, and prints, and had the leisure time to read, collect, and enjoy them. This emerging moneyed and literate class of people developed a voracious appetite, especially for prints and illustrated books. Narratives of moral and social critique, such as *Pamela* (1741), were illustrated by the marketing mastermind William Hogarth (1697–1764). Following Hogarth, a harsher form of social and political critique dominated the subject matter of popular prints in the satirical works of James Gillray (1756–1815) and Isaac Cruikshank (1792–1878) who parodied the avarice and brutality of the slave trade. In Plymouth, for example, M. & B. HAYDON, "Booksellers, Printers and Stationers to His Royal Highness, Prince William Henry," advertised in the *Western Flying Post; or, Sherborne and Yeovil Mercury, and General Advertiser*, a local weekly, that they had "a large and elegant collection of English and foreign Prints, Engravings, Etchings, Chalk and Tinted prints from the most eminent masters, engraved by Bartolozzi, Ryland, Woollett, Hall Cipriani, &c. in plain black and gold, or gold burnished frames. Also some beautiful Drawings, by W. Payne, coloured from romantic views in Devonshire, in sets or single pairs."[42] The abolitionists, however, had avoided illustrative materials, with the exception of maps, charts, and the Abolitionist Society seal.

Headed by bankers, the Plymouth Committee was naturally experienced at raising money, part of which it funneled back to the London Committee and part of which it kept to develop and print its own publications. In this respect, and unlike many of the other country committees, it took an independent, activist role. After applauding a sermon on the slave trade given by Rev. John Bidlake (1755–1814), headmaster of Plymouth Grammar School, on December 28, 1788, the Plymouth Committee arranged to publish it as *Slave Trade: A Sermon Preached at Stonehouse Chapel on 28th December 1788* (1789).[43] Robert Hawker, vicar of Charles Parish, delivered another sermon on the slave trade on January 11, 1789 — resulting in a similar publication.[44] The Plymouth Committee arranged to publish these short tracts with M. & B. Haydon at approximately the same time as the engraving of the plan of the slave ship. On December 29, 1788, the Plymouth Committee announced publication of Bidlake's sermon and authorized "that 1500 plates, representing the mode of stowing slaves on board the African trader with remarks on it, be struck off, and distributed gratis."[45] In its first month of operation, this country committee had displayed an impressive burst of productivity.

Most significantly, the Plymouth Committee was responsible for pioneering a new form of popular visual culture — the political (abolitionist) print. The illustration, titled *Plan of an African Ship's Lower Deck with Negroes in the Proportion of Only One to a Ton*, was a separate copperplate engraving that was attached to a four-page pamphlet (see fig. 1.1). The addition of visual illustrations to written tracts would revolutionize the way that abolitionists fought to end the slave trade. Previous scholars have overlooked this very first printing of the plan of a slave ship, assuming that the second version of this image, published by the Plymouth Committee as a broadside (see fig. 1.10), came first.[46]

Elford, as chairman of the Plymouth Committee, was largely responsible for the descriptive text of the 8⅞ × 8⅞" pamphlet, which was printed by the local firm of Trewman and Haydon.[47] The accompanying 6¾ × 16" plate bears no signature to suggest the name of the artist or the engraver, but scholars generally credit Elford for the design of the plate. He was an artist, in fact an accomplished painter of landscapes in oils and watercolor. As early as 1774, he exhibited his work at the Royal Academy and continued to show his paintings there up until his death in 1837.[48]

In addition, Elford was a banker, someone with a precise and organized mind who dealt with numbers and money on a daily basis. Moreover, he was regarded as an amateur scientist and was nominated a fellow of the Royal Society and the Linnean Society in 1790.[49] Finally, as someone who had deep political, social, business, and family ties to Plymouth, Elford had firsthand knowledge of maritime issues and connections to the Royal Navy.[50] It would appear that the "important intelligence" gained by Elford and the members of the Plymouth Committee concerned early access to the report being prepared by Captain Parrey of the Royal Navy.

Elford studied the meticulous investigative work of Captain Parrey, who was commissioned by the Privy Council of the House of Commons to investigate ships engaged in the slave trade that were docked in Liverpool in early 1788. Parrey interviewed slave ship captains and sailors, took precise measurements of the ships, and examined their sailing records, including muster rolls for slaves and seamen.[51] Most useful to Elford in coming up with an idea for the design of the plan of the slave ship were the small diagrams that Parrey found among slave ship captains, used to indicate where the allotted cargo, *human cargo*, would be stored. These were simple hand drawings of the outline of the ship, indicating the cargo area and the space allotted for the different types of goods to be stowed. They were a type of visual shorthand apparently used to increase the efficiency of packing ships. Along with evidence previously compiled by various abolitionist committees throughout the country, Elford used this information to depict and describe the amount of space allowed to each enslaved man, woman, boy, and girl in claustrophobic detail.

> In the Men's apartment, the space allowed to each is six feet in length, by sixteen inches in breadth.—The Boys are each allowed five feet by fourteen inches.—The Women, five feet ten inches, by sixteen inches; and the Girls, four feet by one foot each.—The perpendicular height between the Decks, is five feet eight inches.[52]

In the engraving, four labeled sections are swollen with shaded figures representing enslaved Africans. Visible are the divided, labeled quarters for men, women, boys, and girls, whose bodies are arranged, flesh pressing against flesh, vertically in rows across the width of the plan. In the bow, there are 120 men in four rows of 30; in the midsection, there are 84 women in four rows of 21 and 60 boys in five rows of 12; and, in the stern, there are 30 girls in three rows of ten, totaling 297. The "Men's room" contains the largest (and most numerous) figures, and the "Girl's room" contains the smallest (and least numerous) figures, referring to the amount of space allotted to each. The men, women, and children represent all of the necessary pieces of a family unit, yet they likely were unrelated, stolen from several different families, villages, and regions.

The plate and the pamphlet represent the measurements and sailing records of an actual ship investigated by Parrey, the *Brooks* of Liverpool, at 297 tons' burden.[53] This number—297 tons *burden*—refers to the amount of space available for stowing cargo, or, in other words, the cargo capacity.[54] The *Brooks* was built at the Liverpool dockyards in 1781 for James Jones and Joseph Brooks Jr. It was used primarily for the triangular trade, sailing between Liverpool, Anamabou (where the slave factory, Fort William, still stands on the present-day Ghanaian coast), and Kingston, Jamaica.[55] Captain Parrey had ascertained that the *Brooks* had inhumanely "packed" and grossly overcrowded its human cargo on many a voyage. To be sure, it was an example of a slaver at its worst, and this is one of the reasons why the Plymouth Committee selected it as the basis for the plan of the slave ship. Moreover, the Plymouth Committee's choice of a notorious Liverpool slaver explicitly implicated that city as Britain's most profitable port involved in the triangular trade.[56]

This first plan of the slave ship reflects a particular moment in the abolitionist struggle. Specifically, the plan represents a graphic depiction of the regulated slave trade, made possible by the adoption of Sir William Dolben's motion to restrict the overcrowding of slave ships. His bill also included a measure requiring each ship to carry a doctor to care for both the enslaved and the crew.[57] Passed in June 1788, the Dolben Act, also known as the Slave Trade Regulation Act, regulated the cargo capacity of slave ships by limiting the number of the enslaved based on the tonnage of each vessel as follows: a ratio of five slaves per three tons up to 200 tons, and then one slave per additional ton thereafter.[58] In short, the Dolben Act aimed to reduce the most heinous abuses as well as slave and seaman mortality by relieving overcrowding.[59] This piece of legislation represented an early political victory for the abolitionists, one in which the role of public agitation played a significant part. That summer, in the first important petition drive, abolitionists collected tens of thousands of signatures around the country calling for an end to the slave trade.

Equiano, for one, was grateful for the Slave Trade Regulation Act. In a letter to Dolben, he and his fellow Sons of Africa wrote: "We beg your permission to lay in this manner our humble thankfulness before you, for a benevolent law obtained at your motion, by which the miseries of our unhappy brethren, on the coast of Africa, may be alleviated, and by which the lives of many, though destined for the present to a cruel slavery, may be preserved, as we hope, for future and for greater mercies."[60] Regulation was only the first step—a victory in part because lawmakers had been mobilized. If they could regulate the slave trade, they could also end it. Yet despite regulation, conditions in the Middle Passage remained inhuman. That the small black figures were squeezed together without any available space for the slightest movement—indeed like "herring in a barrel"—made this argument abundantly clear.

The Abolition Society initially focused on ending the slave trade, rather than ending slavery in the colonies, because the abolition of *slavery* was not only a direct interference with the planters' property (and so it was argued a fundamental challenge to property rights in general), but also an encroachment on the rights of the colonial legislatures. Whereas, the abolition of the *slave trade* was within the jurisdiction of Parliament, which could regulate commerce within the British Empire and enforce its decisions through the Royal Navy and customs officials. In this respect, *Plan of an African Ship's Lower Deck with Negroes Stowed in the Proportion of Only One to a Ton* was brilliantly designed to focus attention on the specific goal of the abolitionist movement at this time. Moreover, it was the first abolitionist publication to succinctly situate the argument for dismantling the slave trade within the discrete confines of the brutal Middle Passage. Other images from this period, such as George Morland's painting *Execrable Human Traffic, or The Affectionate African* (1788), which was subsequently reproduced as an engraving, fail to engage this process in a way that begins to convey the nightmarish dimension of this experience (fig. 1.5).[61] This painting was the first on the subject of the slave trade to be exhibited at the Royal Academy in London in 1788. It shows the sale and separation of an African family on the coast. European slave traders, presumably British, are shown threatening one African man with a stick and pulling an African woman and her child away from the commotion to the awaiting boats. In the background two traders converse, one white, the other black. A coffle of slaves can be seen in the distance coming toward the shore, as can the awaiting slave ship just off the shore. The entire scene is sentimentalized to evoke an emotional response, albeit one that was quite different from that of the slave ship icon.

THE PLYMOUTH COMMITTEE'S FIRST PLAN AND PAMPHLET

The little pamphlet produced by the Plymouth Committee, *Plan of an African Ship's Lower Deck with Negroes Stowed in the Proportion of Only One to a Ton,* was groundbreaking in many significant ways. It was, after all, the first abolitionist publication to combine image and text—and to assert the primacy of visual illustration. Prior abolitionist tracts only consisted of printed text with the possible addition of the Abolition Society seal showing the shackled, kneeling slave encircled by the motto "Am I Not a Man and a Brother?" (after October 1787 when it was designed). It wasn't until the Plymouth Committee added the oblong plate of the slave ship icon that prints became integrated with abolitionist tracts on a regular basis. This innovation of adding an explanatory illustration (or having long explanatory remarks for an illustration) would soon revolutionize the way that abolitionists conducted their campaign of garnering public support when the slave ship icon was printed as a broadside shortly thereafter and posted for public notice.

The plan itself is schematic—a plan and not a realistic representation (fig. 1.6). Indeed, it could be and has been considered crude. But this "crudeness," its simplicity, is part of the engraving's extraordinary power. The lower deck is shaped like a coffin, a metaphor for the death, both physical and spiritual, that came to many of the victims of the Middle Passage. The plan is meant to depict the enslaved Africans in a reclining position, as they were said to be stowed lying down on bare wooden planks, packed in a way that government regulations condoned. Alive, they are forced to assume the position of buried corpses, as if the line between life and death had become so slight that it had become all but indistinguishable. Even though the figures are meant to represent people, they are the human *cargo* and thus are shown stacked like barrels or some other inanimate, nonliving commodity. Here the power is achieved not by some completely new conception but by a classic revelation of economic and human realities. What is invisible and hidden is made visible. Not only does the plan expose what is hidden below decks, it also engages the numerous ship plans/packing lists that label what is placed in the ship's holds but do not show the commodities as they are actually stowed there. In fact, the

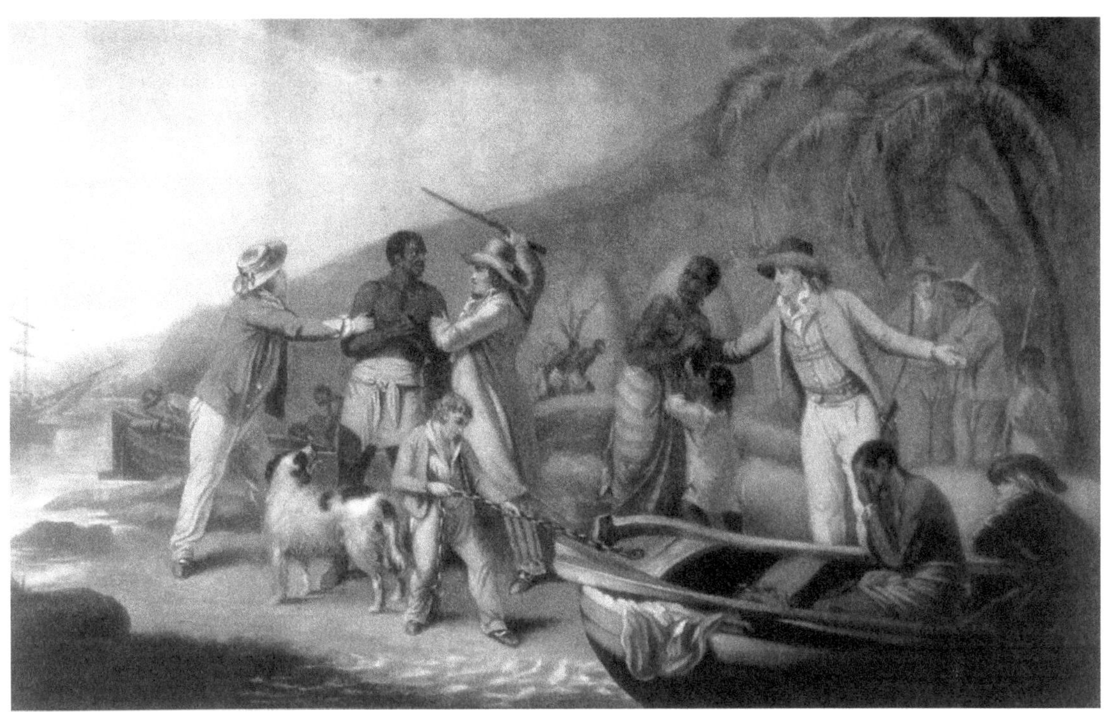

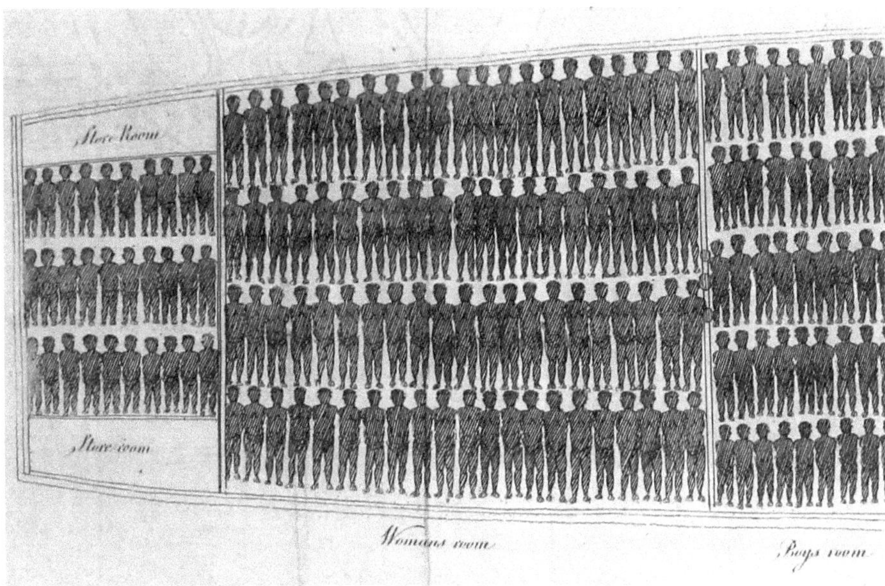

1.5 TOP

George Morland, *Execrable Human Traffic, or The Affectionate African*, 1788, oil on canvas, 85.1 × 121.9 cm.

1.6 BOTTOM

Detail, Plymouth Committee, *Plan of an African Ship's Lower Deck with Negroes in the Proportion of Only One to a Ton*, 1789, copper engraving.

Plymouth Committee's *Plan of an African Ship's Lower Deck* retains two such residual areas labeled simply "Store Room." The descriptive names for the other spaces are now relegated to the exterior area of the ship because the plan just doesn't show what is being stored, but *how*. Labels, words are replaced by representations of people, metaphorically by the people who have been nothing more than abstract, "dead" words. In this way, *Plan of An African Ship's Lower Deck* differs from many of the plans (either of the simple hand-rendered type or of the more detailed naval architectural type) that were gathered by Captain Parrey for his investigation of the slave trade. And it certainly differed from the hand-colored engraving of *La Marie Séraphique*, celebrating its third successful slaving voyage from Angola to Cap-Français in 1773 (fig. 1.7).[62]

The engraving of *La Marie Séraphique* is dominated by a beautifully detailed scene showing the ship on the day that it began to sell its cargo of enslaved Africans at Cap-Français in the West Indies. There is a festive spirit. The sun is shining but it's not too hot. A slight breeze lifts the surface of the deeply hued aquamarine water, setting in motion a sea of rolling waves. Everyone—blacks and whites—is milling about deck as the planters arrive from the shore in approaching boats. It appears to be a glorious day to rejoice a safe passage with no one apparently suffering too much for the experience. Several European women dressed in white contrast with the naked Africans though they seem to mix freely. On the left side of the ship, some of the planters and their ladies are preparing to sit down to an elegantly prepared luncheon at a large white table underneath the protection of a canvas canopy. Meanwhile, nearby and on the right side of the ship just beyond the central barricade, black bodies are being inspected, prodded, poked as objects of sale, chattels. But judging by the calm and merry atmosphere, all this would suggest that the ship is clean of disease, unpleasant smells, death, and danger. What happens in the hold remains safely hidden, though we can surmise that two-thirds of the human cargo is baking below the deck. These unhappy souls remain out of sight, except for the "Coupe du Navire"—the cut of the ship, which reveals the compartmentalized holds in a lateral cross section. In scale, this more schematic rendering is much smaller than the ship it portrays up above, yet it too is elegantly colored and meticulously detailed. It shows how barrels used for drinking water are stored even as other areas are identified for specific functions but the method of stowage is not rendered visually. For instance, the spaces designated as "F" and "G"—those areas that hold the human cargo—are empty, clean—sanitized. In the Plymouth Committee engraving of *Plan of an African Ship's Lower Deck*, Elford reverses the order, choosing to show what is normally shrouded in darkness, filth, and stench.

Elford's plan, with its flat perspective and uniform rows of small human figures, is meant to show the enslaved Africans lying down. At the same time, they appear to be standing up and facing the viewer—staring out at the readers as if they were silently asking for their assistance, begging, demanding to be counted. Yet, as human bodies they are unable to speak, their silence testifying to the shock of their confinement—their temporary powerlessness—and the need for others to act on their behalf. It is a melodramatic image in the way discussed by literary scholar

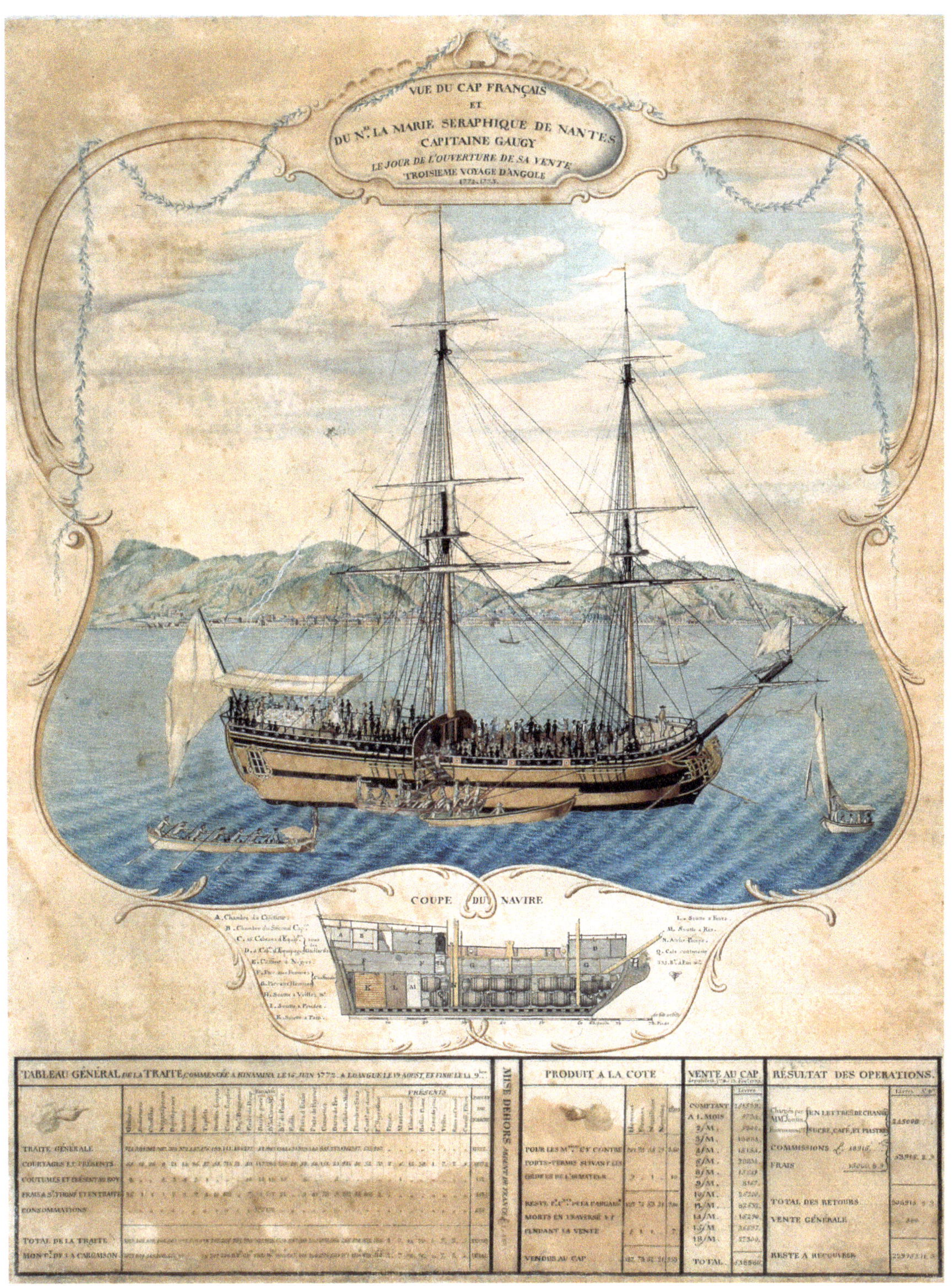

1.7

Anonymous, *Vue du Cap-Français et du Navire
"La Marie-Séraphique"* watercolor engraving from
Capitaine Gaugy, *Troisieme Voyage d'Angole*, 1772–73.

Peter Brooks (b. 1938), where innocents cannot talk because what they need to express is beyond words.[63] These figures that represent enslaved people are also innocents, "torn from their dearest friends and connections, sometimes by force, and sometimes by treachery." Because of its "crudeness," this image has a dialectical power as the spectator oscillates between these different possible frames and responses to the image. But this is only the initial reading, just a glimpse inside the hold of the slave ship at black figures that resemble the stick figures, the icons of contemporary signage.

The engraving is a template that demands an imaginative response even as it bears the imprint of an imaginative mind. The image is a starting point for the viewer—a point of reference while the text enables the reader to elaborate on the image in her mind. The first paragraph simply identifies the image: "The annexed Plate represents the lower deck of an African Ship of 297 tons burthen, with the Slaves stowed on it, in the proportion of not quite one to a ton." The next paragraph provides an explanation for the way the figures are depicted by describing the amount of space allotted to each. Men are each given a space six feet in length by fifteen inches in breadth, boys are allowed five feet by fourteen inches, women, five feet ten inches by fifteen inches, and so forth. Here the reader might find herself returning to the image for a body count. The very number of figures that are shown—just under three hundred—is beyond quick and easy counting and testifies to the scale.

At this point, with the relationship between text and image firmly established, the reader must start to elaborate from the schematic. This immediately becomes evident at the beginning of the third paragraph, which states, "The Men are fastened together, two and two, by hand cuffs on their wrists and by irons rivetted on their legs." What might be the most striking thing about this first plan of the slave ship is the fact that the figures representing the men are drawn *without* shackles, yet these devices of restraint are mentioned more than once in the text. Reading about the shackles but not seeing them in the plan creates a disconcerting tension for the reader. The reader must pause, must focus and question what is not shown—shackles and leg irons, one of the symbols of slavery, of the coffle, of physical restraint, of bodily confinement. If the plan is supposed to be a true representation of what is described in the text, why are the shackles missing? Were they left out intentionally or was their absence a simple oversight? Or might the tension between absence and presence suggest the possibility of liberation—that they should be free, free of shackles? Either in life or death. Nor are their captors anywhere in sight. As silent as they are made to seem in the text, they are invisible in the plan.

The pamphlet now goes on to specify a daily routine for the enslaved Africans in the Middle Passage:

> They are brought up on the main deck every day, about eight o'clock, and as each pair ascend, a strong chain, fastened by ring-bolts to the deck, is passed through their Shackles; a precaution absolutely necessary to prevent Insurrections.— In this state, if the weather is favourable, they are permitted to remain about one-third part of the twenty-four hours, and during this interval they are fed, and their apartment below is cleaned.[64]

The text now turns the static rendering of the slave ship into a narrative. As it sails across the ocean, we are asked to imagine the daily routine. While this paragraph appears to refer only to the experience and treatment of the enslaved Africans, it silently acknowledges the presence of their captors. It was the ship's officers and crew, or in some cases their slaves or servants, who brought the captives up on deck each day, who fed them, who cooked for them, who cleaned their apartments, who fastened and unfastened their shackles, whom they would rebel against. The captors are kept at the periphery of this story. It is the experience of the enslaved that the reader is asked to imagine—the subjectivity of peoples who are daily denied any subjectivity. The reader is, in fact, encouraged to imagine herself in their places. The officers and crew are not rendered lest the focus shifts and this identification process be disrupted.

The text has required the reader to make such an imaginative leap that by the fourth paragraph, its authors (Elford and his associates) imagine the reader to be objecting. The conditions being described must be an extreme case. The reader's instinct is to pull back, looking for a way to discount what she has just encountered.

> It may perhaps be conceived, from the crouded [*sic*] state in which the Slaves appear in the Plate, than an unusual and exaggerated instance has been produced; this, however, is so far from being the case, that no ship, if her intended cargo can be procured, ever carries a less number than one to a Ton, and the usual practice has been to carry nearly double that number.[65]

This becomes an opportunity to underscore the ludicrous inadequacy of the Slave Trade Regulation Act and to return to the template and the scene below deck. We are asked to elaborate still further on the scene below deck, which is far worse than what has been shown. The text takes us one level deeper into this hell.

> And the *Brooks*, of Liverpool, a capital ship, from which the above sketch was proportioned, did, in one voyage actually carry 609 Slaves, which is more than double the number that appear in the Plate.—The mode of stowing them was a follows—Platforms, or wide shelves were erected, between the decks, extending so far from the sides towards the middle of the vessel, as to be capable of containing four additional rows of Slaves, by which means the perpendicular height between each tier, after allowing for the beams and the platforms, was reduced to two feet six inches; for they could not even fit in an erect posture; besides which, in the Men's apartment, instead of four rows; five were stowed by placing the heads of one between the thighs of another.[66]

What has just been described is even worse in smaller ships. Each time we get set to protest, our descent into this hell only deepens. The costs of this horror are now quantified: "of an estimated 100,000 Africans destined for slavery in the New World, 45,000 will die either in transport or in the first two years of their arrival." At this point, the text engages in an intellectual argument to which the outwardly staring figures bear continued witness. The ending of this horror—so redolent with human misery and senseless death—is the sole goal. The icon now acts like a fetish in the classic sense; by focusing on this depiction of the Middle Passage, of the slave ship, the underlying goal of the abolitionists is obscured. This might seem to be a pact with the devil, but just as regulation of the slave trade was a stepping stone to ending the slave trade, its demise would only be a stepping stone to the end of slavery. The commitment to this progression is so transparent that the icon along with these calculated reassurances must arrest the wavering reader-viewer. Indeed, the text finally acknowledges the people who make their living in the slave trade—the seamen who live above deck but die with untold frequency. Now it asks the viewer-reader—moved by the power of the engraving—to intercede. Whatever the nature or depth of their conviction, they have the rare opportunity to act. The end result of this encounter should be a viewer-reader who is committed to the cause of ending the slave trade and who can respond to the opportunities for political action with the same kind of imagination and passion elicited by the image and text.

The Plymouth Committee distributed their initial pamphlet and attached plate locally and to abolition committees in England, including the main organizing London Committee. Upon receiving his copy of the pamphlet, Clarkson shared it with Equiano sometime on or before February 7, 1789, as we have seen. The London Committee, under the direction of Mr. Hoare, then sent a copy of the plate and pamphlet to the New Society for Promoting the Abolition of Slavery in Philadelphia on March 3, 1789. It arrived in the United States somewhere between April 27 and May 11, 1789.[67]

THE PENNSYLVANIA ABOLITION SOCIETY/AMERICAN MUSEUM PLAN

According to its minutes, the executive committee of the New Society for Promoting the Abolition of Slavery (henceforth the Pennsylvania Abolition Society) met on May 11, 1789. Although the organization's august chairman was none other than Benjamin Franklin, he did not as a rule attend these meetings, which were chaired by Richard Wells. On this occasion, "a letter from the Committee of the London Society dated March 3, 1789 was read" and "three pamphlets accompanying it were also laid before the Committee."[68] Also mentioned was "an account of the Manner in which the Africans are accommodated in Vessels when they are stowed in the proportion of one to a Ton by the Plymouth Committee with explanatory copper plate."[69] At the same meeting, the Pennsylvania Abolition Society decided to publish the Plymouth Committee's pamphlet and plate, with "the necessary introduction." Responsibility for this assignment was given to Richard Wells and Caleb Lownes. This was to become the first version of the slave ship icon to be printed and distributed in the United States.[70]

The Pennsylvania Abolition Society worked closely with Philadelphia printer and engraver Mathew Carey, who published a copy of the Plymouth Committee engraving of the slave ship. This was inserted into the May 1789 issue of the *American Museum* magazine and was accompanied by an article titled "Remarks on the Slave Trade," which used modified text from the Plymouth Committee pamphlet[71] (fig. 1.8). A prominent monthly magazine that Carey both edited and published in Philadelphia, the *American Museum* was distributed widely in the United States,

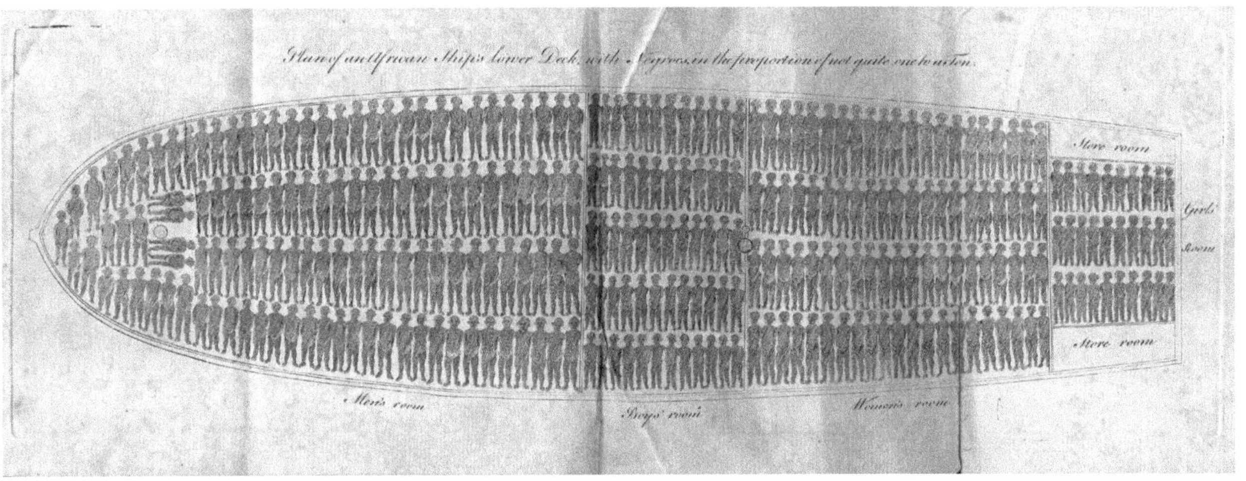

1.8

Mathew Carey, *Plan of an African Ship's Lower
Deck with Negroes in the Proportion of Only
One to a Ton*, copper engraving extracted from
the *American Museum*, May 1789.

Great Britain, and France. Subscribers included senators and congressmen as well
as President George Washington. The president had earlier endorsed the journal,
saying, "I am of the opinion, that the work is not only eminently calculated to disseminate political, agricultural, philosophical, and other valuable information—but
that it has *been uniformly conducted with taste, attention and propriety*."[72] As the
Committee of Correspondence for the Pennsylvania Abolition Society wrote to the
London Committee:

> The small Pamphlet from the Society at Plymouth especially struck our atten-
> tion, & we have had an engraving of the print done here, in order to introduce
> it into one of our monthly publications, entitled the American Museum, which
> hath a very extensive circulation but we shall be obliged to accompany it with
> some additional remarks suited to our more advanced stage of the Business;
> because we observe that publication cautiously avoids the Idea of Emancipation
> & is confined to the abolition of the Slave Trade.[73]

In what sense was Pennsylvania "more advanced"? For one thing, the state had
passed a law in 1780 for the gradual abolition of slavery, and these laws were tight-
ened still further in March 1788.[74] This second bill declared:

> If any person or persons shall build, fit, equip, man or otherwise prepare any
> ship or vessel, within any port of this state, or shall cause any ship or other ves-
> sel to sail from any port of this state, for the purpose of carrying on a trade or
> traffic in slaves, to, from or between Europe, Asia, Africa or America, or any
> places or countries whatever, or of transporting slaves to or from one port or

place to another, in any part or parts of the world, such ship or vessel, her tackle, furniture, apparel, and other appurtenances, shall be forfeited to the commonwealth. . . . And, moreover, all and every person and persons so building, fitting out, etc., shall forfeit £1,000.[75]

A similar bill was passed in neighboring Delaware early in the following year.

Although Pennsylvania had taken a clear-cut stand on the slave trade, the situation was, needless to say, more complex. If slavery was effectively ended in Pennsylvania, that state had now become part of the United States where the constitution recognized slavery and the slave trade. When the United States Constitution went into effect, there were only three states where the transatlantic slave trade was still legal: South Carolina, Georgia, and North Carolina (though North Carolina had a prohibitive duty on the importation of slaves).[76] Nonetheless, as W. E. B. Du Bois has remarked, "In 1787–1788, the New England States forbade the participation of their citizens in the traffic [i.e., the slave trade]. It was this wave of legislation against the traffic which did so much to blind the nation as to the strong hold which slavery still had on the country."[77] The Plymouth Committee's *Plan of an African Ship's Lower Deck with Negroes in the Proportion of Only One to a Ton* reached the United States while the First Congress was in session and as the first debate about slavery (May 13) was imminent.[78] Its principal topic was to be a high tariff designed to discourage and reduce the slave trade where it still operated in the United States. Discussion would be unexpectedly heated as South Carolina and Georgia stood in protest. Unfortunately, action on the proposal was then postponed until the following year.[79]

The Pennsylvania Abolition Society recognized the slave ship icon as a powerful weapon as it sought to lobby against slavery. Since its engraving was a direct copy from the Elford print, the process produced a mirror image with the bow now pointing to the left. The resulting illustration was still the same size and format but printed on paper that measured 5¾ inches by 17¼ inches (slightly narrower and slightly longer). The figures appear to be just as detailed as in the original, while the main identifying caption ("Plan of an African Ship's Lower Deck, with Negroes, in the Proportion of Not Quite One to a Ton") has been slightly changed with the substitution of "not quite" for "only." In fact, this small change made the caption for the engraving conform to the first paragraph of the pamphlet, eliminating a small inconsistency. The labels identifying each of the four sections of the plan ("Men's room," "Boy's room," and such) remain identical. Both the elegant hand lettering on the plate and the type used for the article are similar in style and spirit to that appearing on the pioneering Plymouth Committee engraving and pamphlet. This respect for the Plymouth Committee's work is also evident in Wells's introductory remarks to the Plymouth Committee text, which fully acknowledge the image's provenance. In addition, this republication of *Plan of an African Ship's Lower Deck . . .* retains the original "signature": "By the Plymouth Committee, W. Elford, chairman."

The text for "Remarks on the Slave Trade," the title that Wells and Lownes had given to the *American Museum* article, filled the front page of the magazine and

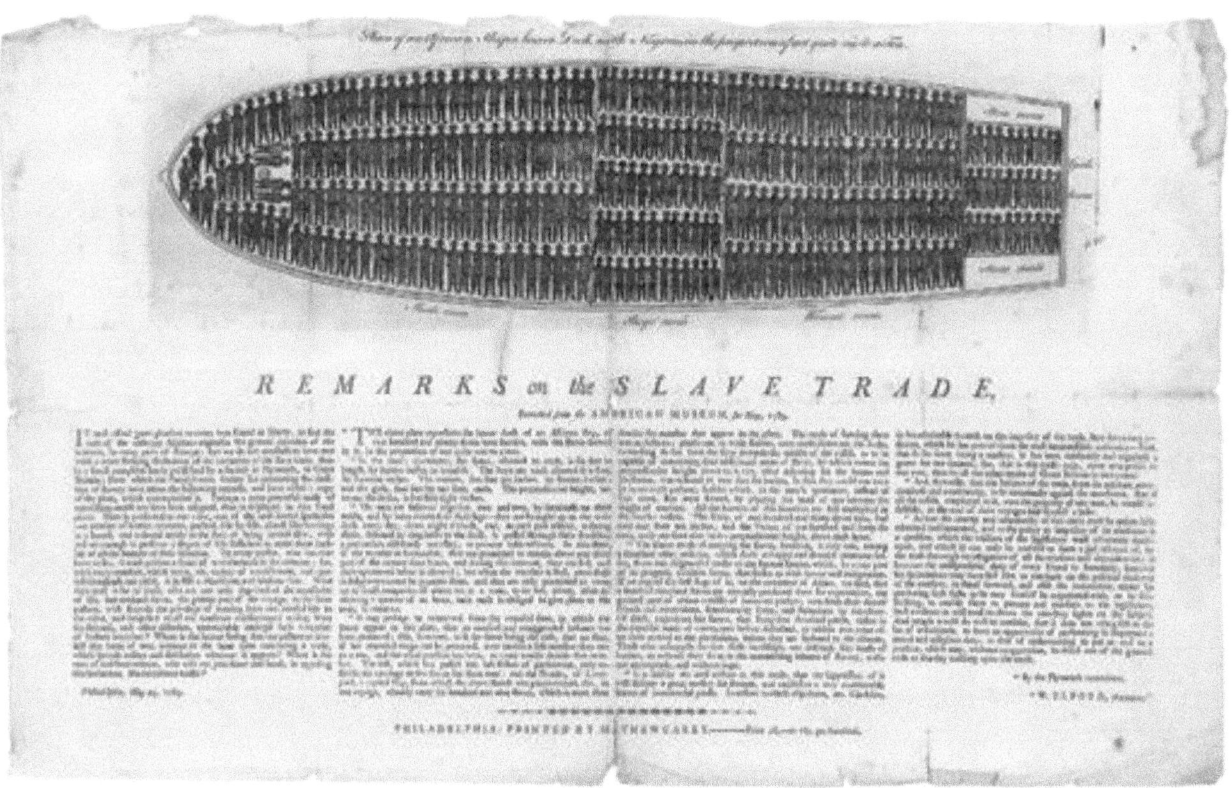

1.9

New Society for Promoting the Abolition
of Slavery, *Remarks on the Slave Trade*
(Philadelphia: Mathew Carey, 1789).

almost the entire second page as well. The illustration was attached to the front
page or cover and opened out to the left in such a way that it was possible to view
the illustration and the first page of text at the same time (fig. 1.9). The pages of the
magazine measured four by eight inches; consequently, when the reader turned the
page only the stern of the slave ship was obscured. Carey thus went to considerable
effort to enable readers to read the text in relationship to the image.

The biggest difference in this first American version and others to follow comes
with the written remarks, which associate the engraving with a different political
purpose, one that calls for the abolition of slavery. To achieve this, Wells and his
colleague added a new introductory paragraph:

> It must afford great pleasure to every true friend to liberty to find the case of the
> unhappy Africans engrosses the general attention of the humane in many parts
> of Europe: but we do not recollect to have met with a more striking illustration
> of the barbarity of the slave trade, than in a small pamphlet lately published by
> a Society at Plymouth, in Great Britain; from which the Pennsylvania Society
> for promoting the abolition of slavery have taken the following extracts, and
> have added a copy of the plate that accompanied it. Perhaps a more powerful

mode of conviction could not have been adopted, than is displayed in this small piece. Here is presented to our view, one of the most horrid spectacles—a number of human creatures, packed, side by side, almost like herrings in a barrel, and reduced nearly to the state of being buried alive, with just air enough to preserve a degree of life sufficient to make them sensible of all the horrors of their situation. To every person, who has been at sea, it must present a scene of wretchedness in the extreme; for, with every comfort, which room, air, variety of nourishment, and careful cleanliness can yield, it is still a wearisome and irksome state. What then must it be to those, who are not only deprived of the necessaries of life, but confined down, the greater part of the voyage, to the same posture, with scarcely the privilege of turning from one painful side to the other, and subjected to all the nauseous consequences arising from sea-sickness, and other disorders, unavoidable amongst such a number of forlorn wretches? Where is the human being, that can picture himself this scene of woe, without at the same time execrating a trade, which spreads misery and desolation wherever it appears? Where is the man of real benevolence, who will not joint heart and hand, in opposing this barbarous, this iniquitous traffic?[80]

This new paragraph replaced the sixth paragraph in the Plymouth Committee pamphlet ("The inhumanity of this Trade…"), designed to attract those in England who might be ready to support the end of the slave trade but were not yet ready to abolish slavery in the colonies.[81] The slave trade was still an issue, but political alignments were different and the goal of ending slavery in the United States seemed achievable. The engraving of the slave ship's lower deck focused attention on the slave trade, but behind it was the larger barbarism of slavery itself. Precisely for this reason it could be—and was—appropriated and repositioned by those whose officially stated goal was more radical—the end of slavery itself—than originally intended.

The new text is notable for several reasons. Not only does it duly credit the Plymouth Committee, it also offers an interpretation of the image that reinforces its iconic appeal. It begins by noting the print's extraordinary power as it shows human beings packed like salted fish in a barrel. Then it notes that they are, in effect, buried alive. Next it encourages reader-viewers to identify with the enslaved Africans represented by these figures. It asks them to recall their own journeys by sea, which in the eighteenth century were still noted for their discomfort, and then asks them to imagine making such a journey under the conditions experienced by those confined in the holds of slave ships. This new text likewise brings the reader back to the image. Finally, it appeals to the reader to oppose this barbarous traffic in souls. In many respects, it rehearses the mental journey that the reader will make in engaging the subsequent text that originated with the Plymouth Committee.

By the time "Remarks on the Slave Trade" had appeared in the *American Museum*, the setback for those arguing for the abolition of slavery in the First Congress had become a reality, reaffirming the need for increased activism. Moreover, the publication itself was doubtlessly well received. In a late May or June meeting of the executive committee for the Pennsylvania Abolition Society, Wells and

Lownes reported that they "had had an engraving of the Plate done and the Editor of the Museum had engaged to publish the whole." They also proposed that a number of separate copies "be procured for distribution among our members and correspondents." The Executive Committee then ordered them to "procure 750 of such copies at the expense of the Society."[82]

These copies took the form of a horizontal broadside measuring approximately 9 by 15 inches. The engraving appears prominently across the top of the broadside, and the remarks are printed in four columns underneath (fig. 1.9).[83] The title for the article in the *American Museum* is now given greater prominence, with large and varied type face ("REMARKS on the SLAVE TRADE"). Credit is also given to the *American Museum* ("*Extracted from the* AMERICAN MUSEUM, for May 1789"). The date of May 29, 1789, was added at the bottom of the left-hand column, which is devoted to the remarks written by Wells and Lownes. The previously selected Plymouth Committee text fills the remaining three columns. A streamer along the bottom states "PHILADELPHIA; PRINTED BY MATHEW CAREY, FOR THE NEW SOCIETY FOR PROMOTING THE ABOLITION OF SLAVERY." This broadside must have been a success, since in the minute for the quarterly meeting of the society on July 6, 1789, the publication committee of Wells and Lownes was "directed to procure 1,500 additional Copies of the Plymouth Pamphlet and also to send a copy to each of the members of the Senate and House of Representatives and to the President of the US."[84] These were printed by July 20, 1789.[85] Although approximately the same size, this latest version of the broadside displays a number of minor adjustments (fig. 1.10). The columns were reduced from four to three—with the column width slightly longer. Carey's name has been removed, along with the streamer along the bottom edge. The fact that the material was extracted from the *American Museum* has been retained but directly underneath in large type has been added: "and published by order of the Pennsylvania Society for promoting the ABOLITION of slavery, &c." The plate that accompanies all three Philadelphia versions of "Remarks on the Slave Trade" continues to show the male figures without shackles.

The shift from a four-page pamphlet with accompanying illustration or a magazine article with a special insert to a broadside or poster was a logical development for several reasons. In general, printers routinely moved between engravings that were meant to be displayed on walls and engravings that were incorporated into books. Often purchasers of books were expected to remove one or more of the illustrations for display. Sometimes these were taken to be hand colored before they were hung on the wall. As J. H. Plumb notes, by the end of the eighteenth century, "the print had been exploited in all its possibilities and was reaching out and responding to an ever widening market."[86] Consequently, these few innovations with the slave ship icon—from plate and pamphlet to magazine insert to broadside—demonstrated how dynamic the possibilities were in the late 1780s. Numerous copies of an image could be reproduced and dispersed to distant points, where they could be copied in different formats. Text could be discretely cut, changed, or recontextualized by introductory remarks. Different versions or printings, with subtle changes often hard to distinguish, could be made. One aspect of this was

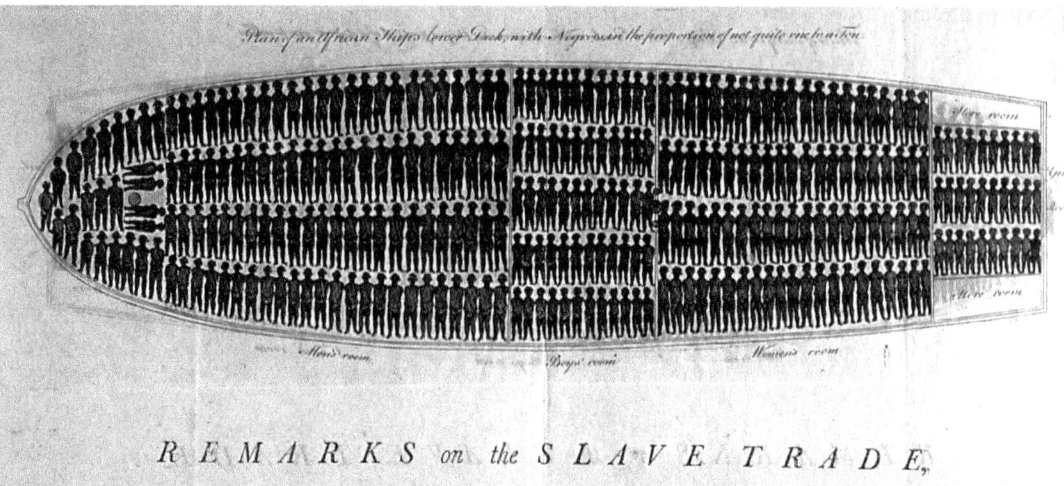

REMARKS on the SLAVE TRADE,

Extracted from the AMERICAN MUSEUM, for May, 1789.

And published by order of the Pennsylvania society for promoting the ABOLITION of slavery, &c.

IT must afford great pleasure to every true friend to liberty, to find the case of the unhappy Africans engrosses the general attention of the humane, in many parts of Europe; but we do not recollect to have met with a more striking illustration of the barbarity of the slave trade, than in a small pamphlet lately published by a society at Plymouth, in Great Britain; from which the Pennsylvania society for promoting the abolition of slavery have taken the following extracts, and have added a copy of the plate, which accompanied it. Perhaps a more powerful mode of conviction could not have been adopted, than is displayed in this small piece. Here is presented to our view, one of the most horrid spectacles—a number of human creatures, packed, side by side, almost like herrings in a barrel, and reduced nearly to the state of being buried alive, with just air enough to preserve a degree of life, sufficient to make them sensible of all the horrors of their situation. To every person, who has ever been at sea, it must present a scene of wretchedness in the extreme; for, with every comfort, which room, air, variety of nourishment, and careful cleanliness can yield, it is still a wearisome and irksome state. What then must it be to those, who are not only deprived of the necessaries of life, but confined down, the greater part of the voyage, to the same posture, with scarcely the privilege of turning from one painful side to the other, and subjected to all the noxious consequences arising from sea-sickness, and other disorders, unavoidable amongst such a number of forlorn wretches? Where is the human being, that can picture to himself this scene of woe, without at the same time execrating a trade, which spreads misery and desolation where ever it appears? Where is the man of real benevolence, who will not join heart and hand, in opposing this barbarous, this iniquitous traffic?

Philadelphia, May 29, 1789.

"THE above plate represents the lower deck of an African ship, of two hundred and ninety-seven tons burden, with the slaves stowed on it, in the proportion of not quite one to a ton.

"In the men's apartment, the space, allowed to each, is six feet in length, by sixteen inches in breadth. The boys are each allowed five feet, by fourteen inches. The women, five feet ten inches, by sixteen inches; and the girls, four feet by one foot, each. The perpendicular height, between the decks, is five feet eight inches.

"The men are fastened together, two and two, by handcuffs on their wrists, and by irons rivetted on their legs—they are brought up on the main deck every day, about eight o'clock, and as each pair ascend, a strong chain, fastened by ringbolts to the deck, is passed through their shackles; a precaution absolutely necessary, to prevent insurrections. In this state, if the weather is favourable, they are permitted to remain about one third part of the twenty-four hours, and during this interval they are fed, and their apartment below is cleaned; but when the weather is bad, even these indulgences cannot be granted them, and they are only permitted to come up in small companies, of about ten at a time, to be fed, where, after remaining a quarter of an hour, each mess is obliged to give place to the next, in rotation.

"It may perhaps be conceived, from the crouded state, in which the slaves appear in the plate, that an unusual and exaggerated instance has been produced; this, however, is so far from being the case, that no ship, if her intended cargo can be procured, ever carries a less number than one to a ton, and the usual practice has been, to carry nearly double that number. The bill, which was passed the last session of parliament, only restricts the carriage to five slaves for three tons; and the Brooks, of Liverpool, a capital ship, from which the above sketch was proportioned, did, in one voyage, actually carry six hundred and nine slaves, which is more than double the number that appear in the plate. The mode of stowing them was as follows: platforms, or wide shelves, were erected between the decks, extending so far from the sides towards the middle of the vessel, as to be capable of containing four additional rows of slaves; by which means the perpendicular height above each tier, after allowing for the beams and platforms, was reduced to two feet six inches, so that they could not even sit in an erect posture; besides which, in the men's apartment, instead of four rows, five were stowed, by placing the heads of one between the thighs of another. All the horrors of this situation are still multiplied in the smaller vessels. The Kitty, of one hundred and thirty-seven tons, had only one foot ten inches; and the Venus, of one hundred and forty-six tons, only one foot nine inches perpendicular height, above each layer.

"The above mode of carrying the slaves, however, is only one, among a thousand other miseries, which these unhappy and devoted creatures suffer, from this disgraceful traffic of the human species, which, in every part of its progress, exhibits scenes, that strike us with horror and indignation. If we regard the first stage of it, on the continent of Africa, we find, that a hundred thousand slaves are annually produced there for exportation, the greatest part of whom consists of innocent persons, torn from their dearest friends and connexions, sometimes by force, and sometimes by treachery. Of these, experience has shewn, that forty five thousand perish, either in the dreadful mode of conveyance before described, or within two years after their arrival at the plantations, before they are seasoned to the climate. Those who unhappily survive these hardships, are destined, like beasts of burden, to exhaust their lives in the unremitting Labours of slavery, without recompense, and without hope.

"It is said by the well-wishers to this trade, that the suppression of it will destroy a great nursery for seamen, and annihilate a very considerable source of commercial profit. In answer to these objections, mr. Clarkson, in his admirable treatise on the impolicy of the trade, lays down two positions, which he has proved from the most incontestable authority—First, that so far from being a nursery, it has been constantly and regularly a grave for our seamen; for that in this traffic only, more men perish in one year, than in all the other trades of Great Britain, in two years: "And, secondly, that the balance of the trade, from its extreme precariousness and uncertainty, is so notoriously against the merchants, that if all the vessels, employed in it, were the property of one man, he would infallibly, at the end of their voyages, find himself a loser.

"As then the cruelty and inhumanity of this trade must be universally admitted and lamented, and as the policy or impolicy of its abolition is a question, which the wisdom of the legislature must ultimately decide upon, and which it can only be enabled to form a just estimate of, by the most thorough investigation of all its relations and dependencies; it becomes the indispensable duty of every friend to humanity, however his speculations may have led him to conclude on the political tendency of the measure, to stand forward, and to assist the committees, either by producing such facts as he may himself be acquainted with, or by subscribing, to enable them to procure and transmit to the legislature, such evidence as will tend to throw the necessary lights on the subject. And people would do well to consider, that it does not often fall to the lot of individuals, to have an opportunity of performing so important a moral and religious duty, as that of endeavouring to put an end to a practice, which may, without exaggeration, be stiled one of the greatest evils at this day existing upon the earth.

"By the Plymouth committee,

"W. ELFORD, chairman."

1.10

Pennsylvania Society for Promoting the Abolition of Slavery, &c, "REMARKS on the SLAVE TRADE," engraved by Matthew Carey, 1789.

not just variation within format but different formats that actually served different functions. A broadside had certain potential advantages over an illustrated pamphlet. Given the tight relationship between image and text, it was awkward for the reader of a bound volume, magazine, or book to flip pages as she looked at the engraving. Yet, with the broadside, one no longer had to worry about the text and the image being separated from each other. Now they were all on the same page. Instead of engaging the individual viewer, the private reader, it became a document that was more open to public discussion and examination. It could be displayed on a wall either in a public space or in a private home. In either case, it enabled group engagement and provided potential access to those who were illiterate or semiliterate, since someone could read the text aloud as others examined the plan of the slave ship. A broadside encouraged a more collective ongoing engagement. A broadside, when placed on a wall, was always there to be perused. It was a constant reminder to all who might encounter it. The shift from pamphlet to broadside was, in this respect, overdetermined. In fact, the same development was occurring in England, where the Plymouth Committee's broadside *Plan of an African Ship's Lower Deck with Negroes in the Proportion of Not Quite One to a Ton* likewise generated attention.

PLYMOUTH COMMITTEE BROADSIDE

The Plymouth Committee's pamphlet and annexed engraving of the hold of a slave ship had generated a powerful reaction in the United States. It was obviously destined to be a persuasive weapon in the battle for abolition being waged on both sides of the Atlantic. Back in England in February and March of 1789, Granville Sharp, chairman of the London Committee, and William Elford held discussions and exchanged letters regarding the future of the plan of the slave ship. Although much of the correspondence is unavailable, these exchanges were heated, even angry. While key members of the London Committee liked the idea of *Plan of an African Ship's Lower Deck*, they felt that it could be improved. Some of their reservations were about the image itself, which Thomas Clarkson later characterized as preliminary; others were about the text. The London Committee, which saw itself at the center of the abolitionist network, was doubtlessly eager to reassert its leadership role over the independent activist "country" committee back in Plymouth. At some point, however, dialogue between the two groups broke down. On March 17, 1789, the London Committee decided to design "its own version of the plan of a slave ship."[87] The London Committee would act independently, printing its own "improved" version of the plan of the slave ship without working with Elford or the Plymouth Committee, and ultimately, without formally crediting his or their achievement. The following day, on March 18, 1789, either not yet aware of the London Committee's decision or trying to repair the breach, Elford wrote to James Phillips, printer for the London Committee:

> Sir—
>
> From a letter of yours which Mr. James Fox has shown me, I am apprehensive that some expressions in my last to the Chairman of the London Committee have been misunderstood by you as intending to convey an idea of your having given offence by your having given by you strictures on the plan of the slave's Deck published by us.—I think it therefore incumbent on me, not as Chairman of the Committee but as from one Gentleman to another to assure you that however strong any expression of mine might be, in my letter to Mr. Sharp, I meant no kind of personal incivility to you—the fact was that as I conceived your Observations to be not well founded, I made use of those arguments as illustration, which I thought most likely to point out the fallibility of your suggestions—I hope therefore you will consider this as an apology for any thing in my letter which may have been offensive to you—

> I trust also your apprehensions that any injury can arise to the cause in which we are engaged from any little misunderstandings among ourselves are without foundation. I doubt not the motives which engaged us in our present pursuit are considered by all of us as of too high a nature to suffer any evil influence from private or personal disagreement—I hope we shall have the heartfelt pleasure of seeing our efforts shortly crowned with success. I am Sir with great regard Your Sincere fellow labourer...
>
> Wm. Elford[88]

From Elford's point of view, the London Committee was not "improving" on his "idea"—as Clarkson would have it in his *History*—but pursuing a different representational approach, one that Elford believed was ill-advised. It is possible to compare the London Committee's resulting *Plan and Sections of a Slave Ship*, and more widely published *Description of a Slave Ship*, to the Plymouth Committee's efforts—to the original pamphlet with annexed illustration as well as to the second Plymouth Committee plan, which was published as a broadside, and almost certainly was the subject of or a response to the exchanges that took place between Elford and his London counterparts. That is, this second Plymouth Committee version has a number of "improvements" that should be noted.

The second Plymouth Committee plan was a broadside twenty-two inches high by fifteen inches wide, consisting of three major components: the plan itself, showing the lower deck of a slave ship; the London Committee seal, depicting the image of a kneeling slave; and a written description (fig. 1.11). The broadside's text is identical to that of the original pamphlet except for one minor change that resulted in the substitution of "The above Plate" for "The annexed Plate" in the very first sentence. The text appears in two columns below the horizontal engraving at the top. The rectangular broadside is thus vertical (in contrast to the two horizontal broadsides produced by the Philadelphia Abolition Society). The title of the engraving has been retained, but moved below the plan itself, switched with the "room" labels that were moved just above the engraving of the slave ship. The title is now situated in a more prominent place, between the engraving and the explanatory text below it. With more varied and elaborate lettering, still done by hand rather than in type, the title commands attention, especially the three key words capitalized in bold, which serve as headlines: Plan of an AFRICAN SHIP'S Lower Deck with NEGROES in the proportion of only One to a Ton.

For the broadside edition, the Plymouth Committee chose an engraver from Bristol, T. Deeble, to render a new, yet similar plate of the plan of the slave ship. At first glance, it looks very much like a copy of the original plate. The number of figures in the plan remains the same and they are drawn in roughly the same positions, with the same level of detail showing facial expressions and fleshy figures. The main difference in this new engraving is the addition of shackles, intricately drawn around the ankles of the figures representing the men (fig. 1.12). What can we make of this addition of such devices of restraint and torture? Does it further signal the brutalization of these innocent figures—that is, a necessary tactic of their

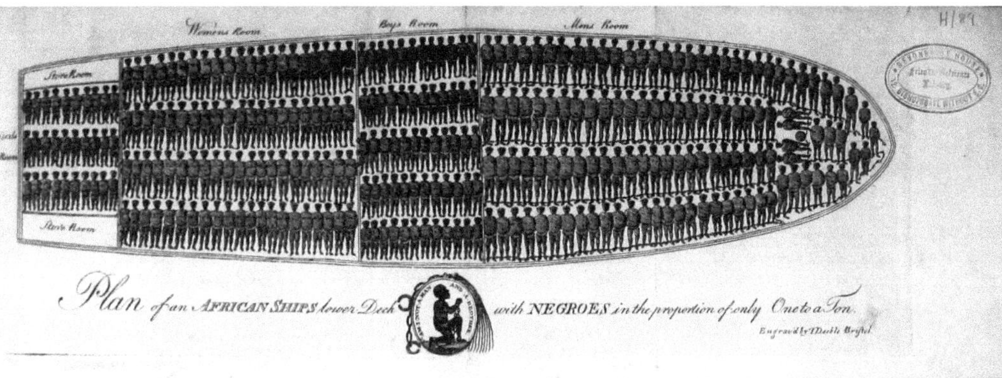

THE above Plate represents the lower deck of an African Ship of 297 tons burthen, with the Slaves stowed on it, in the proportion of not quite one to a ton.

In the Men's apartment, the space allowed to each is six feet in length, by sixteen inches in breadth.—The Boys are each allowed five feet by fourteen inches.—The Women, five feet ten inches, by sixteen inches; and the Girls, four feet by one foot each.—The perpendicular height between the Decks, is five feet eight inches.

The Men are fastened together two and two, by handcuffs on their wrists, and by irons rivetted on their legs.—They are brought up on the main deck every day, about eight o'clock, and as each pair ascend, a strong chain, fastened by ring-bolts to the deck, is passed through their Shackles; a precaution absolutely necessary to prevent insurrections.—In this state, if the weather is favourable, they are permitted to remain about one-third part of the twenty four hours, and during this interval they are fed, and their apartment below is cleaned; but when the weather is bad, even these indulgences cannot be granted them, and they are only permitted to come up in small companies, of about ten at a time, to be fed, where after remaining a quarter of an hour, each mess is obliged to give place to the next in rotation.

It may perhaps be conceived, from the crouded state in which the Slaves appear in the Plate, that an unusual and exaggerated instance has been produced; this, however, is so far from being the case, that no ship, if her intended cargo can be procured, ever carries a less number than one to a ton, and the usual practice has been to carry nearly double that number: The Bill which was passed during the last Session of Parliament, only restricts the carriage, to five Slaves for three tons; and the Brooks, of Liverpool, a capital ship; from which the above sketch was proportioned, did, in one voyage, actually carry 609 Slaves, which is more than double the number that appear in the plate.——The mode of stowing them was as follows—Platforms, or wide shelves were erected, between the decks, extending so far from the sides towards the middle of the vessel, as to be capable of containing four additional rows of Slaves, by which means the perpendicular height between each tier, after allowing for the beams and platforms, was reduced to two feet six inches; so that they could not even fit in an erect posture; besides which, in the Men's apartment, instead of four rows, five were stowed, by placing the heads of one between the thighs of another.—All the horrors of this situation are still multiplied in the smaller vessels.—The Kitty, of 137 tons, had only one foot ten inches, and the Venus, of 146 tons, only one foot nine inches perpendicular height above each layer.

The above mode of carrying the Slaves, however, is only one, among a thousand other miseries, which those unhappy and devoted creatures suffer from this disgraceful Traffick of the Human Species; which in every part of its progress, exhibits scenes that strike us with horror and indignation.—If we regard the first stage of it on the Continent of Africa, we find that a hundred thousand Slaves are annually produced there for exportation, the greatest part of whom consists of innocent persons, torn from their dearest friends and connections, sometimes by force, and sometimes by treachery. Of these, experience has shewn, that five and forty thousand perish, either in the dreadful mode of conveyance before described, or within two years after their arrival at the plantations, before they are seasoned to the climate.—Those who unhappily survive these hardships, are destined like beasts of burthen, to exhaust their lives in the unremitting labours of a Slavery, without recompence, and without hope.

The *Inhumanity* of this Trade, indeed, is so notorious, and so universally admitted, that even the advocates for the continuance of it, have rested all their arguments on the political inexpediency of its abolition; and in order to strengthen a weak cause, have either maliciously or ignorantly confounded together the emancipation of the negroes already in Slavery, with the abolition of the Trade; and thus many well-meaning people have become enemies to the cause, by the apprehensions that private property will be materially injured by the success of it.—To such, it becomes a necessary information, that liberating the Slaves forms no part of the present system; and so far will the prohibition of a future trade be from injuring private property, that the value of every Slave will be very considerably increased, from the moment that event takes place, and a more kind and tender treatment will immediately be insured to them by their Masters, from the necessity every Planter will then be under to keep up his stock, by natural means; a practice which some humane inhabitants of the Islands have pursued with the greatest success, and upon whose estates no new Negroes have been purchased for a number of years, the death vacancies having been supplied by young ones, born and bred in their own Plantations.—Thus then the value of private property will not only suffer no diminution, but will be very considerably inhanced by the abolition of the Trade.—It now only remains to see how the Public and the Slave Merchants will be affected by it.

It is said by the well-wishers to this Trade, that the suppression of it will destroy a great nursery for seamen, and annihilate a very considerable source of commercial profit——In answer to these objections, Mr. Clarkson, in his admirable treatise on the impolicy of the Trade, lays down two positions, which he has proved from the most incontestible authority.—First, that so far from being a Nursery, it has been constantly and regularly a Grave for our Seamen; for that in this Traffick only, more Men perish in ONE Year, than in all the other Trades of Great-Britain, in TWO Years: And, secondly, that the balance of the trade, from its extreme precariousness and uncertainty, is so notoriously against the Merchants, that if all the vessels, employed in it were the property of one Man, he would infallibly, at the end of their voyages, find himself a loser.

As then the *Cruelty* and *Inhumanity* of this Trade must be universally admitted and lamented, and as the policy or impolicy of its abolition is a question which the wisdom of the Legislature must ultimately decide upon, and which it can only be enabled to form a just estimate of, by the most thorough investigation of all its relations and dependencies; it becomes the indispensible duty of every friend to humanity, however his speculations may have led him to conclude on the political tendency of the measure, to stand forward, and to assist the Committees, either by producing such facts as he may himself be acquainted with, or by subscribing, to enable them to procure and transmit to the Legislature, such evidence as will tend to throw the necessary lights on the subject.—And people would do well to consider that it does not often fall to the lot of individuals, to have an opportunity of performing so important a moral and religious duty, as that of endeavouring to put an end to a practice, which may, without exaggeration, be stiled one of the greatest evils at this day existing upon the earth.

By the Plymouth Committee,

W. Elford, Chairman.

1.11

Plymouth Committee, *Plan of an African Ship's Lower Deck with Negroes in the Proportion of Only Une to a Ton*, 1789, steel engraving, 15³/₄ × 22 inches, broadside, engraved by T. Deeble, Bristol, Printed by Trewman and Haydon, Plymouth.

oppressors in order to justify enslaving them? Or is it an attempt to add a realistic detail that might provoke further sympathy for the enslaved Africans? There are no obvious handcuffs and the irons on their legs do not bind them two by two, but in a string—in a manner that suggests how "a strong chain, fastened to ring bolts on the deck, is passed through their Shackles." In this sense, the addition of shackles creates a graphic effect but not, it would seem, of accuracy and verisimilitude.

The London Committee seal of the kneeling slave, situated in the middle of the page, breaks up the broadside's title (fig. 1.13). Thus juxtaposed between the title, the text, and the engraving, the relationship of the seal to the broadside (and especially the plan of the slave ship) is complex. A good place to begin tracing that complexity is with the seal's history. At a meeting of the London Committee on July 7, 1787, it was "Resolved, That a seal be engraved for the use of this society and that Joseph Woods, Dr. Hooper, and Phillip Sansom, be requested to prepare a design for the same, to be laid before the Committee."[89] According to Clarkson, a design for the seal of the London Committee was presented in October 1787 bearing an African "in chains in a supplicating posture, kneeling with one knee upon the ground, and with both his hands lifted up to heaven."[90] Encircling his roughly drawn figure were the words pleading, "Am I not a man and a brother?" Woods, Hooper, and Sansom worked on the design and conception of the seal with William Hackwood, the chief modeler at Josiah Wedgwood's pottery factory at Etruria from 1769 to 1832. Most scholars agree that Hackwood drew the seal. He and Wedgwood, who was an influential member of the London Committee, then adapted it as a medallion in the neoclassical style that was then popular and fashionable among the middle and upper classes.

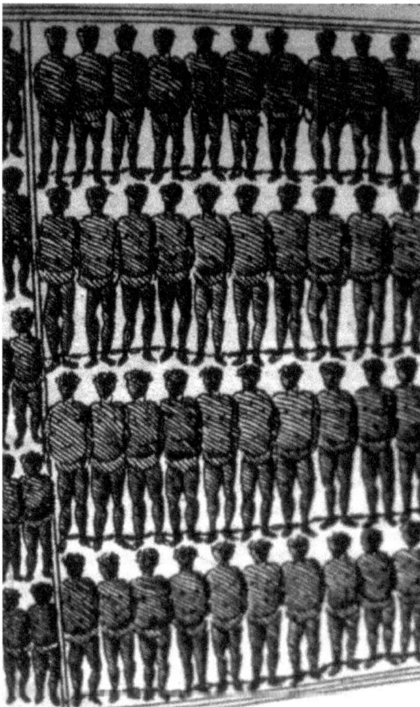

1.12

Detail showing shackles, Plymouth Committee, *Plan of an African Ship's Lower Deck with Negroes in the Proportion of Only One to a Ton*, 1789, engraved by T. Deeble, Bristol, Printed by Trewman and Haydon, Plymouth.

1.13

Detail showing the kneeling slave, Plymouth
Committee, *Plan of an African Ship's Lower Deck
with Negroes in the Proportion of Only One to
a Ton*, 1789, engraved by T. Deeble, Bristol, printed
by Trewman and Haydon, Plymouth.

The image of the kneeling slave suggested religious conversion, promoted
notions of Christian brotherly love, and offered a sentimental appeal to moral-
ity. But at the same time, it showed the chained African in a docile, pitiable state,
one of "supplication," begging for middle-class empathy and acceptance. "Like
the deserving poor, or unfortunate prisoners," David Bindman comments, "it was
intended that they [slaves] would repay the act of magnanimity by eternal devotion to their civilized masters or mistresses, and would, of course, adopt their
masters' religion."[91] Servile and begging for deliverance, the kneeling slave also
throws a challenge to the reader-viewer: "Am I not a man and a brother." The
words are a challenge, asserting equality—albeit in a nonthreatening way. Reflecting on the African figure appearing in Sir John Hawkins's coat of arms, the abolitionist's figure of the kneeling slave is different in many respects. Hawkins's black
figure is dehumanized: an object, which is nothing more than the symbol (also the
source) of Hawkins's status and wealth. The black figure is in fact a demi-moor,
truncated, cut off at the waist, only half a man. In contrast, the London Committee's kneeling slave protests his situation even as he appeals to the decency and
the humanity he shares with the reader. It takes a double form, mixing supplication with assertion. The seal's power comes from the intersection of these two
contradictory positions.

It is important to note that kneeling African figures had been present in religious and secular art of the West well before the end of the eighteenth century.[92]
In fact, the image of the kneeling slave would endure for much of the nineteenth
century, attaching itself to the American abolitionist debate.[93] As the image of
the kneeling slave was endlessly repeated and the words quietly eliminated, what
remained could be seen to condone an inferior status for black people. As Hugh
Honour points out, the kneeling slave "was to be repeated again and again in the art
of the West with such effect that blacks continued to be shown in this posture long

after the abolition of slavery."[94] This image no doubt contributed to the degrading ways in which black people came to be perceived on both sides of the Atlantic.

Like the Plymouth Committee plan of the slave ship, the drawing of the London Committee seal was somewhat unrefined. It depicted a brutish figure with very rough features. But in early 1788, when Wedgwood and Hackwood took the idea of the seal and molded it into a cameo in black on white jasperware, the figure of the kneeling slave experienced a metamorphosis, smoothly changing into a more civilized, palatable image, one poised to be consumed by an ever-fashion-conscious British public (fig. 1.14). Jasperware, a white stoneware that often resembles porcelain, was one of Wedgwood's best-known innovations. As Robin Reilly explains, jasperware was "especially suited to neoclassical ornament and appealed to cultivated taste in the eighteenth century."[95] With Wedgwood's innovation, the kneeling slave became more refined, but he remained kneeling and chained nevertheless.

The cameo, like the plan of the slave ship, was first put to use to foster greater public awareness for Dolben's proposed slave trade regulation bill in 1788. In an initial effort to stimulate interest in the cameos, Wedgwood donated them to friends and allies of the abolitionist movement, including among others Benjamin Franklin, in February 1788. Writing from Philadelphia, Franklin commended Wedgwood on his clever abolitionist propaganda, "the figure of the supplicant…may have an effect equal to that of the best written pamphlet, in procuring favour to those oppressed people."[96] Clarkson, who also received a free supply of the kneeling slave cameos, recalled in his *History* how they made abolitionism fashionable: "Some had them inlaid in gold on the lid of their snuff-boxes. Of the ladies, several wore them in bracelets, and others had them fitted up in ornamental manner as pins for their hair."[97] Illustrations and notices in the pages of *Gentleman's Magazine* and the *Morning Chronicle and Daily Advertiser* reported the growing middle-class taste for the cameos.[98] The production of an array of settings and colors for the kneeling slave cameo emulated the preexisting marketing structures already established by Wedgwood for his popular neoclassical cameos. According to Reilly, the versatility of jasperware meant that it could be "stained to provide a wide variety of colours, ornamented, engine-turned, laminated and lapidary polished." [99]

Like political campaign buttons, the production of the cameo was stimulated by the grassroots efforts of the abolitionist movement to raise interest in its public agitation campaigns. According to Michael Craton, more than 200,000 kneeling slave medallions were sold between 1791 and 1792, to garner public support for the motion for abolition that was being considered by Parliament in 1792.[100] As J. R. Oldfield affirms, "this simple device [the cameo] became a form of abolitionist shorthand, a visual cue that made explicit the relationship between abolition, consumption and popular politics."[101] The image of the kneeling slave was a widely circulated piece of abolitionist propaganda, appearing in Europe and the Americas in the form of prints, pendants, ceramic ware, handiwork (samplers), and commemorative coins.

In the Plymouth Committee broadside, the kneeling slave of the London Committee's seal complements the figures of the enslaved Africans pictured in the plan

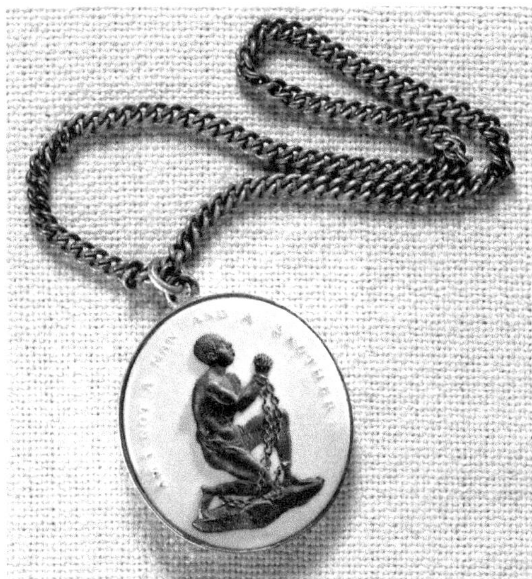

1.14

William Hackwood (for Josiah Wedgwood), *Kneeling Slave Medallion*, white jasperware encased in gold frame, approximately 1 ³/₄ × 1 ¹/₄ inches, ca. 1790.

of the slave ship. The kneeling slave is portrayed in profile, a side view, while all the small figures above are frontal. The kneeling slave is also proportionally larger, as if one of the hundreds of small figures was brought forward and allowed to speak.[102] The figures representing Africans in the ship are the living dead, buried alive. They are mute. They seem to be standing, staring back bearing witness to the written appeal, which speaks for them and their cause. But with the addition of the kneeling slave, one of these Africans is allowed to speak for himself and for all the others, perhaps in terms that Equiano would have used, or at least approved.

One cannot but be struck by the fact that the Plymouth Committee broadside is the only example in which the London Committee's seal and the slave ship icon were combined. The flattened perspective of the engraving, its lack of spatial verisimilitude and absence of three-dimensional renderings allows the spectator to see the figures as both lying down in an overhead view and standing up at the same time. The seal, which offers a profile view of a kneeling slave, would seem to encourage the spectator to see the figures representing enslaved Africans as standing up—standing up to be counted, standing up to protest. They refuse to accept their fate lying down. They confront their tormentors while silently appealing to their potential liberators to take political action on their behalf.

The Plymouth Committee broadside combined what would become the two most popular abolitionist images, the slave ship icon and the kneeling slave. Yet, competing as they did for attention on the same singular broadsheet sent a mixed message that soon would be overruled by the London Committee and its more pragmatic *Plan and Sections of a Slave Ship*. Consequently, few copies of the Plymouth Committee broadside ever were printed. As the second and final version of the slave ship icon to be conceived by the Plymouth Committee, the broadside nevertheless was a prototype that demonstrated how a powerful idea could be transformed into image and text.

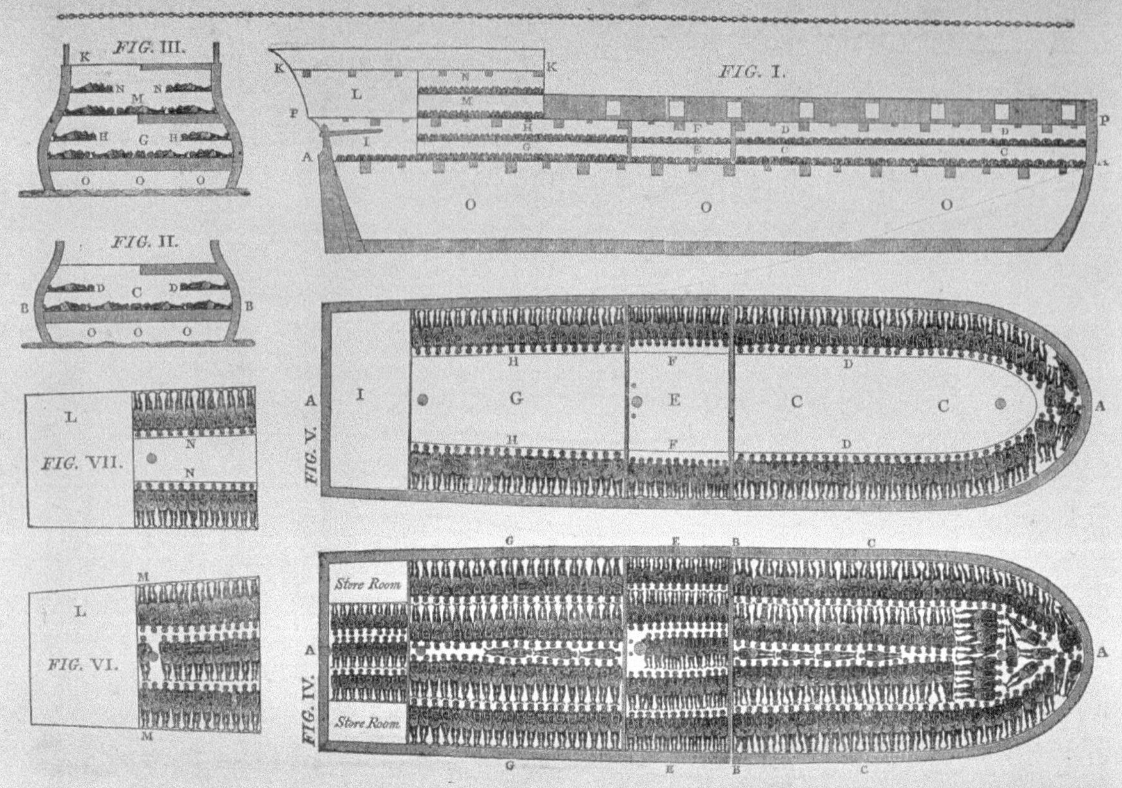

2.1

London Committee, *Description of a Slave Ship*,
1789, wood engraving, 24 × 19 inches.

CHAPTER TWO

FORM: ESSENTIAL ELEMENTS

THE LONDON COMMITTEE'S *DESCRIPTION OF A SLAVE SHIP*

THE PLYMOUTH COMMITTEE AND WILLIAM ELFORD created the archetype for future renderings of the crowded lower deck of a slave ship, which would hold the public's memory of the Middle Passage. But, as we shall see, it was the London Committee's enhancements to the plan as well as its method of distributing it as the "official" abolitionist committee version that enabled *Description of a Slave Ship* to become a leading icon of the movement by 1807, and to continue to be one of the most powerful and prominent images associated with the memory of slavery in our own time (fig. 2.1).

The London Committee decided to print its own plan and sections of a slave ship on March 17, 1789 (see fig. 2.4). The minutes from that date reported the following: "Resolved that it is the opinion of this Committee that a description of a Slave Ship with a plan and sections be prepared and that the following Gentlemen be appointed to execute the same: Mr. James Phillips, Mr. Harrison, Mr. Woods, Mr. Hoare, Rev. Mr. Clarkson."[1] In addition to eighteenth-century advancements in printing technology, having an in-house printer enhanced the ability of the London Committee to produce and disseminate broadsides, pamphlets, testimonies, reports, and books in support of the abolition of slavery. These publications were printed by the thousands and were translated into French among other languages. The simultaneous development of print culture in the eighteenth century combined with the preexisting network of Quaker meetings created a climate in which abolitionist propaganda could circulate widely.

Phillips published the London Committee version of the plan and sections of the slave ship between April 21 and April 28, 1789. According to the minutes of the committee meeting on April 28, "Mr. James Phillips reports that the description of a slave ship with the plan and sections has been prepared and printed."[2] Larger than the Plymouth Committee broadside, it was redesigned with a more succinct and descriptive title, *Plan and Sections of a Slave Ship*, and added cross-section and longitudinal views to reflect the packed hold of the slave ship in three dimensions (see fig. 1.11). A lengthier descriptive text combined with the additional sections produced a print that measured roughly 28 by 18 inches. This initial London Committee version likely was the print that Members of Parliament had available to them when Wilberforce made his first motion for the immediate abolition of the slave trade on May 13, 1789, discussed below. But it was subsequently redrawn with wider public consumption in mind resulting in the more widely distributed broadside *Description of a Slave Ship* measuring 24 by 19 inches. Under the direction of Clarkson, the London Committee broadsides were drawn with greater accuracy, detail, and verisimilitude. This was evident in the revised title, multiple schematics, description, and relational layout.

Consider the London Committee's choice of a title and its placement on the broadside. The London Committee title, *Description of a Slave Ship*, is short, neutral in tone, precise, and almost scientific. It is remarkably modern compared to many of the lengthy titles of books and pamphlets that were then common. Its brevity and precision allows for easy reference and quick memorization. Its brevity also allows for the large lettering, which are in type rather than handwritten. The London Committee's label of its broadside as a "Slave Ship" rather than an "African Ship" is clearer than that of the Plymouth Committee's plan, and more straightforward.

The London Committee sought to render the interior of the slave ship *Brooks* in three dimensions while the Plymouth *Plan of an African Ship's Lower Deck* was rendered in only two (and even then, in a manner that was spatially ambiguous). The London group thus employed state-of-the-art drafting techniques commonly used by naval architects to precisely and more fully visualize the space. Instead of showing only a plan view of the lower deck of a packed slave ship hold, the London Committee used seven numbered figures to illustrate almost every perspective from which to view the contents of the *Brooks* cargo hold. Indeed, it was their addition of cross sections that made the defining difference; these made it possible for viewers to imagine movement (and consequently themselves) within the space previously delineated by the plan view. This "improved version," as Thomas Clarkson would later claim, revealed overhead plan views of the crowded lower deck (IV), platform (V), and quarter decks (VI and VII); lateral cross sections of the lower

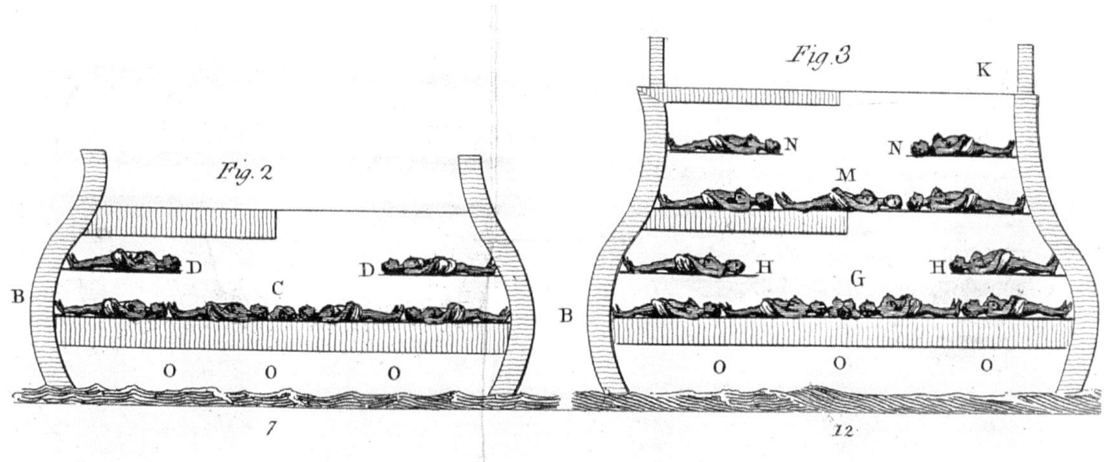

2.2

Detail, showing figures 2 and 3, London Committee, *Description of a Slave Ship*, 1789.

deck and platform (II), and the quarter decks (III); and a longitudinal cross section of the entire hold (I). Each lettered, numbered figure corresponded to a list of
the "Dimensions of the Ship" described in the accompanying text. The platforms to
which the Plymouth broadside only alluded in the text, now had a visual counterpart (fig. 2.2).

Upon first glance, the bodies of the African captives appear to be sketches, uniform black figures, each one adorned with a white loincloth. But closer inspection
reveals distinctions that indicate gender. The men are shackled together by twos,
each pair sharing hand- and leg-irons (see IV, section C, and V, sections C and D).
According to the text, the shackles were "a precaution absolutely necessary to prevent insurrections." The shackles were a clear statement of power and domination,
of violence and inhumanity, of the slavers' own barbarity and savagery. They were
meant to appeal to the viewers' moral and religious convictions and sense of benevolence (fig. 2.3).

Unlike the bodies representing the men, the bodies representing the women are
drawn without shackles, reflecting a perception held by slavers that women posed
less of a physical threat than men. Quite the contrary, however, enslaved women
were known to organize, lead, and assist with rebellions aboard slave ships.[3] In
addition, the figures representing the females' bodies are clearly eroticized, their
breasts forming a series of highly accentuated peaks in the cross-section views
(see, for example, sections G, H, M, and N in I and II). Most of the women's hands
are crossed on top of the loincloths that cover their genitals (IV, section G). The
exaggerated, sexualized physical forms of these women reflect the objectified status of the black female body and the history of rape and sexual abuse to which
black female slaves were subjected by their white male captors. The proximity of
the crew's cabin (I, section L) to the quarter decks of the women's rooms (I, sections G, H, M, and N) further suggests this relationship. Equiano described in his

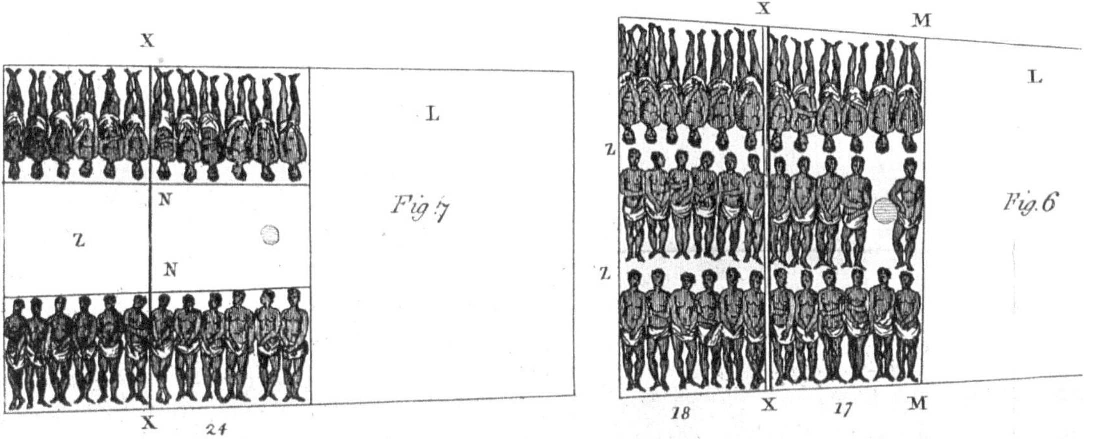

2.3
Detail, showing figures 6 and 7, London
Committee, *Description of a Slave Ship*, 1789.

Interesting Narrative the behavior of the crew members of one slave ship: "I have even known them to gratify their brutal passion with females not ten years old; and these abominations sometimes practised to scandalous excess, that one of our captains discharged the mate and others on that account."[4] Ottobah Cugoano, the author of another noted black Atlantic slave narrative, *Thoughts and Sentiments on the Evil and Wicked Traffic of the Slavery and Commerce of the Human Species*, published in London in 1788, remembered how "it was common for the dirty filthy sailors to take the African women and lie upon their bodies; but the men were chained and penned up in the holes."[5] Former slave ship captain John Newton recalled, "When the women and girls are taken on board a ship, naked, trembling, terrified, perhaps almost exhausted from cold, fatigue and hunger, they are often exposed to the wanton rudeness of white savages.…In imagination the prey is divided on the spot, and only reserved till opportunity offers."[6] The plan of the slave ship, which shows the overt sexualization of the black female body, was created around the same time that descriptions of Africans from European travel accounts and advances in science and technology converged to formulate racist ideologies about black female sexuality and black people as inferior, subhuman.[7] The shackled men and sexual specificity of the women in the plan seem to describe in a schematic but powerful manner a brutal understatement of the system of New World slavery: "We rape the Negro women; we work the savage men." To be sure, men and women experienced slavery and the Middle Passage differently.

Looking closer still, the image offers us a visual intimacy that compels the imagination: It is possible to discern distinct facial expressions and bodily positions among the figures representing the slaves. White lines defining their chests, navels, facial cavities, and postures are drawn meticulously. Some of the captives appear to be wincing from discomfort, while others seem to be in conversation with one another, their bodies gesturing or turned toward each other. The detailed figures provide visual testimony to the evidence gathered by abolitionists and the narratives told by slaves. It was known that African captives were in constant communication with one another during the Middle Passage, despite being contained in different rooms or separated by platforms or distanced by different languages or cultural groups. Indeed, strong ties, often created by being paired two by two or separated by sex, developed between Africans who endured the Middle Passage.[8]

The London Committee versions of the slave ship icon presented a very ordered graphic image, one that structured and sequenced the visualization of the hold that was evidence of a technology of vision and surveillance.[9] These multiple perspectives hold the attention of the viewer, not only as they explore each of the figures but also as they relate the figures to each other until they have established a clear understanding of the architectural dimensions of the ship. These require a sustained encounter with the individual drawings, encourage the referencing of the text, and generally force the viewer to engage the full horror of the subject. Different perspectives also produce a certain redundancy that repeats and reemphasizes the horror. The sense of claustrophobia, for instance, is visually strengthened by the addition of cross and longitudinal sections.

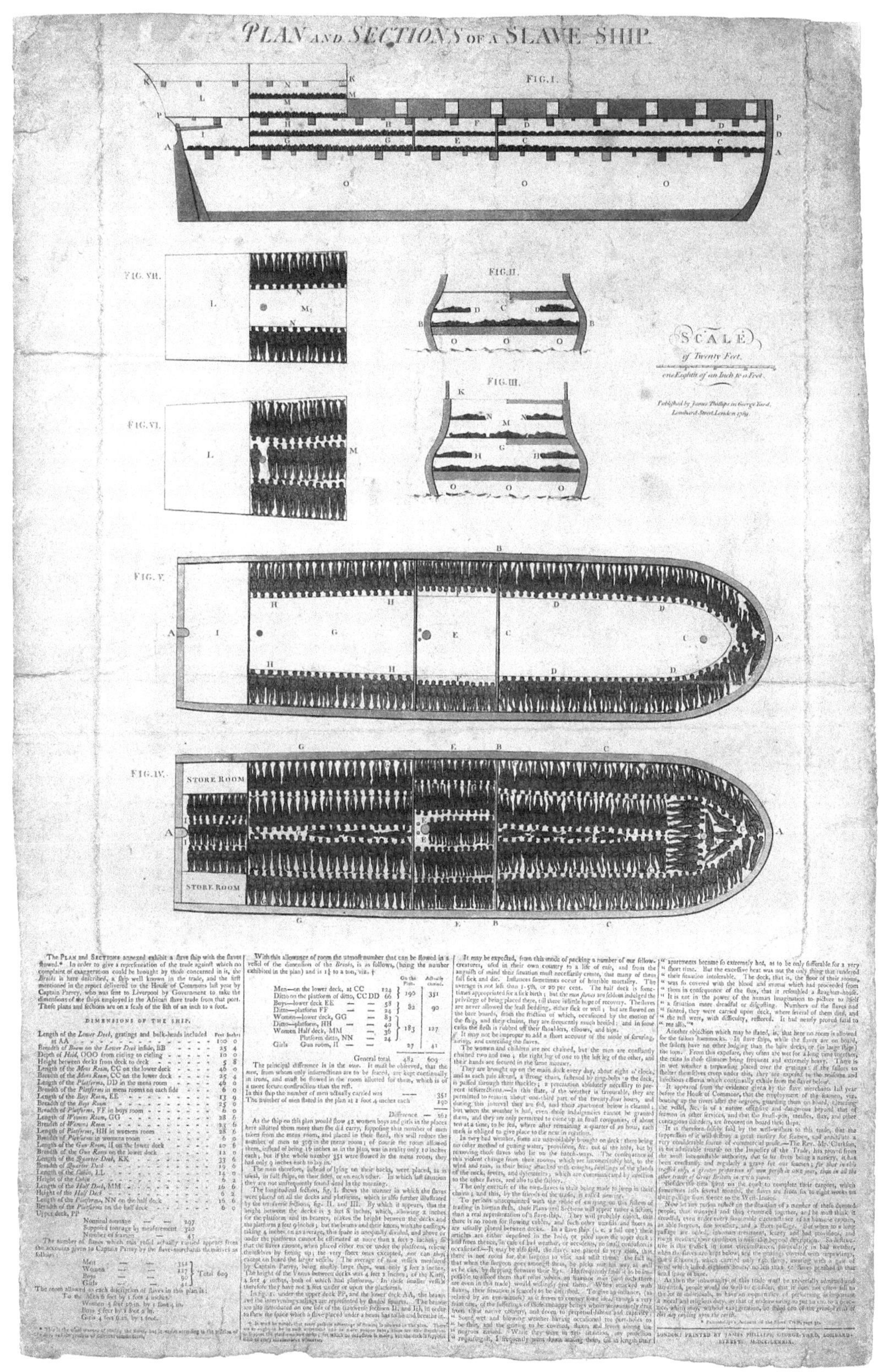

2.4

London Committee, *Plan and Sections
of a Slave Ship*, 1789, 706 × 467 mm
(approximately 28 × 18 inches).

The emphasis on specificity, thoroughness, and precision is evident in the handling of the individual sections. In IV, the bodies are laid out in a precise way, with the heads of the enslaved Africans placed toward the center line of the hold. The tension between Africans lying down and standing up, which characterized the Plymouth plan, is eliminated. The tight packing of bodies is further shown with the addition of several figures laid laterally down the ship's spine. The packing of bodies into the bow is also shown with much greater accuracy. Unlike the Plymouth pamphlet and annexed plate, the African men are shown shackled two by two. Even in the Plymouth broadside where the men are shackled, there is a lack of comparable precision. Here the contortion of the bodies that results from this practice is shown. The realism and immediacy of the schematic is emphasized by the addition and selected tangential details, including the location of the ship's masts, the rudder, beams, and portals for guns in the longitudinal section, the placement of decks and the waterline in the cross sections. *Description of a Slave Ship* became a schematic representation designed to impress on the memory the magnitude of the horror of the Middle Passage—to visually encode that memory for its viewers.

Despite its graphic flourishes and details, this plan was not a realistic representation of the space available or the conditions characteristic of a slave ship hold. Instead it was an abstraction. As with the Plymouth plan, the schematic drawings, easy to grasp and hold in the memory, were elaborated by the descriptive text.

[1] The Plan and Sections annexed exhibit a slave ship with the slaves stowed.*
In order to give a representation of the trade against which no complaint of exaggeration could be brought by those concerned in it, the *Brooks* is here described, a ship well known in the trade, and the first mentioned in the report delivered to the House of Commons last year by Captain Parrey, who was sent to Liverpool by Government to take the dimensions of the ships employed in the African slave trade from that port. These plans and sections are on a scale of the 8th of an inch to a foot.

[2] DIMENSIONS OF THE SHIP.

	Feet	Inches
Length of the *Lower Deck*, gratings and bulk-heads included at AA _	100	0
Beneath the *Beam on the Lower Deck* inside BB _ _ _ _ _ _ _	25	4
Depth of *Hold*, OOO from cieling [*sic*] to cieling [*sic*] _ _ _ _ _	10	0
Height between decks from deck to deck_ _ _ _ _ _ _ _ _	5	8
Length of the *Mens Room*, CC on the lower deck _ _ _ _ _ _	46	0
Breadth of the *Mens Room*, CC on the lower deck _ _ _ _ _ _	25	4
Length of the *Platforms*, DD in the mens room _ _ _ _ _ _ _	46	0
Length of the *Boys Room*, EE_ _ _ _ _ _ _ _ _ _ _ _ _ _ _	6	0
Breadth of the *Boys Room* _ _ _ _ _ _ _ _ _ _ _ _ _ _ _ _	25	0
Breadth of the *Platforms*, FF in boys room _ _ _ _ _ _ _ _	6	0
Length of *Womens Room*, GG _ _ _ _ _ _ _ _ _ _ _ _ _ _	28	6
Breadth of *Womens Room* _ _ _ _ _ _ _ _ _ _ _ _ _ _ _ _	23	6

Length of *Platforms*, HH in womens room _ _ _ _ _ _ _ _   28   6
Breadth of *Platforms* in womens room _ _ _ _ _ _ _ _ _ _   6   0
Length of the *Gun Room*, II on the lower deck _ _ _ _ _ _ _   10   6
Length of the *Quarter Deck*, KK _ _ _ _ _ _ _ _ _ _ _ _   33   6
Breadth of the *Quarter Deck* _ _ _ _ _ _ _ _ _ _ _ _ _ _   19   6
Length of the *Cabin*, LL _ _ _ _ _ _ _ _ _ _ _ _ _ _ _   14   0
Height of the *Cabin* _ _ _ _ _ _ _ _ _ _ _ _ _ _ _ _ _   6   2
Length of the *Half Deck*, MM _ _ _ _ _ _ _ _ _ _ _ _ _   16   6
Height of the *Half Deck* _ _ _ _ _ _ _ _ _ _ _ _ _ _ _ _   6   2
Length of the *Platforms*, NN on the half deck _ _ _ _ _ _ _   16   6
Breadth of the *Platforms* on the half deck _ _ _ _ _ _ _ _   6   0
Upper deck, PP

Nominal tonnage _ _ _ _ _ _ _ _ _   297
Supposed tonnage by measurement _ _   320
Number of seamen _ _ _ _ _ _ _ _   45

[3] The number of slaves which this vessel actually carried appears from the accounts given to Captain Parrey by the slave-merchants themselves as follows:

Men _ _ _ _ _ _ _ _ _ _ _ _ _ _   351
Women _ _ _ _ _ _ _ _ _ _ _ _ _   127
Boys _ _ _ _ _ _ _ _ _ _ _ _ _ _   90   Total 609
Girls _ _ _ _ _ _ _ _ _ _ _ _ _ _   41

[4] The room allowed to each description of slaves in this plan is:

To the Men 6 feet by 1 foot 4 inches.

Women 5 feet by 10 in. by 1 foot 4 in

Boys 5 feet by 1 foot 2 in

Girls 4 feet 6 in by 1 foot

[5] With this allowance of room the utmost number that can be stowed in a vessel of the dimension of the Brooks, is as follows, (being the number exhibited in the plan) and is 1½ to a ton, viz.†

		On the Plan.	Actually carried.
Men–on the lower deck, at CC	124		
Ditto on the platform of ditto, CC DD	66	190	351
Boys—lower deck EE	58		
Ditto—platform FF	24	82	90
Women—lower deck, GG	83		
Ditto—platform, HH	40		
Women Half deck, MM	36	183	127
Platform ditto, NN	24		
Girls Gun room, II		27	41
General total		482	609

[6] The principal difference is in the *men*. It must be observed, that the *men*, from whom only insurrections are to be feared, are kept continually in irons, and must be stowed in the room allotted for them, which is of a more secure construction than the rest.

In this ship the number of men actually carried was   351

The number of men stated in the plan at 1 foot 4 inches each   190

Difference   161

[7] As the ship on this plan would stow 42 women boys and girls in the places here allotted them more than she did carry, supposing that number of men taken from the mens room, and placed in their stead, this would reduce the number of men to 309 in the mens room; of course the room allowed them, instead of being 16 inches as in the plan, was in reality only 10 inches each; but if the whole number 351 were stowed in the mens room, they had only 9 inches each to lay in.

[8] The men therefore, instead of lying on their backs, were placed, as is usual, in full ships, on their sides, or on each other. In which last situation they are not unfrequently found dead in the morning.

[9] The longitudinal section, fig. I. shows the manner in which the slaves were placed on all the decks and platforms, which is also further illustrated by the transverse sections, fig. II. and III. By which it appears, that the height between the decks is 5 feet 8 inches, which, allowing 2 inches for the platform and its bearers, makes the height between the decks and the platform 2 feet 9 inches; but the beams and their knees, with the carlings, taking four inches on an average, this space is unequally divided, and above or under the platforms cannot be estimated at more than 2 feet 7 inches; so that the slaves cannot, when placed either on or under the platform, relieve themselves by sitting up; the very short ones excepted, nor can *they*, except on board the larger vessels. The average of nine vessels measured by Captain Parrey, being mostly large ships, was only 5 feet 2 inches. The height of the Venus between decks 4 feet 2 inches; of the Kitty, 4 feet 4 inches, both of which had platforms. In these smaller vessels therefore they have not 2 feet under or upon the platforms.

[10] In fig. I. under the upper deck PP, and the lower deck AA, the beams and the intervening carlings are represented by shaded squares. The beams are also introduced on one side of the transverse sections II. And III, in order to shew the space which a slave placed under a beam has to lie and breathe in.

[11] It may be expected, from this mode of packing a number of our fellow creatures, used in their own country to a life of ease, and from the anguish of mind their situation must necessarily create, that many of them fall sick and die. Instances sometimes occur of horrible mortality. The average is not less than 1/5th, or 20 per cent. The half deck is sometimes appropriated for a sick birth; but the *men slaves* are seldom indulged the privilege of being placed there, till there is little hope of recovery. The slaves are never allowed the least bedding, either sick or well; but are stowed on the bare boards, from the friction of which,

occasioned by the motion of the ship, and their chains, they are frequently much bruised: and in some cases the flesh is rubbed off their shoulders, elbows, and hips.

[12] It may not be improper to add a short account of the mode of securing, airing, and exercising the slaves.

[13] The women and children are not chained, but the men are constantly chained two and two; the right leg of one to the left leg of the other, and their hands are secured in the same manner.

[14] The are brought up on the main deck every day, about eight o'clock, and as each pair ascend, a strong chain, fastened by ring-bolts to the deck, is passed through their shackles; a precaution absolutely necessary to prevent insurrections. In this state, if the weather is favourable, they are permitted to remain about one third part of the twenty four hours, and during this interval they are fed, and their apartment below is cleaned; but when the weather is bad, even those indulgencies cannot be granted them, and they are only permitted to come up in small companies, of about ten at a time, to be fed, where after remaining a quarter of an hour, each mess is obliged to give place to the next in rotation.

[15] In *very* bad weather, some are unavoidably brought on deck: there being no other method of getting water, provisions, &c. out of the hold, but by removing those slaves who lie on the hatch-ways. The consequence of this violent change from their rooms, which are inconceivably hot, to the wind and rain, is their being attacked with coughs, swellings of the glands of the neck, fevers, and dysenteries; which are communicated by infection to the other slaves, and also to the sailors.

[16] The only exercise of the men-slaves is their being made to jump in their chains; and this, by their friends of the trade, is called *dancing*.

[17] To persons unacquainted with the mode of carrying on this system of trading in human flesh, these Plans and Sections will appear rather a fiction, than a real representation of a slave-ship. The will probably object that there is no room for stowing cables, and such other utensils and stores as are usually placed between decks. In a slave ship (i.e. a full one) these articles are either deposited in the hold, or piled upon the upper deck; and from thence, in case of bad weather, or accidents, no small confusion is occasioned.—It may be also said, the slave are placed so very close, that there is not room for the surgeon to visit and assist them: the fact is, that when the surgeon goes amongst them, he picks out his way as well as he can, by stepping between their legs. He frequently finds it to be impossible to afford them that relief which an humane man (and such there are even in this trade) would willingly give them. When attacked with fluxes, their situation is scarcely to be described. To give an instance, (as related by an eye-witness) as it serves to convey some idea, though a very faint one, of the sufferings of those unhappy beings whom we wantonly drag from their native country, and doom to a perpetual labour and captivity: "Some wet and blowing weather having occasioned the port-holes to be shut, and the grating to be

covered, fluxes and fevers among the Negroes ensued. While they were in this situation, my profession requiring it, I frequently went down among them, till at length their apartments became so extremely hot, as to be only sufferable for a very short time. But the excessive heat was not the only thing that rendered their situation intolerable. The deck, that is, the floor of their rooms, was so covered with the blood and mucus which had proceeded from them in consequence of the flux, that it resembled a slaughter-house. It is not in the power of the human imagination to picture to itself a situation more dreadful or disgusting. Numbers of the slaves had fainted, they were carried upon deck, where several of them died, and the rest were, with difficulty, restored. It had nearly proved fatal to me also.†

[18] Another objection which may be stated, is, that here no room is allowed for the sailors hammocks. In slave ships, while the slaves are on board the sailors have no other lodgings than the bare decks, or (in large ships) the tops. From this exposure, they often are wet for a long time together, the rains in those climates being frequent and extremely heavy. There is in wet weather a tarpawling placed over the gratings: if the sailors to shelter themselves creep under this, they are exposed to the noisome and infections effluvia which continually exhale from the slaves below.

[19] It appeared from the evidence given by the slave merchants last year before the House of Commons, that the employment of the seamen, viz. boating up the rivers after the Negroes, guarding them on board, cleansing the vessel, &c. is of a nature offensive and dangerous beyond that of seamen in other services, and that the small-pox, measles, flux, and other contagious disorders, are frequent on board these ships.

[20] It is therefore falsely said by the well-wishers to this trade, that the suppression of it will destroy a great nursery for seamen, and annihilate a very considerable source of commercial profit.—The Rev. Mr. Clarkson, in his admirable treatise on the Impolicy of the Trade, has proved from the most incontestable authority, that so far from being a nursery, it has been constantly and regularly a grave for our seamen; *for that in this traffick only, a greater proportion of men perish in ONE year, than in all the other trades of Great Britain in TWO years.*

[21] Besides the time spent on the coast to complete their cargoes, which sometimes lasts several months, the slaves are from six to eight weeks on their passage from then to the West-Indies.

Now let any person reflect on the situation of a number of these devoted people, thus managed and thus crammed together, and he must think it dreadful, even under every favourable circumstance of an humane captain, an able surgeon, fine weather, and a short passage. But when to a long passage are added, inhuman treatment, scanty and bad provisions, and rough weather, their condition is miserable beyond description. So destructive is this traffick in some circumstances, particularly in bad weather, when the slaves are kept below, and the gratings covered with tarpawlings, that a schooner, which carried only 140 slaves, meeting with a gale of wind which lasted eighteen hours, no less than 40 slaves perished in that small space of time.

[22] As then the inhumanity of this trade must be universally admitted and lamented, people would do well to consider, that it does not often fall to the lot of individuals, to have an opportunity of performing so important a moral and religious duty, as that of endeavouring to put an end to a practice, which may, without exaggeration, be stiled one of the *greatest evils at this day existing upon the earth*.[10]

*This is the usual manner of placing the slaves, but it varies according to the position of the ship and the practice of different commanders.

†It must be noted, that every advantage of stowing is allowed in the plan. There are or ought to be in each apartment one or more poopoo tubs; there are also stanchions to support the platforms and decks; for which no deduction is made; but the deck is supposed clear of every incumbrance whatever.

This text is meant to be read in conjunction with a close examination of the visual representations of the slave ship—the seven sections and plans of the *Brooks*, which it repeatedly evokes using Roman numerals and letters. Although the title and sections are the first things to engage the viewer, the figure numbers and letters force the individual to turn to the text for explanations. Each is incomplete without the other. Once having moved from the visuals to the text, these two aspects of the broadside virtually require the individual reader to move back and forth between these two elements. As with the Plymouth broadside, it would have been possible for one person to read the text aloud while others explored the wealth of details to be found in the visuals. Nonetheless, excepting the retention of the labels "Store Room" in the section showing the lower deck (IV), the London Committee version has abandoned the use of labels (men's room, women's room), replacing them with letters that are only explicated in the text itself.

This text, for the cognoscenti at least (as well as for today's art historian), could also be read as a commentary on or engagement with the Plymouth Committee's pamphlet and annexed plate—an "improvement" if you will. The London Committee text does not abandon or ignore the Plymouth committee text but rewrites it. *Description of a Slave Ship* elaborates and refines this earlier writing. Significantly, the one word that was changed from the Plymouth Committee pamphlet to the Plymouth Committee broadside—"annexed" (which occurs at the beginning of the text: "the annexed plate" is changed to "the above plate")—is retained in the London Committee version, though other words as well as the phrasing have been changed (that is, "The Plan and Sections annexed"). Since the sections are now "above" the text, it seems logical that the London Committee members would have retained its use if they had been responding to the broadside.

Despite many points of convergence, there are also a wide range of statistical discrepancies between the Plymouth and London committee texts. The first paragraph of both versions begins by identifying the plans as those of a slave ship. But the London Committee immediately identifies the plans as those of the *Brooks*, something that Elford does not do until paragraph 4. It also explains the reasons for and manner in which it was selected—for its typicality. The London broadside then offers a detailed statistical analysis of the *Brooks* in paragraphs 2, 3, and 4. It lists its dimensions in careful detail and notes it "Nominal tonnage" and "Supposed tonnage" (without, however, clarifying the difference between the two). It lists the number of seamen as well as the number of slaves carried according to Captain Parrey's testimony in parliament (609). The idea of stowing slaves "one to a ton" goes unmentioned, dismissed we might speculate as deceptive and irrelevant. In fact, IV through VII are needed to show *all* the Africans who are stowed as so much cargo. This is a visual as well as verbal refutation of the Plymouth approach. At the same time, it requires less imaginative participation by the reader-viewer, who no longer has to conjure up the platforms in her/his mind. But by not showing the platforms and by suggesting that what it did show was a truthful realization, the Plymouth plan could be said to deceive and confuse. In fact, platforms were an essential aspect of the trade, and the *Brooks* under regulation would have carried in the order of 482 and not 297 people in its holds. So the pioneering Plymouth pamphlet and annexed plate, which visualized the truth about the slave trade by revealing what was hidden in the holds, was now shown to offer something less than the truth. The London Committee broadside asserts its own greater accuracy and truthfulness.

The ratio of slaves to tonnage according to *Description of a Slave Ship* is 3 to 2, while for *Plan of an African Ship's Lower Deck* is 5 to 3. The final numbers are little different (36 more according to the London Committee) since the Plymouth figures are based on "Nominal tonnage" while the London figures seemed based on "Supposed tonnage by measurement." The amount of space allotted to each individual according to type (men, women, boys, girls) is identical in both versions (paragraph 4 in the London broadside, paragraph 2 in the Plymouth pamphlet), though the distribution of figures in the schematics does not always correspond. There are, for example, 27 girls in the aft room of the lower deck in the London plan but 30 in the Plymouth plan. What is interesting is that the London version mimes the rhetorical structure of the Plymouth Committee. The Plymouth text starts with 297 figures on the main deck and then jumps to 609. The London Committee starts with 482 and then moves to 609. Platforms, according to the Plymouth Committee, account for the chief differences. According to the London committee, a "full" slave ship (according to the new regulations) was 482, while the additional 127 persons (and a higher percentage of men, who required more space) required techniques of "close packing" described in paragraphs 5 through 8.

According to the London Committee's text, the visual rendering of Africans in the hold of a slave ship falls short of the truth itself. As a footnote in the remarks explains, "It must be noted, that every possible advantage of stowing is allowed in the plan. There are or ought to be in each apartment one or more poopoo tubs; there are also stanchions to support the platforms and decks; for which no deduction is made; but the deck is supposed clear of every encumbrance whatever."[11] It is generous (in the amount of space it gives individuals) or deceptive—indeed, both at the same time. Paragraphs 9 and 10 address aspects of this problem by explaining the longitudinal sections and how the space between the platforms impinges on the living cargo. These paragraphs, like the earlier ones (5 through 8) elaborate on the fourth paragraph from the Plymouth pamphlet with the two references to the slave ships *Kitty* and *Venus* in paragraph 9 essentially the same as those that conclude paragraph 4 of the Plymouth pamphlet (though their order in the text has been reversed). The London broadside then devotes paragraph 11 to describing the level of mortality, illness, and general physical abuse that results from these practices.

In many portions of the text, the same basic material is presented in both the London and Plymouth versions. This is visible in paragraphs 12–15 in which the mode of securing, airing, and exercising the enslaved Africans is detailed. This information is handled much earlier in the Plymouth broadside—in paragraph 3. In the London version, the reader is kept in the hold as the conditions are described for the first 11 paragraphs. There is no escape. This confrontation with the different sections and the detailed written descriptions is purposefully protracted. Once this world below decks has been thoroughly dissected, the commentary declares a sharp break as the reader is now asked to turn to a new scene above deck. Here the London description follows the Plymouth description very closely. The London version uses the beginning of this scene to explain that "the men are constantly chained two and two; the right leg of one to the left leg of the other, and their hands are secured in the same manner." This is, of course, evident in the section plans of the London broadside as opposed to the Plymouth Committee's annexed plate, but it is never explained until this moment. Nonetheless, one might expect it to have been moved up earlier given the extensive and detailed elaborations that proceeded (for instance, in paragraph 6, where it is mentioned that the men are kept continually in irons due to the fear of insurrection). Women and children are said to not be chained, according to this broadside, which reminds us that it is not trying to describe the worst-case situations but a typically good one. Well the reader should be reminded, since shackles for women and children survive, this was not always the case.[12] Paragraph 14 is an almost verbatim transcription from paragraph 3 of the Plymouth pamphlet. Paragraphs 15 and 16 then extended this analysis to detail still further the brutality and inhumanity of even this practice of bringing people onto the deck.

Paragraph 17 begins by appropriating language similar to that at the beginning of paragraph 4 in the Plymouth pamphlet: this account which must as first seem a fiction, in fact grossly understates the case. It thus returns to an issue already raised in a footnote tied to an early section of the text and reiterates the fact that section drawings are simplified, "idealized," and sanitized renderings. The holds must contain various paraphernalia for which the plan makes no allowances. Certainly these engravings do not conform to the conditions described by the ship's doctors, who were required by law to travel onboard slave ships. When attending the sick below decks, one doctor, despite his humane intentions, found himself stepping on his patients as they were so tightly packed. This portion of the London Committee remarks thus excerpts Dr. Alexander Falconbridge's *Account of the Slave Trade*, which describes the state of confusion, suffering, and disarray to be expected in the hold: "The deck, that is, the floor of their rooms, was so covered with the blood and mucus which had proceeded from them in consequence of the flux, that it resembled a slaughterhouse."[13]

The first seventeen paragraphs of the London Committee text focus on the conditions of the enslaved Africans, with virtually no attention given to the crew. Paragraphs 18 through 20 briefly turn the reader's attention to the seamen. The difficult conditions under which they must abide—sleeping on deck, with little protection from the elements, forced to perform tasks that are offensive and dangerous. They do not escape the illnesses of the people they transport, but die more quickly than people in other lines of work. Again, this echoes ideas and phrases found in the Plymouth pamphlet, notably the quotation of Clarkson himself. The London Committee thus quotes the Plymouth Committee quoting its own principal agent.

It is worth noting that there is only one paragraph in the Plymouth pamphlet that is ignored or rejected outright in *Description of a Slave Ship*. This is paragraph 6, calling for a coalition of people to oppose the slave trade—even those who don't oppose slavery. Rather than draw attention to this fault line in the politics of abolition, *Description of a Slave Ship* uses the power of the image to hide it. As with the Philadelphia Abolition Society, this cry for a popular front around this one image may have seemed too transparent, drawing attention to a problem that was best ignored, best hidden. It was the inhumanity of the slave trade they wanted to bring to light, not their own internal differences. In this one area at least, the Plymouth Committee pamphlet suffered from an excess of truthfulness.

Again, following the lead of the Plymouth pamphlet, the London broadside concludes by refocusing attention on the conditions of Africans caught in the machinations of the slave trade. In its penultimate paragraph, the Plymouth Committee calls on readers to provide more information or documentation on the slave trade itself, or to provide the committees with donations (that is, subscriptions). In this same paragraph, the London Committee offers another horrifying account—of a schooner that lost 40 of the 140 slaves it carried over the course of an eighteen-hour storm. More than enough information has been gathered. Indeed, there is no call for financial contributions. As an appeal for donations, the integrity of the broadside might be compromised. Rather, it maintains the air of a disinterested, scientific account that provokes distress and passionate feelings to end the trade among writers and readers alike.

The final paragraphs of each version also have much in common. The Plymouth pamphlet:

> And people would do well to consider that it does not often fall to the lot of individuals, to have an opportunity of performing so important a moral and religious duty, as that of endeavouring to put an end to a practise, which may, without exaggeration, be stiled one of the greatest evils at this day existing upon the earth.[14]

The London broadside:

> As then the inhumanity of this trade must be universally admitted and lamented, people would do well to consider, that it does not often fall to the lot of individuals, to have an opportunity of performing so important a moral and religious duty, as that of endeavouring to put an end to a practice, which may, without exaggeration, be stiled one of the *greatest evils at this day existing upon the earth.*[15]

It is certainly noteworthy that *Description of a Slave Ship* is not a signed document. There is no official author. It is anonymous. On one hand, this reinforces its scientific approach. It is objective. It does not represent any one group's point of view. On another level, however, it would have been very hard to claim this as a document that originated simply with the London Committee. It is not just the idea that was taken by Clarkson, Phillips, and their committee. It was the language as well as visual detail. The broadside can perhaps best be seen as a coauthored effort. The actual collaboration did not go very far, though that might have been Elford and Wilberforce's initial intention. The general move, as already discussed, was toward a more detailed, accurate, and realistic (that is, less "primitive") document.

The London Committee plans of the slave ship nonetheless offered a simplified, schematic view—a template onto which the reader-viewer could map the horrors of the Middle Passage, as described in the text or elsewhere. Lacking the romanticizing tendencies of artists such as British painter George Morland or efforts at fully articulated images that achieved a high level of specificity (naturalism), the London Committee representations offered a dispassionate and apparently scientific approach that, in fact, powerfully captured public sympathy for the human suffering. On the reaction of the British public to the plan of the slave ship, Clarkson wrote, "No one saw it but he was impressed. It spoke to him in a language, which was at once intelligible and irresistible. It brought forth the tear of sympathy in behalf of the sufferers, and it fixed their sufferings in his heart."[16] The detailed cross section rid the ship of its disorganization and the attentively drawn figures were cleansed of the bodily fluids described by doctors and introduced in the text. By choosing a cleverly designed schematic plan that eliminated disorder, the abolitionists condensed the Middle Passage into an icon that would be easily stored in the visual memory. The broadside also provided a level of human detail that deepened the complexity of the image. The text and the pictures worked in a coordinated way. To understand fully the horrors of the Middle Passage, reader-viewers had to synthesize texts and images in their minds.

THE SLAVE SHIP ICON, PUBLICITY, AND PARLIAMENTARY ACTION

The slave ship icon would become a mainstay of the Abolition Society's arsenal. Within three months of its first publication in April 1789, at least 8,700 copies had been printed and distributed by the London Committee alone.[17] The initial print order of broadsides was placed for a very specific use. As a notation in the minute book on April 21, 1789, describes, "Mr. James Phillips is directed to send a Plan and

Sections of the Slave Ship to the Members of both houses of Parliament and to such other persons as may be thought expedient by the Committee of Distribution."[18] The Committee of Distribution intended for this first run of broadsides to reach the Members of Parliament before William Wilberforce introduced his motion for the abolition of the slave trade in the House of Commons on May 13, 1789. Thus, the printing and distribution was timed to coincide with a specific political aim; that is, convincing the Members of Parliament that there was no solution short of the abolition of the slave trade. The Committee of Distribution had hoped that the graphic visualization of the hold of a slave ship would firmly plant this idea in the minds of many Members of Parliament, enough to mobilize a coalition of statesmen in support of abolition. To add to the intensity of their political demands, the abolitionists employed an increasing variety of ammunition; the slave ship icon was joined by the Report of the Privy Council, which had been presented in Parliament in April, and by the thousands of petitions from around the countryside that demanded an end to the slave trade.

The speech that William Wilberforce made on May 13, 1789, is believed to be one of his most eloquent and moving orations, lasting more than three and a half hours, with Members of Parliament riveted to his every word. Wilberforce had returned to Parliament after a grave illness to deliver the speech, and the intensity of his delivery together with the duration of his argument moved his fellow statesmen, friend and foe. His speech was later published in its entirety together with some of the comments it provoked from the Members of Parliament.[19] Wilberforce had carefully studied the Report of the Privy Council, a document with which his fellow Members of Parliament would have been familiar, and wisely chose to tailor the outline of his speech to the six sections of that report: "(1) A detailed description of the different kingdoms along the Slave Coast and the way in which slaves were obtained in each. (2) The carrying of slaves to the West Indies. (3) The treatment of slaves in the West Indies. (4) The extent of the Trade and the population of the West Indies. (5) The advantages said to be enjoyed by the French sugar colonies. (6) The slave Trade as conducted by other countries."[20] Of these six points, Wilberforce placed considerable time and graphic emphasis on the description of the Middle Passage, stating, "This, I confess, in my opinion, is the most wretched part of the whole subject. *So much misery condensed into so little room* is more than the human imagination has ever before conceived."[21]

As one of the key strategists of the London Committee, who carefully coordinated their efforts with legislative action in Parliament, Wilberforce was well aware that his fellow statesmen would have received copies of *Description of a Slave Ship*. Many would have had it before them, and even might have studied it in wonderment, following the contours of its graphic rigidity as Wilberforce tried to animate it, making the situation it portrayed seem all the more real:

> I verily believe, therefore, if the wretchedness of any *one* of the many hundred Negroes stowed in each ship could be brought before their view, and remain within the sight of the African merchant, that there is no one among them, whose

heart would bear it?—Let any one imagine to himself, 6 or 700 of these wretches chained two and two, surrounded with every object that is nauseous and disgusting, diseased, and struggling under every kind of wretchedness!—How can we bear to think of such a scene as this? One would think it had been determined to heap upon them all the varieties of bodily pain, for the purpose of blunting the feelings of their mind; and yet, in this very point (to shew [*sic*] the power of human prejudice), the situation of the slaves has been described by Mr. Norris one of the Liverpool delegates, in a manner, which, I am sure, will convince the House how interest can draw a film over the eyes, so thick, that total blindness could do no more, and how it is our duty, therefore to trust not the reasonings of interested men, or to their way of colouring a transaction.[22]

Wilberforce devoted so much time and effort to the horrific conditions of the Middle Passage because of the opposition he faced from the defenders of the slave trade.

The merchant and planter lobby was not to be taken lightly; like the abolitionists, they were organized in their political assaults. They published newspaper articles, pamphlets, and books that tried to dispel the abolitionists' charges of the inhumanity, grotesqueness, and cruelty of the Middle Passage and plantation life in the West Indies. They ran a marketing campaign of their own that aimed to paint a rosy picture of the Middle Passage and to disclaim the reports of torture, mutilation, and death. In so doing, the Liverpool Delegates, as they were called, gave testimony before the Privy Council in defense of the slave trade, and on one such occasion, the slave merchant Mr. Norris tried to argue that the experience of the African captives in the Middle Passage was commodious, if not pleasurable. This was the type of testimony that Wilberforce set out to disprove in his speech. He began by citing excerpts from Norris's own testimony,

"Their *apartments*," says Mr. Norris, "are *fitted up* as much for their advantage as circumstances will admit." The right ancle [*sic*] of one indeed is *connected* with the left ancle [*sic*] of another *by a small iron fetter*, and if they are turbulent, by another on their wrists. "They have several meals a day; some," as he tells you, "of *their own country provisions, with the best sauces of African cookery*; and, by way of variety, another meal of pulse, & c. according to European taste. After breakfast they have water to wash themselves, while their apartments are perfumed with frankincense and lime-juice. Before dinner, they are amused after the manner of their country. The song and dance are *promoted*"; and, as if the whole was really a scene of pleasure and dissipation, it is added, that games of chance are furnished. "The men play and sing, while the women and girls make fanciful ornaments with beads, which they are plentifully supplied with." Such is the sort of strain in which the Liverpool Delegates, and particularly Mr. Norris, gave evidence before the Privy Council.[23]

If the Abolition Society and Wilberforce had it their way—if their strategy of distributing "a Plan and Sections of the Slave Ship to the Members of both houses of Parliament" had made an impact, it might convince them to see through Norris's tales of ease and merriment. Unrelenting in his cause, Wilberforce proceeded, point by point, to refute the ludicrous details of Norris's storybook account of the Middle Passage:

> What will the House think, when, by the concurring testimony of other witnesses, the true history is laid open. The slaves, who are sometimes described as rejoicing at their captivity, are so wrung with misery at leaving their country, that it is the constant practice to *set sail in the night*, lest they should be sensible of their departure. The *pulse* which Mr. Norris talks of are *horse beans*;...Mr. Norris talks of frankincense and lime-juice; when all the surgeons tell you, the slaves are stowed so close, that there is not room to tread among them: and when you have it in evidence from Sir George Yonge, that even in a ship which wanted 200 of her complement, *the stench was intolerable.* The song and dance, says Mr. Norris are *promoted.* It had been more fair, perhaps, if he had explained that word *promoted.* The truth is, that, for the sake of exercise, these miserable wretches, loaded with chains, oppressed with disease and wretchedness, are forced to dance by the terror of the lash and sometimes by the actual use of it.[24]

Wilberforce warned the Members of Parliament about taking such descriptions at face value. Instead, he argued that the only trustworthy evidence was *death*, that is, the disproportionately high numbers of slaves and seamen who die in the trade each year. As Furneaux explains, "the descriptions of the Middle Passage given by defenders of the Trade could not be reconciled with statistics for the death rates of slaves and seamen."[25]

At the end of his rousing oration, Wilberforce laid before the House twelve detailed measures against the slave trade derived from the Privy Council Report. Member of Parliament Edmund Burke commended Wilberforce's speech: "The House, the nation and all of Europe, were under very great and serious obligations to the hon. Gentleman, for having brought the subject forward in a manner the most masterly, impressive and eloquent. Principles so admirable, laid down with so much order and force, were equal to any thing he had ever heard of in modern oratory."[26] Along with Burke, William Pitt believed that Wilberforce had argued convincingly enough for Parliament to consider his pioneering motion to put an immediate end to the slave trade. But despite these few praiseworthy words of encouragement from powerful voices in Parliament, the coalition of support that the London Committee needed was still elusive. After prolonged debate, Wilberforce's motion was tabled and it was decided that still more evidence needed to be presented before Parliament in the next session. This was the first time that a motion for the abolition of the slave trade had been put before Parliament, and it would take several more motions and nearly twenty years before the Members of Parliament would be convinced to take the necessary legislative action to bring about its demise.

THE FRENCH REVOLUTION, THE SOCIÉTÉ DES AMIS DE NOIRS, AND THE COMTE DE MIRABEAU

On August 7, 1789, members of the London Committee sent Thomas Clarkson to France to promote the efforts of the Société des Amis de Noirs, established in February 1788 by the journalist Jean-Pierre Brissot de Warville and modeled after the Society for Effecting the Abolition of the Slave Trade in England.[27] The London Committee, together with Wilberforce and Clarkson, saw an opportunity in the revolutionary climate that was blossoming in France during the spring and summer of 1789. The creation of a new representative body of the people, the National Assembly, in June was followed by the July 14 storming of the Bastille. Barely three weeks later, Clarkson arrived in Paris.

The Société des Amis de Noirs boasted some of the most outspoken liberal voices of the revolution among its founding members.[28] Clarkson aimed to take advantage of an atmosphere ripe for social and political reform to agitate for the abolition of the slave trade, hoping that it might be counted "among the abuses to be done away."[29] Ultimately, his mission was intended to investigate whether the two rival countries, England and France, might mutually agree to find a way to abolish the slave trade. Both countries remained suspicious that if one abolished the slave trade, the other would benefit by assuming its trading interests.[30] The anti-slave-trade committees in both countries drew fire from their opposition at home for forsaking national interests in pursuit of their lofty goal. Among nonrevolutionary French, the members of the Société were seen as employing the abolition of the slave trade as simply another revolutionary tool: Brissot de Warville and "others associated with the *Société* were accused of forming a conspiracy with England, the object of which was to undermine France by abolishing the slave trade and destroying her colonial power."[31]

The Société des Amis de Noirs was primed for Clarkson's arrival and had already engaged in its own national campaign of distributing educational materials about the injustices of the slave trade and of slavery itself by placing public notices in the newspapers.[32] The Société was in regular communication with the London Committee, receiving news of its most recent agitation efforts and copies of its latest publications. In fact, the exciting news of the development of *Description of a Slave Ship*, communicated in a letter from the London Committee chairman Granville Sharp in May 1789, moved the Société des Amis de Noirs to make their own version of the schematic engraving. As the minutes from a committee meeting held on May 19, 1789, state,

> According to the motion made by the president to have engraved in France, as in England, the plan and sections of the slave ship called Brooks, it is directed that M. de Warville speak to M. de la Fosse, engraver, and that the Committee obtain the easiest and most economical means to make a copy of the engraving when the Society from London [the London Committee] send us some copies.... It is directed that the copies of this gravure will be placed publicly on sale as a manner of producing the biggest impression.[33]

But as the mounting pressures of the brewing revolution in France preoccupied many members of the Société des Amis de Noirs, this French version would not be published until February 1790.

When upon his arrival Clarkson found the French abolitionist visual propaganda lacking, he quickly requested a package from the London Committee, which contained some of its latest anti-slave-trade issues (see fig. 3.4). "It consisted of above a thousand of the plan and section of a slave-ship, with an explanation in French...[and] one thousand of my Essays on the Impolicy of the Slave Trade, which had been translated into the French Language."[34] Clarkson endeavored to make these materials available to members of the Société des Amis de Noirs, especially the powerful Comte de Mirabeau, whom he was lobbying to bring a resolution before the National Assembly for the immediate abolition of the slave trade. Hoping to employ the same aggressive dissemination strategies that he and the London Committee had developed to educate the members of parliament prior to Wilberforce's first appeal for a motion to abolish the slave trade in 1789, Clarkson schemed to have these materials distributed among the members of the National Assembly "as preparatory to the motion of Mirabeau." To do this, he relied upon influential members of the Société des Amis de Noirs—the Archbishop of Aix, the Bishop of Chartres, the Marquis de la Fayette, the Duc de la Rochefoucauld, the Comte de Mirabeau, and Brissot de Warville—who had intimate ties to the National Assembly. Copies were also given to Madame la Marquise de la Fayette and other women members of the Société des Amis de Noirs, who no doubt shared them with other women supporters of abolition.[35]

The circulation of these graphic printed materials, especially the slave ship icon, made Clarkson an immediate success among the advocates for abolition.[36] As he remembers,

> This distribution had not been long begun, before I witnessed its effects. The virtuous Abbe Gregoire, and several members of the National Assembly, called upon me. The section of the slave-ship, it appeared, had been the means of drawing them towards me. They wished more accurate information concerning it. Indeed it made its impression upon all who saw it.[37]

In this passage, Clarkson remembered the "section of the slave-ship" as if it were an animate being capable of certain powers, abilities, and agency—"I witnessed its effects." For Clarkson, the slave ship icon acted as a powerfully charged magnet, drawing "all who saw it" toward him. Those who saw it wanted to believe that it was, in fact, an accurate representation—that what was drawn in the schematic and written in the text was based on something *real*. Even the text of *Description of a Slave Ship* warns, "To persons unacquainted with the mode of carrying on this system of trading in human flesh, these Plans and Sections will appear rather a fiction, than a real representation of a slave-ship."[38] None of the members of the Société des Amis de Noirs had ever been inside of the packed hold of a slave ship. Some, like Brissot, had observed chattel slavery in the United States, and others were well aware of slavery in Saint-Domingue. But as the saying goes, seeing is believing. The requests of some committee members for more "accurate information" were pleas for evidence to substantiate their distinct *need* to believe (to see) that it was a "real representation." The image made an *"impression"*: an imprint, an indelible mark upon the consciousness of "all who saw it."

In fact, the engraving of the slave ship seems to have provoked a range of reactions among those who saw it, from speechlessness, as in the case of the Archbishop of Aix, to clarity for the Bishop of Chartres, who "had not given credit to all the tales which had been related of the Slave-trade, till he had seen this plate; after which there was nothing so barbarous which might not readily be believed."[39] One wonders if they saw themselves—their current revolutionary moment—in those small black figures, a disenfranchised people? Did they perhaps see the potential for an organized uprising, an insurrection, a revolt? It is documented that many people in France connected the cause of the enslaved masses in Saint-Domingue with their own struggle. Looking at the rows and rows of black figures, they might have thought about the revolutionary potential of masses of people, with the taking of the Bastille still fresh in their minds.[40]

The penetration of these printed materials into the French public sphere, including a copy of *Description of a Slave Ship* published as a supplement in *Le Courrier de L'Europe*, also produced reactions from the detractors of the abolitionist cause.[41] Stirred by the mounting activities of the Société des Amis de Noirs and Clarkson, the planter and merchant lobbies filled the newspapers with stories manufactured to incite public suspicions about the activities of the abolitionists. Clarkson recounts, "One of them was, that they [the members of the Société des Amis de Noirs] were going to send twelve thousand muskets to the Negros [*sic*] of St. Domingo, in order to promote an insurrection there."[42] As mentioned, this accusation was not completely unfounded. Shortly after Clarkson arrived in Paris, a delegation of free people of color came from Saint-Domingue to demand their representation in the National Assembly in October 1789. Led by Vincent Ogé, a corresponding member of the Société des Amis de Noirs, they had been inspired by the events of July 14, 1789, and further believed that the Rights of Man belonged to them too.[43] But they were soon enough disenchanted. After repeatedly being denied their request for representation by the National Assembly, Ogé and the delegation from Saint-Domingue returned home to plot their revenge. On October 21, 1790, Ogé led the first notable black revolt in Saint-Domingue. C. L. R. James recounts, "If not at the instigation of the Friends of the Negro, at least with their consent, Ogé left Paris to lead the insurrection at San Domingo. And in this he was aided and abetted by no less a person than Clarkson."[44] However, the French army swiftly quashed the uprising.[45]

The most remarkable reaction to the plan of the slave ship came from its most important intended audience, the Comte de Mirabeau, the noted orator and statesman who was scheduled to bring a resolution before the National Assembly for the immediate abolition of the slave trade. Clarkson recalls,

> When Mirabeau first saw it, he was so impressed by it, that he ordered a mechanic to make a model of it in wood, at a considerable expense. This model he kept afterwards in his dining-room. It was a ship in miniature, about a yard

long, and little wooden men and women, which were painted black to represent the slaves, were seen stowed in their proper places.[46]

Mirabeau's wooden model of the slave ship was fifteen centimeters high by fifty-one centimeters long by approximately seven centimeters wide (fig. 2.5). It bears a remarkable resemblance to what one might expect from a three-dimensional rendering of the plan and sections of the slave ship. The model is made up of two separate pieces, which are fastened together by two hooks, one at the bow and one at the stern, when the model is closed. It is split at the center longitudinally from bow to stern, and opens out to reveal the decks with small black figures arranged according to the plan. The overhead beams, also drawn according to the plan, alternating larger and then smaller, encumber the space available between decks. The only figures in the model are those that are carved in wood and painted black, representing the slaves. Consequently, the space that signifies the captain's quarters is left empty. Fourteen miniature brass cannon line the perimeter of the top deck, with the nose of each cannon pointing out of the square holes in the side of the ship. The sides of the ship are painted gray from the top edge of the deck to the water line, below which they are painted white.

While a model of a slave ship might seem by contemporary standards an eccentric item to have in one's dining room, we should consider how it may have served Mirabeau's abolitionist efforts. Ship model making was not entirely uncommon by the end of the eighteenth century. Once the domain of naval architects, it was evolving into a respected artisan's craft. But the model of a slave ship would have been quite a novelty; it would have exposed the contents beneath the main deck and offered many different perspectives from which to see *and touch* the carved black figures. He planned to use the model as evidence—a dramatic and convincing prop—to add a visual dimension to the speech he planned to give before the

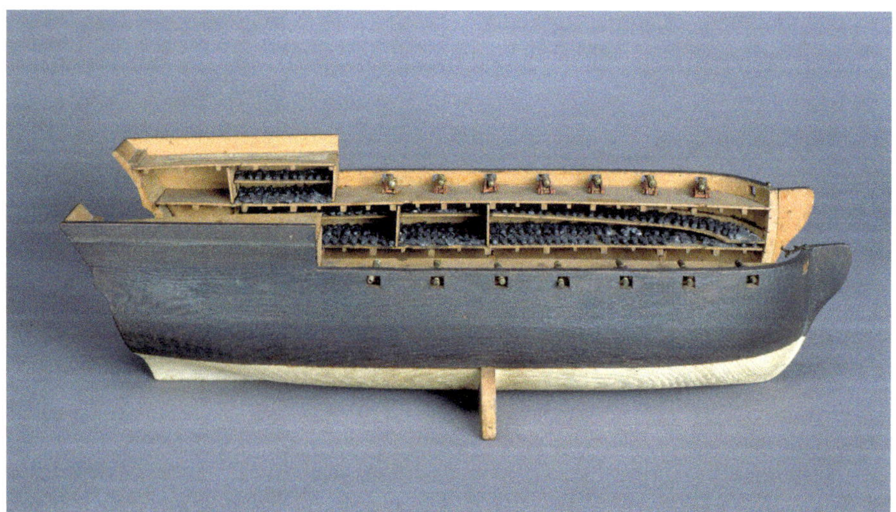

2.5

Comte de Mirabeau, *Model of a Slave Ship*, 1790.

National Assembly. Yet, as a model in his dining room, it became a conversation piece and was somewhat analogous to the way that Quakers hung copies of the slave ship icon in frames in their homes.

In addition to seeing Mirabeau's model, Clarkson had the opportunity to preview the speech. Mirabeau consulted with Clarkson, providing him with outlines to examine and questions to answer regarding "the various evils belonging to the transportation of the Africans from their own country." Dumont remembered how Mirabeau passionately devoted himself to writing it for six months, treating each word "with much affection." And yet the speech was never delivered; the merchant/planter lobby prevented the subject from coming up for debate.[47] Historian Chatillon observes, "It is possibly the best speech that he never gave, above all about the passage that he wrote about the conditions of the crossing (directly inspired by the text that accompanied the engraving of the *Brooks*)."[48] Wrote Mirabeau,

> Behold the model of a vessel laden with these unfortunate beings, and seek not to turn away your gaze! How they are piled one upon the other! How they are crammed into the between-decks! Unable to stand erect: nay, even seated, their heads are bowed. More than that, they cannot move their members, tightly bound, nor even their bodies; for, partakers of all the wants, of all the miseries of him who shares their irons, each man is attached to another: often to a dying one, often to a dead body! Mark how the vessel when it rolls hurts them, mutilates them, bruises them against each other, tears them with their own chains, and presents thus a thousand tortures in a single picture! They crouch themselves down, all the space is filled; and the insensate cupidity which should succour them has not even foreseen that no room for passage remains, but that it is necessary to tread under foot the bodies of the living victims. Have they at the least a sufficient quantity of wholesome air? Let us calculate it together. A space of a little less than six feet in length, and a little more than a foot in breadth, is the base of the column of air, the smallest possible, which has to suffice for the respiration of each one.... The poor wretches! I see them, I hear them gasping for breath: their parched and protruded tongues paint their anguish, and cannot further express it! How they hang to, how they cluster round, the grates! How they endeavor to catch even rays of light, in the vain hope of cooling themselves thereby, were it only for an instant![49]

This portion of Mirabeau's undelivered speech focuses closely on the relationship of space to the human body. He describes that which cannot be seen, but which is taken for granted as a basic human necessity (right)—air—something seemingly evanescent, yet ever present. In the schematic, air is represented (almost unconsciously) by the white areas, appearing only sporadically between the masses of black figures in the confines of the line drawings. The scarcity of space portrays a sense of utter suffocation. The air that Mirabeau so eloquently describes metaphorically embodies that innate right of every man: liberty.

Only a few months before Mirabeau was inspired to write this speech, in August 1789, the National Assembly had adopted the Declaration of the Rights of Man and the Citizen, to serve as the foundation of the new constitution of France. It stated that "all men are born free and equal in rights—rights of liberty, private property, the inviolability of the person, and resistance to oppression." These things are denied the chained mass of black human figures that Mirabeau describes. Their contorted human bodies in submission, with "heads bowed," convey a virtual state of paralysis, rigor mortis, and imprisonment. Alluding to the revolutionary struggles underway in France, Mirabeau's speech not only implied but plainly stated that the enslaved masses in Saint-Domingue deserved to share in the rights of man. In the opening of his speech, he declared,

> I will neither degrade this Assembly nor myself by seeking to prove that Negroes have a right to their liberty! You have already decided that question, because you have declared that *all men* ARE BORN AND DIE EQUAL AND FREE; and it is not on this side of the Atlantic that corrupted sophists will dare to assert that Negroes are not men![50]

If Mirabeau had been able to deliver his great oration, his dramatic performance would have demanded the participation of the audience to listen, look, and feel. His model of the slave ship would have been a key prop, visible in the round for all members of the National Assembly to regard. Mirabeau's wooden model fulfilled a need to imagine the stifling space that the schematic portends in three dimensions.

Even though Mirabeau wasn't able to use his model for the dramatic performance he had planned, it became the talk of many liberals in Paris after he subsequently gave it to the Société des Amis de Noirs at their meeting of March 15, 1790. Before Mirabeau's death, in 1791, Brissot de Warville had planned to publish the undelivered speech.[51] But soon the revolution would take precedence over the abolition of the slave trade for many members of the Société des Amis de Noirs. The

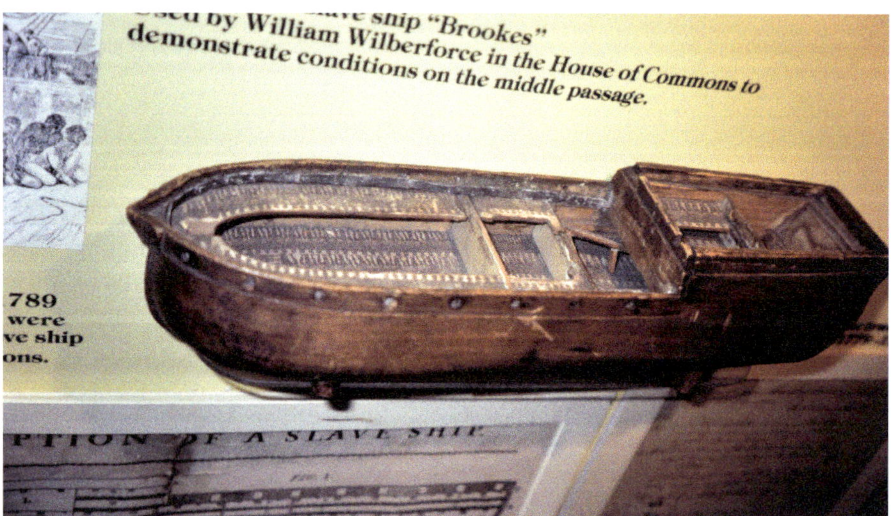

2.6
William Wilberforce, *Model of Slave Ship*, 1790.

first formation of the Société would be silenced by the Terror: in 1793, Brissot and Claviere were guillotined; Concordet took his own life in prison; and Lafayette gave in to the Austrians.[52]

For Mirabeau, the slave ship icon was an arresting image with a powerful text, capable of moving him to craft a wooden model and one of the most captivating orations in abolition history. His model remained in the private collection of the Abbe Gregoire, with the other writings of the second Société des Amis de Noirs, formed after the reign of terror had subsided.[53]

When Clarkson returned from Paris, he shared Mirabeau's idea for a model with the London Committee, including William Wilberforce, who had a wooden model of his own made that measured approximately eighteen inches in length and had the plan of the slave ship laid out on the flat surfaces of the respective decks (fig. 2.6). Small enough to be held, he brought this model to the House of Commons, where it was passed from hand to hand among Members of Parliament that summer. Wilberforce used it to make specific points regarding overcrowding and the inadequacy of the existing regulations of the slave trade. Above all, he wanted to give those Members of Parliament unfamiliar with the interior of the hold of a slave ship another visual aid with which they could imagine it. By these means, he hoped to convince them that the abolition of the slave trade was the only motion that Parliament should consider.

ABSTRACT OF THE EVIDENCE

In the spring of 1791, the London Committee was gearing up for another important parliamentary challenge. According to the minutes of February 1, 1791, "Mr. James Phillips is desired to print 400 Wooden Impressions of the Slave Ship and 500 of the Copperplate Impressions." In the same minute, he was further directed "to send one of the Copperplate Impressions of the Slave Ship to each of the new Members of Parliament."[54] Some of the wooden impressions were distributed to the newer country committees that recently had been established by Clarkson, and others were posted locally.

The publication of *Abstract of the Evidence* was timed to have an impact on the parliamentary debates that were scheduled for later that spring (figs. 2.7, 2.8). As a succinct compendium of the offenses of the slave trade, as well as arguments for its abolition, the London Committee believed it was an indispensable reference for clergy, Members of Parliament, and other people of influence. Thus, it was key to have it printed and distributed to the Members of Parliament in time for them to read it before the hearings on April 18 and 19, 1791. But by the beginning of April, Phillips faced such a backlog of printing jobs that an alternative printer had to be sought. As the minute for April 5 reads, "It is the opinion of this Committee that Mr. Phillips not being able to complete the printing of No. 2 of the Abstract of the Evidence in time to answer the purpose of the Committee some other Printer be employed in that business and that it be referred to Mr. Phillips and Mr. Wedgwood to engage such printer." With the assistance of printers Mr. Cooper of Bond Street and Mr. Marsh of Tower Hill, the *Abstract of the Evidence* was prepared

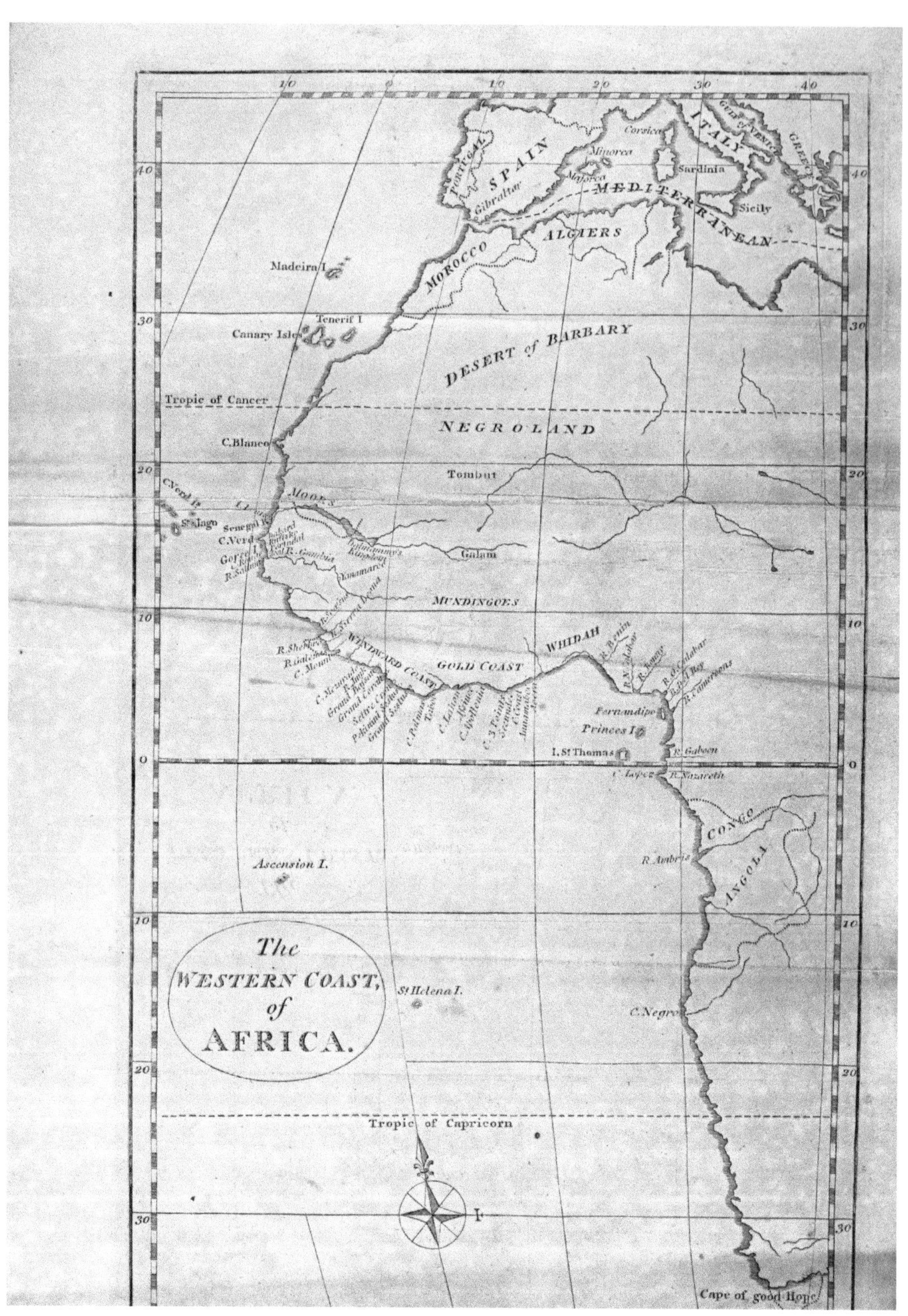

2.7

Map of the Western Coast of Africa, from
Abstract of the Evidence, 1791.

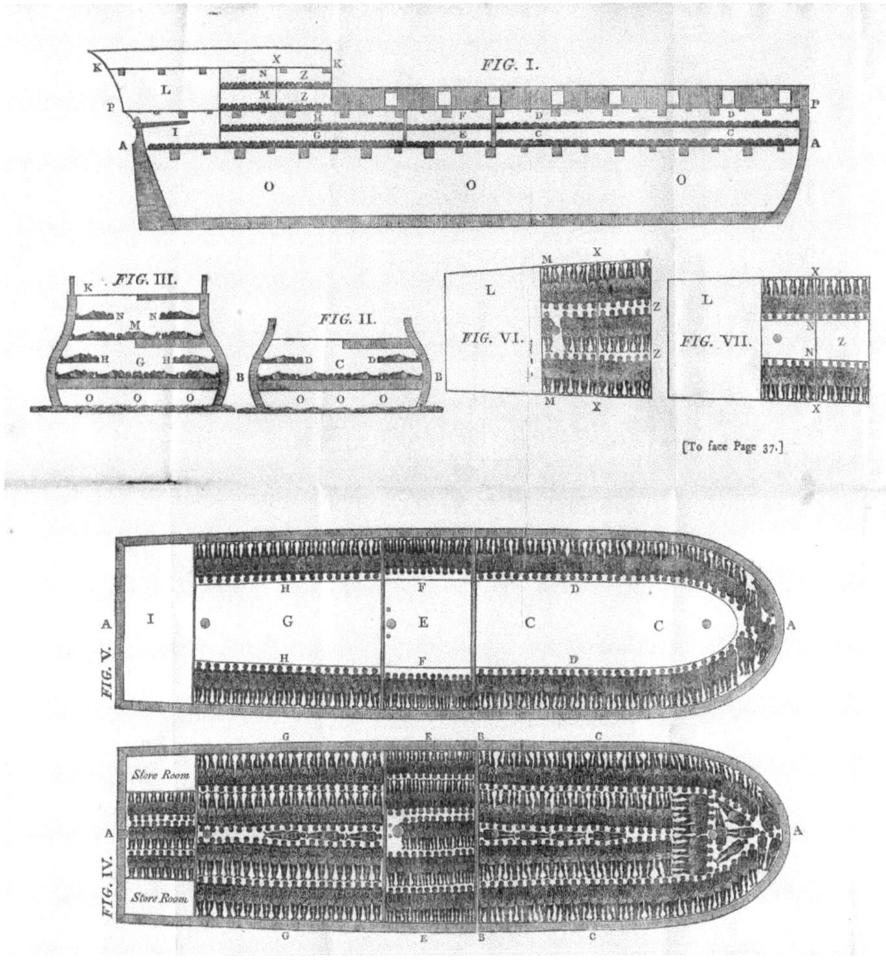

2.8

Description of a Slave Ship, from
Abstract of the Evidence, 1791.

and distributed to the members of the House of Commons just in time for the
hearings.[55] Despite their efforts, however, the House voted against the abolition of
the slave trade.

Although a small volume, *Abstract of the Evidence* became one of the most
important publications of the London Committee. An astounding ten thousand
copies of the book were printed in 1791 alone.[56] This number includes three thousand copies printed in a "cheap edition" that sold for one shilling each.

With the parliamentary setback, the London Committee wasted no time in
renewing its spirit. Clarkson set out once more to encourage the country committees to gather signatures for petitions, as another attempt to convince Parliament to
abolish the slave trade would be made the following year. He traveled as far north
as Edinburgh, where he visited old friends, Katherine and Joseph Plymley. Katherine Plymley kept meticulous diaries of the activities of the Edinburgh Committee,

noting their highly successful petitioning efforts at the grassroots level. Her brother, the Archdeacon Joseph Plymley, was instrumental in leading their petitioning campaigns, gathering only the signatures of "respectable" petitioners who, according to the London Committee, normally did not include women and illiterate people, an indication of increasing middle-class participation in political matters.[57] In order for the campaign for abolition to receive the attention of lawmakers and powerful citizens, it first had to be run and supported by the middle classes (that is, it needed bourgeois validation). The participation of the lower classes in abolitionist activities never received the same attention as that of the middle classes, and only came to play a role after the movement had gained momentum.

The Edinburgh Committee, like the Plymouth Committee, was very active in spreading the word of abolition through its own publications. On October 14, 1791, it decided to print copies of *Abstract of the Evidence* "with all possible dispatch," even though "the Funds of the Society are at present exhausted by prior Publications."[58] Mr. Haliburton, secretary of the Edinburgh Committee, was soon in touch with his London colleagues, asking for their assistance. By December, this had resulted in the publication of another cheap edition of *An Abstract of the Evidence.* The Edinburgh Committee encouraged readers of *Abstract of the Evidence* to share this information freely and to furnish them with comments and suggestions: "When you shall have perused the information now transmitted, and communicated the same to the persons in your neighborhood whom you think best qualified to derive benefit from its perusal, we earnestly request your sentiments on the subject."[59] In her diary from this period, Katherine Plymley remarked, "The committee at Edinburgh have been very active. . . . They have sent an abstract of the evidence to every clergyman throughout Scotland—they paste up a plan of a Slave ship wherever they think it will be seen by many."[60]

Despite the wide circulation of visual propaganda such as the slave ship icon and compilations of convincing evidence such as the *Abstract,* Wilberforce's motions for the immediate abolition of the slave trade were not adopted by the House of Commons in 1790 or 1791. In 1792, William Pitt's motion for gradual abolition (by 1796) was passed in the House of Commons, but it failed to gain approval in the House of Lords. The following year, a bill for the abolition of the foreign slave trade was rejected and several other attempts in the late 1790s to abolish the slave trade were quashed.

CARL BERNHARD WADSTRÖM: *AN ESSAY ON COLONIZATION*

Yet back in 1794, before the ultimate triumphs of the next decade, the slave ship icon would be brought out once more to illustrate a new work on the subject of African colonization.[61] Published in London by the Swedish-born naturalist Carl Bernhard Wadström, it was titled *An Essay on Colonization, Particularly Applied to the Western Coast of Africa, with Some Free Thoughts on Cultivation and Commerce; also Brief Descriptions of the Colonies Already Formed, or Attempted, in Africa, Including Those of Sierra Leona and Bulama.*[62] This massive undertaking was presented in two extensive volumes totaling more than 550 pages, with multiple appendixes on various colonization projects, and six engraved plates, notably a

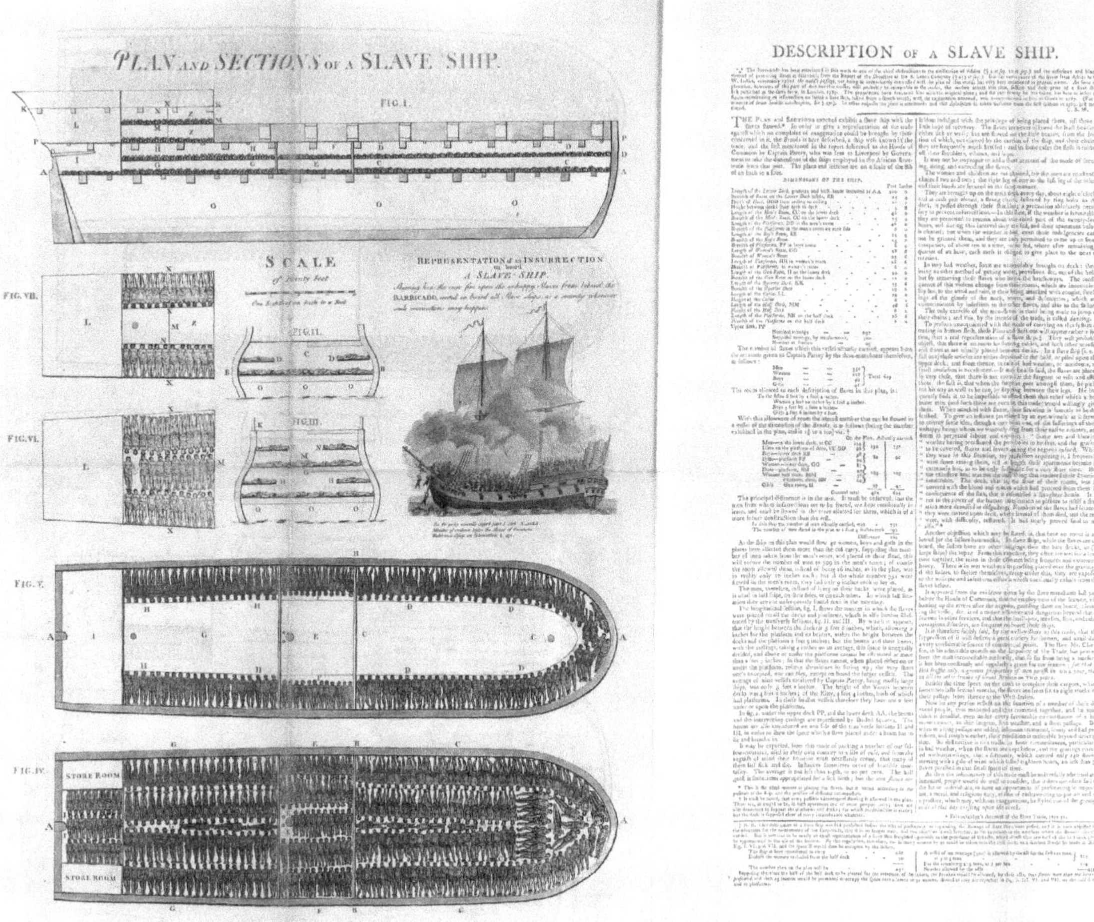

2.9

Carl Bernhard Wadström, *Plan and Sections
of a Slave Ship*, 1794.

new and radical printing of *Description of a Slave Ship* that included an image of
an insurrection (fig. 2.9). Wadström's *Essay on Colonization* offered a perspective
that was informed by his own exploration in Africa, his ties to British abolitionists,
his affiliation with the Sierra Leone Company, and likely knowledge of the Saint-
Domingue revolution.

Wadström's *Essay on Colonization* included six plates: two architectural drawings showing how to build temporary colonial housing structures in Sierra Leone,
a nautical map of the waters in the general region of the Sierra Leone and Gambia River area, two maps of Sierra Leone, and a new version of the slave ship icon.
Wadström chose the engraving of the slave ship icon to support his claim that the
slave trade was a barrier to African colonization. In the preface to his new and
different version of the London Committee plan and sections of a slave ship, Wadström explains,

> The slave-trade has been mentioned in this work as one of the chief obstructions to the civilization of Africa and the nefarious and bloody method of procuring slaves is described, from the Report of the Directors of the S. Leona Company. But the Conveyance of the slaves from Africa to the W. Indies, commonly called *the middle passage*, not being so immediately connected with the plan of this work, has only been mentioned in general terms. As some explanation, however, of *this* part of that horrible traffic, will probably be acceptable to the reader, the author inserts this plan, section and description of a slave ship, first published in the same form, in London, 1789. The proprietors have favoured him with the original plate; and the *only* liberty he has taken, has been to insert the figure representing an insurrection on board a slave ship, taken from a sketch, with the explanation annexed, was communicated to him at Goree in 1787. (For an account of some similar catastrophes, see paragraph 471). In other respects the plate is unaltered: and this *description* is taken *verbatim* from the first edition in 1789, just mentioned.[63]

Instead of a wood or copperplate engraving, Wadström used mezzotint, a printing process that allowed for more even shading of the figures representing the enslaved Africans as well as the lines of the sections of the ship. Overall, a softer look was given to the slave ship icon, which contrasted with the sharper engraving of "Representation of an Insurrection on board a Slave Ship," which was inserted in place of the scale on the original *Plan and Sections of a Slave Ship*. The image caption read, "Shewing how the crew fire upon the unhappy Slaves from behind the Barricado (or barricade), erected on board all Slave Ships, as a security whenever such commotions may happen." According to Wadström, he acquired this image at Gorée Island, presumably during his trip to Africa in 1787–88. It shows the double-masted British frigate, the *Fair Trader*, with a violent battle brewing on deck. The ship's full sails are obscured by large billows of smoky clouds, which rise from the gunfire of British sailors on the mass of revolting slaves. The soldiers are lined up to the right behind the barricade, with their long rifles pointed at the angry group of naked captives on the other side trying to defend themselves. Some of them jump overboard, while others seem to scream and throw their arms up in the air, taunting the sailors, liberating their once-shackled limbs. This is one of the first images to visually assert the revolutionary capabilities of the enslaved—to grant a sense of agency to the still and corpse-like figures trapped in the slave ship icon. The tension between the engraving of the insurrection and the slave ship icon enlivens the figures in the hold of the slave ship and hints at the possibility of their liberation, of their ability to take matters into their own hands. This image has an undeniable revolutionary appeal. It also stands as a warning to those who continue to participate in the slave trade. It stands in stark contrast to the hand-painted engraving of *La Marie Séraphique*, wherein the enslaved and the planters seem to coexist happily on the deck amid a luncheon and the sale and inspection of the cargo (see figure 1.7).

CHAPTER THREE

CIRCULATION: POLITICS AND PUBLICITY

THE SLAVE SHIP ICON circulated in many different versions between 1790 and 1860, a seventy-year period bounded on one side by the French Revolution and on the other by the American Civil War. Although the icon's popularity fluctuated during these decades, marked by a sustained and unprecedented international social movement calling for the end of the slave trade and chattel slavery, it continued to function as the preeminent visual weapon in the abolitionist arsenal. Throughout, the London Committee broadside, *Description of a Slave Ship*, provided the principal, although not exclusive, reference point, and often served as a template for the numerous variants. Victory against the slave trade in the British Parliament and US Congress led to a period of celebration and reflection in which the icon was used as a historical marker, a reminder of past ordeals. Yet it gradually became clear that international laws passed by the United Kingdom in 1807 and the United States in 1808, which made the abolition of the slave trade a legal reality, did not guarantee its demise. Traders sought to circumvent enforcement, and these widespread efforts saw a revival of the icon in new forms. There was increasing recognition that the horrors of the Middle Passage would not end until slavery itself was abolished.

Chapter 2 has shown that from 1789 to 1806, the slave ship icon was used to educate and mobilize adults who might bring an end to the slave trade. As the abolitionist struggle continued over the course of decades, even lifetimes, the importance of educating young adults and even children in the ideology of abolition became recognized. Throughout the revolutionary antebellum period, variations of the eighteenth-century icon were recycled as a form of historical memory. By examining the manner and context in which variants on this icon were conceived and distributed, a clearer picture of how it became so powerful, so memorable comes into focus. We might wonder what it means to endlessly repeat an image over and over again during a seventy-year period such that it threatens to become a familiar cliché. Without necessarily intending to, abolitionists using this image and others no doubt contributed to the hypervisibility of the black body on both sides of the Atlantic. What did it mean for black and white Americans for this image to circulate when the legal status of black people in the United States was still in question? To be sure, the slave ship icon generated a range of multivalent meanings that became associated with it during the period leading to the American Civil War.

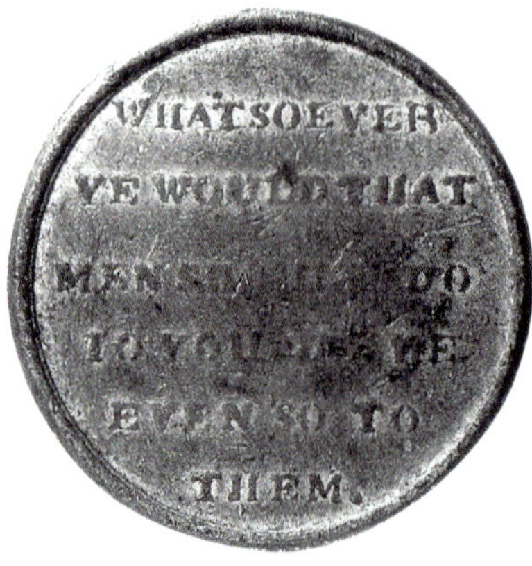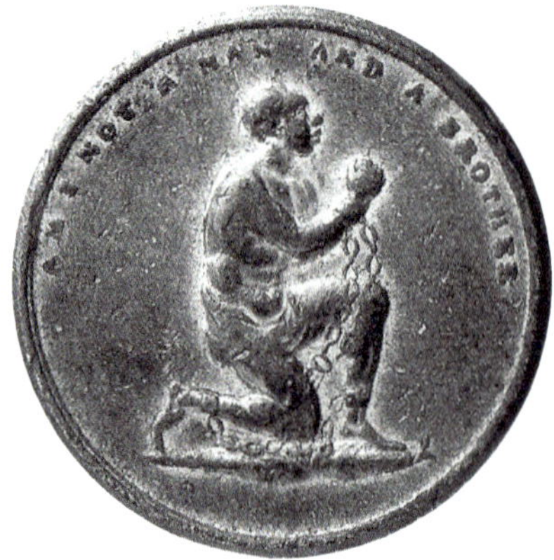

3.1
Coins commemorating the Abolition
of the Slave Trade, 1807.

ABOLITION AND SUPPRESSION

Despite the wide circulation of visual propaganda such as the slave ship icon and compilations of convincing evidence such as the *Abstract*, Wilberforce's motions for the immediate abolition of the slave trade were not adopted by the House of Commons in 1790 or 1791. In 1792, William Pitt's motion for gradual abolition (by 1796) was passed in the House of Commons, but it failed to gain approval in the House of Lords. The following year, a bill for the abolition of the foreign slave trade was rejected and several other attempts in the late 1790s to abolish the slave trade were lost. The parliamentary elections of 1804 resulted in a coalition of pro-abolition supporters and a renewed London Committee, whose collective momentum would result in the passage of the Abolition of the Slave Trade Act on March 25, 1807.[1]

Coins commemorating the abolition of the slave trade were issued that year, showing in some cases the image of the kneeling slave (fig. 3.1). Both Great Britain and the United States agreed that the total abolition of the slave trade would begin in 1808.[2] To mark the occasion after a twenty-year struggle, commemorative coins, pottery, and prints bearing the image of the kneeling slave were issued by independent artisans associated with the Abolition Society in England. In addition to the phrase "Am I Not a Man and a Brother?," which encircled the kneeling slave, these commemorative issues were accompanied by such slogans as "May slavery and oppression cease throughout the world," indicating that there still was something left to fight for—that slavery had yet to be abolished.

CLARKSON'S HISTORY OF THE SLAVE TRADE

To mark this passage from memory into history, Thomas Clarkson issued the very first account of the abolition of the slave trade, titled *History of the Rise, Progress, and Accomplishment of the Abolition of the African Slave-Trade by the British Parliament*. Spanning two large volumes and numbering nearly 1,200 pages, it was published in England and the United States in 1808, coinciding with the year that abolition took effect. Clarkson proclaims in the closing paragraph of volume two:

> Reader! Thou art now acquainted with the history of this contest! Rejoice in the manner of its termination! And if thou feelest grateful for the event, retire within thy closet, and pour out thy thanksgivings to the Almighty for this his unspeakable act of mercy to thy oppressed fellow creatures.[3]

Like the commemorative coins and ceramic wares issued around the same time, Clarkson's *History* was really a celebratory account, a tribute to the Abolition Society and to himself in particular. Told as a personal narrative, he traces his contributions (accomplishments) to abolishing the slave trade and, through his actions, those of the Abolition Society.[4] Clarkson begins his narrative with the first purchase of African slaves by the Portuguese in 1503, in order to give a sense of the events leading up to the establishment of the Abolition Society in 1787, and continues through to 1807, when the British Parliament votes to abolish the slave trade. In keeping with the celebratory nature of his endeavor, Clarkson selected four images to be remembered with his narrative, images that gave a lasting impression of what was at stake in abolishing the slave trade and those people responsible for bringing it to fruition. These key images include an imaginary map of a river that traces the early genealogy of the abolitionism, the Abolition Society seal, mechanical drawings of four devices of torture and restraint, and the slave ship icon (figs. 3.2, 3.3). With the exception of the abolition society seal, which is printed on page 450 of the first volume, all of the illustrations were meticulously engraved by Hemsley from copper plates and inserted as separate sheets.

The first illustration is inserted as a separate engraved plate facing page 259 at the beginning of chapter 11. It is an imaginary map of a river that traces the early genealogy of the abolitionism. Clarkson explains:

> It would be considered by many, who have stood at the mouth of a river, and witnessed its torrent there, to be both an interesting and a pleasing journey to go to the fountain-head, and then to travel on its banks downwards, and to mark the different streams in each side, which should run into it and feed it. So I presume the reader will not be a little interested and entertained in viewing with me the course of the abolition of the Slave-trade, in first finding its source, and then in tracing the different springs which have contributed to its increase.[5]

Beginning in 1650 and ending in 1787, Clarkson's map charts the mostly Quaker, British, and American roots of abolitionism and their intersecting streams and tributaries referring to how ideas were exchanged across the Atlantic and over generations.[6] As a metaphor, Clarkson's river is an apt choice, hinting at the depth of commitment of its supporters and the continuing, living nature of the cause. Moreover, visually and spatially, his map helps to organize the reader's notion of the key players in time and space.

Clarkson's updated, commemorative version of the slave ship icon was one of the most detailed yet to be produced. Engraved from a copper plate, the figures

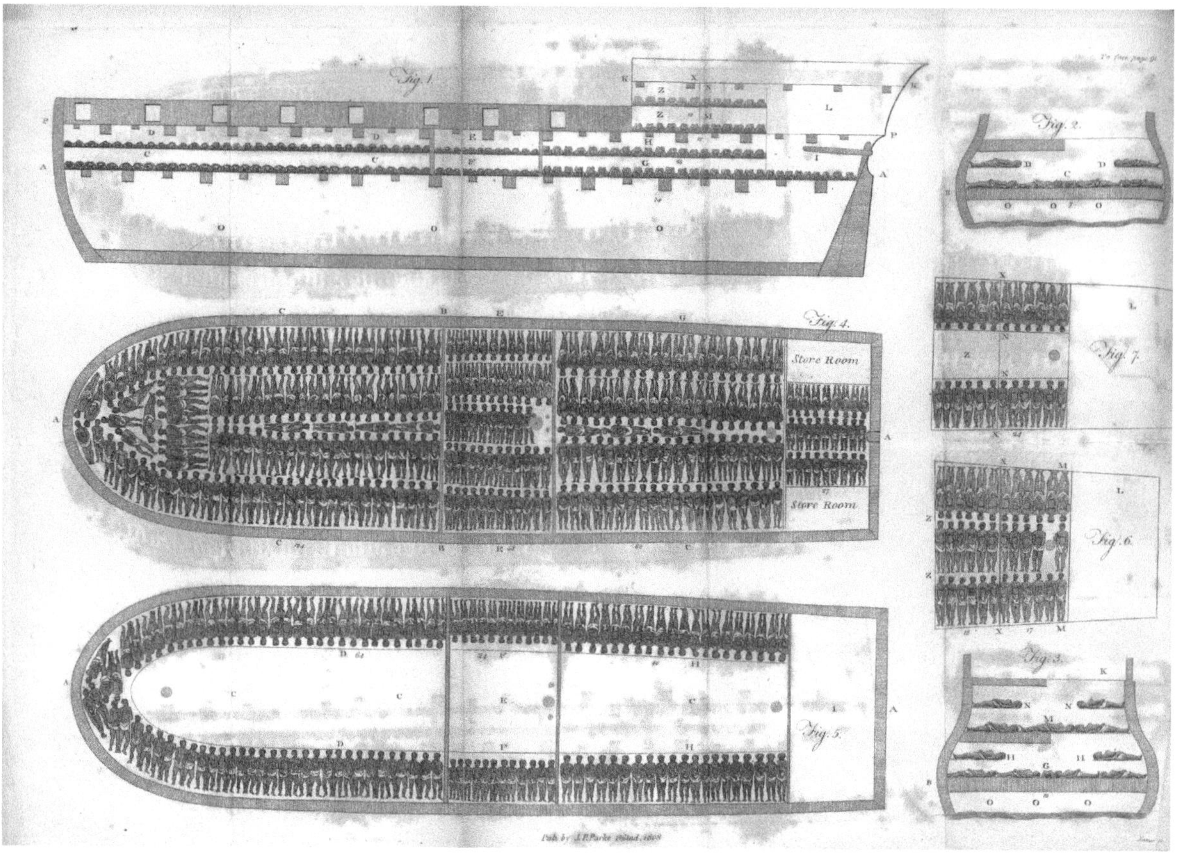

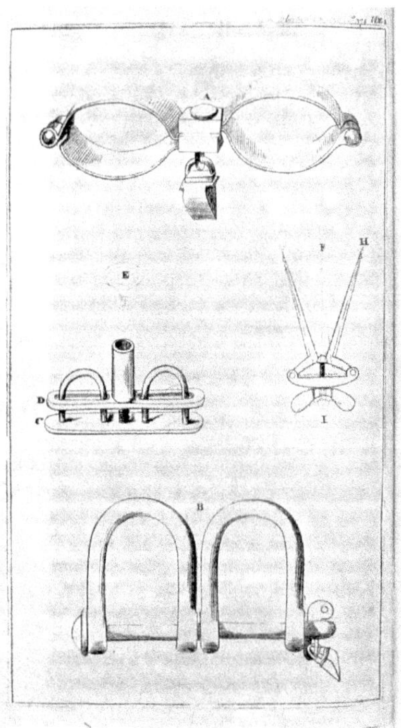

3.2 ABOVE
Description of a slave ship, from Clarkson, *History of the Slave Trade*, 1808.

3.3 LEFT
Mechanical drawings of four devices of torture and restraint, from Clarkson, *History of the Slave Trade*, 1808.

representing the slaves were executed in a painstaking manner, their facial features and the lines marking the contours of the bodies reached the height of refinement. The figures representing the women were hypereroticized, almost to the point of caricature, their breasts in the longitudinal and cross-section views capped with shaded areolas and sharp, blackened nipples. Even more remarkable is the overall change in the physical appearance and posture of each and every one of the figures. A close examination of these will reveal how they now seem to take on a somewhat sculptural appearance, almost resembling miniature Greek statues dating from the early classical period (480–450 BC). Even their crisp, white loincloths are gently draped across their torsos in a manner typical of that period. What is more, their turning gestures reinvent the contrapposto pose, one of the key postures of early classical sculpture. In the contrapposto pose, the weight is shifted slightly, making the axes of the torso uneven, while the head is turned a little as the gaze of the figure looks down. The Kritios Boy (ca. 480–475 BC) is the best-known example of a figure exhibiting the contrapposto pose during this period. According to Jerome Pollitt, contrapposto "concerned the representation of emotions and changing states of consciousness."[7] The shifting weight, turning head, and averted gaze were meant to visually indicate the doubts and inner struggles of the physical and mental man, his changing states of mind, his range of emotions.

What message did Clarkson mean to convey by representing the enslaved Africans in the manner of the classical Greek ideal? First, the abolitionists may have attempted to grant the enslaved African the status of the thinking man that the contrapposto pose represented. Depicting African slaves as figures from classical Greek antiquity supports the popular assertion that many abolitionists compared the state of the slaves in ancient times to that of the slaves in the New World. As Clarkson himself stated, "Slavery had existed from the first ages of the world, not only in Africa, but throughout the habitable globe; among the Persians, Greeks, and Romans."[8] Second, it is important to consider the popularity of the neoclassical style in British art during the Georgian period. The artist who drew the plan of the slave ship for Clarkson's *History* may have made an aesthetic decision, in keeping with the fashion of the times, when he chose the figure of the Greek ideal to represent the body of the African slave. An analogous image is the Wedgwood kneeling slave cameo, itself designed in the neoclassical style.

Despite its highly personal narrative and the criticism it attracted, Clarkson's *History* was a very popular book in its time.[9] It was the first history of the slave trade to be published, and readers were eager to learn more about an important social movement that had captured the public attention for some time. It was reissued several times, translated into French and Spanish, and later abridged in shorter volumes.[10] This is an important point to consider given the fact that images were published with it. These images were afforded even greater circulation when published in Clarkson's *History*. Indeed, because the explanations belonging to the large folding plates were published in the body of the text bound as a book, when the images become separated from the book, the context is removed. In other words, folded plates were often taken out of books and passed around.

As with other earlier versions published in abolitionist tracts, such as the *Abstract of the Evidence*, the engraving of the slave ship icon stands alone on a separate inserted sheet, without the explanatory text, which is printed in the body of the bound book. Sometimes these plates were removed from the bound volumes to be passed on to other people, displayed in frames in the home, or posted publicly. Now divorced from the text, what new meanings do these plates take on? In the version printed for Clarkson's history, another set of numbers appears in the schematic, indicating the number of people stowed in each section. These arabic numbers appear in addition to the lettered, numbered figures. For instance, the number 124 next to figure IV, section CC, indicates that the storage space holds 124 shackled men. With the descriptive text no longer present to elaborate on the meaning and purpose of the image, it becomes used in a variety of new ways after the official abolition of the slave trade. These novel uses include the suppression of the illegal slave trade, children's literature, reformed slave traders' narratives, and other adaptations related to the abolition of slavery.

THE CASE OF THE *VIGILANTE*

By 1823, after nearly all the European countries and the United States had passed laws abolishing the slave trade, it seemed that the illegal slave trade was on the rise, if not flourishing. Newspaper reports citing incidents of illegal slave trading began to appear regularly. The London Committee launched a campaign to publicize the fact that the slave trade was still being conducted using once again its most effective visual propaganda, the slave ship icon. In 1822, Thomas Clarkson published *The Cries of Africa, to the Inhabitants of Europe; or, a Survey of That Bloody Commerce Called Slave-Trade* with Harvey and Darton, the London Committee's choice nineteenth-century printer.[11] This small volume was a "history of the most atrocious crimes, and of the most bitter sufferings" of the slave trade. So shocking were the tales of this fifty-page tract that Clarkson warned, "We anticipate your frequent astonishment while you peruse it…you will therefore be often inclined to doubt the truth of the facts which have passed before you."[12] Throughout the tract, Clarkson tries to quell the anticipated disbelief of his readers. In chapter 4, which describes the horrors of the Middle Passage, Clarkson reminds his readers:

> Horrible as this account may appear, we assert, in the most solemn manner, that we have omitted to mention many circumstance, which would render it still more afflicting; and that we have been cautious, in what we have said, to keep ourselves within the bounds of truth. It is possible, however, that some person may be unwilling to believe us. If there are such, we refer them to the annexed engraving, which represents the shape and dimensions of the places for the slaves, in the English slave-ship *Brookes*. We inform them that these admeasurements were made by order of the English parliament. We invite their particular attention to them; and after this, we shall leave them to regulate their own belief.[13]

The London Committee wood engraving was inserted between pages 26 and 27. As with the *Abstract of the Evidence* and Clarkson's *History* before it, the plate was printed without the text. Instead, some paragraphs of text were reproduced in the body of the tract, along with a table of lettered, numbered dimensions referring to the plan on page 27. Clarkson's assertions for the veracity of his story were not unfounded. By the early 1820s, the defenders of chattel slavery were feeling not only threatened but also regretful that the slave trade had been declared illegal. They aimed to assert that the treatment of slaves on the plantations was humane. Clarkson's *Cries of Africa* would take the reader from the interior of Africa through the Middle Passage, stating the reasons for refuting the slave trade and the reasons why it is contrary to religion.

In 1823, the London Committee published a short tract describing the British capture of an illegal French slave ship, *Case of the Vigilante, a Ship Employed in the Slave Trade; with Some Reflections on That Traffic*. An advertisement on page three explained the purpose of that small volume (fig. 3.4):

> The following narrative is published by a Committee of the Religious Society of Friends in London, who act on behalf of their brethren in this nation and Ireland, to aid in promoting the total Abolition of the Slave-trade. The circumstances of the case are described from official and authentic documents; in publishing which, the Committee wish it to be distinctly understood, that they in no degree compromise the well-known testimony of the Society, against fighting; and the drawing was taken, by an able draftsman, at Portsmouth, whilst the vessel was detained there, previously to the determination of the British government on the way in which it should be disposed of.[14]

The tract gave the details of the capture of the French brig *Vigilante* of Nantes, found to be illegally carrying a cargo of enslaved Africans in the vicinity of the River Bonny. It was illustrated with a foldout engraving by J. Hawksworth that measured 22½ by 17¼ when opened to its full size. As the tract describes,

> The annexed plate is a drawing of a vessel employed in the Slave-trade, which was captured by Lieutenant Mildmay, in the river Bonny, on the coast of Africa, on the 15th of 4th month, (April,) 1822. The brig, named the Vigilante, was from Nantes. It was 240 tons burden, and had on board, at the time it was taken, 345 slaves. It was manned by thirty men, armed with four twelve-pounders, all of which were brought over on one side for the attack.

A table in the beginning of the tract refers the reader to the annexed plate, which indicates the way in which the enslaved were found to be stowed (by corresponding lettered, numbered figures); the number carried; and the number lost in the battle. The plate represents another innovation on the slave ship icon. Now that the slave trade was conducted illegally, the clandestine ships had to be faster in order to outpace the British patrol ships. In many cases, coastal schooners, brigs, and clippers were favored. These ships were lower to the surface of the water and with masts that tilted at an angle to cut through the wind effortlessly. Often the hull was coated with copper to make it easier for the ship to slice through the water, with less buildup of algae and sea life. While this new design afforded speed, it also meant

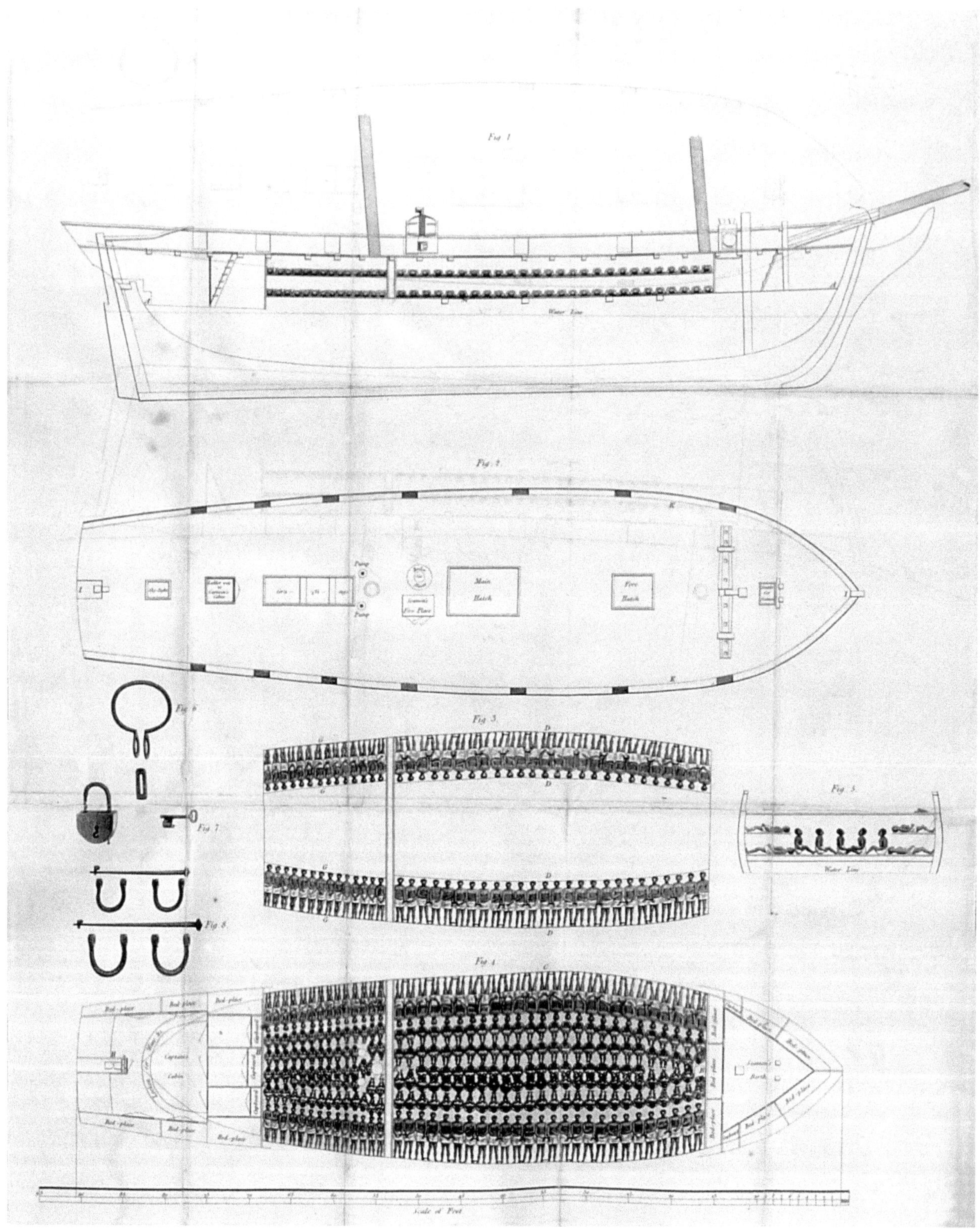

3.4

London Committee, "Case of the *Vigilante*," 1823.

that there was less depth in the storage area, contributing to more overcrowding in the cargo hold. The plans that subsequently were made show how African captives often were found in crouching positions, unable to sit up at all, because of the shallow depth of the hold.

Figure one (of fig. 3.4) is a line drawing showing the longitudinal section with the figures representing men and women lying on their backs with the tops of their heads facing toward the viewer. The two masts of the schooner are drawn halfway and shaded. Also visible are the pump and the staircase leading to the captain's cabin, which is located within close proximity of the women's room. A second staircase to the lower deck is drawn in the bow. It connects to the men's room and the seamen's berth. The waterline is also drawn, below which there are no human figures.

Figure two (of fig. 3.4) is an overhead view of the deck, showing from left to right, the sky light over the captain's cabin, the space for the ladder to his cabin, the gratings over the slave quarters, the pumps, and two separate cooking/heating sources: a boiler for slaves and a seamen's fireplace. The boiler for slaves is fueled with wood or coal and a large cauldron is placed on top of the single burner. There is a large main hatch and a smaller "fore hatch." The "scuttle for seamen" marks the ladder leading to their quarters. Also visible around the perimeter are the fourteen shaded spaces showing where guns would be mounted. There are no figures representing the slaves visible in this section.

Figure three (of fig. 3.4) shows the half deck or the "wings" with male and female figures lining the perimeter. They wear simple white loincloths. The women cross their arms over their laps and wear no shackles. Their bodies are shaded with fine lines. The men are shackled by twos at the wrists and feet. None of the figures wear the iron collars that are described as having been on the captives when they were discovered by the British naval ship. Instead, these devices of torture and restraint are illustrated in figures 6 (iron collar), 7 (padlock and key), and 8 (shackles). Taking a page from Clarkson's *History*, this is the first time that a single broadsheet with the slave ship icon was shown with detailed illustrations of the torture devices.

Figure four (of fig. 3.4) presents the main deck filled with the figures representing the slaves. Section F shows the women and section C shows the men. Around the perimeter, they are lined up as in figure 3, feet facing out, lying on their backs. But in the center rows, they are illustrated in a seated position, with knees bent, their arms wrapped under their thighs, pulling their knees toward their chests, as if rolling their bodies into a ball. The figures in the very center rows are touching at the knees, almost overlapping. Spaces for the masts and pumps are allotted as circles of whiteness, but not emptiness. At the bow, shown at the left end, there are six "bed places," three on either side, the captain's quarters in the center surrounded by a wine locker, and four cupboards, three abutting the section for the women and one close by the captain's quarters. The triangular-shaped bow is reserved for the seamen's berths, including seven bed places and two cupboards. Figure four is positioned above the "scale of feet," to which lines are drawn for easy measurement. This new mode of showing the figures bent over and crouching corresponds directly to innovations in maritime technology that produced the brig, schooner, and clipper style of vessel, with sleek lines for quick passage.

Figure five (of fig. 3.4). The transverse section provides the necessary perspective, when combined with the longitudinal and plan views, to imagine the hold in three dimensions. The mix of doubled-over and prone figures further illustrates the lack of space.

With the *Vigilante*, the slave ship icon was transformed to represent the illegal slave trade. In so doing, it showed how the ship's design afforded it speed and maneuverability. It also revealed the spaces where slave traders and sailors slept for the first time.

The detailed report of the capture of the *Vigilante* described a grisly battle in which many of the enslaved were saved. Some however, were "devoured by sharks" when they jumped overboard. Others were used as "human shields" by the slave traders during the attack. Those who were liberated were "repatriated" to Sierra Leone. This action, while intended to provide those who had been captured with a new life, a fresh start, actually placed them further away from the people and the life they once knew. Instead, in Sierra Leone, they would have to adjust to living in a Christianized, English-speaking colony. This tract was translated into French with the intent of having an impact in France, especially in the popular slaving ports of Nantes and Bordeaux, and her colonies.[15]

THE SPANISH SCHOONER, *JOSEFA MARACAYERA*

A broadside published by Harvey and Darton for the London Committee in 1823 illustrates another such example of a captured illegal slaver, the "Spanish Schooner, Josefa Maracayera, of 90 Tons, 21 Seamen, belonging to the Havannah, Captured by the *Driver*, Capt. Wolrige, in the Bight of Benin, on the Coast of Africa, on the 19th of 8th Mo. (Aug.) 1822, with 216 male Slaves on Board"[16] (fig. 3.5). As the text explained:

> The above representation of the interior of a Slave-ship is taken from a sketch lately received, with an accompanying explanation, from Sir Charles MacCarthy, Governor of Sierra Leone. It is submitted as a striking proof of the dreadful sufferings to which the victims of the Slave-trade are subjected in their passage across the Atlantic.

The broadside, measuring 12 by 15 inches, shows a longitudinal and a cross-section view of the hold with the figures of men in a crouching position in the hold. In the longitudinal view, the extreme shallow depth of the hold becomes visible: "height between deck and platform, exclusive of the beams, 2 feet 6 inches; immediately under the beams, 2 feet."[17] The beams of the upper deck are shown to obstruct their heads and some have to bend even further in order to clear the beams. Below the figures, caskets used to hold water are arranged somewhat haphazardly. This longitudinal view also shows the foremast (F) and the main mast (E). In the coastal schooner, the masts are angled back, for faster speed. Other sections of the ship

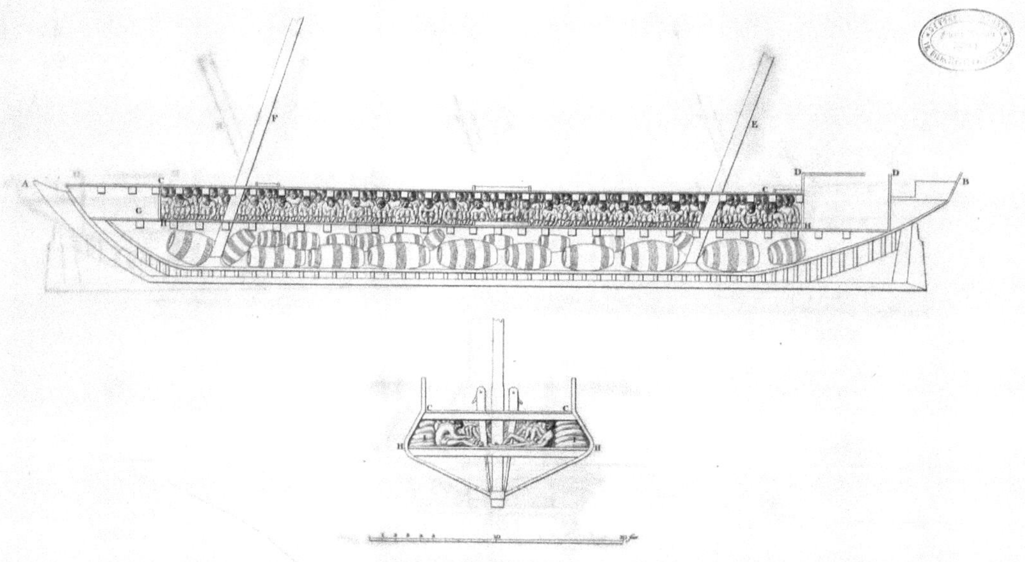

THE SPANISH SCHOONER, JOSEFA MARACAYERA,

Of 90 Tons, 21 Seamen, belonging to the Havannah,

Captured by the DRIVER, Capt. Wolrige, in the Bight of Benin, on the Coast of Africa, on the 19th of 8th Mo. (Aug.) 1822, with 216 male Slaves on board.

DESCRIPTION.

A. Head. B. Stern. CC. Deck. DD. Quarter Deck. E. Main-mast. F. Fore-mast. G. Forecastle. HH. Platform. II. Rice-bags. Length of deck from head to stern, 72 feet. Width of platform 14 feet; namely, 2 feet on each side for the rice-bags, and 10 feet, the intermediate space. Height between deck and platform, exclusive of the beams, 2 feet 6 inches; immediately under the beams, 2 feet. Distance between main-mast and stern, 16 feet; between fore-mast and head, 14 feet. Length of platform, 52 feet. This length will give 6 inches in breadth for each Slave, allowing 104 to have been ranged on each side. The whole number is stated to have been 216; but, of these, a few are understood to have been stowed in the forecastle. By the papers found on board, it appeared that the ship was intended to take 217.

The above representation of the interior of a Slave-ship is taken from a sketch lately received, with an accompanying explanation, from Sir Charles MacCarthy, Governor of Sierra Leone. It is submitted as a striking proof of the dreadful sufferings to which the victims of the Slave-trade are subjected in their passage across the Atlantic. Another authentic description of a Slave-vessel, the French ship *la Vigilante*, of 240 tons, and carrying 345 Negroes, has been recently published, and may be had of the same booksellers as this.

In justice to the Spanish nation it ought to be observed, that the *cedula* or royal decree, in 1817, for the abolition of the Slave-trade in Spain and its dependencies, has been followed up by the introduction of an article into the criminal code adopted by the Cortes, rendering the prosecution of it more widely penal. By some, however, of the subjects of that power, as the present instance evinces, the traffic is still continued. The extent to which, taken in its whole compass, this guilty commerce in the persons of the unoffending natives of Africa is now carried on, is almost inconceivable. Into the harbour of the Portuguese settlement of Rio de Janeiro alone, the number imported during the first six months of 1822, according to official documents recently laid before the British Parliament, was upwards of 17,000!

London: printed, under the direction of a Committee of the Society of Friends appointed to aid in promoting the total Abolition of the Slave-Trade, by HARVEY and DARTON, Gracechurch-street; and sold by them, and by J. and A. Arch, Cornhill; W. Phillips, George yard, Lombard-street; and Hatchard and Son, Piccadilly.

3.5

Spanish schooner *Josefa Maracayera*, 1822.
Printed under the direction of a Committee of
the Society of Friends appointed to aid in
promoting the total abolition of the slave-trade.

are denoted by letters ("A. Head. B. Stern. CC. Deck. HH. Platform"). Below the longitudinal view, a cross-section view shows the contorted figures leaning over and sitting among what are identified as bags of rice (II). The sense of crowding is further amplified by the placement of rice bags and water caskets with the figures representing the enslaved and further clarifies their status as commodities.

That the *Josefa Maracayera* carried only men reflected the state of the market—not only the supply that was available in Africa but also the demand for fresh, strong male laborers, who brought the highest prices in the New World slave markets. By the time this broadside was published, the Spanish had prohibited the slave trade and enacted laws that made it easier to prosecute those who defied the law. As the plate explained:

In justice to the Spanish nation it ought to be observed, that the *cedula* or royal decree, in 1817, for the abolition of the Slave-trade in Spain and its dependencies, has been followed up by the introduction of an article into the criminal code adopted by the Cortes, rendering the prosecution of it more widely penal. By some, however, the subjects of that power, as the present instance evinces, the traffic is still continued.[18]

The slave ship icon was applied to abolition efforts and documentation in Brazil, too, notably in the two-volume *Notices of Brazil in 1828 and 1829* by Robert Walsh (1772–1852), which offered up a different version showing the cramped quarters measuring only "3 Feet 3 In in height," according to the inset cross-section (fig. 3.6). Insurrections on board slave ships had been portrayed with the slave ship icon as we saw in the work of Wadström in the last chapter. But with the huge publicity received by the *Amistad* mutiny in 1839, illustrations appeared in newspapers showing the violence and disorder that took place above decks (fig. 3.7), sometimes with an inset showing the cramped quarters below.

Some of the artists and draftsmen who documented the search and seizure of illegal slavers also drew the interior of the hold of the slave ship from life. One such image in pencil and gouache was made by Lieutenant Francis Meynell in 1846, *View of the Deck of the Slave Ship Albanoz* (fig. 3.8). Meynell's painting presents a jumbled mess of frightened, despondent captives among water caskets, fabric, and other stores. The captives appear languid and emaciated, with so little strength that they can hardly move from their curling and crouched positions. Some sit on beams; others try to find space enough to take comfort in assuming a fetal position

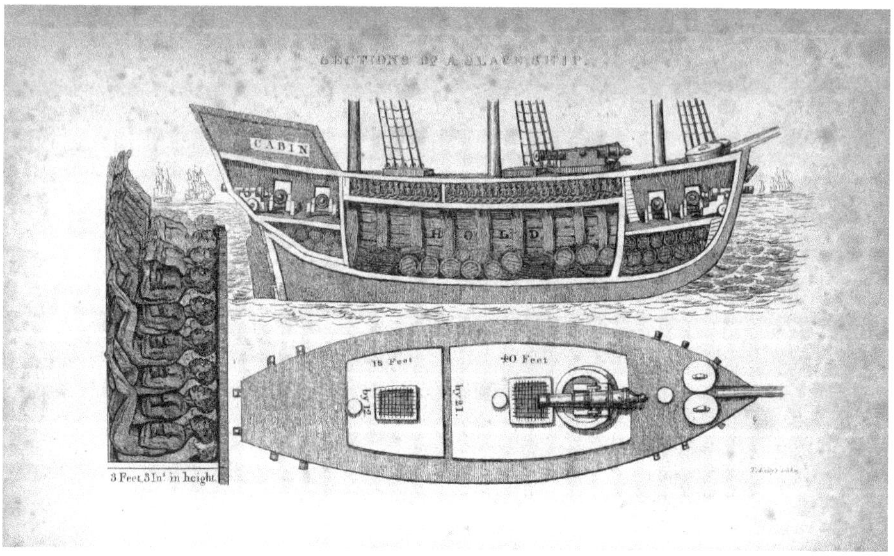

3.6

Sections of a Slave Ship (the *Veloz Passageiro*), 1830, from Robert Walsh, *Notices of Brazil in 1828 and 1829* (London: Frederick Westley and A.H. Davis, 1830), vol. 1, p. 17.

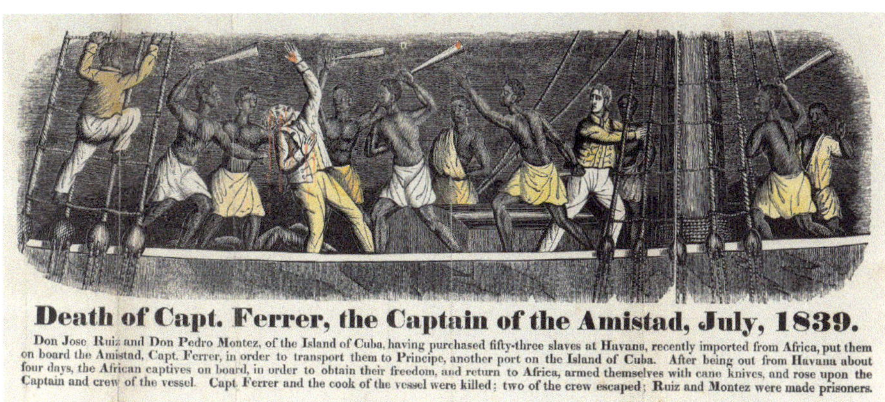

Death of Capt. Ferrer, the Captain of the Amistad, July, 1839.

Don Jose Ruiz and Don Pedro Montez, of the Island of Cuba, having purchased fifty-three slaves at Havana, recently imported from Africa, put them on board the Amistad, Capt. Ferrer, in order to transport them to Principe, another port on the Island of Cuba. After being out from Havana about four days, the African captives on board, in order to obtain their freedom, and return to Africa, armed themselves with cane knives, and rose upon the Captain and crew of the vessel. Capt. Ferrer and the cook of the vessel were killed; two of the crew escaped; Ruiz and Montez were made prisoners.

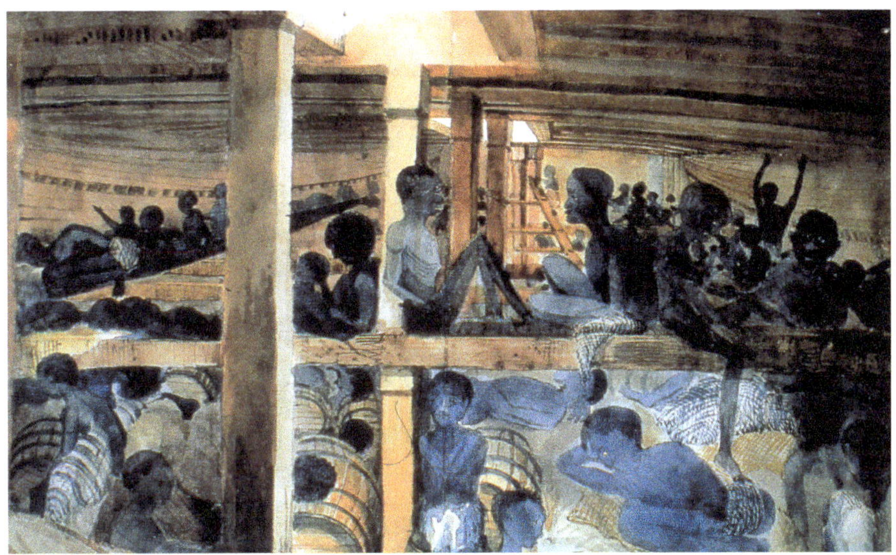

3.7 TOP
Newspaper clipping depicting the *Death of Capt. Ferrer, Captain of the Amistad, July, 1839.*

3.8 BOTTOM
Lieutenant Francis Meynell, *View of the Deck of the Slave Ship Albanoz*, 1846, pencil and gouache.

between the wooden caskets. It seems that women and men are thrown together in the same room, not separated by sex as popularly depicted in the slave ship icon. Two overhead hatches let in blinding sunlight that illuminates the scene in the hold. In the center of the composition, two men seated on a beam face each other and seem to be engaged in conversation. A young woman below them crosses her arms over her bare chest and stares at the viewer with an intense look of fear, longing, and sadness. A man curled up beside her stares blankly. All of the captives are nearly naked, except for the customary loincloth and other striped and patterned fabric, either part of the cargo or possibly their own. Drawn from life, this watercolor is a more realistic view into the hold of a slave ship than the schematic engraving of the *Josefa Maracayera*, wherein the rescued captives were neatly arranged among bags of rice just above the storage area for water caskets. In Meynell's image of the hold, the captives are seen among water caskets and burlap sacks. The utter state of confusion hints at the motion of the ship on the water. Part of a journal that Meynell kept during the patrol documented his experience both visually and textually. His watercolor is but one example of the other types of images that were being presented at this time—those that provided a sense of realism, but also a welcome contrast to the organized diagrammatic of the slave ship icon. Now the once anonymous, monotonous figures of the slave ship icon have distinct facial expressions and differentiated postures. By mapping Meynell's image onto the slave ship icon, it becomes memorable in another sense. Meynell's watercolor did not circulate widely in the mid-nineteenth century. As part of a personal album, it remained unknown to scholars and the public until it was donated to the National Maritime Museum at Greenwich, England.

Other images of the slave ship provided new ways of looking at the history of the abolitionist movement. In 1840, the Anti Slavery Society Convention was held in London, an international gathering of male and female / black and white supporters of abolition. This event became the subject of a painting by Benjamin Robert Haydon (1786–1846) in which the elder Clarkson was shown delivering a speech before 130 of the convention's attendees (fig. 3.9). That same year, the Royal Academy in London exhibited two large history paintings on the subject of the slave trade: Joseph Mailord William Turner's *Slave Ship* and François-Auguste Biard's *The Slave Trade*. Instead of tackling current events, such as the illegal slave trade, these paintings refer back to other historical events or other visual catalogues of the slave trade. For instance, Turner's *Slave Ship* is an abstract depiction of the case of the slave ship *Zong*, defended by Granville Sharp in 1783 (fig. 3.10). In this widely publicized case, slavers attempted to collect insurance for the 130 slaves that they threw overboard prior to reaching their destination in the West Indies.[19] Hugh Honour has suggested that Thomas Clarkson's *Cries of Africa* may have been a source for this painting, as it mentioned the case of the *Zong*, of some fifty years ago. The captives were thrown overboard because many were sick and dying and the ship was running out of fresh drinking water.[20] This painting, with its red and orange fireball sky and a sea awash with shackled limbs and sharks, was shocking for contemporary audiences. The critics who wrote about the Salon of 1840 did not have praise for Turner. The critic for the *Times* declared that Turner's painting was "impossible to look at…without mingled feelings of pity and contempt."[21] Biard's *Slave Trade* received a better reception from critics (fig. 3.11). The author William Makepeace Thackeray called Biard's painting "the best, most striking, most pathetic lecture against the [slave] trade that ever was delivered." It was a virtual inventory of the cruelties of the slave trade acted out on the West African coast. From right to left, it shows the coffle, a European (French) trader seated comfortably with his account book, and a bare-chested woman. The scene continues with an African trader smoking a long pipe, two traders inspecting a man being offered for sale, a young woman being branded by a sailor in a striped shirt who is assisted by a young boy who holds a lantern, and more African traders whipping captives onto the ship waiting in the distance. Biard's *Slave Trade* was pornographic.[22] The slaves wore only

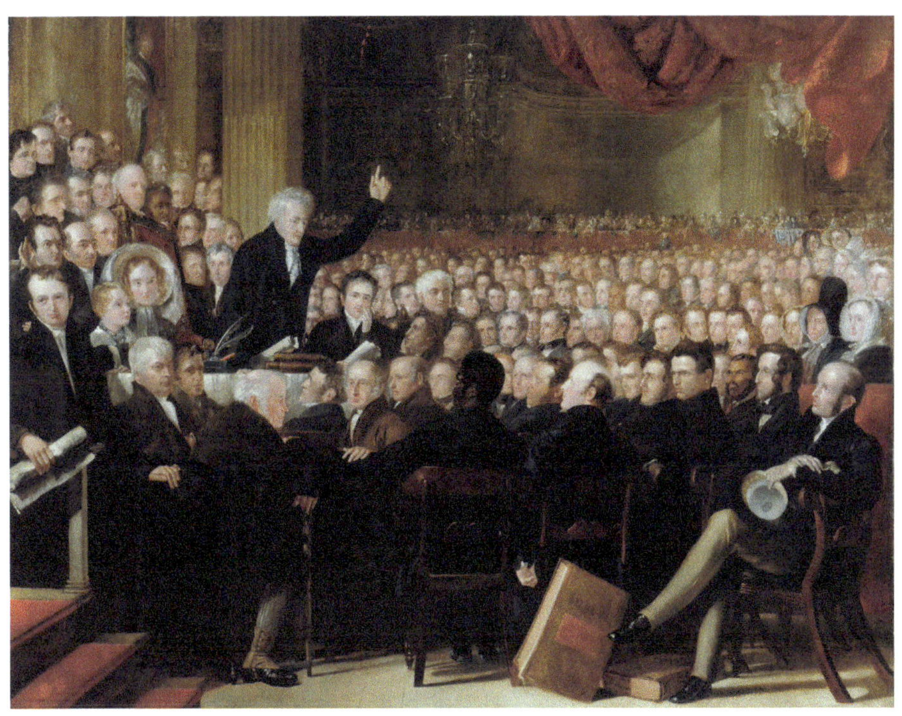

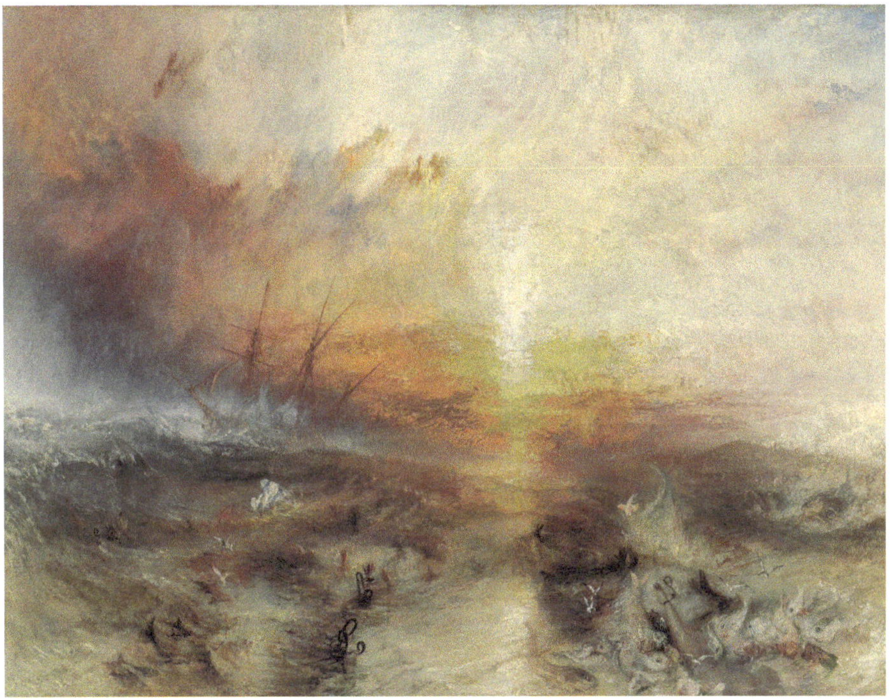

3.9 TOP
Benjamin Robert Haydon, *The Anti-Slavery Society Convention, 1840*, dated 1841, 297 × 383.5 cm.

3.10 BOTTOM
J.M.W. Turner, *The Slave Ship*, 1840, 90.8 × 122.6 cm.

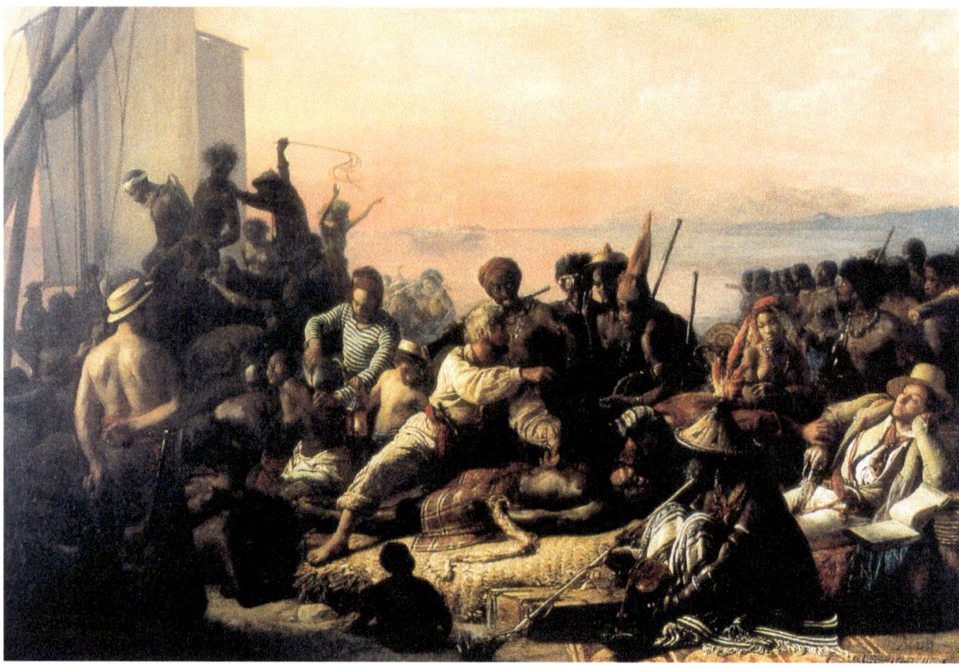

3.11
François-Auguste Biard, *The Slave Trade*,
ca. 1833, 162.5 × 228.6 cm.

loincloths or covered themselves with blankets or swaths of fabric. The European traders, on the other hand, were almost all fully clothed. They performed sadomasochistic acts upon the enslaved with regularity and disinterestedness. There were many onlookers, spectators, some of whom seemed to take pleasure in the performance of violence, while others sit there passively. This scene would be repeated again and again in the second half of the nineteenth century. It was engraved and circulated widely. Even a few small details of this image have been selected to illustrate memoirs of notorious and reformed slave traders, especially the image of the woman being branded and the man being inspected. This image owed a great deal to George Morland's 1788 painting *Execrable Human Traffic*, which shows African/European contact and the sale and separation of African families (see fig. 1.5). Biard's *Slave Trade* was purchased by delegates at the Anti-Slavery Society Convention and presented to Sir Thomas Fowell Buxton, William Wilberforce's successor, to commemorate his work on the abolition of slavery in the British colonies, which took effect in 1834.

CHILDREN'S LITERATURE

In the United States and England, the antislavery campaign developed literature for children. Usually in the form of pamphlets or pocket-size books, these small volumes were heavily illustrated with woodcut engravings and sometimes included a version of the slave ship icon. They are important in the way that they packaged and spread the anti-slavery message to a young audience of future citizens and leaders. Also, because of their small size, they were easily transported, traded, and passed on, thereby increasing the publicity of the abolitionist cause and the images used to illustrate it. Many of these pamphlets were written in verse and thus were intended to be recited by the children as they identified the images. Consequently, another way of reinforcing the immediacy of the cause, especially for children, was through not only oral but also visual repetition.

The New York printer, publisher, and bookseller Samuel Wood was known for his children's books and abolitionist publications. He had a store downtown at 362 Pearl Street with "a large selection of well chosen books in the different departments of science." He also carried a wide variety of schoolbooks, bibles, and writing instruments. An ardent supporter of the abolition of slavery, Wood used his influence as a publisher to spread his simple message: "Slavery must be abolished." In 1807, Wood published two abolitionist "pocket volumes" intended for juvenile audiences, *The Mirror of Misery; or, Tyranny Exposed* (fig. 3.12) and Thomas Branagan's *The Penitential Tyrant*.[23] Both were printed with a small collection of standard abolitionist literature followed by a series of popular abolitionist engravings, including a version of the slave ship icon that gained early notice in the United States when it was published with *Remarks on the Slave Trade*. Intended for a juvenile audience, it was an intimate size, measuring only six by four inches. On the title page, a version of the kneeling slave was printed with the following caption:

> Ah! Pity human mis'ry, human we:
> Tis what the happy to the unhappy owe.

The printed and visual materials published in this volume were "extracted from Authentic Documents, and exemplified by Engravings" and included "The Method of Procuring Slaves, on the Coast of Africa, &c"; "Remarks on the Slave Trade"; eight pages of "Descriptive Plates"; "Essay on Slavery" (by Captain Marjoribanks, belonging to a British regiment which was stationed in the West Indies); "A Subject for Conversation and Reflection at the Tea Table"; a poem extracted from the *New Haven Gazette*; and William Cowper's poem *The Negro's Complaint*.

Wood's illustration of the slave ship icon is printed across two facing pages (fig. 3.13). A simplified rendering of the original Plymouth Committee engraving (which was copied for *Remarks on the Slave Trade*), it lacks that certain unsettling elegance embodied in the fanciful handwritten title and the detailed engraved figures of the original. Instead, printed nearly thirty years after the original, Wood's mass-produced version is not engraved. It has a simple printed title above what now appears to be a visually flattened schematic with rather undefined, undifferentiated blackened figures. Additionally, Wood makes a few minor editorial changes to the text that accompanied *Remarks on the Slave Trade*, aimed at bringing it up to date.[24]

The descriptive plates that follow the reprint of *Remarks on the Slave Trade* have emotional captions, such as: "The husband and wife, after being sold to different purchasers, violently separated; probably never to see each other more," with the illustration below showing a white overseer whipping the separating couple,

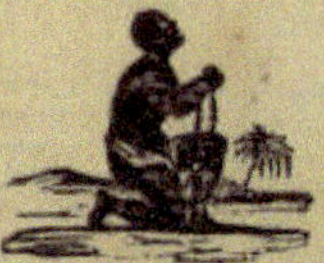

3.12 LEFT
Title page and illustration from Wood,
The Mirror of Misery, 1807.

3.13 BELOW
*Plan of A Slave Ship's Lower Deck with Negroes
Stowed in the Proportion of Only One to a
Ton* from *Remarks on the Slave Trade* by Captain
Major Banks.

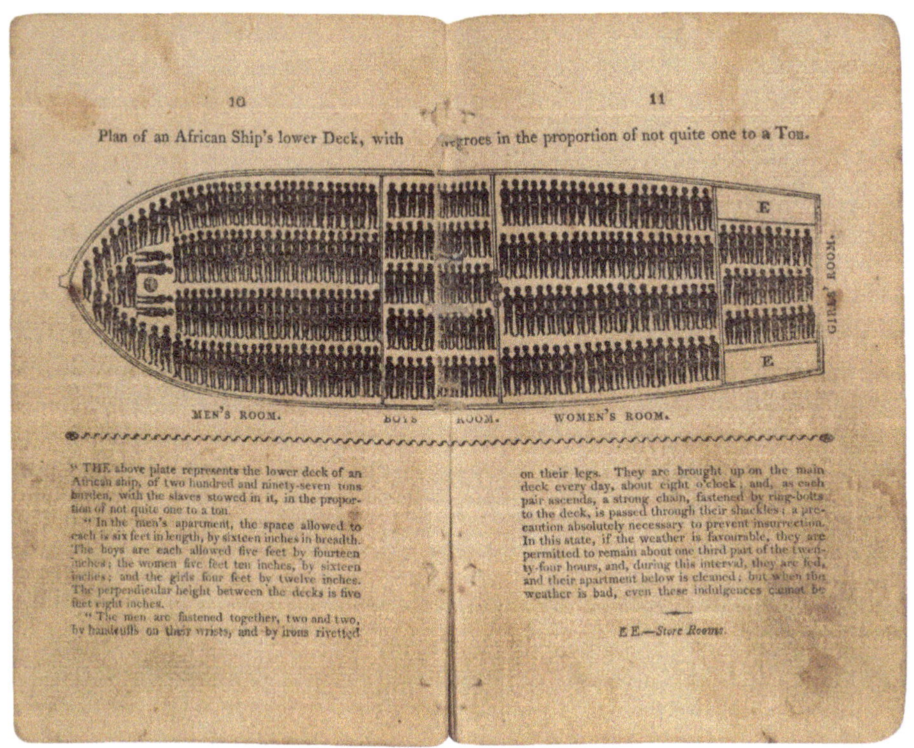

" THE above plate represents the lower deck of an African ship, of two hundred and ninety-seven tons burden, with the slaves stowed in it, in the proportion of not quite one to a ton.

" In the men's apartment, the space allowed to each is six feet in length, by sixteen inches in breadth. The boys are each allowed five feet by fourteen inches; the women five feet ten inches, by sixteen inches; and the girls four feet by twelve inches. The perpendicular height between the decks is five feet eight inches.

" The men are fastened together, two and two, by handcuffs on their wrists, and by irons rivetted on their legs. They are brought up on the main deck every day, about eight o'clock; and, as each pair ascends, a strong chain, fastened by ring-bolts to the deck, is passed through their shackles; a precaution absolutely necessary to prevent insurrection. In this state, if the weather is favourable, they are permitted to remain about one third part of the twenty-four hours, and, during this interval, they are fed, and their apartment below is cleaned; but when the weather is bad, even these indulgences cannot be

E E.—*Store Rooms.*

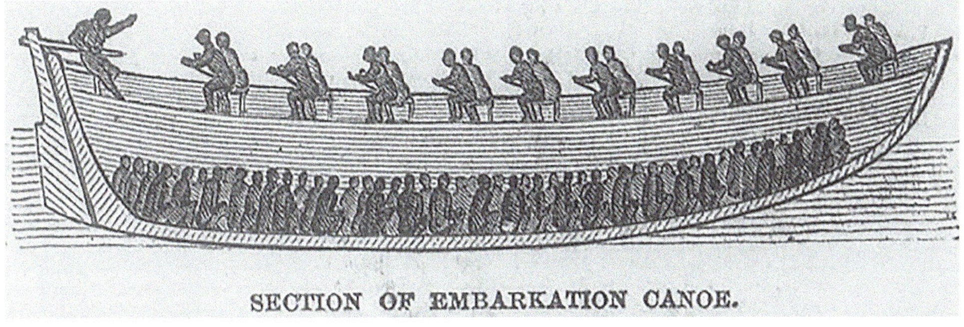

3.14
Section of Embarkation Canoe from Isaac
Taylor, *Scenes in Africa and America: For the
Amusement of and Instruction of Little
Tarry-at-Home-Travellers*, published by Harris
and Sons, London, 1820.

their child looking on at their side. Other descriptive plates illustrate the methods of torture, such as "A representation of a slave at work cruelly accoutered, with a head-frame and mouth piece to prevent his eating—with boots and spurs round his legs, and half a hundred weight chained to his body to prevent his absconding." Here, a male slave is shown wearing the devices described as he labors to hoe a patch of land. With a large palm tree off to one side, this image was distinctly meant to dramatize the cruelty of West Indian slavery. Later works, including the *Uncle Tom's Cabin Almanac* (1853), appealed to juvenile audiences while *Revelations of a Slave Smuggler* (1860), the autobiography of Captain Drake, illustrated now-familiar scenes of torture and cruelty. Other works such as Isaac Taylor's *Scenes in Africa and America: For the Amusement and Instruction of Little Tarry-at-Home-Travellers* were illustrated travelogues that presented images from the abolition period, including a slightly different version of the slave ship icon in the form of an "embarkation canoe" (fig. 3.14).

SUPPRESSION OF THE SLAVE TRADE

What exactly did "abolition of the slave trade" mean, especially to the international community? How would such a wide-sweeping regulation be enforced? How would a once legally sanctioned commerce, one that had flourished and profited for more than two centuries, be expected to stop overnight? How would the other European powers that still condoned the slave trade interfere or cooperate with the British and American plans for abolition? Finally, how would these other countries be made to comply?

W. E. B. Du Bois's PhD dissertation from Harvard, published in 1896 as *The Suppression of the African Slave-Trade to the United States of America, 1638–1870*, remains one of the best accounts of how the slave trade was curtailed after Britain and America declared it abolished in 1807 and 1808 respectively, and finally put it to an end. What is important to remember is that the slave trade did not stop overnight. In fact, the idea of immediate abolition was a complete fallacy. British and American slavers continued to operate illegally alongside slavers from other European nations that still allowed the slave trade, often flying the flag of a foreign nation as a disguise. It would take more than fifty years and several international treaties before the illegal slave trade was finally brought under control. As Du Bois explains, the key to abolishing the slave trade lay in a series of international agreements made between Britain and other European nations between 1806 and 1862.[25]

British laws prohibiting the slave trade were enforced with patrol ships led by the preeminent force of the British Navy with gradual international cooperation. The British Navy's strength enabled the ships to engage in search and seizure on the high seas, but only once they had obtained agreements from other nations that had declared the slave trade illegal. For example, Denmark had been the first country to abolish the slave trade in 1802, yet in order to effectively enforce this declaration, a bilateral agreement with England was signed in 1810. Sweden forbade the trade in 1813, and the Netherlands complied the following year. At the Congress of Vienna, wherein the European powers convened late in 1814 in order to negotiate peace across the continent, it was hoped that an agreement would be reached by all participants to end the slave trade altogether, but Spain and France refused to comply. In 1815, Portugal agreed to abolish the slave trade north of the equator. Spain made the same commitment two years later in 1817. In the same year, Portugal and Spain were the first countries to allow Britain limited Right of Search. In 1818, France put an end to the slave trade, and in the same year, the Netherlands agreed to allow the British Navy the right to search Dutch ships suspected of illegally transporting cargos of slaves. In 1820, Spain declared the slave trade illegal south of the equator, and ten years later Portugal made the same declaration. Over the next ten years, France, Denmark, Austria, Russia, and Prussia would agree to allow Britain the Right of Search.

But the United States held out until 1842, when the Treaty of Washington was signed, in which she joined Britain in jointly policing the high seas. This treaty also extended limited but eventually ineffective search and seizure rights to Great Britain. The Treaty of Washington never was given serious consideration by the United States government. The bold refusal of the United States to comply with laws forbidding the slave trade and the right to search tarnished the reputation of the American flag. As Du Bois remarked, "the stand of the United States really amounted to the wholesale protection of pirates under her flag."[26] In addition to a lax attitude toward suppressing the slave trade, the United States didn't allocate enough resources to provide the necessary number of naval squadrons to make suppression effective. Besides, the geographic area that each ship or group of ships was supposed to monitor was vast. Du Bois concurs, "As the commanders themselves acknowledged, the squadron was too small and the cruising-ground too large to make joint cruising effective."[27] A report from the American naval squadron assigned to Brazil agreed.

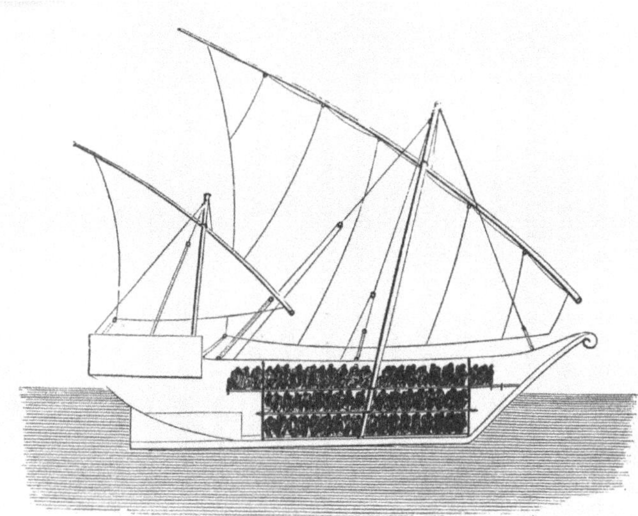

3.15
Section of the Dhow Alluded to at Page 168, Showing the Manner of Stowing Slaves on Board, from Sulivan, *Dhow Chasing in Zanzibar Waters*, 1873.

Nothing effectual can be done towards stopping the slave trade, as our squadron is at present organized.... When it is considered that the Brazil station extends from north of the equator to Cape Horn on this continent, and includes a great part of Africa south of the equator, on both sides of the Cape of Good Hope, it must be admitted that one frigate and one brig is a very insufficient force to protect American commerce, and repress the participation in the slave trade by our own vessels.[28]

Finally, in 1862 with the outbreak of the Civil War, the United States agreed to sign a treaty with Britain, granting a mutual Right of Search and to establish mixed courts. How was this part of the history of the slave trade represented visually? The image of the slave ship would figure prominently, especially that of the slave ship icon. For example, to denote that much of the illegal slave trading was taking place in the Indian Ocean, the type of ship drawn changed from a coastal schooner to a dhow. Examples of illustrations can be found in texts such as *Dhow Chasing in Zanzibar Waters*, detailing the high seas adventures of British naval squadrons charged with catching illegal slavers (fig. 3.15). With the introduction of photography in 1839, and later photographic printing technologies that allowed for enlargements, photographers boarded some of these captured illegal slavers and took pictures, which were later engraved and reproduced in popular illustrated journals such as *Harper's Weekly*.

PART TWO

MEANINGS/ROUTES

1900–present

CHAPTER FOUR

NEGROES: OLD AND NEW

TWENTIETH-CENTURY ARTISTS RECLAIM THE SLAVE SHIP ICON

BY THE EARLY PART OF THE TWENTIETH CENTURY, the slave ship icon had become an artifact, still capable of recreating the horror of the Middle Passage for those who encountered the schematic image, but no longer used for its original purpose, the active promotion of the abolition of the slave trade or of slavery. Those battles had been fought and won in the previous century, yet the social, political, and economic inequities left in their wake continued to crash along the shores of the black Atlantic.

During the twentieth century, an emerging class of professional black artists began to interrogate the history of slavery in light of their political and cultural moment. In their efforts to bring new meaning to how they came to be part of an African diaspora or to understand for themselves the fact—the existence—of an African diaspora, black artists and their white and Latino allies seized on the symbols, sites, and rituals of the past, guarding them as aesthetic tools to be used, in the words of Walter Benjamin (1892–1940), "in times of danger." They realized that these keys to the past could also be keys to the future.

Beginning in the early 1910s, record numbers of black people had started moving from the rural South to the industrial North, Midwest, and West in what became known as the Great Migration, fleeing racial oppression and lynch mobs in search of opportunities for work and for a chance to live in an environment free of the psychological and physical trauma of slavery's past. They craved something new, a fresh start, with jobs in manufacturing, better housing, and educational opportunities for themselves and their children. Within the next decade this urbanization led to a critical mass of the educated and enfranchised people necessary for the development of the New Negro Arts Movement.

The art historian Richard J. Powell argues that Alain Locke (1885–1954), a Howard University philosophy professor, and Charles S. Johnson (1893–1956), a sociologist and the director of research and publicity for the National Urban League, "carefully orchestrated" the New Negro Arts Movement "to place African American social issues at the forefront of the national agenda. They used African American arts and culture as the vehicles for promoting 'the race.'"[1] The term *New Negro* was popularized by Locke in 1925 through the favorable reception of two notable publications that he edited: a special issue of the sociological and political issues magazine *Survey Graphic* called "Harlem: Mecca of the New Negro"; and his groundbreaking book of essays, short fiction, photographs, drawings, and a short play that he called *The New Negro: An Interpretation*. Among the trade publishers who supported and encouraged the art and literature of the New Negro Arts Movement were Alfred A. Knopf and Albert and Charles Boni. Monthly journals and weekly magazines, such as *Opportunity, Crisis*, the *New Yorker*, and *Vanity Fair*, provided additional opportunities for artists and illustrators. Between 1919 and 1929, poetry, short stories, and novels by black writers were published in record numbers, and books previously written about black subject matter were reissued. Many of these publications were lavishly illustrated or presented with bold cover designs by the artists Miguel Covarrubias (1904–1957), Aaron Douglas (1898–1979), and Winold Reiss (1886–1953). Each in his own way pushed the limitations of the highly stylized, modernist primitivist aesthetic popular at the time. In both literature and the arts, Africa was being recast as a symbol of pride and inspiration.

Emerging alongside the aesthetic developments of the New Negro Arts Movement (a.k.a. Harlem Renaissance) were the political activities of the Jamaican-born activist Marcus Garvey (1887–1940), who began a movement to encourage black people in North America and the Caribbean to return to their ancestral homeland. His Pan-Africanist agenda focused on economic and political independence for black people. In 1911, he founded the Universal Negro Improvement Association (UNIA) to assist his cause, leading enormous demonstrations and marches through the streets of Harlem and other locations with large black populations in the northeastern United States. His popularity was aided by favorable reports in the black press and by photographs taken by the popular Harlem photographer James Van Der Zee (1886–1983), whom Garvey hired to document the immense crowds that turned out for Harlem's UNIA rallies. From 1919 to 1922, Garvey also sold shares in the Black Star Line, an international shipping line he hoped would be the vehicle for making his dream come true, to enable commerce between Africa and the Americas and to transport black people on their return to Africa (fig. 4.1).[2] Garvey's dreams of ships and their commercial possibilities coincided with a general sense of longing for seafaring in the public mind at this time. Large ocean liners had long since replaced sailing ships as the primary means of transatlantic travel, and while they would soon be eclipsed by the airplane, for the time being, the lure of the ship and the ocean still exerted a mighty pull on the popular imagination.

MIGUEL COVARRUBIAS AND *ADVENTURES OF AN AFRICAN SLAVER*

Simultaneous with the period of black rediscovery exemplified and capitalized upon by Marcus Garvey, a new wave of mainstream interest in writing about the transatlantic slave trade, which had only officially ended a little over a century before, took shape.[3] In the mainstream American press, historical narratives about the trade were revised for modern audiences, newer ones were fictionalized or dramatized, and historical accounts were written.[4] Nostalgia for a bygone era of sea and sail led to the publication of works that in effect romanticized the slave trade, with authors focusing on the personal narratives and memoirs of slave traders, who were benevolently portrayed as adventurers on the high seas instead of as purveyors

NOW IN AMERICA

S. S. Phyllis Wheatley

LATEST ADDITION TO FLEET OF

BLACK STAR LINE, Inc.

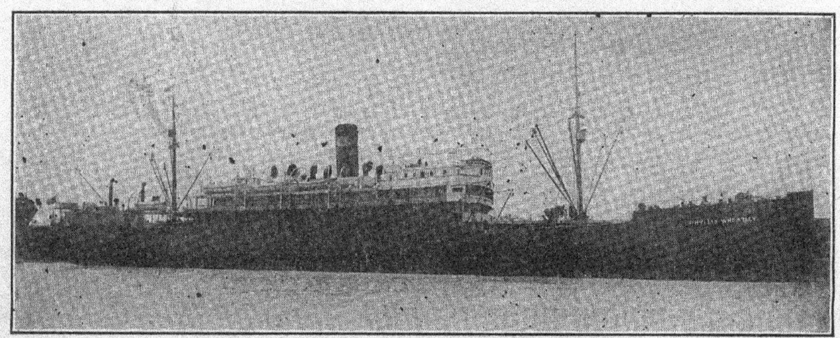

TWIN SCREW BOAT

Carries 4,500 Tons Cargo--nearly 2,000 Passengers ; Electric Lights, Fans, Music Rooms, Smoking Rooms, Refrigerating Machinery--Modern Conveniences

To be Taken Over by Black Star Line After Inspection

MAY 25th

BIGGEST STEAMBOAT DAY in HISTORY of RACE

Dollar Drive for Members of the U. N. I. A.

The proceeds of this Dollar Drive will be used to donate our mother ship all necessary equipments, and make it specially and conveniently fitted for the African Trade.

Universal Negro Improvement Association,   **56 W. 135th Street,   New York**

4.1

Advertisement for Marcus Garvey's
Black Star Line, ca. 1922.

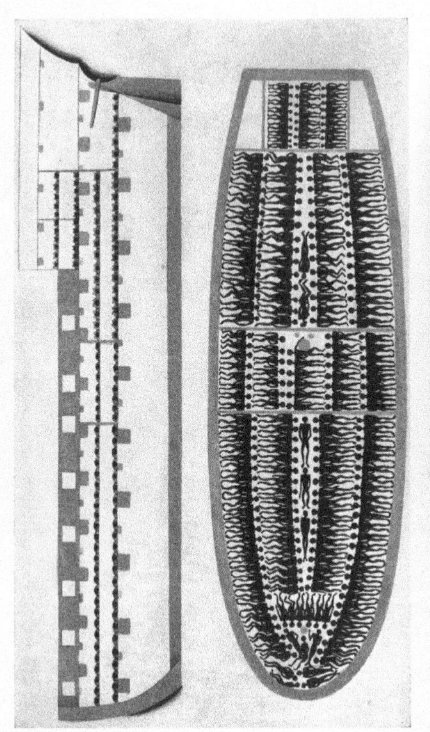

4.2

Miguel Covarrubias, *A Black Cargo Ready for
an Ocean Voyage*, frontispiece and title page from
Adventures of an African Slaver, 1928, gouache.

of human beings. It was in this moment that the freelance writer Malcolm Cowley
(1898–1989) and the Mexican-born artist Miguel Covarrubias embarked on their
substantial revision of the original 1854 publication of the biographical study *Captain Canot; or, Twenty Years of an African Slaver; Being an Account of His Career
and Adventures on the Coast, in the Interior, on Shipboard, and in the West Indies*,
by Brantz Mayer (1809–1879).[5] Cowley's revision of the Mayer book, similarly titled
*Adventures of An African Slaver, Being a True Account of the Life of Captain Theo-
dore Canot, Trader in Gold, Ivory & Slaves on the Coast of Guinea: His Own Story
as Told in the Year 1854 to Brantz Mayer*, appeared at the height of the New Negro
Arts Movement of the late 1920s.[6]

Miguel Covarrubias, as illustrator of Cowley's book, thus became the first artist
to reclaim the slave ship icon in the twentieth century (fig. 4.2). His reinterpretation of the prominent eighteenth- and nineteenth-century abolitionist engraving

appeared in 1928, when the innovative New York publishers Albert and Charles Boni produced the new edition of *Captain Canot*. Covarrubias's newly recast slave ship icon appeared as the frontispiece, the first of nine full-page black-and-white illustrations—a truly striking introductory image for the 376-page book. The artist was riding the wave of the period's revolution in book art, in which illustration was integrated with text in mechanically printed books, journals, and magazines.

The book's original author, Brantz Mayer, was a founder in the United States of the Maryland Historical Society in Baltimore and a journalist who had written several books on the history and culture of Mexico.[7] He relied on his conversations with Canot as well as on Canot's ship logs, journals, and papers to construct a first-person "memoir" of the slaver's "adventures" in a trade that had long since been declared illegal. Dr. James Hall, a leading member of the American Colonization Society, founded in 1816, had introduced Mayer to the idea of writing Canot's memoirs.[8] Mayer himself was a supporter of the American Colonization Society, which sought to establish settlements of free blacks in West Africa and was responsible for the founding of Liberia in 1821. According to Mayer, Hall became intrigued by Canot's story when the physician met Canot in Liberia in the early 1850s. In his introduction, Mayer argues that Canot's memoirs were important for the United States at a time when the "slavery question" was being debated. Mayer explains his reasons for wanting to bring Canot's story to the attention of the public in the book's dedication to the noted American poet and literary editor Nathaniel Parker Willis (1806–1867),

> I thought that the evidence of one who, for twenty years, played the chief part in such a drama, was of value to society, which is making up its mind, not only about a great political and domestic problem, but as to the nature of the race itself. I thought that a true picture of aboriginal Africa,—unstirred by progress,—unmodified by reflected civilization,—full of the barbarism that blood and tradition have handed down from the beginning, and embalmed in its prejudices, like the corpse of Egypt,—could not fail to be of incalculable importance to philanthropists who regard no people as beyond the reach of enlightenment.[9]

Mayer had hoped that Canot's memoirs would encourage voluntary African colonization. "Will our colonial fringe spread its fibres from the coast to the interior," he asks, "and, like veins of refreshing blood, pour new currents into the mummy's heart?"[10] In addition to the interesting and detailed chapters on the business of the slave trade, including the drastic economic and diversionary tactics executed in its illegal operation, there were several chapters describing the climate, people, flora, and fauna of Africa.[11] Mayer's *Captain Canot* sought to portray Africa as an ideal place to live. These ethnographic travel chapters, together with the original engraved illustrations, also suggested to the reader that "repatriating" the enslaved population of the United States to Africa was an alternative answer to the looming question of abolishing slavery. In Mayer's own words, "They who are practically acquainted with the colored race of our country have long believed that gradual colonization was the only remedy for Africa as well as America."[12] More to the point,

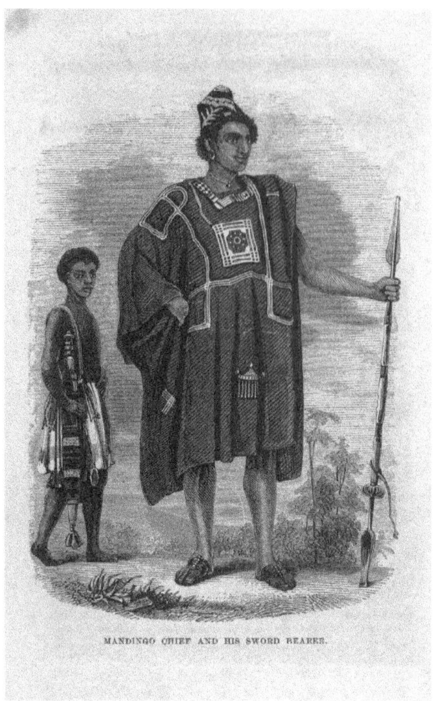

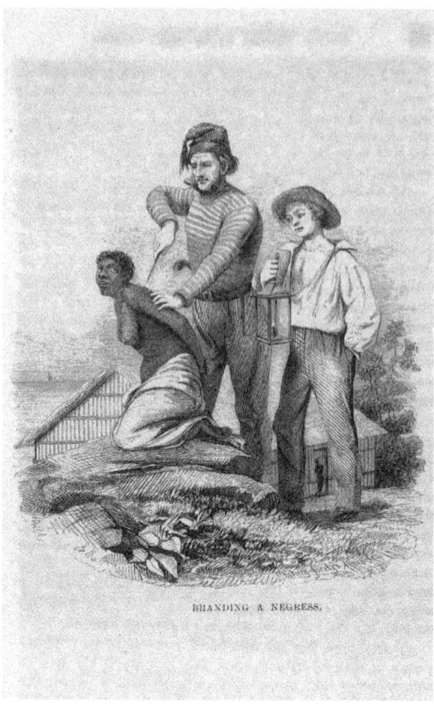

4.3

Brantz Mayer, *Mandingo Chief and His Sword Bearer*, frontispiece engraving from *Captain Canot*, 1854.

4.4

Brantz Mayer, *Branding a Negress*, engraving from *Captain Canot*, 1854.

Mayer and his colleagues at the American Colonization Society argued for colonization in lieu of emancipation.

Captain Canot was published with seven wood engravings from illustrations drawn by Mayer himself, referring to scenes and people described in the narrative: *Mandingo Chief and His Sword Bearer* (frontispiece) (fig. 4.3); an illustrated title page with a jungle motif; *Branding a Negress* (facing page 102) (fig. 4.4); *The Women of Timbo Drawing Water* (facing page 178); *the Inspection and Sale of a Negro* (facing page 189); *the Massacre at Digby* (facing page 384), and *An Elephant Hunt* (facing page 440).[13] The title page is embellished with lush tropical vegetation, including palm trees on either side, one climbed by a monkey, the other encircled by a hissing snake. In the center of the illustration below the ghoulishly lettered title, Mayer has depicted a coffle of four enslaved Africans being led by three whites. These figures are drawn in the flat frontal-profile style of ancient Egyptian mural painting and are placed on a mantle that sits on the shoulders of two sphinxes.

Showing the manner of dress, as in *Mandingo Chief*, or the customs, as in *Women of Timbo Drawing Water*, the ethnographic appeal of Mayer's illustrations proffered a sense of exotic realism. *Women of Timbo Drawing Water* focuses on the activities of a small group of women gathered to draw water for the jugs they carry on their heads. With their bare chests exposed and wearing only boldly patterned fabric draped from their waists, the women assume the classical contrapposto poses of ancient Greek sculpture, but in an imaginary African savanna setting dotted by palm trees and round-house-style thatched huts visible in the distance. *Branding a Negress* reproduces a detail from the famous historical painting *The Slave Trade* by François-Auguste Biard (1799–1882) (see fig. 3.11). Presented to the public in 1840, it was a visual inventory of the brutalities of inspection, branding, and trading on the African coast. Its immediate popularity spurred many imitations and popular prints. Mayer's *Branding a Negress* refers to only a small section of the painting, in which a kneeling, bare-chested woman winces at the pain of being branded with a hot iron by a sailor who is identified by a striped shirt and stocking cap.[14] In Mayer's drawing, the woman, man, and his attendant strike the same poses as in the Biard painting, but the setting is a little farther inland, with the ocean still in view. Together, the seven illustrations offer up an Africa still in need of civilization yet appealing for colonization. It is important to note that Mayer offers no visual representation of the Middle Passage (or the slave ship icon) in *Captain Canot*.

Cowley's revisions to Mayer's 448-page text endeavored to update Mayer's cumbersome mid-nineteenth-century language, making it lively and accessible to readers in 1928. One reviewer of the time praised Cowley's "able introduction" and described the new edition of Canot's autobiography as thrilling, "with a few unavoidable horrors thrown in." Cowley was just beginning what would be a long and distinguished literary career as a poet, editor, critic, and historian.[15] In the early 1920s, he studied French literature and lived in Paris, where he was captivated by the popular European fascination with Africa in vogue during the bohemian era.

Adventures of an African Slaver was published in the midst of Prohibition in America, and in his introduction Cowley points out the analogies between "rum running" and the illegal slave trade: "In both forms of smuggling one finds the swift vessels, the desperate crews, the dash to load or unload a cargo, and the carouse at the end of the voyage when profits were divided."[16] Cowley even deploys visual metaphors linking the illegal slave trade with Prohibition: "In order to make the venture pay, the slaves were packed as tightly as cases of Scotch whiskey."[17] Cowley's interpretation of Mayer's text combined his deep interest in the history of the slave trade with editorial wit to portray what he felt was a true story of adventure and "the romantic side of the slave trade."[18] In contrast, his artistic collaborator, Miguel Covarrubias, illustrated a visual counternarrative, the centerpiece of which is the slave ship icon.

Covarrubias spent his formative years in Mexico during the revolution. His firsthand experience of the country's economic, social, and political upheaval shaped the direction of his art and the tenor of his aesthetic. He drew sharp satirical caricatures of the reactionary leaders of the revolution, which gained him a reputation as a captivating illustrator among his fellow artists and countrymen, including the printmaker Francisco Mora (1922–2002) and the painters José Clemente Orozco (1883–1949) and Diego Rivera (1886–1957). These artists became known in the 1920s and 1930s for their works of social realism, which sought to affect change for the oppressed, challenge dictatorships, and arouse solidarity among the masses.[19]

It was in part through his association with these artists that Covarrubias decided to go to New York in 1923, at the age of eighteen. Both Orozco and Rivera had spent time there, and their stories about the art and entertainment scene, particularly in Harlem, were often recounted at the bohemian artist café Los Monotes, owned by Orozco's family in Mexico City. When Orozco first set out to explore New York on his own in earnest in 1919, he found "the neighborhood of Harlem, where Negroes and Hispanic Americans live" to be one of the most beautiful and entertaining places in the city.[20] Indeed, Harlem in the 1910s, '20s, and '30s was a mixed immigrant neighborhood, known mostly for its black and Latino residents. Having come from a country in the midst of social and political change, it was easy for Covarrubias to recognize revolutionary tendencies in the works and aspirations of the black artists, writers, performers, and musicians he met in Harlem. What is more, both he and his fellow Mexican artists who settled in New York developed an understanding of and affinity for the social position of blacks in the United States and its historical roots.

Covarrubias also learned about black New York through the influential Harlem Renaissance entrepreneur Carl Van Vechten (1880–1964), whom he met within months of his arrival in the city. Van Vechten was chiefly responsible for introducing Covarrubias to the rich and powerful of New York, whom Covarrubias began to caricature with searing wit and a seeming lack of sympathy. As with his earlier work in Mexico, many of Covarrubias's earliest caricatures of American subjects were produced with the cunning simplicity of sly black lines on white paper. These works were published in magazines such as *Vanity Fair* and the *New Yorker* and compiled in a book of caricatures, *The Prince of Wales and Other Famous Americans*, published by Alfred A. Knopf in 1925, with an introduction by Carl Van Vechten. But Van Vechten wasn't Covarrubias's only patron. In 1927, Alain Locke introduced him to Charlotte Osgood Mason (1854–1946), a wealthy Park Avenue benefactor to some of the most respected figures of the New Negro Arts Movement in Harlem. Covarrubias benefited from her largesse, as did Langston Hughes (1902–1967), Aaron Douglas (1899–1979), Zora Neale Hurston (1891–1960), and Locke himself.[21]

During his forays into Harlem, Covarrubias became associated with a coterie of black artists whose stars were also rising. He befriended people like the artist Douglas, who, like Covarrubias, contributed to the rich production of graphically illustrated books for which this period became known. Covarrubias also collaborated with Langston Hughes, designing the cover of the poet's first book, *The Weary Blues*, in 1926. Walter White (1893–1955), head of the NAACP, wrote to congratulate Hughes about the forthcoming publication of *The Weary Blues*, commenting, "It is certainly great to have a foreword by Van Vechten and have Covarrubias to do the jacket."[22] The following year, Covarrubias illustrated *Blues: An Anthology* by W. C. Handy (1873–1958). Meanwhile, beginning in December 1924, his illustrations of black life in the nightclubs, dance halls, and theaters of Harlem had been appearing in *Vanity Fair* to much acclaim; in 1927 these were collected in his second monograph, *Negro Drawings*.[23] The art historian Lizzetta LeFalle-Collins notes, "In a way, *Negro Drawings* was a pioneering volume since it offered a new prominence to representations of African Americans."[24] Covarrubias continued to be sought after for his portrayals of black life.[25] As a consummate observer

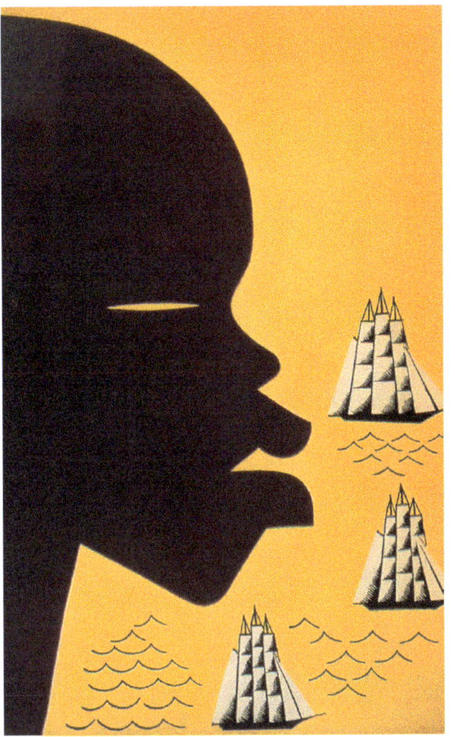

of performance—dance, theater, and song—Covarrubias was able to capture the nuances of black movement, gesture, music, sensuality, and form. His friend Diego Rivera once said, "He discovered and brought to the world of art the marvels of the black inhabitants of the island."[26] Some of Covarrubias's earlier illustrations of black figures were drawn in a minimal yet expressive manner. In later works, he would add shading, texture, and color to further describe his subjects. This is especially evident in his drawings for Handy's *Blues: An Anthology* and his own *Negro Drawings*. These projects would provide the background from which he drew the inspiration for the illustrations for *Adventures of an African Slaver*.

Unlike the "ethnographic travelogue" contained in the text, Covarrubias's drawings for *Adventures of an African Slaver* are instilled with a personal style informed by caricature as well as by the artist's study in Paris, travel in North Africa, and close interactions with members of the Harlem Renaissance. If the reader takes cues from Covarrubias's illustrations alone, beginning with the cover, the entire book may be read through a lens of crossing, displacement, and perpetual movement—of Middle Passage. The bright yellow cover is illustrated with a large profile of a brown face and sailing ships floating in a sea of waves (fig. 4.5). Placed at the left edge of the cover, the elongated profile captures the modernist primitivist moment. Its pronounced features—high forehead, broad nose, full lips—recall a ceremonial African mask. With slits for eyes, this all-seeing ancestral figure spies the three tall clipper ships, sleek slave ships, with their billowing white sails full of fast-moving air. They have been streamlined for quick ocean crossings so as to avoid capture by naval blockades. The flat spatial organization of the cover reads like a symbolic map of the black Atlantic.[27] On the back cover, the brown profile, yellow sea, and sailing ships are repeated, but the image is *reversed*. By flipping the image, Covarrubias allows us to imagine a more specific map, one of the West African coastline and the Gulf of Guinea. Furthermore, Covarrubias's large brown profile puts the figure of the African at the center of the narrative, displacing Captain Canot. From the very beginning, the cover of the book, Covarrubias's illustrations subvert the written narrative.

The depiction of African masks and other symbolic markers of African heritage was a central motif of the illustrators and artists associated with the New Negro Arts Movement. Aaron Douglas in particular employed African motifs and what he called "the Egyptian form" to stylize his black figures. In Egyptian form, he wrote, "the head was in perspective in a profile flat view, the body, shoulders down to the waist turned half way, the legs were done also from the side."[28] This technique produced exaggerated, Africanized profiles for many of the figures depicted on his covers for the NAACP's *Crisis* magazine in the 1920s, as well as in his murals painted for the Works Progress Administration, Fisk University, and myriad institutions in the 1930s.[29] His fellow artists of the 1930s, Wilmer Jennings (1910–1990), Loïs Mailou Jones (1905–1998), and Hale Woodruff (1900–1980), drew African ceremonial masks and ritual figures as a way of recalling their African roots and the historical forces that made them part of the African diaspora. The most notable of these works include the wood engraving *Still Life with Fetish* (1937) by Jennings, the oil painting *Les Fétiches* (1938) by Jones, and the linocut *African Headdress* (1937) by Woodruff.[30] For these artists and for Covarrubias, the act of imaging African art through the depiction of ritual objects became a way of imagining Africa.

The pale-yellow endpapers of *Adventures of an African Slaver* (fig. 4.6) are printed with an enlarged detail of the crowded midsection of the slave ship icon abstracted from Covarrubias's frontispiece. The endpapers are a metaphor for an inner skin—essentially the palm of the hand—of the cover of the book and leave an indelible imprint on the reader's subconscious. They are the connective tissue that links the story from cover to cover. Heavy brown lines draw the outline of the section of the ship, and stylized black figures represent the enslaved Africans. As a crucial design element of the book's construction, these endpapers possess a tantalizing graphic appeal, and one not without consequence. Refashioned as a design motif, the slave ship icon becomes aestheticized in all its horror. Looking closely, one can glean how Covarrubias forms and contorts the figures with an exacting primitivist shorthand, producing recognizable profiles and volumetric shapes. It is important to note that Covarrubias had become well versed in African dance and other native dance forms through the work he did as a costume and production designer for dance and musical theater—in 1925, he designed the sets and costumes for *La Revue Nègre*, in which Josephine Baker made her Paris debut—and he made use of this movement in his stationary art. Their herky-jerky, squirming motions, evocative of African dance movements, add a heightened intensity to the ordered yet rhythmic image.

At the center of the endpapers, one figure holds a bold black circle meant to represent the mast. His arm clutches it between his torso and thigh. Instead of a mast, the circle could also be seen as a drum used to energize—to call to action—the other figures, which are drawn in constant movement. The continuous motion of the boat on the ocean becomes visible in the way that Covarrubias draws the figures in action, shaking them to and fro. Elongated and angular, with sharp, broad shoulders and spherical heads, the figures of the slave ship icon are modernized by Covarrubias in a frenzied moment of aesthetic exaggeration. Instead of the staid or passive appearance of the figures in *Description of a Slave Ship*, Covarrubias's reinterpretation of this historic image has the power of activating the force of the collective. The subsequent illustrations in the book show a people alive, vibrant, responsive, thinking. His slave ship icon affirms that knowledge of African religion, dance, art, and culture did not die in the Middle Passage.

The frontispiece, from which the endpapers are abstracted, is an important interpretive device that helps to visually sequence and set the tone of the book. For Covarrubias, the frontispiece was a central design element in all his illustrated books. He often rendered an image in gouache instead of line for this key placement. For instance, he placed the brightly colored gouache *Negro Mother and Child*, a somber Madonna-and-child image, as the frontispiece for *Negro Drawings* in 1927.[31] Covarrubias's choices in reinterpreting the slave ship icon for both endpapers and frontispiece is critical to understanding the tension between the narrative and the illustration.

Captioned *A Black Cargo Ready for an Ocean Voyage*, the frontispiece is a gouache reproduced for publication in black and white (see fig. 4.2). It shows the

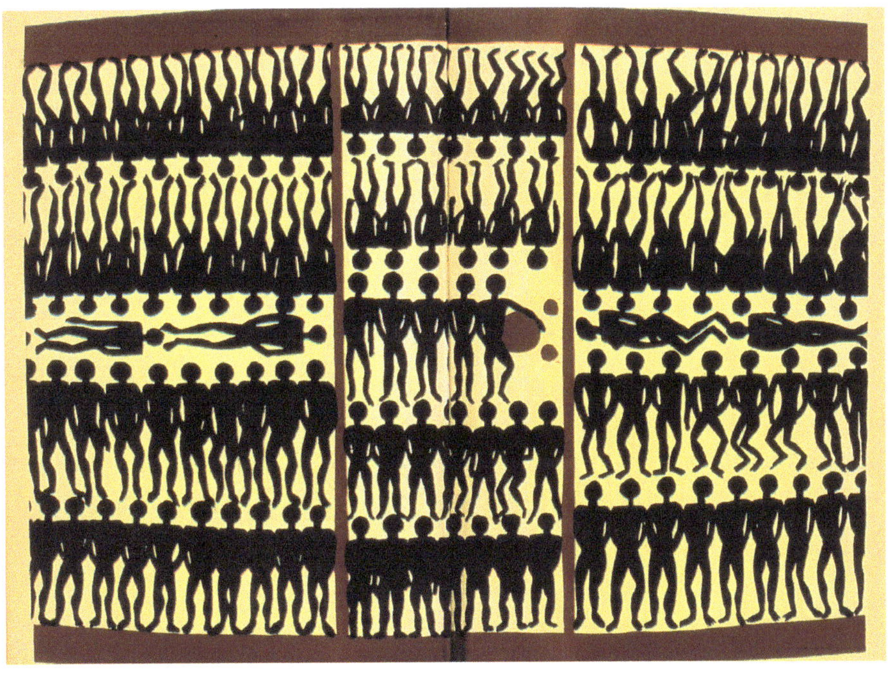

4.6
Miguel Covarrubias, endpapers from
Adventures of an African Slaver, 1928.

longitudinal view of the quarterdecks and the loaded lower deck. Its relative graphic faithfulness to the London Committee version of the slave ship icon reveals that it was no doubt drawn from the original. The gouache lends a softer feeling to this visually harsh and exacting image and dissolves the hard edge of the engraving line.[32] Yet it does not minimize the fact that Covarrubias chose this revolutionary image as the one through which the subsequent illustrations in the book would be visualized.

Nevertheless, we must question the implications of Covarrubias's redesigned slave ship icon as the frontispiece of a book such as this. Why is the slave ship icon the filter through which this book is viewed? Our answers may lie in revisiting the original Mayer publication and rephrasing our question: Why wasn't the slave ship icon part of Mayer's *Captain Canot*? The answer lies in the distinction between support for emancipation and support for colonization: As an image associated with the abolition of the slave trade, the slave ship icon would have been in direct opposition to the pro-colonization politics of Mayer and his adventure story, which makes light of Canot's career as a slaver. Furthermore, as a reminder of the unspeakable horror that millions of enslaved Africans had already endured to reach American shores, and which many thousands more would continue to suffer through the efforts of illegal slave traders like Canot, the slave ship icon had no place in Mayer's book. As an abolitionist image, the slave ship icon by 1854 stood as a symbol of the need to end slavery in the United States. Finally, for anyone contemplating the move to Africa and the transatlantic voyage that it entailed, the slave ship icon would have been an obvious reminder of the psychic trauma that such a return voyage might engender.

Covarrubias's subsequent eight illustrations serve the purpose of humanizing African people and bringing to life figures within the slave ship icon, without the icon itself. They describe specific events, rituals, or anecdotes from the narrative, including *Ivory Caravan, Guinea Princess, Foulah Chief, Inspection and Sale of Slaves* (fig. 4.7), *Pirates Boarding a Vessel, The Smuggling of Slaves* (fig. 4.8), *A Village*, and *African Ritual Dance*. In addition to these full-page illustrations, there is a small image of a black nude female figure reclining on a hammock, which closely resembles a scene from *La Revue Nègre*. Like the original Mayer publication, this new edition has a plate after Biard's *African Slave Trade*, titled *Branding a Negress*. Other plates, such as *Foulah Chief* (fig. 4.9) and *Guinea Princess*, show Covarrubias's adept use of modernist principles in portraying people. Three of Covarrubias's illustrations for *Adventures of an African Slaver* were published in the journal *Creative Art* in 1928, with the titles *Two African Men, African Village*, and *African Dance*.[33]

In contrast to Mayer's illustrations of nearly seventy-five years earlier, Covarrubias tried to instill his African figures with a sense of dignity and history, relying on classic African sculpture as his formal guide for the figures he depicted. While in Paris and New York, he saw collections of African art in museum exhibitions, flea markets, and in the homes of artists and collectors. His association with the artists and innovators of the New Negro Arts Movement as well as his own central position in that artistic and cultural awakening were evident in the visual counternarrative he constructed against Cowley's written text. Moreover, as central as this project was to bringing together Covarrubias's artistic and scholarly interests (as an illustrator,

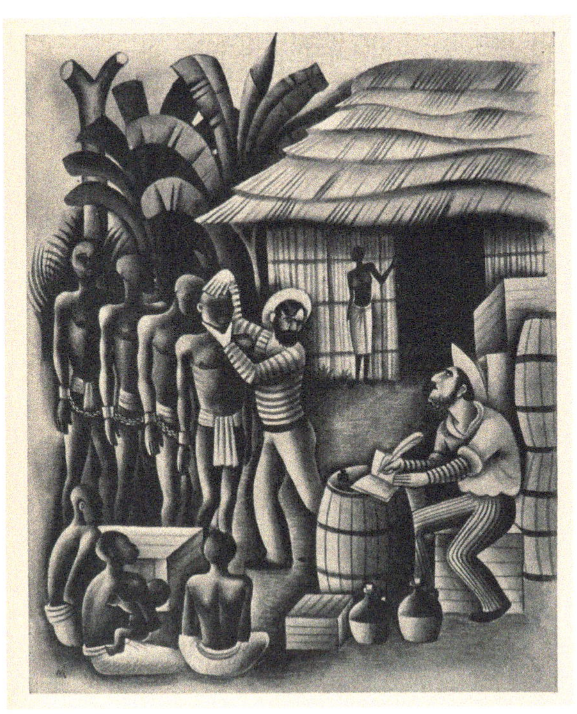

4.7 LEFT
Miguel Covarrubias, "Inspection and Sale of Slaves," from *Adventures of an African Slaver, 1928.*

4.8 BELOW LEFT
Miguel Covarrubias, "The Smuggling of Slaves," from *Adventures of an African Slaver*, 1928, gouache.

4.9 BELOW RIGHT
Miguel Covarrubias, "Foulah Chief," from *Adventures of an African Slaver*, 1928, gouache.

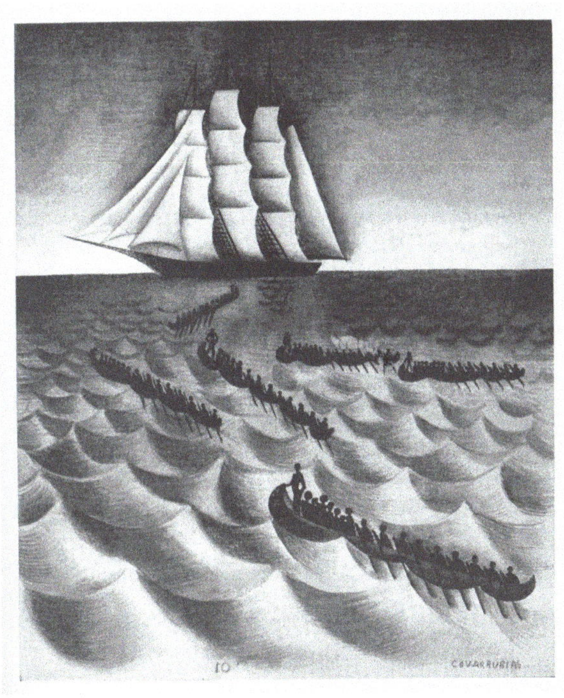

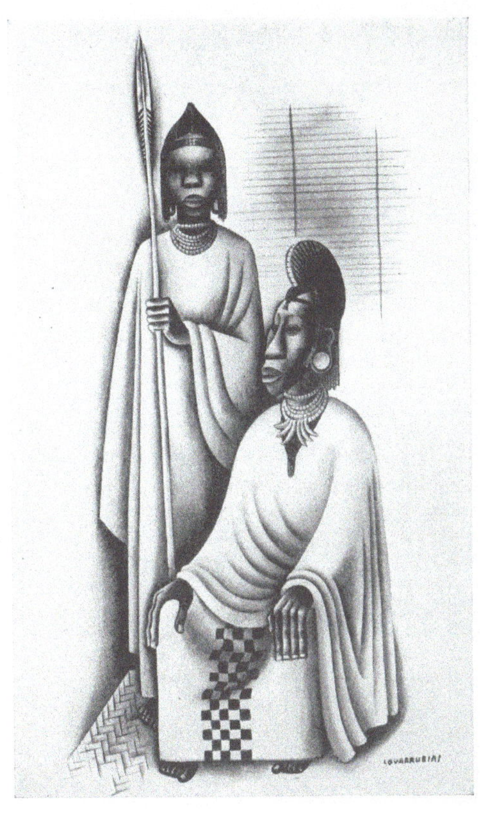

anthropologist, and costume and set designer), few scholars have discussed *Adventures of an African Slaver* in any significant way. This is no doubt due to the subject matter of the book and the complicated relationship of his images to Cowley's text.

THE TIME IN BETWEEN

During this period, there seemed to be a mutual recognition and understanding between Mexicans and blacks of the struggles of the oppressed, so perhaps it is not surprising that the slave ship icon was first resurrected by a Mexican artist born of a revolutionary political climate, one who could relate to and empathize with black struggles for freedom and equality. Furthermore, even seventy-five years after emancipation was still too soon, it seemed, for black artists to reckon with the image of the slave ship and all the history that it implied. As the collective memory scholar Barbie Zelizer has noted, "Visual records at times display a power too difficult to bear at points within the unfolding of memory."[34] During the New Negro Arts Movement and in the decade prior, black artists were creating images of uplift that signified the New Negro. These positive images concentrated on black achievement, performing arts, advancement, and education, not on the dreadful past, a past that was still too difficult to come to grips with, too hard to acknowledge with only two generations between them and the end of slavery. Many artists heeded Alain Locke's famous proclamation on the duty of black artists to incorporate the image of Africa into their work. But this visual and spiritual resurrection of Africa for many did not mean that black artists were ready to mine the Middle Passage or to contemplate the transatlantic voyage to get back to Africa. Marcus Garvey's back to Africa movement had come and gone, despite its initial appeal to millions of African diasporic followers in the United States and the Caribbean to the UNIA. Instead, for black artists, theirs was a metaphorical return that glorified Africa as an ancestral home with the artifacts of classical African civilization as their memory aides.[35]

By the early 1930s, the last people who had been born into the system of chattel slavery were beginning to pass on, and with them the memories of lives lived in fetters and the old "folk" ways. In the early 1930s, the ethnographer Alan Lomax (1915–2002) began his landmark study of the survivor-witnesses of slavery, recording their stories and recollections of their lives under the "peculiar institution."[36] Photographers working for the Department of Agriculture's Resettlement Administration and the Farm Security Administration, including Walker Evans (1903–1975) and Dorothea Lange (1895–1965), captured images of poor blacks in the rural South in the mid- to late 1930s that were published in government brochures and also in the popular and black press. The growing interest in these and other New Deal–era public art initiatives, coupled with the effects of the Great Migration, paved the way for the first significant wave of African American artists and writers to consider the history of slavery as a subject. This period also witnessed the publication of three seminal historical works on African diaspora history: *Black Reconstruction* by W. E. B. Du Bois (1935), *The Black Jacobins* by C. L. R. James (1938), and *Negro Slave Revolts* by Herbert Aptheker (1943).

In 1934, the graphic artist and muralist Aaron Douglas was commissioned by the Public Works Administration (not to be confused with the similarly named, and perhaps better known, Works Progress Administration) to paint a series of murals for the Countee Cullen Branch of the New York Public Library on 135th Street and Lenox Avenue in Harlem (now the Schomburg Center for Research in Black Culture). The murals, known collectively as *Aspects of Negro Life*, consist of four paintings documenting significant moments of transformation in black history and culture: *The Negro in an African Setting, Slavery through Reconstruction, An Idyll of the Deep South*, and *Song of the Towers*. Using a somber palette of earth tones and his typical "Africanized," modernist style, Douglas's murals portray the roots of African American culture in Africa, chronicle the challenges of oppression and terrorism during slavery and its aftermath, dramatize the monotony of plantation labor and the trickery of sharecropping, and critique the promise of a better life in rapidly growing urban centers. The best-known murals of Douglas's oeuvre, *Aspects of Negro Life* were among the outstanding projects of the Public Works Administration, and helped to garner him a national reputation and additional noteworthy commissions. Two years later, Douglas was commissioned to paint four more murals, this time on the occasion of the 1936 Texas Centennial Exposition in Dallas. Installed in the Hall of Negro Life, which opened on the celebration of emancipation that became known as Juneteenth Day (June 19), this series of murals, like *Aspects of Negro Life*, charted the experiences of African Americans from slavery to the present. Of the four murals, only two remain, *Into Bondage* and *Aspiration*. The first shows the march of a coffle of beleaguered Africans, their heads hung low in anticipation of the awaiting slave ship beyond the shore, which is framed by the shackled, raised hands of a female captive in protest (fig. 4.10). Painted in varying shades of pale green and dark blue, Douglas contrasted the environment's lush vegetation against the sorrowful mood. *Aspiration* dramatizes the African American experience in progressive layers from bondage to freedom to possibility in urban centers. At the base of the mural, undulating, shackled hands, suggestive of African American origins in the Middle Passage, reach toward (support) figures representing history, science, and art that yearn for the promise of the bejeweled city on the hill. While both murals make reference to the transatlantic crossing as a defining yet transformative moment in African American history, they do so through their portrayal of certain repeated stylistic elements: manacled hands raised in acts of defiance, and aspiring leaders looking to a star, possibly the North Star, which will deliver them to the promised land. Douglas also painted his signature concentric circles, connoting sound waves, and repeated iconic shapes to signal the spread of hope and triumph over adversity. Like other black visual artists who came of age during the New Negro Arts Movement, Douglas favored images of black struggle, transformation, progress, and achievement over images that conjured up the psychic terror of the Middle Passage or other aspects of the negative past.

In 1939, to mark the one hundredth anniversary of the *Amistad* revolt and to celebrate the political roots of the founding of Talladega College, Hale Woodruff was commissioned to paint a series of three murals for the historically black institution's new center of research and knowledge, Savery Library: *The Mutiny Aboard*

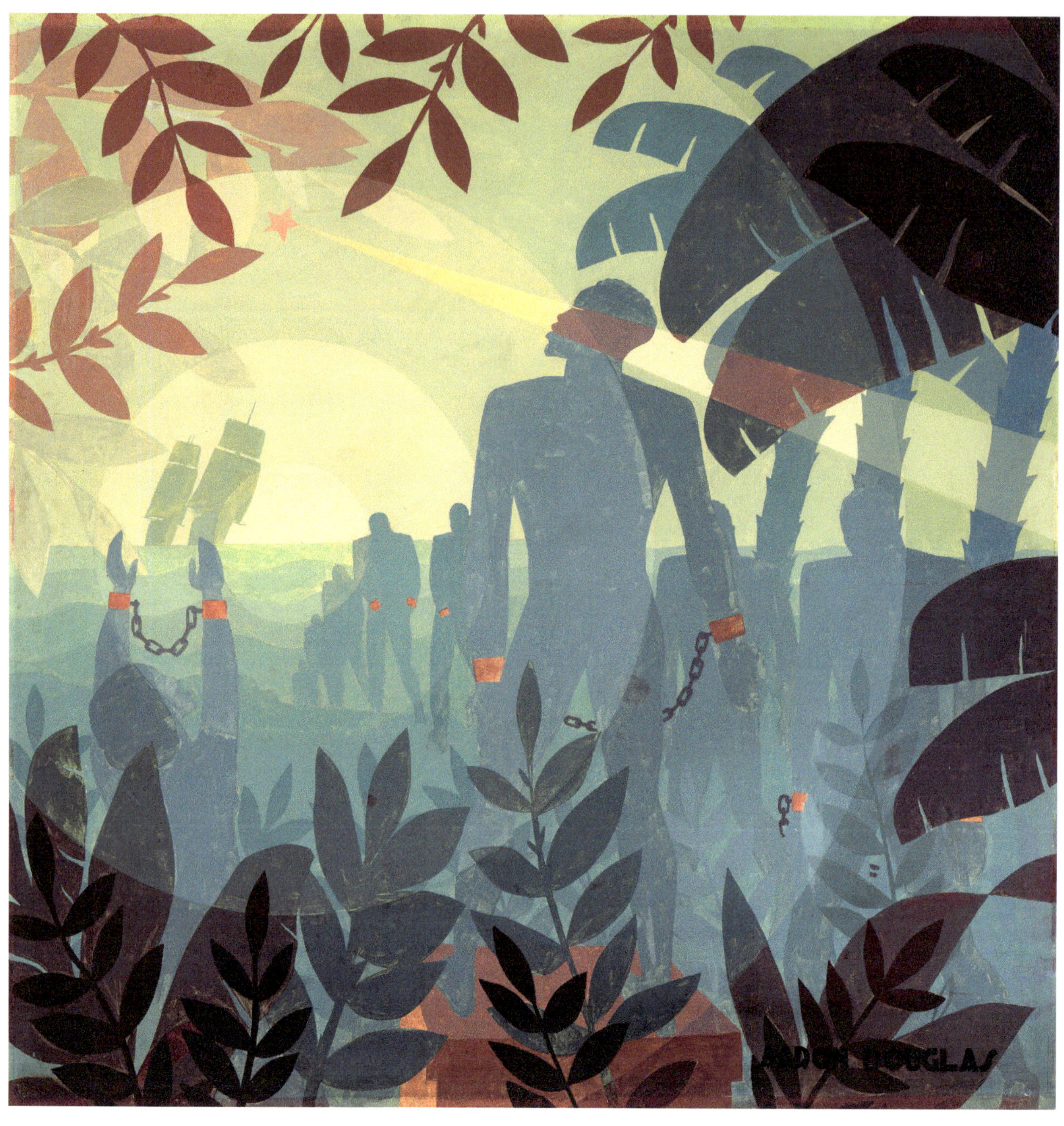

4.10
Aaron Douglas, *Into Bondage*, 1936,
oil on canvas, 60 3/8 × 60 1/2 inches.

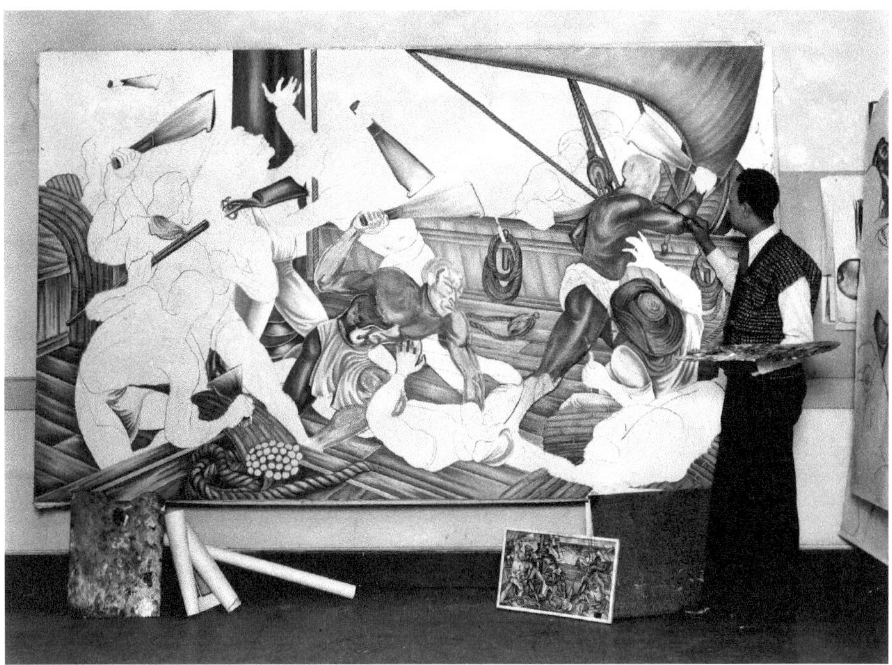

4.11
Hale Woodruff, at work on the *Amistad Murals:*
The Mutiny Aboard the Amistad, 1839, 1939,
oil on canvas, 6 × 10 ¹/₂ feet.

the Amistad, 1839 (fig. 4.11); *The Amistad Slaves on Trial at New Haven, Connecticut, 1840*; and *The Return to Africa, 1842.* Located in Talladega, Alabama, the college was founded in 1867 with the help of the American Missionary Association, an abolitionist group that formed in the wake of the *Amistad* incident. The brightly colored, three-panel mural series highlights the most publicized parts of this international case for human rights, and its tripartite narrative stands as a metaphor for the triangular trade. Because Woodruff had not known of the *Amistad* revolt until he was commissioned to paint the murals, he traveled from Atlanta, where he was teaching at Atlanta University, to New Haven, Connecticut, to conduct research in archives nearby where the *Amistad* captives were held until their trial was successfully won by former President John Quincy Adams, who came out of retirement to argue their case before the United States Supreme Court in 1841. At the New Haven Historical Society and Sterling Memorial Library at Yale, Woodruff gathered documentary evidence for his narrative tableaux by scouring newspaper illustrations, court records, historical accounts, paintings, and engravings, all of which had been widely circulated among supporters of the abolitionist movement, which, by 1839, the year of the sensational story of African resistance and triumph, was fighting vigorously for the end of chattel slavery in the United States.

Stylistically, Woodruff's murals bear the influence of the pioneering Mexican muralists Diego Rivera and David Siqueiros (1896–1974), whom Woodruff had met when he studied in Mexico City in previous years. Their use of rich colors, bold gestures, and exaggerated physical expressions characterized their works that documented the Mexican Revolution and other politically charged events from the country's founding. To emphasize the significance of the *Amistad* case as a politically galvanizing event in the history of the black struggle, Woodruff adopted some of the same aesthetic strategies. The first panel, which shows the brutal and triumphant struggle for freedom on the deck of the *Amistad*, was based on a popular published newspaper engraving that was later reprinted in *A History of the Amistad Captives*, published in 1840 by John Warner Barber (1798–1885). In that version of the image, a small inset engraving shows the packed underbelly of the slave ship, likely copied from an image that appeared in the 1830 book *Notices of Brazil in 1828 and 1829* by Robert Walsh (1772–1852) (see fig. 3.6). Yet Woodruff's version of the struggle on deck focuses only on the victorious uprising. Absent are the portrayals of bloodshed and other compromising images, including the kneeling supplicant, that had been circulated for the cause of abolition. His project was a celebratory one that would ultimately serve an educational function installed in a central space of Talladega's new Savery Library.

The second panel is based on court records, and for his courtroom scene, Woodruff relied on some of the twenty-two courtroom sketches the New Haven artist William H. Townsend made of the captives as they awaited trial. The last panel is based on a well-known oil painting of the rebellion's triumphant leader, Cinqué (ca. 1814–ca. 1879), by Nathaniel Jocelyn (1796–1881), which Woodruff likely saw when he conducted his research in New Haven. Upon completion, notice of Woodruff's *Amistad* murals was publicized widely as Talladega College soon realized their value as a fund-raising tool for the institution, and their national reputation brought visitors from around the country. From the beginning, Woodruff was keenly aware of the importance of this commission, as it marked the first time the *Amistad* incident would be portrayed by an artist—African American or otherwise—in the twentieth century. Given a national audience, his dynamic murals of triumphant black resistance could serve as a catalyst for change at a time when the political climate in the United States still produced mob violence and lynching in the South and viciously denied black people their civil rights. The *Amistad* murals were completed at a decisive moment in the early years of the civil rights movement, when artworks such as his that portrayed triumphant moments in the black struggle became a sign of hope that change was on the horizon. (That same year, 1939, the African American contralto Marian Anderson made civil rights parts of the national conversation when, denied the chance to perform at the Daughters of the American Revolution's segregated Constitution Hall in the nation's capital, she instead held an outdoor concert, at the invitation of First Lady Eleanor Roosevelt—herself a member of the DAR until their discriminatory actions spurred her resignation—against the backdrop of the Lincoln Memorial.) The efforts of Woodruff, Jacob Lawrence, Anderson, and others provided fertile ground for the roots of black artistic activism to sprout in the next generation that came of age in the 1960s.

CHAPTER FIVE

1969: ACTIVISM, ART, AND PERFORMANCE IN THE UNITED STATES

> What is called the imagination (from image, magi, magic, magician, etc.) is a practical vector from the soul. It stores all data, and can be called on to solve all our "problems." The imagination is the projection of ourselves past our sense of ourselves as "things." Imagination (image) is all possibility, because from the image, the initial circumscribed energy, and use (idea) is possible. And so begins that image's use in the world. Possibility is what moves us.
>
> —Amiri Baraka (LeRoi Jones), *The Revolutionary Theatre*[1]

FOR THE BLACK ARTS MOVEMENT IN THE UNITED STATES (1965–76), 1969 was a pivotal year. Beginning on January 9, the Black Emergency Cultural Coalition (BECC), led by the artists Benny Andrews (1930–2006) and Henri Ghent (b. 1926), was formed to protest the absence of black artistic, curatorial, and scholarly participation in the exhibition *Harlem on My Mind: Cultural Capital of Black America, 1900–1968*. That controversial show, on view at the Metropolitan Museum of Art in New York from January 18 to April 6 of that year, was organized by the curator Allon Schoener, noted for his history exhibitions using large-format documentary photography, and was boycotted by members of the BECC and others for its failure to include works by contemporary black artists (especially those living and working in Harlem); involve black curators, art historians, or arts professionals; or present the harsh realities of contemporary black life in Harlem in the 1960s[2] (fig. 5.1). Although its exhibition design, with its mural-size documentary photographs, archival materials, and sound recordings combining to create large-scale installation environments that chronicled seven decades of the neighborhood's transformation, was hailed as innovative, especially for the staid Metropolitan Museum of Art, many critics felt that *Harlem on My Mind* fabricated a distorted, nostalgic image from the distant past of Harlem and its residents and was better suited for a history museum or a venue like the New York Historical Society across Central Park.[3] Protesters decried the exhibition's treatment of Harlem and its residents as artifact when it was still very much alive, though not necessarily well—plagued by poverty, discrimination, decrepit housing, poor schools, urban renewal, white flight, crime, gangs, and drugs. From its inception, *Harlem on My Mind* ignited local and national controversy. Widespread media attention drew to it a continuous stream of visitors, and it would be subsequently recognized as the first-ever

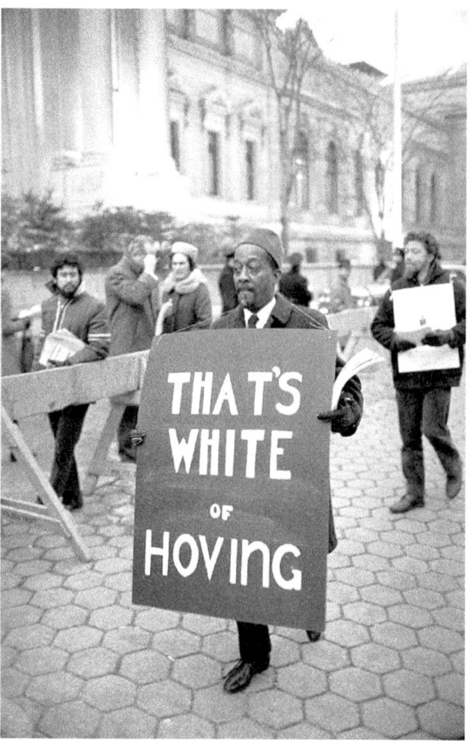

5.1
Protesting *Harlem on My Mind* exhibition
at the Metropolitan Museum of Art in New York,
January 16, 1969. Norman Lewis (FOREGROUND)
and Benny Andrews (BACKGROUND).

blockbuster exhibition in the United States. Its aftermath served to bring to a boil an already simmering pot of black artistic activism protesting the exclusionary practices of elitist, mainstream cultural institutions in cities like New York that reverberated around the country.

The year ended with the founding of a new black arts institution in New York, Cinque Gallery, by the artists Romare Bearden (1911–1988), Ernest Crichlow (1914–2005), and Norman Lewis (1909–1979). Named for the heroic leader of the famed 1839 *Amistad* revolt, Joseph Cinqué (also referred to as Sengbe Pieh), the nonprofit gallery represented the work of young, emerging black artists and provided a platform for aspiring art historians and curators. As Bearden explained, "Our purpose is to provide the encouragement, that serious young artists need, particularly minority artists.... Too many gifted unknowns drop out of painting before they're 30—out of sheer discouragement."[4] With a name chosen from black history, Cinque Gallery had a clear mission and consciousness rooted in the black struggle that the popular albeit patronizing *Harlem on My Mind* lacked. The blockbuster exhibition and the gallery opening served as bookends to a pivotal and poignant year of black creativity that brought an arsenal of images into sharper view and established practices and attitudes that would be used by black artists to define black art and identity in America for years to come. The practice of mnemonic aesthetics would take root in this critical year of black artistic activism with the slave ship icon serving as one of the principal historical images of choice.

To be sure, the Black Arts Movement was the most significant black creative arts explosion since the New Negro Arts Movement or Harlem Renaissance (1919–29). Marked by the formation of artists' collectives, culturally focused institutions, and community-based programming, the Black Arts Movement was a period of intense artistic, social, and political activism that grew out of the civil rights movement of the 1950s and 1960s and valued the civil rights movement's focus on education. The Black Arts Movement mirrored the Black Power struggle of the 1960s and early 1970s and tapped into the black international freedom struggles in Africa, the Caribbean, and Europe (particularly in England and France) of the same period. Encompassing the visual, literary, and performing arts, the Black Arts Movement produced racially focused art that explored the roots and meanings of black identity during an era of black self-determination. As the art historian Mary Schmidt Campbell (b. 1947) observed, "In the face of the extraordinary political and social changes brought about by the Civil Rights Movement, many Black American artists found it necessary to clear away the old symbols of the *ancien regime* and put in their place new metaphors for a new African American identity, an identity that would permanently supplant the 'Negro' in American culture."[5] With activism at its core, artists and writers of the Black Arts Movement demanded social change and political enfranchisement by pioneering new aesthetic forms to counteract if not mute entirely the extreme racial violence of the decade.[6]

For some artists, this meant reworking racist stereotypes from the past in an effort to render them impotent and strip them of their demeaning powers. The sexless, brooding servant embodied by the Aunt Jemima stereotype, for example, was parodied with grenade in hand in Joe Overstreet's (b. 1933) larger-than-life pancake box called *New Jemima* (1964) and revolutionized by the artist Betye Saar (b. 1929), with a rifle and the clenched Black Power fist in *The Liberation of Aunt Jemima*, 1972 (figs. 5.2, 5.3). But for other artists, this meant "remembering" empowering icons and noted figures in black history to shape new works of art that defined identity in social, political, economic, and gendered perspectives. As Campbell explains, "the remembering clarified the distinctiveness of African American history."[7] Using a purposeful aesthetic process that I call *symbolic possession of the past*, these artists found it necessary to reach back in time to reclaim important emblems and icons of history as a way of understanding their relationship to the present.[8] Practicing a form of mnemonic aesthetics, they reinterpreted the symbols of the past in order to bring into focus the uniqueness of black history, identity, and culture, and indeed to define their ongoing struggle *to be* in America.

The Black Arts Movement heralded a time of revolutionary art production and dissemination, where black artists employed innovative and radical means to create, publish, and exhibit their work. This period also produced a black art geared to reach the masses through community-based mural projects, the establishment of neighborhood art centers in urban areas, and the founding of new museums of black art, history, and culture. Using art for political and educational purposes, black artists endeavored to portray black history and black life, often through the depiction of key events and individuals. Others sought new meanings for traditional

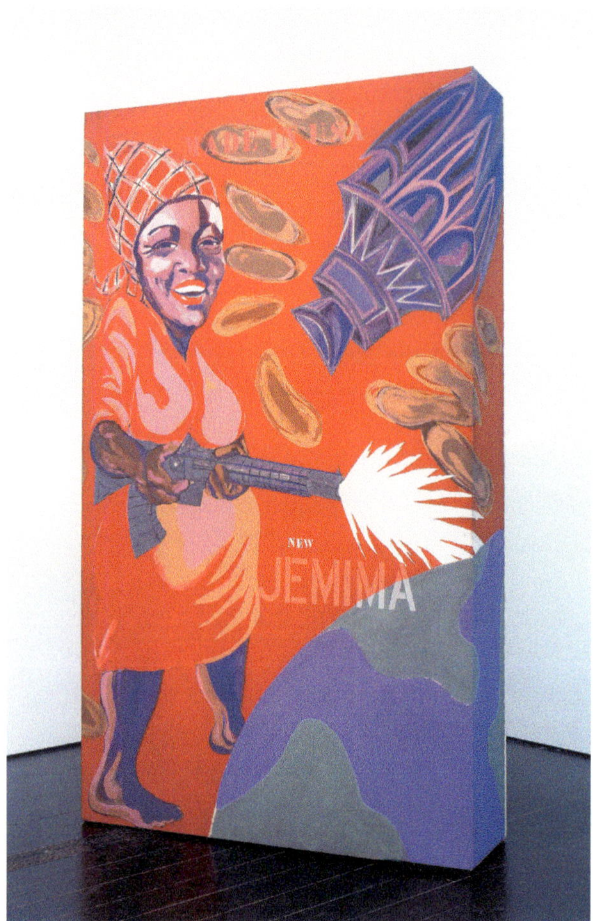

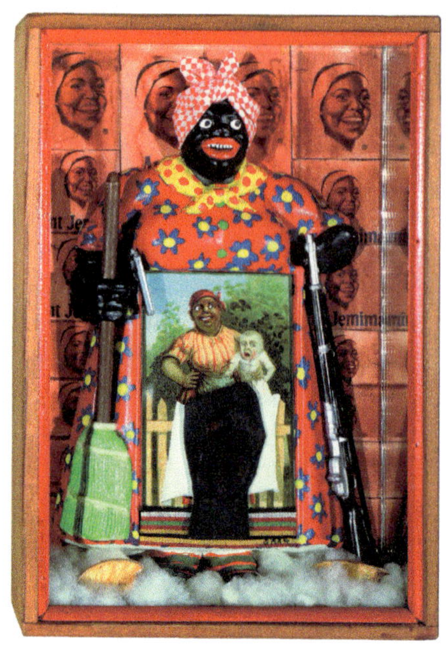

5.2 LEFT
Joe Overstreet, *The New Jemima*, 1964, 1970,
acrylic on fabric over plywood construction.
102³/₈ × 60³/₄ × 17³/₄ inches (260 × 154.3 × 43.8 cm).

5.3 ABOVE
Betye Saar, *The Liberation of Aunt Jemima*, 1972,
mixed media assemblage, 11.6 × 7.9 × 2.5 inches.

art forms, such as painting and photography, through structural and environmental transformation. Stretched canvases were stripped of their supports to form three-dimensional sculptures, wall hangings, and floor pieces. Photographs were enlarged as murals or projected as installation and performance art. Employing clever means of presenting their ideas, such as Revolutionary Theatre, assemblage, public history murals, or experimental music, the artists of the Black Arts Movement frequently relied on the symbols of the past as fodder for their works of activist potential.

SOUL SEARCHING

One of the key images that black artists resurrected during this period of soul searching was the slave ship icon. For these artists, playwrights, and poets of the 1960s, the slave ship icon was pregnant with multiple, useful interpretations, adaptable for black nationalist and integrationist agendas alike. One of the most influential publications responsible for developing mid-twentieth-century black consciousness of the slave ship icon, and forging a purposeful remembering of that influential image, was *A Pictorial History of the Negro in America: 1,000 Illustrations from Prints, Engravings, Photographs, Paintings, Etc.*, published by Langston Hughes and Milton Meltzer (1915–2009) in 1956. Appearing just two years after the historic *Brown v. Board of Education* Supreme Court decision that declared segregation illegal, the book was a rallying cry for black people to wake up and reclaim the images that had shaped their past. *A Pictorial History of the Negro in America* provided visual sustenance for the Black Arts Movement in the form of historical images that Hughes and Meltzer meticulously selected from their own collections as well as from archives around the country. As the book's promotional material claimed:

> This book is far more than a collection of pictures—fascinating as they are. Beginning with the origins of the Negro in Africa, the authors trace in text and picture the story of the Negro as a slave and as a freeman, who he is, where he came from, what he has contributed, how he has affected and, in turn, has been affected by American life and, finally, where he is headed. Included in this absorbing account are reproductions of news editorials, letters, posters, handbills and pamphlets, ranging from the early days of the slave trade to the recent desegregation decision of the Supreme Court.[9]

Accompanying the profusely illustrated pages was a moving text written by Hughes, which conveyed to the reader/viewer the significance of each image in black history. The Hughes-Meltzer collaboration was reminiscent of earlier fruitful partnerships that produced notable photographically illustrated books with integrated and inspiring narratives. Distinguished among these are Richard Wright (1908–1960) and Edwin Rosskam's (1903–1985) *Twelve Million Black Voices* (1941) and Hughes's joint venture with the photographer Roy DeCarava (1919–2009), *The Sweet Flypaper of Life* (1955). *A Pictorial History of the Negro in America* owed a debt of gratitude to historical precursors including the journals *Opportunity, Crisis!, Negro Digest*, and the *Journal of Negro History*. Taken together, the momentum started by these pioneering black history and culture journals, the Hughes-Meltzer collaboration, and popular black-oriented magazines like *Ebony* and *Jet* (launched by the pioneering publishing mogul John H. Johnson [1918–2005] in 1945 and 1951, respectively) set the stage for all manner of educational advances in the emerging field of Black Studies in the 1960s and 1970s, among them the reissue of important black-authored texts from the 1920s and 1930s, the establishment of Black Studies departments in mainstream American colleges and universities, and the integration of black history as part of secondary and elementary school curricula.[10] The first book of its kind to be published after the *Brown v. Board of Education* decision, *A Pictorial History of the Negro in America* made a direct link between the value of knowing one's history and the success of freedom struggles:

> Here, for the first time, is an authoritative, panoramic picture story of the Negro in America, from the arrival of the first African slave ship to present times, covering every aspect of Negro life—social, political, artistic and economic. This unique book, lavishly illustrated with more than 1,000 reproductions of pictures, paintings, broadsides, drawings, woodcuts and cartoons, contains concise pictorial accounts of all the important events in the Negro's dramatic struggle for freedom.[11]

A Pictorial History of the Negro in America inspired an entire cadre of black artists and writers in the 1960s and 1970s, including Alex Haley (1921–1992) (*Roots*, 1976); black artists' collectives such as the Organization of Black American Culture (OBAC), which spearheaded the public mural movement of the late 1960s with the *Wall of Respect* (1967) in Chicago; the poet and playwright Amiri Baraka (formerly LeRoi Jones); and the artists Malcolm Bailey (1947–2011), Larry Rivers (1923–2002), Tom Feelings (1933–2003), and Romare Bearden, among others. By "remembering" and presenting images and documents from the past, this volume "clarified the distinctiveness of African American history."[12] *A Pictorial History of the Negro in America* was thus one of the key progenitors of the black visual arts practice of symbolic possession of the past, and the slave ship icon was one of its essential images.[13]

Two seminal works produced in 1969 reintroduced and recast the slave ship icon: Amiri Baraka's masterpiece of Revolutionary Theatre, *Slave Ship: A Historical Pageant*, and Malcolm Bailey's *Separate but Equal* installation. These celebrated works of performance and installation art demonstrate the function and necessity of mnemonic aesthetics during this crucial period of activism, negotiating the relationship between history, memory, and identity.

AMIRI BARAKA AND THE DEVELOPMENT OF REVOLUTIONARY THEATRE

Amiri Baraka was the chief artist-intellectual of the Black Arts Movement. Through his critically acclaimed poems, plays, jazz operas, and music criticism, he encouraged black artists to abandon the integrationist themes of a raceless, classless society, which had become popular in the previous decade, and to instead embrace an art *and practice* that was grounded in black experience, history, and memory. In Baraka's own words, the Black Arts Movement "declared a need for:

1. An art that is recognizably Afro American
2. An art that is mass oriented that will come out of the libraries and stomp
3. An art that is revolutionary, that will be with Malcolm X and Rob Williams, that will conk klansmen and erase racists."[14]

Shaped by a black nationalist perspective, Baraka asserted that black art was a means for black artists and their audiences to gain deeper understanding of themselves as a people.[15] This necessarily separatist ideology was especially pronounced in the decade spanning 1965 to 1974, when Baraka's poetry, plays, and Black Arts Movement manifestos were concerned with developing an aesthetic strategy for deflecting, overcoming, and eliminating centuries of racism embedded in American society.

For Baraka, who at the time still went by LeRoi Jones, a form of his birth name Everett Leroy Jones (he adopted the Swahili Muslim name Imamu Amiri Baraka in 1967), 1964 was his single most important year in theater.[16] In that year he wrote, published, and produced five one-act plays, including *The Baptism*, *The Toilet*, *Dutchman*, *The Slave*, and *The Eighth Ditch*. As Hughes and Meltzer remark in *Black Magic: A Pictorial History of the Negro in American Entertainment* (1967), their follow-up to *A Pictorial History of the Negro in America*:

> During the 1964 season, Jones became the most talked about dramatist in New
> York when he had five plays performed one after the other in four different
> houses. Each of his dramas depicted the moral and spiritual decay of the United
> States. All these five one-acters attracted such attention pro and con that two of
> them were closed by orders of the police.[17]

Among the three plays that were not shuttered, *Dutchman*, presented at the Cherry
Lane Theatre in Greenwich Village, was the biggest hit, winning Baraka an Obie
Award and receiving critical attention from the American theater establishment.
New York Times theater critic Howard Taubman claimed, "Everything about LeRoi
Jones's *Dutchman* is designed to shock—its basic idea, its language and its murder-
ous rage."[18] Set in a New York City subway car, the thirty-minute, one-act play centers
on the dialogue and interactions between Clay, a well-dressed black man who has
just boarded the car, and Lula, a provocative white woman, who accosts Clay with
suggestive advances while insulting his general appearance and demeanor as inauthentic. Unable to hold his well-mannered composure any longer, Clay unleashes a
pent-up diatribe over the relentlessness of racial oppression, which ends abruptly
when Lula stabs him and enlists the help of other white (complicit) subway riders
to dump his body out of the car when the train pulls into the next station. "If this is
the way even one Negro feels," Taubman's review continues, "there is ample cause
for guilt as well as alarm, and for a hastening of change."[19] Change unfolding around
the nation and in New York in 1964 and 1965 would shape Baraka's concept of
Revolutionary Theatre, and Clay would become one of its first victims.

President Lyndon B. Johnson signed the Civil Rights Act of 1964 into law on
July 2 of that year, putting a legal end to discrimination based on race, color, religion, sex, or national origin in the workplace and segregation in public places. Yet
this key piece of civil rights legislation could not prevent the recurring acts of racial
terror that plagued the nation and especially the Deep South, where the Ku Klux
Klan that summer had declared open war on the civil rights movement. Less than
two weeks before Johnson signed the monumental piece of legislation into law,
what was known as the Freedom Summer had reached its bloody peak with the
murders of three civil rights workers—two white and one African American—at
the hands of the Klan in Philadelphia, Mississippi. Exactly two weeks after the
signing of the bill, on July 16, a black student named James Powell was shot and
killed by a white, off-duty police officer, Lieutenant Thomas Gilligan, on New York
City's Upper East Side. Two days of peaceful demonstrations against Powell's murder turned violent, resulting in six days of rioting in the predominantly black neighborhoods of Harlem in Manhattan and Bedford Stuyvesant in Brooklyn, and before
the end of the long, hot summer other racially motivated riots would cripple the
nearby cities of Newark and Patterson in New Jersey; and the cities of Rochester,
New York; Philadelphia, Pennsylvania; and Chicago, Illinois.

The summer of riots was followed by the winter assassination of Malcolm X on
February 21, 1965, at the Audubon Ballroom in Harlem. These traumatic events
left Baraka profoundly discontented and served to crystallize his thoughts about

Black Arts and Revolutionary Theatre. He disavowed his association with the Beat poets; broke up with his first wife, the poet Hettie Jones; and moved from the East Village to Harlem, where he established the Black Arts Repertory Theatre/School (BART/S) on April 20, 1965. BART/S was financed in part by private donations and Harlem Youth Opportunities Unlimited–Associated Community Teams (HARYOU-ACT), one of hundreds of community-based organizations around the country funded by the Office of Economic Opportunity (OEO), a federal agency established in August 1964 by President Johnson's War on Poverty to deliver social and economic incentives to the disillusioned residents of the nation's shell-shocked inner cities. BART/S fulfilled Baraka's initial craving for something new in art, literature, and theater that would move black people, young and old, to demand change, if not be the change themselves.

The mission of BART/S was to establish "a repertory theatre in Harlem, as well as a school. As a school, it will set up and continue to provide instruction, both practical and theoretical, in all new areas of the dramatic arts."[20] Classes in acting, writing, directing, set design, and production management were offered. BART/S was a black thing. It refused admittance to whites; its productions were performed by black actors for exclusively black audiences (fig. 5.4). Notable among these were *Experimental Death Unit no. 1* (1965), a parody of Samuel Beckett's *Waiting for Godot*, and *J-E-L-L-O* (1966), a satire of the popular television show *The Jack Benny Program*. As the professor of literature and African American studies Werner Sollors (b. 1943) explains, Baraka's "satires of 'white' culture, high and popular, were attempts to 'de-brainwash' Black audiences…from a Black nationalist point of view."[21] Seeking to influence the widest possible audience—the masses—improvisational street-corner performances of *Dutchman* and other plays popped up around Harlem. According to Larry Neal, who worked with Baraka to establish the BART/S, "For three months the theatre presented plays, concerts, and poetry readings to the people of the community. Plays that shattered the illusions of the American body politic, and awakened Black people to the meaning of their lives. Then the hawks from the OEO moved in and chopped off the funds."[22] The Black Arts Repertory Theatre/School only lasted about a year; it was shut down in spring 1966 when New York police claimed to have found a cache of weapons and the OEO withdrew its funding. Baraka moved to his hometown, Newark, New Jersey, where he lived until his death in January 2014. There he established Spirit House, which continued to produce plays for primarily black audiences, while honing the principles of the practice he called Revolutionary Theatre.

Baraka demanded that Revolutionary Theatre, an activist mode of expression for black art, be itself nothing less than a new form of black aesthetics. For him, Revolutionary Theatre was "the force…of twenty million spooks storming America with furious cries and unstoppable weapons…peopled with new kinds of heroes ready to die for what's on their minds."[23] According to Baraka, "The Revolutionary Theatre should force change; it should be change."[24] Revolutionary Theatre was inextricably linked to the political aims of the Black Power movement and, as one of the most social of the performing arts, could be an integral part of the movement's socializing process. "We had to do plays that we saw people needed based on our observation of peoples' struggle," Baraka explained.[25] "Black Theatre," he said, "has gotta gotta gotta raise the dead, and move the living."[26] The activist dimension of Revolutionary Theatre required the involvement and action of audience members; it was designed to elicit a sense of responsibility and awareness through process and participation (fig. 5.5).

Baraka's Revolutionary Theatre resembled the environmental theater of avantgarde New York in the 1960s and 1970s and the burgeoning performance art scene of the same period in that it subverted and overturned the traditional boundaries between audience and performer.[27] But Revolutionary Theatre presented a more profound challenge to the audience. As the theater critic Dan Isaac wrote, "The fluidity of environmental theater encourages new social configurations. As a commercial entertainment, environmental theater simulates political action rather than necessarily initiating it."[28] Baraka's Revolutionary Theatre however, produced a ritual component encouraged by its participatory nature, which reinforced the social processes of memory for actors and audience members alike. Intended to stimulate collective remembering, collective consciousness, and collective action, Revolutionary Theatre called for "new kinds of heroes ready to die for what's on their minds," according to Baraka, and portrayed hidden histories as a way to gain control of the dissemination and interpretation of black images.[29] Bringing contemporary urgency to pressing historical and social issues, such as police brutality and public school busing, Revolutionary Theatre aimed to be a radical artistic intervention directed toward dislocating the white mainstream manipulation of black images and experiences.

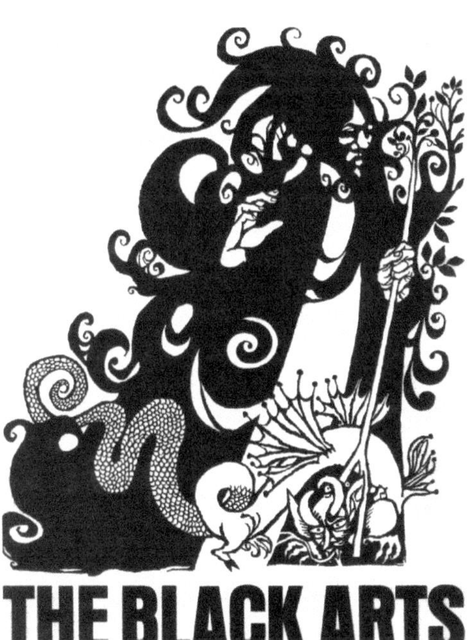

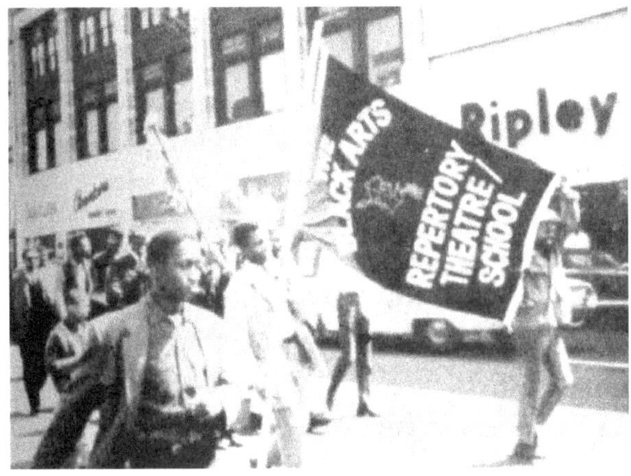

5.4 LEFT
Artists unknown, offset lithographic poster for LeRoi Jones's Black Arts Repertory Theatre/School, 1965.

5.5 ABOVE
LeRoi Jones and members of the Black Arts Repertory Theatre/School, 1965, photograph.

As Sollors describes, "Historical and heroic plays established a past dimension to present struggles and confrontations."[30] Baraka was heavily influenced by his own familial narrative of black history and struggle going back several generations, as told to him by his father and grandfather around the kitchen table when he was growing up. Additionally, the evolution of his dramaturgy and political consciousness was shaped by the repercussions of the 1964 Harlem riots, the assassination of Malcolm X, the 1965 Watts riots, the 1967 Newark riots, and his own repeated mistreatment at the hands of the New York City and Newark police. Revolutionary Theatre served as both a by-product and a catalyst of these collective memories and experiences, forging change out of the castoff irons of the immediate and distant past.

These pressing issues were on the national stage for sure, and national weekly news magazines such as *Newsweek* and *Time* covered them with illustrated photographic news stories. In the January 24, 1969, issue of *Time* magazine, a lengthy article ran that characterized the nation's woes and appealed to then-incoming president, Nixon, with ideas for how he might bring people together. Titled "To Heal a Nation," the article chronicled the nation's ills with statistics and stark documentary photographs, pointing to decades if not centuries of structural racism. In this same issue, a provocative two-page advertisement placed by the Chicago *Tribune* ran. The left facing page showed the crowded main section of the slave ship icon and the right facing page stated, "Not everyone's ancestors came over on the Mayflower." The text that followed appealed to sponsors of *Time* to consider placing ads in the Chicago *Tribune*.

> To understand the Negro's problems, you have to understand his history. We told it like it was, in a special issue, "The Negro in America." And reprint requests for this Sunday special issue came in by the thousands. Requests from schools, universities, and individuals. Black and white. Editorial issues like this help make the *Tribune* crowd what it is: Chicago's biggest crowd of readers and Chicago's first market of advertisers.

The gist of the ad was that stories about hot topics, and in particular, about black history and culture, sell newspapers. Both highly visible and widely circulated in one of the nation's popular weekly magazines, the graphic component of the ad offered insight to Baraka's literary genius and vision to Bailey's artistic promise by the year's end. It also aligned with a scholarly resurgence in black history and culture shaped by the visual culture of slavery.

SLAVE SHIP: A HISTORICAL PAGEANT

"Peace, *Slave Ship*—do your thing" is the closing line of the *New York Times* theater critic Clive Barnes's scathing review of Amiri Baraka's (then LeRoi Jones) *Slave Ship: A Historical Pageant*, performed at the Brooklyn Academy of Music's Harvey Theater from November 21, 1969, to January 13, 1970 (fig. 5.6).[31] Produced by the Chelsea Theater Center in association with Woodie King Jr. (b. 1937), *Slave Ship* was directed by Gilbert Moses (1942–1995) of the Free Southern Theater, who also composed the music along with tenor saxophonist Archie Shepp (b. 1937). Eugene

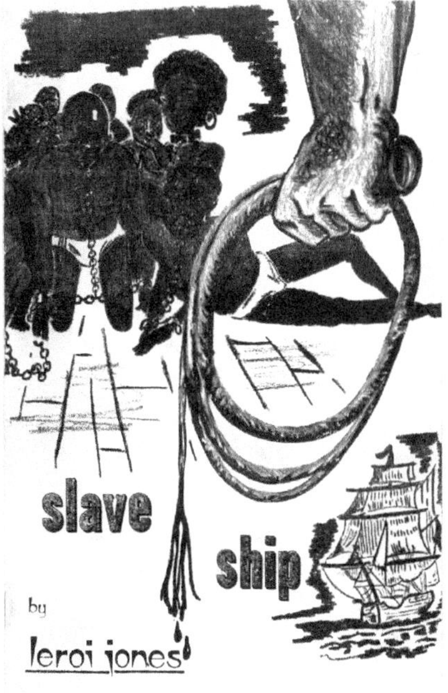

5.6 RIGHT
Program cover for LeRoi Jones's *Slave Ship*,
ca. 1967.

5.7 BELOW
Eugene Lee's set design for the Chelsea Theater
Center's production of *Slave Ship*, ca. 1968–69.

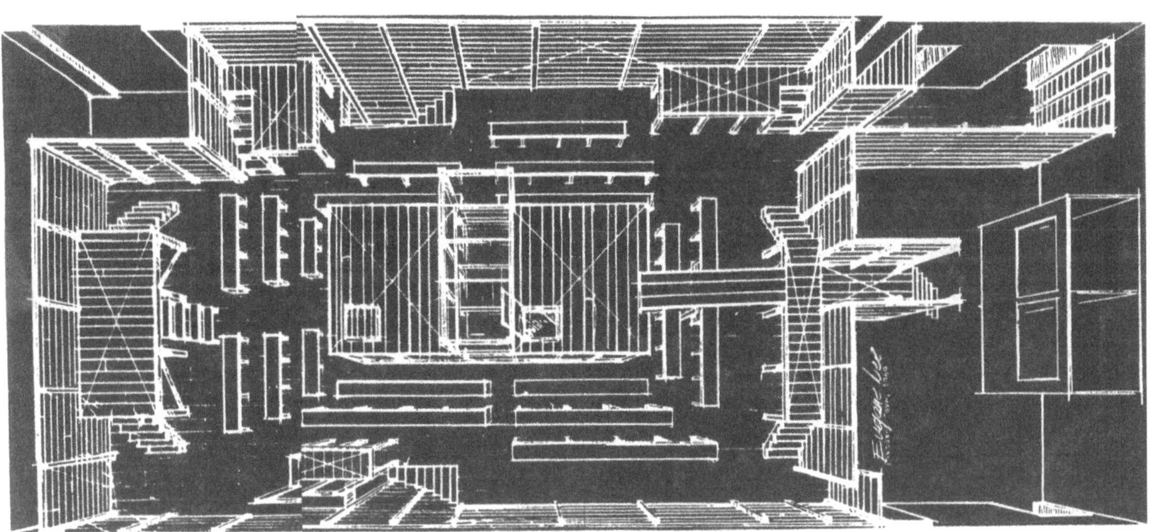

Lee (b. 1937) designed the unforgettable set, a wooden slave ship on rockers with an exposed human cargo hold, after drawings he had seen of the slave ship icon (fig. 5.7). Subtitled *A Historical Pageant*, Baraka's *Slave Ship* was a shocking spectacle of historical tableaux, recreating in ceremonial fashion the progression of black history from Africa to America in a montage of visceral, iconic scenes, all taking place within or atop the ingenious slave ship set design.

Beginning in Africa with ritual dance and rites of passage, the play progresses through the terror of the Middle Passage, the separation of families on the auction block, a plantation uprising foiled by a duplicitous "Uncle Tom" figure, and climaxes in a riot symbolizing the victory of Black Power over white America. *Slave Ship* immersed the audience in a "total *atmosfeeling*," as Baraka's script called it, flashing the images, sounds, and smells of black history in rapid-fire succession, producing a momentum forceful enough to mobilize a revolutionary call to action. And *Slave Ship*, no doubt, to borrow a phrase from the aforementioned theater critic Clive Barnes, did its thing. "The best examples of [environmental theater] in recent New York seasons," writes the theater historian Dan Isaac, "were *Slave Ship* and *Stomp*. Much more than mere entertainment, both works were constantly threatening to overflow the traditional boundaries of theatrical form by mobilizing an audience and urging them toward some action."[32] In Baraka's own words, "I remember feeling, if we want to be really militant, what we should do is try to get ourselves actually back into the state of mind that our people must have been in when they first brought 'em here. I didn't think you could be more militant than that, you know?... We tried to conceive of actally creating the slave ship the way it would be."[33]

The artistic implications of setting the entire play within the hold of a slave ship are of most immediate concern here. That radical choice recognized the centrality of the slave ship as a space of mnemonic proportions in the black psyche. When television talk show host David Frost asked him what he wanted to communicate with *Slave Ship*, Baraka responded, "I wanted to explain naturally to sensitive black people, exactly what the realities of the slave ship were—and how America in a lot of senses is a continuation of the same slave ship, I wanted to explain that America has not changed."[34] The play relied on its novel set design, clever staging techniques, and innovative props to produce and sustain the feeling of being trapped in the chaotic slave ship during the rocky, transatlantic voyage. Set designer Eugene Lee recalled: "Jones' 'Ship' is a metaphor, a symbol, connecting the memory of African roots with the vicious containment of the present. The ship is the fulcrum from which the play moves both backward and forward in time. Gil Moses staged the piece in a very free form theatrical style, action occurred throughout the room."[35] Choosing art over commerce, Lee removed the recently installed, comfortable red seating of the Chelsea Theater and replaced it with a platform on rockers into which a hatch was inserted and around which simple backless benches were arranged for seating.

Claiming the slave ship as the central metaphor or symbol necessarily dictated that the other spaces and elements of black experience depicted in the play—the plantation, insurrection, church, and even the culminating celebration of Black Power—were to be read through the defining experience of the Middle Passage and imagined from within the noisy, stifling decks of the slave ship. Moreover, through the explicit strategies of Revolutionary Theatre, Baraka's play not only attempted to reenact the traumatic transatlantic crossing visualized by the slave ship icon, but it also succeeded in dramatizing it in a very tangible way that tapped into the sensorial dimension of memory possessed by actors and audience members alike. Such a deliberate symbolic possession of the past recast the political possibilities of the abolitionist-era slave ship icon, adding a new and meaningful layer of understanding for a late 1960s race-conscious black revolutionary audience.

The play's script, its set, and the improvisational staging all referenced the appearance of the slave ship icon and the original descriptive texts published with it. On a visual level, the architectural rendering of the set seemed inspired by the cross section and plan views of the slave ship icon. This is no coincidence, as Eugene conducted extensive archival research as he embarked upon the design of the prodcution. Designed to reproduce the feeling of claustrophobia between decks, the creaky wooden set included hatches, platforms, masts, and other architectural details represented in the plan of the slave ship. The set produced a sense of confinement, which was amplified by the extreme contrast between complete and total darkness below decks and blinding light above, suggesting the tension between black and white.

Slave Ship furthermore recreated the suffocating, claustrophobic environment that the diagrammatic abolitionist drawing suggested by giving life to the actual *bodies* it depicted. The actors and audience members crammed together gave real, live physical form to the tiny black figures meticulously drawn in the slave ship's plan. Instead of remaining still or silent (silenced), however, Baraka's slave bodies spoke and moved about, rocked to and fro by Lee's innovative set design. Through them, he inserted the voices, desires, movements, and music of resistance that were absent from the static, two-dimensional drawing, for, as thc American literary scholar Danielle Skeehan reminds us, "ships traveling the pathways of the Middle Passage—and beyond—were anything but silent spaces.... [They] were gigantic, migrating percussionist instruments that carried voices, rhythms, and sounds beyond ship holds and deck barricades."[36] In a bold gesture, Baraka recast the slave ship icon with an updated purpose fitting for revolutionary times.

Baraka's *Slave Ship* was closer to a *reenactment* of the experiences of the Middle Passage and of plantation slavery and revolution than a dramatic production of those events, and audience members were an intimate and necessary part of the play. Their placement on planks around the set situated them in the deepest bowels of the slave ship, which additionally co-opted them as members of the cast, or re-enactors, if you will. In fact, in the script, the audience is listed among the cast as the "voices and bodies in the slave ship."[37] The other members of the cast included the "voices of African slaves," dancers, musicians, children, actors playing an "Old Tom" in the person of a slave and a "New Tom," in the form of a preacher, with other actors playing the "voices of white men"—a captain, a sailor, and a plantation owner.

Audience members were called on to join the actors in generating the soundscape of the play, its cries and screams. With the participation of audience members to fill space and create sound, the sense of claustrophobia and terror in the hold of the slave ship was vividly and memorably reproduced. The art historian Robert Farris Thompson, who attended (and participated in) three consecutive nights of performances of *Slave Ship* in 1969, recalled how the cacophony of screams and the atmospheric sounds and music intensified the design of the set, stage, and seating to create a sense of bcing trappcd in thc space that the slave ship icon depicts. This forced members of the audience to share in the creation of the performance and consequently moved them toward a sense of collective responsibility. As the postcolonial literary theorist Francis Ngaboh-Smart points out, Baraka "assumes that the ritual of the stage consists in situating the events in the hearts of the black audience who, after reliving the memory of the sources of their cultural dislocation, can then work towards remedying their condition.... The collective enactment is supposed to help the community move toward regeneration."[38] As a participatory event, *Slave Ship* operated for many as a cathartic experience: one of confinement, passage, struggle, and release.

The performance space was invaded by the sights, sounds, and smells the abolitionists described as the "poopoo tubs, whips, chains, and cries" through the use of innovative props that assaulted the aural and olfactory perception, including:

Smell effects...incense...dirt/filth
Smells/bodies
Heavy Chains
Drums (African bata drums, and bass and snare)
Rattles and tambourines
Banjo music for plantation atmos. [*sic*]
Ship noises
Ship bells
Rocking and Splashing of Sea
Guns and cartridges
Whips/whip sounds[39]

The impact of the sounds and smells emanating from the set of the slave ship was intensified by careful control of the audience's sensory experience of the space. In particular, darkness—deep, total, consuming darkness—was used in a sustained manner to emphasize the atmosphere of containment experienced during the Middle Passage and throughout hundreds of years of slavery in order to reinforce the feeling of domination. The stage directions called for:

Whole theater in darkness. Dark. For a long time. Just Dark. Occasional sound, like ship groaning, squeaking, rocking. Sea smells. In the dark. Keep the people in the dark, and gradually the odors of the sea, the sounds of the sea, and sounds of the ship, creep up. Burn incense, but make a significant, almost stifling, smell come up. Urine. Excrement. Death. These smells and cries, the slash and tear of the lash, in a total atmos-feeling gotten some way.[40]

A large part of the play was, in fact, performed in darkness. Baraka's use of lighting was specific and intentional. In some cases, dim lights were shone toward parts of the set from which voices or spoken dialogue emanated: "There is just dim light at top of the set, to indicate where voices are."[41] In other instances, bright lights starkly illuminated the characters of the slave traders and sailors or reproduced the effect of blinding sunlight coming from open hatches above deck. The stage directions specify, for example, "Lights flash on white men in sailor suits grinning their vices...voices down...hummmmmmmmmmmmmmmmmmmmmmmmm mmmmmmmm. Lights to light white people are sudden, very bright and blinding."[42]

Through an intentional use of lighting and improvisational dialogue, white audience members were made to feel complicit in if not responsible for the historical narrative that unfolded. As the literary theorist Mike Sell explains, "In the Chelsea Theatre's production of *Slave Ship*, the eye of whiteness was literally cast into the hold of racism's epitomous metaphor, the slave ship, and struggled like the captured Africans in the play, to find a place to stand, a place to breathe, a place from which to make sense of the sensory assault."[43]

Baraka's play effectively rewrites the descriptive text of the eighteenth-century broadside to include the voices of the enslaved and their stories of pain and suffering as well as their tactics of resistance and survival. For example, their accounts of suicide and infanticide are enacted here:

MAN 1.   God, she's killed herself and the chi [*sic*] child.

Oh, God. Oh, God....

WOMAN 1.   She strangled herself with the chain. Choked the child.

Oh, Shango! Help us, Lord. Oh, please."[44]

The well-documented history of rape and sexual abuse depicted in the schematic drawing and remarks of the slave ship icon is also portrayed in the play...

WOMAN 2.   Oh, please, please don't touch me...Please...

MAN 1.   What you doing? Get away from that woman.

That's not your woman. You turn into a beast, too.

...as are the sounds of insanity:

MAN 3.   Devils, Devils. Cold walking shit. (All mad sounds together.)[45]

The actors vividly convey the psychological trauma of confinement, sensory assault, and sustained captivity as enduring legacies of the Middle Passage that continue to haunt black communities in the United States. Refusing any semblance of linear structure and forsaking any reference to plot, *Slave Ship*'s free-form improvisational structure defies American and European avant-garde political drama by disrupting the boundaries of narrative.

In dialogue and stage directions that imagine the conversations between captives in the hold of the slave ship, Baraka created characters who reflected a deep belief in African, particularly Yoruba, religion. Some of the stage directions call for "African Drums like the worship of some Orisha. Obatala, Mbwanga rattles of the priests. BamBamBamBamBoom BoomBoom BamBam."[46] During the Middle Passage sequence, Shango, the Yoruba thunder god, and Obàtálá, the Yoruba creator god, father of the orishas, or deities, are called upon as sources of strength through the ritual beating of drums (fig. 5.8).

MAN 1.   Shango, Obatala, make your lightning, beat the inside bright with paths for your people. Beat. Beat. Beat (Drums come up, but they are walls and floors being beaten. Chains rattled. Chains rattled. Drag the chains).[47]

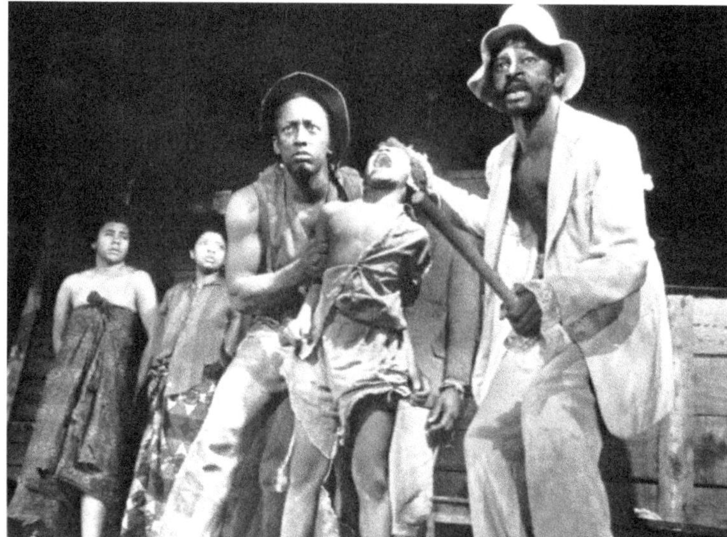

5.8
Production still from *Slave Ship*, ca. 1968–69.

In addition to drawing on spiritual strength, conversations between African captives during the harrowing journey created new possibilities and frequently led to attempts at freedom. As Skeehan notes, "The combined record of noise and revolt suggests that cargoes of captive men and women speaking a number of different languages and dialects who began their journey to ships coasting off the shores of Western Africa from vastly different regions and cultures began to communicate with each other and to act en masse."[48] Toward the end of the play, the plantation revolt is brought on by summoning Ogun, the Yoruba warrior god of iron.

> OGUN. Give me weapons. Give me iron. My spear. My bone and muscle make them tight with tension of combat. Ogun, give me fire and death to give to these beasts.[49]

Slave Ship was not alone among artworks in its attempt to practice a "form of spiritual renaissance" that was by no means simply religious in nature, but also political and historical in inspiration. According to Geneviève Fabre (b. 1936), a historian of African American theater, "[*Slave Ship*] also locates the mythical basis that sanctions its relationship with religion and allows them [the actors] to master both a 'disquieting and feverish agitation' and 'an inordinately vagrant artistic imagination.'"[50] Beginning in the 1950s with the surge of liberation movements in Africa, many black Americans expressed a sense of pride and solidarity with the continent through their study of African languages, religions, customs, and beliefs. Artists, writers, intellectuals, activists, and musicians journeyed to Africa to experience the revolutionary fervor of those seminal black independence movements as they mobilized their own civil rights movement in the United States. The novelist Richard Wright traveled to the Gold Coast, now Ghana, in 1953, to observe Kwame Nkrumah's (1909–1972) rise to power and eventual election as the first prime minister of that country in 1957. Soon thereafter the activists Martin Luther King Jr.

(in 1957), W. E. B. Du Bois (in 1961–63), Maya Angelou (in 1962–64), and Malcolm X (in 1964) followed, all of whom were inspired by Ghana's pioneering example as the first African nation to gain independence from colonial rule and encouraged by Nkrumah's vocal support of black Americans' efforts to gain full and equal citizenship rights.

Two months after Nkrumah was deposed by a military coup in February 1966, the 1er Festival Mondial des Arts Nègres (FESMAN) was convened in Dakar from April 1 to April 24 by Senegal's first president, the poet Léopold Sédar Senghor (1906–2001), to demonstrate the achievements of Négritude, a literary and intellectual movement led by francophone Africans that promoted pride in and affirmation of African cultural identity and artistic innovation as a means to overcome the oppressive effects of European colonialism on Africa and the African diaspora.[51] With the financial backing of UNESCO, FESMAN brought upwards of two thousand artists, writers, poets, musicians, and performers from more than thirty countries on the African continent and the African diaspora to showcase traditional and contemporary black art and culture on a global stage. Amiri Baraka, along with the dancer Katherine Dunham (1909–2006), Langston Hughes, the Alvin Ailey Dance Theater, and the painters Teixeira Nash (1931–2007) and Hale Woodruff, was part of the US delegation. Traveling with the US delegation was the documentary filmmaker William Greaves (1926–2014), who was tasked by the United States Information Agency with filming the *First World Festival of Negro Arts*. Narrated by Langston Hughes, the forty-minute documentary begins (and ends) with the poet reciting one of his most celebrated poems, "I've Known Rivers," as the camera follows him walking in the sand, waves crashing upon the Senegalese shore. With this cinematic framing device, Greaves identified a poignant visual legacy of the transatlantic slave trade, the West African coastline, which would figure as a site of memory in later works by the artists Romare Bearden and Tom Feelings; the filmmakers Julie Dash (b. 1952), Isaac Julien (b. 1965), and Kevin MacDonald (b. 1948); and the photographer Carrie Mae Weems (b. 1953). A key cultural event of the postcolonial era, FESMAN had roots in the ideological and intellectual yearnings of Négritude, which no doubt influenced how the Black Arts Movement unfolded in Baraka's hands.

Improvisational music served as a catalyst for action in the play when Baraka enlisted the talents of the pioneering Afro-futurist Sun Ra, known for his experimental and improvisational electronic music, and the tenor saxophonist Archie Shepp. Repeated sounds and musical riffs orchestrated a compelling mnemonic aesthetic that engaged the call and response of the aural and oral, wherein ritual beats called on actors and audience to respond and remember. The following lines, the last of the script, are first chanted and then accompanied by music:

Rise, Rise, Rise
Cut these ties, Black man rise
We gon' be the thing we are...
(Now all sing, "When we gonna Rise")

When we gonna rise/up
When we gonna rise/up
When we gonna rise/up…
When we gonna rise/up, brother
When we gonna rise/up above the sun
When we gonna take our own place, brother
Like the world had just begun?
Drum—new sax—voice arrangement.[52]

Throughout the play, drumming, dancing, and music channel a deep African memory while sowing the seeds of resistance and later, revolt. As the play opens, the sound of African drums dominates, whereas the plantation scene begins with the lazy sound of the banjo, but later crescendos to a drummed call to revolt. In his pioneering text on black music, *Blues People*, Baraka claimed that music presented itself as one of "the most important legacies of the African past, even to the contemporary black American."[53] In 1967's *Black Magic: A Pictorial History of the African American in the Performing Arts*, Hughes and Meltzer also trace this musical legacy back to the continent of Africa through the Middle Passage and on to the plantation:

> The White sailors on the Middle Passage found these Africans and their rhythms highly entertaining, as did the planter ashore who purchased black imports to work on their American plantations. The syncopated beat which the captive Africans brought with them—and which perhaps lightened a little of the burden of their servitude—quickly took root in the New World. Now that beat has been for generations a basic part of American musical entertainment.[54]

Throughout the play, the musical symbols of an African past are never silenced, but only transformed, reshaped into popular forms of black American music. The culminating celebration of Black Power is punctuated by a fusion of jazz, soul music, and popular black dances of the late 1960s.

> Lights come up abruptly, and people on stage begin to dance, same hip Boogalo-ruba, fingerpop, skate, monkey, dog.…Enter audience; get members of audience to dance. To same music Rise Up. Turns into an actual party.[55]

Theater historians, critics, and audience members alike have discussed the power of *Slave Ship* to elicit Baraka's desired "revolutionary" effect on some audiences. During a tour of the play in Mississippi produced and directed, as in the aforementioned New York production, by Gilbert Moses of the Free Southern Theater, some Greenville theatergoers were ready to revolt. According to Val Ferdinand, writing in the *Black World* in April 1970, they "were only reluctantly persuaded to go home. And then there was the entire audience in West Point, Mississippi, which rose to its feet, waving fists and singing, 'When We Gonna Rise Up!'"[56] Later that year, when *Slave Ship* was performed in Europe, audience members became so agitated that they rendered the set useless, according to Baraka, and its fragmented pieces were left behind as a reminder of the generative power of Revolutionary Theatre. Baraka employed everything at his disposal to "accuse and attack anything that can be accused and attacked" to force audience members to summon the "wisdom and strength in their own minds and bodies."[57] This approach made white liberals and some middle-class and integrationist-minded blacks extremely uncomfortable if not antagonized, as noted by Clive Barnes's *New York Times* review of *Slave Ship*.

In *Slave Ship*, Baraka crafted a unique blend of "double voicing" that was richly nuanced, in which the different layers of the senses and the spatial levels of the set collided and conversed with the actual voices of the cast and the audience, their co-opted reenactors. This process of shaping and reshaping the experience of black Americans prompted the literary theorist Lloyd W. Brown to call *Slave Ship* "one of Baraka's more successful experiments in ritual drama," where "history itself becomes a succession of rituals."[58] In *Slave Ship*'s triumphal conclusion, then, "the Black masses symbolically expunge the visible and invisible hegemony of the dominant culture."[59] Baraka's practice of mnemonic aesthetics is thus revealed in his ritual of shaping and reshaping the experience of black Americans. As a defining element of the mnemonic aesthetic, ritual—characterized by repetition with revision—drives the impulse to remember in the dramatic as well as the visual arts.

MALCOLM BAILEY: *SEPARATE BUT EQUAL*

A little over a month after the premiere of Baraka's *Slave Ship*, the young painter Malcolm Bailey (b. 1947) garnered mainstream critical attention for his *Separate but Equal* series, an installation of monumental paintings and drawings inspired by the slave ship icon and the ongoing civil rights struggle. These works were featured in the inaugural exhibition of Cinque Gallery at 425 Lafayette Street bordering New York's East Village on December 22, 1969, for which the twenty-two-year-old artist created an arresting installation environment with life-size, black and white crouching figures painted in uniform rows across the soaring gallery walls. The *New York Times* art critic Grace Glueck praised the daring new direction signaled by Bailey's exhibition: "The works that impressed me in that show were those devoted to themes of the African slave trade—schematic renderings of transport vessels and a recurrent form, the peculiar semifoetal position forced on slaves so that the ships could be packed to capacity. Mr. Bailey's offerings were interesting for, among other things, his fresh feeling for shape and pattern, his skill at schematic drawing and—in the larger works—an overall compositional vigor."[60] A striking installation photograph by Don Hogan Charles showing the artist in front of his mural-size painting *Separate but Equal* accompanied Glueck's article, "Minority Artists Find a Welcome New Showcase," announcing the establishment of Cinque Gallery (fig. 5.9). Dressed in all black and sporting a neatly trimmed Afro, mustache, and tinted glasses, Bailey was the vision of cool—and with good reason. Not only was this his first one-man gallery show in New York, he also had a painting on view uptown in the Whitney Museum's *1969 Annual Exhibition of Contemporary American Painting*, which had opened just the week before. Yet a closer look at the

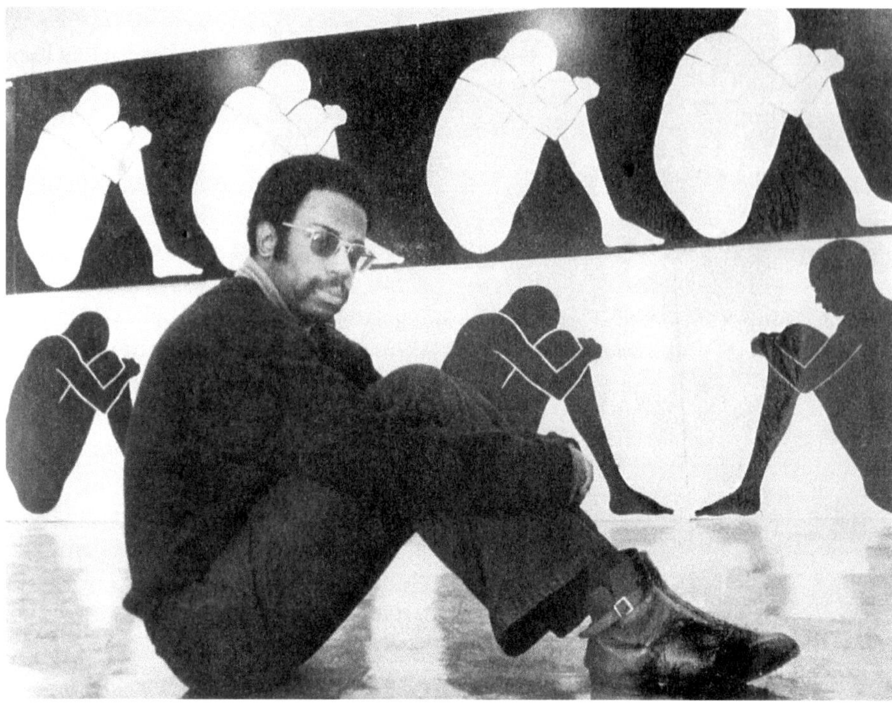

5.9

Don Hogan Charles, portrait of Malcolm Bailey
at Cinque Gallery, New York, 1969.

photograph of Bailey at Cinque Gallery, with his body mimicking the doubled-over slave figures, exposes the tenuous position that he and other black artists occupied in the art world as they sought opportunities to exhibit their work. "[I doubt] I'd get very far," he acknowledged, "if I tried the Uptown dealers."[61] Bailey's confession reinforced the need for institutions like Cinque Gallery.

With Cinque Gallery, its founders Romare Bearden, Ernest Crichlow, and Norman Lewis determined to mentor the next generation of black artists and arts professionals, and to provide entrée to the mainstream art world by "helping artists in such areas as contracts, and training personnel in gallery management."[62] Begun with a $30,000 seed grant from the Urban Center at Columbia University, which had backing from the Ford Foundation, Cinque Gallery was located in an expansive renovated space on the second floor of the New York Shakespeare Festival Public Theater, directed by Joseph Papp. According to Bearden, "Norman wanted the place to be very well kept, so it would have all the appearances of a professional gallery you might find on 57th Street"[63] (fig. 5.10). Joseph Papp, whose innovative approach to the arts was inclusive of the performing and visual arts, welcomed the addition of Cinque Gallery: "This location is a natural for a gallery—the audiences that we draw here for other events will flow right into it."[64] According to Myron Schwartzman, who conducted extensive interviews with Romare Bearden toward the end of the artist's life, Bailey's exhibition was "augmented by some of Papp's

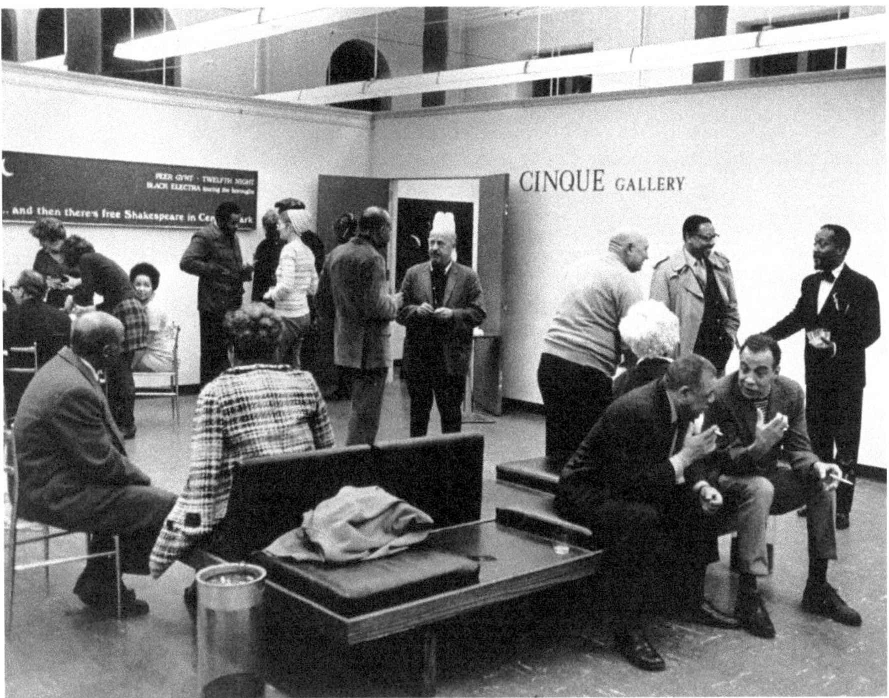

5.10
Exhibition opening at Cinque Gallery, ca. 1970,
with Bearden, Lewis, Crichlow, and others.

mise-en-scenes—chains, pieces of wood, which Bearden remembered, 'gave it a
kind of ambiance.'"[65] Presented in a gallery that was housed within a theatrical
institution, Bailey's installation exerted, not surprisingly, a corporeal grip on many
visitors, who paused in the gallery to contort their own bodies into the fetal or
rigor-mortis-like poses of the artist's repeating figures.

Uptown at the Whitney Annual, on view from December 16, 1969, to February 1,
1970, Bailey's large-scale, mixed-media painting, *Hold, Separate but Equal*, showed
black and white figures, primarily contorted but two prone, within the confines of
the cross section and plan of a slave ship in the manner of the famous British abolitionist engraving that began circulating around the black Atlantic in 1789 (fig. 5.11).
The painting's blue background and placement of the spare schematic drawings
bear resemblance to the *Time* magazine ad that appeared in January 1969 (see
fig. 5.5). Remarkably, the black and white male figures painted in the diagrams are
divided by "race," not gender: on one side, white figures mirror an equal number of
black figures on the other. The diagram on the left shows one side of a plan view.
The diagram on the right pictures the plan view of the half deck with two rows of
uniform black figures systematically arranged on one side and the same number
of white figures on the other. This section is labeled with the letter *H* in black at
the top, and the letter *E* in white at the bottom. The diagram in the center shows
a cross-section view of the hold, with an equal number of black and white figures

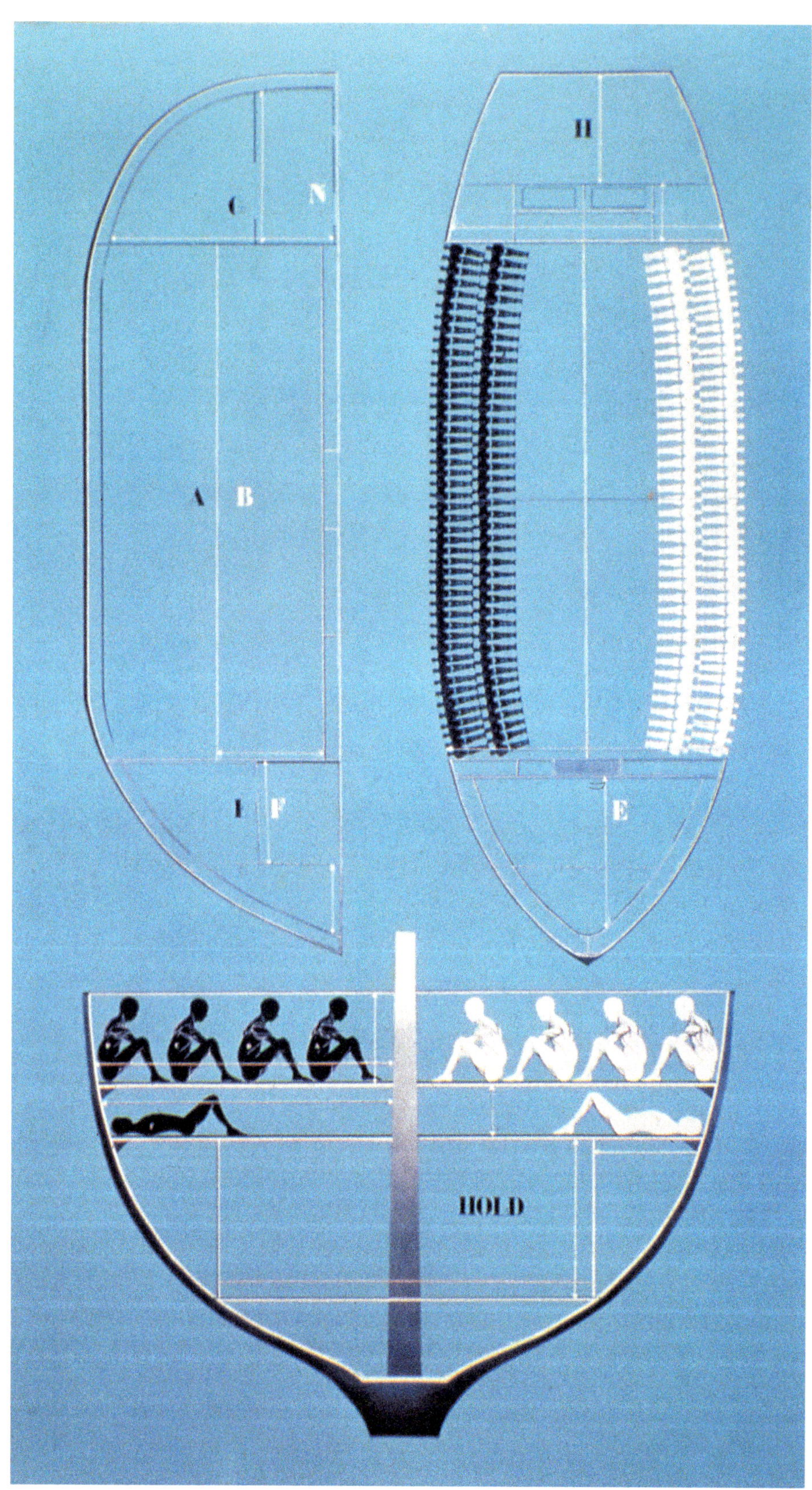

5.11

Malcolm Bailey, *Hold, Separate but Equal*, 1969,
mixed media, 7 × 4 feet.

separated by a bold vertical line at center that represents the mast. The figures on the upper deck bend into contorted seated positions in order to fit into the shallow space. Each of the figures is labeled with a letter (*A*, *B*, and so on) that corresponds to a location specified on the plan views above. The artist drew black and white contour lines to define the musculature of these figures doubled over in distress. His skillful use of shading renders the figures as anatomical drawings. The black and white figures in the lower deck are allotted even less space and are reduced to a reclining position with legs bent. Instead of being labeled with single letters, this diagram is marked "HOLD" in bold, black letters in the "white" section of the boat.

Bailey's choice of materials is integral to the viewer's experience of the painting. He applied synthetic polymer paint to composition board in order to achieve a slick blue background. He used press type to demarcate the hard lines of the diagrams and the fine, white directional lines that divide spaces within the sections. Press type also labeled the sections with bold, uniform letters. The art historian Kellie Jones (the daughter of Amiri Baraka) has pointed out how some of the exciting new materials of the space age, such as acrylic paint, synthetic polymers, and mixed media, were used by black abstract artists to achieve revolutionary effects.[66] Together, these materials lent a crisp, mechanical look to the painting that reduced it to its barest essentials and enhanced its minimalist, blueprint appearance, referencing the naval architectural origins of the slave ship icon. The use of a minimalist aesthetic accentuated the starkness of the plan view on the left and gave the sense that the other sections weren't quite filled to capacity. This visual strategy revealed a clear contrast between many of the late eighteenth-century drawings by abolitionists of slave ship plans, filled to capacity with tiny figures to emphasize overcrowding and inhumane conditions on board. With its apparent sense of openness and attention to spatial dynamics, Bailey's blueprint-like painting conjures up larger questions of freedom and equality for blacks and whites alike. *Hold, Separate but Equal* was purchased by the Museum of Modern Art in 1970.

Hold, Separate but Equal addressed the popular national debate over integration that came to a head at the end of the 1960s with the emergence of the Black Power movement. It should be obvious that the title, *Separate but Equal,* refers to the landmark school desegregation case, *Brown v. Board of Education,* argued by Thurgood Marshall (1908–1993) before the Supreme Court in 1954, which overturned *Plessy v. Ferguson,* the 1896 ruling that amounted to government-sanctioned segregation and created the doctrine of "separate but equal" for blacks and whites.[67] The triumph of *Brown v. Board of Education* marked a turning point for the civil rights movement and ushered in greater government control over the integration of public facilities, public schools, and government workplaces. Malcolm Bailey was only eight years old when the Supreme Court handed down its decision in the *Brown v. Board of Education* case, and he benefited from its promises of equal access to education. Born in Harlem in 1947, he won a fellowship to attend an integrated private secondary school before going on to study art at the High School of Art and Design in New York and Pratt Institute in Brooklyn, where he earned a Bachelor of Science in Art in 1969. The following year Bailey was selected for the competitive residencies at the predominantly white artist communities of Yaddo, in Silver Springs, New York, and the MacDowell Colony in Peterborough, New Hampshire.[68] He was a prime example of the kind of artist Bearden, Crichlow, and Lewis hoped to help with the founding of their Cinque Gallery. "There were a number of young minority artists out of the whole 'uplift' thrust of the Johnson years who were on scholarships to various colleges, art schools," Bearden recalled. "Many of these young people had graduated with academic degrees; others had come out of art school and felt that they were ready to paint, and we found there was very little outlet for their work."[69] In addition to educating young black artists about the business strategies that would serve them well in the art world, the founders of Cinque Gallery provided numerous platforms on which these newcomers could exhibit their work.

FIFTEEN UNDER FORTY: PAINTINGS BY YOUNG NEW YORK STATE BLACK ARTISTS

Perhaps the most notable of these opportunities was in *Fifteen under Forty: Paintings by Young New York State Black Artists*, on view at the Gallery Museum, Hall of Springs, Saratoga Springs Performing Arts Center, July 1 through July 31, 1970.[70] Ernest Crichlow, as director of the exhibition, selected the artists, who included Emma Amos (b. 1938), Ellsworth Ausby (1942–2011), Malcolm Bailey, Betty Blayton (b. 1937), John Edward Chandler (b. 1943), Calvin Douglass (b. 1931), Alvin C. Hollingsworth (1928–2000), James G. Pappas (b. 1937), Louise Adele Parks, Betty J. Pitts-Foster, Alvin Smith, Vincent D. Smith (1929–2003), Raymond Saunders (b. 1934), Eldridge Suggs III (b. 1939), J. Philip White, and Benjamin Leroy Wigfall (b. 1930). Romare Bearden designed the attractive, illustrated catalog with John Mochon and, in the role of consultant, wrote the foreword and compiled the biographical notes. Sponsored by the New York State Education Department, *Fifteen under Forty* was "planned because of a deep conviction that the arts, more than any other of man's expressions, depict the human struggle to achieve the dream of personal and universal freedom," offered Ewald B. Nyquist (1914–1987), president of the university and commissioner of education.[71] "They [the arts] are an essential grace in a civilized people," he concluded.[72]

Bearden's foreword began with a personal anecdote about the difficulty faced by young black artists seeking to show their work, echoing the impetus for founding Cinque Gallery. "To deny the artist the possibility of exhibiting is to deny a great essential in his or her development," he warned.[73] Providing further historical context for *Fifteen under Forty*, Bearden traced the roots of black artists' isolation from "an active artistic community" in the United States to the 1930s, and championed their use of political and social themes as motivating change agents. Turning to the "varying concerns of young Black artists of this era," he described three differing but not necessarily competing themes: "artists whose works are a direct adjunct to the Black Liberation Movement" that aim to destroy an oppressive social structure; "artists who seek to create a definitive black aesthetic," whose community-based mural paintings depict heroic figures designed to instill pride and self-respect; and "those Black artists whose challenges are either purely aesthetic, and allied with various movements within the mainstream of contemporary art."[74]

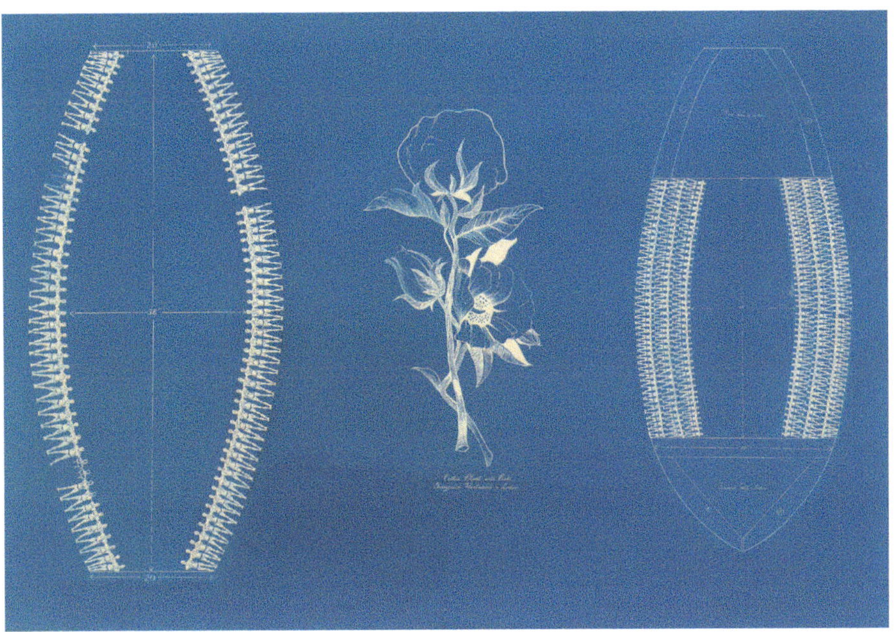

5.12
Malcolm Bailey, *Untitled, 1969*, 1969. Acrylic on composition board, 48 × 71 15/16 inches (121.9 × 182.7 cm).

Fifteen under Forty was in conversation with current debates about the meaning of black art and the purpose of black art shows. For example, in the exhibition catalog of *Afro American Artists: New York and Boston*, on view earlier that spring at the Museum of Fine Arts, Boston, from May 19 to June 23, Edmund Barry Gaither (b. 1944), curator of Boston's Museum of the National Center of Afro-American Artists, stated, "Black art is a didactic art form arising from a strong nationalistic base and characterized by its commitment to a) use the past and its heroes to inspire heroic and revolutionary ideals, and b) use recent political and social events to teach recognition, control and extermination of the 'enemy,' and c) to project the future which the nation can anticipate after the struggle is won."[75] Not surprisingly, Gaither was aligned with the aesthetic principles and political aims of the Black Arts Movement during this period. Like *Fifteen under Forty, Afro-American Artists: New York and Boston*, represented a successful partnership between black artists (or a black art entity) and a mainstream cultural institution. Bailey was one of sixty-nine artists shown in Gaither's exhibition.

Crichlow chose three works Bailey executed in 1969 for *Fifteen under Forty*, including two large-scale paintings and one print, all of which likely had been exhibited with the *Separate but Equal* series. Of these works, Bearden observed, Bailey "looked to Africa…the Middle Passage, that frightful route followed by the slave ships. His blue and white paintings are handsome and forceful."[76] In *Untitled, 1969* (fig. 5.12), which was purchased by the Whitney Museum, Bailey centered a depiction of enormous flowering cotton buds between two similarly painted plan views of the slave ship. The cotton buds are elegantly rendered in the style of eighteenth-century drawings of botanical specimens made popular by European itinerant naturalist botanists who traveled aboard sailing vessels bound for Africa, Asia, the Caribbean, and the Americas to document the flora and fauna of faraway lands that were soon to become colonial possessions. Their detailed drawings were meticulously hand colored and later engraved as sumptuous aquatints annotated with a newly developed scientific classification system that sought to control knowledge production by naming each specimen in Latin. Below the two interlacing stems of flowering cotton, Bailey delicately painted the words "Cotton Plant" and then below that the Latin translation, *Gossypium barbadense*, in white acrylic, using cursive lettering typical of botanic drawings. On either side of the cotton specimen, white line drawings of slave ship plans and their human cargo subtly transform the richly colored cyan background into a blueprint and a cyanotype specimen. The duality of this reading—at once blueprint and scientific specimen—reflects both the layered meanings of this work and the historical uses of early photographic printing processes developed in 1839 by the British inventor William Henry Fox Talbot (1800–1877).[77] An 1853 publication by the pioneering British photographer Anna Atkins (1799–1871) demonstrated how the cyanotype printing process could portray scientific specimens of plant life with unparalleled accuracy and enter them into a system of classification. The shape and design of the slave ship plans in Bailey's painting furthermore resemble the engraving of the French schooner *Vigilante* printed in an abolitionist tract that publicized the British naval squadron's capture of the illegal slaver in 1823 (see fig. 3.4). Like that engraving, the rooms indicated in Bailey's plans are labeled as to their use in cursive writing and systematically filled with seemingly uniform figures around the edges, which from a distance resemble interlacing paper dolls or the iconic stick figures used in public signage. Upon closer inspection, however, some of the figures are missing altogether or appear to be fading away. A deliberate choice of the artist, these missing and disappearing figures suggests the debilitating toll that confinement has on the body and the psyche (chronicled in abolitionists' tracts and slavers' journals) or radical acts of resistance, including self-emancipation.

At the pinnacle of the Black Power and Black Arts movements, Bailey created a series of paintings that visually engaged the national debate over integration and racial equality. He did so by placing white figures alongside black figures in a number of paintings and drawings that portray repeating and recurring minimalist reiterations of the slave ship icon to draw connections between a long history of suffering and racial strife and the political urgency that characterized the contemporary moment: civil unrest, assassinations, and antiwar demonstrations alongside black student protests and the establishment of black cultural institutions. As Bailey put it in an interview with Elsa Honig Fine in 1972, "Real revolution won't occur until poor whites as well as poor blacks realize they are oppressed."[78] His iconic black and white figures were a visual affirmation of that ideology: they mirror and double each other, duplicating the painful postures of a continuing race-class divide that produces unequal access to education, housing, health care, jobs, and natural resources. As the first visual artist to insert white figures in the slave ship icon,

Bailey exposed their glaring absence in the original eighteenth- and nineteenth-century schematics.

The medium and the message of Bailey's reclaimed slave ship icon differed greatly from that of Amiri Baraka's as brought to life in his Revolutionary Theatre production of *Slave Ship* staged at roughly the same time, at the close of 1969. Bailey's clean, crisp line drawings evoke symmetry, pattern, calculation, and uniformity, whereas Baraka's one-act play presents the opposite: filth and foul odors, disorder, rancor and revolution. That such a range of ideas could be expressed with an evocation of the same image was a reminder of the interpretive possibilities of the slave ship icon and an indication of its multivalent afterlife. But these two projects also stand as examples of how different philosophies circulated among black artists and innovators of this period.

CONTEMPORARY BLACK ARTISTS IN AMERICA

Efforts to define black art, black artists, and a black aesthetic coincided with artists' demands to be exhibited in mainstream art institutions. These produced a number of group shows in the early 1970s, the most successful of which were often organized by or in partnership with black curators, art historians, and artists, frequently at mainstream institutions. Yet it took some of these institutions and curators more than one attempt to learn from the shortcomings of *Harlem on My Mind*. The Black Emergency Cultural Coalition (BECC) sought to exert pressure on the art establishment when it negotiated a set of demands with the Whitney Museum in 1968 that would produce twelve exhibitions focusing on contemporary black art and artists over a six-year period, including eleven solo exhibitions and one survey show. Malcolm Bailey's solo show was on view in the Lobby Gallery when the much anticipated survey show *Contemporary Black Artists in America* opened amid black artists protesting the absence of a black curator.[79] Curated by Robert Doty and on view from April 6 to May 16, 1971, the exhibition included painting, sculpture, and mixed-media works by contemporary artists who were loosely grouped together in the catalog's essay by the curator's brief discussion of the ideals of black intellectuals as diverse as Richard Wright and Alain Locke. Contemporary artists as far-reaching as the sculptor Barbara Chase-Riboud (b. 1939) and Malcolm Bailey (who wasn't even in the show) were cited in the catalog regarding their feelings on "black art." Chase-Riboud offered, "Nobody should attempt to limit artists in their response to the world," while Bailey stated, "There is no definition of black art. It is absurd to take a group of painters, whose various works and concepts differ, and categorize this group as exponents of black art just because of their skin color."[80] Both black art shows at the Whitney—Bailey's solo show and *Contemporary Black Artists in America*—were panned by critics. Prior to its opening, fifteen of the seventy-five artists pulled their work from *Contemporary Black Artists in America*, while Romare Bearden waited to remove his work from the walls after the opening. Running concurrently, *Black Artists in Rebuttal to the Whitney Museum* was planned in advance at the black-owned Acts of Art Gallery in the West Village and included, among others, paintings by two of the artists who had withdrawn from the Whitney show: Richard Mayhew and Betty Blayton. Echoing the sentiments of Chase-Riboud and Bailey, art critic John Canaday, in his review of both shows concluded, "With luck—or, better yet, with any common sense—these may be the last shows in which we will be forced to think of an artist's skin color as a factor of his accomplishment."[81]

SOME AMERICAN HISTORY

In 1971, the Menil Foundation in Houston commissioned the white American artist Larry Rivers to produce *Some American History*, an exhibition about the history of slavery and race relations in America.[82] Rivers, who started out as a jazz musician, later turned to painting and mixed-media installations that often criticized and appropriated classic images and themes of Western art history. In an effort to avoid the mistakes and criticisms of *Harlem on My Mind*, Rivers invited six black painters to collaborate with him: Daniel LaRue Johnson (b. 1938), Peter Bradley, William T. Williams (b. 1942), Frank Bowling (b. 1936), Joe Overstreet (b. 1933), and Ellsworth Ausby. *Some American History* was organized by the Institute for the Arts at Rice University in Houston. The film *Slavery: The Black Man and the Man*, conceived by June Jordan (1936–2002) and directed by John Chandler, was circulated with the exhibition.

A central work of art in the exhibition was Rivers's own installation, titled *Slave Ship*. The artist Charles Childs described it as "magnificently appointed with its large expanse of sail and languorous jigsaw fashioned waves."[83] Rivers's installation shared a feeling of openness similar to that of Malcolm Bailey's *Separate but Equal*. Constructed of wood and painted panels, Rivers's *Slave Ship* shows only a skeletal form of the ship—the ribs, sails, bow, and stern. The ribs expose silhouettes of black bodies connected by shackles, which are mounted to the wall side by side. Instead of imposing a sense of confinement, the installation provided space for viewers to walk around (and possibly in) the waves—to peer between the ribs of the ship at the variously posed and contorted bodies. As Childs wrote, "*Slave Ship* has none of the chilling grimness, the iron shackles and wall-to-wall crowding one usually associates with the Atlantic crossing."[84] The way in which Rivers focused on the figurative representation of the bodies—some sitting cross-legged, others reclining, others holding onto one another, some squatting—provided sharp contrast to the uniformity of Bailey's iconic figures and those of the slave ship icon. Instead, Rivers's installation seemed to riff on the spatial disarray and emphasis on individual suffering dramatized in the watercolor and pencil painting by Lieutenant Francis Meynell, *View of the Deck of the Slave Ship Albanoz* (1846) (see fig. 3.8).

In all, *Some American History* comprised forty-nine works of art, ranging from paintings in oil and charcoal to works on paper to mixed-media constructions and elaborate installations. The vast majority of the works were by Rivers, including his parody of Manet's painting *Olympia* (1865), *I Like Olympia in Black Face* (1970), created for the show, while the contributions of the black artists he invited amounted to one or more works each. The range of themes addressed by the artists included Africa, the slave market, lynching, black stereotypes, and important black leaders. Of particular note were Frank Bowling's large-scale, abstract map painting *Middle Passage* (1970); Joe Overstreet's life-size pancake-mix box, *The New Jemima* (1964) (see figure 5.2); and Ausby's pastel portraits on paper each dating from 1969: *Portrait of Sojourner Truth*, *Portrait of Harriet*, and *Madonna and Child*.

WOMEN AND THE BLACK ARTS MOVEMENT

In its own time and since, the Black Arts Movement was criticized for its male-dominated leadership and lukewarm support for black female artists. Yet this did not deter black women from making significant contributions to black visual arts production and political activism during this period. They formed their own groups, such as Where We At: Black Women Artists, staged their own exhibitions, and made works of art from a perspective rarely considered by their black male counterparts. Faith Ringgold (b. 1930) is one such artist whose prolific output in multiple genres, including performance, painting, sculpture, and quilt making, addressed issues of racial and gender inequality, sexual violence against women, and the black woman's place in art history. In 1965, she met Amiri Baraka at the Black Arts Repertory Theater/School in Harlem and later exhibited her work in an exhibition there. This encounter, along with her recent acquaintance with Bearden, Lewis, Crichlow, and other veteran black artists, would have a lasting impact on her art and activism. By 1967, her *American People* series was well underway, and she produced three impressive murals that year: *Die*, depicting the violence and disarray of rioting; *The Flag Is Bleeding*, about how the struggle over integration was hurting the nation; and *U.S. Postage Stamp Commemorating the Advent of Black Power*. A dynamic champion of women and black artists, she spearheaded the organization Women Students and Artists for Black Art Liberation (WSABAL) in 1970 to protest the exclusion of women and black artists from the Venice Biennale show at the School of Visual Arts in New York. WSABAL continued its pressure against the art establishment in protests at the opening of the Whitney Museum's Sculpture Annual the same year, resulting in the inclusion of Barbara Chase-Riboud and Betye Saar, the first black women artists to be exhibited there. Around the same time, Ringgold began work on the *Slave Rape Series*, in which the artist boldly painted black female nudes as strong, courageous, and invincible, able to defend themselves against the sexual and physical abuse of slave catchers on the shores of Africa. Presenting a narrative of black female resistance, this series showed the black female nude in positions of power as they had never been portrayed in the history of art. These works, rendered in warm skin tones and verdant greens, presented the black female in unfamiliar poses and sought to defy popular stereotypes of the Aunt Jemima or the Jezebel. In doing this, Ringgold's women are active, confronting the viewer with a sense of knowing. They contrast with Bailey's schematic paintings in their portrayal of frontal poses, bright eyes, curious expressions, and unfettered determination. Yet they complemented some of the characters of Baraka's Revolutionary Theatre production of *Slave Ship*. The vitality of Ringgold's paintings presented an alternative image and an unacknowledged narrative in the history of the slave trade and slavery yet to be addressed by artists during the Black Arts Movement.

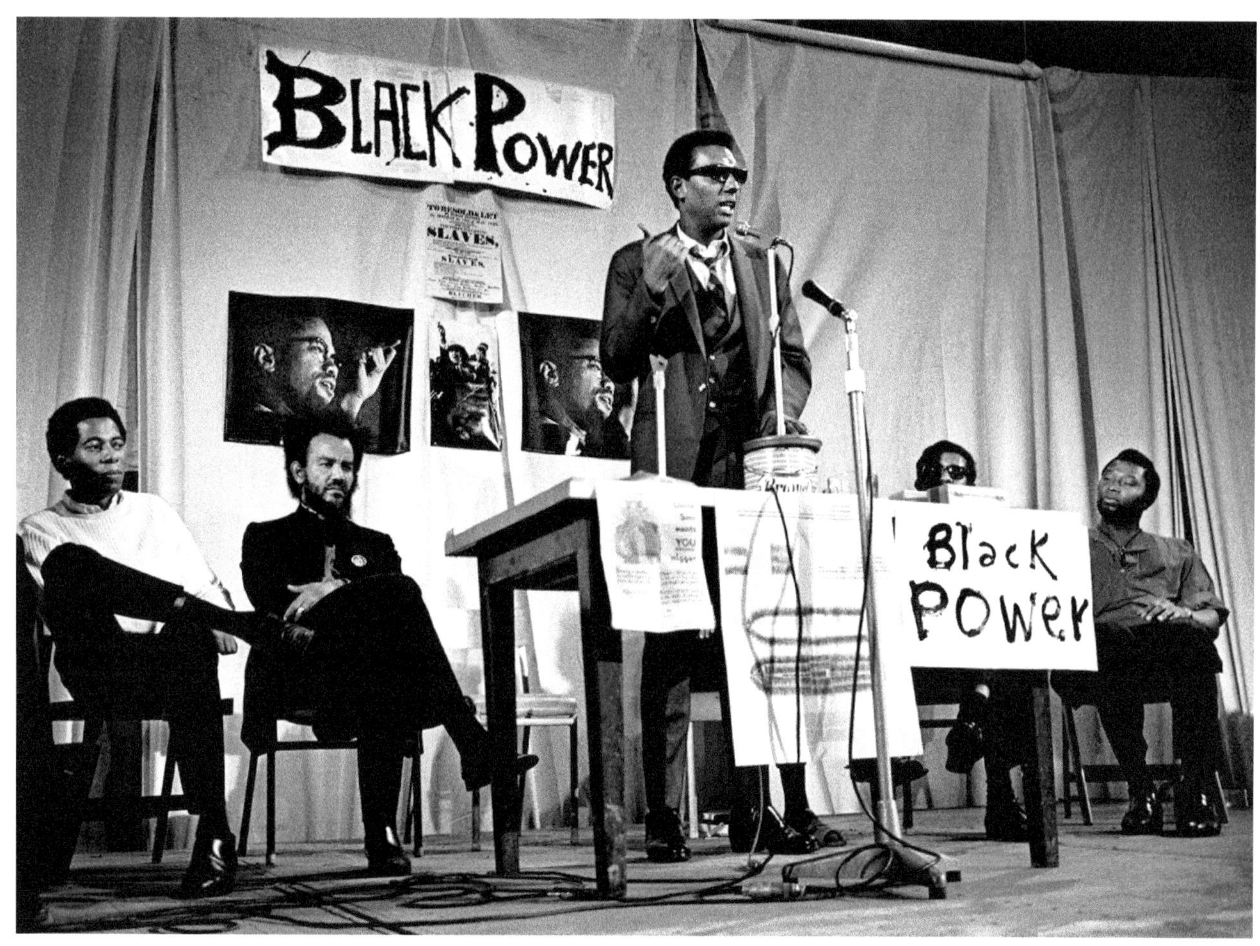

6.1
Horace Ové, *Stokely Carmichael Addresses the Black Power Conference*, The Roundhouse, Camden Town, London, 1968. Silver gelatin print.

CHAPTER SIX

ART AND ACTIVISM IN BRITAIN: 1960s–1990s

IN 1968, the civil rights activist and organizer Stokely Carmichael (1941–1998) traveled to London from the United States to spread news of the increasingly international Black Power movement. Just the year before, he had stepped down as chairman of the Student Nonviolent Coordinating Committee (SNCC) and penned the book *Black Power* with Charles V. Hamilton (b. 1929), clarifying the meaning behind the term he had coined. Speaking at the Roundhouse in Camden Town, the charismatic and stylish Carmichael donned dark sunglasses and a three-piece suit. On the podium with him were assorted community leaders, including Michael X (1933–1975), the organizer of the newly established branch of the Black Panther Party in London. Behind Carmichael, a number of iconic visual aids from historic sources were displayed: agitprop, such as photographs of the slain Malcolm X (1925–1965); copies of nineteenth-century slave sale posters; the famous nineteenth-century engraving of a slave's whipped back; and the slave ship icon, front and center. Referring to these archival images as he spoke, Carmichael identified the roots of Black Power in the current international struggles for freedom and liberation taking place on the African continent, in the Caribbean, and in the United States. This scene, documented by the Trinidadian-born photographer and filmmaker Horace Ové (b. 1939), foreshadowed the Black Arts Movement that would unfold nearly fifteen years later in Britain (fig. 6.1). Mirroring the way eighteenth- and nineteenth-century British abolitionists sent their visual propaganda across the Atlantic to agitate in the United States, Carmichael introduced an arsenal of images, many of which had been out of circulation in England for more than one hundred years. These would inform some of the themes black artists and activists in Britain would later address in light of social, political, and economic transformations of the 1970s and 1980s, including the anti-immigration stance of Prime Minister Margaret Thatcher, increased surveillance and policing of black men and women, and the 1981 Brixton riots. The social and intellectual work of cultural studies as framed by Stuart Hall, Paul Gilroy, Hazel Carby, and Kobena Mercer would offer foundational theoretical texts regarding identity formation, diaspora, memory, sexuality, and gender that would pave the way for the Black Arts Movement.

THE BLACK ARTS MOVEMENT

Cultural Studies theorist Stuart Hall (1932–2014) identified many of the artists who came to Britain from her former colonies in the post–World War II era as the "first generation" of black British artists. Among them were the painters Aubrey Williams (1926–1990), Frank Bowling (b. 1936), and Rasheed Araeen (b. 1935), who worked in abstract and conceptual modes. They created paintings that often recalled physical and political aspects of the homeland they left behind, if not a spatial and metaphorical notion of diaspora itself, which Hall discussed as "a landscape in the process of becoming abstract."[1] This process is visible in the work of the painter Frank Bowling, who was born in Guyana and whose large, abstract canvases, such as *Night Journey* (1968–69), faintly trace the land masses of the Americas, the Caribbean, Europe, and Africa, providing a sense of coming and going, but no definitive destination.

The artists that Hall spoke of as the "second generation" were the British-born children of Caribbean, African, and South Asian parents who immigrated to the cosmopolitan centers of London, Leeds, Birmingham, and Manchester in the late 1940s, 1950s, and 1960s. By the 1980s, they were poised to fight for educational training and exhibition opportunities that artists of their parents' generation did not have. Many became professional artists, receiving MFA degrees from art schools around the country. The works of art that they produced engaged the turbulent 1980s, a time when the body and its signifiers of identification often took center stage during a period of civil rights struggle characterized by rioting in Brixton, Bristol, South London, and Liverpool in reaction to the stifling conservatism of the government of Prime Minister Margaret Thatcher.[2] Photographer/media artist Roshini Kempadoo (b. 1959) describes the 1980s and 1990s as

> a period of time in which we were re-defining representations of the black subject. It was an exciting period of time where photography and film moved away from traditional visual arts studies and became more radically linked to cultural studies and criticism. Photography of this kind became situated outside fine art studies, and this broader interdisciplinary field allowed me to consider photography in relation to notions of psychoanalysis, post-colonialism and feminist studies, drawing on the seminal texts of Stuart Hall, Susan Sontag, Laura Mulvey and John Berger to think about photography.[3]

The works of the "second generation" were characterized formally by photography, graphic arts, and documentary styles that used autobiography, (self-)portraiture, and other strategies of visualizing black people in relation to the talked-about issues of the day: racism, politics, empire, culture, immigration, identity, and sexuality. Many of their works incorporate historical prints and photographs as well as striking graphic materials to produce mixed-media works that challenge and critique past and present struggles faced by black people in Britain and her former colonies. For example, the collage of historical prints and photographs from the *Oceans Apart* series (1989) by the photographer Ingrid Pollard (b. 1953) presents three horizontal bands of images toned red, white, and blue respectively—the colors of the Union Jack—from top to bottom (fig. 6.2). The top band shows the washed-out portraits of centuries-old British and European men once heralded as explorers and navigators, including Sir John Hawkins, whose travels fueled the slave trade

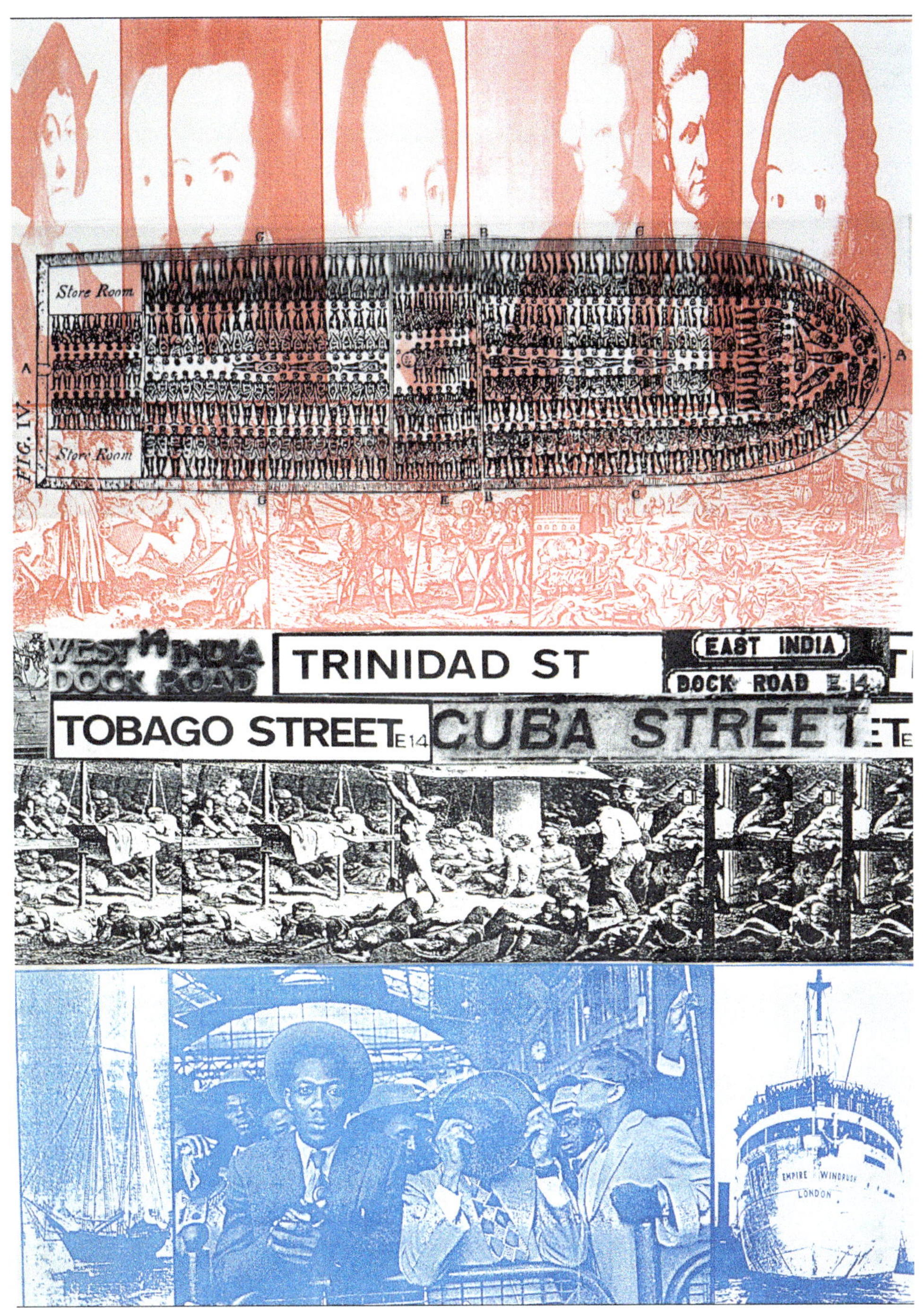

6.2
Ingrid Pollard, *Untitled*, from *Oceans Apart*, 1989,
printed Xerox, acetate, printed text, 24 × 20 inches.

and the expansion of the British Empire, referenced by historical prints of the African coastline and an overlay of the slave ship icon. The middle band overlaps an array of spatial signposts whose names betray the legacy of the slave trade—East India Dock Road, Trinidad St., Tobago Street, and Cuba Street as well as branding irons that spell West India Dock Road—and Johann Moritz Rugendas's depiction of a slave ship hold. The bottom band, colored with the blue of a cyanotype photograph, shows documentary images of the arrival of the *Empire Windrush*, the ship that brought the first wave of hopeful immigrants from Britain's former colonies to her shores in 1948. Pollard posits her collage of historical images with a critique Britain's unfair policies under Thatcher, restricting waves of immigration from her former colonies in the West Indies and Africa.

In another work, *The Attendant* (1993, 8 min.), by artist filmmaker Isaac Julien, the brutality of the slave trade is foregrounded to shed light on the contemporary politics of race, sexuality, and disease. Taking François-Auguste Biard's famous history painting *The Slave Trade* (ca. 1833) (see fig. 3.4) as inspiration, Julien's short film follows a black museum guard at work until he arrives at that painting in a quiet gallery of Wilberforce House in Hull, dedicated to the legacy of William Wilberforce and the antislavery movement. As he observes the painting, it is transformed from a historical scene on the coast of Africa to a contemporary photograph of homoerotic pleasure in which white and black men dressed in black leather and chains engage in an S&M fantasy imagined by the guard. Sounds of a whip followed by the cries of agony and ecstasy find the bare-bottomed museum guard on the floor as a leather-clad assailant from the painting whips him (fig. 6.3). Filmed

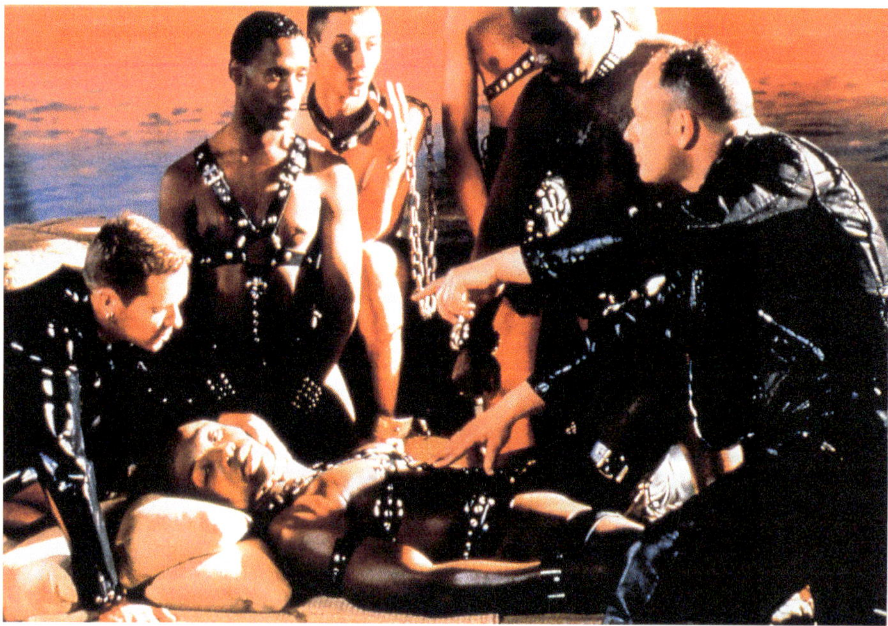

during the height of the AIDS crisis, Julien's film also serves as a requiem. By the mid-1980s, artistic, political, educational, and social opportunities converged to create a climate in which many black artists would focus their creative energies on overturning 150 years of racial discrimination and social oppression inextricably linked to the history of British colonialism and the transatlantic slave trade. Access to education and newly opened archives coupled with rapid changes in printing and digital technologies steered a handful of black British artists to reassign meaning to the slave ship icon as they began to address the past.

KEITH PIPER AND THE BLK ART GROUP

With a passion for social issues and the historical archive, Keith Piper was a founding member of the BLK Art Group, a pioneering collective of black artists, activists, and critics noted for spearheading the Black Arts Movement of the 1980s.[4] Born in Birmingham, England, in 1960 to British Caribbean immigrant parents, Piper came of age amid the decline of manufacturing industries and steady job opportunities in the West Midlands and the rise of Thatcher's conservative government. As a student, he designed the poster for the first National Black Art Convention held at the Polytechnic at Wolverhampton in 1982, where Rasheed Araeen gave the keynote address, "Art and Black Consciousness." In it, he called for black artists to unite in political unity as postcolonial subjects, noting the generative power of being on the periphery.[5] The poster's asymmetric design and use of documentary photographs appealed to both aesthetic and political interests. It read: "Calling all black artists and art students: We, a group of black art students based in the West Midlands are planning...the first national black art convention...to discuss the form, functioning and future of black art."[6] Financial assistance from West Midlands Arts was available for artists to attend the conference, where an exhibition of work by black artists from across the country was organized. One of Piper's aims as an artist, activist, and educator was to make the history of the slave trade relevant to larger contemporary narratives of British history, of which it is a formative and integral part.

To do this, Piper researched the archives for historical documents and images that unabashedly recounted Britain's role in the slave trade and colonialism on the one hand, and broadcast the political activism and protest of postcolonial nations on the other. As early as 1984, Piper began to use one of these historical images, the slave ship icon, in his work. One of its earliest appearances was in the striking exhibition poster *Past Imperfect, Future Tense*, announcing his first solo exhibition at the Black Art Gallery in London from June 7 to July 22 (fig. 6.4). With its bold use of color and intentional placement of carefully chosen words, the poster's collage of historical images of protest hints at the necessarily activist stance of Piper, the BLK Art Group, and the Black Art Gallery. The poster is also an example of "a body of aggressively didactic work which sought to articulate its content through the conscious employment of overtly politicised imagery and textural slogans," according to Piper, a strand of influence characteristic of black art in the early 1980s.

At the close of the following year, Piper's close friend and collaborator, Donald Rodney (1961–1998), had his first solo exhibition, *The First White Christmas and*

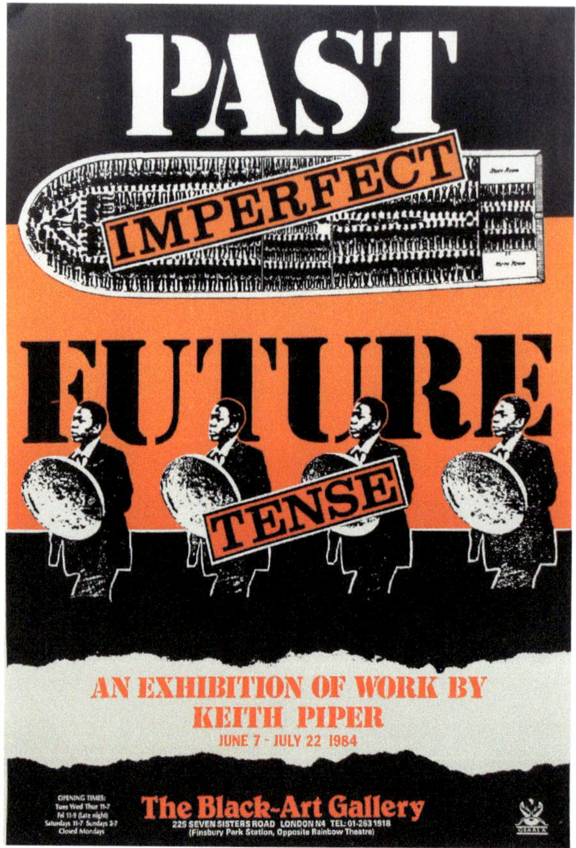

6.4

Keith Piper, *Past Imperfect, Future Tense*, Black Art Gallery, London, 1985, offset lithographic poster.

Other Empire Stories, at Saltley Print and Media in Birmingham, which opened on December 9, 1985. Conceived as an installation, the works "were executed directly on to the walls," according to fellow BLK Art Group member, the artist and art historian Eddie Chambers (b. 1960), and engaged the visual archive of slavery and the slave trade.[7] Rodney, who met Piper in 1981 at Trent Polytechnic, shared many of the same philosophies about black art and collaborated with him in the coming years on exhibitions and writings as a form of artistic activism. Throughout much of his career, Rodney kept sketchbooks for recording ideas, designing art works, drafting installations, and generally taking notes. Now archived at the Tate Modern in London, the notebooks bear the record of his genius. In *Sketchbook number 7* from 1984, he included a torn image of the slave ship icon pasted to a black card with the inscription "travel broadens the mind" written below (fig. 6.5). This was likely incorporated into some part of his first solo exhibition.

Born in Birmingham in 1961 to parents of Caribbean and African descent, Rodney suffered from the genetic blood disorder sickle-cell anemia, which frequently landed him in the hospital for treatment and ultimately brought his life to a premature end in 1998. At times, Rodney's artistic output was informed if not shaped by his illness. In *Sketchbook number 26* from 1989 he returned to the slave ship icon; this time it seemed to complete the half of the picture that was missing from the

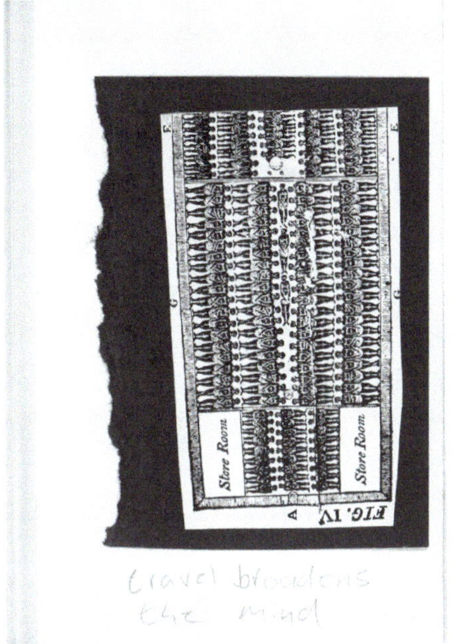

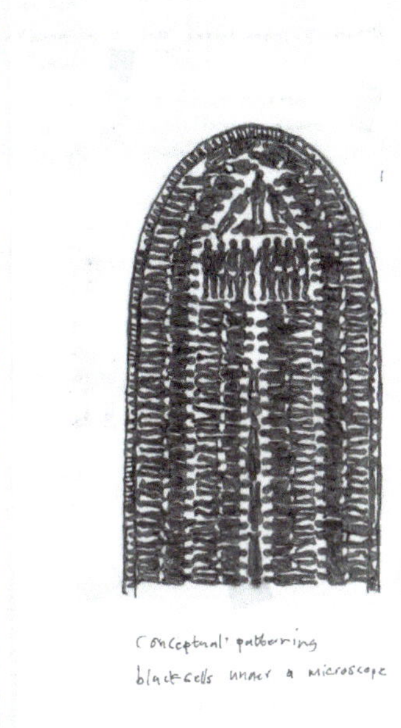

6.5

Donald Rodney, photocopied image of slave
ship mounted on card attached to page inscribed
in pencil, "travel broadens the mind," from
Sketchbook number 7, 1984, 210 × 144 mm.

6.6

Donald Rodney, sketch titled "conceptual patterning black cells under a microscope," attached to
page from *Sketchbook number 26*, January 1989,
210 × 145 mm.

page in *Sketchbook number 7* (fig. 6.6). Instead of pasting a copy of the print as he
did previously, Rodney meticulously drew that second half in black ink. Below it,
he wrote, "black cells under a microscope," an obvious reference to the fragility of
his own body that had larger implications for black subjects in Britain. In another
work, the mixed media *Visceral Canker* (1990), Rodney again pulls from the archive
of slavery, but this time he chooses to update the coat of arms of slaver John Hawkins discussed in chapter 1 (fig. 6.7). In this work, two wooden plaques adorned
with heraldic imagery are connected by a network of plastic tubing, through which
synthetic blood circulates to other nodal points referencing British history. Its title
Visceral Canker critiques how celebrated figures and histories related to the slave
trade remain a sore on the nation's pride and legitimacy. Like Piper, Rodney was
one of the earliest artists during this period of activism to engage the archive of
slavery and the slave trade to make poignant and hard-hitting works about the
state of black Britain.

GO WEST YOUNG MAN

In 1987, the slave ship icon became the cover image of Piper's *Go West Young Man*, a
two-dimensional image and text series made up of fourteen panels with photomon-
tages (fig. 6.8). Taking as its title a popular slogan for manifest destiny coined in the

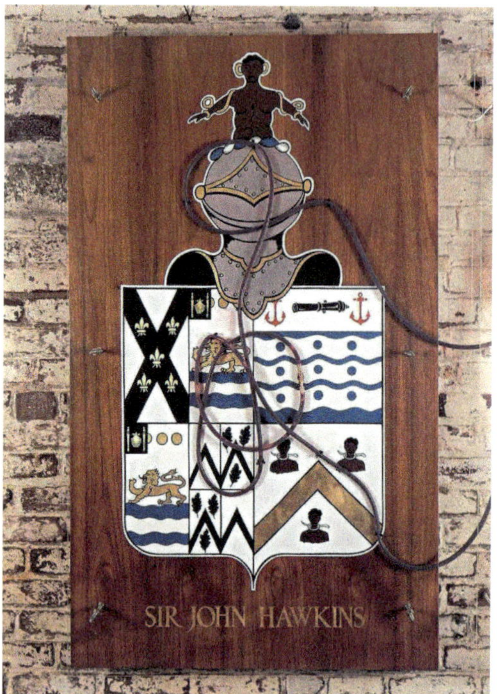

6.7
Donald Rodney, detail, *Visceral Canker*, 1990,
Perspex, wood, silicon tubing, gold leaf, plastic
bags, and electrical pump.

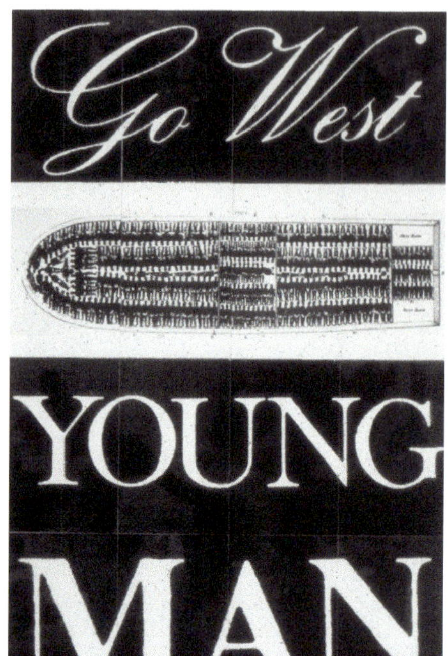

6.8
Keith Piper, detail, *Go West Young Man*, 1987,
photomontage and text.

United States in the mid-nineteenth century, Piper's work suggests much earlier articulations of westward expansion through the triangular trade. Text panels viscerally recall the artist's own experiences of racism in Britain with these words of caution from his father: "When the European says MUGGER, LOOTER, RAPIST, he sees you.... These people have carved out a very special place for you in their nightmares." In another panel, the residue of the slave trade plays out in the politics of fear and mixes signs of cultural subjectivity and social interaction in Britain: "We had made the transition from humanity to commodity.... We had been reduced to objects of fear and fantasy." A seminal series in Piper's evolution as an artist and activist, *Go West Young Man* took center stage in the group exhibitions *Afro-Modern: Journeys through the Black Atlantic* (2010) at Tate Liverpool and *Migrations: Journeys into British Art* (2012) at Tate Britain, where it was acquired for the permanent collection. *Go West Young Man* was animated by Piper in 1995, when he was commissioned by the Arts Council of England and Channel 4 to produce a three-minute forty-second computer animated video. In it, the slave ship icon is layered over multiple images of water, ships, and physical forms as it moves westward (that is, left-pointing) across the screen. Piper was a pioneer in his use of digital media and interactive technologies to merge historical images and issues with contemporary social concerns in the United Kingdom.

A SHIP CALLED JESUS

In 1991, the slave ship icon was a recurring element in the presentation of Keith Piper's first multimedia installation, *A Ship Called Jesus*, at the Ikon Gallery in Birmingham, England (fig. 6.9).[8] Arranged in three sections, the installation refers to the experiences of dislocation, migration, and recovery for artists of the African diaspora. In one section of the installation, eighteen photo transparency panels evoking stained-glass windows are framed on the wall in the shape of a Christian cross. The montage of images that fill each panel consists of layers of pictures: the blue sea, a circular stained-glass window, crisscrossing chains laid over stained glass, the artist's feet marked by stigmata, the crowded lower deck of the slave ship, and dancing

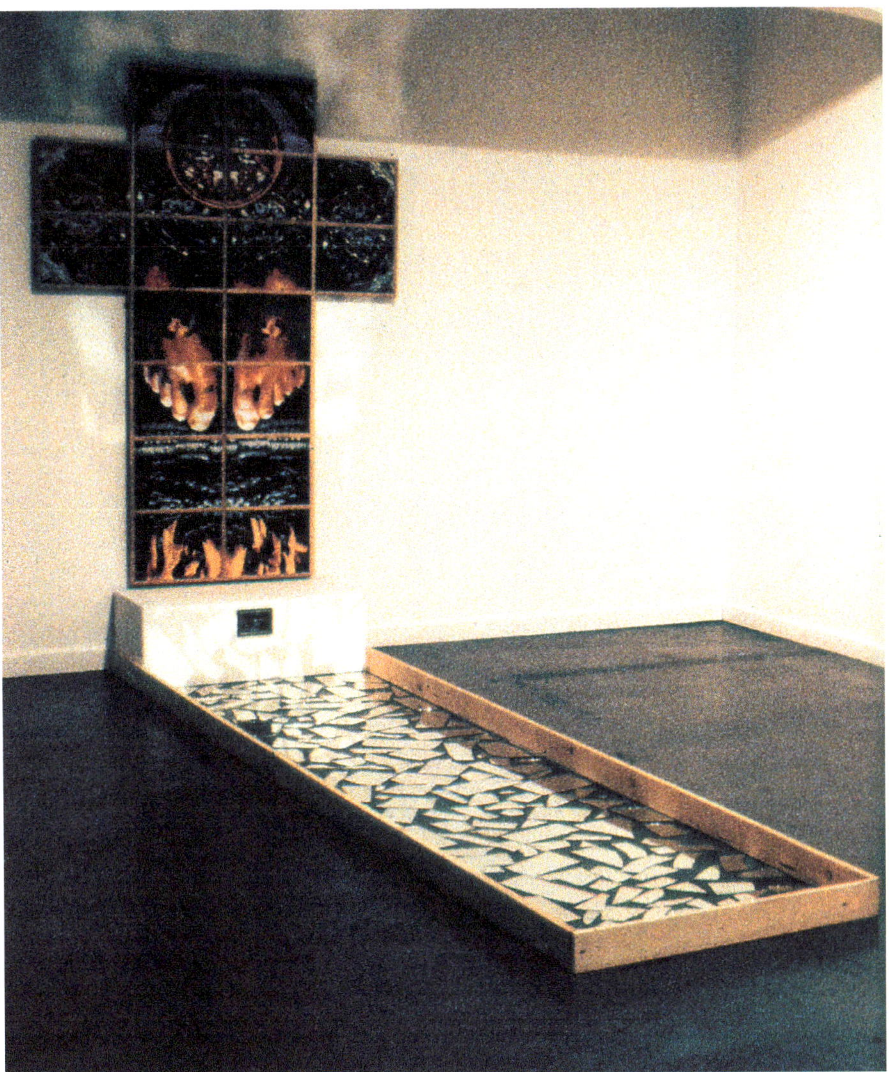

6.9
Keith Piper, *A Ship Called Jesus*, 1991,
mixed media, installation view.

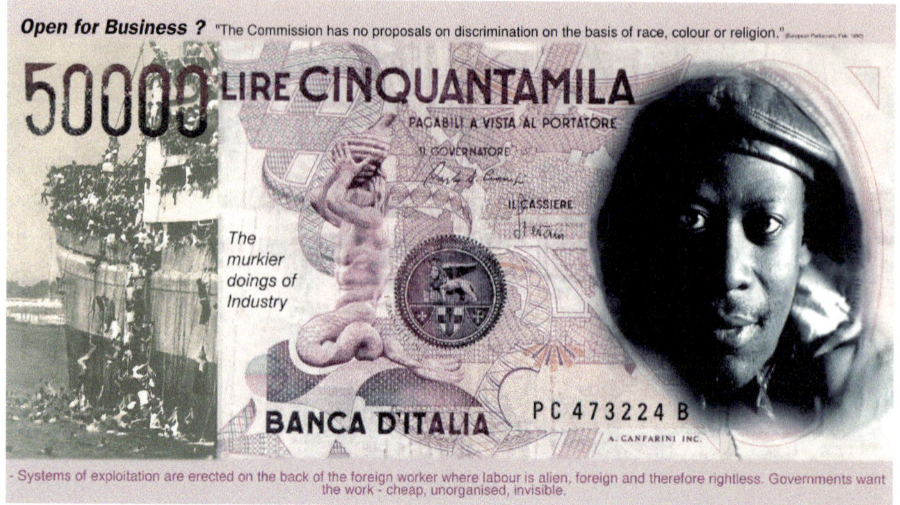

6.10

Roshini Kempadoo, *ECU: European Currency Unfolds 03* (Italian Lira) 1992, digital print.

flames. Arranged on the floor in front of the panels that make up the cross, shards of broken mirror provide a visual reference to the perilous transatlantic crossing with reflective flashes of light that summon the spirits of African captives lost at sea. The multiple layers of pictures and repeating patterns of the cross coalesce in the shimmering sea, offering a visual counterpart to Stuart Hall's notion of cultural identity and diaspora theorized in 1989 as a continual process of becoming.[9]

The title of the installation, *A Ship Called Jesus*, recovers the history of the *Jesus of Lubeck*, an English naval ship loaned by Queen Elizabeth I to Sir John Hawkins for his second slaving voyage to the coast of Africa and the Caribbean in 1564 (discussed in chapter 1). An unforgiving indictment of both the church and the queen of England for their promotion of the slave trade, *A Ship Called Jesus* also offered a searing critique of the conservative government of Prime Minister Margaret Thatcher, which had introduced a renewed sense of oppression for many West Indian and South Asian immigrants living in England by the late 1980s. By the early 1990s, Piper had fully embraced digital photography and printing technologies, which led to aesthetic transformations in both his artistic production and methods of display. Photographic prints became larger and more intricate, as noted by the colorful, layered panels of the stained-glass window, and 3-D installations adopted sound and other elements. The computer-driven innovations in photography, film, and media were a hallmark of the Black Arts Movement.

Roshini Kempadoo, a contemporary of Piper and Pollard, also adopted digital printing technologies for still and moving images. In the series *European Currency Unfolds* (1992), Kempadoo collaged photographs and prints from disparate historical sources to make digital prints resembling various European paper currencies (fig. 6.10). Produced in 1992, Kempadoo's series critiques the history of colonialism and conquest, which was marked by the five-hundredth anniversary of Columbus's exploits that year with exhibitions and works of art that protested the anniversary of the arrival of Columbus.[10] In *European Currency Unfolds*, she produced ten computer-generated banknotes, layering images relating to colonial exploitation and the labor of colonial subjects, the unwilling source of the wealth represented by the banknotes. Employing images and text, her new banknotes resemble those that were in circulation for each country at the time. Other works by Kempadoo and Piper used websites of their own making and other tools on the Internet to bring their works closer to the viewer and to allow others to interact with them.

RELOCATING THE REMAINS

Piper famously redeployed the slave ship icon in his 1997 touring mid-career retrospective, *Relocating the Remains,* organized by the Institute of International Visual Arts (inIVA), an important London-based arts institution arising in the early 1990s with intellectual direction of Stuart Hall and curator Gilane Tawadros and funding from the Heritage Lottery Fund and the Arts Council of London.[11] Noted for its interactive, multimedia installation-based environment, *Relocating the Remains* used state-of-the-art technologies to draw the viewer into the exhibition experience. One novel innovation came in the form of an interactive CD-ROM (which was sold with the exhibition catalog) that viewers could access at different research stations throughout the exhibition. In one instance, viewers were able to pull up a chair to a large wooden desk to begin to explore the CD-ROM at the computer monitor. Their actions, going step by step through the CD-ROM, were guided by an image of the slave ship icon that charted the movement of Africans in the Middle Passage and other New World black experiences and projected them onto a large screen above the desk. For casual viewers and scholars alike, there was empowerment in being able to access and project historical information that had been suppressed, if not elided, from popular narratives in a public exhibition space. By projecting these visual images on a large screen, viewers had the sense that other visitors to the exhibition could share in the learning experience. Their actions, furthermore, were recorded by Piper's computer program and entered into a database of visitor interaction with the exhibition that were incorporated into later versions of the show.

For Piper, the slave ship icon has remained an important thematic symbol that has functioned almost as a signature, marking much of his artistic production. It also appeared in his works for the group exhibitions *Race in Digital Space*, curated by Erika Muhammad at the Studio Museum in Harlem (2002), and the *Black Atlantic* organized by Paul Gilroy at the Haus der Kulturen der Welt in Berlin (2004). In Piper's digital video installations, the slave ship icon flits across the screen, sometimes only for a split second, but its impact is penetrating nonetheless, as its unforgettable schematic, through its reference to legacies of the Middle Passage, stirs up implicit histories related to surveillance that are embedded in the built environment, the contemporary landscape, and the experiences of diasporic people.[12]

Such works as Joy Gregory's multimedia installation *Memory and Skin* (1997) (fig. 6.11) address similar themes of the environment/place of diasporic memory.

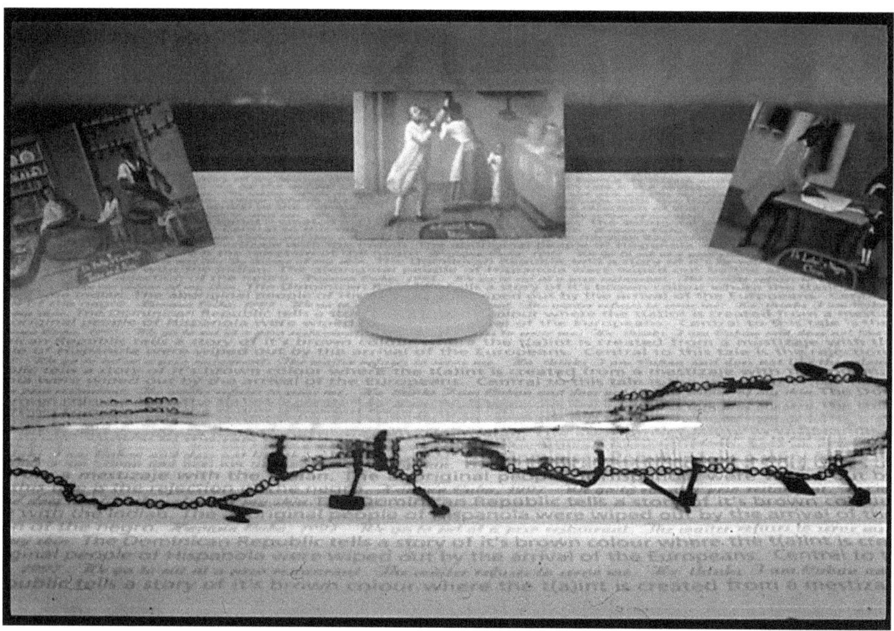

6.11
Joy Gregory, *Memory and Skin*, 1997,
multimedia installation.

"Diaspora always involves dissemination, but not necessarily a return home, to go back," Hall reminds us. "It is a one-way journey, where home is a place of the imagination, a place to understand the current trauma and globalization of Africa (of home) and the cosmopolitan centers of Europe and the West."[13] In *Memory and Skin*, Gregory arranges found objects thematically in vitrines—a chain, postcards, sugar, tobacco—to stand in as symbolic markers of the sites of memory for diasporic Africans in the Caribbean. She determines the immersive installation environment, including sound, projected video, and vitrines, through a combination of two aesthetic processes: collecting historical data and using that data to create a visual narrative. In this way, Gregory listens to, witnesses, and records the desires of others and draws upon their stories to create a narrative that resists containment. Much like her photographic series *Autoportraits* (1989) and *Objects of Beauty*, in these works Gregory suggests how the overpolicing of black bodies during this period produces a politics of hypervisibility that ironically renders them invisible and politically disenfranchised.

Objects of Beauty (1992–95), a series of twenty-one hand-pulled calotypes of the devices and trimmings that are used to define, shape, and enhance women's physical appearances—literally their bodies and body parts—references the female body without picturing it (fig. 6.12). These alluring yet specimen-like images of stockings, false eyelashes, combs, bustiers, and hairnets resituate for a contemporary audience the ways in which black women like Sarah Baartman (1788?–1815), referred to by Europeans as the Hottentot Venus, were subjected to scientific study and humiliating public exhibition in their lifetime.[14] Emulating an ethnographic-scientific style, which in Baartman's time created a physical "norm" and ascribed inferiority to those who deviated from it, Gregory photographed tape measures with corsets and bustiers to reinforce this constant struggle with public perceptions of beauty and the pressures of conformity. In this critique of the fashion industry and its promotion of unattainable and unhealthy ideals of beauty, Gregory argues for the normalcy of the full-figured woman, and *Objects of Beauty* could be an unacknowledged homage to the legacy of Sarah Baartman and the countless other women who have suffered in her wake. Gregory explains, "People in different societies and historical periods have pursued radically different ideals and many of the most remarkable women of history have been well built, middle aged or elderly. Yet in contemporary

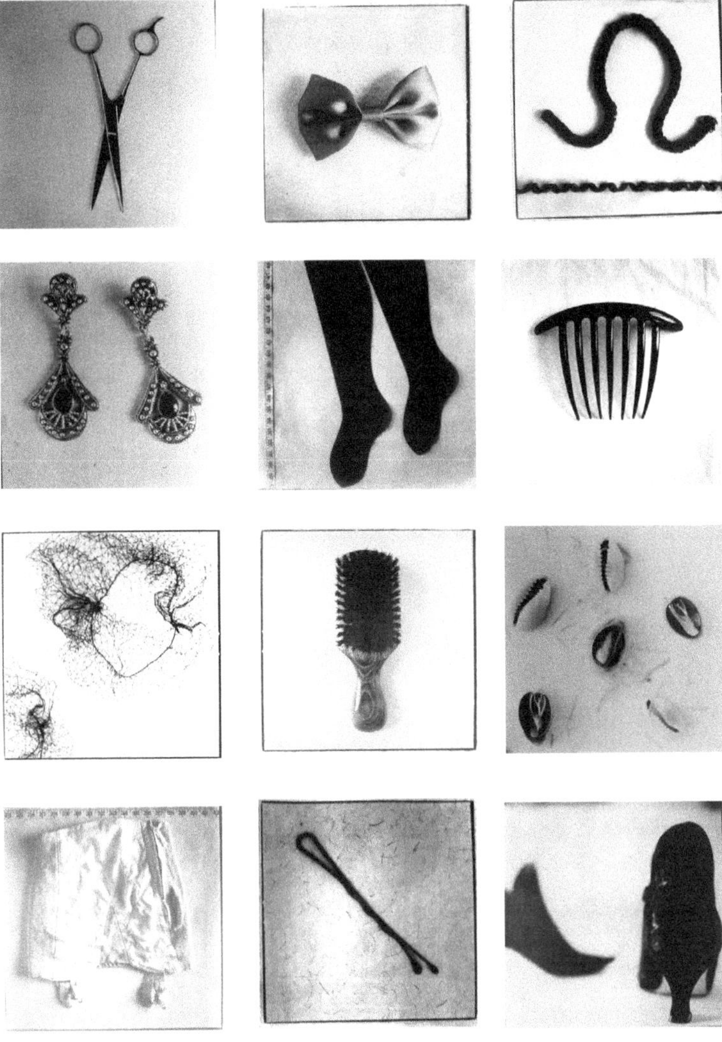

6.12
Joy Gregory, *Objects of Beauty*, 1992–95,
Calotype prints.

Western society the issue of beauty negatively affects almost all women, young and old regardless of race or social position."[15] The viewer is left to imagine the physical and psychological constraints that these objects of beauty conjure up.

GODFRIED DONKOR

In contrast to the work of Gregory, especially as it pertains to the policing and subsequent hypervisibility of black bodies, Godfried Donkor (b. 1964), a British artist of Ghanaian descent, created a series of works on paper that criticized the history and legacy of commoditization of the black male body since the era of the slave trade, notably in the arena of boxing.[16] One of the first examples in this ongoing series is *The Harder They Come*, 1994, a mixed-media work in which the artist appropriates the iconic image of reggae sensation Jimmy Cliff, the star of the Jamaican cult film of the same title and pictures him, pistols drawn, poised to do battle as he straddles an airplane marked by the slave ship icon (fig. 6.13). His head is topped with a halo, a device that Donkor would use in later versions of his imagery that incorporates the slave ship icon. In his celebrated series *From Slave to Champ* (1995), Donkor valorizes the legendary African American boxer Jack Johnson (1878–1946), the son of former slaves (fig. 6.14). In these striking prints, Johnson, larger than life, bare-chested, and dressed in boxing shorts, boots, and gloves, straddles a nineteenth-century print of a slave ship (see fig. 3.6). Poised to win the fight over racism, commoditization, and poverty, he became the first black heavyweight champion of the world (1908–15), remarkably so, at the height of the Jim Crow era, when boxing rings, like all other public spaces, were loath to allow any crossing of the color line.[17]

Donkor returned to a similar visual arrangement in 2004, straddling bodies on top of slave ships, but this time his victors are females who appear to be conquering the slave ships, perhaps even sinking them. In works like *Browning Madonna* (2004), the artist uses collage to transform contemporary newspaper photographs of West Indian dance hall queens into Madonna figures illuminated with golden halos (fig. 6.15). Set against the warm background of the pages of the *Financial Times*, numbers hypnotize in columns, seemingly repeating endlessly, to create a visual illusion of wealth and expenditure. Collaged together, monetary connections between the circulation of these images of nearly bare black beauties in the present and black female bodies in the era of the slave trade reveal age-old pathways to the exploitation of the black female body.

DECODING THE INSTALLATIONS OF MARY EVANS

The medium of 3-D installation is a popular aesthetic strategy for contemporary artists, as its involvement of place and, often, site-specificity lends additional layers of meaning to both the artwork and the space in which it is installed. In many instances, the artist seeks to intervene in if not disrupt normative readings of the space in which the artwork is installed. This manner of presentation and mode of creative practice defines the art of Mary Evans (b. 1963), a Nigerian-born artist working in London, whose "interest in pattern, semiotics and language, particularly

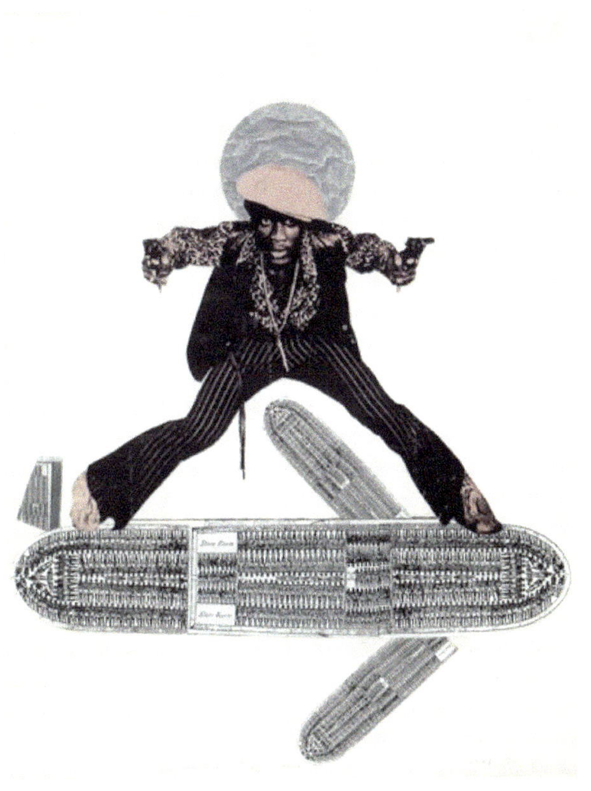

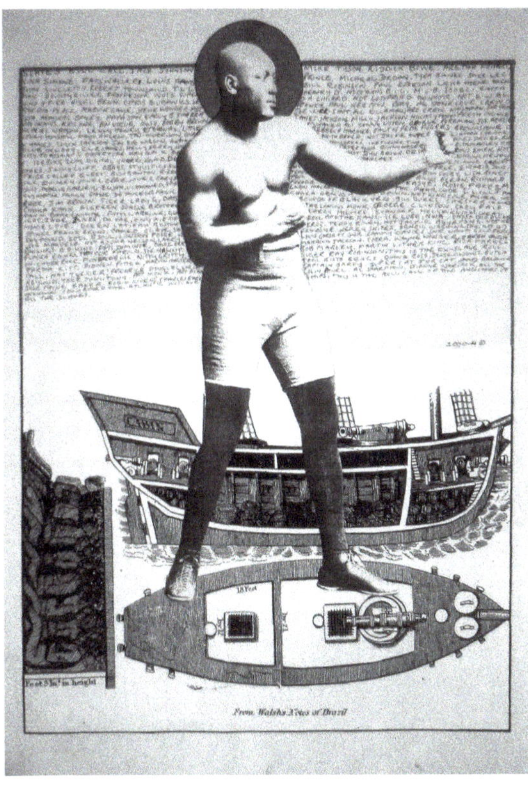

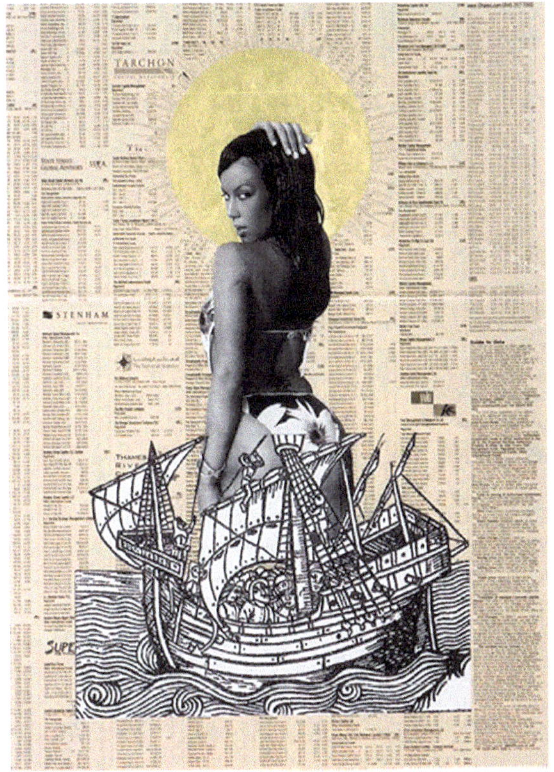

6.13 ABOVE LEFT
Godfried Donkor, *The Harder They Come*, 1994,
mixed media collage.

6.14 ABOVE RIGHT
Godfried Donkor, *From Slave to Champ (Roll Call)*,
1998, mixed media collage.

6.15 LEFT
Godfried Donkor, *Browning Madonna I*, 2009,
mixed media collage on digital print, 85 × 110 cm.

in relation to pictographic images," has produced multiple works that reclaim the slave ship icon. Having grown up in Lagos and London, Evans is "involved in articulating the emblematic devices of two cultures by using equally emblematic methods of image production: stenciling, pasting, printing and stamping."[18] Her patterns appear mesmerizingly decorative, with the repetitive sensibility of wallpaper, mosaic tiles, and other types of ornamental design that often remain in the background. But Evans's attention to detail, choice of cutouts, and arrangement of patterns refer back to specific cultural and historical contexts and the location in which they are placed as installation. Evans's installations of cut-paper murals are strictly site-specific and cannot be moved to another space. As Olu Oguibe (b. 1964), a fellow Nigerian-born artist and art historian reared in the United States, put it, "For Evans, the work is one with the location in which it is executed.... there is only one way to separate them; by destroying the work."[19] Evans's delicately cut paper patterns are adhered to interior or exterior facades and function very much in the same way as murals. They thus possess a certain ephemeral quality, not in the least part attributable to her choice to "paint" with figurative cutouts from nonarchival paper products, such as brown craft paper. Comparable to the murals of Kara Walker, Evans's installations are also fleeting and their themes are similar. However, Evans's murals are based on pictograms as opposed to the silhouettes of Walker.

In her installation *Wall Hanging* (1995), Evans uses the iconic stick figures seen in popular, everyday pictograms that denote male and female spaces (lavatories, accommodations, and so on) to set up an elaborate and oversized example of the classic game of Hangman. As the artist explains, "The images in my work are based on signs, symbols and pictograms culled from popular culture."[20] Her figures, cut from brown craft paper, were applied to the stark white walls of the life-drawing studio at the Norwich School of Art and Design (now called Norwich University of the Arts) in East Anglia, which had commissioned the piece. Her male and female icons, ranging from child-size to life-size to larger-than-life-size, were placed at different levels available to the viewing eye. In the context of the educational setting of the life-drawing studio, where students practice and develop their skills of interpreting the human form, Evans's minimal male and female pictograms pointed to "the continuing tension in art education between traditional skills (life drawing and figurative representation) and a more theoretical and conceptual approach to fine art practice."[21] But the deeper meaning of *Wall Hanging* (even taking note of the title) recalls the violent history of the lynching of black people in the United States, which began as a terror tactic in the South in the aftermath of the Civil War, during the Reconstruction era, and lasted through the mid-twentieth century. The uniformity of Evans's pictograms, similar to the figures depicted in the slave ship icon, emphasized the seeming anonymity and facelessness of the victims and the perpetrators, while hinting at the collective responsibility for that history. Writing about Evans's oeuvre in *Filter*, a catalog and CD-ROM produced in London by the Institute of International Visual Arts at the culmination of her residency at Leighton House Museum (1997), the curator Gilane Tawadros suggests, "The artist compels us to shift our attention away from the fate of specific individuals to the broader implications of human agency. Without creating a simplistic divide between the presentation of black people as 'victims' and white people as 'monsters,' Evans seems to be addressing here the question of how a visual artist can represent the horror of racial violence and its ramifications for all of us."[22] Indeed, the artist's concern for "systems of coding and recoding…[and the] bitter-sweet legacy of colonialism and cultural imperialism" is a thematic mainstay of her installations.[23]

Evans continued her evocation and exploration of the slave ship icon in 1997's *Wheel of Fortune*. Drawing three identical mirror images of the slave ship icon, Evans traced them onto craft paper and used scissors to cut them out (fig. 6.16). She then arranged them in a circular pinwheel pattern and glued them to the wall. The cross sections of the slave ship are paired as positive/negative reflections of the other—implicating both black and white figures—and the repetitiveness of her

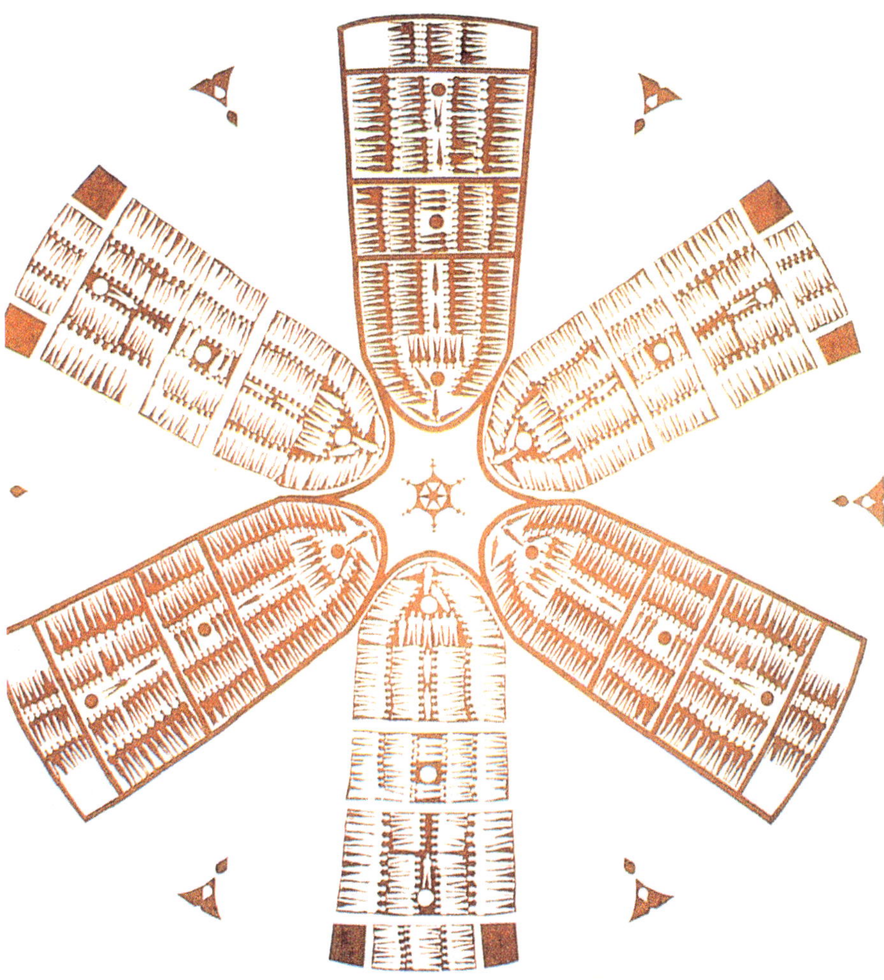

6.16
Mary Evans, *Wheel of Fortune*, craft paper, 250 cm
diameter, 1996, studio installation, London.

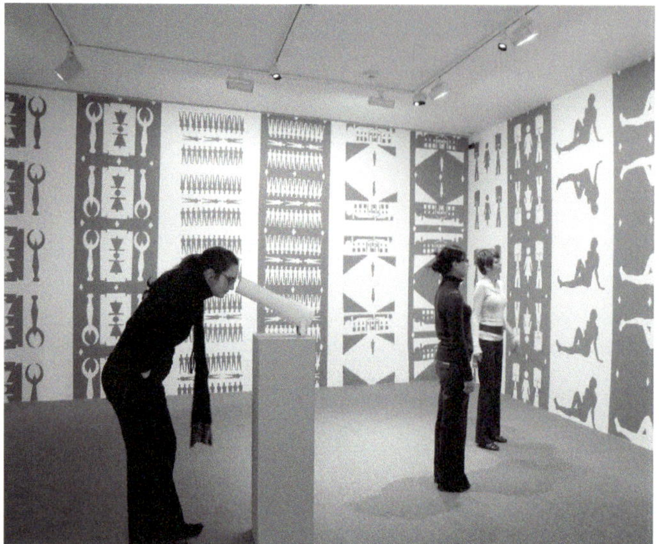

6.17
Mary Evans, *Schema*, craft paper, dimensions variable, 2008, *Meditations on Pattern*, Baltimore Museum of Art, 2008.

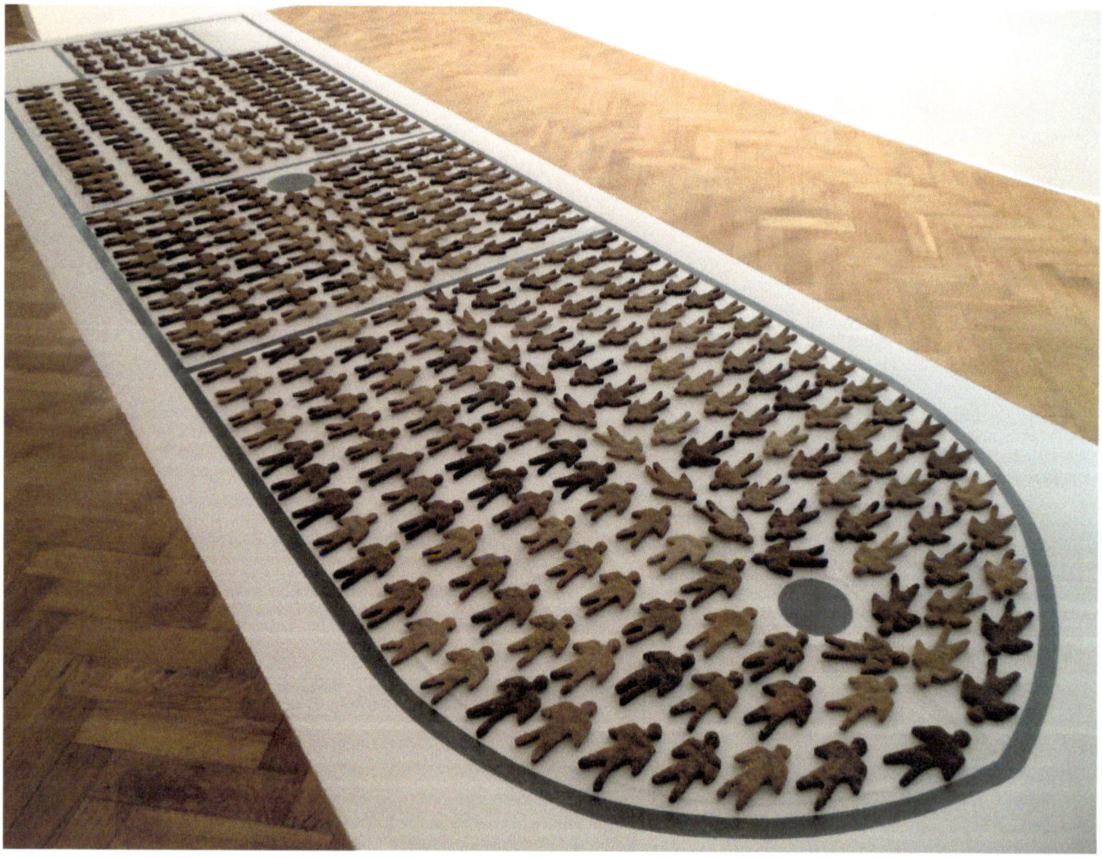

6.18
Mary Evans, *Gingerbread*, mixed media, 60 × 200 cm, 2012, *Cut and Paste*, Tiwani Contemporary, London.

almost-decorative patterns takes a cue from the schematic appearance of the slave ship icon with its multiple sections of rows upon rows of figures. As Evans explains, "The imagery and concepts in the work deal with the characterizations which are often devised by our society to contain people, sexes and races."[24] At the center of the piece, there is a design that resembles a ship's steering wheel, and the bullet-shaped sections of the hold point toward it. Evans cleverly harnesses the pleasure of pattern and design as a subversive strategy to embed references to slave ships and their cargo. As she put it, with *Wheel of Fortune*, "I wanted to generate a pattern with the image that would turn it [the slave ship icon] into something aesthetically pleasing to look at whilst belying its loaded content and implications."[25] The title of the installation, *Wheel of Fortune*, is an ironic play on words that refers not only to the visual appearance of the installation but also to the random nature of selection—of fate—that was part and parcel of the slave trade. Evans's installations are often darkly satirical and disturbing at the same time. She sets up an uncomfortable tension by presenting a seductively decorative pattern that with each repetition becomes all the more intoxicating to the eye. In installations such as *Scope* (2005) and *Schema* (2008) (fig. 6.17), Evans includes a kaleidoscope in the center of the room, filled with pictographic images that suggest the patterns on the surrounding walls but do not duplicate them exactly. The kaleidoscope, a childhood fascination, references the random combination of images and the act of looking/surveillance. Yet when the meaning behind the pattern comes through, revealed by her insistence on repetition and the multiple ways of seeing, the viewer is often exposed to an unsettling truth of the past.

In another work titled *Gingerbread*, the artist decided to bake gingerbread biscuits in the shape of the pictogram figures she culled from the slave ship icon for the fringe exhibition *Itinerants*, which was part of the first Liverpool Biennale in 1999. She packaged the biscuits in transparent plastic wrap and inserted a label bearing an imprint of the slave ship icon inside with the ingredients listed: "sugar, butter, flour, molasses, allspice, ginger, blood, sweat and tears." Evans brought them to be sold at the Tate Museum café and instructed the sales staff to give the money to charity. When she called to inquire about how they were selling, she was told that they "sold like hotcakes." Most buyers apparently didn't realize what they had bought until they were nearly to their tables. Evans returned to baking gingerbread biscuits for another iteration of *Gingerbread* (2012) (fig. 6.18), in which she lays the uniform gingerbread men in the shape of the slave ship icon two meters long on the floor. While she doesn't consider herself a performance artist, she described the act of baking the gingerbread biscuits as one that ultimately can be emotionally cathartic.

In this chapter, we have seen how artists' repeated deployment of the slave ship icon—in multiple formats, media, and exhibitions—demonstrates its power as a mnemonic device and validates the black Atlantic visual practice of mnemonic aesthetics wherein relevant themes of origin and struggle are reinforced and reworked in order to illustrate their importance for contemporary audiences. Through this practice, the art of memory becomes a powerful mode of generating and experiencing art.

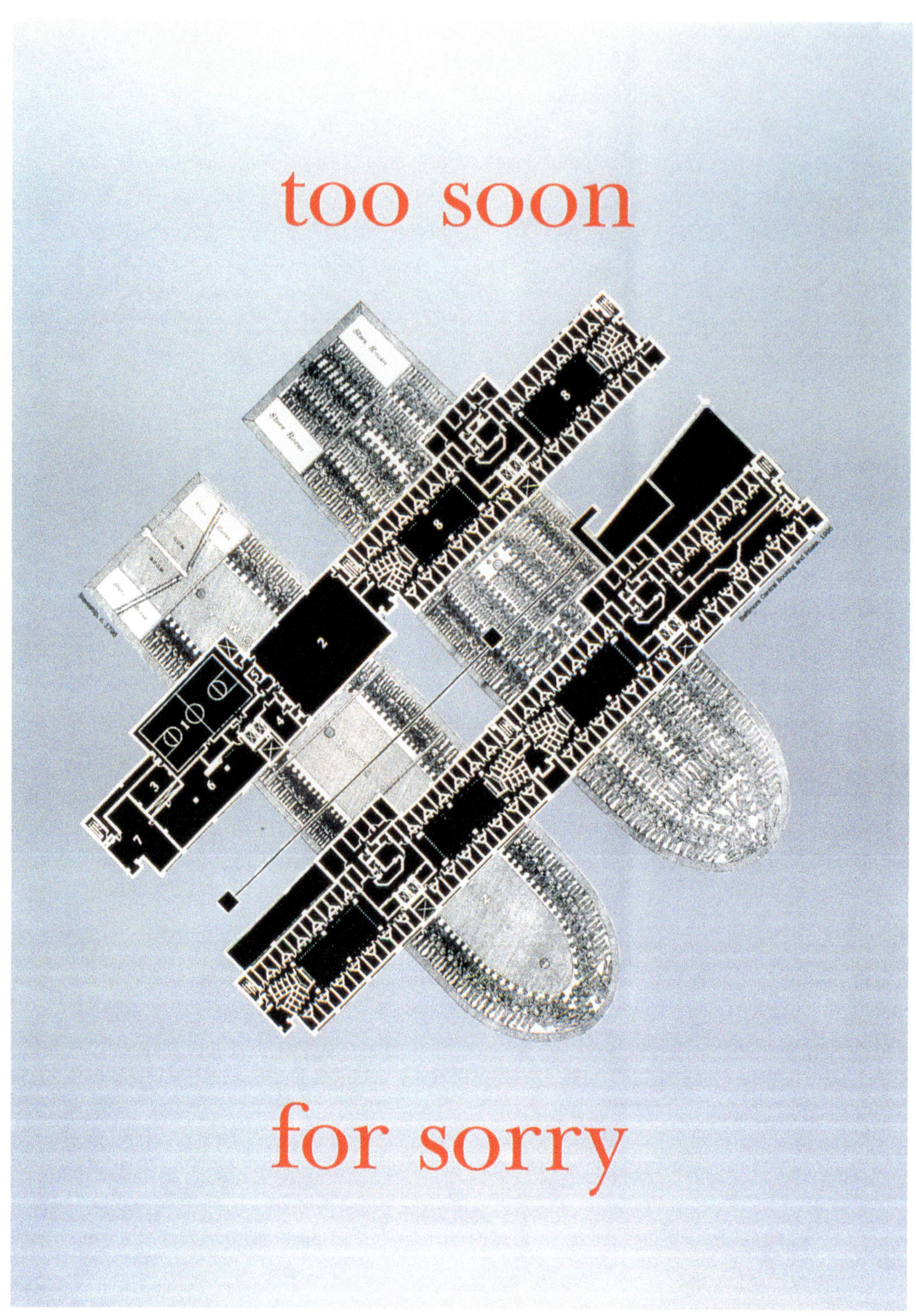

7.1

David Thorne and Resistant Strains, *Too Soon
for Sorry* (*Maximum Security Democracy* series),
photolithographic lithographic poster, 1998.

CHAPTER SEVEN

BODIES: COMMODITIZATION AND BRANDING

Racism is the most successful advertising campaign of all time. Africans have…
thousands of years of culture. Having all of these people packed into ships
and then told they're all the same, reducing them to a single identity—that's
absolute power.
—Hank Willis Thomas

IN THIS CHAPTER, we turn to the (re)commodification of the black body in the late twentieth century and today by examining artists who have recast the slave ship icon to interrogate this centuries-old problem of exploitation and dehumanization. The grassroots artist activist collective Resistant Strains, the filmmaker Marc Levin, and the installation artist Stephen Hayes deploy the slave ship icon to draw genealogical lines between the legacy of its innovative carceral technologies and architecture and those developed by and practiced in the contemporary prison system in the United States, especially in the last twenty years. Using media as diverse as agit-prop prints, independent guerilla filmmaking, and multimedia installation, these artists demonstrate an unrelenting mnemonic aesthetic practice that reveals the roots of structural racism in the diagram of the slave ship icon and a coercive system of "free labor" that produces black bodies as highly sought after commodities. This spectacle of containment, of captive free black labor potential leads us to consider the hypervisibility of the black body in both abolitionist-era propaganda and in contemporary marketing and advertising media, notably sports, entertainment, and alcohol branding. Contemporary artist Hank Willis Thomas takes up the issue of advertising, branding, and marketing and how it has had detrimental effects on black communities, and especially young black men in his *B®anded* series and subsequent works that meditate on the visual catalog of the history of slavery. Employing a savvy didactic mode of exposing the mutability of signs, Thomas mines the archive of the history of slavery and cleverly enmeshes its most familiar images with well-known advertising campaigns to expose the underlying racist tendencies of brand marketing in black communities and their exploitative, sometimes deadly effects. In both instances—that of the prison industrial complex and that of marketing and branding blackness in commercial advertising—the commoditization of the black body reproduces it as a hypervisible raw material ripe for exploitation and consumption.

THE PRISON INDUSTRIAL COMPLEX

Since the late 1990s, resistance movements against the growing industrialization and commercialization of the criminal justice system have gained momentum in the United States. One of the boldest emblems to emerge from this struggle is the slave ship icon, which has been symbolically resurrected by poets, activists, artists, and filmmakers who are vigorously advocating for prison reform. They have found it a viable image for calling attention to the inequalities in the criminal justice system that have led to a disproportionate number of people of color (black, Native American, and Latino) and women, held behind bars—essentially a modern-day equivalent of the slave ship—and to centuries of "racial profiling" that have produced neoconservative policies of "stop and frisk" and "shop and frisk" in New York City and other racially diverse urban environments in the United States. As former political prisoner and scholar-activist Angela Y. Davis put it in her seminal 1998 article "Masked Racism: Reflections on the Prison Industrial Complex":

> To deliver up bodies destined for profitable punishment, the political economy of prisons relies on racialized assumptions of criminality—such as images of black welfare mothers reproducing criminal children—and on racist practices in arrest, conviction, and sentencing patterns.[1]

The previous year, Davis, along with scholar-activist Ruth Wilson Gilmore, prison reform activist Rose Braz, and others founded the grassroots advocacy organization Critical Resistance. Drawing from the strategies and legacies of the antislavery movement, Critical Resistance calls for the abolition of the prison industrial complex, a term coined by Davis, who explained:

> Taking into account the structural similarities of business-government linkages in the realms of military production and public punishment, the expanding penal system can now be characterized as a "prison industrial complex."[2]

In September 1998, "Critical Resistance: Beyond the Prison Industrial Complex," the first grassroots, scholar-activist conference to address the prison industrial complex, was held at the University of California, Berkeley. It brought more than 3,500 activists, former prisoners and their families, scholars, artists, poets, and musicians together to develop strategies for prison reform through grassroots political action. Davis, Gilmore, and other scholars, former prisoners, and leading advocates for prison reform headlined the conference. The poets Sonia Sanchez (b. 1934) and Nikki Giovanni (b. 1943) held spoken-word performances. The conference was successful in organizing a local and national network of activist groups that still continues to agitate at the prisons, in the halls of government, and in the boardrooms of the prison conglomerates.

TOO SOON FOR SORRY

David Thorne, of the West Coast artist activist collective Resistant Strains, designed the *Maximum Security Democracy* series (1998), a set of striking photolithographic posters that were available for purchase at the Berkeley conference to support the then-fledgling organization Critical Resistance.[3] The poster *Too Soon for Sorry* was one of the popular prints from the series.[4] Featuring a bold crisscrossing design that resembles a swastika, *Too Soon for Sorry* includes the two essential plan views of the slave ship icon (figures 4 and 5 of fig. 7.1) interlaced with two oblong floor plans showing the cellblocks of the Baltimore County Jail Central Booking circa 1995 (fig. 7.1). The juxtaposition of these two different configurations of confined space alludes to a tension between individual and collective suffering, while suggesting that the slave ship's pioneering forms of torture, social control, and psychic/sensory deprivation are also practiced in the space of the present-day prison cell block. The silver background of the photolithographic poster references iron shackles, prison bars, and other forms of bodily confinement. The title, *Too Soon for Sorry*, printed in blood-red letters, suggests that the wounds of the past, still fresh, are festering in the prison system, and that an apology for slavery, which had been a topic of current events when it was widely speculated that then President Bill Clinton would issue such an admission of national guilt when he visited La maison des esclaves at Gorée Island in Senegal in April 1998, was premature at best, when the American prison system was merely taking over where chattel slavery left off.

Another version of the poster, titled "PRISON: AMERIKKKA'S NEW PLANTATIONS," crosses the plan views of the slave ship with the cell block plans to form a grid that suggests the monotony of free labor enforced upon prison inmates. The spelling the word America with three *K*'s is an obvious reference to the white supremacist group, the Ku Klux Klan, founded in Pulaski, Tennessee, on December 24, 1865, by six ex-Confederate soldiers to resist Reconstruction efforts after the Civil War by terrorizing and brutalizing newly freed slaves. Invoking the KKK in the spelling of the name of our nation, here reiterates the white supremacist organization's foundation upon and promulgation of racial terror and its long-standing collusion with law enforcement, and by extension, the prison system, in order to administer its brutal tactics of fear and intimidation. Below the diagrams, the text exclaims, "To A Slave A 'Real' Payday Never Comes!" exposing the profit motives of the prison industrial complex while perhaps also acknowledging the allied work of the reparations movement that was taking hold anew nationally at the very same time. The poster concludes with, "The Fight For Freedom Is Never Ending," and asks, "What Have You Done Today?" By aligning the plan of the slave ship with the plan of Baltimore County Jail Central Booking, the poster's clever design further situates the legacy of the slave ship's novel forms of carceral confinement, terror, control, monotonous routine, and punishment in the design of the modern-day prison and the more recent growth of the prison industrial complex. The scholar-activist, UC Berkeley professor of ethnic studies, and founding member of Critical Resistance Dylan Rodríguez argues this point powerfully in the concluding chapter of his book, *Forced Passages: Imprisoned Radical Intellectuals and the U.S. Prison Regime*, where he states:

> There is material and historical kinship between the prison as a contemporary regime of violence and the structures of racialized mass incarceration and disintegration prototyped in the chattel transfer of enslaved Africans…this process

underwrote the innovation of a distinctive maritime architecture, literally a sea-borne and shipbound geography, devoted to the accumulation, storage, and biological preservation of an enslaved human "cargo."… This portable and moving confinement was invested with an intensive and sophisticated—and profoundly brutal—technology of incarceration.[5]

Thorne's posters for the *Maximum Security Democracy* series offer illuminating graphic detail in blueprint form of the idea that, although developed centuries apart, the carceral technologies of the slave ship (Middle Passage "chattel transfer of enslaved Africans") intersect and overlap with the modern-day prison.

SLAM

Like Thorne and the collective Resistant Strains, other artists have been compelled to represent these ideas. The director Marc Levin made some of the same observations in his timely 1998 prison film *Slam*: the inmates are "slaves," the wardens the "slave drivers," the prison the "slave ship," the experience of doing time nothing less than "the Middle Passage." This critically acclaimed independent film also made important links between the power of art and memory, the slave ship, and the state of the prison system at the end of the twentieth century. *Premiere* magazine described the film in a promotional statement as "an unlikely mix of cinema verité visuals and colorful verse [that] makes this fight-the-system message movie a visceral look at art's redemptive powers."[6] *Slam* won the Grand Jury Prize at the Sundance Film Festival and the Camera d'or at the Cannes Film Festival in 1998, the same year in which David Thorne's *Maximum Security Democracy* debuted. An ensemble of socially conscious writers, poets, and rappers, including Bonz Malone, Sonja Sohn (b. 1964), Saul Williams (b. 1972), and Richard Stratton (b. 1946), wrote the script. Stratton, a former editor and writer for *Prison Life* magazine, who served eight years in federal prison for smuggling marijuana, also produced the film.[7] The film's title, *Slam*, dually references the popular urban spoken-word contests called "poetry slams" and "slammer," and the slang term meaning prison (fig. 7.2).

Slam was filmed during a two-week *guerrilla shoot*—where the actors and film crew had limited time and resources to produce the film—at the notorious DC Jail (officially the DC Central Detention Facility) in a crime-ridden, low-income black neighborhood of Anacostia in southeast Washington, DC. Stratton explained the reason for setting the film in one of the worst neighborhoods in the nation's capital:

> I learned that if you want to see where and how racism lives on in full blown horror in this country, you need only look at the criminal justice system.… Washington, D.C., with its gleaming white monuments to liberty and justice for all, has an incarceration rate four times that of the rest of the nation, making the District the undisputed incarceration capital of the world. The rate of black to white prisoners in D.C. is greater than ten to one.[8]

The actor-poets wrote most of their own dialogue and improvised many scenes with Levin's direction as the camera rolled. The film tells the story of Ray Joshua,

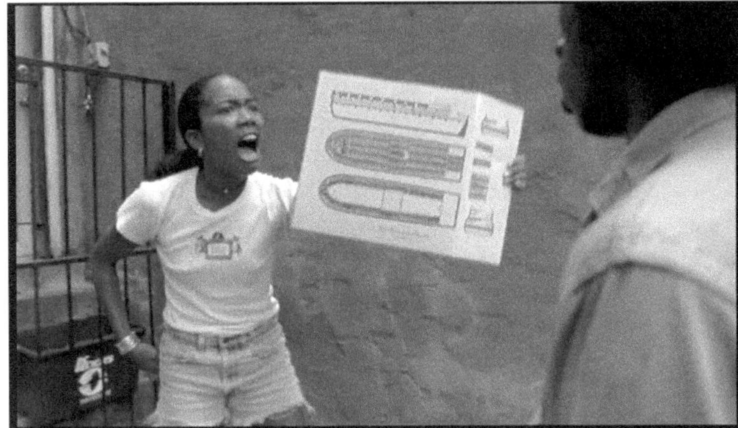

7.2
Film still, *Slam*, 1998, Marc Levin, director.

played by the award-winning poet and actor Saul Williams.[9] Ray, a talented, young poet-rapper, is regarded as a role model by the boys and girls in the Anacostia housing project where he lives, but he is also a low-level marijuana dealer. One night, he gets caught by the police and is sent to jail for selling a small "nickel bag" of marijuana (only five dollars' worth) to a friend. While in the DC Jail awaiting arraignment, he instinctively uses the power of the spoken word to defend himself against in-house gangs and to keep his wits about him. His gift for rapping is noticed by Lauren, a prison volunteer who teaches creative writing and poetry to the inmates. The New York–based performance poet Sonja Sohn plays Lauren, who encourages Ray to never lose faith in his writing.

When Ray is released from the DC Jail on bond pending a hearing, he is invited to Lauren's apartment for an evening of spoken-word poetry. Their friendship turns amorous, and the next afternoon they stroll through the vibrant and colorful Eastern Market. Hand-held tracking shots follow Lauren and Ray past vendors' stalls and young street musicians, who drum the rhythmic sounds of the popular Washington, DC "Go Go beat" pioneered by native son, Chuck Brown. As they are drawn to the stall of a vendor selling African American history books, prints, and memorabilia, "The camera zooms in on a print of the slave ship *Brookes*, taking in the 'decks and gallows.'"[10] Lauren purchases the print and they make their way home. Seeing this image spurs Ray to think about his recent jail experience and the hearing he must stand for the next day. It provokes one of the most heated exchanges in the film, which sheds a harsh and illuminating light on the relationship between the slave ship, the prison, and black Atlantic memory:

RAY.   Yesterday, I woke up in a fucking prison. I woke up on a fucking ship. I woke up there, you know? I woke up there! (*he says, pointing to the print of the Brookes*) And then, I went home. And I saw that for what it was. And then, I came here…and it was like a fucking new world to me. It was a new world. [referring to Lauren's world] And I was like, Ah, this is fucking home, this is where I need to be, this is the shit that I've dreamt about. This is the shit that I can do, this is the new world that I want…*(desperate)* but I don't want to have to go through the fucking middle passage to get to the new world! That's not for me.

LAUREN. *(quiet)* Look, Ray. All I'm saying is you made a mistake, baby. We all make mistakes, I've made mistakes. All you got to do is just walk up in that court with your head up high, and accept responsibility for what you've done. Go to jail, do your time, make the most of your time, read, write, do whatever it is you gotta do—

RAY. My only responsibility is to my fucking dreams. That's my responsibility…

LAUREN. I know about your dreams. And I know about not being able to get your dreams, and wanting them and having them and all these road-blocks in your way. I know something about that shit, Ray. I haven't been in jail, I haven't done time, but I know something about that, Ray. And all I'm saying is, this thing that you're going through right now is what is going to catapult you into the fucking dream. You can't see that right now because you haven't been there. I've been there—

RAY. You haven't fucking been there!

LAUREN. Don't you fucking tell me I haven't been there before! You don't know me! You don't know my fucking life story, motherfucker!

RAY. And you know mine.

LAUREN. Oh yeah, baby. You just spilled it all right here. You don't know what kind of prisons I've been a part of. You don't know what it's like to sell you ass on the street for a hit of crack. You don't know what that's like, motherfucker. I've been a slave! Fuck being a prisoner! Oh, don't come for me, motherfucker. Let me tell you something. You don't know me. Remember that. You don't know where I come from. But everything you tell me right now? I know it. I know it like the back of my motherfucking hand.

RAY. What the fuck do you mean, I don't know.

LAUREN. You don't know!

RAY. You've been a fucking slave, what do you think I've been? Where do you think I was in that fucking metaphor? Where do you think I was? When you were the fucking slave, who was the fucking over-seer? Where do you think I was then? Who was the one giving it to you, who was the one selling that shit? That was me!

LAUREN. Say it again, goddamnit. Say it again. Who was it? Who was it? Who was it that put me in my prison? Who was it that enslaved me? Who was it, goddamnit?

(holds up the slave ship picture; screaming)

Who the fuck was it?! Who was it!

(throws the picture down; voice caught)

It was you. It was you. It was you.

(a long moment)

It's not easy, baby. Escaping it. It hasn't been easy. It hasn't been easy for none of us. You ain't the first motherfucker to be up in this piece like this, and you won't be the last. All I'm trying to do, Ray, is help you, baby. Because I've been there, that's all. That's all I'm trying to say. That's all that was. That was just to show you that I've been there. I know what it's like. I know what the fear is like…I know what the pain is like, I know what it's like…I know what it's like to be cornered. I know what it's like.

(slowly moving toward him; almost a whisper)

Just trust me, baby. Just trust me. All you gotta do is go forward. Don't fall into their traps, don't fall into their games. Please. Just go. 'Cause if you run away from it, you just gonna get caught up later. Trust me. Your freedom is there, it's waiting for you. It's waiting for you. And oddly enough, baby, it's waiting for you in the goddamn prison. It is.

(reaches for him; holds him tightly)

I know you can't see it. I know you can't see it, but it's there. It's there. It's there.

(It's too much for Ray. He pulls back, picks up his bag, starts to walk away.)[11]

In this scene, the slave ship icon acts somewhat like a truth serum that forces both Ray and Lauren to take a close look at themselves, how they have lived their lives, and what the future holds for them. Ray realizes that he has found his dream element, that of poetry and writing, in which he desperately wants to immerse himself. He admits to having done the drug deal, but does not want to have to serve what he feels is an unjust sentence in order to get to the other side—to where he wants to be, both spiritually and professionally. He equates the prison with the slave ship and the experience of serving time with that of the Middle Passage, a journey that he cannot take. Lauren figures otherwise. She suggests that the Middle Passage, embodied in the image of the slave ship to which she points, is part of every black person's subconscious, psychic memory, or dream space. She further associates him with the slave ship, but in two different roles, as both overseer and slave: as an overseer for selling the marijuana (and thus making a new generation of young black people beholden to the drug); as a slave imprisoned in the jail, now caught and living in bondage—whether on the slave ship or in the prison—until his time is up, until he regains his freedom.

The inferences within this exchange are multilayered. By implicating Ray as both overseer and slave, Lauren is suggesting the relationship between Africans who sold their kin as slaves and who were later captured and also sold into slavery, or enslaved Africans on plantations who also served as overseers, enforcers, "Uncle Toms," or spies. At the same time, this exchange brings to mind the tragic and perplexing issue of black-on-black crime. Furthermore, by admitting to having been addicted to crack, and having had to sell her body to get a fix, Lauren insinuates herself into the equation as a slave to the drug and doubles back on Ray's analogous role as an overseer/enforcer. They both use their gifts of language and metaphor to get at the heart of a lingering presence that the slave ship icon makes evident: the institutional structures that still exist to maintain the status quo, which are complicit in the physical and psychic control over black people in America. As Davis argues, "The prison industrial complex has thus created a vicious cycle of punishment which only further impoverishes those whose impoverishment is supposedly 'solved' by imprisonment."[12] This scene also reveals how difficult it is to forget about the slave ship or to escape its history, its burdensome legacy. In Lauren's words, "it hasn't been easy" to take responsibility for that past—to symbolically seize hold of it, to claim it as one's own. The issues that Levin's film raises still resonate twenty years later, with aging, overpopulated prisons, the expansion of the private prison industry, and the psychic and physical effects of a carceral state more evident than ever with the rise of the black lives matter movement and the spectacle of black death in art, film, music videos, and everyday life. Moving away from independent film, the artist Stephen Hayes employs the medium of 3-D installation, including sculpture and printmaking, as he meditates on the legacy of slavery and its connection to these pressing issues in his impressive debut work, *Cash Crop* (2010).

CASH CROP

Stephen Hayes (b. 1983) is among a coterie of contemporary artists who have found an urgent need to make sense of the present by redeploying the slave ship icon. In the artist's riveting installation *Cash Crop* (2010), life-size totems—half human figures, half slave ship icons—fan out across the gallery floor (fig. 7.3).[13] Ranging in size from about four-and-a-half to seven feet, these totems confront the viewer head on, charged with the weight of the past. The human figures (men, women, children, and one of Hayes himself) are cast in concrete, and each represents 1 million of the 12.5 million enslaved Africans estimated to have survived the Middle Passage during the transatlantic slave trade.[14] As life-size figures, they stand eye to eye with the viewer, their expressions of pain and despair demanding an emotional connection with anyone who walks into the gallery. Their hands and feet are bound by shackles connected to chains, which snake across the floor, linking each totem to a central wooden pallet with the official seal of the United States of America carved onto its surface. To complete the installation, Hayes created large-scale prints from the wood engravings of the slave ship, illustrating how he, like the abolitionists of the eighteenth and nineteenth centuries, and artists and innovators of the twentieth century and today, was attracted to the deliberate repetition of figures and numbered sections that reiterate the schematic icon's mnemonic aesthetic.

Cash Crop boldly displays Hayes's genius as a conceptual artist and his skillful training in multiple fine art practices: welding, casting, printmaking, carving, drawing, and 3-D installation. The process of casting the human figures was especially

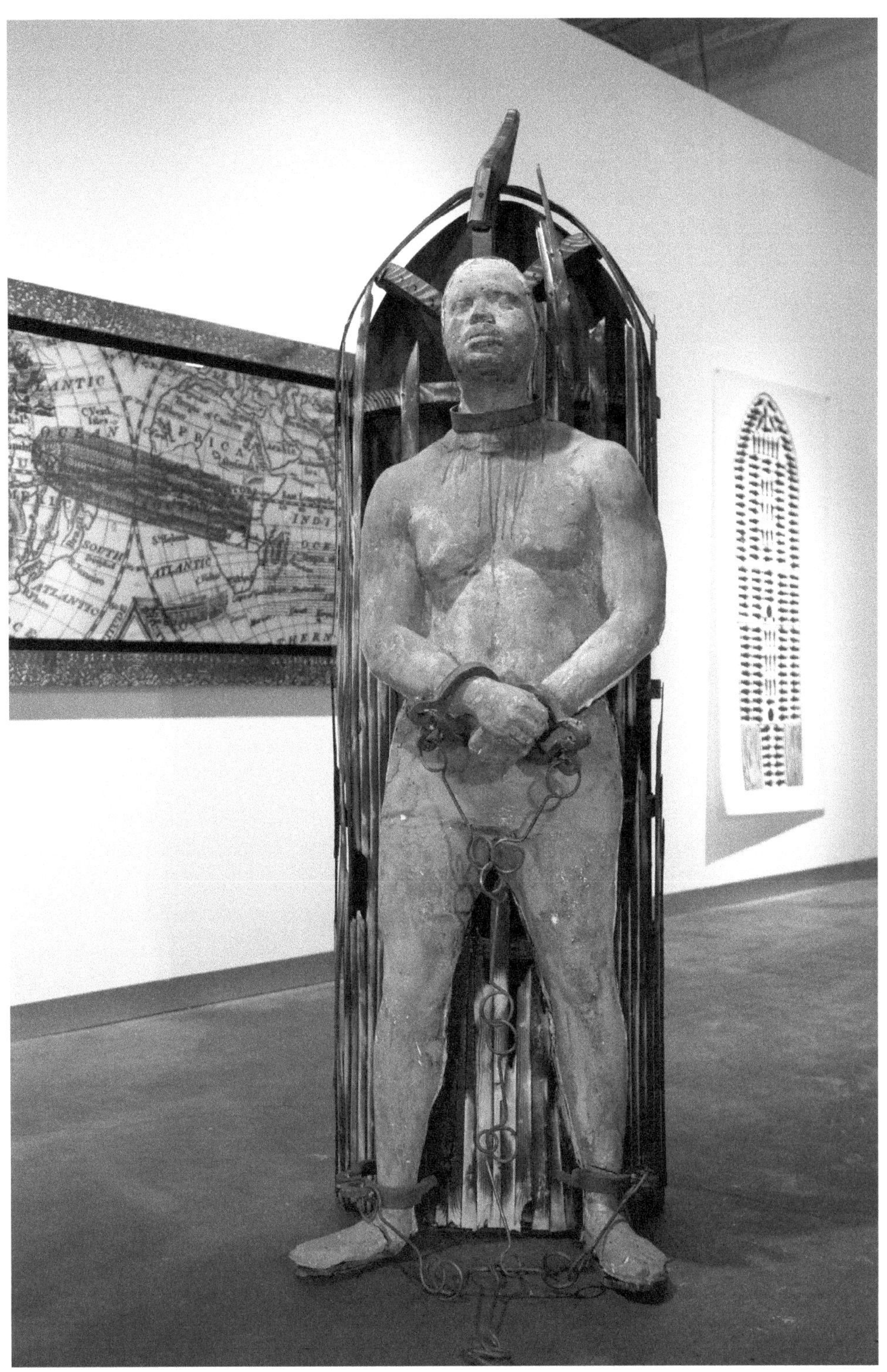

7.3
Stephen Hayes, *Cash Crop*, 2011, installation view, cast cement, chains, wooden palate, prints, variable dimensions.

painstaking for both the artist and those who volunteered their bodies. Initially, Hayes found it difficult to recruit anyone for his project. Those who came forward resisted the idea that their bodies would not only be cast in concrete, but that each concrete figure would also represent 1 million of the 12.5 million enslaved Africans estimated to have survived the Middle Passage. The weight of history was simply too much for some to bear, and in the end, he had to rely on friends, relatives, and himself to complete the number of figures needed for the installation. He enlisted younger cousins and a niece for the figures of the small children. To cast his own body, Hayes asked a friend to help with the laborious process: first the legs, then the torso, and finally the head; fifteen minutes to apply the wet, heavy substance and ten minutes for it to dry. "I got lightheaded from the process," he recalled.[15] Metal rods and hooks were used to connect the torso, head, and limbs. It was challenging to hold a still pose while the cast was applied to their bodies, and the internal struggle with imagining how enslaved Africans endured the eight- to twelve-week Middle Passage in slightly similar poses added a layer of psychic discomfort.

Considering the arduous nature of the casting process, one wonders why Hayes was motivated to work with concrete. Concrete is not a precious metal, such as bronze, nor a more desirable stone like marble, both commonly used materials for sculptures of the human form. Quite the contrary: concrete is an abundant, if not redundant, building material. The sidewalks of cities and suburbs, the foundations of even the smallest buildings and the highest skyscrapers, are made of concrete. Concrete is visible in just about everything the eye can see in the built environment. As Hayes puts it, "You can come across it any day, all day long."[16] The ubiquitous nature of this building material and its ability to withstand time also point to one of the key metaphors of *Cash Crop*: you can confront or be confronted by legacies of the transatlantic slave trade "any day, all day long."

All in all, it took Hayes five months to complete *Cash Crop*. While he fabricated most of the components, the tactile nature of found objects such as the large wooden pallet and some of the chains and scraps of wood lend an immediacy and urgency to the installation. The ship plans were made of two-by-fours and other strips of salvaged wood that were carved and then scorched around the edges.[17] The shackles and chains that connect the concrete totems to each other and to the central wooden pallet join to create a space of purpose with the prints that adorn the walls surrounding the installation, mural-size prints made from woodblocks Hayes carved to create the slave ship plans the size of human beings. The installation environment itself encourages interactions between the visitors and the totems, and the visitors and each other.

Like other artists before him who have forged a vital canon that addresses the visual culture of slavery, Hayes employs the formal details of the slave ship icon—the shackles; the coffin-shaped schematic; the uniform, darkened figures—as a way of honoring its uncompromising visual legacy. Yet he also makes use of the shortcomings of this powerful icon, notably its inability to humanize the mass of those darkened figures. The artist thereby fills in the gaps in the official abolitionist narrative of the transatlantic slave trade and offers new avenues of interpretation through the strategies of installation. By creating the cast concrete figures of friends, family, and himself, Hayes seeks to humanize the mass of anonymity in the engraving. Each figure is unique and commands the viewer's attention. Unlike the chalky gray cast-bronze figures of Detroit city residents (men, women, boys, and girls) that were designed by Ralph Appelbaum Associates for the highly criticized minimalist representation of a slave ship hold in the main exhibition *Of the People: The African American Experience* at the inaugural installation at the Charles H. Wright Museum of African American History in 1997 (see fig. 11.4), Hayes's gray concrete figures have a direct relationship to the slave ship icon, which is literally strapped to their backs. Moreover, the individual fashioning of Hayes's cast concrete figures puts a recognizable face on the obscurity of the uniform, faceless figures on the slave ship icon, enabling viewers to essentially step onto the ship themselves, and, for black audiences, to make their ancestral connection personal. With the weight of their ancestors literally carried upon their backs in the form of the slave ship icon, the relationship of the cast concrete figures to the ship's hull suggests a sort of transgenerational memory that connects a faraway past to the present.

Hayes's desire to involve viewers as participants in his installation activates the exhibition space and demonstrates an urgency to bring a tangible, visceral sensibility to African American history that evokes and demands a human presence. In an interview, he recalled, "The first time I encountered the *Brooks* slave ship plan was in the *Rights of Passage*, a program driven to teach young black men about their past, to show them brotherhood, and how to be a man."[18] Hayes was about eleven or twelve years old at the time and remembers how the image stuck with him over the years. The oversized pallet to which the human/slave ship totems are chained makes explicit the culpability of the United States in the history of transatlantic slavery. Made of cast concrete and wood, two ubiquitous and foundational construction materials, Hayes's totems reference the millions who built the foundation of the American South, indeed, the foundation of the nation. As unpaid laborers confined by the economic system of chattel slavery, they represented a cash crop, referring to an agricultural product that is sold for the purposes of turning a profit. With the seal of the United States emblazoned on the wooden pallet, the artist suggests that the slave ships of yore are, in fact, the sweatshops and the prisons of today—where free labor is performed and millions of African American men and women remain disenfranchised. As Davis explains:

> Many corporations whose products we consume on a daily basis have learned that prison labor power can be as profitable as third world labor power exploited by U.S.-based global corporations. Both regulate formerly unionized workers to joblessness and many even end up in prison.[19]

Not just a critique of the United States trade, labor, and incarceration policies, *Cash Crop* also references the negative impact of the globalized economy. The installation calls to mind the dangerous, clandestine nature of illegal human trafficking, notably the trucks, container ships, and makeshift boats used by refugees seeking asylum and better living conditions in North America and Europe in recent years.

Hayes invokes the slave ship icon as an acknowledgment of the often-oppressive weight of history on the present-day lives of African Americans.

BRANDING THE BLACK MALE BODY

Few contemporary artists have made the connection between the slave ship icon and commodity culture as incisively as Hank Willis Thomas (b. 1976). His work with archival images and the semiotics, or the theory behind how signs and symbols communicate, of advertising has brought to the fore many necessary conversations about commodity culture, violence, class, race, gender, and sexuality, and their intertwined visual representations throughout history. Working in a variety of media, from photography to film and installation, to traditional silk-screen printing and painting, Thomas has brought much-needed understanding to the ways in which historic archival and contemporary popular images circulate and function. While his early works examine the way advertisers use the black male body to target their products to black audiences (and in turn the detrimental consequences of this type of advertising for the black male psyche), his larger body of work calls into question the way advertisers capitalize on the "mythology" of a singular black identity or a so-called black "community." His claim for the individual layers, shades, and nuances of black identity is where the artist's work stands to change visual and social perceptions of blackness henceforth.

Thomas's MFA thesis exhibition, *B®anded* (2004), formed the kernel of his first critically acclaimed series, which catapulted him to the attention of critics, curators, and collectors as well as advertisers, sports writers, and cultural theorists.[20] Using the language of advertising and seductive imagery, he designed an exhibition that revealed the rapacious nature of alcohol, sports, and athletic marketing in black communities. Feeding off the muscular and voluptuous bodies of young black men and women, advertisers and sports recruiters alike specializing in urban markets have promoted/fueled the hypervisibility of black bodies in contemporary commodity culture, sometimes to the detriment of their corporeal existence. In the *B®anded* series, Thomas harnesses the tools of glossy print advertising and savvy brand marketing to create a blistering critique of this phenomenon. Drawing links between contemporary images known as popular brands and commodities and those of earlier historical periods in which black bodies were on frequent, often demeaning display, laboring, serving, sparring, performing, hanging from trees, or standing on the auction block, his sleek designs mimic the look of real ads. *Absolut Power* (2003) turns the Absolut vodka advertising campaign on its head by filling the now recognizable shape of the bottle with the crowded black bodies of the slave ship icon (fig. 7.4A). According to the artist, "Absolut Power is…the residue. It's about how something that could have begun half a millennium ago can still be directly affecting the minds of everyone in the world. But it's this very intentional action that shifted the course of the world's frame of mind, which is interesting to me. I'm not ready to let it go."[21] Another work, *Branded Head* (2003), reveals the clean-shaven head of a young black man with the Nike logo branded on his scalp, the brand (both meanings) creating a raised scar in the shape of the familiar

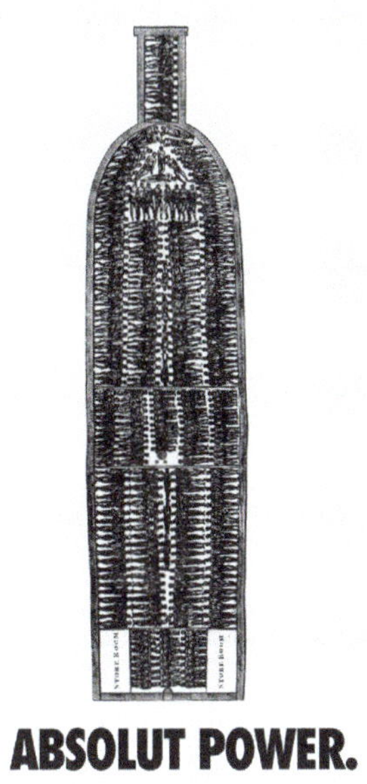

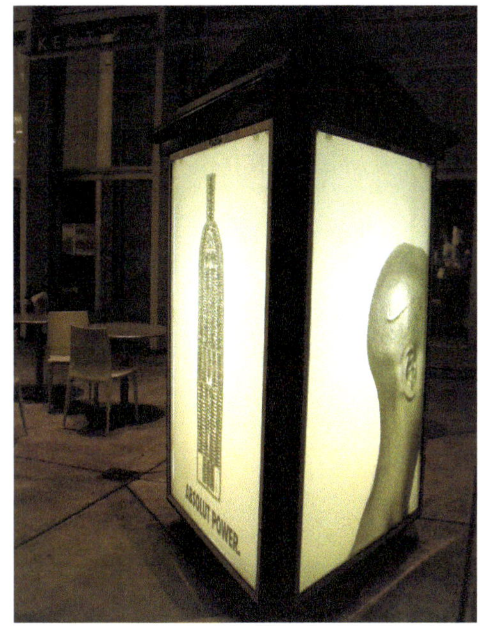

7.4
(A) Hank Willis Thomas, *Absolute Power*, 2003,
inkjet print on canvas, 30 × 40 inches, and
(B) *Branded Head*, 2003, California College of
the Arts thesis exhibition.

swoosh (fig. 7.4B). Referencing the brutal history of lynching, another work, *Jordan and Johnnie Walker in Timberland Circa 1923* (2004) combines recognizable logos—for Nike, the jump-man; for Johnnie Walker, a top-hatted man in mid-stride; and for Timberland, a barren tree in the landscape—into one easily decoded message about the detrimental and life-threatening effects of alcohol and sports advertising and recruitment on black males. So seamless was the artist's presentation of this work, set up in rented illuminated advertising kiosks in the courtyard outside the gallery on the California College of the Arts campus, that passersby took these works to be *real* print ads for the depicted brands. Thomas ran with it and took the ruse even further, imitating marketing tactics of brand management by printing poster-size inkjet prints and black-and-white T-shirts emblazoned with the logos, which were sold in a pop-up shop, as well as designing a series of credit cards, their famous corporation names slightly altered, that took design elements from the visual catalog of slavery and the slave trade collaging them with clever snippets of text. (His mother, the award-winning photography historian, curator, and artist Deborah Willis [b. 1948] was his source for many of these images, which had been an established part of his frame of reference since childhood. In addition, the renowned archival collections of institutions such as the Schomburg Center for Research in Black Culture, the Library of Congress, and Johnson publications [*Ebony* and *Jet* magazines], which he frequented with his mother as a

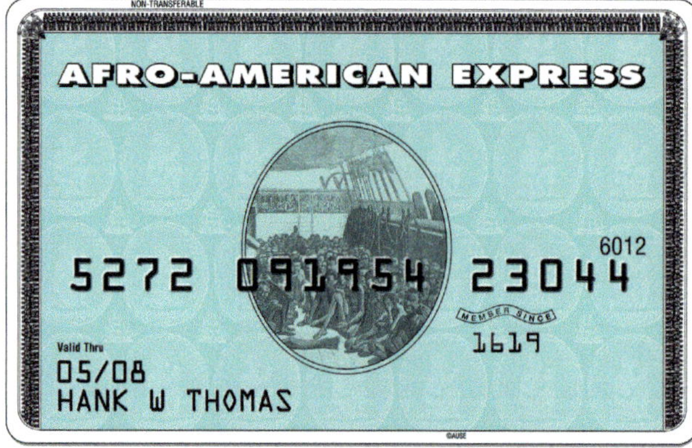

7.5

Hank Willis Thomas, *Afro-American Express*, 2004, digital print and Lucite, 2¹/₂ × 3¹/₂ inches.

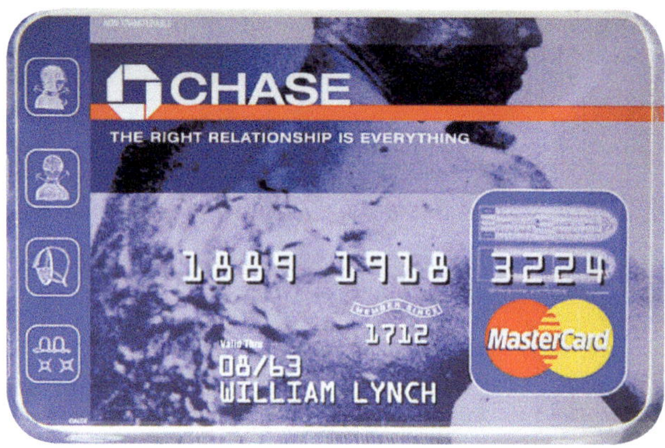

7.6

Hank Willis Thomas, *The Chase Mastercard*, 2004, digital print and Lucite, 2¹/₂ × 3¹/₂ inches.

child, have provided previously untouched fodder for the artist's working methodology.) The American Express card, in the hands of Thomas, becomes the *Afro-American Express* (2004) (fig. 7.5). A shadow image of the kneeling slave creates a repeating watermark pattern on the green background, while a famous antislavery engraving (first published in *Harper's Weekly* in 1860) of captives on the deck of a captured illegal slave ship occupy the foreground, centered in an oval frame. Around the border of the card, what looks like black trim is actually a repeating band of tiny black figures excerpted from the slave ship icon. Now a familiar visual trope of his *B®anded* series, the slave ship icon becomes the reflective strip above the Mastercard logo in *Chase Mastercard* (2004), where the "Right Relationship Is Everything" (fig. 7.6). The scarred and tortured back of Gordon, the whipped slave made famous in an image widely circulated by the American abolitionist movement of the mid-nineteenth century, appears under the lettering, and to the left sits a series of designs for torture and restraint devices published in Thomas Branagan's abolitionist primer, *The Penitential Tyrant*, published in 1807 by Samuel Wood.[22]

Like the slave ship icon, the abolitionist seal featuring the kneeling slave would be reconceptualized by Thomas in the handcrafted, gold pendant, *Ode to the CMB: Am I Not a Man and a Brother* (2004) (fig. 7.7). This gold pendant serves as a companion piece to the billboard-sized digital photograph, *Priceless #1*, 2004, inspired by the memory of his best friend and first cousin, Songha Willis, who, in 2000, was shot to death while visiting his native Philadelphia by a black man attempting to steal his gold chain. Appropriating the Mastercard company's popular "Priceless" ad campaign, the artist superimposed the costs of the every-day objects that figured so prominently in his cousin's death—"a three-piece suit: $250; new socks: $2; gold chain: $400; 9 mm pistol: $80; bullet: 60 cents"—over the mournful photograph of his family members at the funeral. Installed on the facade of the Oakland Museum, where an exhibition of his artwork was on view inside, the billboard-sized *Priceless #1*, 2004 miffed many viewers, who took it for an advertisement (fig. 7.8). The theme of black-on-black crime characterized another work by Thomas, *Absolut 187: A Memorial for the 183 Victims of Homicide in San Francisco and Oakland in 2003* (2005), in which 183 brass bullets assume the shape of an oversized Absolut vodka bottle (fig. 7.9). Installed on the floor of a dimly lit gallery across from an illuminated *Absolut Power* projected as an adver-tising transparency, this jarring sculpture says something about the mutability of signs, the ability of icons to enfold new and different meanings. *Absolut 187* is also a critique of the underreported and underacknowledged incidents of lethal violence that plague black communities in black-on-black gun violence and institutional-ized police brutality.

In 2005, Thomas and his artist friends formed the group Cause Collective, which creates socially responsible public artworks that are accessible to all.[23] Their first commission in 2007, *Along the Way*, is a digital video projection comprising a mosaic of over one hundred individual thirty-second video portraits of Oakland area residents. Tasked with making a portrait about the city's historic economic and ethnic diversity, the twenty-minute digital projection presents individual vignettes and personal narratives shot in various neighborhoods that together

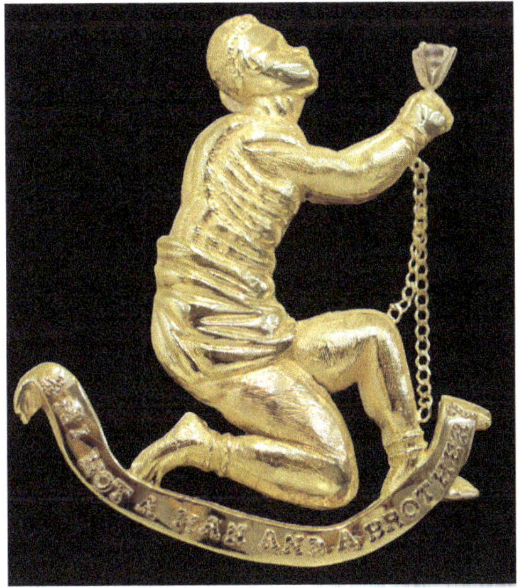

7.7
Hank Willis Thomas, *Ode to the CMB: Am I Not a Man and Brother?* 2004, 14-karat gold and cubic zirconia, 4 × 2¹/₂ inches.

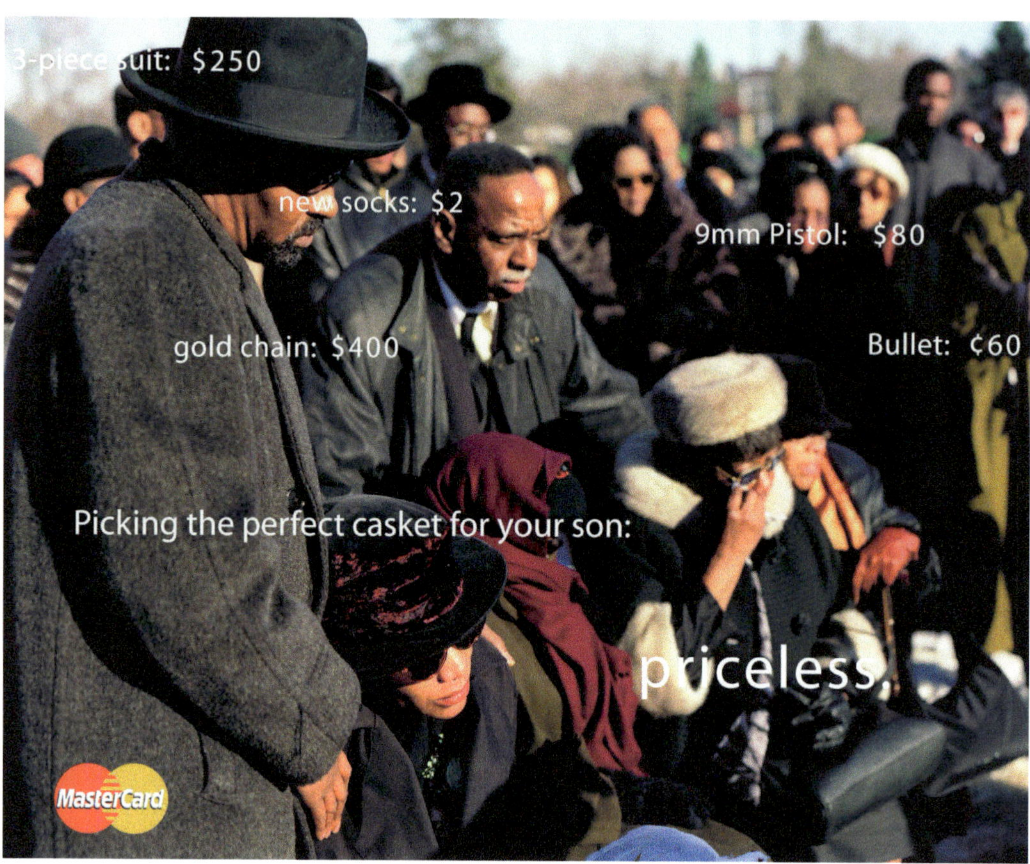

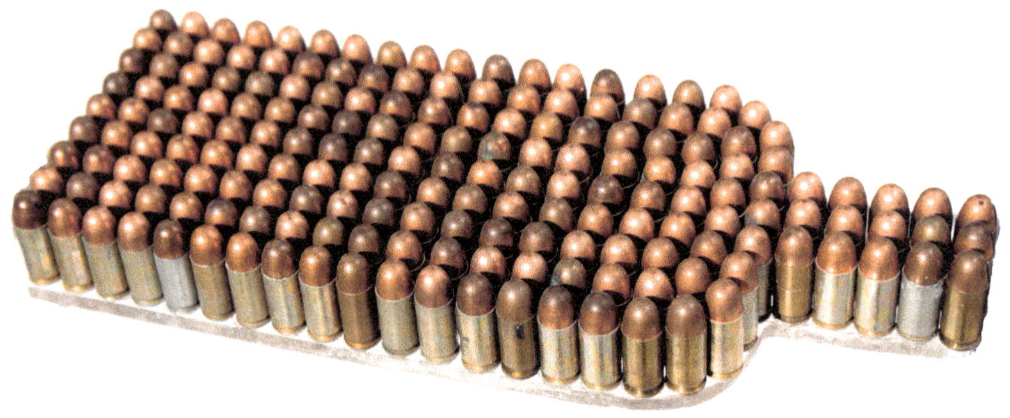

7.8 TOP
Hank Willis Thomas, *Priceless #1*, 2004,
LightJet print, variable sizes.

7.9 BOTTOM
Hank Wills Thomas, *Absolut 187: A Memorial for
the 183 Victims of Homicide in San Francisco
and Oakland in 2003*, 2004, bullets and plexiglass.

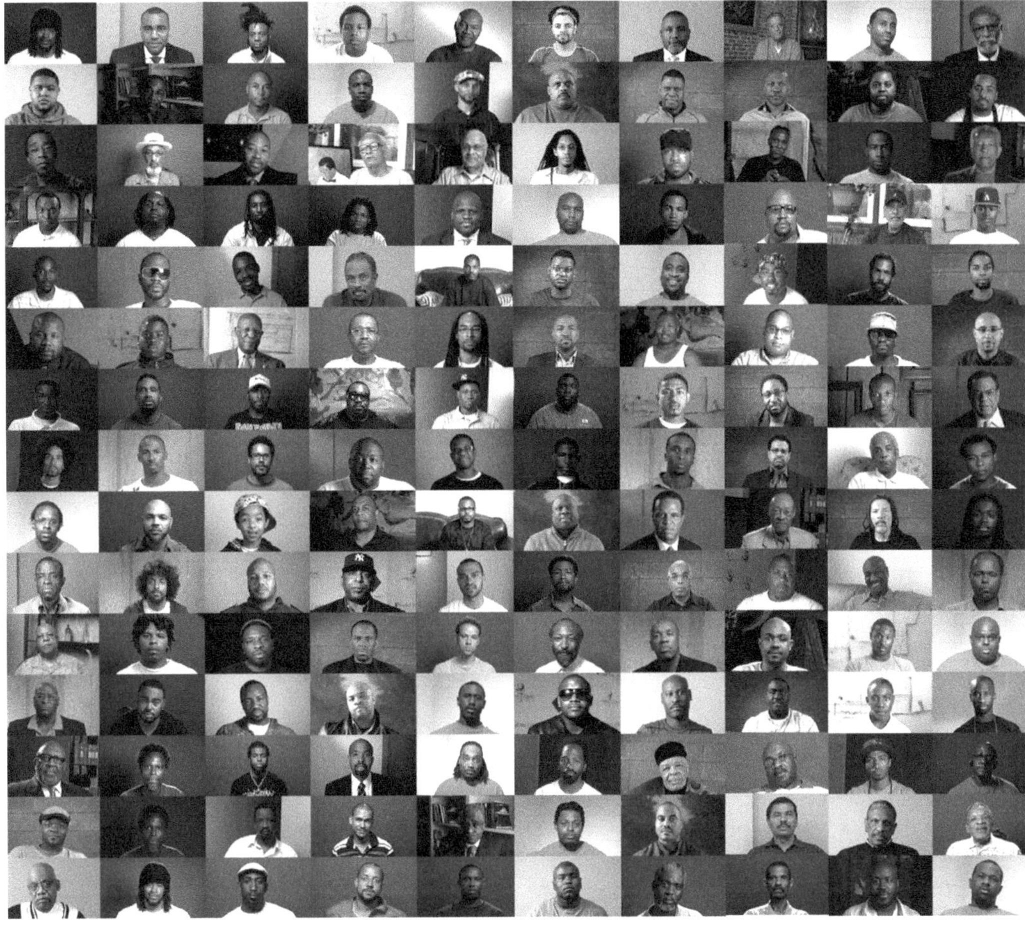

7.10

form an urban mosaic. Another work, *Question Bridge: Black Males*, was begun with a Kickstarter campaign in 2011 (fig. 7.10). On view in the inaugural installation of the National Museum of African American History and Culture on the Mall in Washington, DC, *Question Bridge* is an interactive digital video platform made up of up-close and personal interviews with black men based on a set of questions that engage a national conversation about critical issues affecting black male identity in the United States. Previous iterations of *Question Bridge* were shown in a three-channel video installation format that traveled nationally, beginning with the Brooklyn Museum, while the project also has an accessible online presence.

RITES/REINVENTIONS

1990s–present

PATTERN: BEHIND THE FACE OF AN IRON

The image is a trickster. From a distance it looks beautiful, until you realize that the little patterns are bodies.
—Betye Saar[1]

HAVE YOU EVER STOPPED to contemplate the face of a common, household steam iron—that flat, shiny, metal surface in the shape of a bowed triangle, embedded with small holes arranged in a graphic pattern? By now, its formal connections to the slave ship icon might be easy to see. The curved triangular shape of the iron hints at the outline of the plan of the slave ship. The steam holes—some circular, others elongated—reference the small black bodies laid out in the plan. The formal similarities between these two iconic shapes have not been lost on three African American artists working in the late 1990s: Willie Cole, Marianetta Porter, and Betye Saar. Each in his or her own way took hold of the iron, or its counterpart the ironing board, to shape and reshape the slave ship icon. Their actions and artwork provide key examples of the practice of mnemonic aesthetics, as each artist uses the strategies of repetition and revision in producing a series of works inspired by this pattern and shape.

WILLIE COLE

The New Jersey–based printmaker and sculptor Willie Cole (b. 1955) has made prolific use of the steam iron as a domestic symbol, an art object, and an aesthetic tool. In fact, it would not be unfair to suggest that his initial career as an artist was defined by his repeated use of these objects, creating a body of work with its own visual language, naming practices, personal mythology, and embedded rituals. In the early 1990s, Cole began making innovative works of art using ironing boards and the scorch produced when a hot iron burns the fabric cover or another surface (paper, canvas, or wood), and with this procedure, he engineered a new printing process. Curator Wendy Weitman described Cole's method: "Using heat as a kind of ink and an iron as a stamping device, he created elaborate compositions out of repeated printed forms."[2] In a 1997 interview with the art critic Jacqueline Brody, Cole recalled his initial attraction to working with irons: "The iron and scorch pieces started…with my seeing an iron on the street for many days and noticing it had a face on it that looked like a West African mask, a Dan. I brought it here and photographed it and put the picture on the wall."[3]

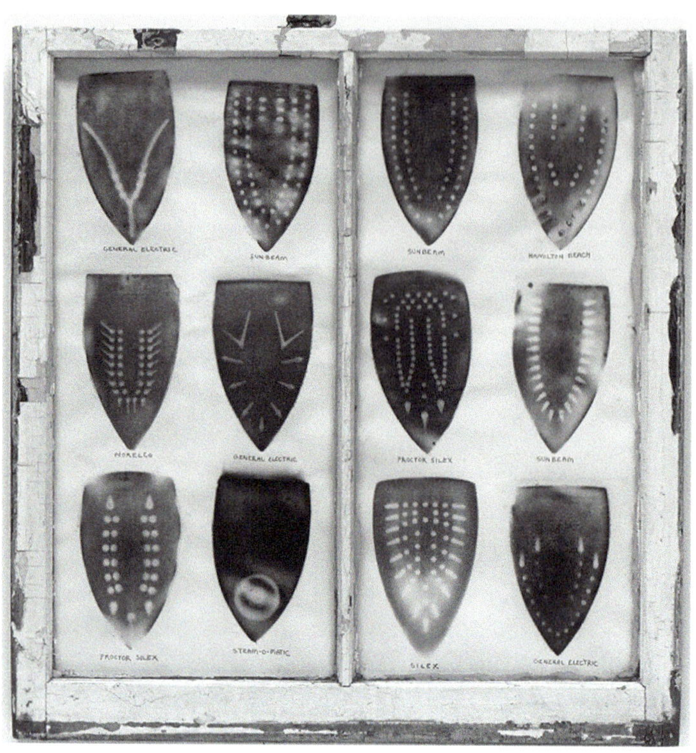

8.1 LEFT
Willie Cole, *Domestic Identity, IV*, 1991, steam iron scorch and pencil on paper, mounted in recycled wooden window frame, composition (including frame): 35 × 32 × 1³/₈ inches.

8.2 BELOW
Willie Cole, *Household Guardians*, 1991, scorched ironing boards.

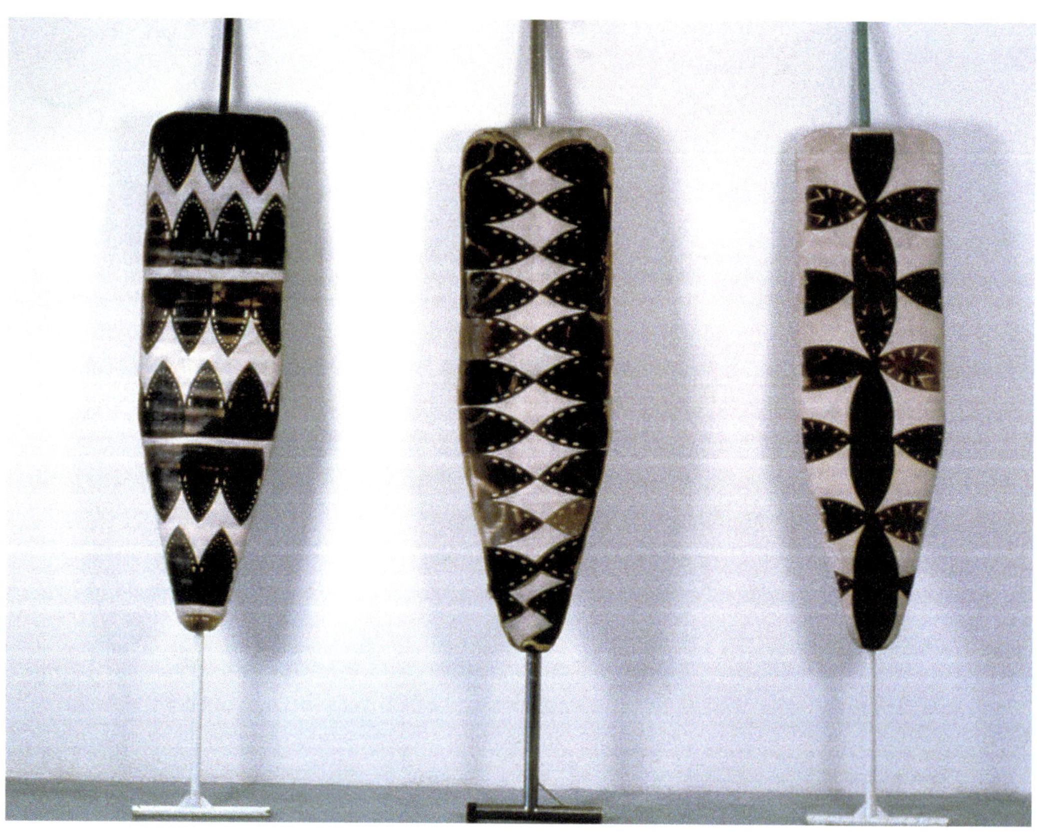

Cole's earliest works combined the process of assemblage with the medium of printmaking to produce pieces that vaguely recall the formal iconography of West African art (masks, figurines, and shields) and ritual scarification of the face and body. Yet the symbolic resonance of this work simultaneously references the branding of slaves, engravings of packed slave ships, and menial domestic labor performed by generations of enslaved and free black women. In short, Cole's works bear signs of a collective black Atlantic memory.

Further motivation for working with irons and ironing boards came from the women who raised Cole—his mother, grandmother, and great-grandmother—who earned their living by performing wearisome domestic tasks in the homes of white people in and around Newark, New Jersey. Cole was born in Somerville, New Jersey, in 1955 and grew up in postindustrial Newark during the progressive years of the Black Arts Movement. As a young man, he often repaired the irons the women in his family used, and his fascination with their function, design, and utility later grew into an art practice. The titles and visual references of his early works, such as *Domestic Identity IV* (1991) (fig. 8.1) and *Household Guardians* (1992) (fig. 8.2), pay tribute to his ancestors and the legacy of black women domestic workers.

With its visually appealing, easy-to-read format, Cole produced art that was accessible to mainstream audiences as well as to museums and collectors of the 1990s, who were not only eager to disseminate and digest this innovatively presented information but also to buy into the hype of multiculturalism in an era that embraced artists whose work sought to explain positions of cultural identity, gender, and sexuality. The message of Cole's work was short, simple, and easy to grasp, offered up on the face of an iron, a familiar domestic object. Cole even developed his own form of hieroglyphics, a writing system designed to further aid in the understanding of his work. As he explained, "When the ironing board is horizontal, it represents a ship. When it's vertical, it's a shield. And the iron, when the point is up, represents a house, and when the point is down, a face."[4] Thus, *Domestic Identity IV* and *Household Guardians* can be read using Cole's system of signs.

Domestic Identity IV consists of iron scorches on paper, mounted in a recycled, painted wooden window frame. The iron scorches are made with different brands of steam iron, including Proctor Silex, General Electric, and Hamilton Beach. Each brand bears a different marking made by the arrangement or shape of the steam holes on the face of the iron. The iron scorches point down, referencing "household faces" or, more precisely, the different markings of social or group identity, branded by domestic labor. Cole and his critics have described these social groupings as "tribes of Silex and General Electric," reinforcing through Cole's invented naming mythology the analogies to African people and culture. The names of the "tribes" are handwritten beneath each iron scorch. The wooden window frame is an added reference to the domestic realm, yet in today's consumer society, it also recalls the distressed artifacts of flea markets that were copied and mass-produced most famously by the domestic home furnishings chain Pottery Barn in the 1990s. Nowhere else but in the malls of America was such inauthentic authenticity so easily had.

In the series of twelve assemblage sculptures titled *Household Guardians*, Cole scorches the surface of ironing boards with designs that hint at West African textile patterns, ritual scarification, or carved wooden masks. Each ironing board measures 96 by 16 inches and is padded and covered with canvas. The ironing boards lean in a vertical position against the wall, and, according to Cole's own iconography, are meant to represent shields. As their title suggests, they stand to protect and defend domestic laborers. But they also may be seen as weapons to be deployed to liberate black women from the drudgery of domestic labor.

A master printmaker, Cole is renowned for his use of the iron scorch to produce intricate, overlapping patterns. In 1991, after more than a decade of exhibiting his work as an art student, the exhibitions *Household Gods and Domestic Demons* at the Peter Miller Gallery in Chicago and *From Our House to Your House* at the Mint Museum of Art in Charlotte, North Carolina, were his first one-person shows in which Cole fully integrated his works using the iron and ironing board iconography.[5] In these and other exhibitions held through the mid-1990s, Cole seemed to exploit the superficial visual similarities of his work with classical African art and pattern, and critics could not get enough of the perceived exoticism of his work. In their reviews, essays, and interviews, they praised the iconographic similarities between the artist's assemblage sculptures or prints and African art, and made analogies between African rituals and the ritual process Cole used in creating sculptures from found objects. The art critic Grace Glueck of the *New York Times*, for example, referred to how his works "suggest a cluster of African tribal shields."[6] Yet, as he admitted in a 1997 interview, "The closest I've been to Africa is Harlem."[7]

It wasn't until 1996 that Cole shifted the focus of the iron/ironing board symbolism to adhere more directly to the visual similarities between the shape and pattern of the scorch and the slave ship icon. That year, he combined his trademark scorching technique with the traditional medium of woodcut to produce the monumental fifty- by ninety-five-inch print *Stowage*, which was based on a plan of a slave ship that he remembered from a book he had as a child (fig. 8.3). To print this work, Cole collaborated with Maurice Sanchez and James Miller at Derriere L'Etoile Studios in New York. Because of the combination of elements that made up the wooden printing block, the artist had to devise a new printing technology: he cut holes in the oversize wooden planks that compose the printing block and inserted twelve different irons. Each iron "face," highlighted by a circle, suggests a different African ethnic group, such as the Mandingo, Fullah, or Igbo, for instance, whose members might have been forced into the hold of a slave ship. The enormous central plank of the printing block was cut to accommodate the ironing board. The dots that make up the patterned surface of the ironing board refer back to the iron faces surrounding it. Cole describes his choice of the iron and ironing board in *Stowage*:

> These symbols have been recognized by a lot of people. It looks like a slave ship. It looks like a mask, whether it's African, Native American, Tibetan. A triangle will always make a face, and people recognize that. I think this print will definitely force the idea of these objects as symbols in a highly graphic form. The

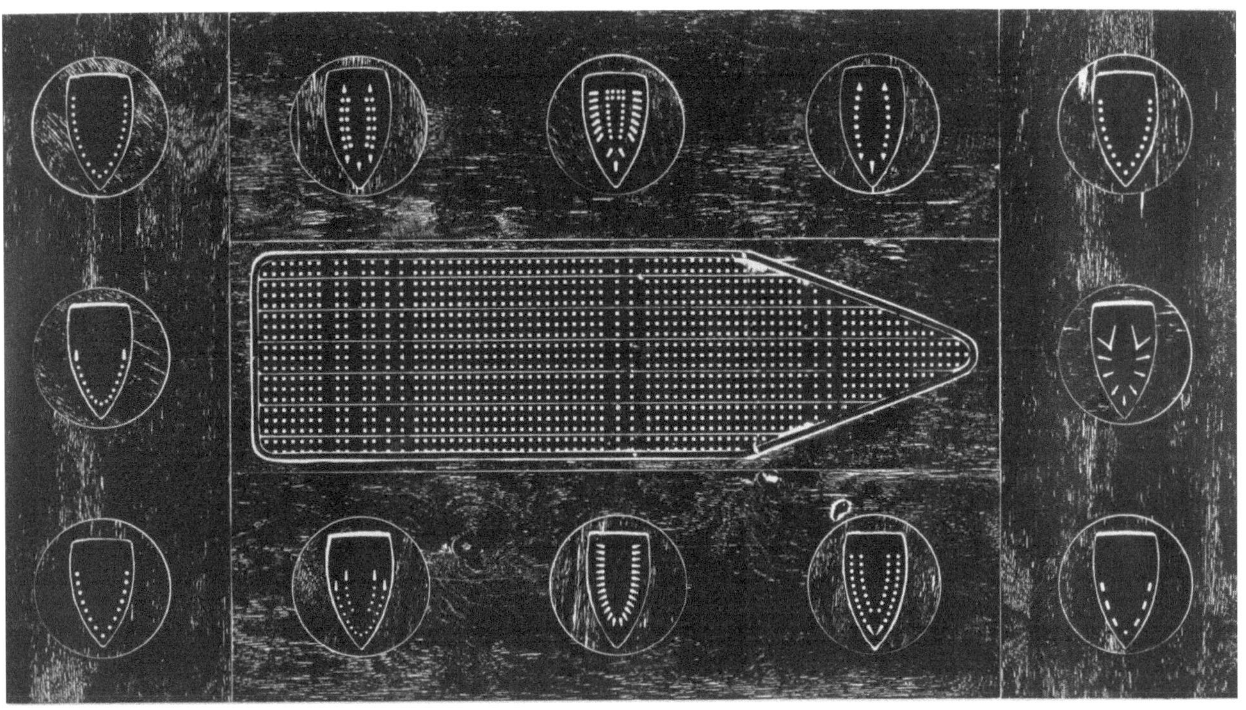

8.3
Willie Cole, *Stowage*, 1997, woodblock
composition, 49 9/16 × 95 1/16 inches.

patterns in an ironing board are not normally seen as little cubbies. People will
ponder. And the title—*Stowage*—will push them in a direction.[8]

In *Stowage*, pattern, geometry, and shape, together with a suggestive title, provide
meaning and metaphor for the work.[9]

In *Stowage*, the meaning of the scorch more emphatically refers to the torturous branding of Africans prior to boarding slave ships to mark them for their owners. If we recall that *Description of a Slave Ship* was most frequently reproduced
as a woodblock print, then Cole's *Stowage*, consciously produced in the woodcut
medium, is a nod, if not homage, to the slave ship icon in its medium as well.[10] Cole
explains that fact in an interview with Ned Oldham in 1998:

> There's a piece called *Stowage*, a large print. I viewed it with David [Moos] and a
> collector he knows. And this collector has no image in his mind of the image that
> inspired the piece—and a lot of people don't—all he saw was an ironing board
> with irons around it. But when I made the piece, I saw something completely
> different. And that incident helped me to realize that if you don't already have
> the image in your mind, then it won't be put in your mind by the piece. You'll just
> see the objects.[11]

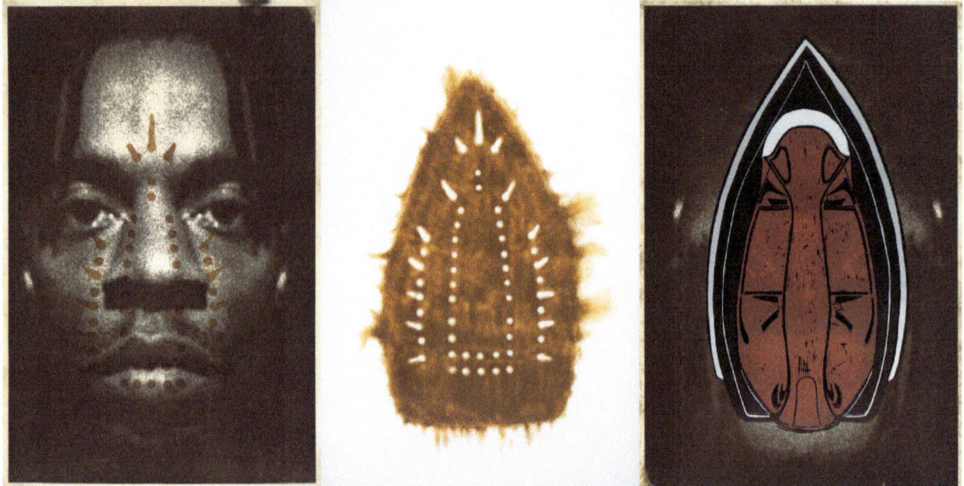

Cole's anecdote is a reminder that his works possess greater underlying meanings that are often tied to images evocative of both historical and contemporary moments, for viewers to decipher amid the patterns, shapes, and arrangements of iron scorches and ironing boards.

In later works, such as *Unmasked Journey* (1999), Cole continues to use the horizontal ironing board to stand in for the slave ship icon. This composition combines wax, a metal ironing board, and paper on an oversized scorched canvas. The outline of the continental United States is placed above the ironing board/slave ship on the picture plane, an outline of the continent of Africa below, quite obviously suggesting the Middle Passage.

In another work from 1999, the triptych *Man, Spirit, Mask*, Cole once again showcases his mastery of printmaking, using a different printing technique for each panel (fig. 8.4). The first panel, "Man," embosses a photo etching of the artist with scorch marks from the steam holes of an iron that resemble an intentional pattern of scarification on his face. The second panel, "Spirit," is a silkscreen on paper of the scorch of the iron that was used to produce the pattern of steam-hole marks on his face. Coating the print with lemon juice and then placing it in a photographic dry-mount press produces its brown color and bleeding edges, suggestive of the spirit of the man. Indeed, in Cole's personal visual lexicon, the scorch of the iron represents the spirit. In the last panel, "Mask," Cole returns to the photo etching of his face, which is turned upside down and layered with a photograph of the iron taken from above, to produce a masklike appearance. All in all, the three images together present a man who is possessed by a spirit through ritual practice involving a mask as the mediator for the spirit. Like *Stowage*, this work was produced in a limited edition and has been collected by prominent museums, notably on American college and university campuses, where it is frequently shown as an example of innovative printing techniques and an expression of cultural identity. While the print medium lends itself to the contemporary marketing strategy of limited editions, it also points to the commercial side of the art world and the brand of populism that some artists have refused, such as Mary Evans in her one-off, site-specific installations (see chapter 6). But given the historical reference of the slave ship icon, Cole's limited editions instead invoke the multiples that were necessarily part of disseminating this popular political print in its original eighteenth-century context.

MARIANETTA PORTER

In 1999, the Michigan-based artist Marianetta Porter (b. 1953) made a series of three assemblage sculptures using antique wooden ironing boards, titled *Slaver, No Time to Die*, and *Aunt Hagar's Child* (fig. 8.5).[12] These works are part of a larger, ongoing series in which she contrasts artifacts of restraint with stories of African American resistance. The impetus for this series was, in part, Porter's first visit to Ghana, in 1995, to study textile design.[13] At the culmination of her stay, Porter spent two days touring the slave castles of Cape Coast and Elmina, an experience that led her to study intensely the historical documents and visual resources of slavery upon her return to the United States. In Porter's experience, the history of African American resistance to slavery had been hidden from popular narratives and left out of the personal stories told even within her own family. Coming of age in the South in the late 1950s and early 1960s, Porter was not taught about slavery in the schools she attended, at least not from the perspective of the enslaved.[14] The residue

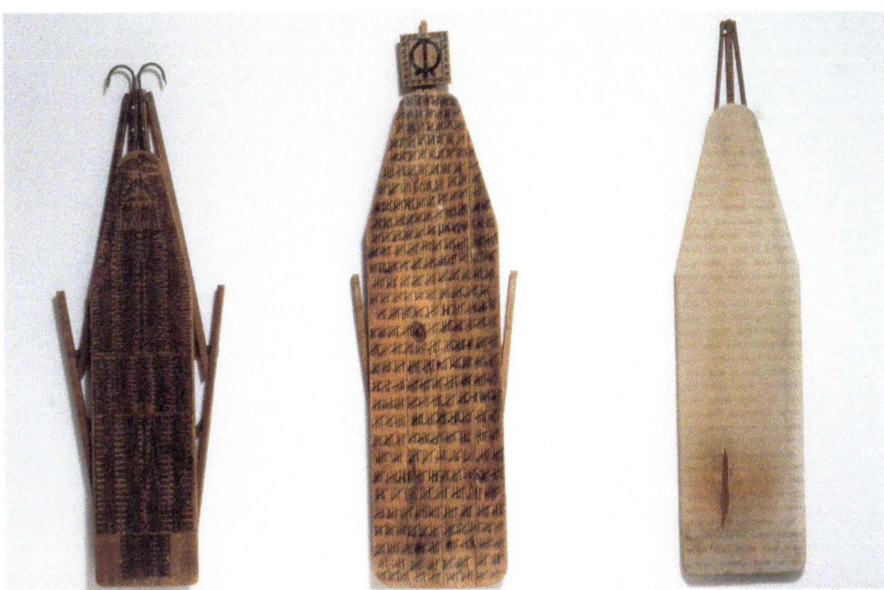

of slavery continued to haunt the Southern landscape, visible to Porter in the legacy of Jim Crow (separate "colored" and "white" drinking fountains, for example) and in the ongoing system of sharecropping that she witnessed during summer visits to her grandparents' home in South Carolina. Her sculpture *Sharecropper's Song* is inspired by that history, a miniature, indigo-dyed woven bag, reminiscent of the kind sharecroppers might drag alongside themselves as they harvest the crops. In her family, the subject of slavery was still taboo and only broached with the greatest reluctance, shrouded by the shadow of shame.

During the course of her research, Porter encountered for the first time an illustration of the slave ship icon in a textbook. With it were other historical illustrations of devices of restraint—iron muzzles, shackles, and intricate contraptions engineered to punish and deter runaway slaves (fig. 8.6). Porter confessed that she actually found "a lot of those artifacts beautiful, in terms of their form." "You are seduced by the beauty of the piece, the craftsmanship," she elaborated. "Then almost secondarily, you are reminded that this was used to hurt someone or to kill something."[15] Similarly, her initial response to the slave ship icon was one that expressed on the surface a fascination with the design, and only after a concern for the underlying, deeper meaning. Porter explains:

> I was really drawn to the diagram as a pattern. If you see it from a distance, you don't see the figures. You see the pattern first. That's how we visualize things. We make sense of the world by seeing a pattern and then putting that pattern into some kind of cohesive structure that then has meaning for us. I was really drawn to the fact that from a distance you see this beautiful pattern and as you get up close to it, you realize, oh, those are figures, and they're black figures, and they're crunched together. I was interested in the various levels of reading that pattern and then the history behind it.[16]

As it did with Willie Cole, Porter's attraction to the pattern and shape of the slave ship icon led her to the ironing board, which she chose as the central platform for the series of three sculptures. Preferring to work with artifacts and found objects, she sought out antique ironing boards in flea markets and in secondhand stores. Describing her process, Porter notes, "I like to work with found objects because they have a history—their own memory embedded in them in a sense." In the case of the ironing boards, she explains that "when you tear off the cover, there are marks that people have made—carved names and initials" belonging to the women who used them.[17] Porter's belief in the inherent ritual power of the found object (derived from its previous use, its "embedded" memory), is shared by other artists who work in assemblage, including Cole and Betye Saar. The past life of the recycled object charges the new work with a ritual power. Thus, rooted in the form and symbolic meaning of the ironing board are the stories of the drudgery to which black women were subjected, and their resistance against it.

In Porter's solo exhibition at the University of Michigan Art Gallery in 1999, these sculptures were hung vertically side by side, with the pointed end of the collapsed ironing board at the top. For *Slaver*, the first in the series, Porter treats the

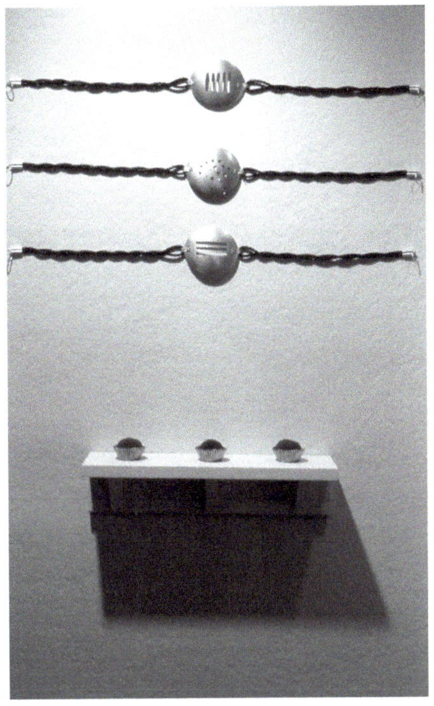

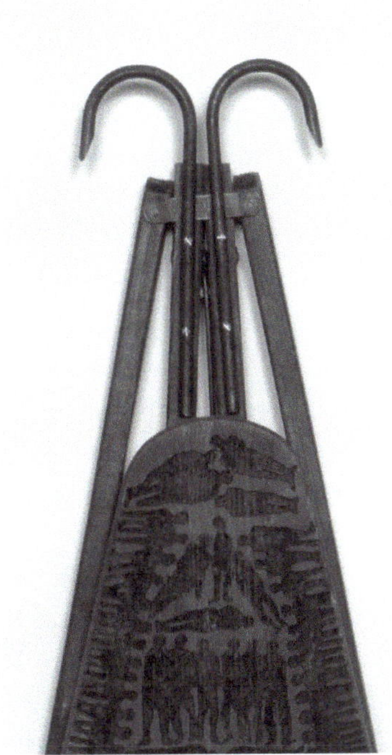

8.6
Marianetta Porter, *Silver Muzzles*, 1999, silver
and leather.

8.7
Marianetta Porter, detail, *Slaver*, 1999, wooden
ironing board and steel, 57 × 19 × 2 inches.

face of the ironing board as the container of restraint that the slave ship represents
(fig. 8.7). On the bare, wooden surface, she draws the pattern of the slave ship icon,
using black to outline the bodies and reddish-brown to shade them. Porter's subtle
use of color—reddish-brown on blond wood—makes the image of the slave ship
faint, almost ghostly, but no less powerful. At the top of the ironing board, two
attached iron meat hooks suggest grappling hooks used to pull bodies out of the
water. The hooks are a palpable reference to those enslaved Africans who chose to
liberate themselves during the Middle Passage by jumping overboard. Using form
to establish the relationship between the slave ship and the ironing board, *Slaver*
initiates a system of meaning that is carried throughout the series. It also sets up a
tension between restraint and release that the two other works continue.

In *No Time to Die*, Porter uses charcoal to inscribe the bundled tally marks for
ticking off time onto the raw surface of the wooden ironing board. The natural burls
in the wood create an underlying layer of pattern that draws the viewer's attention to
certain bundles of time, possible nodal points in African American history. In fact,
burls in wood are indicators, marks, or scars left behind from past wounds, traces of
experience in the life of the tree, the "embedded memory" that Porter has discussed.
The bold, repeating pattern of black tally marks replaces the schematic of the slave
ship icon, yet is still referential. The marks also make a visual allusion to the icon of
the stick figure, sticks as groups of people. If we think of the tally marks for marking

off the past as simultaneously anticipating a future, then *No Time to Die* is clearly about the tension between the past, present, and future. These marks counter the past against the future while referring to the act (in the present) of keeping time. The tally marks also imply a kind of bitter resignation, a deep patience, or a determined optimism within a given confined circumstance. *No Time to Die* pictures a space in which enslaved Africans (or, alternatively, today's black prison population—whom we also saw alluded to in the discussion of Stephen Hayes's *Cash Crop* in chapter 7) imagine and perhaps prepare for their own destinies, bearing in mind all the while that they are barred from the freedom to act as they mark time. Both *No Time to Die* and *Slaver* demonstrate the physical and psychic torture of confinement that the experience of the slave ship (and the prison) constantly enforced on black bodies.

Onto the torn, scorched, and stained cover of the ironing board in *Aunt Hagar's Child* (fig. 8.8) Porter stenciled the names Ruby, Sadie, Bessie, Beulah, and others. What first might appear to be just a random gathering of women's names is instead a compilation of names from a collection of ads for runaway slaves in South Carolina. Porter became interested in the frequency with which the slave women's names took on diminutive forms and meanings. For instance, as Porter explains, "You weren't called Rebecca; you were called Bessie."[18] This pattern of naming, she surmises, was an intentional part of the overarching power system of Southern slavery that maintained psychological and physical control over black women. Such names were assigned to slave women by their masters as reminders of their "subordinate status." *Aunt Hagar's Child* resurrects and reinscribes these names in a powerful way. The stencil design of Porter's names references a popular nineteenth-century typeface used in headstone engravings. For the artist, these are the names of survivors, of the women who persevered, despite the lot given to them. As she explains, the names also presented a surprising personal connection. "When I had the lists compiled [I realized] these were names of my aunts, my grandmother, their friends, people that I could put faces to today.... This was my family."[19] *Aunt Hagar's Child* is a veritable roll call of the significant women in the artist's life.

The title, *Aunt Hagar's Child*, refers to something that Porter's mother used to say when it was time for her to come in and wash up from playing in the red earth of South Carolina: "Hurry in here before you look like Aunt Hagar's child," referring to the biblical figure Hagar from the book of Genesis, an Egyptian slave who was cast out into the desert with her son Ishmael by her Hebrew master Sarah.[20] Many enslaved people in the United States identified with Hagar's plight during the eighteenth and nineteenth centuries. In illustrations and in sculpture, she is often depicted as determined and resilient, yet weathered by not only the harsh elements but also by her fate. The noted nineteenth-century Native American and African American sculptor Edmonia Lewis (1847–1907) chose to depict Hagar as a subject twice, once in 1870 and again in 1875. The surviving sculpture, *Hagar in the Wilderness* (1875), is carved in white marble in the neoclassical style popular at the time and displays a female figure with classical European features and flowing straight hair (fig. 8.9). Standing upright, a forlorn expression on her face and her hands clasped, Lewis's Hagar symbolizes both the trials and tolls that slavery has

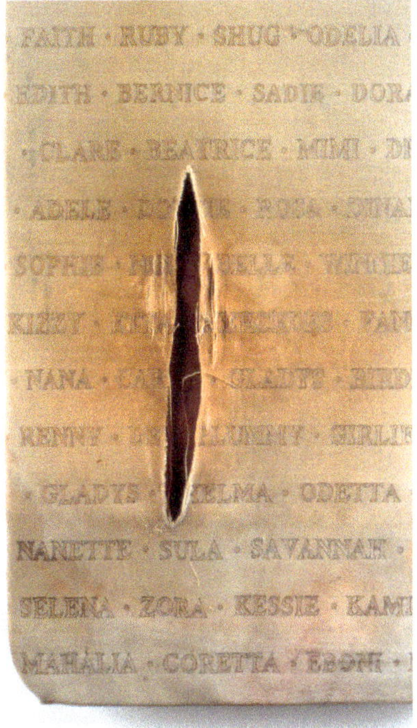

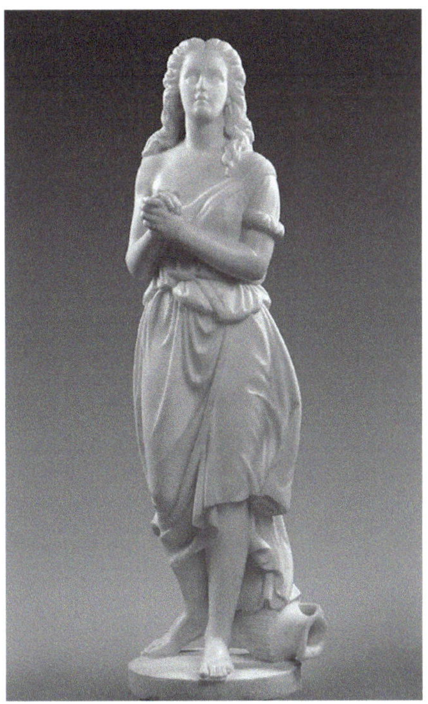

8.8
Marianetta Porter, detail, *Aunt Hagar's Child*,
1999, cotton covered vintage ironing board.

8.9
Edmonia Lewis, *Hagar in the Wilderness*, 1875,
carved marble, 52⁵/₈ × 15¹/₄ × 17¹/₈ inches
(133.6 × 38.8 × 43.4 cm).

presented for African American women and families. A staunch supporter of the
abolitionist and feminist causes of her time, Lewis exhibited her first sculpture of
Hagar in Chicago in 1870, exclaiming, "I have a strong sympathy for all women who
have struggled and suffered."[21] At the turn of the twentieth century, the novelist
Pauline Hopkins (1859–1930) wrote *Hagar's Daughter: A Story of Southern Caste
Prejudice*, which was first serialized in *Colored American Magazine*.[22] By the 1930s,
the slang terms "Aunt Hagar" and "Hagar's Children" were commonly understood
to refer to black people. The folklorist and novelist Zora Neale Hurston even listed
it in her "Glossary of Harlem Slang," published at the end of her short story "Story
in Harlem Slang": "Aunt Hagar—Negro race (also Aunt Hagar's chillun)."[23]

Porter's assemblage sculptures combine folklore, artifacts, personal narratives,
and historical research.[24] Her process is a prime example of the practice of mnemonic aesthetics in contemporary African American art. She describes her work as
"sculptural and mixed media constructions [that] fuse found objects with contemporary forms and idioms to serve as a point of departure for a remembered past."[25]
Porter takes symbols and relics of the past, such as the slave ship icon, the grappling
hook, or the names of slave women, and reinscribes them with new meaning. The
repetitive pattern in the slave ship icon leads her to consider other patterns—among
them patterns of marking time and of naming. With the sensibility of a textile

designer, Porter finds in the ironing board a symbolic marker for the series of three sculptures and a way of suggesting the stories of resistance told by black women. While the ironing board recalls the backbreaking menial labor inherent to the low-paying jobs—often the only jobs—open to black women, it also represents a source of income that fed families, clothed children, and sent them to school. Thus, as we saw in the case of Willie Cole's *Household Guardians*, the ironing board could be perceived as a double-edged tool, one of resistance and at the same time determination. Using the palette of antique ironing boards, Porter imposed new patterns of memory—patterns that humanize, patterns that suggest what enslaved people might have been thinking, patterns that try to retrieve lost histories, patterns of perseverance.

BETYE SAAR

The renowned Los Angeles–based collage and assemblage artist Betye Saar (b. 1926) first came across a reproduction of the slave ship icon in the late 1960s, a period during which the number of books being published on black history and African art and culture was skyrocketing, and she began to collect them voraciously.[26] It was in Langston Hughes and Milton Meltzer's *Black Magic: A Pictorial History of the African American in the Performing Arts* (1967) that Saar was first struck by the slave ship icon "as a visual pattern" as well as by how it seemed to express the "pain of the Diaspora."[27] At around the same time, Saar became immersed in creating the mystical style that is now associated with her collages and assemblage sculptures, works of art that resonate with spiritual and ancestral might. Incorporating symbolic forms with found objects and painting, Saar developed a ritualistic art practice that has been compared to that of a conjurer. One of her best-known works is *The Liberation of Aunt Jemima* (1972), from her *Workers and Warriors* series (see fig. 5.3), the assemblage of a rifle-toting Aunt Jemima whose torso is made out of a Black Power fist. In other works from this noteworthy series, Saar takes the easily recognizable, derogatory stereotype of Aunt Jemima and empowers her with revolutionary meaning. Saar chose to "recycle" both the image of Aunt Jemima and the slave ship icon "to jab the memory—to remind people of their history."[28] Saar admits there was a political motivation behind these works. Both blacks and whites need to come to grips with the history behind these images, she has expressed, if racism is ever to fade from the American landscape.

Thirty years after she first saw the slave ship icon in *Black Magic*, Saar conceived an entire exhibition with it in mind.[29] The result was the show *Crossings*, which premiered at the Jan Baum Gallery in Los Angeles in 1998. Nearly all the works in the show included a visual reference to that schematic bullet-shaped print. *I'll Bend but I Will Not Break*, for example, incorporates that now familiar stand-in for the slave ship icon, the ironing board. But instead of leaning folded up flat against the wall, as in the work of Willie Cole and Marianetta Porter, Saar opens the ironing board to stand as if in use (fig. 8.10). Two images adhere to the surface of the board: a replica of the original broadsheet image of the slave ship icon and a print of a black woman ironing. As part of her ritual process, Saar actually ironed these images onto the surface of the board using a photo transfer. According to Saar, "There is a lot

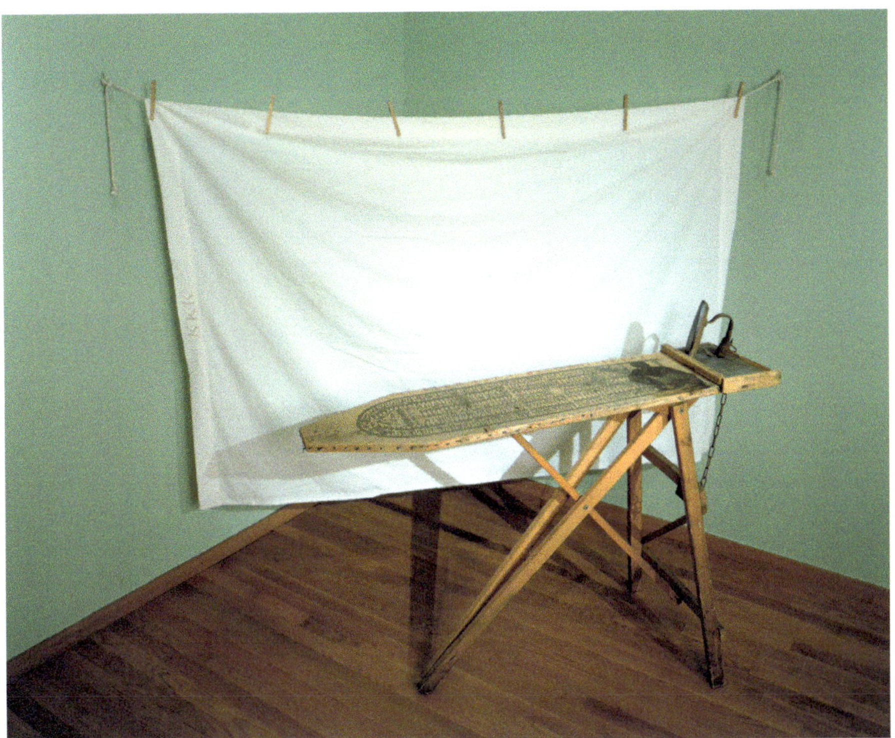

8.10
Betye Saar, *I'll Bend but I Will Not Break*, 1998,
vintage ironing board and iron installation,
33 × 19 × 48 inches.

of symbolism in the process of putting things together that has to do with building
the power of the piece—the accumulation of the spirit of something, both living
and dead."[30] Both the ironing board and the iron chained to it were antique finds
from a flea market, not unlike the vintage ironing boards Porter reclaimed that had
been used, *worked*, by others, or the irons that Cole used to make his impressions.
Behind the ironing board, a crisp white sheet is stretched out on a clothesline, presumably the product of the labor of the black woman pictured in the photo transfer.
On closer inspection, however, the sheet bears three blood-red letters, "KKK," that
taint the supposed purity of its whiteness. "Black women were considered dirt," Saar
explains, "but they kept the white people clean."[31] Placing this tableau in the corner
of a room painted an institutional green reinforces the monotony of domestic labor
and institutional settings both. Furthermore, the ritual involved in ironing recalls
the posture of bending over found among the small black figures in the slave ship
icon, but also among the enslaved picking cotton in the fields. Together with the title
I'll Bend but I Will Not Break, Saar's installation illuminates how these iconic postures support the workaday will to survive.

Other works from the *Crossings* exhibition make further references to posture,
such as the mixed-media painting *Maiden Voyage* (fig. 8.11). The basis of this work

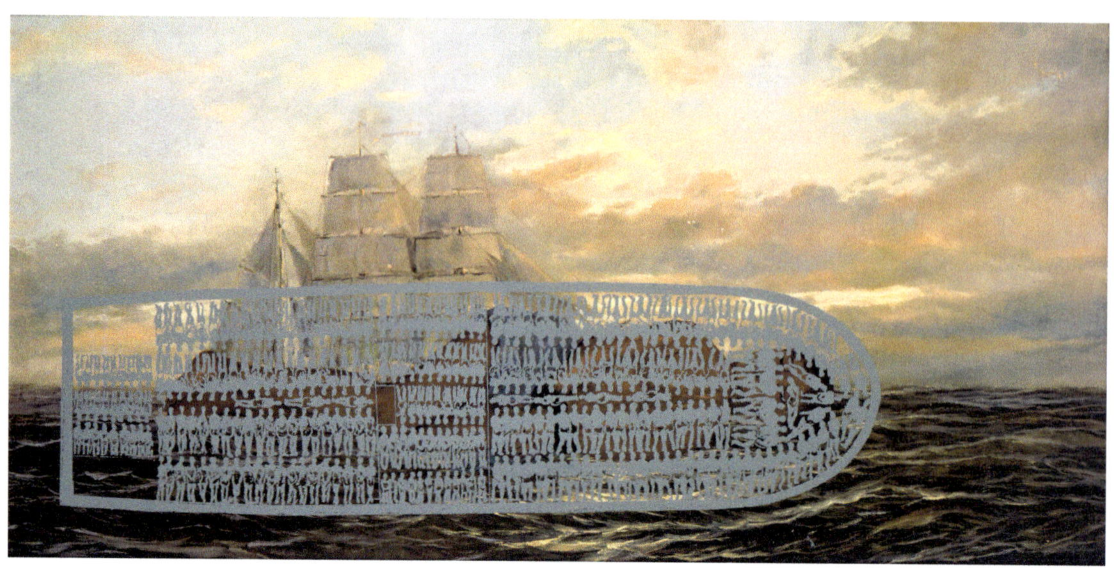

is a commercially manufactured painting of a clipper ship at sea that Saar found in a flea market. Perhaps it reminded her of the vanity paintings commissioned by slave merchants to celebrate successful slaving voyages, such as the painting of *La Marie Séraphique*, discussed in chapter 1 (see fig. 1.7). As oil paintings, they were expensive to commission and served as an overt display of the owner's wealth. Yet the black bodies responsible for producing that wealth were hidden in the hold of the slave ship. Abolitionists working more than 230 years ago likely took some measure of inspiration from those vanity paintings, as the slave ship icon was designed to expose the valuable contents of the hold. With *Maiden Voyage*, Saar exposes the horror masked by the beauty of the ship at sea with a pastel sunset as a backdrop. On top of the image of the ship lies a painted figure of an "African maiden," depicted in a fetal position, her hands bound and tied; on top of the figure of the woman is silk-screened the bullet-shaped slave ship icon. The title of the work, *Maiden Voyage*, is a play on words referring to the birth of the African diaspora in the belly of the slave ship.

Two works on paper that are part of *Crossings* also incorporate the slave ship icon. The mixed-media collage *The Dark Past, the Grey Future* includes both slave ships and canoes, a reference to Saar's mixed African American and Native American heritage. *The Fragility of Smiles (of Strangers Lost at Sea)*, a serigraph on blue rice paper, once again presents the unrelenting figural repetition of the slave ship icon.[32] "The image is a trickster," observes Saar, echoing Marianetta Porter's sentiments. "From a distance it looks beautiful, until you realize that the little patterns are bodies."[33]

In addition to collecting slave ship imagery, Saar also seeks out vintage items that depict African Americans in demeaning and stereotypical ways. By reinvigorating the items through processes of reclamation and reappropriation, in a sense

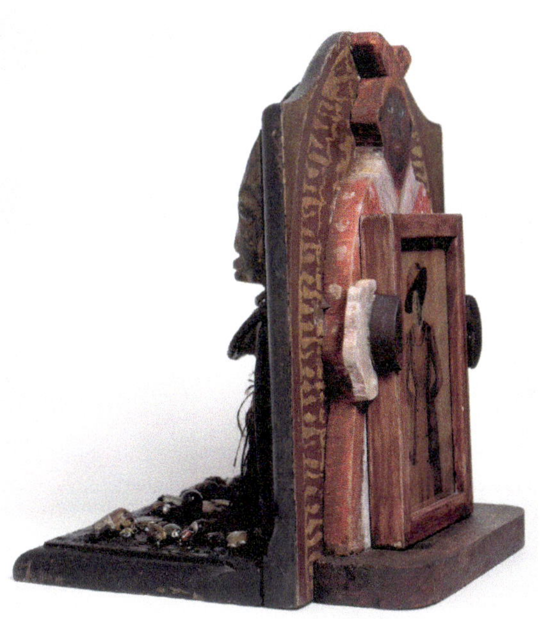
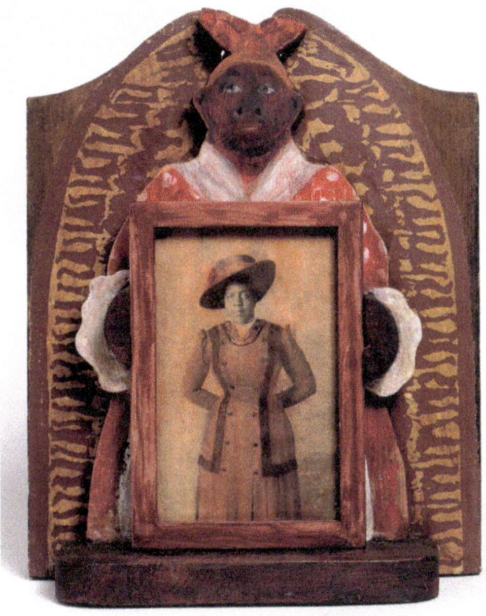
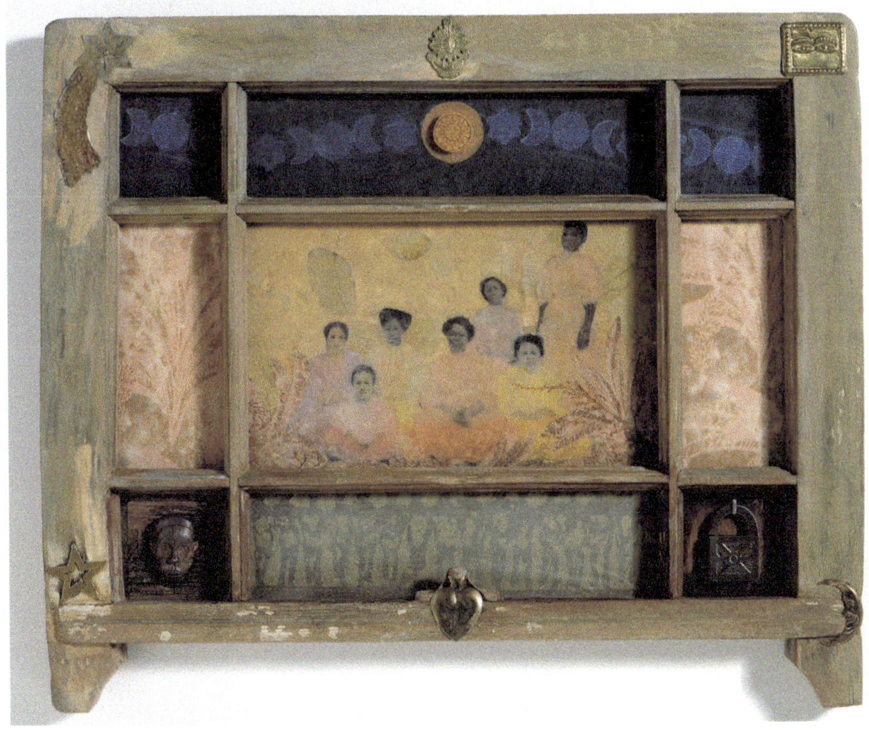

8.12 TOP
Betye Saar, *Migration: Africa to America II*,
2006, mixed media assemblage.

8.13 BOTTOM
Betye Saar, *Yesteryear*, 2006, mixed media
assemblage.

arming them to engage in an anachronistic battle, Saar stakes a claim on a symbolic possession of the past. The importance of these "derogatory images of African Americans, now called Black Collectibles" that Saar began to collect in the late 1960s is their "documentation of how Whites have historically perceived African Americans and how we have been portrayed as caricatures, as objects, as less-than-human."[34] Reclaiming these objects allows her to disempower them, taking them out of circulation as agents of racism. She has enlisted these collectibles and their images in some of her mixed-media assemblages from the *Migrations/Transformations* series (2005–6), which imagine historical journeys of Africans in the Middle Passage to becoming African Americans. In *Migration: Africa to America II* (2006), a two-sided work, a wooden African ancestral figure is placed back to back with an Aunt Jemima figure and sandwiched between the pointed hull of the slave ship icon and a vintage photograph of a nicely dressed black woman (fig. 8.12). In the shape of a bookend, this Janus-faced, mixed-media work combines the symbols and images of the past to ameliorate, in Saar's words, "the struggle of memory against the attraction of forgetting."[35] The Aunt Jemima figure serves as a reminder to the woman in the photograph of the struggles she and her ancestors have overcome in their journey to becoming African Americans.

Saar has repeatedly made use of the Aunt Jemima figure, old photographs, and the imprint of bodies from the slave ship icon, to the point of further embedding in her assemblage process of combining shapes, forms, and objects, a ritualized practice. This aspect of her work, visible in *Migration: Africa to America II* and another work from the *Migrations/Transformations* series, *Yesteryear* (2006) (fig. 8.13), demonstrates how ceremony can be a part of symbolic possession of the past. Saar, like other artists including Cole and Porter who revisit certain key themes in black Atlantic history through the use and reuse of specific symbolic images and gestures, emulates, if not engages in, a ceremonial practice. For example, the mixed-media assemblage *Yesteryear* takes a vintage window frame, like Cole's *Domestic Identity IV* (see fig. 8.1), to juxtapose her familiar mystical lexicon of celestial objects with a miniature African mask, a padlock, a painted hand, and an early twentieth-century photograph of seven black women. The photograph not only rests upon but also rises above the small, yet recognizable imprint of slave bodies excerpted from the slave ship icon. The women in the photograph are awash in a golden hue, presumably emanating from the heavens above, suggesting their triumph over adversity and hope for a transformed future.

Saar, Porter, and Cole effectively used the ironing board or the iron to conjure the shape and pattern of the slave ship icon. Evoking themes of women's domestic work, Middle Passage, carceral traumas, laboring postures, self-determination, and transformation, their works are marked by an aesthetic practice that involves the use of found objects, repetition, and ritual practice. In prints, assemblages, and series, these artists invoke the slave ship icon repeatedly as part of a ceremonial practice defined by a mnemonic aesthetic. Taking on an almost religious connotation, their works and practices prefigure the artists discussed in the next chapter, which probes the spiritual dimension of the slave ship icon in twenty-first-century installation art.

SPIRITS: FROM CHANGÓ TO ICONOCLASM

NEARLY SINCE ITS CONCEPTION in 1788, the slave ship icon has embodied religious meaning. The committee of abolitionists who conceived it consisted of Quakers and radical Christians who found its visual impact an able weapon in their arsenal of images arrayed to win popular support for ending the slave trade. To be sure, in their hands the image was circulated and invoked as a sacred icon. Contemporary artists in the late twentieth century and more recently have recognized its spiritual connotations, too. In works citing religious traditions as diverse as Christianity, Santería, and Buddhism, these artists, including María Magdalena Campos-Pons, Manuel Mendive, Nari Ward, Tom Feelings, and Sanford Biggers, have presented the slave ship icon as an emblem of religious reverence. Notably, each of the artists discussed in this chapter incorporates some element of 3-D installation, conjuring up the slave ship icon's ties to worship, reverence, devotion, and meditation in contemporary art and culture. In generating these spaces, the artists encourage viewers to experience the image of the slave ship in sensorial and emotional ways; by entering these works of art they are encouraged to commune with the past. The artists' three-dimensional installations become necessary spaces for people to come together to meditate on the multiple meanings, lessons, and interpretations told to us by this history.

THE SEVEN POWERS COME BY THE SEA

The multimedia installation and performance artist María Magdalena Campos-Pons was born in the small town of La Vega, a former sugar plantation in the province of Matanzas, Cuba, in 1959, the year that Fidel Castro came to power.[1] Known today for its still potent African culture, which survived the Middle Passage and the terror of forced labor on sugar plantations, Matanzas is home to the largest population of slave descendants in Cuba. Campos-Pons grew up there in a former slave quarters that had been renovated as an apartment. Ironically, while interviewing her mother for the installation *History of a People Who Were Not Heroes* (1994), Campos-Pons discovered that their apartment "was the very place where my great-great-grandpa had lived when he was brought as a slave to Cuba from Nigeria."[2] The installation environment created by the artist was shaped by her family's transgenerational attachment to and experience of the place they called home. Hence, she deployed place memory as an aesthetic strategy, summoning the slave barrack and other architectural symbols of the former sugar plantation to convey her family's historical attachment to Matanzas. More broadly speaking, *History of a People Who Were Not Heroes* acknowledges the personal narratives of Afro-Cubans that have been overlooked by the official historical record and offers up a vital revisionist narrative.

Many of Campos-Pons's early works incorporated photographic portraiture and self-portraiture and were tied to her memories of the place, the people, and the customs she left behind in Cuba. As she remembers, "During the time I've spent in America, I've thought a lot about what Cuba means to me historically, geographically and socially."[3] According to the performance artist and cultural critic Coco Fusco, this type of reflection is not uncommon for artists and intellectuals who fled Cuba in the last fifty or more years, a result in part of the dictatorship of Fidel Castro and isolationism resulting from the long-standing United States economic embargo.[4] Many of these artists, in light of their dislocation from Cuba, began to use installation, performance, and video to articulate the effects of their migration and exile on diasporic identity formation, transcultural religious artistic freedom, and traumatic memory. Fusco's scholarship, moreover, uncovers the ways in which these performance art practices are considered dangerous criminal activity by the government. The subsequent criminalization of performance artists has in turn rendered contemporary performance art necessarily clandestine and transgressive, and led to technological innovations that have allowed the work to thrive under a state of censorship. In the case of Campos-Pons, the threads of meaning that run through her work produced in the United States recall family (especially the female members of her family), Santería rituals (a syncretic combination of New World Yoruba, Catholic, and indigenous religious traditions), and her Afro-Cuban roots, which she traces to Nigeria through the transatlantic slave trade.

Campos-Pons's installation *The Seven Powers Come by the Sea* was conceived for the 1992 exhibition *Ways to See: New Art from Massachusetts* at the Institute for Contemporary Art in Boston and acquired by the Seattle Art Museum in 1994 (fig. 9.1). This large-scale work poignantly comments on the remembered history of the Middle Passage, Yoruba religious practices in the Caribbean, and contemporary African diasporic identity formation. Her installation presents seven large wooden tablets with black stick figures carved into them, in patterns resembling the figures from the slave ship icon. The bottom of each wooden tablet (or ship) is labeled with the name of a Yoruba orisha, or deity, brought to the Caribbean and the Americas by Africans in the Middle Passage. As the art historian Robert Farris Thompson describes:

> The Yoruba remain the Yoruba precisely because their culture provides them with ample philosophic means for comprehending, and ultimately transcending, the powers that periodically threaten to dissolve them. That their religion and their art withstood the horrors of the Middle Passage and firmly established themselves in the Americas (New York City, Miami, Havana, Matanzas, Recife, Bahia, Rio de Janeiro) as the slave trade effected a Yoruba diaspora—reflects the triumph of an inexorable communal will.[5]

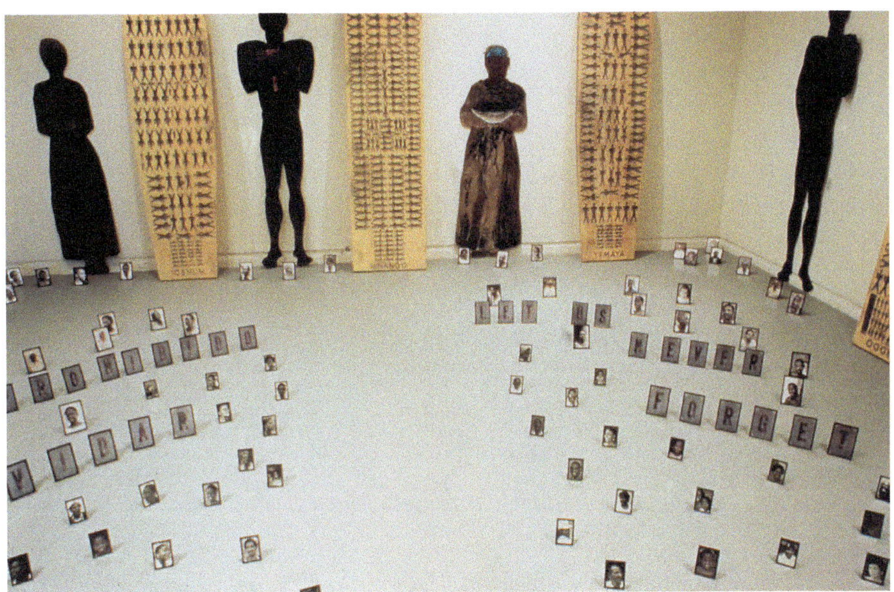

9.1
María Magdalena Campos Pons, installation
view, *The Seven Powers Come by the Sea*, 1992,
mixed media.

Traveling by historical patterns of capture during the slave trade, the Yoruba deities came to Cuba from the city-states of Oyo and Ketu in Yorubaland, which is in present-day Nigeria.[6] The pantheon of orishas that are worshiped today in the Americas was influenced by the migration of different Yoruba-practicing groups within West Africa and in the transatlantic slave trade. The seven major orishas observed in Cuba are Changó, Yemayá, Ogún, Obàtálá, Eshu, Oshun, and Osayin. "Especially in Cuba and Brazil," explains Thompson, "New World Yoruba were introduced to the cult of Roman Catholic saints, learned their attributes, and worked out a series of parallelisms linking Christian figures and powers to the forces of their ancient deities."[7] Thus, in Cuba, Changó is often associated with the Catholic Saint Barbara, and Oshun is linked with the Virgin Mary. These "seven powers" were incorporated into the creolized religion of Santería practiced in Cuba among other New World African diaspora communities. The artist Charo Oquet's acrylic-on-canvas painting, *The Two Queens—Elizabeth I and Yemayá* (1997), exposes the links between Britain's early involvement in the slave trade, Christianity, and the creation of African-inspired saints in New World practices of Santería (fig. 9.2). In *Barco Negrero (Slave Ship)* (1976), Manuel Mendive (b. 1944) uses the icons of Santería in his longitudinal view of a Spanish slave ship at sea with its human cargo exposed (fig. 9.3). In this vibrantly detailed work, Mendive also paints white sailors on the deck, one of whom, standing at the bow, looks over the edge to see a captive—one of the black figures—tumbling into the sea. Other black figures in the hold below are portrayed in prone positions or, if upright, barely erect.

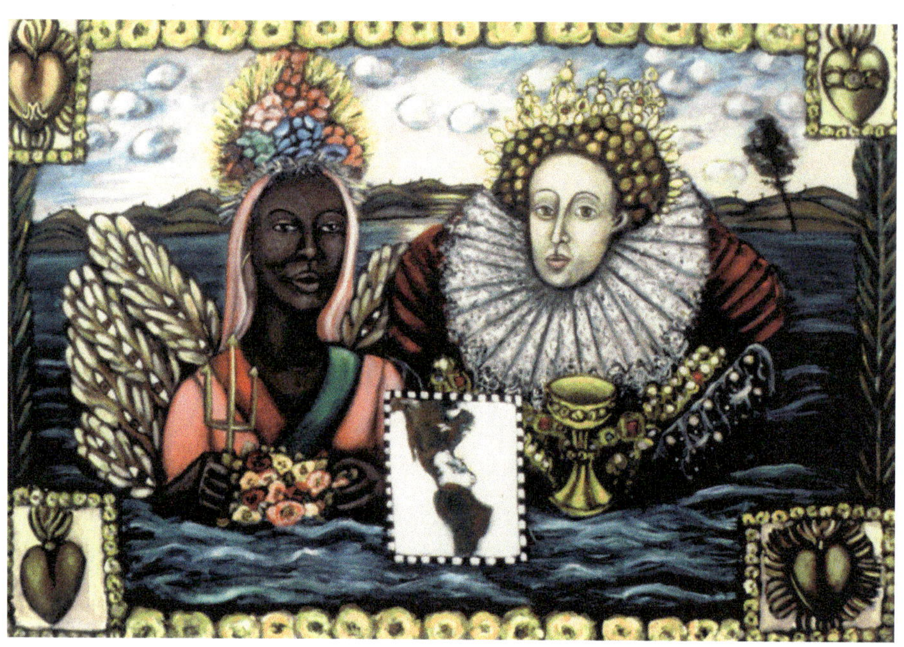

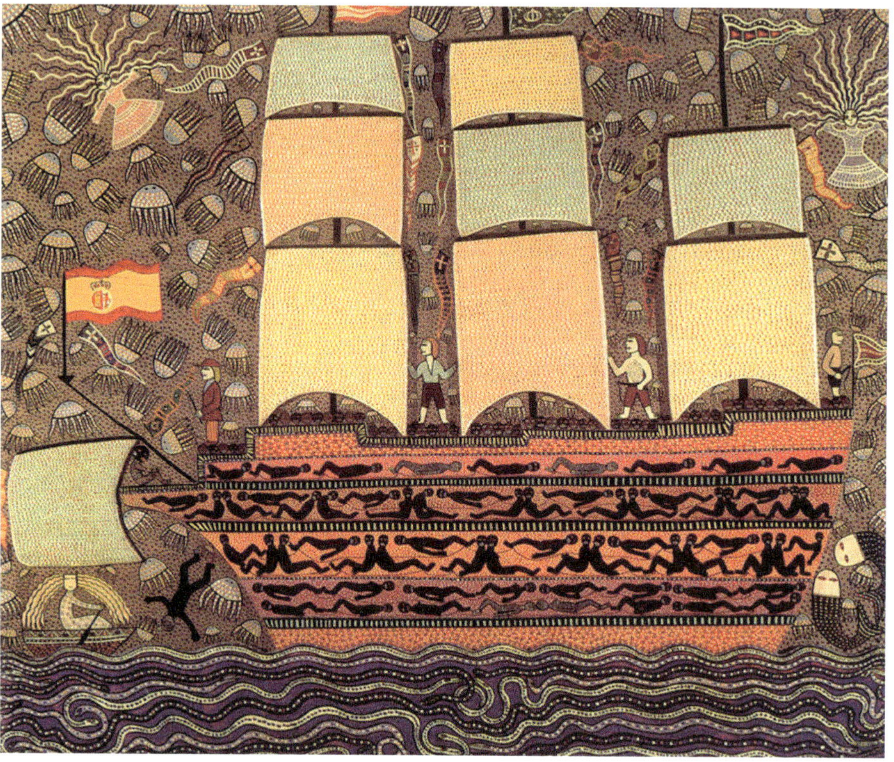

9.2 TOP
Charo Oquet, *The Two Queens — Elizabeth I and Yomayá*, 1997, acrylic on canvas.

9.3 BOTTOM
Manuel Mendive, *Barco Negrero*, 1976, acrylic on canvas.

Campos-Pons has described how she came to incorporate the slave ship icon into *The Seven Powers Come by the Sea*:

> When I did this work, I found an illustration of the bottom of slave ships. I was interested in how the bodies of the slaves were distributed in the ship. It's poignant—that illustration of the actual bottom of the ship—there is such beauty in that awful thing. It was like looking at a computer hardchip. It's mathematically distributed, absolutely, with a total sense of saving space [on the part of the slave owners]—more money with little room. And I was struck with that, but also I was struck with the pattern. And this was why I decided to do the carving in the plank with this pattern.[8]

In 2010 *The Seven Powers Come by the Sea* was exhibited at the Indianapolis Museum of Art for Campos-Pons's midcareer retrospective, *Everything Is Separated by Water*. Leaning vertically against the wall, the wooden tablets resemble gravestones, reminders of the catastrophic loss of life in the Middle Passage, but they also take on the shape of gothic church windows. Between each of them are seven life-size silhouettes, both male and female, that correspond to the seven Yoruba orishas whose names are carved at the bottom of each wooden plank. In Yoruba religion, personal orishas guide, nourish, and protect the believer. Specific colors, objects, and character traits symbolize each orisha. In the installation, Campos-Pons has given each figure an offering that symbolizes his or her unique character trait. At the center is Changó, the powerful thunder god of passion and creativity, who is symbolized by the lightning-charged double ax and red, the color of pomegranates. The silhouettes of the orishas add human form, as if the artist had put a magnifying glass over the black stick figures, yet they also embody the spiritual powers seen as protectors of the enslaved Africans who made it to Cuba.

The silhouetted figures also mediate between past and present, symbolizing memory's ability to straddle both worlds, both times, and the sustaining force of spiritual belief. Representing the protective forces of the orishas, these silhouetted figures watch over the artist's African descendants from Cuba and North America, who are pictured in the black-and-white photographs arranged on the floor as if they are floating across the sea. Numbering one hundred in all, the photos are arranged in clusters at the feet of each orisha and in two large groups marked by the framed letters that spell out "Let Us Never Forget" on one side of the space, repeated in Spanish, "*Prohibido Olvidar*," on the other (see fig. 9.1).

Language is an important part of Campos-Pons's oeuvre and is characteristic of her works conceived with postmodernist practices. Upon her arrival in the United States in 1991, her works began to incorporate text in both English and Spanish. In her installations, language is both visual and narrative. It doubles the meaning of the work, adding a textual layer to its visual understanding. A bilingual conversation takes place that emphasizes another form of double voicing. As Campos-Pons put it, "When I exhibit in North America, this is the audience [primarily English-speaking] that I am interested in reaching. I play with language visually but I also use it as an exact means of communication. Home is here and there—so I use

Spanish and English in my work; I use the African language too—that is home for me."[9] It is no coincidence that *The Seven Powers Come by the Sea* was conceived just a year after Campos-Pons migrated to the United States from Cuba. In addition to the Middle Passage, this work recalls other, more recent migrations of diasporic Africans from the Caribbean, specifically those made by Cubans following the rise of Castro in 1959 and decades later in the 1980s. It also alludes more generally to the unresolved trauma of exile in the successive waves of African diasporic migration from the Caribbean (notably Haiti and the Dominican Republic) to North America for political reasons or following a natural disaster.

The Afro-Caribbean religion Santería, with its blending of Yoruba and Roman Catholic traditions, has been a formative influence on the work of Campos-Pons, guiding the creation of the form and content as well as the bodily experience of the installation. Her understanding of the centrality of the body to the ritual practices of Santería is crucial to the power of her installations. As the art historian Kellie Jones explains, "If we mediate on an immediate history of installation art (one dating from the 1970s) we find that its activation of 'place,' on both the cerebral and corporeal planes, was an activation of context. Through installation, artists could create a space of intentionality."[10] Installation art invites viewer interaction with the objects in the 3-D space. It thus relies on an interactive form of place memory that summons the kinesthetic relationship of the viewer to the objects in the installation as well as the viewer's experience of the installation environment. As a postmodernist strategy of deconstruction, artists often create multimedia installations to interrogate social, cultural, and political juxtapositions.

But Santería's hold on the body in ritual is also integral to why Campos-Pons began to fold performance art into her installations. The curator Julia Herzberg argues:

> The subject of the body is central in Campos's explorations, linking her to other contemporary women artists who also use their own body and/or the female body in general as a landscape upon which memory is resuscitated, ancestral linkages are established, creation and survival are affirmed, and individual and collective histories are inscribed.[11]

For the opening of *The Seven Powers Come by the Sea* at the Institute of Contemporary Art in Boston, Campos-Pons decided to do a spontaneous performance (fig. 9.4). "It was a very large opening, maybe three thousand people, and I just walked through this many people and stood in the center of my installation."[12] She stood barefoot, wearing a long white dress gathered at the waist. The style of the dress resembled the simple garments worn by Cuban slave women, but it also referenced a type of dress worn in Santería initiation ceremonies. "I was there forty-five minutes without saying a word," she recalled. "It was very charged."[13] White numbers were painted on the smooth brown skin of the artist's neck and arms. These numbers consolidated many aspects of the historical omissions she aimed to illuminate in her installation and referred back to her depictions of the slave ship icon—to the business of the slave trade, the number of lives lost or transplanted, the space

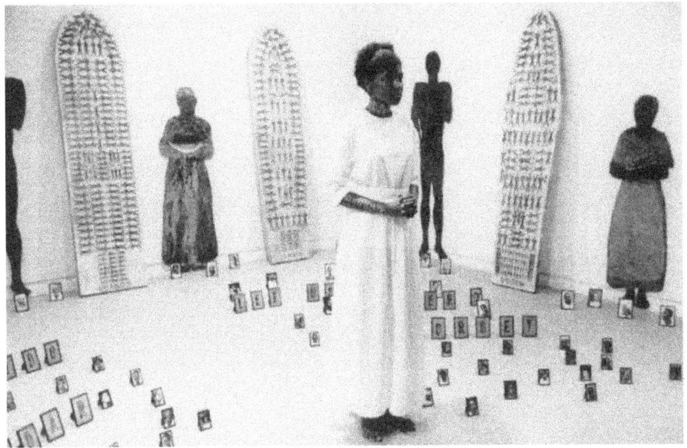

9.4
María Magdalena Campos Pons, photo-
documentation of performance, the
Seven Powers Come by the Sea, Institute
of Contemporary Art, Boston, 1992.

between decks, the closeness of bodies, the profits earned, the days of waiting, the anonymity of the loss.[14] The curator Sally Berger has described the performances of Campos-Pons as having "the intensity equal to that of a shamanic trance."[15]

Together, the arrangement of the elements of the installation—the large wooden planks, the silhouette figures, and the photographs—reference an altar. This grouping is a conscious act on the part of the artist, stemming from her lived experience of the creolized ceremonial ties of altar making and ancestor worship that bind Santería and its African and European cousins. "The altar appears as an art form throughout history," explains curator Berger, "but its contemporary manifestations are most apparent in the work of artists referencing their roots in Latino and Caribbean cultures that are a fusion of Spanish, African, and indigenous elements."[16] For example, the Afro-Chinese photographer and installation artist Albert Chong (b. 1958) constructs ceremonial altars out of chairs and ritual objects in his *Ancestral Thrones* series. Works such as his 1987 *Throne for the Ancestors* are first conceived in a ritual setting and then photographed, producing two separate but related works of art (fig. 9.5). Chong's thrones envision a space that serves a dual purpose: as a seat for the ancestors and as an altar for offerings. The altar form is repeated in other works by Campos-Pons, such as the critically acclaimed multimedia installation *Softly Spoken with Mama*, on view at the Museum of Modern Art New Projects gallery in 1997, where it served both a design and a memorial function.

Observe how in *The Seven Powers Come by the Sea*, Campos-Pons represents the slave ship icon not just once, but seven times, each time renaming it with a different Yoruba deity, each time reconfiguring the arrangement of the black figures carved into the wood. Her choice to repeat the iconic form of the slave ship more than once works on many different levels. It points to the magnitude of the slave trade by referencing the multiple human cargos stowed in ships that traveled the Middle Passage as well as the vast number of ships engaged in the industry. Its relentless, repetitive schematic form functions as a mnemonic device to imbed the immensity of the catastrophic legacy of the slave trade into the viewer's psyche, producing

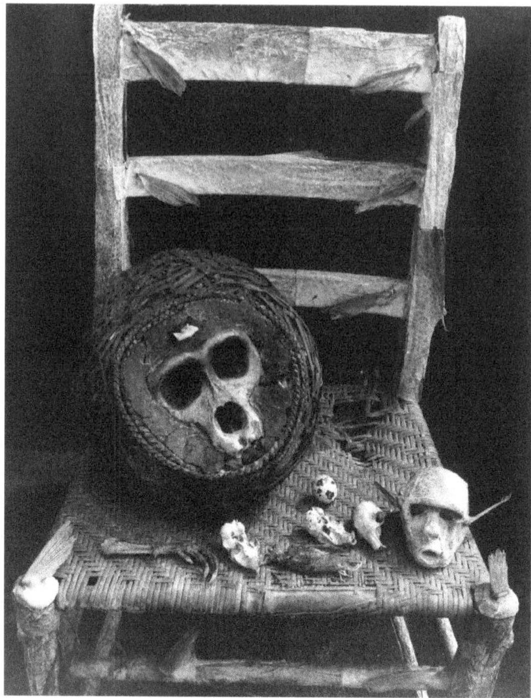

9.5
Albert Chong, *Throne for the Ancestors*, 1987, gelatin silver print, 1996–98, 23 ³/₄ × 19 ³/₈ inches.

a sense of haunting familiarity. Still, the seven tablets and figures reinforce the capacity of religious and cultural practices to flourish and sustain life in Cuba and other societies in the Caribbean and the Americas where Santería is practiced.

The Seven Powers Come by the Sea was not Campos-Pons's first installation to rely heavily on the slave ship icon as its primary symbol. Instead, *The Seven Powers Come by the Sea* draws on an earlier work, *Tra…*, conceived in Canada while Campos-Pons was a visiting artist at the Banff Center for the Arts in Alberta (1990–91) (fig. 9.6). At the Fourth Havana Biennial in 1991, where *Tra…* was exhibited at the National Museum of Fine Arts, the work was called "one of the most effective and succinct statements" to address the biennial's theme, *Challenge to Colonization*.[17] The title refers both to the Spanish word *travesía* ("crossing" in English) and metaphorically to the Middle Passage; it also makes reference to other Spanish words that begin with "*tra*," such as *trata* (trade) and *tragedia* (tragedy). Combining photographic portraits printed on canvas of three generations of Afro-Cubans from Matanzas, their testimonies etched in marble, the installation emphasizes the lingering legacies of slavery in Cuba, especially for people of African descent. As a symbolic measure, the photographs are collaged in the shape of the letter *T*, which also could be read as a cross. Stressing the corporeal experience of racism, exclusion, and marginalization, the artist's haunting self-portrait adorns her rendering of a pulsating heart and the main arteries that connect the flow of blood throughout the body. Campos-Pons draws connections between the personal stories of the people in the photographs and to the broader legacy of transatlantic slavery by using a representation of the slave ship icon, repeated three times (a reference to the three

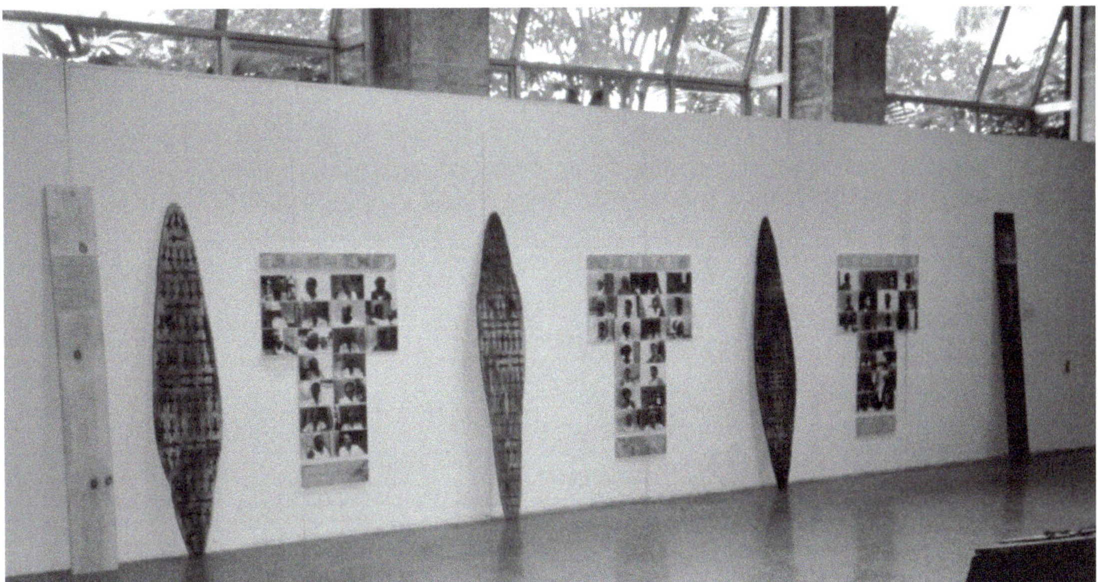

generations of the Matanzas Afro-Cubans portrayed as well as to the triangular trade, the transatlantic slaving route that took as its vertices Europe, Africa, and the Americas) as life-size wooden planks carved with simple black stick figures. Also connecting *Tra...* and *The Seven Powers Come by the Sea* is Campos-Pons's use of photography to recall ancestral memories—in particular the use of portraits, sometimes even of people unknown to the artist. By enlarging the slave ship icon and the corresponding *T*-shaped collages of portraits the artist uses a mnemonic aesthetic to memorialize if not monumentalize the lingering echoes of the slave trade in the Caribbean. For her, the slave ship icon is a potent source for making claims for the survival and transformation of Yoruba religious beliefs in Cuba and the Americas. Her installations centered on the unforgettable schematic diagram convey a sense of spiritual and familial will, transformation, and renewal.

AMAZING GRACE

In 1993, the Studio Museum in Harlem's annual artists-in-residence exhibition included a large-scale installation by the Jamaican-born artist Nari Ward (b. 1963). Titled *Amazing Grace*, the work included more than three hundred abandoned baby carriages collected by the artist in and around the Harlem neighborhood during his one-year residency (fig. 9.7). He installed them in a defunct firehouse not far from the museum in a curved shape that referenced the slave ship icon. For the artist, the abandonment of these vessels of transport, meant to carry the most precious form of life, presented a huge conundrum: Why had they been left behind? Where were the children that they once carried? To what purpose might they be put? An artist accustomed to using found objects and urban detritus in his sculptures, Ward was keenly aware of the raging crack epidemic and AIDS crisis that had hollowed out much of the Harlem community, producing growing numbers of homeless people. The baby carriages, instead of carrying babies, he observed, were being used by the homeless population to transport, store, and protect their few worldly goods.

Installed in the firehouse, the baby carriages were pushed close together and often stacked upon each other. Old fire hoses, used to tie the carriages together, helped to create the curvaceous shape, crisscrossing and winding across the floor, as did the shape of the firehouse itself. "The space was long and narrow, and that's how the shape evolved," Ward explains. To Ward, the cramped and crowded baby carriages "looked like a slave ship," referring to the slave ship icon. Through this haunting shape from history, the artist found a way to honor the lost souls, to offer a way to redemption.

Ward added a sound element to the installation, Mahalia Jackson's rendition of the spiritual "Amazing Grace" wafting throughout the otherwise hollow, cavernous space. Today, a popular spiritual sung in African American congregations, this song was originally penned by a once notorious slave ship captain, Reverend John Newton, who later reformed and joined the church. Ward's exhibition received strong reviews, and the work was later installed in five other venues before being purchased by a collector. In 2013, *Amazing Grace* was reinstalled at the New Museum, and again its reception was tremendous. By this time, it was widely known in scholarly circles that "Amazing Grace" had been written by a former slave trader, and a

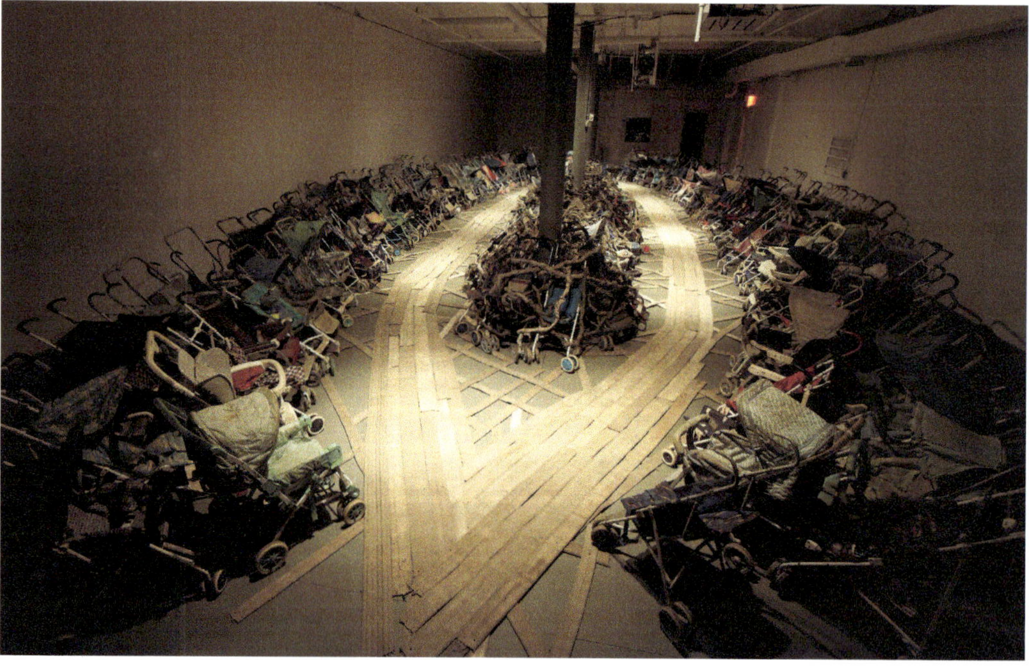

9.7
Nari Ward, *Amazing Grace*, 1993, 310 baby strollers and fire hoses, dimensions variable, installation view, New Museum of Contemporary Art, 2013.

Broadway musical based on the book *Amazing Grace* was in the works with Eugene Lee, who designed the set for Amiri Baraka's *Slave Ship*, as production designer (see fig. 5.7).[18]

"A THEOLOGY OF REMEMBRANCE"

A few days before Christmas in 2000, a stained-glass rose window with an image of the slave ship icon was dedicated to mark the fiftieth anniversary of the New Mount Pilgrim Missionary Baptist Church, an African American congregation in the West Garfield Park neighborhood of Chicago's West Side (fig. 9.8). The commanding twenty-five-foot-diameter rose window stands out amid the nineteenth-century European biblical scenes favored by the Irish American parishioners who formerly occupied the Romanesque revival building before New Mount Pilgrim purchased it from the Catholic Archdiocese of Chicago in 1993. Installed on the east side of the building, the morning sunlight illuminates the somber shades of blue and gray that color the central figure of the rose window: an African man with outstretched arms whose torso is filled with the crowded central section of the slave ship icon. With chains descending from his outstretched arms and angular pieces of stained glass forming currents of water, he seems to be pushing up, propelling his body through

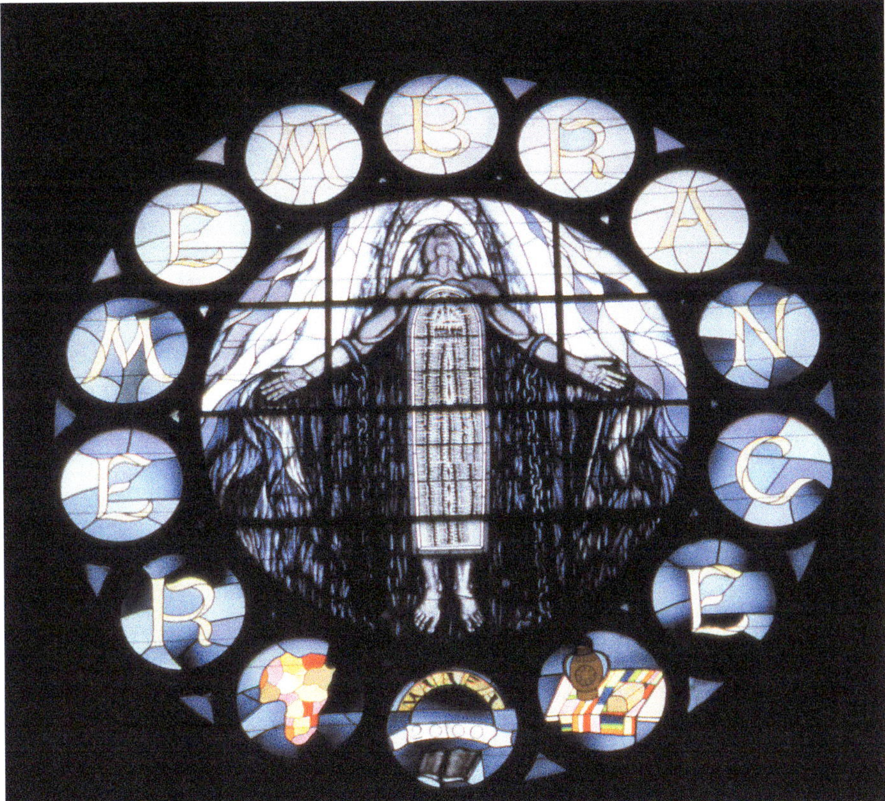

9.8

Maafa Remembrance Rose Window, New Mount Pilgrim Missionary Baptist Church, West Garfield Park, Chicago, 2000, 25 feet diameter.

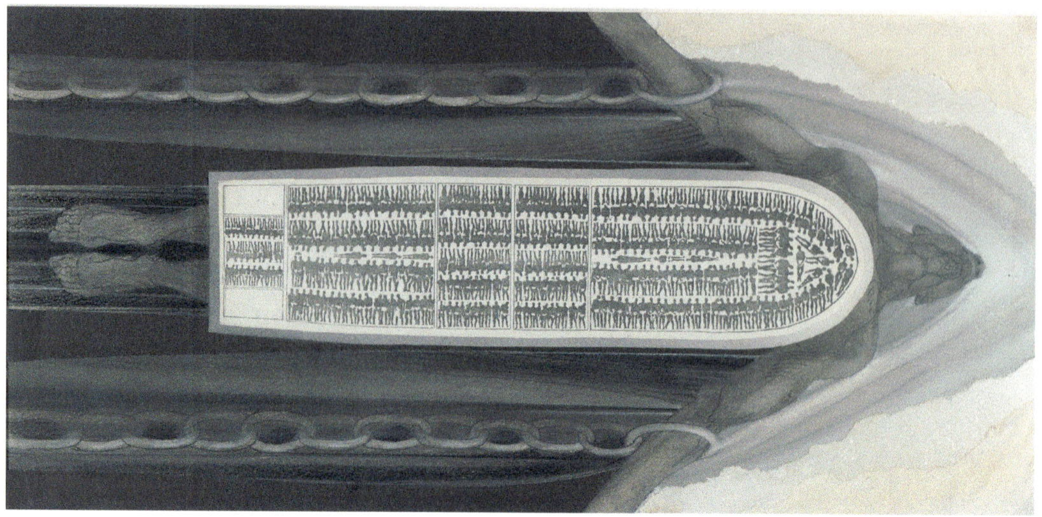

9.9
Tom Feelings, illustration from *The Middle Passage*, 1995, pen and ink drawing.

the water, rising from the depths of an unspeakable struggle. With such iconography, it would be hard not to mistake the body of this African man for a Christ figure, albeit one who has been updated for an African American congregation poised to take control of the images that align their historic struggle with those of biblical narratives. As the Reverend Dr. Marshall E. Hatch, pastor of the New Mount Pilgrim Missionary Baptist Church, explains, "That's a Christ figure for us, an African Man. He's ascending with the bodies and suffering of the slave ship."[19]

The idea for the window was inspired by a drawing in the children's book *The Middle Passage: White Ships/Black Cargo* (1995) by the illustrator Tom Feelings (1993–2003) (fig. 9.9), which caught the attention of the Reverend Dr. Hatch while he was a scholar-in-residence at Harvard Divinity School in 1998.[20] Since its publication, Feelings's book has been hugely popular with black audiences in the United States as an accessible visual narrative that depicts a formative part of their collective experience with easy-to-read, yet excruciatingly painful, visceral images. In all, the book has fifty-four pen-and-ink tempera drawings with an introduction by the historian John Henrik Clarke (1915–1998). Feelings did not include a written narrative, choosing instead to empower the images to tell the story themselves. A self-proclaimed graphic griot, Feelings once said, "As a storyteller in picture form, as an African who was born in America, how could I do anything else but try and live up to that legacy and become a vehicle for this profound, dramatic history to pass through?"[21]

Feelings, a native of the Bedford-Stuyvesant neighborhood of Brooklyn, New York, moved to Ghana in 1964, following college, stoked by a growing black consciousness and interest in Africa.[22] He became part of a wave of African American artists, intellectuals, educators, and activists who traveled or settled there—many at the invitation of President Kwame Nkrumah (1909–1972), who reached out to this cohort in an effort to fuel the nascent country's growth—in the blush Ghana's new-found independence. Feelings taught classes in illustration and worked as a graphic artist for the Ghana Government Publishing House's *African Review Magazine* until 1966, when Nkrumah was ousted in a coup d'état. The artist's experiences in Ghana fueled his desire to create pictorial narratives of black life and black history. As he recalled, "Africa helped make my drawings more fluid and flowing; rhythmic lines started to appear in my work."[23] The idea for *The Middle Passage: White Ships/ Black Cargo*, was first sparked by a question a Ghanaian friend asked of him: "What happened to all of you when you were taken away from here?"[24]

After his years in Ghana, Feelings was drawn back to New York, where the burgeoning Black Arts Movement had opened new opportunities for black artists and arts professionals. He began to illustrate Afrocentric children's books that were instructive by nature (taking on subjects of black history or teaching moral lessons) and filled with figural illustrations characterized by a rare luminosity and corporeal integrity. Appealing to an underserved juvenile market, and communicating to an overlooked young black readership a sense of physical and spiritual beauty, his books received national acclaim and helped to carve out a new and vital niche in the publishing industry.[25] It was around this time that he first encountered the work of the young artist Malcolm Bailey, whose *Separate but Equal* series had premiered at the opening of Cinque Gallery in 1969 and had been lauded by the mainstream art world at the Whitney Annual the following year (see figs. 5.11 and 5.12). Feelings's assessment of Bailey's paintings was, in effect, the fuel that fed a burning desire to produce his masterpiece, *The Middle Passage*.[26] In his opinion, Bailey's stark minimalist aesthetic lacked the compassion needed to treat the subject of the Middle Passage. He questioned Bailey's use of the slave ship icon to interpret polarizing contemporary issues of race relations and integration over the history it most commonly represents. An image of reverence and respect for Feelings, the slave ship icon not only lost its historical relevance deployed by Bailey as an oversized graphic blueprint, but it also became "just a diagram." Feelings began to make the illustrations for his book *The Middle Passage: White Ships/Black Cargo* in 1974, with the idea that the publication might serve as a memorial to the horrific voyage, but it would take him twenty years to complete it. In the end, Feelings admitted, "I clearly did this book for black people so it would be something that inspires them. This book is also for whites who claim they can't recognize what racism feels like."[27] With their long reach into American culture, Feelings's illustrations occupy a place of visual reverence in the American imagination, both black and white. Noted for their understated if not muted tonal range, these illustrations were used for the cover of Charles Johnson's popular novel *Middle Passage* (1990), and as storyboard illustrations for Steven Spielberg's 1997 film *Amistad*.[28]

The place of reverence for Feelings's *Middle Passage* illustrations would be translated to a place of worship in the New Mount Pilgrim Missionary Baptist Church's new stained-glass rose window. In 2001, it was dedicated by the Reverend Jesse Jackson, the founder of Rainbow Coalition/Operation Push, a Chicago-based civil rights organization that, among other things, lobbies the United States Congress to pass legislation that grants reparations to the descendants of slaves and to create a memorial dedicated to the history of slavery on the National Mall in Washington, DC. The church is closely aligned with the Jackson's organization, not only because of its proximity in Chicago, but also because of a shared outlook regarding reparations. The stained-glass window, dedicated as the *Maafa Remembrance 2000 East Communion Window*, is part of a larger discussion surrounding the importance of paying tribute to the legacy of the Middle Passage. As the Reverend Dr. Hatch has commented, "It's more than just church art, it's part of contemporary discourse—political and moral—on how to repair African People."[29] To the New Mount Pilgrim community, the Swahili word *Maafa* (pronounced may-AY-fa), meaning "great struggle," carries a similar heft to that of the word *Holocaust* for Jews.

The *Maafa Remembrance* window is part of a larger contemporary wave of iconoclasm, where predominantly black congregations around the country have been replacing white figures with black figures in biblical art and stained glass since about 1990. The Reverend Dr. Gregory E. Thomas, the pastor of the 140-year-old historically black congregation at Calvary Baptist Church in Haverhill, Massachusetts, affirms, "It's very important for people of color, but also others, to see that there are other icons and that they see themselves within those images. These are just pictures, but they have powerful meanings.... That's why the Middle Passage picture is so important and we need to tell our children what this means."[30]

The impetus for replacing the rose window was not merely aesthetic. When New Mount Pilgrim purchased the nearly one-hundred-year-old church building from the archdiocese in 1993, it was in a state of disrepair. Severe structural issues plagued its three magnificent twenty-five-foot rose windows, which had been designed in Munich by the famed stained-glass artist F. X. Zettler (1841–1916) in 1910 for the former Catholic church of Saint Mel. But the occasion to repair the windows also provided an opening to reshape the congregation's outlook. "Surrounded by European Catholic characters, the church took the opportunity to look beyond mere repairs to restoration," offers Pastor Hatch. "We envisioned new art to tell our own faith stories and to transform the worship space."[31] In a historic preservationist-minded negotiation with the Smith Museum of Stained Glass Windows, which opened on Navy Pier in Chicago in 2000, New Mount Pilgrim donated the three storied rose windows in exchange for the cost of fabricating and installing comparable replacement windows of the congregation's choosing.[32]

The Great Migration, the first rose window to be fabricated and installed at New Mount Pilgrim in early 2000, celebrates the self-determination of African Americans to transform their lives from mere survival in slavery to living and thriving in freedom by moving from the South to the North. Bursting with vibrant blues, reds, greens, and yellows, a family unit composes the main scene above the words "Lift Holy Hands"; its central figure is a father dressed in a 1970s-era Afrocentric robe, his Afro hairstyle accentuated by muttonchops sideburns (fig. 9.10). His bodily gesture, that of lifting a newborn baby to the heavens, recalls the scene in Alex Haley's television miniseries *Roots* (1977), when Toby (the slave name of the older Kunte

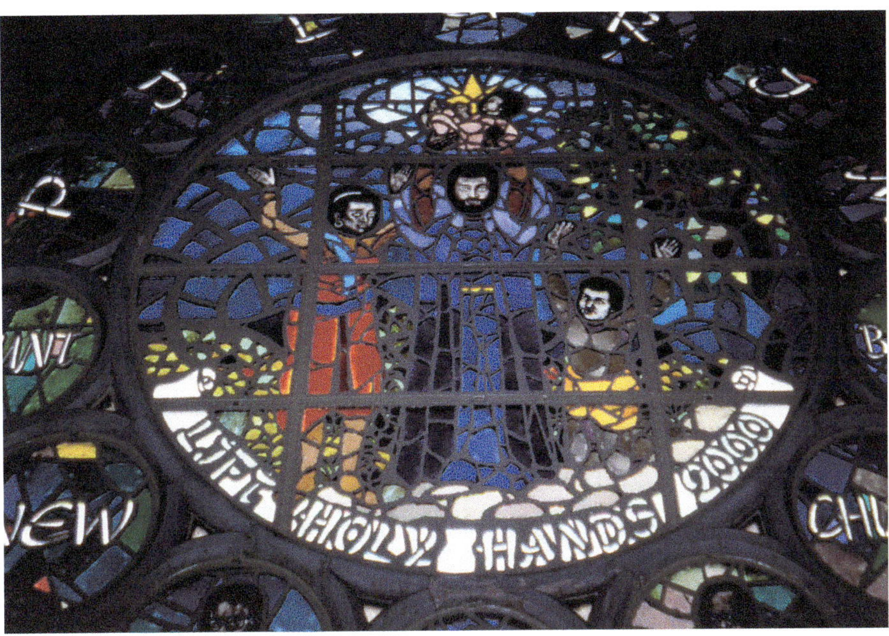

9.10
The Great Migration Rose Window, New Mount
Pilgrim Missionary Baptist Church, West Garfield
Park, Chicago, 2000, 25 feet diameter.

Kinte), played by John Amos, raises his firstborn child to God and the heavens in an act of baptism. The star-studded sky is reminiscent of the star charts escaping slaves (and migrating free blacks in the late nineteenth and early twentieth centuries) used to propel themselves northward, especially by the guiding light of the North Star, which shines bright yellow above the child, casting an ethereal light. Situated on the north side of the sanctuary across from the pulpit and visible above the main entrance to the church on 4301 W. Washington Boulevard, the smaller rosettes of *The Great Migration* window spell out the name of the church and showcase portraits of its three founding pastors.

The third and final rose window will be installed on the west side of the sanctuary across from the *Maafa Remembrance* window. Tentatively called the *Sankofa Peace* window, it combines the Akan word (derived from the language spoken by the Akan people of Ghana) *sankofa*, meaning "to go back and retrieve it," with the circularity of life in Christian theology, symbolized by the geometry of the rose window. Still in the planning and design stages, the *Sankofa Peace* window pays tribute to African tradition, youth, and victims of violence. Memorialized in the window are young African Americans sacrificed in the civil rights movement, notably Addie Mae Collins, Denise McNair, Carole Robinson, and Cynthia Wesley, the four little girls who perished in the Birmingham, Alabama, church bombing of 1963, as well as more recent victims of Chicago gun violence, whose images will appear in the rosettes.

In the *Maafa* stained glass window, surrounding the central image of the arisen black Christ figure, rosettes spell out the word "remembrance." At the very bottom, three rosettes depict an image of Africa, the Communion ritual with wine and bread, and the dedication panel with the words "Maafa 2000." The stained-glass window, then, is clearly meant as a memorial, but it also resembles the contemplative spiritual reflection and call to worship that traditional Christian iconography serves, and as the largest example of the slave ship icon that I have observed or located to date, it is an impressive memorial indeed. Returning to Feelings's seminal illustration in his book *Middle Passage: White Ships/Black Cargo*, the slave ship icon rests in the abdomen of the African man as a constant reminder of the humanity of the enslaved during the Middle Passage: "You begin to see it just as diagram. You forget that these are human beings. That's why I included the figure in the back," Feelings explained in an interview when the window was dedicated. The massive rose window faces east, symbolically toward the Atlantic Ocean, with the figures of the African captives literally embodied in a risen black Christ. As the Reverend Dr. Hatch announced in his dedication speech, "*Maafa Remembrance 2000* not only acknowledges their humanity, but the memorial acknowledges their loss to humanity, and declares that we can neither be whole, healed, or reconciled without their remembrance as part of our consciousness."[33]

As a memorial, the *Maafa Remembrance* window has been responsible for attracting not only new parishioners but also tourists. According to the Reverend Dr. Hatch, such widespread appeal was part of the goal. After all, the window is part of a larger project that involves educating people about the history of slavery and the Middle Passage—"a contribution to the twenty-first century work of reconciliation."[34]

Reiterating the dual instructional messages of Feelings's seminal Middle Passage illustration and that of stained-glass church imagery, the Reverend Dr. Gregory Thomas concurs: "The children will need to know that this symbol, this window, is but a representation of not only the pain, but the possibilities, of a great and mighty God."[35] Feelings's window reclaims Christian iconography for a primarily black congregation, offering narratives of tragedy and triumph as a way of channeling the trials and aspirations of its parishioners in the surrounding West Side Chicago neighborhood.

MEDITATING ON THE CIRCULARITY OF LIFE

In Buddhist tradition, the lotus flower symbolizes not only creation but also the timeless and continual process of birth and rebirth. In nature, the lotus flower sleeps at night. With the waking of the sun it returns to life, once again renewed. In the natural world, life is born and reborn. Similarly, the Buddha rises above all earthly pleasures and desires to a new world of enlightenment. In the shape of a mandala, the lotus flower is thus a key focal point of meditation in the practice of spiritual enlightenment. In the 2007 installation *Lotus*, the performance and installation artist Sanford Biggers (b. 1970) transforms the sections of the slave ship icon into the petals of a lotus flower, where they are repeated in etched glass (figs. 9.11, 9.12). Commissioned by New York's Rubin Museum of Art, a dynamic

Sanford Biggers, *Lotus*, 2007, steel, etched glass, colored LEDs, 7 feet diameter, installation view, Rubin Museum of Art, New York.

Sanford Biggers, detail, *Lotus*, 2007, steel, etched glass, colored LEDs.

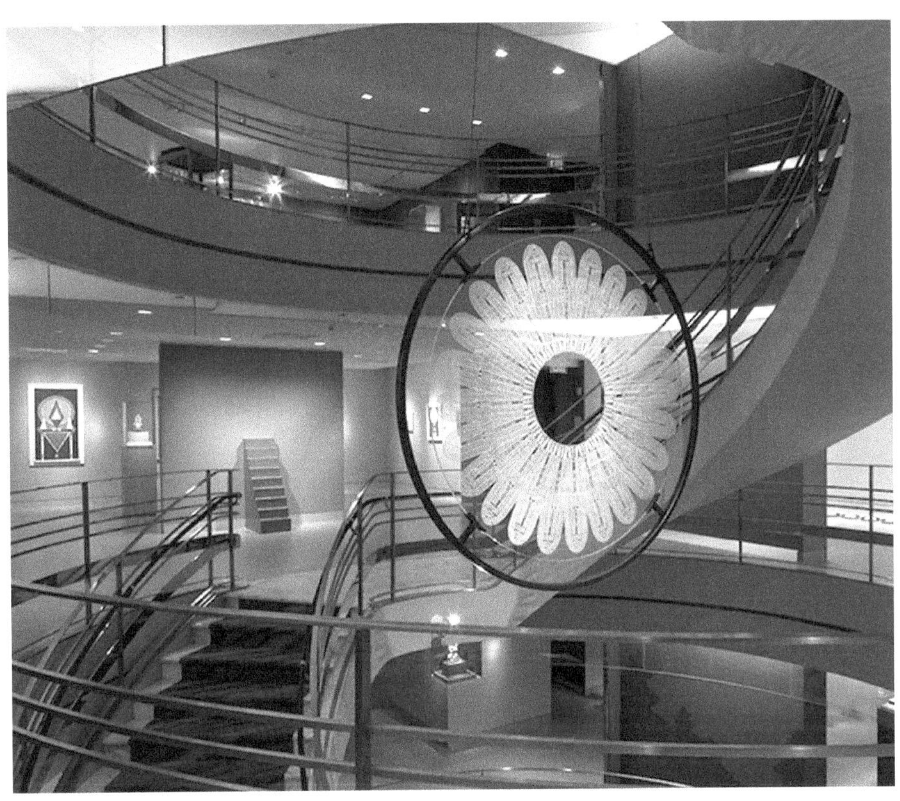

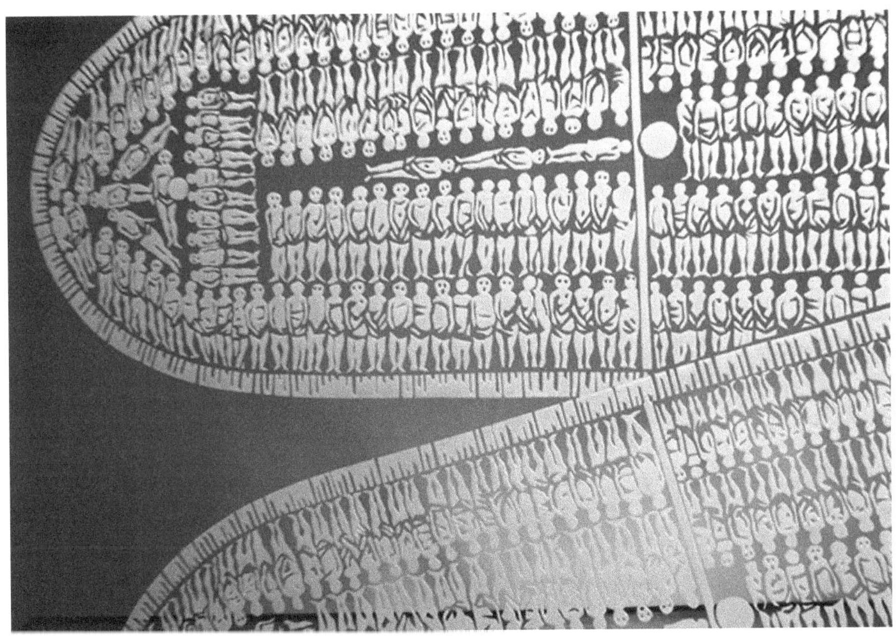

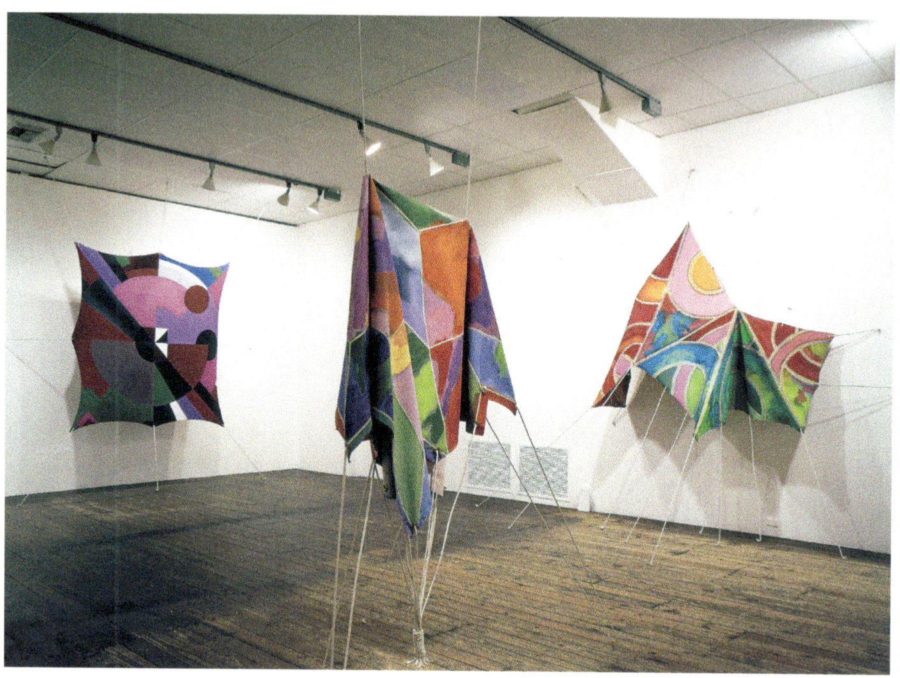

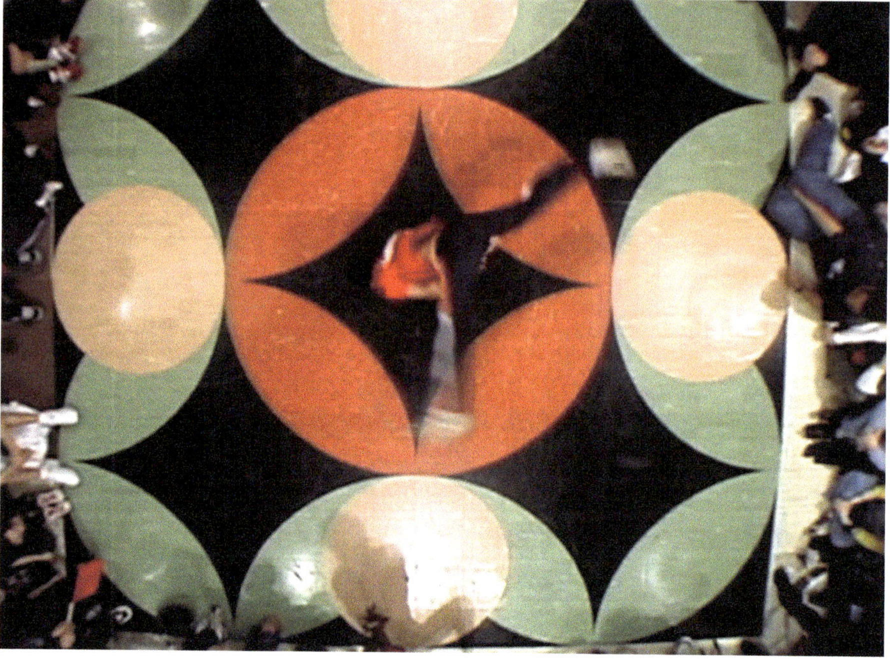

9.13 TOP
Installation view of Joe Overstreet exhibition at
the Menil Collection, 1970, showing (left to right):
Hoodoo Mandala, 1970; *We Came from There
to Get Here*, 1970; and *For Happiness*, 1970. All
works acrylic on canvas with rope.

9.14 BOTTOM
Sanford Biggers with David Ellis, aerial installation
view of *Mandala of the B-Bodhisattva II*, 2002,
silkscreen on hand-carved rubber tiles, Formica
backing, 16 × 16 feet.

exhibition space dedicated to the art and culture of Himalayan Asia, *Lotus* was installed in a central staircase, affording visibility from multiple viewpoints and through surrounding works of art. Its location high up in the museum references the concept of the lotus flower rising through the density of pond waters to produce long-lasting, powerfully beautiful blooms. Through *Lotus*, Biggers suggests that perhaps a different form of enlightenment can be gained from meditating on the schematic forms and tiny bodies, one that considers the spiritual transformation of a people birthed into African diasporas through the transatlantic slave trade.

Seven feet in diameter, the work is not the first by an African American artist to consider the influence of Hinduism and Buddhism on African-derived religions and cultural practices. This visual analogy was observed by Joe Overstreet as early as 1970 in his painting *Hoodoo Mandala*, which infuses the circular shape of the mandala with references to Vodún, the ancient West African religion also known as Voodoo, in which *véve*, the diagrammatic instructions to the *loa*, or spirits, create directional patterns of landing strips (fig. 9.13). Prior to *Lotus*, Biggers created large red, black, and green dance floors in the shape of the circular mandala and then choreographed performances upon them with hip-hop and other music genres, such as *Mandala of the B-Bodhisattva II*, 2002 (fig. 9.14). Photographed from above, Biggers also takes as inspiration the geometric, kaleidoscopic choreography of Busby Berkeley in Depression-era Hollywood musicals, noted for their large-scale dance extravaganzas filmed from above. *Lotus* led to another commission in 2010 by the Percent for Art program of the New York City Department of Cultural Affairs, in which the 110 × 60′ diameter *Lotus II*, made of galvanized steel, was installed on the red brick facade of Eagle Academy for Young Men, a school for black and Latino students in New York City's Harlem neighborhood.

In his 2011 retrospective at the Brooklyn Museum of Art (*Sweet Funk—An Introspective*, September 23, 2011–January 8, 2012), *Lotus* was installed with a suite of quilts that Biggers tagged with smaller fabric versions of the slave ship lotus shape as circular discs dotting the quilts, stitched by the artist with painstaking precision. Biggers compares the slave ship icon as a central motif in his work to a "jazz standard," a composition that becomes universally associated with a musician's repertoire, that like the slave ship icon is often performed (repeated) with revision, as improvisation. It's not incidental that Biggers himself is also a musician and performance artist. His 2012 MASS MoCA exhibition, *The Cartographer's Conundrum*, included quilts with miniature round mandalas that took on the appearance of geometric patterns and mathematical problems (fig. 9.15). This large-scale installation was inspired in part by the work of his cousin, the noted painter John Biggers, who reveled in Afro-futurist works painted with mathematical precision. Sanford Biggers's 2012 exhibition *Codex* at the John and Mable Ringling Museum of Art in Sarasota, Florida, offered additional layers of meaning to a series of new quilts by hanging large bales of cotton in the exhibition space (fig. 9.16). Linking the fabric of traditional American quilts to the cotton industry that fueled the slave trade, the miniature lotus mandalas serve as signposts, points of meditation and reverie, while recalling the African American quilting tradition, notably the inspirational

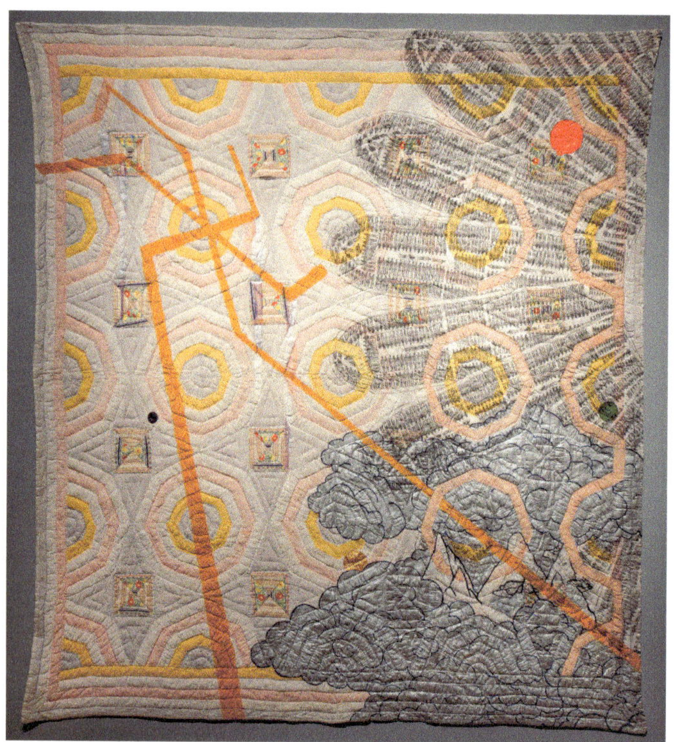

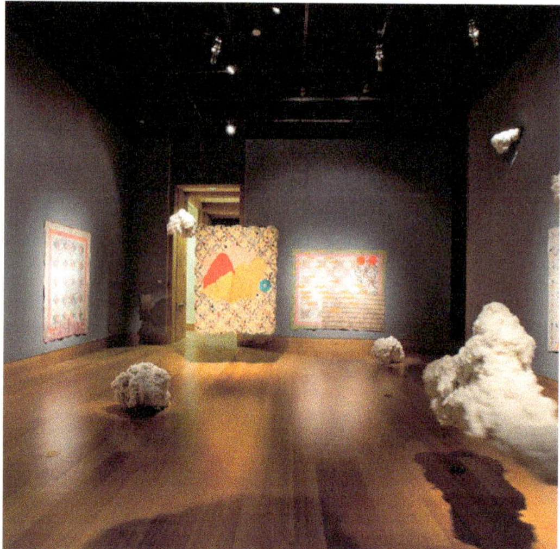

Pictorial Quilt (1895–98), created by Harriet Powers (1837–1910) (fig. 9.17). Born a slave near Athens, Georgia, Powers is known to have assembled two quilts, depicting biblical scenes using an appliqué style resembling textiles from Benin: the *Bible Quilt*, exhibited in the Athens Cotton Fair of 1886, and the former, commissioned for Dr. Charles Cuthbert Hall, President of Union Theological Seminary in New York, by the faculty ladies of Atlanta University, where he served as chairman of the board of trustees.

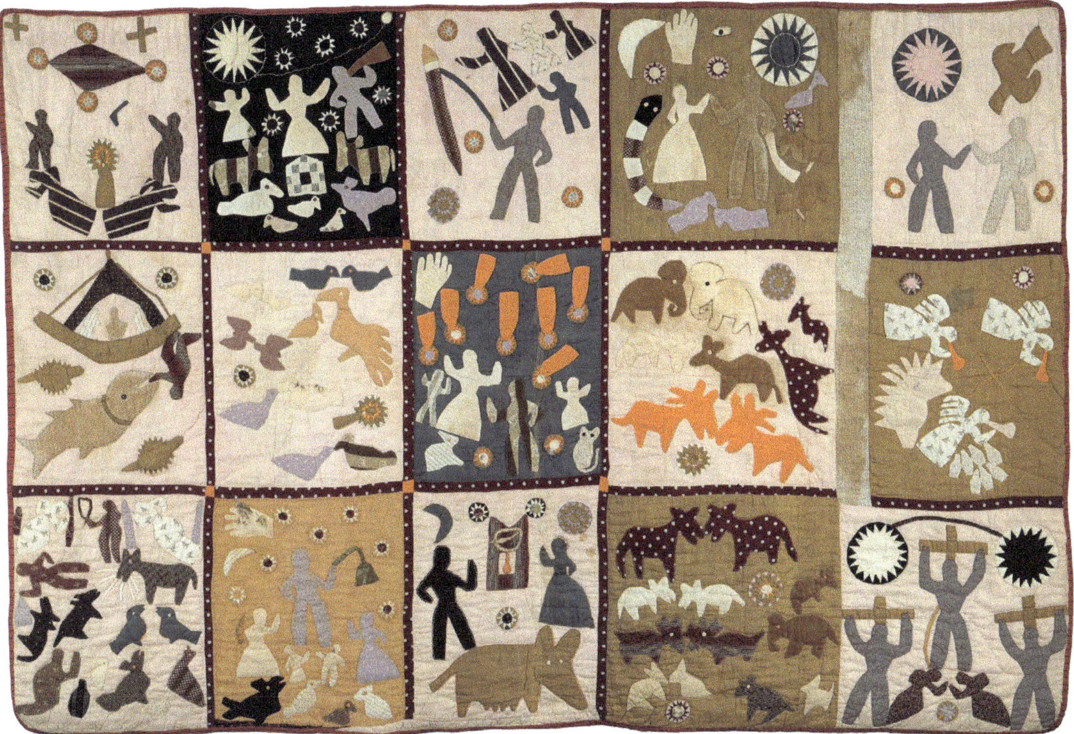

9.17
Harriet Powers, *Pictorial Quilt*, American (Athens, Georgia), 1895–98, cotton plain weave, pieced, appliquéd, embroidered, and quilted, 175 × 266.7 cm (68 7/8 × 105 inches).

RELIGIOUS REVERENCE

The artists discussed in this chapter recreated the slave ship icon not just once, but multiple times. As used by Sanford Biggers, Tom Feelings, Nari Ward, and María Magdalena Campos-Pons, their act of repetition with revision has contributed to the iconic nature of this image and to its ability to stand as a recurring trope in the work of black Atlantic artists. Although they each have shaped and reshaped the slave ship icon, their faithfulness to the original black-and-white schematic print has rendered it an image of religious reverence. For these artists, the very practice of repetition, of faithfully invoking this image repeatedly, is in itself a sacred act.

The fact that these artists have chosen to create works that lend new meaning to the slave ship icon necessarily implies both an artistic practice of mnemonic aesthetics and a dedication to social change. Performing a necessary type of rescue work, these artists work out of the same sense of duty as those freed slaves who bought their own kin on the auction block; they liberate history from oblivion. Their works of art not only evoke the slave ship icon, they also offer the tools to understand the contemporary relevance of this unforgettable image through a creative means that enables it to remain an active part of the black Atlantic imagination.

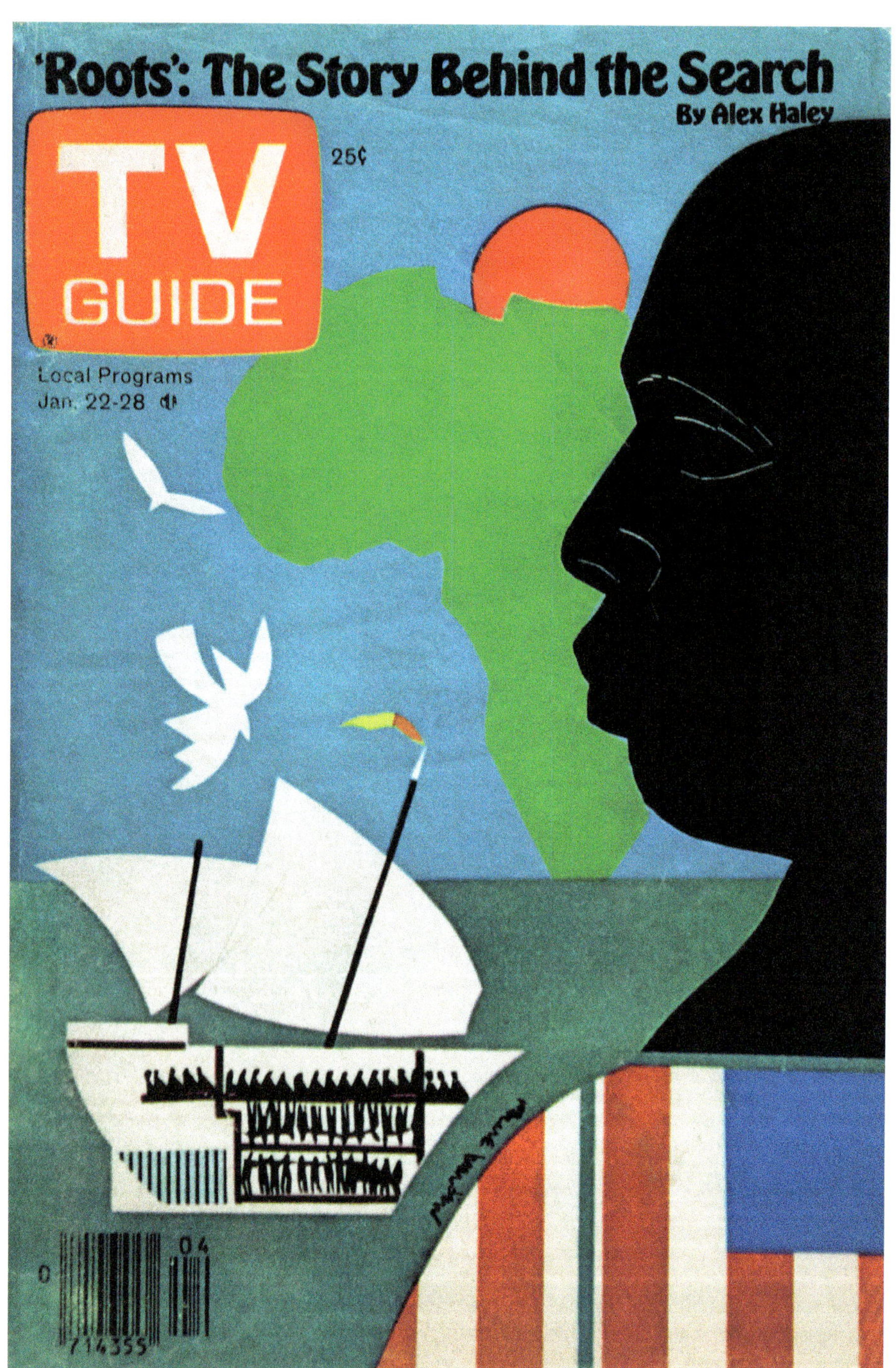

10.1

Romare Bearden, *Roots*, 1977 (cover of *TV Guide*).

CHAPTER TEN

ROOTS TOURISM AND THE SLAVE SHIP ICON

ROOTS

IN 1977, Romare Bearden was commissioned by *TV Guide* to illustrate its cover story announcing the premiere of *Roots: An American Family Saga*, based on Alex Haley's best-selling novel of the previous year (fig. 10.1). As Haley explained in the dedication to his novel, "It wasn't planned that *Roots'* researching and writing finally would take twelve years. Just by chance it is being published in the Bicentennial Year of the United States. So I dedicate *Roots* as a birthday offering to my country, within which most of *Roots* happened."[1] Tracing his family's lineage all the way back to mid-eighteenth-century Africa, specifically to the tiny village of Juffure in The Gambia, *Roots* was television's first miniseries, broadcast in two-hour segments over a period of eight nights.[2] Its unprecedented popularity breathed life into the study of African and African American subjects and inspired art that followed the lines of black genealogy. Furthermore, it encouraged another wave of black Americans to begin conducting genealogical research in Africa, especially in places like The Gambia (where Haley's story begins), Ghana, Senegal, and Liberia.[3] Such personal and familial quests for identity and place of origin in Africa had grown since the mid-1960s, when black Americans connected to African liberation movements by adopting African naming practices, wearing African fashions, and styling their hair in the Afro and other natural hairstyles. Their frequent sojourns have produced a thriving albeit controversial "roots," or heritage, tourism industry in Ghana, Senegal, South Africa, and The Gambia today (despite the rise in genetic testing and DNA research by companies such as 23andMe and popular US public television series, such as *Finding Your Roots*, which often suggest that the science may not lead to these symbolic heritage sites).

The miniseries genre marked an innovation in television marketing that initially was met with doubt. *TV Guide* considered the network's showing of *Roots* for eight consecutive nights a gamble, but it eventually paid off. *Roots* was a runaway success with the American viewing public. Not only was the format of the miniseries new to the nation's TV audience, but the idea of presenting such a potentially explosive theme as slavery with a predominantly black cast of actors in the homes of mainstream America was a first. *Roots'* favorable reception paved the way for more black-oriented television programming, especially dramas, and created a new profit model for television, the miniseries, which frequently relied on suspense to keep the viewers coming back day after day.[4]

Prior to taking on the commission for *Roots*, Bearden had made other collages in which he used the silhouette of a slave ship, notably the strikingly similar *Prince Cinque* (1971) (fig. 10.2). In that work, Bearden introduced two key iconographic elements that would make their way into other of his works: the deck of a slave ship with an active slave revolt and the map of Africa, which Bearden used to position the three-quarter profile of the heroic figure Cinqué, leader of the 1839 *Amistad* revolt. This is the first work in which Bearden references the *Amistad* revolt, and he does so by clearly riffing off of both the 1839 newspaper illustrations that first publicized this now-legendary slave revolt (see fig. 3.7) and the Nathaniel Jocelyn (1796–1881) portrait of Cinqué, just as Hale Woodruff had done in 1939 with the third panel of the *Amistad* murals; by 1969, however, Bearden had opened the Cinque Gallery with Ernest Crichlow and Norman Lewis, named after the Senegalese prince (see fig. 5.10).

Another work, a large-scale appliqué quilt called *Captivity and Resistance* (fig. 10.3), was commissioned to mark the founding of the Philadelphia African American Museum and the nation's two-hundredth anniversary in 1976. In that work, Bearden again depicts the slave ship icon in dhow style with silhouetted slave figures below. But he also includes the *Amistad* version of a nineteenth-century clipper ship, in which the human cargo has taken to the deck in an intense battle to win over the ship below a large portrait of Cinqué. Inset in the quilt, it confronts the dhow-style ship, and serves as a focal point of the overall work. Bearden's repeated use of certain patterns—the dhow-style ship, the *Amistad* revolt, Cinqué—recalls Harriet Powers's repetition of familiar images in her *Pictorial Quilt* (see fig. 9.17). This is contrasted with a version of the kneeling slave, the scales of justice, and multiple verdant patches alluding to the shores of Africa and America. Bearden also pictures representations of moments in black history and of seminal black leaders like Frederick Douglass and Sojourner Truth in conversation. The establishment of African American history museums during the late 1960s and early 1970s built on the interest in African history and genealogy that had begun to take root during the initial period of the African liberation movement in the 1960s and produced a second wave of roots tourism.

The collage that Bearden created for *TV Guide, Roots Odyssey*, shows a slave ship with its human cargo exposed in silhouette as it sails toward the map of Africa and the bust of a man in profile. Wearing red, white, and blue striped fabric, suggesting African textiles dressed up for the Bicentennial, the man seems to welcome the beleaguered ship. Quoting the map of Africa is a visual strategy employed by many artists, especially during the Black Arts Movement; for example, the Guyanese-born painter Frank Bowling, discussed in chapters 5 and 6, became known for his large acrylic canvases dripping with colorful map forms of Africa and the Americas, such as *Night Journey* (1968–69) and *Texas Louise* (1971). While black artists' use of maps and spatial charting hinted at a growing interest in their individual origins and the personal journey to find one's place in the world, it was

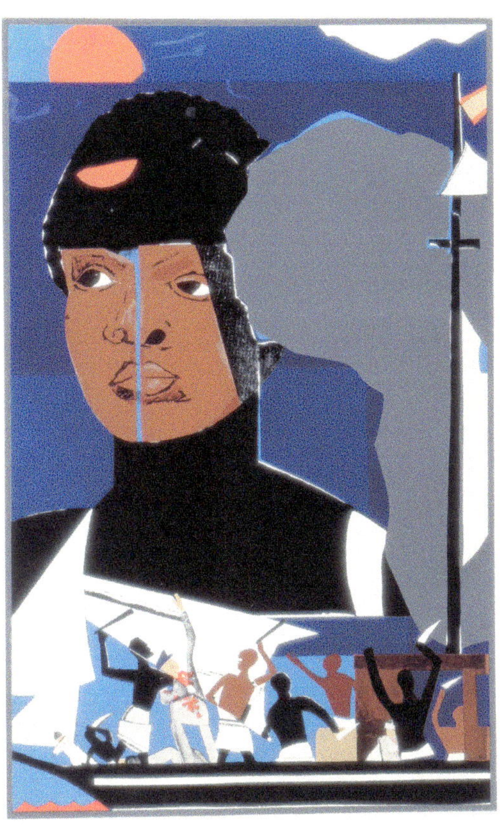

10.2 LEFT
Romare Bearden, *Prince Cinque* (Slave Ship), 1971,
screen print.

10.3 BELOW
Romare Bearden, *Captivity and Resistance*, 1976,
fabric collage on canvas, Philadelphia African
American Museum.

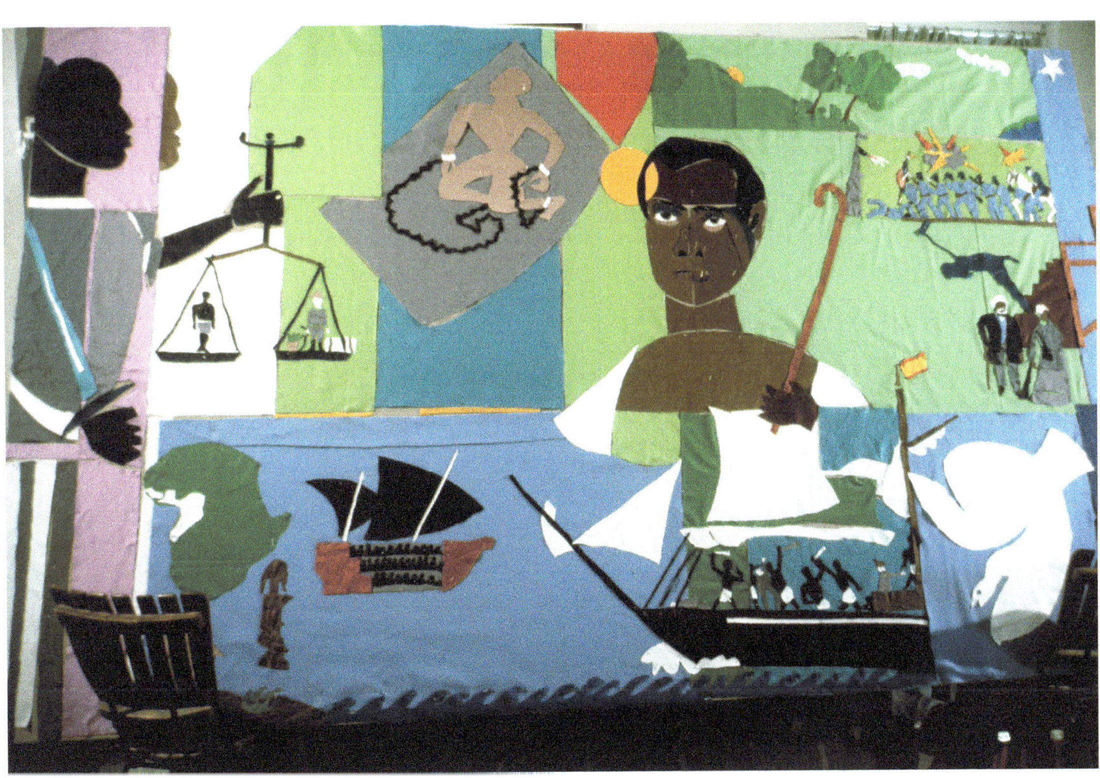

also part of a larger visual tradition. Bearden's *Roots Odyssey* also resonates with Covarrubias's brown and gold cover for *Adventures of an African Slaver*, discussed in chapter 4. Bearden's collage vibrantly dons the Pan-Africanist colors—red, black, and green—against a sea of blue. The somewhat ambiguous position of the ship, modeled after the mid-nineteenth-century diagrams of dhows caught illegally transporting human cargo, references both the Middle Passage and the return voyage to Africa, or, in personal terms, alludes to Haley's own discovery of his family's genealogy and his eventual homecoming to Africa in search of his roots.

SURVIVAL

In 1979, the internationally acclaimed Jamaican reggae artists Bob Marley (1945–1981) and the Wailers produced the album *Survival*, the first of a trilogy of hard-hitting resistance albums that included *Uprising* (1980) and *Confrontation* (1983). According to Marley's biographer David Vlado Moskowitz, "Philosophically, the *Survival* album was part of a larger puzzle that Bob was trying to construct. With the sounds and messages of the album, Bob laid the groundwork for his 'call to action' for all black people.... The first step was to survive four hundred years at the hands of white oppressors; next the disenfranchised black population must band together and shake loose their shackles (either literally or figuratively); and third, they should make the move to a location where they could be free to live in peace (Africa)."[5] With *Survival*, Marley affirmed the Rastafari roots of reggae music as an ideology of resistance, liberation, and emancipation to Africa as espoused by the Jamaican activist Marcus Garvey in the early twentieth century. As the Jamaican-born political scientist Horace Campbell explains, "The Rastifari song—reggae—was the highest form of self-expression, an expression which was simultaneously an act of social commentary and a manifestation of deep racial memory."[6] Reggae thus performs a mnemonic aesthetic, through which lyrics and melody conjure impressions of past freedom struggles on the African continent and across the black diaspora as a call to action.

But it is the art on the front of the album sleeve, designed by Neville Garrick, a graphic artist born in Jamaica and based in Los Angeles, that offers an overt visualization of the ideology of reggae music and its ties to resistance and liberation movements in Africa. A student of graphic design at UCLA in the early 1970s, Garrick became close friends with Marley after returning to Kingston to become art director for the *Daily News*. He later became the artistic director for Marley's Tuff Gong record label and designed some of the artist's most iconic album covers. For *Survival*, the flags of forty-eight postcolonial African nations (and Papua New Guinea) circa 1979 adorn the cover, an elongated, horizontal graphic of the famous crowded section of the slave ship icon serving as a banner. The word "SURVIVAL" is printed in white block letters over the schematic banner, setting off the vibrant colors of the flags—red, black, green, and gold—to form a Pan-Africanist collage of unity, shared struggle, and liberation.

With songs such as "We are the Survivors," the album linked the historical narratives of African survival in the transatlantic slave trade to contemporary struggles for the survival of African nations. The song "Zimbabwe" became a rallying anthem for the ZANLA freedom fighters, and on the backside of the album cover a small picture of the classical civilization Great Zimbabwe demands, "Let us fight and rebuild Zimbabwe."[7] At the invitation of Zimbabwe's newly elected leader, Marley traveled there from Kingston to perform at the independence ceremonies.

But, as Campbell notes, *Survival* also had a very personal meaning to Marley, who was shot and injured in a politically motivated assassination attempt at his home in 1976. The song "Ambush in the Night" is a direct reference to that incident, after which Marley went into hiding for nearly a year, taking the time to reflect on life and write the lyrics and music for most of the songs on the *Survival* album.

With its colorful flags resembling the patterned strips of kente cloth, the album cover also situates the symbolic importance of Africa as a site of memory for Marley and other diasporic Africans in search of their own roots. This connection between Africa and its new world diasporas was reiterated in the opening scenes of the acclaimed 2012 documentary *Marley*, directed by Kevin Macdonald with stills photography by Garrick. The film opens at the site of the Elmina slave castle in coastal Ghana; the camera then takes off across the Atlantic Ocean before settling in the Green Hills of Jamaica, Marley's birthplace, to begin the story. The first sub-Saharan nation to gain freedom from colonial rule in 1957, Ghana stands out as an object lesson. Recent studies of that country's tourism industry as well as efforts to maintain and update some of its historic forts and castles suggest how installations that seek to recreate or simulate the hold of the slave ship became a popular means of promoting public history exhibits about slavery in certain sites around the black Atlantic.

ROOTS TOURISM

For centuries, the castles and forts of coastal Ghana have been important sites of African-European contact and cultural exchange. Built between 1482 and 1784 by rival European nations, these rare examples of late medieval, fortified architecture in sub-Saharan Africa are remembered today for their fundamental role in facilitating the notorious transatlantic slave trade, though their descriptions as *castles* may imply otherwise. In all, there are some sixty remaining structures in varying states of disrepair along Ghana's coast alone, whose rocky and treacherous promontories provided both defense from enemies approaching by land and sea and the lime-rich natural resources necessary to build structures that would withstand centuries of battering by the salty seaside air as well as human suffering at the hands of other humans. The paradoxical combination of the shocking history of these man-made sites, the natural beauty of the seashore, and the physical grandeur of the architecture has produced the most popular tourist attractions in contemporary Ghana.

According to the Ghana Museums and Monuments Board, there are only three structures designated as castles among the sixty colonial forts that remain on Ghana's coast: Elmina, built by the Portuguese in 1482; Cape Coast, erected by the Swedish in 1653; and Christiansborg, built by the Danish in 1661 at Osu in the capital city of Accra and now the official residence of Ghana's president. Of the three,

Cape Coast and Elmina are the most popular with tourists and within visible distance of each other, just three hours' drive from Accra. Over the past several hundred years, Elmina and Cape Coast have been classified as castles for their style of architecture, enormous size, and multiplicity of function. Distinguished from the more numerous but smaller forts, the castles have a larger surface area, a more intricate complex of connecting structures, and the ability to house a large number of people. This is evident in the way the space inside the castle walls was designated and used as governors' quarters, officers' barracks and mess halls, servants' cooking facilities, male and female slave dungeons, trading and sales rooms, prison cells, ammunitions storage, churches, schools, courtyards and terraces, lookout towers, and defense.

Sankofa is an Akan word, deriving from modern Ghana's most widely spoken language, meaning "one must return to the past in order to move forward." Diasporic Africans have been inspired by Ghana's example to do just that since Kwame Nkrumah came to power in the mid-1950s. W. E. B. Du Bois made the country his home toward the end of his life; his gravesite is a national landmark in Accra. After 1972, when UNESCO designated the slave trade castles of Cape Coast and Elmina as World Heritage Monuments, Africans from the continent and the diaspora began to make pilgrimages to these sites to make sense of their past. Galvanized initially by the social and political advances won by the Black Arts and Black Power movements of the late 1960s and early 1970s, and later bolstered by the popularity of the novel and subsequent miniseries *Roots*, a steady flow of African Americans has participated in, if not shaped, a type of tourism that has at its center the need to uncover and validate an authentic cultural heritage. This brand of tourism has been called *roots tourism*, its practitioners often seeking a symbolic "return" to an ancestral homeland made visible by the idea or racial memory of Africa as a familial place of origin in the transatlantic slave trade. Roots tourism, however, isn't confined to Africa, and many roots tourists have found meaningful sites of memory across the black Atlantic in places like Salvador da Bahia, Brazil, where African traditions have survived among large black populations and indeed where corollaries to the dungeons also exist as physical monuments.

Beyond the notion of Africa as a symbolic motherland, roots tourists claim the physical and imposing sites of Cape Coast and Elmina as tangible and necessary memorials, among the very few places where material evidence of the legacy of slavery—the legacy of their ancestors—still stands before their eyes to be touched, walked through, and experienced with all of their senses and with the movement of their bodies through the space. Cape Coast and Elmina are profound examples of the historian Pierre Nora's influential and useful term *"lieux de memoire,"* or sites of memory, "where memory crystallizes and secrets itself."[8] European sailors aboard slave ships, like the French First Lieutenant Robert Durand aboard the *Diligent* in 1731, drew on paper and in journals their impressions of the Ghanaian coastline, including illustrations of Elmina and Cape Coast castles (fig. 10.4) that are still recognizable today.[9] Likewise, a century earlier, European sailors and traders had rendered their own impressions of the fishing boats sometimes used to transport

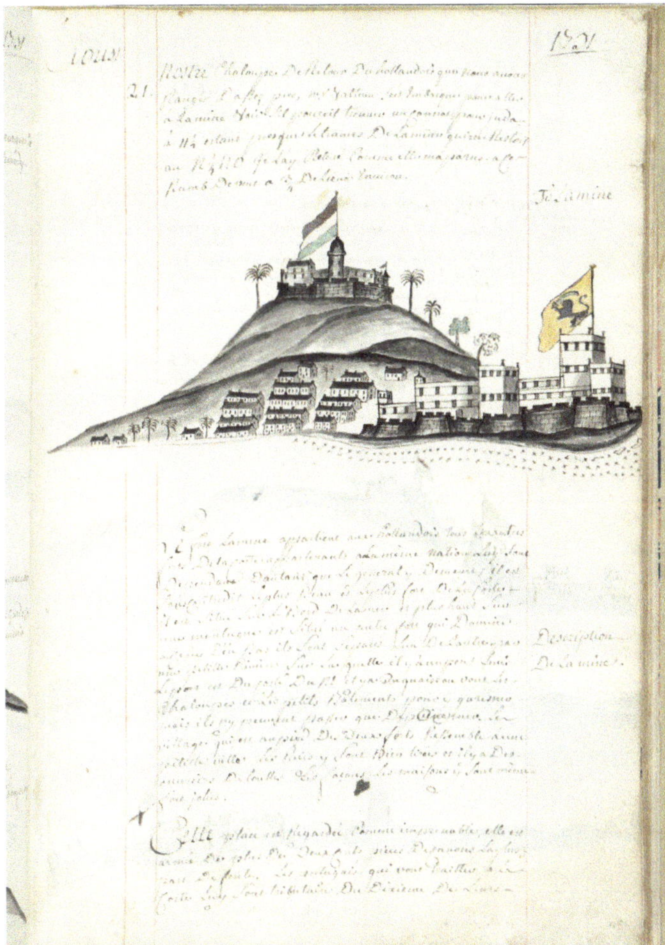

10.4
Robert Durand, view of Fort St. Jago (top)
and Elmina Castle, 1731, pen and ink drawing
on journal page.

human cargo to the awaiting slave ships in the harbor.

Ghanaian Asafo company (the warrior group of the Fante people who traditionally inhabit the coastal regions) flags dating from the early twentieth century illustrate scenes of European-African contact at Cape Coast (fig. 10.5). These brightly
colored banners combine both Fante and European designs and textile practices, a
bricolage that dates back to European contact, where Fante warriors observed and
incorporated the heraldry, royal arms, and regimental colors of Europeans into their
own system of representation to produce textiles of extraordinary presence. Using
patchwork, appliqué, and embroidery, the designs tell narratives using local folklore
and symbols while interpreting buildings and sites of memory, such as this example
depicting Cape Coast Castle. Other commonly seen elements in Asafo flags, especially those that predate Ghanaian independence, include a representation of the
British Union Jack, usually in the upper left, and the Asafo company number. More
recently, contemporary Ghanaian artists have made a number of attempts to visualize their relationship to the history and presence of the forts and castles. A series
of late twentieth-century fantasy coffins, burial vessels commissioned by Ghanaians

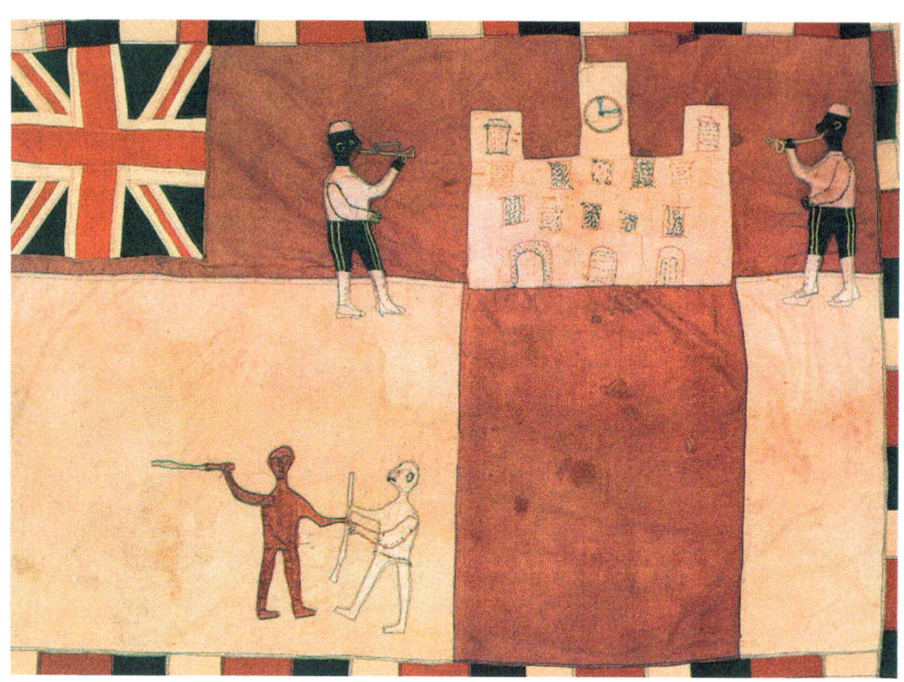

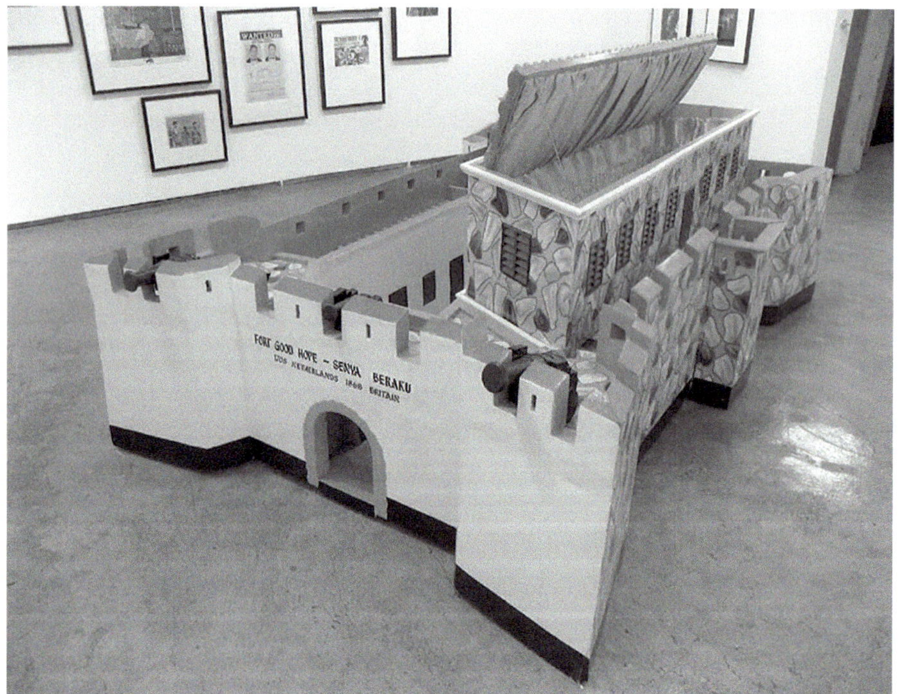

10.5 TOP
Asafo Flag, twentieth century, Ghana
(showing Cape Coast Castle), cotton appliqué.

10.6 BOTTOM
Paa Joe, *Fort Good Hope Fantasy Coffin*,
ca. 2006, mixed media.

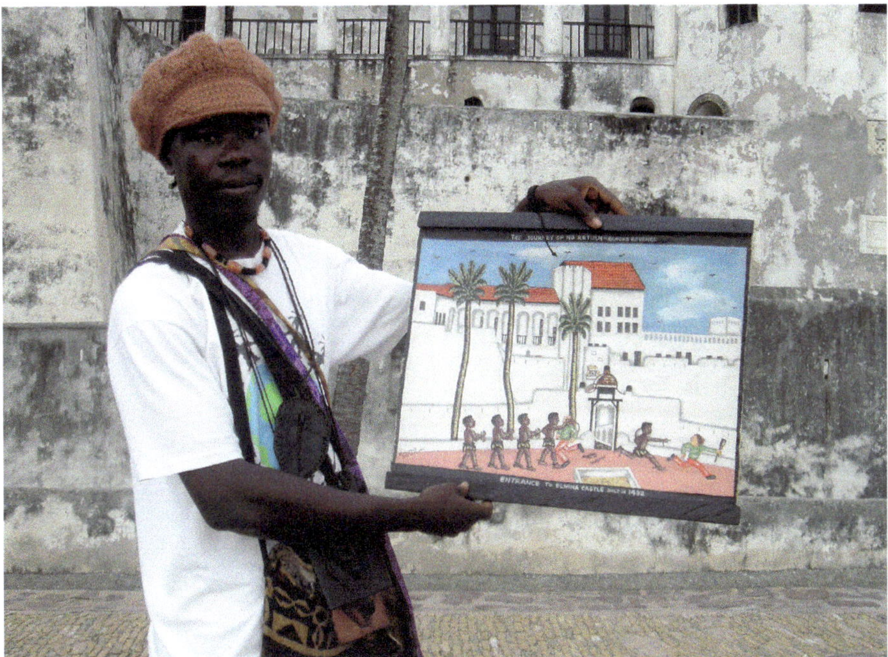

10.7
Local artist sells his depiction of history
in front of Elmina castle, 2005.

to symbolize important places, buildings, or forms of transportation, designed by the artist Paa Joe (b. 1947), feature three-dimensional "coffin-size" models of the prominent forts, including Fort Good Hope (fig. 10.6). Responding to the desire of roots tourists and capitalizing on their frequent sojourns to Cape Coast and Elmina, local artists converge just outside of the forts and castles, where they sell their own interpretations of historical events in paintings and sculpture. In this Elmina-based artist's series, he has two paintings that tell a story of African-European contact outside the entrance to Elmina Castle (fig. 10.7). In one version, the enslaved Africans are shown in a coffle, walking solemnly, heads down, followed by a red-faced European man with a raised whip. In another version (pictured here), the tables are turned and he shows the coffle of once-manacled Africans broken free of their shackles as they chase the European men who tried to enslave them.

The need to offer alternative visual narratives is also the province of African diaspora artists who have made installations, quilts, and other works of art to piece together the history of the forts and their relationship to them on their own terms. In 2009, the painter and installation artist Radcliffe Bailey (b. 1968) created a series of works commemorating his first trip to Ghana, including watercolors of Elmina and other forts painted in lush, verdant colors over sheet music, and a large-scale installation, *Windward Coast*, of piano keys in disarray suggesting the scurrilous history of the rocky coast and ships and bodies washed up against its shores (fig. 10.8). The photographer and quilt maker Deborah Willis (b. 1948)

10.8 TOP
Radcliffe Bailey, *Windward Coast*, 2009,
piano keys, painted bust, glitter.

10.9 BOTTOM
Deborah Willis, *Middle Passage*, 1992, appliqué
quilt with runaway ads, fringe, and ribbon.

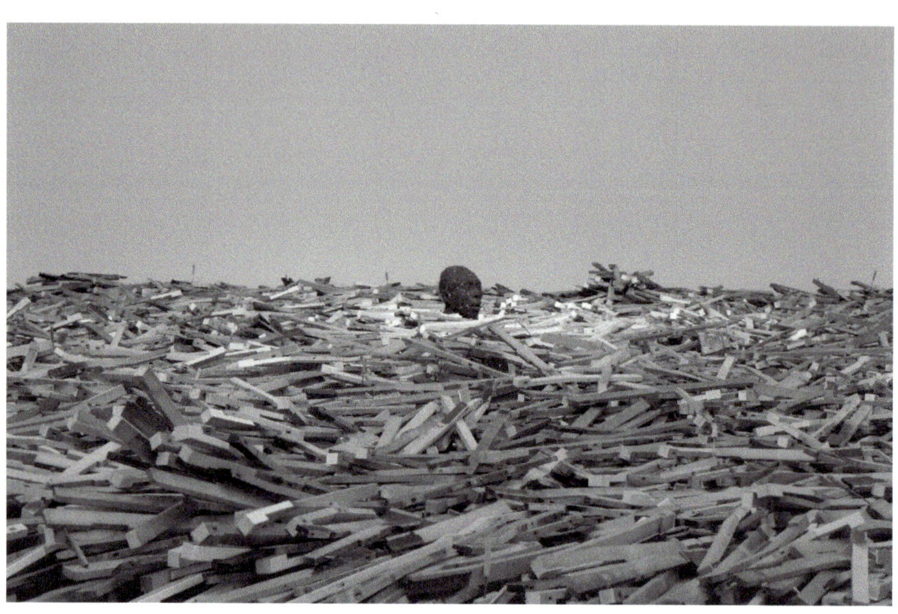

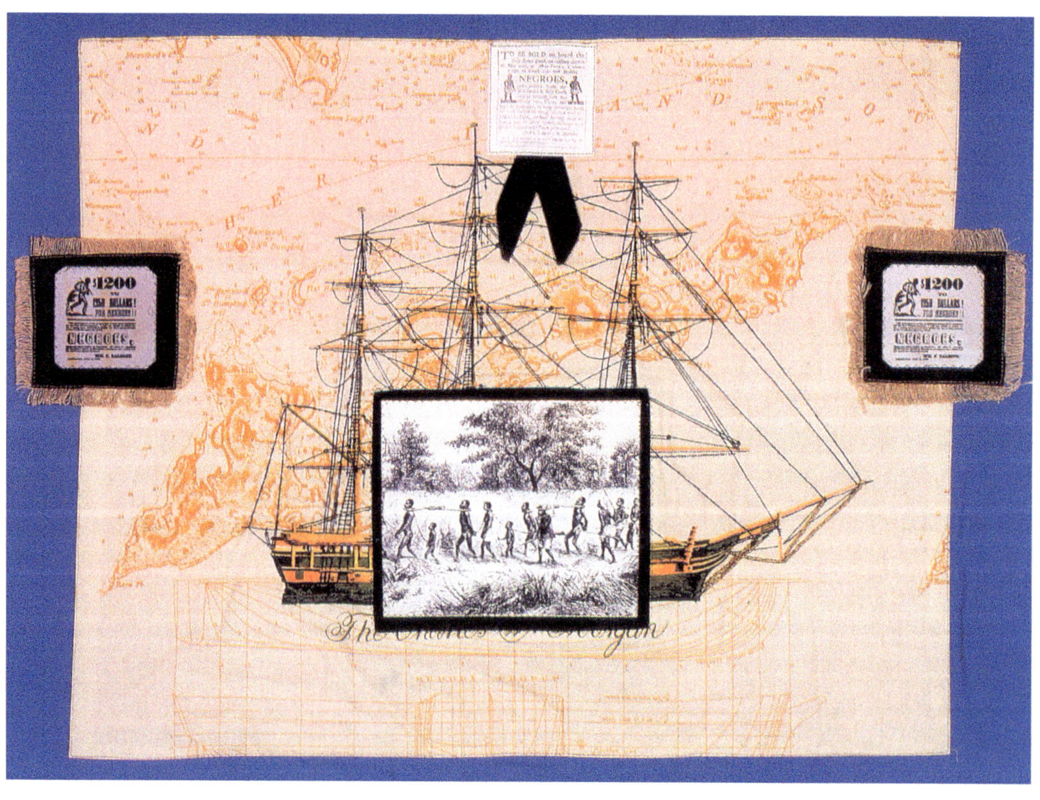

extends Bailey's work to the transatlantic crossing in *Middle Passage*, 1992, an appliqué quilt that uses as its base a found piece of fabric depicting a line drawing of a ship over a nautical map (fig. 10.9). Pieced over this illustrated fabric are small patchwork squares of iconic archival images of coffles of slaves and slave sale posters, suggesting the contents of the ship.

A range of controversial issues arises when monuments fraught with such historical tension and cultural import become objects of global tourism. Many roots tourists feel that the use of the term *castle* elides the history of the dungeons beneath Cape Coast and Elmina and that of their ancestors' experience, allowing their stories to become lost. In their place, fairy-tale notions of European architectural grandeur associated with a popular understanding of the term *castle* sugarcoat the fact that enslaved Africans were held captive in them in unimaginably inhumane conditions. This is more than a wholesale rejection of the term *castle*, however, which is largely used for militaristic strongholds born out of the medieval period. Some roots tourists disagree with the renovation efforts being made in the name of historic preservation. They claim that renovations privilege high architecture and transform the castles into "make-believe" places. Referring to coats of fresh white paint on the bastions, the addition of potted plants and flowers at the entrance, and the effort to clean and paint the inside of the dungeons, one visitor from Jamaica lamented, "It is horrible to watch this dungeon being turned into a Walt Disney castle!"[10] The double-edged phrase "Stop whitewashing our history!" appears frequently in the visitor comment books at Cape Coast and Elmina.[11] Instead of the regular program of painting, upkeep, and renovation, some roots tourists and local African American expatriates argue that these monuments should be left alone to crumble and fall into the sea.

PERFORMANCES OF MEMORY, RACE, AND AUTHENTICITY

Memory serves a central function in roots tourism. Like heritage, it is something of an intangible commodity and a social construct that mediates the experiences, actions, and expectations of individuals. Memory is offered to the tourist for consumption; it is what tourists themselves rely on to authenticate and make meaningful their experiences at the sites. Memory also shapes the *expectations* of roots tourists, guiding their hopes for some sort of connection with and resolution of their ancestral past. Memory lures them to places like Cape Coast and Elmina, offering a real and symbolic link to their ancestors via the physical monuments from whence they became part of a diaspora. Memory thus functions in the creation of a shared racial historical consciousness that roots tourists employ to make sense of their past, to sift through the historical elements—the trauma and the triumph—tied to the lived experience of modern racial formation. At the destinations of roots tourists, such as the monuments of Cape Coast and Elmina, the concept of memory is active and fluid as in the performative, human function of *re-membering*: putting back together, restoring, healing, making whole the body politic. As an embodied practice, memory performed at these sites serves a temporal-spatial function by incorporating the awareness of sight, sound, smell, touch, and taste to fully experience the physical space of the memorial.

Complexities of memory and identity politics are at play among tourists, museum officials, and local inhabitants who frequent the castles and dungeons of Cape Coast and Elmina. Practices of remembering at these sites are further politicized along racial, national, ethnic, class, and gender lines, and are evidenced by the way individuals and groups *perform* memory in the physical space of the monuments. Just whose history and what history is being interpreted at these sites? Most African Americans and black people from the diaspora stress that the history of the slave trade, made tangible by the presence of the dungeons beneath the castles, should be the focal point. To the contrary, some Ghanaians feel that the long history and multiple uses of the sites should take precedence. Tourists more concerned with medieval architecture or European colonial history concentrate on the aesthetic quality and architectural splendor of the whitewashed buildings. Can we ethically condone the architectural and interpretive changes to Cape Coast and Elmina castles that have been made in the name of facilitating tourism? The truly authentic moment offered to the tourist is the *memory* of the enslaved Africans who left the dungeons centuries ago—the now absent black men, women, and children who have become part of the allure of these monuments. It is a perplexing problem that some visitors to the castles have passionately vocalized. As one African American tourist demanded, "Don't turn our memories into a tourist attraction."[12] In the current age of global tourism, memory itself becomes a commodity—a thing to be bought, sold, and traded.

Upon entering Cape Coast or Elmina, visitors unknowingly participate in several different layered and nuanced performances of memory, race, and authenticity. First, they become aware of themselves as a particular type of tourist—Ghanaian national or non-Ghanaian national—based on the price of the admission ticket. Non-Ghanaian nationals pay ten times more than Ghanaian nationals. This designation affects the way that they interact with other tourists and the experience of the guided tour itself.

Each tour guide takes a group of about twenty people, who are usually racially and ethnically diverse and of different ages and nationalities. On occasion, however, some members of the tours have complained that they were made to feel uncomfortable, if not unwelcome, by other members of the group. The comments of a tourist who distinguished himself as a white American from Connecticut described his uneasy experience during the hour-long tour of Elmina Castle:

> Very impressive castle. Tour was very good. Great views toward the city, beach and ocean. One concern—a man during the tour was distracting and I felt offended by his anti-white sentiments, as he kept saying, "white people this…" I couldn't understand exactly, but he should respect other people more who are trying to follow the tour guide. Overall, I enjoyed my visit here.[13]

A Ghanaian member of the same tour group added, "It should be strictly forbidden for visitors in the group to keep making offensive comments which directly or indirectly concern individuals in the group."[14] Yet incidents such as this one are examples of the pervasive effects of racial inequality and the legacy of slavery enacted on the world stage today.

Organized tour groups defined either racially, ethnically, or by school, church, or social affiliation often request to have their own guide. Many African American groups ask that no whites accompany their tour. Similarly, many organized groups of roots tourists demand that whites be barred from participating in their tour, especially when they descend into the sacred spaces of the dungeons for the first time. It is there that roots tourists seek to claim a privileged status, a certain aura of authenticity. They rebuff the presence of whites, citing that they do not wish to experience the pain of their ancestors with descendants of their oppressors in their midst. If some groups exclude outsiders, then are these excluded outsiders not allowed to *mourn*? Are roots tourists, Europeans, or Ghanaians equally permitted their grief?

The guided tours at both Cape Coast and Elmina focus on the points of pain and suffering or strength and resistance to lend a sense of authenticity to the historical and contemporary significance of the sites. Indeed, the notion of authenticity is central to the allure of tourism as an industry. When choosing a vacation destination, the average tourist goes in search of the authentic ethnic experience, the authentic white sand beach, or the authentic ancient ruins. Cape Coast and Elmina combine all of these notions of authenticity. In an effort to show "This is how it *really* was," the principal highlights of the castle tours, while somber and inviting, perform an authenticating function. Thus, visitors learn about sensational and brutal acts that were all too commonplace, including the rape of enslaved women at the hands of European traders, governors, and officers; the types of torture inflicted upon defiant captives; the presence of the churches inside of the castles (one Anglican, the other Catholic); points of architectural interest; the spacious governors' and officers' quarters on the upper levels; the stench and horror of the underground dungeons; and the door of no return.

Most if not all of the rooms that tourists pass through are empty. The churches have no pews, and the governors' and officers' quarters lack decoration with period furniture. Visitors are expected to imagine what it might have been like to live in these spaces. One visitor at Cape Coast demanded: "Please authenticate the Governor's residence to look exactly the way it was then. I think that will make the necessary contrast with the dungeons."[15]

But how might the dungeons be "authenticated"? A visitor to Elmina had one possible solution: "Renovate with models of slaves, sound effects, [and] smells to give authenticity and real feel for what it was like for our ancestors."[16] But would such an attempt to recreate a sensorium of the unspeakable go too far, especially when the physical architecture of the dungeons themselves is still there to be experienced? How would the curators and designers choose the models to represent the enslaved men and women, and which actors might be asked to create the sound effects?

Some of the changes to the female dungeons at Elmina aim at authenticity, especially the metal bars that were placed in the arched window openings. But the fresh coats of white paint inside of some of the male dungeons have left many visitors in a state of outrage. As one person commented, "The Jews would not paint the ovens in Germany!"[17] Similarly problematic was the renovation of one of the male dungeons at Elmina into a gift shop, replete with merchandising shelves and walls painted with coats of fresh yellow paint. So many visitors complained about the gift shop that it was eventually dismantled and moved to an outer service area across from the castle restaurant, the presence of which also has not gone without criticism.

In general, the dungeons have been left hauntingly bare, with the exception of the wreaths, flowers, notes, and burning candles left by visitors on a daily basis. And most tourists seem to prefer the dungeons that way. They feel that the emptiness best signifies the absence of the many millions gone, and for them, that is the only authentic way for the dungeons to be represented. Visitors regularly choose the hallowed dungeons as sites in which to perform rituals of tribute and commemoration or to participate in reenactments of the kidnapping of African captives. In one such reenactment staged by local Ghanaian actors at Panafest 1999, the biennial Pan-African Festival of Performing Arts, the actors donned masks of American presidents, including Richard Nixon and Ronald Reagan, to portray the slave catchers, an overt criticism of American involvement in the slave trade with a decidedly politicized contemporary reference to how their policies have affected African Americans.

PHOTOGRAPHIC MEMORIES

Photography is the leading authenticating action among tourists. Individuals, armed with cell phones and digital movie cameras, engage in intense and constant photographic activity that documents historical points of interest, details of architectural or aesthetic curiosity, or members of their group. At Elmina, the courtyard is a popular place for photography, offering visitors views of the Portuguese church and the surrounding dungeons, an aesthetically pleasing backdrop for taking photographs of individuals and groups. The most picturesque photographic site at Cape Coast is the balustrade walkway framing the angular row of cannons pointed toward the sea. But photographic activity also reinforces the most perplexing of paradoxes, as one tourist noted, "The disparity between the horrific history of the castle and the natural and physical beauty of the seashore is a difficult mix for the present day visitor."[18] In 1993, the renowned African American artist Carrie Mae Weems (b. 1953) produced black-and-white photographs of Cape Coast, Elmina, and Gorée Island in Senegal for her *Slave Coast Series*. These filmic diptychs and triptychs combine image and text to quietly memorialize the history of slavery while acknowledging the popular phenomenon of roots tourism (fig. 10.10). In *Grabbing, Snatching*, Weems's documentary-style images capture the iconic dungeons and door of no return of the Maison des esclaves (House of Slaves) on Gorée Island in Senegal. In contrast, Iké Udé's (b. 1964, Nigeria) *Conde Nast Traveler* (1994), a digitally manipulated photograph that appropriates the cover and stylings of the popular travel magazine, foregrounds the slave ship icon to criticize the popularity of travel and tourism focused on these sites of memory.

Even fashion photographers have chosen the castles as stylish backdrops for their glossy magazine work. Inspired by this perverse phenomenon, the noted Ethiopian-born filmmaker Haile Gerima (b. 1946) set the opening scenes of his

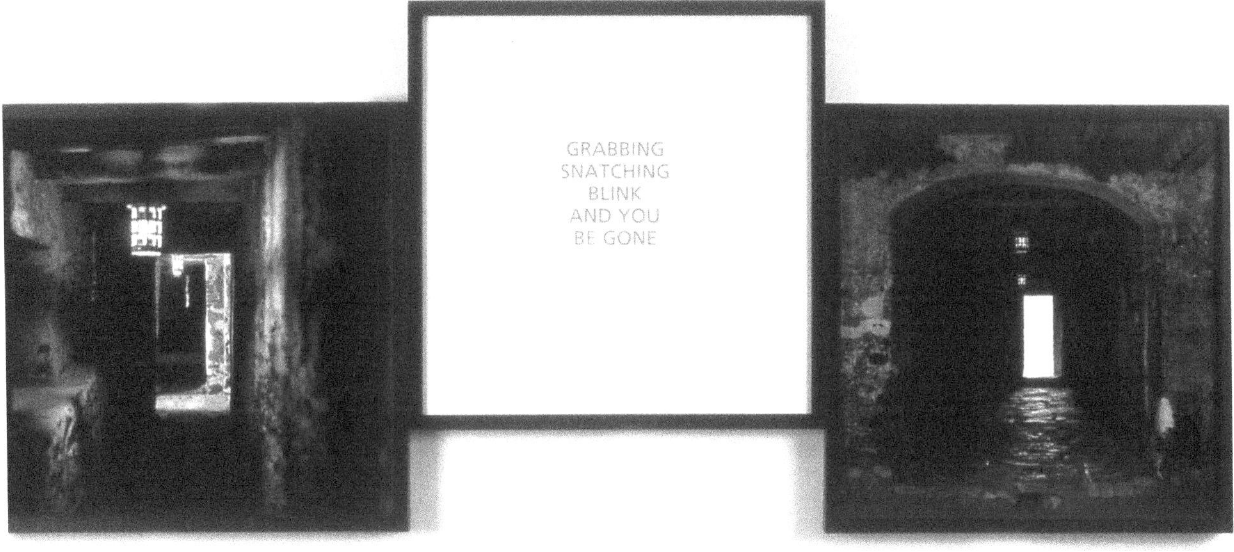

10.10
Carrie Mae Weems, *Slave Coast Series: Grabbing,
Snatching,* 1993, two gelatin silver prints and
one screen printed panel, 20 × 20 inches.

critically acclaimed film *Sankofa* (1993) among a crowd of tourists about to enter the dungeons at Cape Coast Castle. Told as a flashback, the film follows a black fashion model on location for a photo shoot (wearing a blond wig and Western clothing) as she is psychically taken backward in time through the dungeon to relive the horrors of slavery as a lesson not to forget her roots. *Sankofa* seeks to expose some of these issues when the spirits in Cape Coast Castle subsume a fashion shoot that takes place on this most unlikely runway (fig. 10.11). In a strange way, the horror of these monuments becomes aestheticized in the act of recording them on film. The African American novelist and photographer Richard Wright recalls with biting sarcasm the sublime beauty of Elmina Castle in his 1954 novel *Black Power*: "Towers rise two hundred feet in the air. What spacious dreams! What august faith! How elegantly laid-out the castle is! What bold plunging lines! What, yes, taste."[19] His black-and-white photographs document its balustrades, courtyards, cannons, and the door of no return prior to Ghana's independence from Britain in 1957.

The dynamics of picture taking at the castles could be a study in and of itself. In the case of roots tourism, though, it has a special commemorative function and unique familial appeal. As roots tourists gather in groups in front of the cannons at Cape Coast Castle or with the backdrop of the Portuguese church at Elmina, they are participating in an act of remembering—symbolically taking possession of the past, some smile, some weep, others look straightforward at the camera with solemn expressions on their faces. Authenticating actions such as these signal the practice of mnemonic aesthetics as a novel form of African diasporic ritual

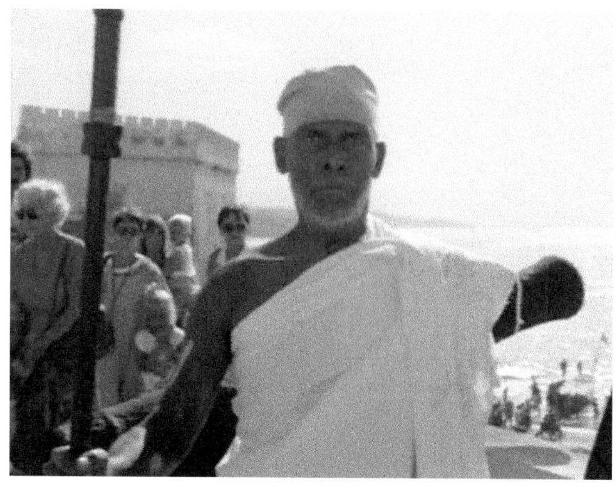

10.11 LEFT
Film still, Haile Gerima, *Sankofa*, 1993.

10.12 BELOW
Cape Coast Castle, *Door of No Return and Door of Return*, 2005.

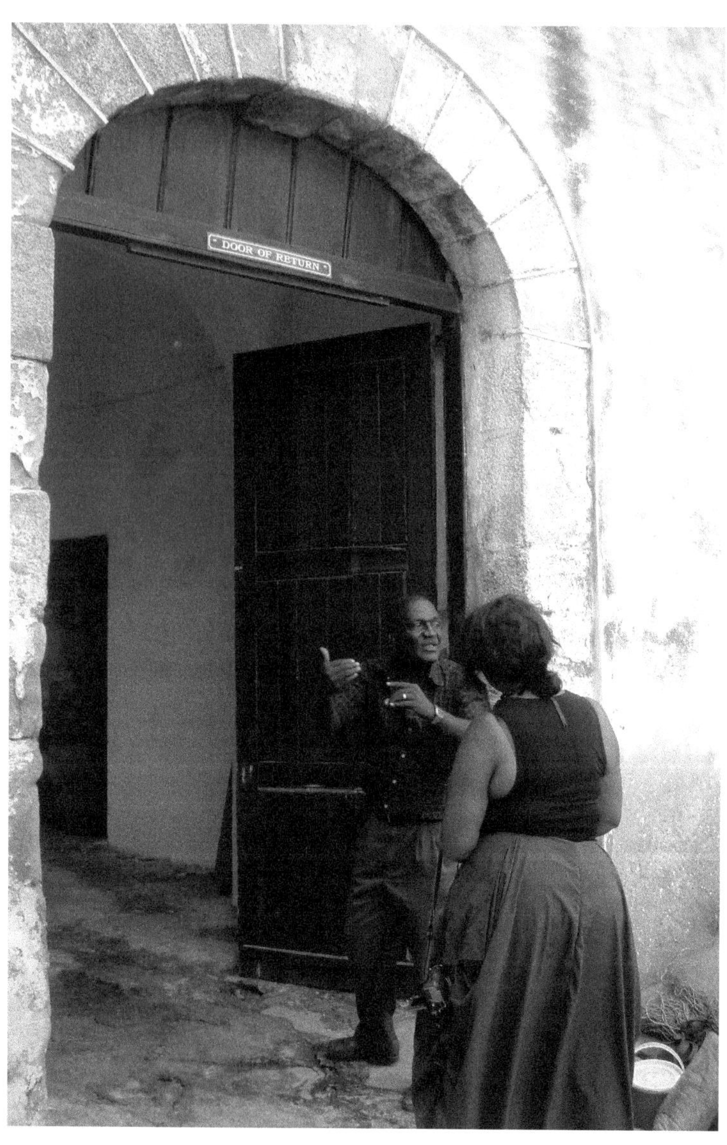
" DOOR OF RETURN "

and performance. These photographs are evidence of a return to the ancestral homeland, of the buildings that still stand as a reminder of the birth of the African diaspora in the transatlantic slave trade. Back home, roots tourists share their photographs with family and friends as proof of having been there, of having walked through the *door of no return* (fig. 10.12).

The door of no return is the most popular site that roots tourists choose to record on film. At Cape Coast Castle, the door of no return is located at the base of the central courtyard, just beyond the female dungeons. At the top of the doorframe, a standard Ghana Museums and Monuments Board sign labels the door in neat white letters, DOOR OF NO RETURN, marking it as a site of special interest. Other such signposts can be found around the castle labeling other important places of interest such as the MALE SLAVE DUNGEON, PALAVER HALL, CONDEMNED CELL, BASTION, and so on. During one of the climactic moments of the tour, visitors watch in quiet anticipation as the guide opens the heavy, black wooden door for the first time, revealing the expanse of a motionless sea where African captives were led to awaiting slave ships. Waiting there on the tiny strip of sandy beach are local children, who know the opening door will reveal a new group of tourists, whom they engage in conversation and sometimes ask for money. This culminating moment of the tour possesses a theatrical feeling as the group timidly walks across the threshold to the beach, where some roots tourists pour libations, place memorials, or say prayers to the ancestors.

Finally, as the guide motions to the group that it is time to go back inside, he points out another sign above the door of no return, which is visible only from the outside, upon reentry. This time, the now recognizable neat white lettering reads, DOOR OF RETURN. The guide explains that the sign is meant as a gesture of reconciliation, one that welcomes back the thousands of African diaspora tourists who make pilgrimages to the monuments each year. But is such a "return" to an ancestral homeland that they as individuals never before set foot on really possible? Think about it: What does the new sign, DOOR OF RETURN, really mean? What is lost or gained by renaming the infamous DOOR OF NO RETURN? Does such an act signify an attempt to erase the brutal history of the castles and the dungeons beneath them in the name of facilitating tourism? Does it mean that time—four hundred years—has healed the wounds? Is it asking us to forget and move on? To most thoughtfully reflect on an issue of tremendous complexity and weight, we might return to the Akan word *sankofa*: "one must return to the past in order to move forward."

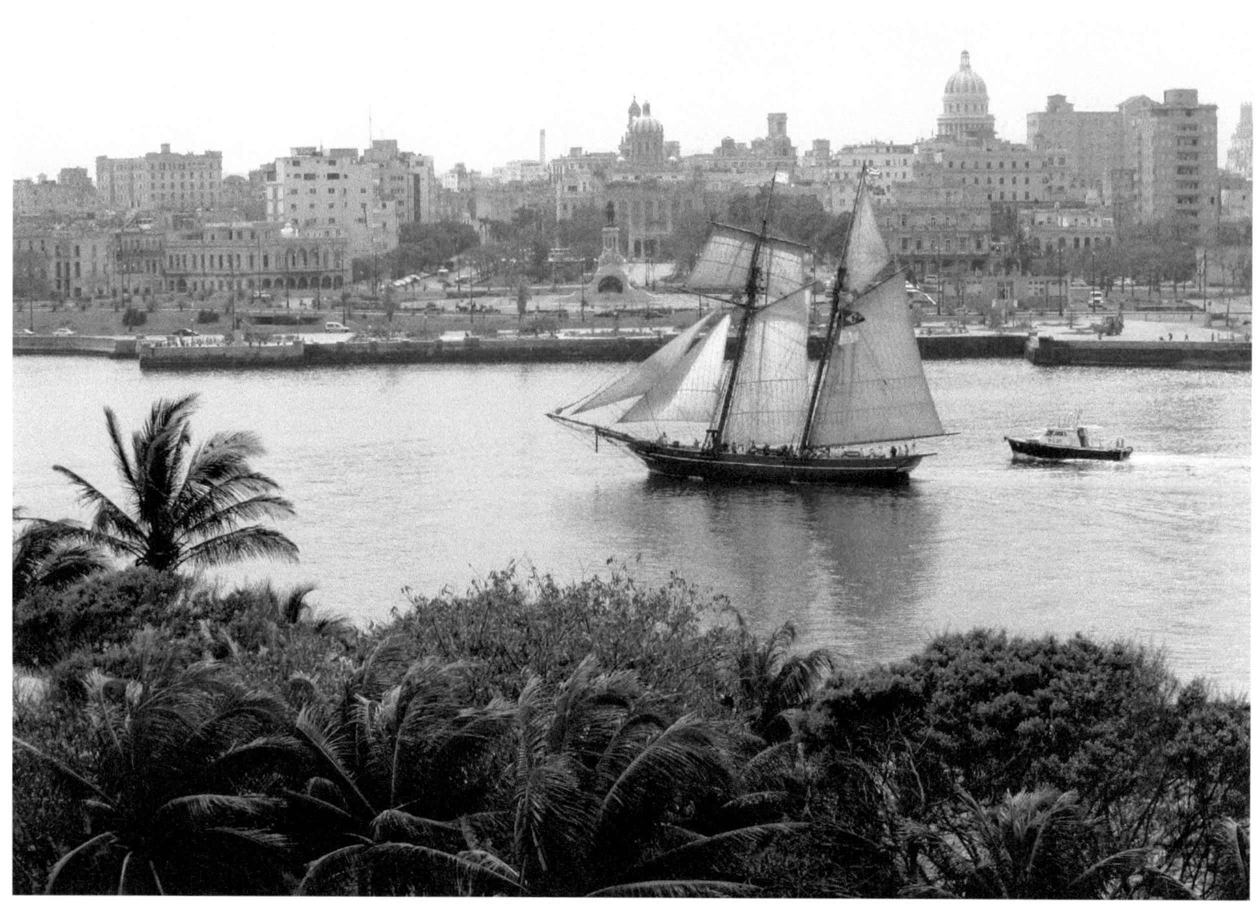

11.1
Franklin Reyes, *Replica of La Amistad Coastal Schooner in Havana Harbor, Cuba*, 2010.

MUSEUMS, MONUMENTS, AND MEMORIALS

IN 2000, Amistad America Inc. launched a novel memorial, the *Freedom Schooner Amistad*, a floating replica of *La Amistad* (*The Friendship*), the coastal schooner that was taken over by a group of fifty-three captive Africans who were being transported from Havana to nearby coastal sugar plantations for a life of chattel slavery (fig. 11.1). The story of the *Amistad* mutiny has been well documented and celebrated in scholarship, literature, and the cinema of the 1980s and 1990s.[1] The forty-nine men, three girls, and one boy had been brought to Havana in 1839 aboard the *Tecora*, an illegal slaver sailing under a Spanish flag from Sierra Leone. They revolted, killing the captain and the cook, and demanded that the remaining crew sail the ship back to their native land. After sixty-three days, the ship was seized by the United States Coast Guard in Long Island Sound and brought into the harbor at New London, Connecticut. Her human cargo was taken to New Haven, jailed, and charged with murder, where a bronze memorial created by Ed Hamilton (b. 1947) stands in front of City Hall today. A long, closely watched trial ensued. Two years after the *Amistad*'s capture, in 1841, former President John Quincy Adams came out of retirement to argue the case before the United States Supreme Court and finally won the *Amistad* Africans' freedom that year. The court case attracted international attention and caused intense legal and diplomatic strife between the United States and Spain. In the end, as the students aboard the *Freedom Schooner Amistad* learn, the triumph of the *Amistad* captives set precedents for an international understanding of human rights and the use of the law on an international scale.

When I first viewed the *Freedom Schooner Amistad* shortly after it was launched, I was impressed by the detail with which the shipwrights in Mystic Seaport, Connecticut, had created such a convincing nineteenth-century replica, noting the expert craftsmanship of the woodwork, masts, rigging, and sails. But when I was led below deck on my tour, I was somewhat surprised not to see some reference to the slave ship icon in the design. Instead, below decks the ship seemed relatively modern, with a state-of-the-art kitchen, sleeping quarters, and tables and other furniture for recreation and educational purposes. On one side, there were reproductions of documentary images of the *Amistad* captives that had appeared in newspapers at the time of the trial, but there were no shelves, shackles, or other devices of restraint that one might expect to see on a replica of a slave ship. In 2007, a replica of the scandalous British slave ship *Zong* included wooden shelves, numbered and empty,

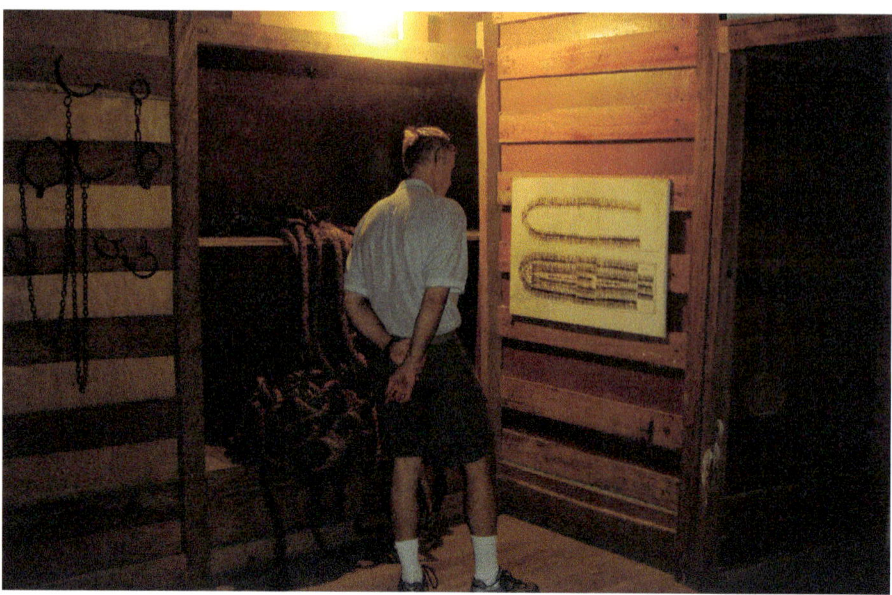

11.2

Installation view of slave ship hold, *Crossroads
of a People, Crossroads of Trade*, Cape Coast
Castle Museum, Cape Coast, Ghana, August 1999.

representing the spaces where enslaved Africans would be held below decks. It was launched as part of the commemorative celebrations marking the two hundredth anniversary of the Abolition of the Slave Trade Act by Britain.

The *Amistad* captain and crew told me that there were no plans for an installation of shelves with mannequins of prone, shackled slave bodies. Installations such as these (some with and others without the addition of the figures) had been realized at the Cape Coast Castle Museum in Ghana (fig. 11.2); in Great Britain at the Wilberforce House in Hull (fig. 11.3), the Transatlantic Slavery Gallery at the Merseyside Maritime Museum in Liverpool, the International Slavery Museum also in Liverpool, and the National Maritime Museum in Greenwich; the Field Museum in Chicago, the Charles H. Wright African American Museum in Detroit (fig. 11.4), the Blacks in Wax Museum in Baltimore, and the Heinz History and Culture Center in Pittsburgh; and in traveling exhibitions of salvaged slave ships, such as *A Slave Ship Speaks: The Wreck of the Henrietta Marie* (2002) (fig. 11.5). These installations contrast with the design below decks of the New Haven–based *Amistad* replica: with a mission of international understanding and reconciliation, such a didactic installation would not be necessary. Instead, the work of education, of memorialization, of reconciliation, and of understanding was taking place through the act of sailing the boat, not so much as a reenactment of the mutiny but more so as an act of reclamation, of symbolic possession of the past, of reclaiming the spaces and histories that such a sailing replica might actually touch and transform by charting a practice of mnemonic aesthetics.

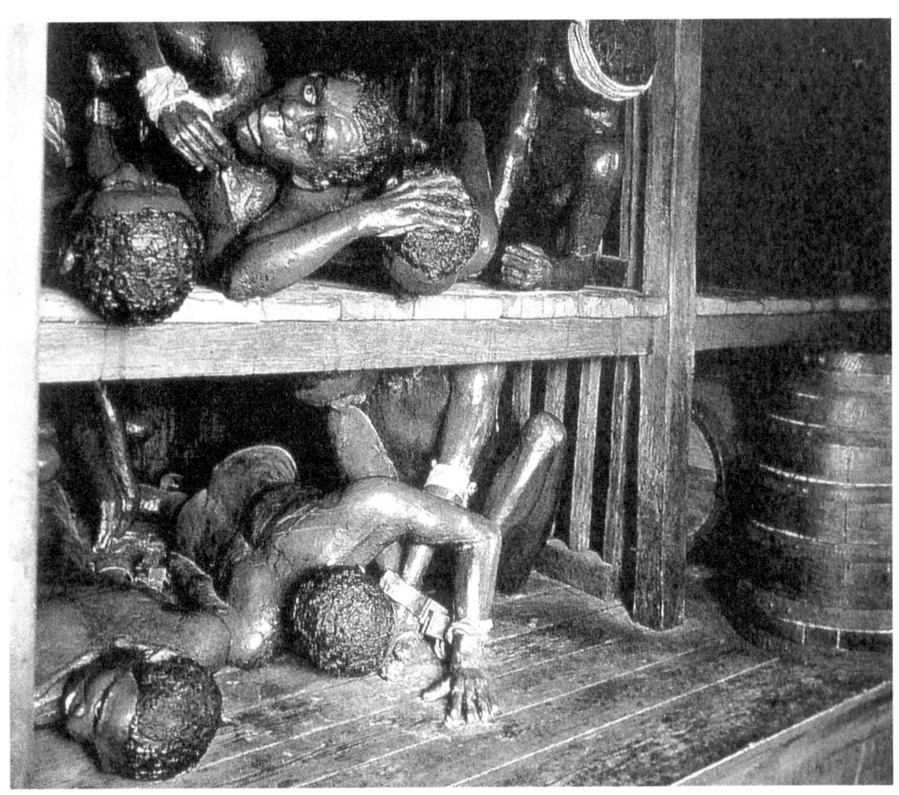

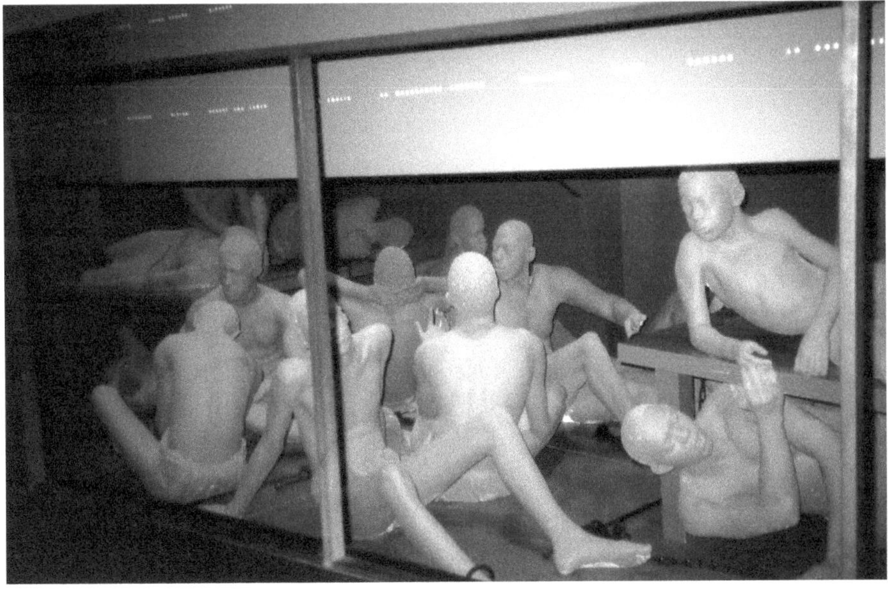

11.3 TOP
Installation view of slave ship hold, Wilberforce
House Museum, Hull, ca. 1999. Dismantled
ca. 2006.

11.4 BOTTOM
Installation view of core exhibition, *Of the
People: The African American Experience*,
Charles H. Wright National African American
Museum, Detroit, 2000. Dismantled 2003.

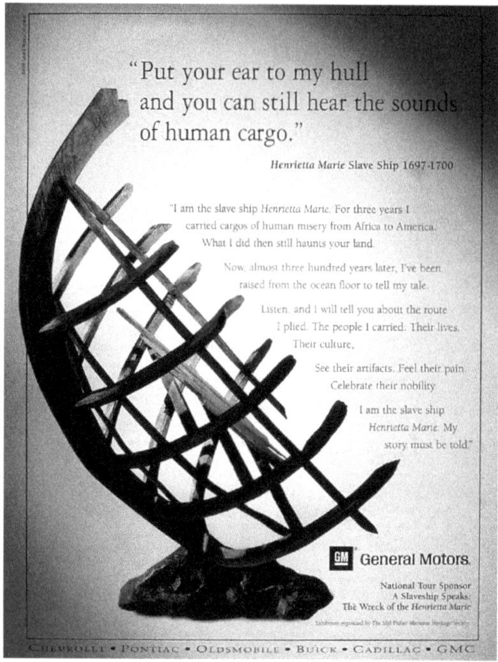

11.5
Magazine advertisement for the exhibition
A Slave Ship Speaks: The Wreck of the Henrietta Marie, ca. 2002.

The tradition of making ship models goes back to the beginning of maritime architecture. Initially, they served as prototypes of actual sailing vessels, but as time went on, ship models were also made for sailing enthusiasts as well as for commemorative purposes. In 1984, the book *Traite Negrier L'Aurore* (Plan of the Slave Ship *Aurore*) was published on the occasion of the two hundredth anniversary of the ship's manufacture (fig. 11.6). A notorious slave ship with European ports of embarkation in Nantes and La Rochelle, the *Aurore* made several voyages in the triangular trade touching the coast of West Africa and the French colonies in the West Indies. This volume tells the history of the *Aurore* and also includes line drawings and plans for a scale model. Published by a fine art naval architectural press, the plans are profusely illustrated, but with the most unexpected and remarkable images: brown figures representing the emaciated enslaved Africans whose bodies would be squeezed between the decks and other spaces of the architectural plans. This shocking and contrary volume leaves much to consider when the craft of ship model making is combined with telling the history of the slave trade and remembering the difficult past. Perhaps in the hands of contemporary artists of the African diaspora, such as Yinka Shonibare MBE (RA) (b. 1962), similar projects might produce a different result. His *Wanderer*, a wooden one-quarter model with colorful sails using his characteristic "African" textiles, was made during the wave of frenetic artistic activity in the United Kingdom leading up to the 2007 commemoration of the Abolition of the Slave Trade Act (fig. 11.7). The *Wanderer* was built in 1857 as a pleasure ship and racing yacht, but later changed hands and was converted to be used in a clandestine slaving voyage that left Port Jefferson, New York, just one year later. The ship carried 457 enslaved Africans to Jekyll Island, Georgia, where they were disembarked and

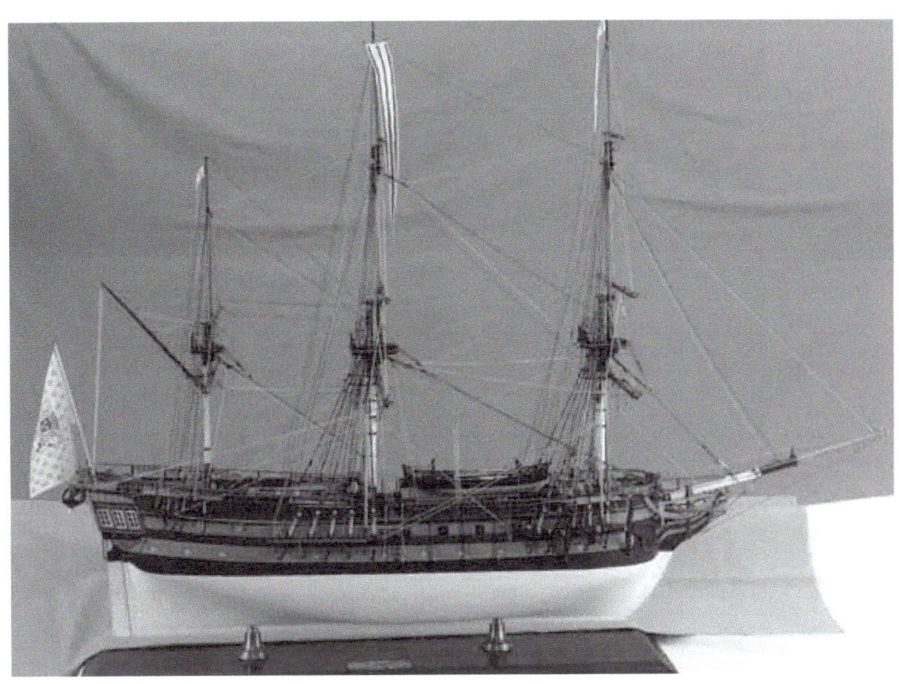

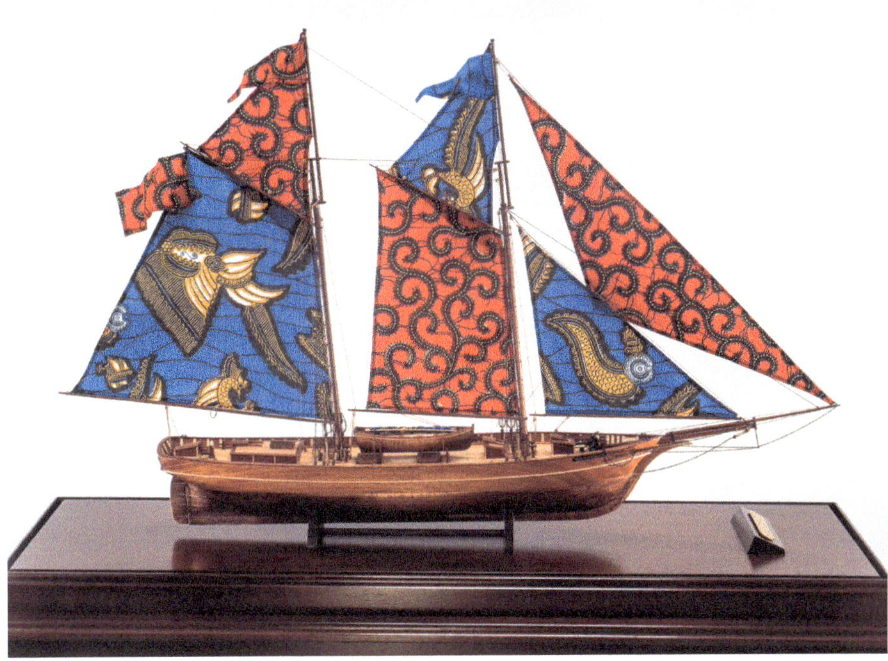

L'Aurore, 1984, contemporary wooden model.

Yinka Shonibare, *The Wanderer*, 2006–7, wooden
model, wax printed cotton. Model: 71 × 101.6 × 22.9 cm
(28 × 40 × 9 inches); vitrine: 77.5 × 111.8 × 31.8 cm
(30 1/2 × 44 × 12 1/2 inches).

quickly hidden due to rumors that attracted the interest of the US Coast Guard and Navy, who suspected a case of illegal slaving. The owners of the ship were brought to trial but none of their prosecutions produced sentences. Finally, during the Civil War, the ship was seized to be used as a gunboat. Shonibare's *Wanderer* was produced in an edition of seven, and the example pictured here was collected in 2016 by the Addison Gallery of American Art in the United States. Known for its sizable holdings of quarter models, the Addison Gallery acquired Shonibare's *Wanderer* as a counterpoint to the gallery's example of the *Mayflower*, one of the ships that first brought European settler colonists to the shores of North America.

Since its launch nearly twenty years ago, the *Freedom Schooner Amistad* has made several voyages, including a notable journey in the 2007 bicentenary year to key points in Europe, West Africa, and the Caribbean. The *Freedom Schooner Amistad* sailed to Haiti following the devastating earthquake of January 12, 2010, to deliver humanitarian aid. Two months later, on March 25, 2010, she sailed into the harbor at Havana for the very first time to mark the International Day of Remembrance for the Victims of Slavery as part of the UNESCO Slave Routes Project.

With a name meaning "friendship," the symbolic return of the *Freedom Schooner Amistad* to Havana raises significant questions about the political implications of its mission and the redemptive possibilities of return foreshadowing the warming of US-Cuban relations in the last years of the Obama administration. As the ship sailed into the harbor at Havana, it flew three flags to symbolize the international nature of its journey and the work of reconciliation: the US flag, the flag of Cuba, and the flag of the United Nations. Public tours of the ship were arranged during its week-long stay in Cuba, along with simulcast educational television for school-age children in Cuba, Trinidad and Tobago, Guyana, Jamaica, and Britain, and in the United Nations headquarters in New York. Wherever she sails, the students and crew of the *Freedom Schooner Amistad* participate in a novel form of edu-tourism aboard a vessel that serves as a symbol of freedom, an international ambassador of human rights, and a museum of conscience through its teaching of the *Amistad* incident.

On March 25, 2015, the United Nations dedicated a memorial to the slave trade to mark the International Day of Remembrance and to introduce the next decade in which the focus of remembrance will be on Africans and their descendants who were affected by the transatlantic slave trade. The memorial, called the *Ark of Return*, was designed by Haitian American architect Rodney Leon (b. 1970), known for the African Burial Ground National Memorial in Downtown New York (2010). The *Ark of Return* sits prominently on UN Plaza in New York City, a gleaming white marble structure. It has three sides, in homage to the triangular trade, and inside, the figure of a man with jet black skin lies supine. Engraved on the facade, the schematic designs of the slave ship icon's most prominent cross sections, figures 4 and 5, mark its inescapable presence. More prevalent today than ever, memorials such as these show how the art of the slave ship icon connects the urgency of the past to contemporary struggles in the black Atlantic.

THE SHAPE OF THINGS...
DOESN'T ALWAYS APPEAR AS IT SEEMS

IN FALL 2001, the exhibition and book *Words for Images: A Gallery of Poems* were presented at the Yale University Art Gallery in New Haven, Connecticut, to mark the yearlong celebration of the university's three-hundredth anniversary.[1] For the exhibition, twenty-two alumni poets were commissioned to write about works of twentieth-century art in the gallery's collection. This innovative project was the brainchild of the poet and professor John Hollander and the curator and art historian Joanna Weber. *Words for Images* was a cross-disciplinary artistic collaboration and a chance to commemorate the university, its poets, and its art collections.

Elizabeth Alexander (b. 1962), a graduate of the class of 1984, was among the poets asked to contribute.[2] Known for her witty, soulful lyricism, she often reaches back in time to her 1960s- and 1970s-era Washington, DC, childhood, or to the people and events that have shaped African American history, to reveal a profound symbolic possession of the past. Occasionally, her poems take on an epic length, layered with the vivid images and expressive music of her astute historical consciousness, making the not too distant past meaningful for present generations. Of her poem "Praise Song for the Day," delivered on the occasion of the inauguration of President Barack Obama on January 20, 2009, the poet E. Ethelbert Miller (b. 1950) noted, "This is a praise song in which the words of remembrance do the heavy lifting."[3] Like the poets Robert Hayden (1913–1980) and Ntozake Shange (b. 1948), or the writers Toni Morrison (b. 1931) and Caryl Phillips (b. 1958), Alexander continues the practice of mnemonic aesthetics in literature.

Free to choose from the gallery's impressive collection of twentieth-century art, Alexander decided upon *Islands No. 4*, a small, square painting by the minimalist artist Agnes Martin (1912–2004) from around 1961 (fig. A.1).[4] According to Alexander, finding a work of art to write about wasn't simple. "I settled on the painting after first looking to find something by a black artist," she recalled. "At the time, there was basically NOTHING."[5] Then she perused the gallery's permanent collection on display and found herself attracted to abstract works such as those by Paul Klee, Joan Miró, Constantin Brancusi, and Mark Rothko. Abstract works, she felt, "left lots of room to 'feel' the poem."[6] Ultimately, for Alexander, the process of discovering Martin's painting in the museum's basement storage was akin to fate, or perhaps destiny: "The painting was so wee, so tucked away in that drawer, so protected and secreted, and waiting for me, it seemed."[7]

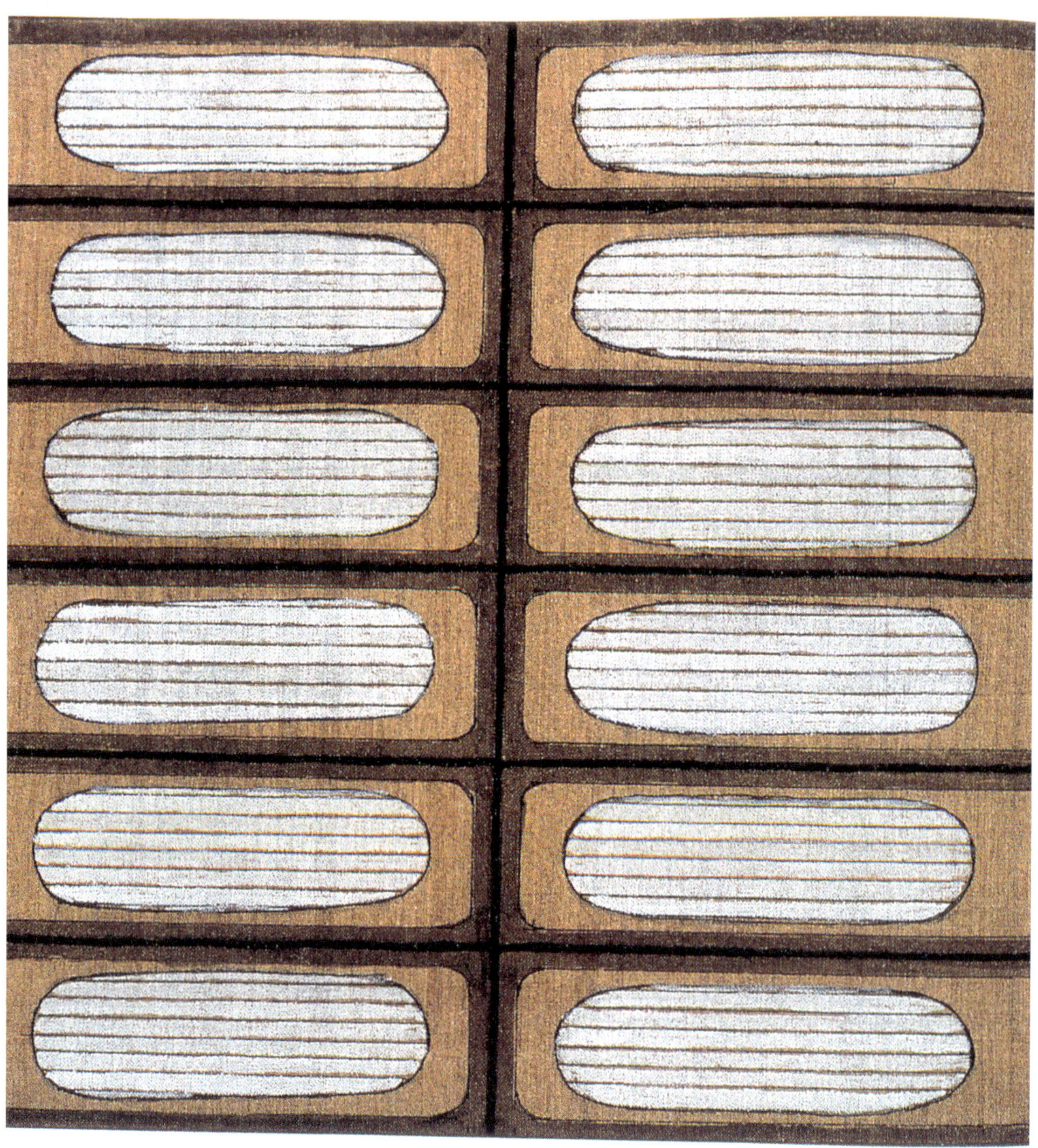

Agnes Martin, *Islands No. 4*, ca. 1961, oil on canvas,
37.8 × 37.8 cm (14⁷/₈ × 14⁷/₈ inches).

The small format of *Islands No. 4*, measuring only approximately fifteen by fifteen inches, is atypical of Martin's canvases, which are usually rendered as large as six by six feet. The abstract minimalist subject matter, however, is reminiscent of the vast majority of her works, which often repeat simple geometric forms in grid-like fashion. The practice of repetition and the unadorned quietude of her works evoke a meditative state of mind and a deep spiritual awareness. This is no coincidence. Martin studied Taoism and Eastern religion after moving to New Mexico in 1946, and art critics and scholars have noticed its influence on her compositions. The art critic Michael Kimmelman has called her paintings "nature's mystical poetry."[8] *Islands No. 4* dates from the period shortly after she had her first noteworthy New York showing at the Betty Parsons Gallery in 1958, which coincided with the height of minimalism as a popular force in the art world of that era.

On the surface, Martin's painting is seemingly as simple as its title: a neutral, sand-colored canvas with twelve elongated white ovals arranged in recurring compartments within a grid, two to each side. Viewed more closely, it is anything but simplicity and exactitude. Fine black lines transform the ovals into wood grain and demarcate their borders and the grid that encloses them. The surface of the canvas glistens and shimmers ever so slightly depending on the light and the angle at which it is viewed. These fleeting sparkles add texture and simulate light rays that might reflect off the water and onto highly polished grains of sand on an island shore.

Joanna Weber commented that Martin's repetition of the "[horizon] line within the simple geometric form of oval capsules encased in a grid shows an archipelago of islands organized as neatly as if they were in an ice cube tray."[9] This simple visual analogy suggests the ways in which the artist's spare use of line and form brings to mind other objects that share a similar geometric appearance. When I first saw *Islands No. 4*, I conjured up the image of a squat, rectangular version of the popular African game of memory, Mankala, usually played by two people on an elongated wooden board, with small stones dropped successively into parallel concave hollows or pits on either side of the board.[10]

Alexander's poem, titled "Islands Number Four," completely disrupts the painting's visual balance of endless, hypnotic horizon lines, setting it forever off-kilter:

Islands Number Four

1.
Agnes Martin, *Islands Number Four*,
Repeated ovals on a grid, what appears
To be perfect is handmade, disturbed.
Tobacco brown saturates canvas to burlap,
Clean form from a distance, up close, her hand.
All wrack and bramble to oval and grid.
Hollows in the body, containers for grief.
What looks to be perfect is not perfect.
Odd oval portholes that flood with light.

2.

Description of a Slave Ship. 1789:
Same imperfect ovals, calligraphic hand.
At a distance, patter. Up close, bodies
Doubled and doubled, serried and stacked
In the manner of galleries in a church.
In full ships on their sides or on each other.
Isle of woe, two-by-two, spoon-fashion,
Not unfrequently found dead in the morning.
Slave-ships, the not-pure, imperfect ovals,
Portholes through which they would never see home.
The flesh rubbed off their shoulders, elbows, hips.
Barracoon, sarcophagus, indestructible grief
Nesting in the hollows of the abdomen.
The slave-ship empty, its cargo landed
And sold for twelve ounces of gold a-piece.
Or gone overboard. Islands. Aftermath.[11]

Alexander's poem uses the language of vision and memory, of closeness and distance, of shape and line to reveal a remembered history and a familiar, indelible image. She takes Martin's predominant geometric form, the recurring oval, and astutely recognizes specific objects that share the same (or similar) shape: slave ships and portholes as well as a barracoon, sarcophagus, abdomen—each in its own way a container for grief. For the poet, Martin's seemingly free-floating oval islands escape any notion of liberty. Caught up in the crisscrossing matrix that is the history of the slave trade, these islands could signify Gorée off the coast of Senegal, Jamestown off the coast of The Gambia, or the collection of Caribbean islands on the other side of the Atlantic, all famous for the embarkation and disembarkation of enslaved people. What is more, the black lines that traverse each curvilinear form could suggest iron bars that keep freedom at bay on the floating coffins, the slave ships.

In the first stanza, Alexander uses color and metaphor to describe the painting, subtly dropping hints that flood the senses with a feeling, an impression of the Middle Passage and the history of slavery. In the first stanza, Alexander writes, "Tobacco brown saturates canvas to burlap." Tobacco was one of the biggest cash crops that enslaved people were forced to produce in the southern United States. Burlap was used to make the bags in which they carried tobacco and cotton from the fields. In the leanest of times, their clothing also was made from burlap. The colors "tobacco brown" and "burlap" bring to mind the color of skin, the texture of sand, the smell of wood, and the stench of feces, all realities of the Middle Passage that Alexander references in the second stanza.

The power of Alexander's poem lies in her ability to remember *and* imagine *Description of a Slave Ship* in Martin's work. Through clever uses of the mnemonic devices of repetition, comparison, and visual analogy, the poem emphasizes the spatial dynamics of both images. Martin's painting is made up of some of the basic geometric shapes: a square canvas, rectangles that form a compartmentalized grid, and ovals repeated within the graphic matrix. Just the mere suggestion of Martin's "odd ovals" jarred Alexander's memory of *Description of a Slave Ship*. Like Martin's islands, this engraving is made up of basic geometric shapes: a naval architectural plan, divided by squares and rectangles that section off compartments containing repeated figural forms, "imperfect ovals," within the schematic template. Alexander's insistence on seeing the slave ship icon in Martin's painting is further proof of how deeply embedded this image is within our personal psyches, how much it is one of the visual aftershocks that continues to rock the black Atlantic.

Alexander's poems frequently address works of art and artists.[12] As John Hollander explains in the introduction to *Words for Images*, poems about works of art hark back to the beginnings of literature. Indeed, this fundamental urge to combine image and text can also be traced to the very first works of art, both natural and man-made. This type of writing is generally known as *ekphrastic*, after the Greek *ekphrasis*, meaning "to speak."[13] Traditionally, such descriptive writing has taken two forms: that of a *notional* ekphrasis, a poem about an imaginary image, or that of an *actual* ekphrasis, a poem about a real image or work of art.[14] Most actual ekphrases contain some element of the notional or the imaginary. All in all, this sort of interpretive writing usually brings out something more about the form and content of a work of art—something that the artist did not consider, something that is not readily visible upon casual observation, or something that places the work of art within a social or historical context.

Alexander's poem takes the form of an ekphrasis within an ekphrasis. The poem is an actual description of Martin's painting as well as a notional illustration, in which Alexander sees and imagines *Description of a Slave Ship* in the minimal shapes of Martin's painting. Similarly, the explanatory text of *Description of a Slave Ship* is also an ekphrasis in the most traditional art-historical sense. Not only does the text explain the actual graphic image, it also describes the interior space of the slave ship, which was purely imagined by the artist and the author of the text based on evidence gathered by the London Committee.

In preparation for writing "Islands Number Four," Alexander studied an original example of *Description of a Slave Ship* in the collection of Yale University's Beinecke Rare Book and Manuscript Library. There she read the descriptive text of the 1789 broadside—the ekphrasis—and selected a few phrases, which she later excerpted in the second stanza of the poem:

> In full ships on their sides or on each other.
> Not unfrequently found dead in the morning.
> *The flesh rubbed off their shoulders, elbows, hips.*[15]

The poet also conducted a careful examination of the schematic engraving. The visual exercise of looking at such a detailed print required patiently going back and forth, focusing and refocusing on the ways in which the image changes when viewed from a distance or up close. The rigor of such visual analysis, of "squinching," as Alexander described this exercise of sustained looking, also found its way into the poet's writing. Certainly, her poem urges us to look deeper at both images, beyond a simple description or a formal analysis. About Martin's painting she writes, "Clean form from a distance, up close, her hand." Alexander shrewdly noticed that no oval in the painting is quite the same: "Repeated ovals on a grid, what appears to be perfect is handmade, disturbed." In *Description of a Slave Ship*, Alexander first caught a glimpse of the "same imperfect ovals, calligraphic hand. At a distance, patter," and then, focusing, "up close, bodies doubled and doubled, serried and stacked." This back-and-forth method of looking also mimics the tossing and turning, up-and-down rhythm of a slave ship at sea.

The last line of Alexander's poem suggests a release from the confines of the slave ship, of liberty even if by death: "Or gone overboard. Islands. Aftermath." The islands here could be floating corpses, set free from a future life of perpetual servitude. The final word of the poem, "Aftermath," is a reminder of what is still at stake for the descendants of slaves and slave traders alike. If anything, Alexander's prescient work is evidence that the consequences of transatlantic slavery still haunt the black Atlantic imagination. She admits, "It was one of the hardest poems I ever wrote."[16]

As this book has illustrated, contemporary artists' representations of the slave ship icon have repeated the basic shape of an "imperfect oval." This is no coincidence; rather, it has something to do with the ways in which icons function, a point that Alexander's poem reiterates again and again through its focus on the interpretive possibilities of the oval. The oval is a frequently occurring form in nature and a commonly seen shape in man-made objects. Take, for instance, the egg, the womb, and the three-quarter moon, or the "barracoon, sarcophagus," and bier. Icons usually assume simple geometric forms, memorable shapes, and easily recognizable images (people, flora, and fauna) that tend to appear again and again either by force of nature or the human hand. Alexander's poem demonstrates how the imperfect oval is the basic template for the way we remember the slave ship icon. She thus brings us back, full circle, to the ways in which the slave ship icon has been committed to memory.

Notes

INTRODUCTION

THE PRACTICE OF MNEMONIC AESTHETICS

1. The Yoruba are an important ethnic group living in southwestern Nigeria and parts of neighboring Benin. Boasting one of the highest rates of twin births in the world, twins occupy a special place in Yoruba belief systems. This is due in part to the high mortality rate associated with such pregnancies, which contributed to the integration of a unique twin belief system within Yoruba religion.

2. William Wilberforce, who led the abolitionist movement from his place as a leading member of Parliament was from Hull, and his home is now a museum dedicated to his life story and abolition; Liverpool and Bristol were notorious slave trading ports; English trade goods sent aboard slave ships were produced in New Castle; and London was initially a key port of embarkation for slave ships. *La Bouche de Roi* previously was exhibited at the Menil Collection, Houston (2005) and the Musée du Quai Branly, Paris (2006).

3. Durham University (2007), "Palace Green Transformed into A Slave Ship," http://www.dur.ac.uk/durham.first/winter07/slaveship/, accessed February 2, 2008.

4. Paul Gilroy, *The Black Atlantic: Modernity and Double Consciousness* (Cambridge, MA: Harvard University Press, 1993), 4.

5. Jesse Jackson in a live interview with Anderson Cooper on CNN, September 1, 2005. Cultural commentator Michael Eric Dyson noted that during Hurricane Katrina the residents of New Orleans "were treated like slaves in the ship" in an interview for Spike Lee's film, *When the Levees Broke* (2007).

6. The compelling story of the life of the slave ship icon and its crucial role in bringing an end to the slave trade has received attention from British and American scholars who primarily focus their studies on the eighteenth and early nineteenth centuries. See Marcus Reideker's *The Slave Ship: A Human History* (2007); Adam Hochschild's *Bury the Chains: Prophets and Rebels in the Fight to Free an Empire's Slaves* (2005); art historical scholarship on the slave ship icon is also largely limited to the eighteenth and nineteenth centuries. See the surveys: Hugh Honour's *The Image of the Black in Western Art, Volume 4, Part 1* (1996) and Albert Boime's *The Art of Exclusion: Representing Blacks in the Nineteenth Century* (1990). Marcus Wood's *Blind Memory: Visual Representations of Slavery in England and America, 1780–1865* (2000). From the perspective of social movement theory, J. R. Oldfield's *Popular Politics and British Anti-Slavery: The Mobilisation of Public Opinion against the Slave Trade, 1787–1807* (1995) analyzes the early printing history of the slave ship icon and its relationship to the visual propaganda of the abolitionist movement. These and other scholars have shied away from explaining the contemporary relevance of the slave ship icon, especially with regards to thinking about modern racial formation.

7. By "historical memory," I mean the oral, written, and visual accounts that document and transmit the memory of a past event to an individual or group in the present that did not experience it. Autobiographical memory refers to the memory of an event that was experienced firsthand by an individual or a group. See Lewis A. Coser, "The Revival of the Sociology of Culture: The Case of Collective Memory," *Sociological Forum* 7, no. 2 (1992): 371–73.

8. Robert Farris Thompson, *Flash of the Spirit: African and Afro-American Art and Philosophy* (New York: Vintage, 1983), xiii.

9. Ibid.

10. See Robert Farris Thompson, *Flash of the Spirit*; "The Song That Named the Land: The African Impulse in African American Art," in *Black Art: Ancestral Legacy* (Dallas: Dallas Museum of Art, 1989); and *Face of the Gods: Art and Altars of Africa and the African Americas* (Munich: Prestel, 1993).

11. Gilroy, *Black Atlantic*, 16–17.

12. Paul Gilroy, "Living Memory: A Meeting with Toni Morrison," in *Small Acts: Thoughts on the Politics of Black Cultures* (New York: Serpent's Tail, 1993), 179–81.

13. Vivian Sobchack, "Nostalgia for the Digital Object," *Millennium Film Journal* 34 (Fall 1999): 14.

14. Walter Benjamin, "Theses on the Philosophy of History" (1950), in *Illuminations*, trans. Harry Zohn (New York: Schocken Books, 1968), 264.

15. Pierre Nora, "Between History and Memory: *Les Lieux de Memoire*," *Representations* 26 (Spring 1989): 15.

16. Thomas Clarkson, *The History of the Rise, Progress, and Accomplishment of the Abolition of the African Slave-Trade by British Parliament*, 2 vols. (London: Longmans, 1808), 2: 11.

17. Robert Farris Thompson, *African Art in Motion: Icon and Act* (Los Angeles: University of California Press, 1974), xiv.

18. Ibid.

19. Ibid., 47.

20. Arthur Jafa, "The Notion of Treatment: Black Aesthetics and Film; An Interview with Arthur Jafa," in *Oscar Micheaux and His Circle: African American Filmmaking and Race Cinema of the Silent Era*, ed. Pearl Bowser, Jane Gaines, and Charles Musser (Bloomington: Indiana University Press, 2001), 12.

21. Huston Baker Jr., *Modernism and the Harlem Renaissance* (Chicago: University of Chicago Press, 1987), 56.

22. Ibid.

23. Henry Louis Gates Jr., *The Signifying Monkey: A Theory of African American Literary Criticism* (New York: Oxford University Press, 1988), 110.

24. Ibid.

25. Marianne Hirsch, *The Generation of Postmemory: Writing and Visual Culture after the Holocaust* (New York: Columbia University Press, 2012).

26. Jafa, "Notion of Treatment," 11. Jafa refers to "shaping and reshaping Black artistic expression and creativity" as a theory of black aesthetics in film.

27. Gilroy, *Black Atlantic*, 198.

28. My discussion of mnemonic aesthetics is also grounded in the work of pioneering theorist of the arts of memory Frances Yates, in *the Art of Memory* (Chicago: University of Chicago Press, 2001) as well as leading scholars whose works have given shape to cultural memory studies, including Maurice Halbwachs on collective memory in *On Collective Memory* (Chicago: University of Chicago Press, 1992); Cathy Caruth on traumatic memory in *Trauma: Explorations in Memory* (Baltimore: Johns Hopkins University Press, 1995); Paul Ricoeur on memory and forgetting in *Memory, History, Forgetting* (Chicago: University of Chicago Press, 2006); Paul Connerton on social ritual in *How Societies Remember* (Cambridge: Cambridge University Press, 1989); Marianne Hirsch on postmemory and photography in *Family Frames: Photography, Family, and Postmemory* (Cambridge, MA: Harvard University Press, 1997); and Joseph Roach on memory and performance in *Cities of the Dead: Circum-Atlantic Memory and Performance* (New York: Columbia University Press, 1996).

CHAPTER ONE

IDEA: IMAGE AND TEXT

1. Olaudah Equiano to the Committee for the Abolition of the Slave Trade at Plymouth, *The Public Advertiser*, February 14, 1789, reprinted in Olaudah Equiano, *The Interesting Narrative and Other Writings*, edited with an introduction and notes by Vincent Carretta (New York: Penguin Classics, 1995), 343. In approximately 1755 at about the age of ten, Olaudah Equiano was captured in an area of West Africa now known as Igboland in southeastern Nigeria. After serving as a slave for a British Royal Navy officer and later as a slave on a West Indies plantation, Equiano purchased his own freedom in 1766 and settled in London. He frequently published letters (sometimes with the Sons of Africa, a group of free black men descendant of Africa living in London) in *The Morning Chronicle*, *The Daily*, and *The Public Advertiser*, all London newspapers, voicing his opinion on the slave trade, slavery, and the treatment of black people in England and the colonies. See Vincent Carretta, *Equiano, The African: Biography of a Self-Made Man* (Athens: University of Georgia Press, 2005). Carretta's biography disputes Equiano's African birth origins, suggesting instead that he was born in the Carolinas. However, many scholars of African American studies and literature still find Equiano's autobiography a foundational slave narrative.

2. Art historian Kellie Jones has suggested that Equiano and his Sons of Africa contemporaries helped to develop a style of public oratory in which recounting the "personal" slave experience became a central trope of a genre of public performance that served to keep the topic of abolition in the public consciousness. In the mid-nineteenth century, noted African American orators, such as Sojourner Truth, Frederick Douglass, and William Wells Brown, continued this tradition of "performing identity" in the United States and Great Britain. Equiano might be considered a noteworthy forerunner of later-day Race men. See Hazel Carby, *Race Men* (Cambridge, MA: Harvard University Press, 1998), 2–5.

3. Equiano traveled throughout England selling copies of his *The Interesting Narrative of the Life of Olaudah Equiano or Gustavus Vassa, The African* and speaking at public meetings organized to arouse interest in the abolitionist cause. His slave narrative was a popular piece of abolitionist literature; the book's initial subscribers included such influential British abolitionists as Thomas Clarkson and noted potter Josiah Wedgwood, both members of the London Committee (Equiano, *Interesting Narrative and Other Writing*, 317–21). Equiano's book, first published in March 1789, went through nine editions during his lifetime, each expanded and revised. The ninth edition (London, 1794) is reprinted in Equiano, *Interesting Narrative and Other Writings*, edited by Vincent Carretta. All quotations are from this edition. The publication histories of Equiano's autobiography and the abolitionist engraving of a slave ship have many interesting parallels.

4. Equiano, *Interesting Narrative and Other Writings*, 58.

5. Since the mid-1990s, this passage has been used in museum exhibitions in England and in texts on the history of slavery. The pioneering *Trans-Atlantic Slavery Gallery:*

Against Human Dignity, installed at the Merseyside Maritime Museum in Liverpool in 1994, played an audiotape version of this passage during the exhibition that simulated the hold of a slave ship. See Anthony Tibbles, ed., *Transatlantic Slavery: Against Human Dignity*, National Museums and Galleries on Merseyside (London: HMSO, 1995), and Madeline Burnside and Rosemarie Robotham, *Spirits of the Passage: The Transatlantic Slave Trade in the Seventeenth Century* (New York: Simon and Schuster, 1997), 130.

6. Plymouth Committee of the Society for Effecting the Abolition of the Slave Trade, *Plan of an African Ship's Lower Deck with Negroes in the Proportion of Only One to a Ton* (Plymouth, England, 1789).

7. Equiano to the Committee for the Abolition of the Slave Trade at Plymouth, *The Public Advertiser*, February 14, 1789, in Equiano, *Interesting Narrative and Other Writings*, 343.

8. See Cheryl Finley, "Committed to Memory: The Slave Ship Icon in the Black Atlantic Imagination," *Chicago Art Journal* (Spring 1999): 2–22.

9. According to Seymour Drescher, the efforts of the British abolitionists formed "the prototype of the modern social reform movement." See Seymour Drescher, *Capitalism and Antislavery: British Mobilization in Comparative Perspective* (Oxford: Oxford University Press, 1987), 67.

10. Roger Anstey, *The Atlantic Slave Trade and British Abolition, 1760–1810* (Atlantic Highlands, NJ: Humanities Press, 1975); Michael Craton, *Sinews of Empire: A Short History of British Slavery* (Garden City, NY: Anchor/Doubleday, 1974); David Brion Davis, *The Problem of Slavery in the Age of Revolution, 1770–1823* (Ithaca, NY: Cornell University Press, 1976); Drescher, *Capitalism and Antislavery*; Daniel P. Mannix in collaboration with Malcolm Cowley, *Black Cargoes: A History of the Atlantic Slave Trade, 1518–1865* (New York: Viking Press, 1962); Phillip Lapsansky, "Graphic Discord: Abolitionist and Antiabolitionist Images," in *The Abolitionist Sisterhood: Women's Political Culture in Antebellum America*, ed. Jean Fagan Yellen and John C. Van Horne (Ithaca, NY: Cornell University Press, 1994), 201–30; James A. Rawley, *The Transatlantic Slave Trade: A History* (New York: W. W. Norton, 1981); Bernard F. Reilly Jr. "The Art of the Anti-Slavery Movement," in *Courage and Conscience: Black and White Abolitionists in Boston*, ed. Donald M. Jacobs (Bloomington: Indiana University Press for the Boston Athenaeum, 1993); Hugh Thomas, *The Slave Trade: The Story of the Atlantic Slave Trade, 1440–1870* (New York: Simon and Schuster, 1997).

11. Thomas Clarkson, *History of the Rise, Progress, and Accomplishment of the Abolition of the African Slave-Trade by British the Parliament*, 2 vols. (London: Longmans, 1808). I would even suggest that with the publication of Clarkson's *History*, the London Committee becomes not only the focus but also the beginning (and the end) of some scholarly investigations of this image. See Hugh Honour, *The Image of the Black in Western Art, Volume 4, Part 1* (Houston: Menil Foundation, 1996).

12. See Clarkson, *History*, 2: 111–15. Like J. R. Oldfield, I agree that Clarkson's claim for the superiority of the London Committee version of the slave ship icon, *Description of a Slave Ship*, is overstated. See Oldfield, *Popular Politics and British Anti-Slavery: The Mobilisation of Public Opinion against the Slave Trade, 1787–1807* (Manchester: Manchester University Press, 1995), 182n34. More recently, Marcus Wood has characterized the January 1789 Plymouth Committee version as a crude and simple precursor of *Description of a Slave Ship*. See Wood, *Blind Memory: Visual Representations of Slavery in England and America, 1780–1865* (New York: Routledge, 2000), 25–26.

13. Oldfield, *Popular Politics and British Anti-Slavery*, 165.

14. Ibid., 182n34.

15. Wood, *Blind Memory*, 25–26.

16. Only Oldfield mentions the textual additions to the London Committee version. See Oldfield, *Popular Politics and British Anti-Slavery*, 165. Wood reproduces only the images, not the text.

17. Elizabeth Donnan, *Documents Illustrative of the History of the Slave Trade to America*, vol. 5, *1441–1700* (1930; New York: Octagon Books, 1969), 1: 45–46.

18. Other investors in Hawkins's voyages included men who held high government or social standing, as well as the Queen's advisors. See Donnan, *Documents Illustrative of the History*, 1: 45n3; 1: 47n6, 1: 63n2.

19. Keith Piper, *A Ship Called Jesus* (London: Ikon Gallery, 1991), n.p.

20. Collection of the city of Plymouth Museums and Art Gallery. See Michael Duffy et al., eds., *The New Maritime History of Devon*, vol. 1, *From Early Times to the Late Eighteenth Century* (London: Conway Maritime Press in association with the University of Exeter, 1992), 113 (plate 12.7).

21. John Prince, *Danmonii orientales illustres; or, The worthies of Devon. A work, wherein the lives and fortunes of the most famous divines, statesmen, swordsmen, physicians, writers, and other eminent persons, natives of that most noble province, from before the Norman conquest, down to the present age, are memorized ... out of the most approved authors, both in print and manuscript ...* (London: Rees and Curtis, Plymouth, 1810), cited in Robert Southey, *English Seamen: Howard, Clifford, Hawkins, Drake, Cavendish*, edited and with an introduction by David Hannay (Chicago: Stone and Kimball, 1895), 189–90.

22. See Donnan, *Documents Illustrative of the History*, 1: 66–67.

23. Only two of Hawkins's six ships escaped the Spanish fleet after an intense skirmish in the Bay of Vera Cruz on September 24, 1568. In the previous month, Hawkins had traded by force in other parts of the Spanish colonies and was

attempting to sell his remaining cargo. He and approximately two hundred crewmen, including the famous explorer Sir Francis Drake, also of Plymouth, escaped with their lives to return home to England in early 1569. See "Deposition of John Hawkins, of the City of London, Gentleman, 23 April 1569," reprinted in Donnan, *Documents Illustrative of the History*, 1: 70–71, and *Dictionary of National Biography* (Oxford: Oxford University Press, 1921–22), 12: 215.

24. Other noted English explorers associated with the Royal Navy and Plymouth in the late sixteenth century include Sir Francis Drake, who completed the first voyage of circumnavigation, and Sir Walter Raleigh. See Southey, *English Seamen*, 170–358, and C. W. Bracken, *A History of Plymouth and Her Neighbours* (Plymouth: Underhill [Plymouth], 1931), 74–105. For more on the subsequent development of Plymouth as a naval stronghold, see Nigel Tattersfield, *The Forgotten Trade, Comprising the Log of the Daniel and Henry of 1700 and Accounts of the Slave Trade from the Minor Ports of England, 1698–1725* (London: Jonathan Cape, 1991), 22–24, 195–96, 298–304; J. D. Davies, "Devon and the Navy in the Civil and Dutch Wars, 1642–88," in Duffy, *New Maritime History of Devon*, 173–76; and Jonathan Coad, "The Development and Organisation of Plymouth Dockyard, 1689–1815," in Duffy, *New Maritime History of Devon*, 192–200.

25. In a series of seven separate wars, England remained at war with France for 67 of the 127 years from 1689 to 1815. See Michael Duffy, "Devon and the Naval Strategy of the French Wars," in Duffy, *New Maritime History of Devon*, 182–91.

26. Nigel Tattersfield discusses Plymouth's early role in the slave trade along with other lesser ports in the southwest. See Tattersfield, *Forgotten Trade*, 22–24, 195–96, 298–307, 372–74, and 380–82.

27. Kenneth Morgan, "Convict Transportation from Devon to America," in Duffy, *New Maritime History of Devon*, 153–54.

28. Oldfield, *Popular Politics and British Anti-Slavery*, 99.

29. Abolition Committee Minutes, May 22, 1787, vol. 1, Add MSS 21,254, British Library, Department of Manuscripts, London.

30. The Somerset case decided by Lord Mansfield in 1772 gave the false impression that slavery was illegal on English soil. Mansfield's purposely vague judgment only meant that enslaved black people could not be removed from England by force. Nevertheless, Mansfield's ruling was interpreted widely, both in the contemporary popular imagination and in subsequent scholarly works, as setting the slaves free in England. To the contrary, slavery continued to exist in England throughout the eighteenth century and into the nineteenth century as evidenced by newspaper advertisements for the sale of slaves, as well as additional court battles testing the liberty of immigrant slaves to British soil. See F. O. Shyllon, *Black Slaves in Britain* (London: Oxford University Press for the Institute of Race Relations, 1974), ix–x.

31. The organizational structure of the Society of Friends and their network of yearly and local meetings set them apart from other religious groups perhaps prone to antislavery work, and lay the foundation for the system of abolition societies throughout England and North America. The committee system subsequently set in place by the Abolition Society seems to have been derived largely from the provincial composition of the Committee for Sufferings established by the London Yearly Meeting in 1783. See Anstey, *Atlantic Slave Trade*, 260, and Oldfield, *Popular Politics and British Anti-Slaver*, 42–43.

32. The three other members of the London Committee were Anglicans, including Thomas Clarkson, Granville Sharp, and Philip Samson. The nine Quakers were Joseph Hooper, John Barton, Richard Phillips, James Phillips, Samuel Hoare, Joseph Woods, George Harrison, William Dillwyn, and John Lloyd. The previous five men listed as Quakers were part of a more radical six-member branch of the Quaker Committee of Sufferings established in 1783 (including Dr. Thomas Knowles). Together, they formed the core of the Society for Effecting the Abolition of the Slave Trade, overseeing many of its day-to-day operations. Abolition Committee Minutes, May 22, 1787, Add MSS 21,254. Judith Jennings, *The Business of Abolishing the British Slave Trade, 1783–1807* (London: Frank Cass, 1997), 45–51.

33. Jennings, *Business of Abolishing the British Slave Trade*, 51. By "country abolitionists," Jennings is referring to the local abolition committees of the countryside and in the provinces.

34. According to Lenore Loft, the work of the Quaker Committee for Sufferings established in 1783 influenced the topic for the Latin Dissertation prize proposed by the vice chancellor of Cambridge in 1785. See Lenore Loft, "Quakers, Brissot, and Eighteenth-Century Abolitionists," *Journal of the Friends' Historical Society* 55 (1989): 279.

35. Thomas Clarkson, *An Essay on the Slavery and Commerce of the Human Species, Particularly the African; Translated from a Latin Dissertation Which Was Honoured with the First Prize in the University of Cambridge for the Year 1785* (London: James Phillips, 1786). Clarkson first became acquainted with the Quaker abolitionists when he sought out the Quaker printer and later London Committee member James Phillips to publish his award-winning Cambridge University dissertation in 1786.

36. Ellen Gibson Wilson, *Thomas Clarkson: A Biography* (London: Macmillan, 1989), 1.

37. Ibid.

38. Between 1788 and 1792, Clarkson traveled some 35,000 miles around the English countryside and in France to establish committees and to campaign for the abolition of the slave trade.

39. "Slave Trade," *Western Flying Post; or, Sherborne and Yeovil Mercury, and General Advertiser*, December 8, 1788.

40. Ibid.

41. Abolition Committee Minutes, August 12, 1788, vol. 2, Add MSS 21,255, British Library, Department of Manuscripts, London. The list of publications included in the expense report with the number printed is as follows: "100 Resolutions of Committee; 250 Letters; 4,750 Lists; 15,050 Summary View; 15,026 Reports of the Committee; 14,000 Dean of Middlehams Letter; 2,325 Clarksons Essay on the Inhumanity etc.; 6,025 Falconbridges Account etc.; 3,000 Stanfields Observations; 1,500 Benezets Guinea; 4,000 Ramsay's Objections & Answers; 252 Letters of Africanus; 375 Letters to Mayors of Corporation; 750 Commonses to Committees; 3,580 Newtons Thoughts; 2,000 Clarkson on the Impolicy, etc.; 1,500 Morning Chronicles containing Debates of Parliament on the Subject; 10,000 Extracts from the Morning Chronicle containing part of said Debates; Observations of CB Wadstrom (not yet published); 1 Long's History of Jamaica; Sundry Small tracts."

42. *Western Flying Post*, December 29, 1788. M. and B. Haydon was located in the heart of Plymouth on Whimple Street, just opposite the Old Guild Hall, a sociable place where all the local celebrities gathered. See Bracken, *A History of Plymouth and Her Neighbours*, 258.

43. John Bidlake, *The Slave Trade: A Sermon Preached at Stonehouse Chapel on 28th December 1788* (Plymouth: M. and B. Haydon, 1789). This popular tract went through two editions in just one year.

44. *Western Flying Post*, January 5, 1789, January 19, 1789, February 2, 1789, and February 16, 1789; Oldfield, *Popular Politics and British Anti-Slavery*, 99. Robert Hawker published a later short tract (twenty-four pages) about slavery in the West Indies: *An Appeal to the Common Feelings of Mankind in Behalf of the Negroes in the West-India Islands...* (London, 1823).

45. *The Western Flying Post*, 5 January 1789.

46. See Oldfield, *Popular Politics and British Anti-Slavery*, 163–65, and Wood, *Blind Memory*, 17–21.

47. They were among the best printer-publishers in Plymouth and the same printers who published the sermons by Bidlake and Hawker.

48. Algernon Graves, *Royal Academy of Arts: Complete Dictionary of Contributors and Their Works from Its Foundation, 1769–1904*, vol. 3 (London: Graves and George Bell and Son, 1905), 38. Elford's work can be found in the collections of the British Museum, Windsor Castle, and Oxford University. Plymouth developed a reputation for its flourishing artistic community in the last half of the eighteenth century and through the first half of the nineteenth century. Noted painter, Sir Joshua Reynolds (1723–1792), the first president of the Royal Academy in London (1768), hailed from nearby Plympton in Plymouth. James Northcote studied with Reynolds in London for five years.

49. Shortly before his death he published his research into a substitute for yeast. See *Dictionary of National Biography* (Oxford: Oxford University Press, 1921–22), 4: 600.

50. Oldfield, *Popular Politics and British Anti-Slavery*, 100.

51. In all, Captain Parrey inspected eighteen slave ships docked in Liverpool. For a discussion of all the ships and their dimensions see his Report to the Privy Council in Add MSS 38,416, 208–12.

52. Plymouth Committee, *Plan of an African Ship's Lower Deck with Negroes Stowed in the Proportion of Only One to a Ton* (Plymouth, 1789), 1.

53. The name of the slave ship *Brooks* often has been misspelled since the publication of Thomas Clarkson, *An Abstract of the Evidence Delivered before a Select Committee of the House of Commons, in the Years 1790 and 1791; on the Part of the Petitioners for the Abolition of the Slave Trade* (Edinburgh: J. Robertson, 1791), which included a folding plate of the London Committee version of the slave ship icon with the erroneous spelling: Brookes. See Clarkson, *An Abstract of the Evidence*, 41–43 and plate. Subsequent scholarly works and numerous other publications that have reprinted the slave ship icon also have committed this same error.

54. "Tonnage is a term which has caused some confusion down the years," as Nigel Tattersfield explains. "It does not describe the weight of the vessel; this is known as displacement and varies with the amount of cargo or ballast being carried. It does describe the volume of the vessel available for stowing cargo or accommodating passengers—its burden." A ship's burden is calculated by a formula that takes into consideration the length, beam, and depth of the ship. Tattersfield, *Forgotten Trade*, 49.

55. Fort William at Anamabou was built by the British between 1753 and 1770 as a fortified coastal trade-post and factory with deep cavernous dungeons for keeping enslaved Africans. Since Ghanaian independence in 1957, it has served alternatively as a guesthouse, post office, and prison. Today, its primary use as a prison is the subject of heated debate between prison administrators, the Ghana Tourist Board, the Ghana Museums and Monuments Board, local residents, and tourists.

56. Philip D. Curtin, *The Atlantic Slave Trade: A Census* (Madison: University of Wisconsin Press, 1969), 133–36.

57. The doctor was required to keep a roster of the enslaved people, noting any deaths. Financial incentives were given to the doctor and the captain of the ship if the mortality was kept below 3 percent. See Thomas, *Slave Trade*, 510.

58. Herbert S. Klein and Stanley L. Engerman, "Slave Mortality on British Ships, 1791–1797," in *Liverpool, the African Slave Trade, and Abolition: Essays to Illustrate Current Knowledge and Research*, ed. Roger Anstey and P. E. H. Hair (Bristol: Historic Society of Lancashire and Cheshire, 1976), 119.

59. Investors and underwriters required slave traders to keep records of slave mortality. Abolitionists used this information, along with data they collected on seamen mortality onboard slave ships, to plead their case for abolition.

60. Sons of Africa to the Honourable Sir William Dolben, *The Morning Chronicle and London Advertiser*, July 15, 1788, in Equiano, *Interesting Narrative and Other Writings*, 341.

61. This detail is from a copy made by Morland in 1789, which measures 85.1 × 121.9 cm, Houston Menil Foundation Collection. Morland painted a companion to *Execrable Human Traffic* between 1778 and 1790, titled *African Hospitality*. This painting also shows a scene on the coast of Africa, where a group of European travelers (including a woman and small child) are being comforted, aided, and saved from a stormy shipwreck. In both paintings, the Africans are depicted seminaked, wearing the essential loincloth, and thus visually portray the African as the noble savage. Morland relied upon literary references in order to paint these scenes of African/European contact, including poetry and journals written by slave traders. In 1791, John Raphael Smith made engravings of these paintings, which became popular abolitionist prints. See Honour, *Image of the Black in Western Art*, 68–72; Oldfield, *Popular Politics and British Anti-Slavery*, 168–72.

62. From *Troisième voyage d'Angole, 1772–1773* (Paris, 1778), in Madeleine Burnside, *Spirits of the Passage: The Transatlantic Slave Trade in the Seventeenth Century* (New York: Simon and Shuster, 1997), 124. *La Marie Séraphique* can be found in this rare book. It is a hand-colored engraving and not an "anonymous watercolor" as the caption reads in *Spirits of the Passage*.

63. Peter Brooks, *The Melodramatic Imagination* (New Haven, CT: Yale University Press, 1974).

64. Plymouth Committee, *Plan of an African Ship's Lower Deck*, 2.

65. Ibid.

66. Ibid.

67. Presumably, *Plan of an African Ship's Lower Deck* arrived after the previous meeting of the New Society for Promoting the Abolition of Slavery on April 27, 1789. See Minutes of the New Society for Promoting the Abolition of Slavery, April 27, 1789, in *Manuscript Collection Belonging to the Pennsylvania Society for Promoting the Abolition of Slavery, for the Relief of Free Negroes Unlawfully Held in Bondage, and for Improving the Condition of the African Race* (Philadelphia: n.p., 1876), 2: item 1.

68. Minutes of the New Society for Promoting the Abolition of Slavery, May 11, 1789, in *Manuscript Collection Belonging to the Pennsylvania*; Ramsay's address on the "Proposed Bill for the Abolition of the Slave Trade" was one of the pamphlets.

69. Minutes of the New Society for Promoting the Abolition of Slavery, May 11, 1789, in *Manuscript Collection Belonging to the Pennsylvania Society*.

70. Philip Lapsansky, Hugh Honour, and Marcus Wood give brief mention of the fact that this is the first version of the slave ship icon to appear in the United States, yet none of them is able to trace it back to this source—to the very first Plymouth Committee engraving. Instead, it is called an even "cruder" version of the Plymouth Committee broadside produced afterward.

71. "Remarks on the Slave Trade," *American Museum*, May 1789, 429–30.

72. George Washington to Mathew Carey, June 25, 1788, printed in the preface to *American Museum*, vol. 5 (1789).

73. Pennsylvania Abolition Society to London Committee, June 24, 1789.

74. W. E. B. Du Bois, *The Suppression of the African Slave-Trade to the United States of America, 1638–1870* (New York: Longmans, Green, 1896), 225, 231–32.

75. Dallas, *Laws*, II. 586 cited in Du Bois, *Suppression of the African Slave-Trade*, 232.

76. Du Bois, *Suppression of the African Slave-Trade*, 69.

77. Ibid., 52.

78. By coincidence or by design, May 13, 1789, was the same day that Wilberforce presented his first motion for the abolition of the slave trade in Parliament.

79. Du Bois, *Suppression of the African Slave-Trade*, 75; see also "Proceedings of Congress," *American Museum*, June 1789, 614.

80. "Remarks on the Slave Trade," *American Museum*, May 1789, 429. Although the title and introductory paragraph were presumably written by Wells and Lownes, their authorship remained anonymous or uncredited. This paragraph had the editorial force of the *American Museum* behind it.

81. Plymouth Committee, *Plan of an African Ship's Lower Deck*.

82. Minutes of the New Society for Promoting the Abolition of Slavery, [late May–June 1789], in *Manuscript Collection Belonging to the Pennsylvania Society*.

83. New Society for Promoting the Abolition of Slavery, *Remarks on the Slave Trade* (Philadelphia: Mathew Carey, 1789), Collection of the Historical Society of Pennsylvania.

84. Ibid.

85. Minutes of the New Society for Promoting the Abolition of Slavery, July 20, 1789, in *Manuscript Collection Belonging to the Pennsylvania Society*.

86. Neil McKendrick, John Brewer, and J. H. Plumb, *The Birth of a Consumer Society: The Commercialization of Eighteenth-Century England* (Bloomington: Indiana University Press, 1982), 269. See also Walter Benjamin, who focuses on the introduction of lithography as a key moment for the ways in which original works of art are manipulated, transformed, and made available by techniques of mechanical reproduction at the beginning of the nineteenth century. As he explains, "With the woodcut, graphic art became mechanically reproducible for the first time, long before script became reproducible by print.... With lithography, the technique of reproduction reached an essentially new stage. This much more direct process was distinguished by the tracing of the design on a stone rather than its incision on a block of wood or its etching on a copperplate and

permitted graphic art for the first time to put its products on the market, not only in large numbers as hitherto, but also in daily changing forms. Lithography enabled graphic art to illustrate everyday life, and it began to keep pace with printing. But only a few decades after its invention, lithography was surpassed by photography." See "The Work of Art in the Age of Mechanical Reproduction," in Walter Benjamin, *Illuminations*, ed. Hannah Arendt, trans. Harry Zohn (New York: Schocken 1968), 218–19.

87. Abolition Committee Minutes, March 17, 1789, Add MSS 21,255.

88. William Elford to James Phillips, Thompson/Clarkson MSS, 2: 93, Religious Society of Friends Library, London.

89. Abolition Committee Minutes, July 7, 1787, Add MSS 21,254.

90. Clarkson, *History*, 1: 450.

91. David Bindman, "Am I Not a Man and a Brother? British Art and Slavery in the Eighteenth Century," *Res 26* (Autumn 1994): 79.

92. Honour, *Image of the Black in Western Art*, 63.

93. The image of the kneeling slave labeled many abolitionist tracts and literary works, including, for example, an American edition of Equiano's *The Interesting Narrative of the Life of Olaudah Equiano*, dating from 1827. The frontispiece of this late American edition bears an engraved portrait of Equiano, and the title page has a version of the kneeling slave. The other six illustrations, all from wood engravings, include the slave ship icon and three additional examples of the kneeling slave.

94. Honour, *Image of the Black in Western Art*, 64.

95. Robin Reilly, *Josiah Wedgwood, 1730–1795*, 2 vols. (London: Macmillan, 1992), 2: 517.

96. Franklin to Wedgwood, May 15, 1788, #3927-1, Benjamin Franklin Collection, Yale University Library.

97. Thomas Clarkson, *History*, 2: 192. See also Reilly, *Josiah Wedgwood*, 199.

98. *Gentleman's Magazine* (London) 56 (March 1788): 161, 208 (illustration of London Committee Seal), 209; *Morning Chronicle and Daily Advertiser*, London, April 3, 1788.

99. Reilly, *Josiah Wedgwood*, 2: 517.

100. Michael Craton, *Sinews of Empire: A Short History of British Slavery* (Garden City, NY: Anchor/Doubleday, 1974), 262.

101. Oldfield, *Popular Politics and British Anti-Slavery*, 179.

102. Encircled by the rounded edge of the seal, it is as if a magnifying glass had been put over one of the figures portrayed in the ship.

CHAPTER TWO
FORM: ESSENTIAL ELEMENTS

1. Abolition Committee Minutes, March 17, 1789, Add MSS 21,255. Mr. Hoare was the London Committee's treasurer. Mr. James A. Phillips of London, who would print the resulting broadside, was the Quakers' official printer.

2. Abolition Committee Minutes, April 28, 1789, Add MSS 21,255.

3. See Deborah Gray White, *Ar'n't I a Woman: Female Slaves in the Plantation South* (New York: W. W. Norton, 1985), 63–64.

4. Equiano, *Interesting Narrative and Other Writings*, 75.

5. Ottobah Cugoano cited in John Pope-Hennessy, *Sins of the Fathers. A Study of the Atlantic Slave Traders, 1441–1807* (New York: Knopf, 1968), 100.

6. Sir John Newton cited in Pope-Hennessy, *Sins of the Fathers*, 100–101.

7. Sander L. Gilman, *Difference and Pathology: Stereotypes of Sexuality, Race, and Madness* (Ithaca, NY: Cornell University Press, 1985), 81–143.

8. According to Sidney W. Mintz and Richard Price, "In widely scattered parts of Afro-America, the 'shipmate' relationship became a major principle of social organization and continued for decades or even centuries to shape ongoing social relations…. In Jamaica, for example, we know that the term 'shipmate' was synonymous in their [the slaves'] view with 'brother' or 'sister.'" See Sidney W. Mintz and Richard Price, *The Birth of African American Culture: An Anthropological Perspective* (Boston: Beacon Press, 1992), 42.

9. John Charnock, *An History of Maritime Architecture… from the Earliest Period to the Present*, 3 vols. (London, 1800), 1: 114; 2: 220.

10. *Description of A Slave Ship* (London: James A. Phillips for the London Committee for the Abolition of the Slave Trade, 1789).

11. Ibid.

12. In this respect, *Description of A Slave Ship* acts like a modern documentary. When making a documentary about an institution such as a high school or hospital, filmmaker Frederick Wiseman is always careful to show us an example that is well above average to avoid accusations that he chose an easy and so unrepresentative target. (I thank Charles Musser for bringing this parallel to my attention.)

13. Alexander Falconbridge, *Account of the Slave Trade on the Coast of Africa* (London: 1788), 31, cited in *Description of a Slave Ship*. Such commentary would later be enhanced by Dr. Thomas Trotter, who served as surgeon aboard the "Brooks" in 1783 and testified before a committee of the House of Commons investigating the abuses of the slave trade in 1790 and 1791. Excerpts of that testimony were described in the *Abstract of the Evidence*, which also published a two-page fold-out pamphlet of the *Brooks'* cargo hold: "On the subject of the stowage and its consequences, Dr. Trotter says, that the slaves in the passage are so crowded below, that it is impossible to walk through them, without treading on them. Those who are out of irons are locked spoonways (in the technical phrase) to one

another." See Thomas Clarkson, *An Abstract of the Evidence Delivered before a Select Committee of the House of Commons in the Years 1790 and 1791* (London: James A. Phillips, 1791), 34. See also Clarkson, *History*, 2: 187.

14. Plymouth Committee of the Society for Effecting the Abolition of the Slave Trade, *Plan of an African Ship's Lower Deck.*

15. *Description of A Slave Ship* (London, 1789).

16. Bernard F. Reilly, "The Art of the Anti-Slavery Movement," in *Courage and Conscience: Black and White Abolitionists in Boston*, ed. Donald M. Jacobs (Bloomington: Indiana University Press for the Friends of the Boston Athenaeum, 1993), 62–63.

17. Abolition Committee Minutes, April 21, 1789, July 28, 1789. A "report of the Committee" was recorded in the minute of July 28, 1789, wherein the printing orders were stated as follows: 1,700 Description of a Slave Ship with copper plate; 7,000 ditto with wood cuts." The copperplate engravings, which produced a more detailed impression of a higher quality than the woodcut engravings, would have been distributed to "the members of both houses of Parliament" and other men of influence, including clergy. The woodcut engravings were sent to affiliate abolition committees around the country and abroad. The Pennsylvania Abolition Society received a package dated October 8, 1789, containing twenty different publications produced by the London Committee, including, "1 doz description of a Slave Ship" and "1 Plan and Section of ditto." See Minutes of the New Society for Promoting the Abolition of Slavery, July 20, 1789, in *Manuscript Collection Belonging to the Pennsylvania Society.*

18. Abolition Committee Minutes, April 21, 1789, Add MSS 21,255.

19. *The Speech of William Wilberforce, Esq. Representative for the County of York, on Wednesday the 13th of May, 1789, on the Question of the Abolition of the Slave Trade. To Which Are Added the Resolutions Then Moved, and a Short Sketch of the Speeches of the Other Members* (London: Logographic Press, 1789).

20. Section Headings, Report of the Privy Council in Robin Furneaux, *William Wilberforce* (London: Hamish Hamilton, 1974), 86.

21. *Speech of William Wilberforce*, 12.

22. Ibid., 12–13.

23. Ibid, 13–14.

24. Ibid., 14–15.

25. Furneaux, *William Wilberforce*, 86.

26. Ibid., 90.

27. Marcel Chatillon, "La Diffusion de la Gravure du Brookes par la Société des Amis des Noir et son Impact," in *De la Traite a L'Esclavage: Actes du Colloque international sur la traite de Noirs, Nantes, 1985*, ed. Serge Daget (Nantes: Centre de Recherches sur L'Histoire du Monde Atlantique, 1988), 2: 135–47.

28. Unlike its British counterpart, the Société des Amis de Noirs was made up of an elite membership of high-ranking government officials, dukes, counts, and marquises, who found little need for the popular support of the people. By 1789, the society boasted ninety-four members. See *Tableau des Membres de la Société des Amis des Noirs: Année 1789* (Paris: Société des Amis de Noirs, 1789); Lawrence C. Jennings, *French Anti-Slavery: The Movement for the Abolition of Slavery in France, 1802–1848* (Cambridge: Cambridge University Press, 2000), 2. Some of their members had close ties with American revolutionaries, such as Benjamin Franklin, who moved among the leading liberal circles in Paris during the eight and a half years he spent there from December 1776 to July 1785. Upon his return to the United States, Franklin founded the Pennsylvania Society for Promoting the Abolition of Slavery and the Relief of Free Negroes Unlawfully Held in Bondage in 1784. La Fayette was a supporter of the American Revolution, as were many of the French revolutionaries. Mirabeau developed a close friendship with Franklin during his stay in Paris and delivered a brief but moving eulogy before the National Assembly at the time of Franklin's death in 1790. For the text of the eulogy, see John Stores Smith, *Mirabeau: A Life History; In Four Books* (Philadelphia: Lea and Blanchard, 1848), 284.

29. In fact, the subject of slavery and the slave trade were among the grievances enumerated in the petitions presented to the Estates General at the beginning of the French Revolution. See Rawley, *Transatlantic Slave Trade*, 143.

30. This was not far from the truth. During the French Revolution and with abolition of the slave trade seeming more probable, the British stepped up their involvement in the slave trade. Similarly, the French actively participated in the slave trade after British abolition in 1807.

31. Lenore Loft, "Quakers, Brissot, and Eighteenth-Century Abolitionists," 282.

32. Unlike the Abolition Society in England, many members of the Société des Amis de Noirs openly advocated for abolition of slavery, which upset Clarkson and other members of the London Committee, who wanted to keep the public attention narrowly focused on the abolition of the slave trade. See Clarkson, *History*, 2: 159.

33. Register of the Society Instituted in Paris for the Abolition of the Slave Trade, 132, Private Collection, quoted in Chatillon, "La Diffusion de la Gravure du Brookes," 137–38.

34. Ibid., 2: 151. The French translations were carried out in London by Dr. Frossard of Lyon by February 1790. See Abolition Committee Minutes, February 2, 1790.

35. Other female members of the Société des Amis de Noirs in 1789 were: Madame la Marquise de Bauffans, Madame Poivre, Madame Claviere, and Madame la Duchesse de la Rochefoucault. See *Tableau des Membres de la Société des Amis des Noirs: Année 1789.* (Paris: Société des Amis de Noirs, 1789).

36. Thus inviting the ire of the opposition, Clarkson acquired many enemies in France. He was denounced as a spy by the powerful planter and merchant lobbies, which played upon the historic rivalry between England and France. Clarkson wasn't unfamiliar with this type of reception. While collecting evidence in Bristol and Liverpool, he was similarly denounced and even received threats upon his life. See Clarkson, *History*, 2: 153–54.

37. Clarkson, *History*, 2: 152.

38. London Committee of the Society for the Abolition of the Slave Trade, *Description of a Slave Ship* (London: James A. Phillips, 1789).

39. According to Clarkson, it was deemed unsuitable viewing material for the beleaguered King Louis XVI, who was by that time a virtual prisoner in his own country. See Clarkson, *History*, 2: 153. In a much later trip to Paris, in 1815, Clarkson shared *Description of a Slave Ship* with Czar Alexander I of Russia, who had long admired the work of the abolitionists. Ellen Gibson Wilson, *Thomas Clarkson: A Biography* (London: Macmillan, 1989), 145.

40. C. L. R. James, *The Black Jacobins: Toussaint L'Ouverture and the San Domingo Revolution* (1935; New York: Vintage Books, 1963), 60–61. James Rawley adds, "The revolution, with its libertarian slogans, encouraged black insurrection in the islands and effected abolition of slavery and the slave trade." See Rawley, *Transatlantic Slave Trade*, 143. As C. L. R. James explains, the atmosphere in Saint-Domingue was ripe for rebellion by the end of 1789, "The enormous increase of slaves was filling the colony with native Africans, more resentful, more intractable, more ready for rebellion than the Creole Negro. Of the half-a-million slave[s] in the colony in 1789, more than two-thirds had been born in Africa." See James, *Black Jacobins*, 55–56.

41. The London Committee likely was responsible for the appearance of *Description of a Slave Ship* in *Le Courier de L'Europe* on June 2, 1789. A French-language journal published in England, *Le Courier de L'Europe* was distributed in France as well as the rest of Europe. It therefore would have put the *Description of a Slave Ship* in the hands of a wide audience and produced a strong impact, especially as a broadside that could be removed from the paper and posted publicly or privately. See Chatillon, "La Diffusion de la Gravure du Brooks" in Daget, *De la Traite a L'Esclavage*, 139.

42. Clarkson, *History*, 2: 129–30.

43. For a detailed history of these events, see James, *Black Jacobins*, 68–75.

44. James further asserts that Ogé went to Saint-Domingue via London, where he met secretly with Clarkson, who arranged for him to get money and letters of credit to purchase arms in the United States. See James, *Black Jacobins*, 73.

45. Ogé subsequently was captured and publicly executed in a brutal form known to the French sugar islands: his body was drawn and quartered, literally broken apart on the wheel. Other participants in the revolt were likewise executed. Despite this vicious display of capital punishment, not to mention the violence of the insurrection itself, Vincent Ogé's brave attempt was not altogether a failure. Instead, it foreshadowed the heroic Saint-Domingue slave revolt led by Touissant L'Ouverture in 1792, which produced the first independent black state, Haiti.

46. Clarkson, *History*, 2: 129–30. Mirabeau's model is in the collection of the Bibliothèque de l'Arsenal, Bibliothèque Nationale de France.

47. Mirabeau's oration on the slave trade ultimately numbered more than one hundred pages. As Smith speculates, "Had it been delivered, it could hardly have failed to have gained the reputation of being Mirabeau's most triumphant oratoric achievement, as it would have indubitably been his longest." See Smith, *Mirabeau*, 276.

48. Chatillon, "La Diffusion de la Gravure du Brookes," 143.

49. Smith, *Mirabeau*, 277–78. Mirabeau relies upon the function of kinesthetic memory, that is, the relationship between bodily movement—bodily reception to sensory stimulation—to memory, the way we remember and experience space. Thus, the "columns of air" and shafts of light that he refers to affect a sense of bodily memory, the way we remember being in a specific place at a specific time. Rare was it that the chained masses on slave ships saw the light of day or even the darkness of the night sky, the stars and constellations. These feelings of experiencing one's body in space of light or air, carved out of the surrounding environment, is something that Mirabeau wanted his audience to think about, to think back to and remember, as a way of putting themselves in the confines of the place that the black figures occupied. See Joseph Roach, *Cities of the Dead: Circum-Atlantic Performance* (New York: Columbia University Press, 1996).

50. Excerpt from the opening of Mirabeau's undelivered speech on abolition. Quoted in Smith, *Mirabeau*, 276.

51. Chatillon, "La Diffusion de la Gravure du Brookes," 145.

52. Known as Girondins and closely tied to the Brissotin faction, these members of the Société des Amis de Noirs were dispersed by the Robespierrists. See Jennings, *French Anti-Slavery*, 3.

53. Michel Dorigny, *Les Bieres flotantes des negriers*, n.p. (frontispiece).

54. Abolition Committee Minutes, February 1, 1791, Add MSS, 21,255, British Library. Department of Manuscripts. London.

55. Having secured printers, the minute of April 12, 1791 stated, "Mr. James Phillips reports that Mr. Cooper of Bond Street and Mr. Marsh of Tower Hill are engaged to print No. 2 of the Evidence which is continued under the care of Mr. Phillips and Mr. Wedgwood." Abolition Committee Minutes, April 12, 1791.

56. Abolition Committee Minutes, March 23, April 26, November 29, December 28, 1791. Oldfield, *Popular Politics and British Anti-Slavery*, 77.

57. Drescher, *Capitalism and Antislavery*, 219n58.

58. Thomas Clarkson, *An Abstract of the Evidence Delivered before a Select Committee of the House of Commons, in the Years 1790 and 1791; on the Part of the Petitioners for the Abolition of the Slave Trade* (Edinburgh: J. Robertson, 1791), preface.

59. William Forbes, Appeal, December 1, 1791, supplemental page to Clarkson, *An Abstract of the Evidence* (Edinburgh, 1791), insertion at the end of the book.

60. Diary of Katherine Plymley, 1066/4, October 30, 1791–February 9, 1792, in Oldfield, *Popular Politics and British Anti-Slavery*, 102.

61. In 1790, Charles Crawford published a revised version of *Observations upon Negro-Slavery* with a 5-by-15-inch oblong plate of the slave ship icon printed by Carey. See Crawford, *Observations upon Negro-Slavery*, a new edition (Philadelphia: Eleazer Oswald, 1790). The original publication was 44 pages with no illustrations. See Crawford, *Observations upon Negro-Slavery* (Philadelphia: Joseph Crukshank, 1784).

62. Carl Bernhard Wadström, *An Essay on Colonization, Particularly Applied to the Western Coast of Africa, with Some Free Thoughts on Cultivation and Commerce; also, Brief Descriptions of the Colonies Already Formed, or Attempted, in Africa, Including Those of Sierra Leona and Bulama*, 2 vols. (London: Darton and Harvey, 1794–95).

63. Wadström, *Essay on Colonization*. "Description of a Slave Ship," plate 6, is inserted at the end of volume 2 as one of several illustrations.

CHAPTER THREE
CIRCULATION: POLITICS AND PUBLICITY

1. The foreign slave trade was banned in 1806. See Du Bois, *Suppression of the African Slave-Trade*, 131–33.

2. On March 2, 1807, the US Congress passed "an Act to prohibit the importation of Slaves into any port or place within the jurisdiction of the United States, from and after the first day of January, in the year of our Lord on thousand eight hundred and eight," effectively banning the slave trade. *Statues at Large*, II, 426, in Du Bois. *Suppression of the African Slave-Trade*, 245–46. On March 25, 1807, the British Parliament voted to abolish the slave trade, forbidding any ship engaged in the slave trade from clearing out of any British port after May 1, 1807, and banning the importation of slaves in the colonies after March 1, 1808. See *Statute 47 George III*. I sessions, chap. 36. Slave Trade Papers, PRO.

3. Clarkson, *History*, 2: 587. Clarkson began writing his *History* well before the abolition of the slave trade at the suggestion of friends, such as Pitt.

4. As Wilson notes, Clarkson's *History* also served as an autobiography, albeit one that covered only a short and specific period of his long life. See Wilson, *Thomas Clarkson*, 117.

5. Clarkson, *History*, 2: 30.

6. It is important to note that maps are very powerful visual tools, and Clarkson was well aware of this fact. By marking and delineating space, maps visually organize surface areas, such as landscapes, for the human mind to follow and memorize. As much as they leave in, there is other material left out. Thus, Clarkson's map is not entirely inclusive of all the voices that shouted out for the abolition of the slave trade.

7. Jerome J. Pollitt, *Art and Experience in Classical Greece* (London: Cambridge University Press, 1972), 6.

8. Clarkson, *History*, 2: 545.

9. Clarkson's *History* was criticized for its scanty coverage of the last years of abolition, from 1804 to 1807, a period when he was increasingly alienated by the Abolition society, which had newer members comprised mostly of a Parliamentary lobby. The criticism especially came from members of the Clapham Sect, who were closely connected to Wilberforce, and in later years from Wilberforce's sons, who felt that Clarkson had minimized his role in the history of abolition. See Wilson, *Thomas Clarkson*, 117–19. Clarkson collected subscriptions for his *History* prior to its publication. According to Wilson, "Nearly 4,000 copies were bought before it was advertised." See Wilson, *Thomas Clarkson*, 117.

10. For example: abridged by Brinsmade, Augusta, PA, 1830; reissued in three volumes by J. S. Taylor, New York, 1836; issued as a new edition by John W. Parker, London, 1839.

11. Thomas Clarkson, *The Cries of Africa, to the Inhabitants of Europe; or, a Survey of That Bloody Commerce Called Slave-Trade* (London: Harvey and Darton, 1822).

12. Ibid., 3.

13. Ibid., 27.

14. London Committee, *Case of the Vigilante, a Ship Employed in the Slave Trade; with Some Reflections on That Traffic* (London: Harvey, Darton, 1823), 3.

15. *Affaire de La Vigilante, Batiment Negrier de Nantes* (Paris: Crapelet, 1823). The plate measures 19¾ × 18½ in.

16. London Committee, *The Spanish Schooner, Josefa Maracayera…* London: Harvey, Darton, 1823.

17. Ibid.

18. Ibid. In 1839, with the notorious case of the *Amistad* revolt, a similar engraving was made to show how the enslaved were likely carried beneath the hold.

19. They could not collect insurance for captives killed by disease.

20. She accidentally overshot the island in the West Indies, where the ship was meant to disembark.

21. "Exhibition of the Royal Academy," *The Times* (London), May 6, 1840, 6.

22. The painting inspired the Isaac Julien short film *The

Attendant (1991), about a homoerotic orgy that takes place in a museum after hours.

23. Samuel Wood, *The Mirror of Misery; or, Tyranny Exposed* (New York: Samuel Wood, 1807, 1811, and 1814); Thomas Branagan, *The Penitential Tyrant* (New York: Samuel Wood, 1807).

24. These minor changes include the insertion of the date for which the Slave Trade Regulation Act was passed by parliament, "1789." The actual date for the first passage of the bill to which the text refers is 1788. The bill was renewed several times, including once in 1789. Finally, in the last paragraph, where there is an appeal to individuals to assist the committee, it states that the committee will attempt to "transmit to the legislature, such evidence as will tend to throw the necessary lights on the subject," thus reflecting an American context.

25. Du Bois, *Suppression of the African Slave-Trade*, 133–50. See page 144 for a succinct table that lists the dates of when the slave trade was abolished by country with dates for when the Right of Search was granted.

26. Ibid., 148.

27. Ibid., 159.

28. Ibid., 159.

CHAPTER FOUR
NEGROES: OLD AND NEW

1. Richard J. Powell, *Black Art and Culture in the 20th Century* (London: Thames and Hudson, 1997), 41–42.

2. Garvey was convicted of mail fraud and sentenced to five years in prison in 1922. He was deported to Jamaica, his country of origin, in 1927. See Judith Stein, *The World of Marcus Garvey: Race and Class in Modern Society* (Baton Rouge: Louisiana State University Press, 1986), and Rupert Lewis, *Marcus Garvey* (Trenton, NJ: Africa World Press, 1988).

3. As we have seen in chapter 2, the slave trade continued illegally throughout much of the nineteenth century.

4. See, for example, the novel by Mary Johnston, *The Slave Ship* (Boston: Little, Brown, 1924); the illustrated collection of adventure tales of the slave trade in George Francis Dow, *Slave Ships and Slaving* (Salem, MA: Marine Research Society, 1927); and the groundbreaking collection of historical documents compiled by Elizabeth Donnan, *Documents Illustrative of the Slave Trade to America*, 4 vols. (Washington, DC: Carnegie Foundation, 1930–34).

5. Brantz Mayer. *Captain Canot; or, Twenty Years of an African Slaver, Being an Account of His Career and Adventures on the Coast, in the Interior, on Shipboard, and in the West Indies* (New York: D. Appleton, 1854).

6. Malcolm Cowley, *Adventures of an African Slaver, Being a True Account of the Life of Captain Theodore Canot, Trader in Gold, Ivory, and Slaves on the Coast of Guinea: His Own Story as Told in the Year 1854 to Brantz Mayer* (New York: Albert and Charles Boni, 1928).

7. Mayer's books on Mexico include *Mexico as It Was and as It Is* (New York: J. Winchester, 1844); *History of the War between Mexico and the United States, with a Preliminary View of Its Origin* (New York: Wiley and Putnam, 1848); *Mexico, Aztec, Spanish, and Republican: A Historical, Geographical, Political, Statistical, and Social Account of That Country from the Period of the Invasion by the Spaniards to the Present Time; With a View of the Ancient Aztec Empire and Civilization; A Historical Sketch of the Late War; And Notices of New Mexico and California* (Hartford, CT: S. Drake, 1851); *Observations on Mexican History and Archaeology, with a Special Notice of Zapotec Remains, as Delineated in Mr. J. G. Sawkins's Drawings of Mitla* (Washington, DC: Smithsonian Institution, 1856).

8. Hall was the founder and first governor of the Maryland Colony along the southern border of Liberia, which was incorporated into Liberia as its fourth county in 1856. See Mayer, *Captain Canot*, iii, and Lamin Sanneh, *Abolitionists Abroad: American Blacks and the Making of Modern West Africa* (Cambridge, MA: Harvard University Press, 1999), 222. For an excellent discussion of the American Colonization Society and the founding of Liberia, see Sanneh, 182–237.

9. Mayer, *Captain Canot*, iv. Mayer and supporters of the American Colonization Society argued that repatriating former slaves to Africa would facilitate legitimate commerce between Africa and America, civilize and Christianize Africans, and nullify the question of emancipation for America's enslaved masses. Members of the American Colonization Society shared a firm belief in the separation of the races.

10. Mayer, *Captain Canot*, v.

11. Furthermore, Mayer's book is bound with advertisements for two other books on colonial occupation and exploration of Africa: Mansfield Parkyns, *Life in Abyssinia: Being Notes Collected during Three Years' Residence and Travels in That Country* (London: John Murray, 1853); and Commander Andrew Foote, *Africa and the American Flag* (New York: D. Appleton, 1854).

12. Mayer, *Captain Canot*, vii.

13. Mayer also provided the illustrations for one of his previous books, *Mexico as It Was and as It Is* (New York: J. Winchester, 1844).

14. This same detail of the torturous practice of branding from François-Auguste Biard's *The Slave Trade* (1840) was repeated again and again in nineteenth-century prints, including the cover and plates opposite pages 60 and 74 of Richard Drake's *Revelations of a Slave Smuggler* (New York: Robert De Witt, 1860), another memoir of an illegal slave captain (see plate 2.29).

15. In 1929, Malcolm Cowley published his first book of poems, *The Blue Juanita*, which was praised for its "genuine and refreshing lyrical gift." Cowley, *The Blue Juanita* (New York: J. Cape and H. Smith, 1929). Cowley was a longtime

literary editor for the *New Republic*, from 1929 to 1944, and a literary adviser for Viking Press for more than thirty years. Several of his books and edited collections of American writing focus on the 1920s and 1930s. See Diane U. Eisenberg, *Malcolm Cowley: A Checklist of His Writings, 1916–1973* (Carbondale: Southern Illinois University Press, 1975). Cowley's papers can be found in the collection of the Newberry Library, Chicago.

16. Cowley, *Blue Juanita*, xv.

17. Ibid.

18. At some point during his career, Cowley undertook extensive research on the slave trade in preparation for a book that was never written. However, the fruits of his research were not lost. In 1962, he collaborated with Daniel P. Mannix on a history of the slave trade, to which he contributed the introduction and three chapters. See Daniel P. Mannix and Malcolm Cowley, *Black Cargoes: A History of the Atlantic Slave Trade, 1518–1865* (New York: Viking, 1962).

19. Raquel Tibol, "In the Land of Aesthetic Fraternity," in *In the Spirit of Resistance: African-American Modernists and the Mexican Muralist School*, Lizzetta LeFalle-Collins and Shifra M. Goldman (New York: American Federation of Arts, 1996), 9.

20. Jose Clemente Orozco, *Autobiografía* (1945; Mexico City: Ediciones Era, 1970), 51. During his second stay in New York City in 1927, Orozco took a room on Riverside Drive in Spanish Harlem near Columbia University. From there he frequented the cabaret and theater scene a little farther uptown in Harlem and became immersed in Negro life.

21. Mason's patronage came in the form of financial assistance and her own particular brand of controlling advice. Infatuated with primitivism and ethnology, she tried to convince her protégés of the benefits of making these issues thematic and stylistic parts of their work. She strongly urged many of the black artists and writers under her wing to seek out affinities with the cultures and peoples of so-called primitive Africa. See Mason to Locke, ca. August–November 1927, Locke Papers, Moorland-Spingarn Research Center, Howard University, Washington, DC. Quoted in Amy Helene Kirschke, *Aaron Douglas: Art, Race, and the Harlem Renaissance* (Jackson: University Press of Mississippi, 1995), 46. The extent to which Mason supported Covarrubias is unclear, but it is possible that his association with Covarrubias impacted his second and long-lasting career as an anthropologist and ethnographer in Bali in 1930 and 1931, and later in his native Mexico from 1936, where he resided until his death in 1957. He received two Guggenheim Fellowships to study in Bali in the 1930s and also studied the native peoples and cultures of Mexico and the Americas. His published books of anthropology include *Island of Bali*, with photographs by Rosa Covarrubias (New York: Alfred A. Knopf, 1937); *Mexico South: The Isthmus of Tehuantepec*, with photographs by Miguel and Rosa Covarrubias (New York: Alfred A. Knopf, 1946); *The Eagle, the Jaguar and the Serpent, Indian Art of the Americas: North America, Alaska, Canada, the United States* (New York: Alfred A. Knopf, 1954); and *Indian Art of Mexico and Central America*, 2 vols. (New York: Alfred A. Knopf, 1957).

22. Walter White to Langston Hughes, January 1925, Langston Hughes Papers, Beinecke Rare Book and Manuscript Library, Yale University, New Haven, Connecticut.

23. Miguel Covarrubias, *Negro Drawings* (New York: Alfred A. Knopf, 1927). For Covarrubias's drawings in *Vanity Fair*, see "Enter the New Negro, a Distinctive Type Recently Created by the Coloured Cabaret Belt in New York," *Vanity Fair*, 23, no. 4 (1924): 60–61; "The Increasing Vogue of the Negro Revue on Broadway," *Vanity Fair* 23, no. 6 (1925): 61; "6 Derisions from a Mexican Pencil," *Vanity Fair* 23, no. 7 (1925): 46; and "America's Newest Citizens," *Vanity Fair* 30, no. 5 (1928): 56–57.

24. Lizzetta LeFalle-Collins and Shifra M. Goldman, *In the Spirit of Resistance: African-American Modernists and the Mexican Muralist School* (New York: American Federation of Arts, 1996).

25. Covarrubias illustrated the autobiography of the musician Taylor Gordon, a one-time Van Vechten protégé, in 1929, René Maran's *Batouala* in 1932, Zora Neale Hurston's *Mules and Men* in 1935, and a Book of the Month Club reissue of Harriet Beecher Stowe's *Uncle Tom's Cabin* in 1938.

26. Diego Rivera, *Miguel Covarrubias* (New York: Valentine Gallery, 1932). Diego Rivera wrote the preface to the catalog for this exhibition, which featured Covarrubias's drawings from Bali.

27. As a youth in Mexico, Covarrubias worked briefly as a map designer. In 1939, Covarrubias created six murals of illustrated maps of the islands and culture of the South Pacific for the San Francisco Golden Gate Exposition.

28. Douglas interview, Collins, BOH, Fisk quoted in Kirschke, *Aaron Douglas*, 77.

29. See, for example, "NAACP Cover," *The Crisis*, January 1930; and "The Young Black Hungers," *The Crisis*, May 1928.

30. After spending some time in Ghana and Senegal in the mid-1960s, Lois Mailou Jones once again included African masks in her work, making them a central motif in the paintings from this period. In comparison to *Les Fetiches*, which she painted while studying in Paris, her paintings from the 1960s were more psychedelic in hue and stylization. Other African American artists continued this theme in the 1960s, including Jacob Lawrence and Romare Bearden.

31. Miguel Covarrubias, *Negro Drawings* (New York: Alfred A. Knopf, 1927).

32. It is interesting that Covarrubias, who was known for his facility with the single black line, chose to render the slave ship icon in gouache, a medium known for its graphic rigidity and impact when reproduced in black and white.

33. Miguel Covarrubias, "Two African Men for Canot," *Creative Art* 2, no. 5 (1928): ix; "African Village for Canot," *Creative Art* 3, no. 1 (1928): xii; "African Dance for Canot," *Creative Art* 3. no. 3 (1928): viii.

34. Barbie Zelizer, "Reading the Past against the Grain: The Shape of Memory Studies," *Critical Studies in Mass Communication* 12, no. 3 (1995): 234.

35. Like the European modernists, many of these artists relied on the wealth of colonial exports (exploits) of sacred African ritual objects that poured into the metropolises of Paris, Berlin, London, and New York.

36. Most of his fieldwork was done in the rural South. See Alan Lomax archives at the Library of Congress.

CHAPTER FIVE
1969: ACTIVISM, ART, AND PERFORMANCE IN THE UNITED STATES

1. LeRoi Jones, "The Black Revolutionary Theatre," *Liberator* 5 (July 1965): 4–6, http://nationalhumanitiescenter.org/pds/maai3/protest/text12/barakatheatre.pdf, accessed August 23, 2015.

2. In 1966, Allon Schoener organized the critically acclaimed exhibition *Lower East Side: Portal to American Life, 1870–1924* at the Jewish Museum in New York. That exhibition was noted for its innovative use of historical photographs of immigrants to the United States as mural-size enlargements along with film footage and sound to create a novel installation environment and experience for museum visitors. See Allon Schoener, *Portal to American Life: The Lower East Side, 1870–1924* (New York: Henry Holt, 1967).

3. See Bridget R. Cooks, *Exhibiting Blackness: African Americans and the American Art Museum* (Amherst: University of Massachusetts Press, 2011); and Susan E. Cahan, *Mounting Frustration: The Art Museum in the Age of Black Power*, Art History Publication Initiative (Durham, NC: Duke University Press, 2016).

4. Grace Glueck, "Minority Artists Find a Welcome at New Showcase," *New York Times*, December 23, 1969, 22.

5. Mary Schmidt Campbell, *Tradition and Conflict: Images of a Turbulent Decade, 1963–1973* (New York: Studio Museum in New York, 1985), 64.

6. The 1960s witnessed the assassinations of Patrice Lumumba, John F. Kennedy, Malcolm X, Robert Kennedy, and the Rev. Dr. Martin Luther King Jr. Wanton and calculated acts of racial terrorism characterized the decade. Notable examples include the bombing of the Sixteenth Street Baptist Church in Birmingham, Alabama, on September 15, 1963, which killed four little girls; the murder of three student activists in Philadelphia, Mississippi, during 1964's Freedom Summer; and the murder of the Black Panther Party leader Fred Hampton by Chicago police. (Hampton was shot while asleep in his bed.)

7. Campbell, *Tradition and Conflict*, 65.

8. Cheryl Finley, "The Door of No Return," *Common Place* 1, no. 4, http:/www.common-place.org/vol-01/no-4/finley.

9. Langston Hughes and Milton Meltzer, *A Pictorial History of the Negro in America* (New York: Crown Publishers, 1956), book jacket flap.

10. On April 18, 1969, one hundred black students took over Willard Straight Hall at Cornell University for thirty-six hours, demanding African American and African studies curricula, faculty who could teach the burgeoning field, and other resources for black students. This led to the first African studies department, the Africana Studies and Research Center, at an Ivy League research institution. That same year, at the University of California, Berkeley, students rallied to demand courses and funding for ethnic studies. In 1969, Arno Press began to reprint classic literary and historical texts by black authors published earlier in the century. Similarly, academic journals dedicated to black studies were begun, and popular periodicals, such as *Ebony* and *Jet*, saw their subscriptions rise astronomically.

11. Hughes and Meltzer, *Pictorial History*, book jacket flap.

12. Campbell, *Tradition and Conflict*, 65.

13. See the hugely influential pictorial tribute, *The Middle Passage: White Ships/Black Cargo*, conceived by book illustrator Tom Feelings with pen and ink drawings, including a frequently reproduced illustration of the slave ship icon (page 30). Tom Feelings with and introduction by John Henrick Clarke, *The Middle Passage: White Ships/Black Cargo* (New York: Dial Books, 1995).

14. Amiri Baraka quoted in William J. Harris, *Amiri Baraka, The LeRoi Jones/Amiri Baraka Reader* (New York: Thunder's Mouth Press, 1991), xxi.

15. In 1974, Baraka rejected Black Nationalism and converted to a form of international socialism, which he calls Third World Marxism (Harris, *Amiri Baraka, The LeRoi Jones/Amiri Baraka Reader*, xii–xxxii).

16. Perhaps the strongest assertion of the Black Power and Black Arts movements' dictum that African Americans should reclaim their lost (or stolen) African spirituality and African heritage, and redefine themselves through it, was in the lifting of the "slave name." As an increasing number of prominent black figures began to reject their American birth names in favor of African names, the mainstream white reaction ranged from mockery to consternation to fear.

17. The two plays that were closed were *The Eighth Ditch*, about a gay rape in an army tent, produced by the Poets' Theatre in early March 1964 and performed at the New Bowery Theatre, and *The Baptism*, presented at the Writers Stage Theatre, about a black priest and an interracial congregation and with sexual overtones, including a "chorus of pregnant virgins." See Langston Hughes and Milton Meltzer, *Black Magic: A Pictorial History of the Negro in American Entertainment* (New York: Crown Publishers, 1967), 251.

18. Howard Taubman, "The Theater: 'Dutchman,'" *New York Times*, March 25, 1964. Philip Roth, writing in the May 28, 1964, edition of the *New York Review of Books*, asserted, "I believe this play is written [for a white audience]—not so that they should be moved to pity or to fear, but to humiliation and self-hatred. For that purpose, nothing but a black innocent and a white devil will do." Philip Roth, "Channel X: Two Plays on the Negro Conflict," *New York Review of Books*, May 28, 1964, 10–13 (on James Baldwin's *Blues for Mr. Charlie* and LeRoi Jones's *Dutchman*). Baraka wrote a letter in response to Roth's review, which was published along with a response from Roth to his letter, in the July 9, 1964, edition of the *New York Review of Books*.

19. Taubman, "The Theater: 'Dutchman.'"

20. LeRoi Jones, "The Black Arts Repertory Theatre/School," *The Liberator*, May 1965.

21. Werner Sollors, *Amiri Baraka/LeRoi Jones: The Quest for a Populist Modernism* (New York: Columbia University Press, 1978), 205.

22. Larry Neal, "The Black Arts Movement," in *Black Fire: An Anthology of Afro-American Writing*, ed. Amiri Baraka and Larry Neal (New York: Morrow, 1968), 18.

23. Amiri Baraka, *Home: Social Essays* (New York: William Morrow, 1966), 214–15.

24. Ibid., 210.

25. Woodie King Jr., producer, Black Theater: The Making of a Movement (San Francisco: California Newsreel, 1978), 110 min.

26. Amiri Baraka, *Raise, Race, Rays, Raze: Essays since 1965* (New York: Random House, 1971), 115.

27. Dan Isaac, "The Death of the Proscenium Stage," *Antioch Review* (Summer 1971): 242.

28. Ibid., 245.

29. Baraka, *Home: Social Essays*, 215.

30. Sollors, *Amiri Baraka/LeRoi Jones*, 205.

31. Clive Barnes, "The Theater: New LeRoi Jones Play," *New York Times*, November 22, 1969, 46. The first production of *Slave Ship* was directed by Amiri Baraka at Spirit House in Newark, New Jersey, and ran from March 1967 to an undetermined closing date, and received little, if any, mainstream critical attention. A community-based theater arts center established by Baraka in 1966 in an old warehouse in Baraka's home town, Spirit House and its production company, the Spirit House Movers, were modeled after Baraka's community-based Black Arts Repertory Theatre/School, which produced plays, concerts, and poetry readings with black subject matter for "the education and cultural awakening of the Black People in America" and for exclusively black audiences in the streets of Harlem from spring 1965 to spring 1966, when it was forced to close. The Black Arts Repertory Theatre/School was financed with federal funds through the HARYOU-ACT and the Office of Economic Opportunity. The poets Yusuf Iman and Ed Spriggs, the musicians Pharoah Sanders (b. 1940) and Sun Ra (1914–1993),

and the playwrights Ben Caldwell (b. 1937) and Ed Bullins (b. 1935) were associated with Spirit House early on. Jihad was the publishing house founded by Baraka associated with Spirit House.

32. Isaac, "Death of the Proscenium Stage," 245. Subtitled *A Multimedia Rock Musical Environment Entertainment*, the original Off-Broadway musical *Stomp* opened at the Joseph Papp Public Theatre on November 16, 1969, and ran for 161 performances. Produced and written collectively by the Combine, a group of former University of Texas students, it lamented their alienation as self-described hippies in Texas. The Joseph Papp Public Theatre production of *Stomp* is not related to the 1994 *Stomp*, a hugely successful, percussive performance piece, which is still running Off-Broadway as of this writing. See Dan Dietz, *Off-Broadway Musicals, 1910–2007: Cast, Credits, Songs, Critical Reception, and Performance Data of More Than 1800 Shows* (Jefferson, NC: McFarland, 2010).

33. Woodie King Jr., producer, *Black Theater: The Making of a Movement* (San Francisco: California Newsreel, 1978), 110 min.

34. Charlie Reilly, ed., *Conversations with Amiri Baraka* (Jackson: University Press of Mississippi, 1994), 62.

35. James Schevill, *Breakout!: In Search of New Theatrical Environments* (Chicago: Swallow Press, 1973), 266.

36. Danielle Skeehan, "Deadly Notes: Atlantic Soundscapes and the Writing of the Middle Passage," *The Appendix*, "Out Loud," July 2013, vol. 1, no. 3. http://theappendix.net/issues/2013/7/deadly-notes-atlantic-soundscapes-and-the-writing-of-the-middle-passage, accessed September 15, 2014.

37. Amiri Baraka, *Slave Ship: A One Act Play* (Newark, NJ: Jihad Productions, 1969), 1. Permission by Chris Calhoun Agency, © Amiri Baraka.

38. Francis Ngaboh-Smart, "The Politics of Black Identity: Slave Ship and Woza Albert!," *Journal of African Cultural Studies* 12, no. 2 (1999): 181–82.

39. Baraka, *Slave Ship*, 1.

40. Ibid.

41. Ibid., 2.

42. Ibid., 5.

43. Mike Sell, "The Black Arts Movement," in *African American Performance and Theater History: A Critical Reader*, ed. Harry J. Elam Jr. and David Krasner (New York: Oxford University Press), 56–80, at 70.

44. Ibid.

45. Ibid., 6.

46. Ibid., 1.

47. Ibid., 3.

48. Skeehan, "Deadly Notes."

49. Ibid.

50. Geneviève Fabre, *Drumbeats, Masks, and Metaphors: Contemporary Afro-American Theatre* (Cambridge, MA: Harvard University Press, 1983), 120, translation mine.

51. Francophone African intellectuals, writers, and politicians, including Senghor, the Martinican poet Aimé Césaire (1913–2008), and the poet and politician Léon Damas (1912–1978) of French Guyana developed the literary and ideological philosophy of Négritude in Paris in the early 1930s. Senghor was elected president in 1960 when the Republic of Senegal proclaimed its independence from France. The idea for the 1er Festival Mondial des Arts Nègres was first discussed at the 1956 Conference of Black Writers in Rome, convened by Alioune Diop (1910–1980), the editor of the influential Négritude journal *Presence Africaine*, and at which Césaire and Senghor were present.

52. Baraka, *Slave Ship*, 13–14.

53. Baraka, *Blues People: Negro Music in White America* (New York: William Morrow, 1963), 123.

54. Hughes and Meltzer, *Black Magic*, 1967, 3.

55. Baraka, *Slave Ship*, 16.

56. Val Ferdinand, "On Black Theater in America: A Report from New Orleans," *Black World*, April 1970, 28.

57. LeRoi Jones, "In Search of Revolutionary Theatre: New Heroes Needed," *Black World*, April 1966, 21.

58. Lloyd W. Brown, *Amiri Baraka* (Boston: Twayne Publishers, 1980), 161.

59. Harry Elam Jr., "Social Urgency, Audience Participation, and the Performance of *Slave Ship* by Amiri Baraka," in *Crucibles of Crisis: Performing Social Change*, ed. Janelle Reinelt (Ann Arbor: University of Michigan Press), 22.

60. Grace Glueck, "Black Artist Shows in Whitney Lobby," *New York Times*, March 20, 1971, 25.

61. Ibid.

62. Ibid.

63. Romare Bearden quoted in Myron Schwartzman, *Romare Bearden: His Life and Art* (New York: Harry N. Abrams, 1990), 222–23.

64. Grace Glueck, "Minority Artists Find a Welcome at New Showcase," *New York Times*, December 23, 1969, 22.

65. Schwartzman, *Romare Bearden*, 225.

66. Kellie Jones, *Energy/Experimentation: Black Artists and Abstraction, 1964–1980* (New York: Studio Museum in Harlem, 2006), 17.

67. *Plessy v. Ferguson*, 163 U.S. 537, introduced the "separate but equal doctrine" in public transportation, not education. Nevertheless, "separate but equal" was applied to all areas of black civil rights in the United States, especially in the area of education in the South.

68. Elsa Honig-Fine, *The Afro-American Artist: A Search for Identity* (New York: Holt, Rinehart and Winston, 1973), 62.

69. Romare Bearden quoted in Schwartzman, *Romare Bearden*, 222–23.

70. Ernest Crichlow and Romare Bearden, *Fifteen under Forty: Paintings by Young New York State Black Artists* (Saratoga Springs, NY: New York State Education Department/Division of the Humanities and the Arts, 1970).

71. Ibid., inside flap.

72. Ibid.

73. Ibid., foreword.

74. Ibid.

75. Edmund Barry Gaither, *Afro-American Artists: New York and Boston* (Boston: Museum of the National Center of Afro-American Artists and the Museum of Fine Arts, Boston, 1970).

76. Crichlow and Bearden, *Fifteen under Forty*, foreword.

77. See William Henry Fox Talbot, *The Pencil of Nature*, 1839, which demonstrated how his pioneering photographic paper-printing process could be used for scientific purposes.

78. Honig-Fine, *Afro-American Artist*, 272.

79. See Kellie Jones's clever critique of this troubled exhibition and mainstream institutions' failed attempts at appeasing black artists, in Kellie Jones, *EyeMinded: Living and Writing Contemporary Art* (Durham, NC: Duke University Press, 2011), 415–16.

80. Robert Doty, *Contemporary Black Artists in America* (New York: Whitney Museum of American Art, 1971), 6.

81. John Canaday, "Black Artists on View in 2 Exhibitions," *New York Times*, April 7, 1971, 52.

82. Larry Rivers, *Some American History* (Houston: Institute for the Arts, Rice University, 1971).

83. Charles Childs, "Larry Ocean Swims the Nile: Mississippi and Other Rivers," in Rivers, *Some American History*, 19.

84. Ibid.

CHAPTER SIX

ART AND ACTIVISM IN BRITAIN: 1960s–1990s

1. Stuart Hall, "Three Moments in the History of Black Diaspora Visual Artists," the Raphael Samuel Memorial Lecture, Conway Hall, University of East London, London, November 19, 2004, notes taken by the author.

2. The right-wing policies of Margaret Thatcher and Ronald Reagan served to victimize and disenfranchise large numbers of black people. In the United States, many people felt that the strides of the civil rights and Black Power movements were slipping away. In both countries, funding for the arts was under attack as was the content of the art produced, notably that which engaged the AIDS crisis, gender, and sexuality.

3. Nalini Mohabir, "An Interview with Roshini Kempadoo," *exPLUSultra* 2 (December 2010), accessed August 15, 2016.

4. Piper earned a bachelor of arts degree in 1983 from Trent Polytechnic in Nottingham. The following year he enrolled in the Royal College of Art in London, where he received a master of arts in environmental media in 1986.

5. See http://www.blkartgroup.info/82conference.html, accessed October 28, 2013.

6. Ibid.

7. Eddie Chambers, *Black Artists in British Art: A History since the 1950s* (London: I. B. Taurus, 2014), 112.

8. Keith Piper, *A Ship Called Jesus* (London: Ikon Gallery, 1991).

9. See Stuart Hall, "Cultural Identity and Diaspora," in *Identity, Community, Culture, Difference*, ed. Jonathan Rutherford (London: Lawrence and Wishart, 1990).

10. See Coco Fusco and Guillermo Gómez-Peña, *Couple in the Cage*, photo documentation of a performance piece, 1992.

11. Keith Piper, *Relocating the Remains* (London: inIVA, 1997). I saw the critically acclaimed show in London in 1997 at the Royal College of Art and then again two years later in New York at the New Museum of Contemporary Art. The viewer experiences described in the lines that follow were mine.

12. Kobena Mercer, "Witness at the Crossroads: An Artist's Journey in Post-Colonial Space," in Keith Piper, *Relocating the Remains* (London: inIVA, 1997).

13. Stuart Hall, "Three Moments in the History of Black Diaspora Visual Artists," The Raphael Samuel Memorial Lecture, Conway Hall, University of East London, November 19, 2004.

14. Baartman was a member of the Khosian people of southern Africa, brought to England in 1810 by a Dutch farmer who exhibited her as a "freak" and a curiosity across Britain. To white European eyes, with her pronounced buttocks and labia, she was the physical embodiment of the heightened sexuality they ascribed to blacks. Whether she was brought as his slave is the subject of speculation but has never been confirmed.

15. Joy Gregory, *Objects of Beauty* (London: Autograph/Chris Boot, 2004), 28.

16. In addition to fine arts study at Central St. Martins College of Art and Design in London, the artist received an MA in African art History from the renowned School of Oriental and African Studies in London.

17. Fully aware of the impact of his black skin on a white public, Johnson used his fame to flout convention, most notably (and notoriously) in his many public—and consensual—romances with white women, one of which landed him in a courtroom in 1913, where he was convicted on poorly substantiated but nonetheless effective charges of violating the Mann Act (ironically also known as the White-Slave Traffic), which prohibited the transportation across state lines of women for "the purposes of prostitution, debauchery, or for any other immoral purpose." The women in question were not prostitutes, nor was Jack Johnson part of a prostitution ring, but the jury found him guilty as charged regardless, and he was sentenced to a year in prison. Johnson's physicality riled whites and gave them fodder for the stereotypes of black men that pervaded American society at the time.

18. Mary Evans, *Filter* (London: Institute of International Visual Arts, 1997), n.p.

19. Olu Oguibe, "Studio Call: Mary Evans," *Nka Journal of Contemporary African Art* 10 (Spring/Summer 1999): 38.

20. Evans, *Filter*, n.p.

21. Gilane Tawadros, "Bitter Sweet," in Evans, *Filter*, n.p.

22. Ibid.

23. Ibid.

24. Ibid.

25. Mary Evans, *Filter*, n.p.

CHAPTER SEVEN
BODIES: COMMODITIZATION AND BRANDING

1. Angela Y. Davis, "Masked Racism: Reflections on the Prison Industrial Complex," *Colorlines* (Fall 1998).

2. Ibid.

3. See https://www.prisonactivist.org.

4. I was in attendance at *Critical Resistance: Beyond the Prison Industrial Complex*. I thank my friend and colleague, Leigh Raiford, who was in residence at Berkeley in fall 1998, for suggesting that I attend the conference and for showing me the work of *Resistant Strains*.

5. Dylan Rodríguez, *Forced Passages: Imprisoned Radical Intellectuals and the U.S. Prison Regime* (Minneapolis: University of Minnesota Press, 2006), 223–56.

6. Promotional advertisement, *Premiere*, reprinted on the back cover of the book *Slam*, which includes the screenplay, poetry, and essays by the filmmakers. Richard Stratton and Kim Wozencraft, *Slam* (New York: Grove Press, 1998), back cover.

7. Ibid., 11. Richard Levin is known for the documentaries *What's Going On*, *Acid Test*, and *Beyond JFK*. Bonz Malone is an urban street legend and writer for *Vibe* magazine.

8. Ibid., 14.

9. Ibid., 48. Saul Williams was the Nuyorican Poets Cafe's Grand Slam Champion in 1996. His poetry has been published in the *New York Times* and *Bomb* as well as the anthologies *In Defense of Mumia* and *Catch the Fire*. His first book of poetry was *The Seventh Octave*. Williams is a graduate of Morehouse College in Atlanta and New York University Drama School. He has performed with the popular hip-hop singer Erykah Badu (b. 1971) and the poets Allen Ginsberg (1926–1997), Amiri Baraka, and Sonia Sanchez (b. 1934), among others.

10. Ibid., 246.

11. Ibid., 249–53. Excerpts from SLAM by Richard Stratton. Copyright © 1998 by Offline Entertainment Group. Used by permission of Grove/Atlantic, Inc. Any third party use of this material, outside of this publication, is prohibited.

12. Davis, "Masked Racism."

13. *Cash Crop* was first exhibited in 2010 at Atlanta's Mason Murer Gallery (now Mason Fine Art) after Hayes earned a master of fine arts degree from the Savannah College of Art and Design in 2006. A hugely popular exhibition, *Cash*

Crop was subsequently shown in Atlanta as well as in Durham, North Carolina, and Birmingham, Alabama.

14. Joseph E. Inikori and Stanley L. Engerman, eds., *The Atlantic Slave Trade: Effects on Economies, Societies, and Peoples in Africa, the Americas, and Europe* (Durham, NC: Duke University Press, 1992), 12–13.

15. Stephen Hayes interview with Cheryl Finley, October 6, 2011.

16. Ibid.

17. Ibid.

18. Stephen Hayes interview with Cheryl Finley, October 6, 2011.

19. Davis, "Masked Racism."

20. In 1998, Hank Willis Thomas received his BFA from New York University's Tisch School of the Arts in photography and Africana studies. He went on to study at the California College of the Arts in Oakland, earning an MA in criticism and an MFA in photography in 2004. The following year, Thomas was included in the critically acclaimed *Frequency* exhibition at the Studio Museum in Harlem curated by director Thelma Golden (b. 1965) to introduce the works of cutting-edge artists.

21. Interview with Cheryl Finley, September 2005.

22. Thomas Branagan, *The Penitential Tyrant; or, Slave Trader Reformed: A Pathetic Poem in Four Cantos* (New York: Samuel L. Wood, 1807). This small chapbook was one of a handful of illustrated antislavery books printed by the noted New York City–based abolitionist publisher in 1807, the year that the abolition of the slave trade became law in the UK and in which it was voted by congress to become law in the United States, effective 1808. Thomas likely studied the second edition of this book, now in the collection of the Schomburg Center for Research in Black Culture, where his mother, Dr. Deborah Willis, established and headed the Division of Prints and Photographs for more than a decade. The cover of this edition has an engraving of the kneeling slave with the motto, "Am I Not a Man and a Brother," below it.

23. *Cause Collective* was established in 2005 by Thomas and fellow artists from the California College of the Arts in Oakland. Some of its members have included Bayeté Ross Smith, Ryan Alexiev, and Eric Gottesman. See CauseCollective.org.

CHAPTER EIGHT
PATTERN: BEHIND THE FACE OF AN IRON

1. Interview with Cheryl Finley, March 13, 2002.

2. Wendy Weitman, "New Concepts in Printmaking 2: Willie Cole," *Museum of Modern Art Calendar* (June 1998): 32.

3. Jacqueline Brody, "Every Action Is Political and Spiritual: An Interview with Willie Cole," *Artnet*, February 14, 1997, 2.

4. Ibid., 2.

5. Cole studied graphic design at the Boston University School of Fine Arts from 1974 to 1975 and at the School of Visual Arts in New York, where he earned a bachelor of fine arts degree in 1976. He undertook further training in painting at the Art Students League of New York in the late 1970s, but it wasn't until he was selected for the prestigious artist-in-residence program at the Studio Museum in Harlem in 1989 that he began to receive art-world recognition.

6. Grace Glueck, "Willie Cole: New Concepts in Printmaking 2," *New York Times*, July 10, 1988, E37.

7. See Brody, "Every Action Is Political and Spiritual," 1.

8. Ibid., 4.

9. *Stowage* was published by Cole's New York gallery representatives, Alexander and Bonin, in an edition of fourteen with four artist's proofs. It was exhibited at the gallery upon publication and then included in the Museum of Modern Art exhibition *New Concepts in Printmaking 2* in 1998.

10. Cole is one of a handful of contemporary artists who have used this eighteenth-century printing technique to recast the slave ship icon into new works of art.

11. Ned Oldham, "Open to Interpretation," *Black and White*, no. 92 (Birmingham, AL: Birmingham Museum of Art, 1998), 26.

12. Marianetta Porter is a professor of art in the Department of Sculpture at the School of Fine Arts at the University of Michigan, Ann Arbor. These works were exhibited in a one-person show of the artist's work at the University of Michigan Art Gallery in spring 1999 and in the exhibition *Places without Proper Names* in 2001.

13. Interview with Cheryl Finley, October 18, 2001.

14. Ibid.

15. Ibid.

16. Ibid.

17. Ibid.

18. Ibid.

19. Ibid.

20. Ibid.

21. Kirsten P. Buick, "The Ideal Works of Edmonia Lewis," in *American Art* 9, no. 2 (1995): 11.

22. See Pauline Elizabeth Hopkins (a.k.a. Sarah A. Allen), *Hagar's Daughter: A Story of Southern Caste Prejudice*, first published in serial form in *Colored American Magazine* 2, nos. 5, 6 (March and April 1901);3, nos. 1–6 (May–October 1901); 4, nos. 1–4 (November–December 1901); (January, March, 1902), University of Pennsylvania Digital Library, http://digital.library .upenn.edu/women/hopkins/hagar/hagar.html, accessed July 31, 2013.

23. Zora Neale Hurston, "Story in Harlem Slang," *American Mercury*, July 1942, 94.

24. In 2001, Porter became the first visual artist to be awarded a fellowship from the Smithsonian Institution in Washington, DC, which enabled her to study artifacts in the American Folk Life Collection of the Museum of American History.

25. Marianetta Porter, artist statement, 2001, n.p.

26. Interview with Cheryl Finley, March 13, 2002. Betye Saar was born in Los Angeles, California, in 1926. She earned a bachelor of arts degree from the University of California, Los Angeles, in 1949 and has undertaken graduate studies at California State University, Long Beach; the University of Southern California; and California State University, Northridge. In recent years, Saar has collaborated with her daughter, Alison Saar, a sculptor, on public art installations, artist videos, and other projects. Since the early 1970s, Betye Saar has built her career to become one of the leading black artists in the United States, with important one-person exhibitions at major institutions including the Whitney Museum of American Art in New York; the Detroit Institute of Arts; the Museum of Contemporary Art, Los Angeles; and the Studio Museum in Harlem. Simultaneously, her reputation has been acknowledged by the acquisition of her work by important museums and private collectors, including the Metropolitan Museum of Art, New York; the Philadelphia Museum of Art; the Walker Art Center in Minneapolis; and the Smithsonian American Art Museum in Washington, DC.

27. Ibid., and Langston Hughes and Milton Meltzer, *Black Magic: A Pictorial History of the African American in the Performing Arts* (New York: Bonanza Books, 1967).

28. Ibid.

29. Saar's interest in the slave ship icon at this moment was inspired in part by her awareness of the reinvigorated reparations movement in the late twentieth century, which took shape anew with the introduction in 1989 of H.R. 40, Representative John Conyers's reparations bill, and gained momentum with Randall Robinson's popular book, *The Debt: What America Owes to Blacks* (New York: Penguin, 2000), which outlined the reasons why black Americans (and other diasporic Africans) should demand compensation for slavery, and lawsuits filed in state courts by Harvard law professor Charles Ogletree (et al.), cochair of the Reparations Movement Coordinating Committee. See Charles J. Ogletree Jr., "Repairing the Past: New Efforts in the Reparations Debate in America," *Harvard Civil Rights – Civil Liberties Law Review* 38, no. 2 (2003): 279–320. Demands for reparations date back to before the Civil War with roots in abolitionism, such as David Walker's Appeal published in 1829, notably calling for compensation for the labor of slaves. See *David Walker's Appeal to the Coloured Citizens of the World, but in Particular and Very Expressly, to the United States of America* (rpt.: Black Classics Press, 1997). As Saar put it, "Until this country claims this history—takes responsibility for it—there will always be the issue of racism in America." Interview with Cheryl Finley, March 13, 2002. The question of whether the United States should apologize for slavery also figured in discussions of the day. When President Bill Clinton went on a tour of la Maison des Esclaves during his visit to Senegal in April 1998, it was widely speculated that he might offer an apology for the US participation in the Atlantic Slave Trade; see Howard W. French, "On Both Sides, Reasons for Remorse: The Atlantic Slave Trade," *New York Times*, April 5, 1998 (illustrated with the slave ship icon, see fig. I.2). This apology didn't come until 2008, when the US House of Representatives issued an apology for 246 years of slavery and the subsequent decades of demeaning and demoralizing Jim Crow laws.

30. Interview with Cheryl Finley, March 13, 2002.

31. Ibid.

32. On a personal level, her motives for taking charge of the slave ship icon, she told me in the same interview, relate to her very being. "I even feel like it's part of my DNA."

33. Ibid. Betye Saar's personal revelation, connecting the slave ship icon to her DNA, is fitting to the larger discussion of the role of visual patterning, shape, and repetition has played in contemporary artists' iterations of the slave ship icon. If we take the visual cue that her statement suggests, scientific drawings of an elegantly twisting, color-coded double helix come to mind representing DNA's chemical composition. Found in every cell, deoxyribonucleic acid (DNA) contains the biological instructions that make each species—not to mention each person—unique. Part of the genetic code, DNA and its instructions are passed from adult organisms to their offspring during reproduction. Saar's rather prescient personal revelation foresaw the next decade of scientific debates around genetic testing and ancestor research, scientific tools used to help with genealogical research, especially in black families, where historical records often do not exist or are incomplete. The thirst for this kind of genealogical search has produced the television shows *African American Lives* (2006, 2008) and *Finding Your Roots* (2010, 2015); scholarly books: Henry Louis Gates Jr., *In Search of Our Roots: How 19 Extraordinary African Americans Reclaimed Their Past* (2009); Keith Wailoo, Alondra Nelson, and Catherine Lee, *Genetics and the Unsettled Past: DNA, Race, and History* (New Brunswick, NJ: Rutgers University Press, 2012); Alondra Nelson, *The Social Life of DNA: Race, Reparations, and Reconciliation after the Genome* (New York: Beacon Press, 2016); academic conferences and exhibitions such as the *African Diaspora: Integrating Culture, Genomics, and History*, sponsored by the Smithsonian Institution and the National Institutes of Health National Human Genome Project, http://www.cvent.com/events/the-african-diaspora-integrating-culture-genomics-and-history-symposium/agenda-36a8f2740f0644409dc1c0a3d0d8b5ac.aspx, accessed September 12, 2013.

34. Betye Saar, "Unfinished Business: The Return of Aunt Jemima," in *Unfinished Business: Workers + Warriors, the Return of Aunt Jemima* (New York: Michael Rosenfeld Gallery, 1998), 3.

35. Ibid.

CHAPTER NINE
SPIRITS: FROM CHANGÓ TO ICONOCLASM

1. Prior to immigrating to North America in 1990, Campos-Pons studied photography, drawing, and printmaking at the Escuela Nacional de Arte and the Instituto Superior de Arte in Havana, receiving degrees in fine arts in 1980 and 1985 respectively. Settling in Boston after a year's residency at the Banff Center for the Arts in Alberta, Canada, she pursued an MFA at the Massachusetts College of Art and began to work intensely in 3-D installation, producing works with autobiographical and biographical themes.

2. Lynne Bell, "History of People Who Were Not Heroes: A Conversation with Maria Magdalena Campos-Pons," *Third Text* 43 (Summer 1998): 34. *History of a People Who Were Not Heroes* is an installation in three parts: (1) *Town Portrait*, about how her family visits anew its memories of La Vega. It was first presented at the Norton Gallery in West Palm Beach, Florida, in 1994; (2) *Spoken Softly with Mama* recreated the rituals that were significant to her family. It was first presented at the Museum of Modern Art, New York, in 1998; and (3) *Sugar*, a work in progress, is an examination of issues of migration and displacement of the artist who has left La Vega and Cuba.

3. Bell, "History of People Who Were Not Heroes," 33.

4. Coco Fusco, *English Is Broken Here: Notes on Cultural Fusion in the Americas* (New York: New Press, 1995), 11. While living in Cuba, Campos-Pons was an artist-activist responding to the dictatorship of Fidel Castro. As she recalled, "There were things that I cared about, issues of social justice and the desire to make Cuba a modern country with a voice in the international scene." See Bell, "History of People Who Were Not Heroes," 38.

5. Thompson, *Flash of the Spirit*, 16. Horace Campbell has further asserted that enslaved Africans "resisted the cultural and ideological domination of their colonizers and the religious and artistic self expressions of dignity represented resistance." Horace Campbell, *Rasta and Resistance* (Trenton, NJ: Africa World Press, 1987), 23.

6. Thompson, *Flash of the Spirit*, 17.

7. Ibid.

8. Linda Wong, "Interview with Magdalena Campos-Pons," *Sojourner: The Women's Forum* (September 1997): 29.

9. Ibid., 38.

10. Kellie Jones, "Life's Little Necessities: Installations by Women in the 1990s," in *Trade Routes: History and Geography: 2nd Johannesburg Biennale 1997* (Johannesburg: Greater Johannesburg Metropolitan Council, 1997), 286.

11. Julia P. Herzberg, *Let Me Tell You* (New York: Intar Gallery, 1993), n.p.

12. Bell, "History of People Who Were Not Heroes," 42.

13. Ibid.

14. Campos-Pons did a similar performance at the opening of her installation at the Vancouver Art Gallery in Canada in 1993. Interview with Cheryl Finley, August 29, 2001.

15. Sally Berger, "Magdalena Campos-Pons, 1990–2001," in Salah M. Hassan and Olu Oguibe, *Authentic/Ex-Centric: Conceptualism in Contemporary African Art* (Ithaca, NY, and Venice: Forum for African Arts and la Biennale di Venezia, 2001), 122. The artist's performances have been recorded in still photographs and on film or have taken place spontaneously.

16. Berger, "Magdalena Campos-Pons, 1990–2001," 135.

17. Jan Murphy, "Art Challenges Colonization: The IV Havana Biennial" and "Testing the Limits," *Cuba Update*, March/April 1992, 49–50, 64.

18. See Steve Turner, *Amazing Grace: The Story of America's Most Beloved Song* (New York: Harper Collins) 2009. The musical, *Amazing Grace*, with lyrics and music written by Stephen Smith, was based on the life of English slave trader cum Anglican priest, Sir John Newton, who is credited with penning the famous spiritual. The musical played in Chester, Connecticut, in 2012, had a pre-Broadway run in Chicago in 2014, and played on Broadway in 2015. With a production design by Eugene Lee, the central action of the play takes place on the deck of a slave ship inspired by his designs for Baraka's 1969 Chelsea Theatre production of *Slave Ship*, which Lee also designed.

19. Sabrina Walters, "Glass Recalls Slavery's Horror," *Chicago Sun Times*, December 17, 2000, 24.

20. Tom Feelings, *The Middle Passage: White Ships/Black Cargo* (New York: Dial Books, 1995).

21. Rudine Sims Bishop, "Tom Feelings and *The Middle Passage*," *Horn Book Magazine*, July/August 1996, http://archive.hbook.com/magazine/articles/1990_96/jul96_bishop.asp, accessed October 25, 2013.

22. Feelings (1933–2003) began his formal study of art in high school and upon graduation received a scholarship to the Cartoonists' and Illustrators' School in New York City. He enlisted in the US Air Force in 1953 and was stationed in London, England, where he worked as a staff artist in the graphics division. Eager to hone his skills as an illustrator, Feelings returned to New York in 1957 to attend the School of Visual Arts while working as a freelance graphic artist.

23. Tom Feelings quoted in Horn Book Magazine, 1985.

24. Ibid.

25. In 1969, Julius Lester's *To Be a Slave* (New York: Dial Press), illustrated by Feelings, was chosen as a Newberry Honor Book, the first time a black author received this award. In 1972, Feelings was the first black artist to receive a Caldecott Honor Award for *Moja Means One: A Swahili Counting Book* (New York: Dial Press, 1971), and in 1975 he received a second Caldecott Honor Award for *Jambo Means Hello: A Swahili Alphabet Book* (New York: Dial Press, 1974), both written with Muriel Feelings. Tom Feelings also illustrated Maya Angelou's

Now Sheba Sings the Song (New York: E. P. Dutton, 1987) and invited poets Angelou, Haki R. Madhubuti, Walter Dean Myers, Lucille Clifton, and others to compose poems to his illustrations for *Soul Looks Back in Wonder* (New York: Dial, 1993).

26. Interview with Tom Feelings, New York University, King Juan Carlos I of Spain Center, 1999.

27. Tom Feelings quoted in "Tom Feelings, 70, an Illustrator Who Portrayed Black History," *New York Times*, August 30, 2003.

28. *The Middle Passage: Drawings by Tom Feelings* was exhibited at the McKissack Museum at the University of South Carolina, March 12 – December 3, 2000. The exhibition included fifty-two pen-and-ink and tempera drawings on rice paper used to make the book. The Beinecke Rare Book and Manuscript Library at Yale University purchased the drawings, along with other works by Feelings, in 2009, and added them to the James Weldon Johnson Collection. From 1998 until his death in 2003, Feelings frequently presented the origins of his seminal book project in slide-illustrated lectures to packed audiences where the nationally touring exhibition of his book's drawings was shown.

29. Sabrina Walters, "Glass Recalls Slavery's Horror," *Chicago Sun Times*, December 17, 2000, 24.

30. John W. Fountain, "Church's Window on the Past, and the Future," *New York Times*, February 9, 2001.

31. Marshall E. Hatch, "African American Church Stained Glass: Pointing to Our Past and Our Future," in *Little Black Pearl,* Summer 2013, http://blackpearl.org/wp-content/uploads/LBP-Magazine-Summer-2013.pdf, accessed October 17, 2013.

32. The *Maafa Remembrance* window was fabricated at a cost of $30,000 by the 150-year-old Botti Studio of Architectural Art in nearby Evanston, Illinois, a family-run business specializing in design, restoration, conservation, and fabrication of leaded stained glass and ecclesiastical art.

33. The Reverend Marshall E. Hatch, "Maafa Remembrance 2000 Dedication Speech," www.newmountpilgrim.org.

34. Ibid.

35. The Reverend Dr. Gregory Thomas quoted in Mickey Ciokajlo, "Church Recalls Slavery with Stained Glass Window," *Chicago Tribune*, December 18, 2000, http://articles.chicago tribune.com/2000-12-18/news/0012180051_1_stained-glass -window-slave-trade-middle-passage, accessed October 25, 2013.

CHAPTER TEN
ROOTS TOURISM AND THE SLAVE SHIP ICON

1. Alex Haley, *Roots* (Garden City, NY: Doubleday, 1976), v.

2. Juffure was the name of the village in The Gambia from whence Kunta Kinte and Haley's maternal side of the family came. It has now been turned into a tourist destination for roots-seeking black Americans, even though some of Haley's research has since been disputed. Haley retired from the US Coast Guard in 1959 as its chief journalist and began writing for magazines such as *Playboy* and *Reader's Digest*, the latter of which published portions of *Roots* in 1974. His first book was *The Autobiography of Malcolm X*.

3. African Americans conducted much of their genealogical research in English-speaking West African countries. The first great wave of African American roots seeking began during the Black Power movement.

4. The success of the *Roots* television miniseries came as the hugely profitable blaxploitation film era (1971–77), popularized by Hollywood producers, was coming to an end.

5. David Vlado Moskowitz, *Bob Marley: A Biography* (Westport, CT: Greenwood Publishing Group, 2007), 56.

6. Horace Campbell, *Rasta and Resistance: From Marcus Garvey to Walter Rodney* (Trenton, NJ: Africa World Press, 1987), 6.

7. Some of the lyrics to the songs, such as "a people without the knowledge of past history, origin and country is like a tree without roots" make the direct connection to the album illustration that includes the slave ship icon.

8. Pierre Nora, "Between Memory and History: Les Lieux de Mémoire," *Representations* 26 (Spring 1989): 9.

9. Long-time Yale University history professor Robert W. Harms discovered Lieutenant Durand's journal in the Beinecke Library and brilliantly chronicled the history they tell in *The Diligent: A Voyage through the Worlds of the Slave Trade* (New Haven, CT: Yale University Press), 2007.

10. Visitor Comment Books, Cape Coast Castle, 1998.

11. Ibid. The phrase "Stop Whitewashing Our History" was popularized in the writings and activism of the influential expatriate African American Imahkhus Vienna Robinson. See Imahkhus Vienna Robinson, "Is the Black Man's History Being Whitewashed?" *Uhuru* 9 (1994): 48–50.

12. Visitor Comment Books, Cape Coast Castle, 1998.

13. Ibid.

14. Visitor Comment Books, Cape Coast Castle, 1999.

15. Ibid.

16. Ibid.

17. Ibid.

18. Ibid.

19. Richard Wright, *Black Power: A Record of Reactions in a Land of Pathos* rpt. 1954 (New York: Harper Perennial, 1995), 384.

CHAPTER ELEVEN
MUSEUMS, MONUMENTS, AND MEMORIALS

1. See for example Howard Jones, *Mutiny on the Amistad: The Saga of a Slave Revolt and Its Impact on American Abolition, Law, and Diplomacy* (New York: Oxford University Press, 1987); Alexis D. Pate, *Amistad: A Novel* (New York:

Dream Works, 1997); David Pesci, *Amistad: The Thunder of Freedom* (New York: Marlowe and Co., 1997); Walter Dean Myers, *Amistad: A Long Road to Freedom* (New York: Dutton Juvenile, 1998); and film and video works including *The Voyage of La Amistad* (Oak Forest, IL: MPI Home Video, 1998) 70 min. VHS; and Stephen Spielberg, *Amistad* (Universal City, CA: Dream Works, 1998) 155 min. feature film. Earlier works, such as William A. Owens, *Black Mutiny: The Revolt on the Schooner Amistad* rpt. 1953 (Black Classics Press, 1997) and Robert Hayden's classic poem *Middle Passage* (1954), inspired by the events of the *Amistad*, were reissued during the flurry of publishing in the late 1990s fueled in part by growing interest in the reparations movement developing around the same time (see Robert Hayden, *Collected Poems*, edited by Frederick Glaysher with an introduction by Arnold Rampersad [New York: Liveright reprint edition, 1997]).

AFTERWORD
THE SHAPE OF THINGS...
DOESN'T ALWAYS APPEAR AS IT SEEMS

1. John Hollander and Joanna Weber, eds., *Words for Images: A Gallery of Poems* (New Haven, CT: Yale University Art Gallery, 2001). The exhibition was on view from August 21 to November 4, 2001.

2. Elizabeth Alexander received an MA from Boston University, and a PhD in English from the University of Pennsylvania. An acclaimed poet, essayist, and playwright, she is best known for delivering the poem "Praise Song for the Day" at the inauguration of President Barack Obama. Alexander has published five books of poems and two collections of essays, including *The Venus Hottentot* (1992), *The Black Interior* (2003), *American Sublime* (2005), and *Power and Possibility* (2007).

3. E. Ethelbert Miller, 1/20/09, http://eethelbertmiller1 .blogspot.com/2009_01_01_archive.html-70447341691364 52908, accessed January 10, 2010.

4. Agnes Martin was born in the town of Maklin in the western province of Saskatchewan, Canada, in 1912. She moved to the United States in 1931 and became a United States citizen in 1950. After earning a BS (1942) and an MA (1952) from Teachers College at Columbia University, she moved to New Mexico, and dedicated herself to painting. Martin moved back to New York in 1957 and lived there for ten years before settling in New Mexico again, where she lived and worked until her death in 2004. The Whitney Museum of American Art organized a major traveling retrospective of her work in 1992.

5. E-mail correspondence from Elizabeth Alexander to Cheryl Finley, November 16, 2001. Shortly after Alexander searched the Yale Art Gallery collection for works by African American artists, several major acquisitions were made in May 2000 in conjunction with the exhibition *Imaging African Art: Documentation and Transformation*. These included works by Romare Bearden, Lorna Simpson, Carrie Mae Weems, Albert Chong, and Hale Woodruff, among others. Since then, other substantial acquisitions have been made, including paintings by John Wilson and Jacob Lawrence. See Daniell Cornell and Cheryl Finley, *Imaging African Art: Documentation and Transformation* (New Haven, CT: Yale University Art Gallery, 2000).

6. E-mail correspondence from Elizabeth Alexander to Cheryl Finley, November 16, 2001.

7. Ibid.

8. Michael Kimmelman, "Nature's Mystical Poetry Written in Paint," *New York Times*, November 15, 1992, 35. The art critic Holland Cotter has suggested that her works have a heavenly presence. See Holland Cotter, "Agnes Martin: All the Way to Heaven," *Art in America* (April 1993): 86–97, 149.

9. Hollander and Weber, *Words for Images*, 82.

10. A Mankala (or Mancala) board, usually has fourteen pits: six parallel on either side, and a depository at either end. It was modeled after ancient African memory boards used to track and monitor the passing of an event. Mankala is game of strategy that tests an opponent's ability to remember a series of actions. In some areas of West Africa, Mankala is called Oware or Ayo; in South Africa, it is called Ohoro. Mankala (or Mancala) is the popular, East African name of the game.

11. Hollander and Weber, *Words for Images*, 80. "Islands Number Four" © 2001, by Elizabeth Alexander, first appeared in *Words for Images: A Gallery of Poems*, published by Yale University Art Gallery, reprinted in *Antebellum Dream Book* © 2001, published by Graywolf Press. Used with permission of Elizabeth Alexander and Graywolf Press.

12. See, for example, Alexander's five-part poem *Fugue*, in which part one is named after Charles Alston's civil rights–era painting *Walking* from 1963. The last three lines of part one read,

> The painting was made after marching
> in Birmingham, walking
> into a light both brilliant and unseen.

Elizabeth Alexander, *Antebellum Dream Book* (Saint Paul, MN: Graywolf Press, 2001), 3. The front cover of this collection of poems is illustrated with the painting *Garden of Music* (1960) by Bob Thompson.

13. According to the *Oxford English Dictionary*, an ekphrasis is "a plain declaration or interpretation of a thing." *Oxford English Dictionary* (Oxford: At the Clarendon Press, 1933), Vol. 3, D–E, 36.

14. Hollander and Weber, *Words for Images*, xi–xii.

15. Ibid., 80.

16. E-mail correspondence from Elizabeth Alexander to Cheryl Finley, November 16, 2001.

References

ARCHIVAL SOURCES AND MUSEUM COLLECTIONS

Boston Public Library, Boston
British Library, Department of Manuscripts, London
Minute Books of the London Abolition Committee,
    Additional MSS, 21,254–21,256
Religious Society of Friends Library, London
Thompson/Clarkson MSS
Cape Coast Castle Museum, Cape Coast, Ghana
Elmina Castle, Elmina, Ghana
Ghana National Archives, Accra, Ghana
Ghana National Archives, Cape Coast, Ghana
Ghana National Museum, Accra, Ghana
Historical Society of Pennsylvania
Library Company of Philadelphia
Library of Congress, Washington, DC
Maison des Esclaves, Dakar, Senegal
Musée Historique de Gorée, Dakar, Senegal
Public Record Office, Kew, Richmond, Surrey,
    England (PRO)
Schomburg Center for Research in Black Culture,
    New York Public Library
W. E. B. Du Bois House and Museum, Accra, Ghana
West African Historical Museum, Cape Coast, Ghana
Wilberforce House Museum, Hull City Art Galleries,
    United Kingdom
Yale Libraries
Benjamin Franklin Collection, Sterling Memorial Library
Elizabeth Donnan Papers, Manuscripts Collection,
    Sterling Memorial Library
Beinecke Rare Book and Manuscript Library

NEWSPAPERS AND PERIODICALS

American Museum (1789–90)
The Western Flying Post; or Sherborne and Yeovil
    Mercury, and General Advertiser (1788–89)

SELECTED BIBLIOGRAPHY

Affaire de La Vigilante, Batiment Negrier de Nantes. Paris:
    Crapelet, 1823.
Alexander, Elizabeth. *Antebellum Dream Book.* Saint Paul,
    MN: Graywolf Press, 2001.
Amistad: A Celebration of the Film by Steven Spielberg. Essays
    by Steven Spielberg, Maya Angelou, and Debbie Allen.
    Paintings by Kadir Nelson and photographs by Andrew
    Cooper. New York: Newark Press, 1998.
Anderson, Benedict. *Imagined Communities: Reflections on
    the Origins and Spread of Nationalism.* London: Verso,
    1991.
Anstey, Roger. *The Atlantic Slave Trade and British Abolition,
    1760–1810.* Atlantic Highlands, NJ: Humanities Press,
    1975.
Anstey, Roger, and P. E. H. Hair. *Liverpool, the African Slave
    Trade, and Abolition: Essays to Illustrate Current Knowl-
    edge and Research.* Bristol: Historic Society of Lancashire
    and Cheshire, 1976.
Aptheker, Herbert. *American Negro Slave Revolts.* New York:
    Columbia University Press, 1943.
Bailey, Anne. *African Voices of the Atlantic: Beyond the Silence
    and Shame.* Boston: Beacon Press, 2005.
Balibar, Etienne, and Immanuel Wallerstein. *Race, Nation,
    Class: Ambiguous Identities.* London: Verso, 1991.
Baraka, Amiri. *Home: Social Essays.* New York: William Mor-
    row, 1988; rpt. Hopewell, NJ: Ecco Press, 1998.
———. *Raise, Race, Rays, Raze: Essays since 1965.* New
    York: Random House, 1971.
———. *Slave Ship: A One Act Play.* Newark, NJ: Jihad Pro-
    ductions, 1969.
Baraka, Amiri and Larry Neal, eds. *Black Fire: An Anthology of
    Afro-American Writing.* New York: Morrow, 1968.
Barker, Anthony J. *The African Link: British Attitudes to the
    Negro in the Era of the Atlantic Slave Trade, 1550–1807.*
    London: Frank Cass, 1978.
Barnes, Clive. "The Theater: New LeRoi Jones Play." *New York
    Times,* November 22, 1969.

Barson, Tanya, and Peter Gorschlüter, eds. *Afro Modern Journeys through the Black Atlantic*. Liverpool: Tate Liverpool, in association with Harry N. Abrams, 2010. Published in conjunction with *Afro Modern Journeys through the Black Atlantic* exhibition shown at the Tate Liverpool, International Modern and Contemporary Art.

Baucom, Ian. *Specters of the Atlantic: Finance, Capital, Slavery, and the Philosophy of History*. Durham, NC: Duke University Press, 2005.

Beauchamp-Byrd, Mora J., and M. Franklin Sirmans, eds. *Transforming the Crown: African, Asian, and Caribbean Artists in Britain, 1966–1996*. New York: Caribbean Cultural Center/African Diaspora Institute, 1997.

Bell, Lynne. "History of People Who Were Not Heroes: A Conversation with Maria Magdalena Campos-Pons." *Third Text* 43 (Summer 1998): 33–42.

Benjamin, Walter. *Illuminations*. Edited with an introduction by Hannah Arendt. Translated by Harry Zohn. New York: Schocken Books, 1968.

Berger, Sally. "Magdalena Campos-Pons, 1990–2001." In Salah M. Hassan and Olu Oguibe, *Authentic/Ex-centric: Conceptualism in Contemporary African Art*. Ithaca and Venice: Forum for African Arts and la Biennale di Venezia, 2001.

Berlin, Ira, Marc Favreau, and Steven F. Miller, eds. *Remembering Slavery: African Americans Talk About Their Personal Experiences of Slavery and Emancipation*. New York: New Press, 1998.

Bidlake, John. *The Slave Trade: A Sermon Preached at Stonehouse Chapel on 28th December 1788*. Plymouth: M. and B. Haydon, 1789.

Bindman, David. "Am I Not a Man and a Brother? British Art and Slavery in the Eighteenth Century." *Res 26* (Autumn 1994): 68–82.

Blk Art Group. http://www.blkartgroup.info/82conference.html, accessed October 28, 2013.

Boime, Albert. *The Art of Exclusion: Representing Blacks in the Nineteenth Century*. Washington, DC: Smithsonian Institution Press, 1990.

Bolster, W. Jeffrey. *Black Jacks: African American Seamen in the Age of Sail*. Cambridge, MA: Harvard University Press, 1997.

Boudriot, Jean. *Traite, Négrier L'Aurore, Navire de 280 tx., 1784*. Paris: Collection Archeologie Navale Francaise, 1984.

Bracken, C. W. *A History of Plymouth and Her Neighbours*. Plymouth: Underhill, 1931.

Braidwood, Stephen J. *Black Poor and White Philanthropists: London's Blacks and the Foundation of the Sierra Leone Settlement, 1786–1791*. Liverpool: Liverpool University Press, 1994.

Branagan, Thomas. *The Penitential Tyrant*. New York: Samuel Wood, 1807.

Brewer, John, and Roy Porter, eds. *Consumption and the World of Goods*. London: Routledge, 1993.

Brienen, Rebecca Parker. *Visions of Savage Paradise: Albert Eckhout, Court Painter in Colonial Dutch Brazil*. Amsterdam: Amsterdam University Press, 2006.

Brody, Jacqueline. "Every Action Is Political and Spiritual: An Interview with Willie Cole." *Artnet*, February 14, 1997, 2.

Brooks, Peter. *The Melodramatic Imagination*. New Haven, CT: Yale University Press, 1974.

Brown, Lloyd W. *Amiri Baraka*. Boston: Twayne Publishers, 1980.

Bryden, Inga, and Janet Floyd, eds. *Domestic Space: Reading the Nineteenth-Century Interior*. Manchester: Manchester University Press, 1999.

Buick, Kirsten P. "The Ideal Works of Edmonia Lewis." In *American Art*, vol. 9, no. 2 (Summer 1995): 11.

Burnside, Madeline, and Rosemarie Robotham. *Spirits of the Passage: The Transatlantic Slave Trade in the Seventeenth Century*. New York: Simon and Schuster, 1997.

Byfield, Judy, and Anthea Morrison, eds. *Gendering the African Diaspora: Women, Culture, and Historical Change in the Caribbean and Nigerian Hinterland*. Bloomington: Indiana University Press, 2010.

Cahan, Susan E. *Mounting Frustration: The Art Museum in the Age of Black Power*. Art History Publication Initiative. Durham, NC: Duke University Press, 2016.

Campbell, Horace. *Rasta and Resistance: From Marcus Garvey to Walter Rodney*. New York: Africa World Press, 1987.

Campbell, James T. *Middle Passages: African American Journeys to Africa, 1787–2005*. New York: Penguin Press, 2006.

Campbell, Mary Schmidt. *Tradition and Conflict: Images of a Turbulent Decade, 1963–1973*. New York: Studio Museum in New York, 1985.

Carby, Hazel V. *Cultures in Babylon: Black Britain and African America*. New York: Verso, 1999.

———. *Race Men*. Cambridge, MA: Harvard University Press, 1998.

———. *Reconstructing Womanhood: The Emergence of the Afro-American Woman Novelist*. New York: Oxford University Press, 1987.

Carter, Edward C., II. "The Political Activities of Mathew Carey, Nationalist: 1760–1814." PhD diss., Bryn Mawr College, 1962.

Certeau, Michel de. *The Practice of Everyday Life*. Translated by Steven Rendall. Los Angeles: University of California Press, 1984.

Chambers, Eddie. *Black Artists in British Art: A History since the 1950s*. London: I. B. Taurus, 2014.

Charnock, John. *An History of Maritime Architecture…from the Earliest Period to the Present*. 3 vols. London, 1800.

Chase, Henry. *In Their Footsteps: The American Visions Guide to African-American Heritage Sites*. New York: Henry Holt, 1994.

Clarkson, Thomas. *An Abstract of the Evidence Delivered before a Select Committee of the House of Commons, in the Years 1790 and 1791*. London: James A. Phillips, 1791.

———. *An Abstract of the Evidence Delivered before a Select Committee of the House of Commons, in the Years 1790 and 1791; On the Part of the Petitioners for the Abolition of the Slave Trade*. Edinburgh: J. Robertson, 1791.

———. *The Cries of Africa, to the Inhabitants of Europe; or, a Survey of That Bloody Commerce Called Slave-Trade*. London: Harvey and Darton, 1822.

———. *An Essay on the Slavery and Commerce of the Human Species, Particularly the African; Translated from a Latin Dissertation Which Was Honoured with the First Prize in the University of Cambridge for the Year 1785*. London: James Phillips, 1786.

———. *The History of the Rise, Progress, and Accomplishment of the Abolition of the African Slave-Trade by British Parliament*. 2 vols. London: Longmans, 1808.

———. *A Portraiture of Quakerism, as Taken from a View of the Moral Education, Discipline, Peculiar Customs, Religious Principles, Political and Civil Economy, and Character of the Society of Friends*. 3 vols. London: R. Taylor, for Longman, Hurst, Rees and Orme, 1806.

Cobley, John. *The Crimes of the First Fleet Convicts*. Sydney: Angus and Robertson, 1970.

Coldham, Peter Wilson. *Emigrants in Chains: A Social History of Forced Emigration to the Americas, 1607–1776*. Stroud, UK: Alan Sutton, 1992.

Connerton, Paul. *How Societies Remember*. Cambridge: Cambridge University Press, 1989.

Cooks, Bridget R. *Exhibiting Blackness: African Americans and the American Art Museum*. Amherst: University of Massachusetts Press, 2011.

Coombes, Annie E. *Reinventing Africa: Museums, Material Culture, and Popular Imagination*. New Haven, CT: Yale University Press, 1994.

Covarrubias, Miguel. "African Dance for Canot." *Creative Art*, vol. 3. no. 3 (September 1928): viii.

———. "African Village for Canot." *Creative Art*, vol. 3, no. 1 (July 1928): xii.

———. "America's Newest Citizens." *Vanity Fair*, vol. 30, no. 5 (July 1928): 56–57.

———. *The Eagle, the Jaguar and the Serpent. Indian Art of the Americas: North America, Alaska, Canada, the United States*. New York: Alfred A. Knopf, 1954.

———. "Enter the New Negro, a Distinctive Type Recently Created by the Coloured Cabaret Belt in New York." *Vanity Fair*, vol. 23, no. 4 (December 1924): 60–61.

———. "The Increasing Vogue of the Negro Revue on Broadway." *Vanity Fair*, vol. 23, no. 6 (February 1925): 61.

———. *Indian Art of Mexico and Central America*. New York: Alfred A. Knopf, 1957, 2 vols.

———. *Island of Bali*, with photographs by Rosa Covarrubias. New York: Alfred A. Knopf, 1937.

———. *Mexico South: The Isthmus of Tehuantepec*, with photographs by Miguel and Rosa Covarrubias. New York: Alfred A. Knopf, 1946.

———. *Negro Drawings*. New York: Alfred A. Knopf, 1927.

———. "6 Derisions from a Mexican Pencil." *Vanity Fair*, vol. 23, no. 7 (March 1925): 46.

———. "Two African Men for Canot." *Creative Art*, vol. 2, no. 5 (May 1928): ix.

Cowley, Frank. *Colonial Australia, 1788–1840*. Vol. 1. Melbourne: Nelson, 1980.

Cowley, Malcolm. *Adventures of an African Slaver, Being a True Account of the Life of Captain Theodore Canot, Trader in Gold, Ivory & Slaves on the Coast of Guinea: His Own Story as Told in the Year 1854 to Brantz Mayer*. New York: Albert & Charles Boni, 1928. Illustrated by Miguel Covarrubias.

Craton, Michael. *Sinews of Empire: A Short History of British Slavery*. Garden City, NY: Anchor/Doubleday, 1974.

Crawford, Charles. *Observations upon Negro-Slavery*. Philadelphia: Joseph Crukshank, 1784.

———. *Observations upon Negro-Slavery*, new ed. Philadelphia: Eleazer Oswald, 1790.

Crichlow, Ernest, and Romare Bearden. *Fifteen under Forty: Paintings by Young New York State Black Artists*. Saratoga Springs, NY: New York State Education Department/Division of the Humanities and the Arts, 1970.

Critical Resistance. https://www.prisonactivist.org.

Crossroads of People, Crossroads of Trade. Cape Coast: Cape Coast Castle Museum, 1995.

Curtin, Philip D. *The Atlantic Slave Trade: A Census*. Madison: University of Wisconsin Press, 1969.

Daget, Serge, ed. *De la Traite a L'Esclavage: Actes du Colloque international sur la traite de Noirs, Nantes, 1985*. Vol. 2. Nantes: Centre de Recherches sur L'Histoire du Monde Atlantique, 1988.

D'Anjou, Leo. *Social Movements and Cultural Change: The First Abolition Campaign Revisited*. New York: Aldine de Gruyter, 1996.

Davis, Angela Y. "Masked Racism: Reflections on the Prison Industrial Complex." *Colorlines* (Fall 1998).

Davis, David Brion. *Ante-bellum Reform*. New York: Harper and Row, 1967.

———. "The Enduring Legacy of the South's Civil War Victory." *New York Times*, August 26, 2001, 1D, 6D.

———. *From Homicide to Slavery: Studies in American Culture*. New York: Oxford University Press, 1986.

———. *In the Image of God: Religion, Moral Values, and Our Heritage of Slavery*. New Haven, CT: Yale University Press, 2001.

Davis, David Brion. *The Problem of Slavery in the Age of Revolution, 1770–1823*. Ithaca, NY: Cornell University Press, 1975.

———. *The Problem of Slavery in Western Culture*. New York: Oxford University Press, 1988.

———. *Slavery and Human Progress*. New York: Oxford University Press, 1984.

———. *The Slave Power Conspiracy and the Paranoid Style*. Baton Rouge: Louisiana State University Press, 1970.

DeCorse, Christopher R. *An Archaeology of Elmina: Africans and Europeans on the Gold Coast, 1400–1900*. Washington, DC: Smithsonian Institution Press, 2001.

Description of a Slave Ship. London: James A. Phillips for the London Committee of the Society for Effecting the Abolition of the Slave Trade, 1789.

Diedrich, Maria, Henry Louis Gates Jr., and Carl Pedersen, eds. *Black Imagination and the Middle Passage*. New York: Oxford University Press, 1999.

Donnan, Elizabeth. *Documents Illustrative of the History of the Slave Trade to America, 1930–1935*. 4 vols. New York: Octagon Books, 1969.

Doty, Robert. *Contemporary Black Artists in America*. New York: Whitney Museum of American Art, 1971.

Dow, George Francis. *Slave Ships and Slaving*. Salem, MA: Marine Research Society, 1927.

Drake, Richard. *Revelations of Slave Smuggler: Being the Autobiography of Capt. Richard Drake, an African Trader for Fifty Years—From 1807 to 1857; during which period he was Concerned in the Transportation of Half a Million Blacks from African Coasts to America*. New York: Robert M. DeWitt, Publisher, 1860.

Drescher, Seymour. *Capitalism and Antislavery: British Mobilization in Comparative Perspective*. Oxford: Oxford University Press, 1987.

Du Bois, W. E. B. *The Suppression of the African Slave-Trade to the United States of America, 1638–1870*. New York: Longmans, Green, 1896.

Duffy, Michael, et al., eds. *The New Maritime History of Devon*. Vol. 1, *From Early Times to the Late Eighteenth Century*. London: Conway Maritime Press in association with the University of Exeter, 1992.

Eisenberg, Diane. *Malcolm Cowley: A Checklist of His Writings, 1916–1973* Carbondale: Southern Illinois University Press, 1975.

Elam Jr., Harry. "Social Urgency, Audience Participation, and the Performance of *Slave Ship* by Amiri Baraka." In *Crucibles of Crisis: Performing Social Change*, edited by Janelle Reinelt. Ann Arbor: University of Michigan Press.

Eltis, David. *Economic Growth and the Ending of the Transatlantic Slave Trade*. Oxford: Oxford University Press, 1987.

———. Transatlantic Slavery Database. http://www.slavevoyages.org/about/team.

Equiano, Olaudah. *The Interesting Narrative of the Life of Olaudah Equiano or Gustavus Vassa, The African*. 2 vols. London: Printed for and sold by the author, No. 20, Union-Street, Middlesex Hospital, 1789. Facsimile of the first edition with an introduction and notes by Paul Edwards. London: Dawsons of Pall Mall, 1969.

———. *The Interesting Narrative of the Life of Olaudah Equiano or Gustavus Vassa, The African*. 6th ed. London: 1793.

———. *The Interesting Narrative of the Life of Olaudah Equiano or Gustavus Vassa, The African*. 9th ed. 1794. Reprinted in Olaudah Equiano, *The Interesting Narrative and Other Writings*. Edited with an introduction and notes by Vincent Carretta. New York: Penguin Classics, 1995.

———. *The Interesting Narrative and Other Writings*. Edited with an introduction and notes by Vincent Carretta. New York: Penguin Classics, 1995.

———. *The Life and Adventures of Olaudah Equiano; or, Gustavus Vassa, The African. From an Account Written by Himself*. Abridged by A. Mott to which are added some remarks on the slave trade, &c. New York: Samuel Wood and Sons, 1829.

Evans, Mary. *Filter*. London: Institute of International Visual Arts, 1997.

Fabre, Geneviève. *Drumbeats, Masks, and Metaphors: Contemporary Afro-American Theatre*. Cambridge, MA: Harvard University Press, 1983.

———. *Jambo Means Hello: A Swahili Alphabet Book*. New York: Dial Press, 1974.

———. *Moja Means One: A Swahili Counting Book*. New York: Dial Press, 1971.

Fabre, Geneviève, and Robert O'Meally, eds. *History and Memory in African American Culture*. New York: Oxford University Press, 1994.

Falconbridge, Alexander. *Account of the Slave Trade on the Coast of Africa*. London: J. Philips, 1788.

Fanon, Frantz. *Black Skin, White Masks*. New York: Grove Press, 1967.

Feelings, Tom. *The Middle Passage*. New York: Dial Books, 1995.

Felman, Shoshana, and Dori Laub. *Testimony: Crises of Witnessing in Literature, Psychoanalysis, and History*. New York: Routledge, 1992.

Ferdinand, Val. "On Black Theater in America: A Report from New Orleans." *Black World*, April 1970.

Finley, Cheryl. "Committed to Memory: The Slave Ship Icon in the Black Atlantic Imagination." *Chicago Art Journal* 9 (Spring 1999): 2–22.

———. "The Door of No Return," *Common Place* 1, no. 4, http://www.common-place.org/vol-01/no-4/finley.

Fladeland, Betty. *Abolitionists and Working Class Problems in the Age of Industrialization*. Baton Rouge: Louisiana State University Press, 1984.

Foote, Commander Andrew. *Africa and the American Flag.* New York: D. Appleton & Co., 1854.

Foucault, Michel. *The Order of Things: An Archaeology of the Human Sciences.* New York: Vintage Books, 1994.

Fountain, John W. "Church's Window on the Past, and the Future." *New York Times,* February 9, 2001.

French, Howard W. "On Both Sides Reasons for Remorse: The Atlantic Slave Trade." *New York Times,* April 5, 1998.

Friedlander, Saul, ed. *Probing the Limits of Representation: Nazism and the "Final Solution."* Cambridge, MA: Harvard University Press, 1992.

Furneaux, Robin. *William Wilberforce.* London: Hamish Hamilton, 1974.

Fusco, Coco. *English Is Broken Here: Notes on Cultural Fusion in the Americas.* New York: New Press, 1995.

———. "Magdalena Campos-Pons at Intar, Review." *Art in America* (February 1994).

Fyfe, Christopher, ed. *Anna Maria Falconbridge: Narrative of Two Voyages to the River Sierra Leone with Alexander Falconbridge: An Account of the Slave Trade on the Coast of Africa.* Liverpool: Liverpool University Press, 2000.

Gaines, Kevin K. *American Africans in Ghana: Black Expatriates and the Civil Rights Era.* Chapel Hill: University of North Carolina Press, 2006.

Gaither, Edmund Barry. *Afro-American Artists: New York and Boston.* Boston: Museum of the National Center of Afro-American Artists and the Museum of Fine Arts, Boston, 1970.

Gates Jr., Henry Louis. *In Search of Our Roots: How 19 Extraordinary African Americans Reclaimed Their Past.* New York: Crown Publishers, 2009.

———. *The Signifying Monkey: A Theory of African-American Literary Criticism.* New York: Oxford University Press, 1988.

Gillis, John. "Memory and Identity." In *Commemorations: The Politics of National Identity,* edited by John Gillis, 3–26. Princeton, NJ: Princeton University Press, 1994.

Gilman, Sander L. *Difference and Pathology: Stereotypes of Sexuality, Race, and Madness.* Ithaca, NY: Cornell University Press, 1985.

Gilroy, Paul. *Against Race: Imagining Political Culture beyond the Color Line.* Cambridge, MA: Harvard University Press, 2000.

———. *The Black Atlantic: Modernity and Double Consciousness.* Cambridge, MA: Harvard University Press, 1993.

———. *Small Acts: Thoughts on the Politics of Black Cultures.* New York: Serpent's Tail, 1993.

Glueck, Grace. "Black Artist Shows in Whitney Lobby." *New York Times,* March 20, 1971, 25.

———. "Minority Artists Find a Welcome at New Showcase." *New York Times,* December 23, 1969, 22.

———. "Willie Cole: New Concepts in Printmaking 2." *New York Times,* July 10, 1988.

Gorée: The Island and the Historical Museum. Dakar: IFAN–Cheikh Anta Diop and the Historical Museum, 1993.

Gould, Philip. *The Barbaric Trade: Commerce and Antislavery in the 18th-Century Atlantic World.* Cambridge, MA: Harvard University Press, 2003.

Graves, Algernon. *Royal Academy of Arts: Complete Dictionary of Contributors and Their Works from Its Foundation, 1769–1904.* Vol. 3. London: Graves and George Bell and Son, 1905.

Green, James N. "Mathew Carey (1760–1839)." In *American Museum Journalists, 1741–1850,* edited by Sam G. Riley. Ann Arbor: Bruccoli Clark Layman, 1988.

Gundaker, Grey. *Signs of Diaspora, Diaspora of Signs: Literacies, Creolization, and Vernacular Practice in African America.* Oxford: Oxford University Press, 1998.

Gwynne, James B., ed. *Amiri Baraka: The Kaleidoscopic Torch.* New York: Steppingstones Press, 1985.

Halbwachs, Maurice. *On Collective Memory.* Edited and translated by Lewis A. Coser. Chicago: University of Chicago Press, 1992.

Haley, Alex. *Roots.* Garden City, NY: Doubleday, 1976.

Hall, Stuart. "Cultural Identity and Diaspora." In *Identity: Community, Culture, Difference,* edited by Jonathan Rutherford, 222–37. London: Lawrence and Wishart, 1990.

———. "The Question of Cultural Identity." In *Modernity and Its Futures,* edited by. S. Hall, D. Held, and T. McGrew, 273–326. Cambridge: Polity Press, 1992.

———. "Subjects in History: Making Diasporic Identities." In *The House That Race Built,* edited by Wahneema Lubiano, 289–300. New York: Pantheon, 1997.

———. "Three Moments in the History of Black Diaspora Visual Artists." The Raphael Samuel Memorial Lecture, Conway Hall, University of East London, November 19, 2004.

Hamilton, Douglas, and Robert J. Blyth, eds. *Representing Slavery: Art, Artefacts, and Archives in Collections of the National Maritime Museum.* Burlington, VT: Lund Humphries; London: In association with the National Maritime Museum, 2007.

Hanway, Jonas. *Defects of Police.* London: 1775.

Harmon, Katharine. *You Are Here: Personal Geographies and Other Maps of the Imagination.* New York: Princeton Architectural Press, 2004.

Harms, Robert W. *The Diligent: A Voyage through the Worlds of the Slave Trade.* Yale University Press, 2007.

Harper, Michael S. *Debridement.* Garden City, NY: Doubleday, 1973.

Harris, William J. *Amiri Baraka, The LeRoi Jones/Amiri Baraka Reader.* New York: Thunder's Mouth Press, 1991.

Hartman, Geoffrey, ed. *Holocaust Remembrance: The Shapes of Memory.* London: Blackwell, 1994.

Hartman, Saidiya. *Lose Your Mother: A Journey Along the Atlantic Slave Route.* New York: Farrar, Straus & Giroux, 2007.

Hartman, Saidiya V. *Scenes of Subjection: Terror, Slavery, and Self-Making in Nineteenth Century America*. New York: Oxford University Press, 1997.

Hatch, Marshall E. "African American Church Stained Glass: Pointing to Our Past and Our Future." In *Little Black Pearl* (Summer 2013). Accessed 10/17/2013. http://blackpearl .org/wp-content/uploads/LBP-Magazine-Summer-2013.

Hawker, Robert. *An Appeal to the Common Feelings of Mankind in Behalf of the Negroes in the West-India Islands: More especially addressed to the subjects of the British Empire, through the medium of a letter to William Wilberforce.…* London: Printed and sold by A. A. Paris, 1823.

Hayden, Dolores. *The Power of Place: Urban Landscapes as Public History*. Cambridge, MA: MIT Press, 1995.

Hochschild, Adam. *Bury the Chains: Prophets and Rebels in the Fight to Free an Empire's Slaves*. Boston: Houghton Mifflin, 2005.

Hollander, John, and Joanna Weber, eds. *Words for Images: A Gallery of Poems*. New Haven, CT: Yale University Art Gallery, 2001.

Honig-Fine, Elsa. *The Afro-American Artist: A Search for Identity*. New York: Holt, Rinehart and Winston, 1973.

Honour, Hugh. *The Image of the Black in Western Art*. Vol. 4, *From the American Revolution to World War*, part 1, *Slaves and Liberators*. Houston: Menil Foundation, 1996.

Hughes, Langston, and Milton Meltzer. *Black Magic: A Pictorial History of the Negro in American Entertainment*. New York: Crown Publishers, 1967.

———. *A Pictorial History of the Negro in America*. New York: Crown Publishers, 1956.

Hurston, Zora Neale. "Story in Harlem Slang." *The American Mercury*, July 1942, 94.

Hyland, A. D. C. "Monuments Conservation Practice in Ghana: Issues of Policy and Management." *Journal of Architectural Conservations* 2 (1995): 45–62.

Inikori, Joseph E., and Stanley L. Engerman, eds. *The Atlantic Slave Trade: Effects on Economies, Societies, and Peoples in Africa, the Americas, and Europe*. Durham, NC: Duke University Press, 1992.

Isaac, Dan. "The Death of the Proscenium Stage." *Antioch Review* (Summer 1971).

Jacobs, Donald M., ed. *Courage and Conscience: Black and White Abolitionists in Boston*. Bloomington: Published for the Boston Athenaeum by Indiana University Press, 1993.

James, C. L. R. *The Black Jacobins: Toussaint L'Ouverture and the San Domingo Revolution*. 1935. New York: Vintage Books, 1963.

Jennings, Judith. *The Business of Abolishing the British Slave Trade, 1783–1807*. London: Frank Cass, 1997.

Jennings, Lawrence C. *French Anti-Slavery: The Movement for the Abolition of Slavery in France, 1802–1848*. Cambridge: Cambridge University Press, 2000.

Johnson, Walter. *Soul by Soul: Life inside the Antebellum Slave Market*. Cambridge, MA: Harvard University Press, 1999.

Johnston, Mary. *The Slave Ship*. Boston: Little, Brown and Company, 1924.

Jones, Hettie. *How I Became Hettie Jones*. New York: E. P. Dutton, 1990.

Jones, Kellie. *Energy/Experimentation: Black Artists and Abstraction, 1964–1980*. New York: Studio Museum in Harlem, 2006.

———. *EyeMinded: Living and Writing Contemporary Art*. Durham, NC: Duke University Press, 2011.

———. "Life's Little Necessities: Installations by Women in the 1990s." In *Trade Routes: History and Geography. 2nd Johannesburg Biennale 1997*. Johannesburg: Greater Johannesburg Metropolitan Council, 1997.

Jones, LeRoi. "The Black Arts Repertory Theatre/School." *Liberator*, May 1965.

———. "The Black Revolutionary Theatre." *Liberator* 5 (July 1965): 4–6.

———. *Blues People: Negro Music in White America*. New York: William Morrow, 1963.

———. "In Search of Revolutionary Theatre: New Heroes Needed." *Black World*, April 1966.

Jones, Lisa. *Bulletproof Diva: Tales of Race, Sex & Hair*. New York: Doubleday, 1981.

Kirschke, Amy Helene. *Aaron Douglas: Art, Race, and the Harlem Renaissance*. Jackson: University Press of Mississippi, 1995.

Kowaleski-Wallace, Elizabeth. *Consuming Subjects: Women, Shopping, and Business in the Eighteenth Century*. New York: Columbia University Press, 1997.

Kriz, Kay Dian. *Slavery, Sugar and the Culture of Refinement: Picturing the British West Indies, 1700–1840*. New Haven, CT: Yale University Press, 2008.

Kuchler, Susanne, and Walter Melion. *Images of Memory: On Remembering and Representation*. Washington, DC: Smithsonian Institution Press, 1991.

Lacey, Henry C. *To Raise, Destroy, and Create: The Poetry, Drama, and Fiction of Imamu Amiri Baraka (LeRoi Jones)*. Troy, NY: Whitston Publishing, 1981.

Lester, Julius. *To Be a Slave*. Illustrated by Tom Feelings. New York: Dial Press, 1969.

Lettsom, John Coakley. *The Works of John Fothergill, M.D.* 2 vols. London: Charles Dilly, 1783.

Lewis, Rupert. *Marcus Garvey*. Trenton, NJ: Africa World Press, 1988.

Lewis, Sarah. "Vision and Justice." *Aperture* (June 1, 2016): 13.

Liss, Andrea. *Trespassing through Shadows: Memory, Photography, and the Holocaust*. Minneapolis: University of Minnesota Press, 1998.

Linebaugh, Peter. *The London Hanged: Crime and Civil Society in the Eighteenth Century*. London: Penguin, 1991.

Linebaugh, Peter, and Marcus Rediker. *The Many-Headed Hydra: Sailors, Slaves, Commoners, and the Hidden History of the Revolutionary Atlantic*. Boston: Beacon, 2000.

Lipsitz, George. *Time Passages: Collective Memory and American Popular Culture*. Minneapolis: University of Minnesota Press, 1990.

Loft, Lenore. "Quakers, Brissot, and Eighteenth-Century Abolitionists." *Journal of the Friends' Historical Society* 55 (1989): 277–89.

London Committee. *Case of the Vigilante, a Ship Employed in the Slave Trade: With Some Reflections on That Traffic*. London: Harvey, Darton, 1826.

———. *The Spanish Schooner, Josefa Maracayera…* London: Harvey, Darton, 1823.

London Committee of the Society for the Abolition of the Slave Trade. *Description of a Slave Ship*. London: James A. Phillips, April 1789.

Lowenthal, David. *Possessed by the Past: The Heritage Crusade and the Spoils of History*. New York: Free Press, 1996.

Lury, Celia. *Prosthetic Culture: Photography, Memory, and Identity*. London: Routledge, 1998.

Mannix, Daniel P., in collaboration with Malcolm Cowley. *Black Cargoes: A History of the Atlantic Slave Trade, 1518–1865*. New York: Viking Press, 1962.

Manuscript Collection Belonging to the Pennsylvania Society for Promoting the Abolition of Slavery, for the Relief of Free Negroes Unlawfully Held in Bondage, and for Improving the Condition of the African Race. Philadelphia, 1876.

Mayer, Brantz. *Captain Canot; or Twenty Years of an African Slaver, Being an Account of His Career and Adventures on the Coast, in the Interior, on Shipboard, and in the West Indies*. New York: D. Appleton & Co., 1854.

———. *History of the War between Mexico and the United States, with a Preliminary View of Its Origin*. New York: Wiley and Putnam, 1848.

———. *Mexico as It Was and as It Is*. New York: J. Winchester, 1844.

Mayhew, Henry, and John Binny. *The Criminal Prisons of London and Scenes of Prison Life*. London: Frank Cass, 1862.

McKendrick, Neil, John Brewer, and J. H. Plumb. *The Birth of a Consumer Society: The Commercialization of Eighteenth-Century England*. Bloomington: Indiana University Press, 1982.

Mercer, Kobena. "Witness at the Crossroads: An Artist's Journey in Post-Colonial Space." In *Relocating the Remains*, edited by Keith Piper. London: Institute of International Visual Arts, 1997.

Midgeley, Clare. *Women against Slavery: The British Campaigns, 1780–1870*. London: Routledge, 1992.

Miller, Christopher. *The French Atlantic Triangle: Literature and Culture of the Slave Trade*. Durham, NC: Duke University Press, 2008.

Mintz, Sidney W., and Richard Price. *The Birth of African American Culture: An Anthropological Perspective*. Boston: Beacon Press, 1992.

Mitchell, W. J. T. *Iconology: Image Text, Ideology*. Chicago: University of Chicago Press, 1986.

Mohabir, Nalini. "An Interview with Roshini Kempadoo." *exPLUSultra*, vol. 2, December 2010. Accessed August 15, 2016.

Mollerup, Per. *Marks of Excellence: The History and Taxonomy of Trademarks*. London: Phaidon, 1997.

Morrison, Toni. "The Site of Memory." In *Inventing the Truth: The Art and Craft of Memoir*, edited by William Zinsser. Boston: Houghton Mifflin, 1987.

Mortimer, Russell. "Quaker Printers, 1750–1850." *Journal of the Friends' Historical Society* 50, no. 3 (1962–64): 100–114.

Moskowitz, David Vlado. *Bob Marley: A Biography*. Greenwood Publishing Group, 2007.

Murphy, Jan. "Art Challenges Colonization: The IV Havana Biennial" and "Testing the Limits." *Cuba Update*, March/April 1992.

Myers, Norma. *Reconstructing the Black Past: Blacks in Britain c. 1780–1830*. London: Frank Cass, 1996.

Neal, Larry. *Visions of a Liberated Future: Black Arts Movement Writings*. New York: Thunder's Mouth Press, 1989.

Neill, Peter, ed. *Maritime America: Art and Artifacts from America's Great Nautical Collections*. New York: Balsan Press, in affiliation with Harry N. Abrams, 1988.

Nelson, Alondra. *The Social Life of DNA: Race, Reparations and Reconciliation after the Genome*. New York: Beacon Press, 2016.

Neo-Hood Doo: Art for a Forgotten Faith. Edited by Franklin Sirmans. Long Island City, NY: P.S. 1 Contemporary Art Center and Menil Collection, in association with Yale University Press, 2008. Published on the occasion of the exhibition *Neo-Hood Doo: Art for a Forgotten Faith*, shown at the P.S. 1 Contemporary Art Center, the Menil Collection in Houston, and the Miami Art Museum.

New Society for Promoting the Abolition of Slavery. *Remarks on the Slave Trade*. Philadelphia: Published by Mathew Carey, 1789.

Newton, John. *The Journal of a Slave Trader (John Newton), 1750–1754, with Newton's Thought upon the African Slave Trade*. Edited by Bernard Martin and Mark Spurrell. London: Epworth Press, 1962.

Ngaboh-Smart, Francis. "The Politics of Black Identity: *Slave Ship* and *Woza Albert!*" *Journal of African Cultural Studies* 12, no. 2, 1999.

Nora, Pierre. "Between Memory and History: Les Lieux de Memoire." *Representations* 26 (Spring 1989): 9.

Ogletree Jr., Charles J. "Repairing the Past: New Efforts in the Reparations Debate in America." *Harvard Civil Rights-Civil Liberties Law Review*, vol. 38, pp. 279–320.

Oguibe, Olu. "Studio Call: Mary Evans." *Nka Journal of Contemporary African Art* 10 (Spring/Summer 1999): 38–39.

Oldfield, J. R. *Popular Politics and British Anti-Slavery: The Mobilisation of Public Opinion against the Slave Trade, 1787–1807.* Manchester: Manchester University Press, 1995.

Oldham, Ned. "Open to Interpretation." *Black & White*, no. 92. Birmingham, AL: Birmingham Museum of Art, 1998.

Omi, Michael, and H. Winant. *Racial Formation in the United States: From the 1960s to the 1990s.* New York: Routledge, 1994.

Oostindie, Gert, ed. *Facing Up to the Past: Perspectives on the Commemoration of the Slavery from Africa, the Americas, and Europe.* Kingston: Ian Rand Publishers, 2001.

Orozco, Jose Clemente. *Autobiografia.* 1945 rpt. Mexico City: Ediciones Era, 1970.

Pederson, Carl. "Sea Change: The Middle Passage and the Transatlantic Imagination." In *The Black Columbiad: Defining Moments in African American Literature and Culture.* Edited by Werner Sollors and Maria Diedrich. Cambridge, MA: Harvard University Press, 1994.

Perkins, T. E. "Rethinking Stereotypes." In *Ideology and Cultural Production*, edited by Michèle Barrett et al., 135–59. London: Croom Helm, 1979.

Phillips, Caryl. *The Atlantic Sound.* New York: Alfred A. Knopf, 2000.

Piper, Keith. *Relocating the Remains.* London: inIVA, 1997.

———. *A Ship Called Jesus.* London: Ikon Gallery, 1991.

Plymouth Committee of the Society for Effecting the Abolition of the Slave Trade. *Plan of an African Ship's Lower Deck with Negroes in the Proportion of Only One to a Ton.* Plymouth, England, 1788, annexed plate and four-page pamphlet.

———. *Plan of an African Ship's Lower Deck with Negroes in the Proportion of Only One to a Ton.* Plymouth, England, 1789, broadside.

Pollitt, Jerome J. *Art and Experience in Classical Greece.* London: Cambridge University Press, 1972.

Pope-Hennessy, John. *Sins of the Fathers: A Study of the Atlantic Slave Traders, 1441–1807.* New York: Knopf, 1968.

Postma, Johannes. *The Dutch in the Atlantic Slave Trade, 1600–1815.* Cambridge: Cambridge University Press, 2000.

Rawley, James A. *The Transatlantic Slave Trade: A History.* New York: W. W. Norton, 1981.

Reidiker, Marcus. *The Slave Ship: A Human History.* New York: Viking, 2007.

Reilly, Robin. *Josiah Wedgwood, 1730–1795.* 2 vols. London: Macmillan, 1992.

Resistant Strains. *Maximum Security Democracy.* Glover, VT: Resistant Strains, 1998.

Rivera, Diego. *Miguel Covarrubias.* New York: Valentine Gallery, 1932.

Rivers, Larry. *Some American History.* Houston: Institute for the Arts, Rice University, 1971.

Roach, Joseph. *Cities of the Dead: Circum-Atlantic Performance.* New York: Columbia University Press, 1996.

Robinson, Imahkus Vienna. "Is the Black Man's History Being Whitewashed?" *Uhuru*, no. 9 (1994): 48–50.

Robinson, Randall. *The Debt: What America Owes to Blacks.* New York: Penguin, 2000.

Rodríguez, Dylan. *Forced Passages: Imprisoned Radical Intellectuals and the U.S. Prison Regime.* Minneapolis: University of Minnesota Press, 2006.

Saar, Betye. "Unfinished Business: The Return of Aunt Jemima." In *Unfinished Business: Workers + Warriors, the Return of Aunt Jemima.* New York: Michael Rosenfeld Gallery, 1998.

Samb, Djibril, ed. *Gorée et L'Esclavage: Actes du Seminaire sur Gorée dans la Traite atlantique; Mythes et réalités.* Gorée, Senegal, April 7–8, 1997. Dakar: Université Cheikh Anta Diop, 1997.

Sanneh, Lamin. *Abolitionists Abroad: American Blacks and the Making of Modern West Africa.* Cambridge: Harvard University Press, 1999.

Schama, Simon. *Rough Crossings: Britain, the Slaves, and the American Revolution.* New York: Harper Collins, 2006.

Schevill, James. *Breakout! In Search of New Theatrical Environments.* Chicago: Swallow Press, 1973.

Schoener, Allon. *Portal to American Life: The Lower East Side, 1870–1924.* New York: Henry Holt, 1967.

Schwartzman, Myron. *Romare Bearden: His Life and Art.* New York: Harry N. Abrams, 1990.

Sharp, Granville. *Free English Territory in AFRICA.* London, 1790.

Shaw, A. G. L. *Convicts and the Colonies: A Study of Penal Transportation from Great Britain and Ireland to Australia and Other Parts of the British Empire.* London: Farber and Farber, 1966.

Shyllon, F. O. *Black Slaves in Britain.* London: Oxford University Press for the Institute of Race Relations, 1974.

Sims, Lowery Stokes, ed. *Legacies: Contemporary Artists Reflect on Slavery.* New York: New York Historical Society, 2007. Published after the exhibition *Legacies: Contemporary Artists* shown at the Historical Society.

Skeehan, Danielle. "Deadly Notes: Atlantic Soundscapes and the Writing of the Middle Passage." *The Appendix*, "Out Loud," vol. 1, no. 3 (July 2013).

Smallwood, Stephanie. *Saltwater Slavery: A Middle Passage from Africa to American Diaspora.* Cambridge, MA: Harvard University Press, 2007.

Smeathman, Henry. *Substance of a Plan of a Settlement, to be made near Sierra Leona, on the Grain Coast of Africa, intended more particularly for the service and happy establishment of Blacks and people of colour to be shipped as freemen, under the direction of the Committee for reliev-ing the black poor, and under the protections of the British Government.* London: 1786.

Smith, Adam. *An Inquiry into the Nature and Causes of the Wealth of Nations.* London: Printed for W. Strahan and T. Cadwell, 1776.

Smith, John Stores. *Mirabeau: A Life History; In Four Books.* Philadelphia: Lea and Blanchard, 1848.

Soderlund, Jean. *Quakers and Slavery: A Divided Society.* Princeton, NJ: Princeton University Press, 1985.

Sollors, Werner. *Amiri Baraka/LeRoi Jones: The Quest for a "Populist Modernism."* New York: Columbia University Press, 1978.

Southey, Robert. *English Seamen: Howard, Clifford, Hawkins, Drake, Cavendish.* Edited and with an introduction by David Hannay. Chicago: Stone and Kimball, 1895.

The Speech of William Wilberforce, Esq. Representative for the County of York, on Wednesday the 13th of May, 1789, on the Question of the Abolition of the Slave Trade. To Which Are Added the Resolutions Then Moved, and a Short Sketch of the Speeches of the Other Members. London: Logographic Press, 1789.

Spillers, Hortense J. "Mama's Baby, Papa's Maybe: An American Grammar Book." *Diacritics*, vol. 17, no. 2, *Culture and Countermemory: The "American" Connection* (Summer 1987).

Spirits of the Passage: The Transatlantic Slave Trade in the Seventeenth Century. Edited by Rosemarie Robotham, with foreword and text by Madeline Burnside and Cornel West. New York: Bernhardt Fuyma Design Group, in association with the Mel Fisher Maritime Heritage Society and Simon and Schuster Editions, 1997.

Stein, Judith. *The World of Marcus Garvey: Race and Class in Modern Society.* Baton Rouge: Louisiana State University Press, 1986.

Stratton, Richard, and Kim Wozencraft, eds. *Slam.* New York: Grove Press, 1998.

Substance of the Debates on a Resolution for Abolishing the Slave Trade, which was moved in the House of Commons on the 10th June, 1806, and in the House of Lords on the 24th June, 1806. With an Appendix, Containing Notes and Illustrations. London: Phillips and Fardon, 1806.

Svalesen, Leif. *Fredensborg.* Translated by Pat Shaw and Selena Winsnes. Kingston: Ian Rand Publishers, 2000.

Tableau des Members de la Société des Amis de Noirs: Année 1789. Paris: Société des Amis de Noirs, 1789.

Tattersfield, Nigel. *The Forgotten Trade, Comprising the Log of the Daniel and Henry of 1700 and Accounts of the Slave Trade from the Minor Ports of England, 1698–1725.* London: Jonathan Cape, 1991.

Tawadros, Gilane. "Bitter Sweet." In Mary Evans, *Mary Evans: Filter.* London: Institute of International Visual Arts, 1997.

Taylor, Isaac. *Scenes in Africa and America: For the Amusement and Instruction of Little Tarry-at-Home-Travellers.* London: Harris and Sons, 1820.

Thomas, Hugh. *The Slave Trade: The Story of the Atlantic Slave Trade, 1440–1870.* New York: Simon and Schuster, 1997.

Thompson, E. P. *The Making of the English Working Class.* Rev. ed. London: Penguin Books, 1968.

Thompson, Robert Farris. *African Art in Motion: Icon and Act in the Collection of Katherine Coryton White.* Los Angeles: University of California Press, 1974.

———. *Black Gods and Kings: Yoruba Art at UCLA.* Los Angeles: University of California, Museum and Laboratories of Ethnic Arts and Technology, 1971.

———. *Face of the Gods: Art and Altars of Africa and the African Americas.* New York: Museum for African Art, 1993.

———. *Flash of the Spirit: African and Afro-American Art and Philosophy.* New York: Vintage, 1983

———. *Soundings: An Exhibition of Sculpture by Ed Love.* Washington, DC: Gallery of Art, Howard University, 1986.

Tibbles, Anthony, ed. *Transatlantic Slavery: Against Human Dignity.* National Museums and Galleries on Merseyside. London: HMSO, 1995.

Tibol, Raquel. "In the Land of Aesthetic Fraternity." In Lizzetta LeFalle-Collins and Shifra M. Goldman, *In the Spirit of Resistance: African-American Modernists and the Mexican Muralist School.* New York: The American Federation of Arts, 1996.

Trachtenberg, Alan. *Brooklyn Bridge: Fact and Symbol.* Chicago: University of Chicago Press, 1979.

———. *Reading American Photographs: Images as History, Mathew Brady to Walker Evans.* New York: Hill and Wang, 1989.

Trapp, Jean. "The Liverpool Movement for the Abolition of the English Slave Trade." *Journal of Negro History* 13 (July 1928): 265–85.

Trouillot, Michel-Rolph. *Silencing the Past: Power and the Production of History.* Boston: Beacon Press, 1995.

Turner, Steve. *Amazing Grace: The Story of America's Most Beloved Song.* New York: Harper Collins, 2009.

The Uncle Tom's Cabin Almanac or Abolitionist Memento for 1853. London: J. Cassell, 1853.

Wadström, Carl Bernhard. *An Essay on Colonization, Particularly Applied to the Western Coast of Africa, with Some Free Thoughts on Cultivation and Commerce; also, Brief Descriptions of the Colonies Already Formed, or Attempted, in Africa, Including Those of Sierra Leona and Bulama.* 2 vols. London: Darton and Harvey, 1794–95.

Wailoo, Keith, Alondra Nelson, and Catherine Lee. *Genetics and the Unsettled Past: DNA, Race and History.* Rutgers University Press, 2012.

Walker, David. *David Walker's Appeal to the Coloured Citizens of the World, but in Particular and Very Expressly, to Those of the United States of America.* Rpt. Black Classics Press, 1997.

Walters, Sabrina. "Glass Recalls Slavery's Horror." *Chicago Sun Times*, December 17, 2000, 24.

Walvin, James. *Black and White: The Negro in English Society, 1555–1945.* London: Penguin, 1973.

Weitman, Wendy. "New Concepts in Printmaking 2: Willie Cole." *Museum of Modern Art Calendar* (June 1998): 32.

White, Deborah Gray. *Ar'n't I a Woman: Female Slaves in the Plantation South.* New York: W. W. Norton, 1985.

Williams, Gomer. *History of the Liverpool Privateers and Letters of Marque with an Account of the Liverpool Slave Trade.* London: William Heinemann, 1877.

Wilson, Ellen Gibson. *Thomas Clarkson: A Biography.* London: Macmillan, 1989.

Wise, Steven M. *Though the Heavens May Fall: The Landmark Trial That Led to the End of Human Slavery.* Cambridge, MA: Da Capo Press, 2005.

Wong, Linda. "Interview with Magdalena Campos-Pons." *Sojourner: The Women's Forum* (September 1997).

Wood, Marcus. *Blind Memory: Visual Representations of Slavery in England and America, 1780–1865.* New York: Routledge, 2000.

Wood, Samuel. *The Mirror of Misery; or, Tyranny Exposed.* New York: Samuel Wood, 1807, 1811, and 1814.

Yates, Frances. *The Art of Memory.* Chicago: University of Chicago Press, 1966.

Yellen, Jean Fagan, and John C. Van Horne, eds. *The Abolitionist Sisterhood: Women's Political Culture in Antebellum America.* Ithaca, NY: Cornell University Press, 1994.

Young, James. *The Art of Memory: Holocaust Memorials in History.* New York: Prestel-Verlag, 1994.

———. *The Texture of Memory: Holocaust Memorials and Meaning.* New Haven, CT: Yale University Press, 1993.

Zelizer, Barbie. "Reading the Past against the Grain: The Shape of Memory Studies." *Critical Studies in Mass Communication* 12, no. 3 (1995): 214–39.

SELECTED INTERVIEWS

Terry Adkins
Amiri Baraka
Sanford Biggers
Maria Magdalena Campos-Pons
David C. Driskell
Godfried Donkor
Mary Elliott
Mary Evans
Joy Gregory
Reverend Dr. Marshall E. Hatch
Marshall E. Hatch Jr.
Stephen Hayes
Romuald Hazoumé
Roshini Kempadoo
Keith Piper
Ingrid Pollard
Marianetta Porter
Betye Saar
Hank Willis Thomas

Index

Image Credits

fig. I.3. The British Museum. Acquired with contributions from the British Museum Friends and the Art Fund. © Romuald Hazoumé.

fig. I.5. Photograph: Cheryl Finley.

fig. I.6. AP Photo/The Times, Jessica Leigh.

fig. I.7. Massimo Sestini/Polaris.

fig. I.9. Photograph: Rodney D. Moore.

fig. 1.1. © Religious Society of Friends (Quakers) in Britain.

fig. 1.3. © Religious Society of Friends (Quakers) in Britain.

fig. 1.4. By permission of the College of Arms, London. Photograph: Plymouth City Council (Arts & Heritage Service), England.

fig. 1.5. Access. #: 1983–110 DJ. The Menil Collection, Houston.

fig. 1.6. © Religious Society of Friends (Quakers) in Britain.

fig. 1.7. © Château des ducs de Bretagne, Musée d'histoire du Nantes, Alain Guillard.

fig. 1.8. The Library Company of Philadelphia.

fig. 1.9. Historical Society of Pennsylvania.

fig. 1.10. © Religious Society of Friends (Quakers) in Britain.

fig. 1.11. © Religious Society of Friends (Quakers) in Britain.

fig. 1.12. © Religious Society of Friends (Quakers) in Britain.

fig. 1.13. © Religious Society of Friends (Quakers) in Britain.

fig. 2.1. Beinecke Rare Book and Manuscript Library, Yale University.

fig. 2.4. National Maritime Museum, Greenwich, London, Michael Graham-Stewart Slavery Collection. Acquired with the assistance of the Heritage Lottery Fund.

fig. 2.5. Bibliothèque nationale de France.

fig. 2.6. © Hull City Art Museums. Photograph: Cheryl Finley.

fig. 3.5. © Religious Society of Friends (Quakers) in Britain.

fig. 3.8. National Maritime Museum, Greenwich, UK.

fig. 3.9. © National Portrait Gallery, London.

fig. 3.10. Museum of Fine Arts, Boston, Henry Lillie Pierce Fund.

fig. 3.11. © Hull City Museums and Art Galleries, Wilberforce House.

fig. 4.10. Corcoran Collection. Museum purchase and partial gift from Thurlow Evans Tibbs Jr., The Evans-Tibbs Collection. National Gallery of Art, Washington, DC.

fig. 4.11. © Granger Historical Picture Archive, the Granger Collection.

fig. 5.1. Photograph: Jack Manning/The New York Times/Redux.

fig. 5.2. © Joe Overstreet. Access. #: 1970–156 DJ. Photograph: Paul Hester. The Menil Collection, Houston.

fig. 5.3. Courtesy of the artist. Collection of University of Califronia, Berkeley Art Museum; purchased with the aid of funds from the National Endowment for the Arts (selected by The Committee for the Acquisition of Afro-American Art). Courtesy of Michael Rosenfeld Gallery LLC, New York, NY. Photograph by Joshua Nefsky.

fig. 5.6. James Weldon Johnson Collection in the Yale Collection of American Literature, Beinecke Rare Book and Manuscript Library.

fig. 5.9. Photograph: Don Hogan Charles/The New York Times/Redux.

fig. 5.10. Archives of American Art, Smithsonian Institution.

fig. 5.11. Museum of Modern Art, New York, NY. Gift of Barbara Jakobson and John R. Jakobson. Digital image © The Museum of Modern Art/Licensed by SCALA/Art Resource, NY.

fig. 5.12. Whitney Museum of American Art, New York; purchase, with funds from the Larry Aldrich Foundation Fund 69.77.

fig. 6.1. Courtesy of the artist and Zak Ove. © Horace Ove.

fig. 6.2. Courtesy of the artist. © Ingrid Pollard.

fig. 6.3. Courtesy of the artist. © Isaac Julien.

fig. 6.4. Courtesy of the artist. © Keith Piper.

fig. 6.5. © Tate, London 2016. © Estate of Donald Rodney.

fig. 6.6. © Tate, London 2016. © Estate of Donald Rodney.

fig. 6.7. © Tate, London 2016. © Estate of Donald Rodney.

fig. 6.8. © Tate, London 2016. © Keith Piper.

fig. 6.9. © Keith Piper. Courtesy of the artist and the African and Asian Visual Artist Archive.

fig. 6.10. Courtesy of the artist. © Roshini Kempadoo.

fig. 6.11. Courtesy of the artist. © Joy Gregory.

fig. 6.12. Courtesy of the artist. © Joy Gregory.

fig. 6.13. Courtesy of the artist. © Godfried Donkor.

fig. 6.14. Courtesy of the artist. © Godfried Donkor.

fig. 6.15. Courtesy of the artist. © Godfried Donkor.

fig. 6.16. Photograph credit: P. Gorman. Courtesy of the artist. © Mary Evans.

fig. 6.17. Photography credit: M. Hood. Courtesy of the artist. © Mary Evans.

fig. 6.18. Courtesy of the artist. © Mary Evans.

fig. 8.1. © 2017 Willie Cole. The Museum of Modern Art. Acquired through the generosity of Agnes Gund.

fig. 8.2. © 2017 Willie Cole. Courtesy of the artist and Alexander and Bonin.

fig. 8.3. © 2017 Willie Cole. The Museum of Modern Art. Jaqueline Brody Fund and the Friends of Education Fund.

fig. 8.4. © 2017 Willie Cole. Herbert F. Johnson Museum, Cornell University. Acquired through the generosity of Truman W. Eustis III, Class of 1951. Photography courtesy of the Herbert F. Johnson Museum of Art, Cornell University.

fig. 8.5. Courtesy of the artist.

fig. 8.6. Courtesy of the artist.

fig. 8.7. Courtesy of the artist.

fig. 8.8. Courtesy of the artist.

fig. 8.9. Smithsonian Museum of American Art. Gift of Delta Sigma Theta Sorority, Inc. 1983.95.178.

fig. 8.10. Courtesy of the artist and Michael Rosenfeld Gallery LLC, New York, NY.

fig. 8.11. Courtesy of the artist and Michael Rosenfeld Gallery LLC, New York, NY.

fig. 8.12. Courtesy of the artist and Michael Rosenfeld Gallery LLC, New York, NY.

fig. 8.13. Courtesy of the artist and Michael Rosenfeld Gallery LLC, New York, NY.

fig. 9.1. Courtesy of the artist and the Vancouver Art Gallery.

fig. 9.2. Courtesy of the artist.

fig. 9.3. Courtesy of the artist.

fig. 9.5. Yale University Art Gallery. Janet and Simeon Braguin Fund.

fig. 9.6. Courtesy of the artist.

fig. 9.7. Courtesy of the New Museum, New York.

fig. 9.8. Photograph: Cheryl Finley.

fig. 9.9. Tom Feelings, illustration from *The Middle Passage: White Ships, Black Cargo*, 1995, pen and ink drawing. With special permission granted by Dianne Johnson-Feelings and the Tom Feelings Collection, LLC. Tom Feelings Artwork, James Weldon Johnson Collection in the Yale Collection of American Literature, Beinecke Rare Book and Manuscript Library.

fig. 9.10. Photograph: Cheryl Finley.

fig. 9.11. Courtesy of the artist and Grand Arts, Kansas City.

fig. 9.12. Courtesy of the artist and Grand Arts, Kansas City.

fig. 9.13. The Menil Archives. Courtesy of the Menil Collection, Houston.

fig. 9.14. Courtesy of the artists.

fig. 9.15. Courtesy of the artist.

fig. 9.16. Courtesy of the artist and the John and Mable Ringling Museum of Art. Photograph: Giovanni Lunardi.

fig. 9.17. Museum of Fine Arts, Boston. Bequest of Maxim Karolik, 64.619.

fig. 10.1. Art © Romare Bearden Foundation/Licensed by VAGA, New York, NY.

fig. 10.2. Art © Romare Bearden Foundation/Licensed by VAGA, New York, NY.

fig. 10.3. Art © Romare Bearden Foundation/Licensed by VAGA, New York, NY.

Fig.10.4. Courtesy Bob Marley Foundation.

fig. 10.4. Beinecke Rare Book and Manuscript Library, Yale University.

fig. 10.6. Courtesy of the artist and Jack Shainman Gallery.

fig. 10.7. Photograph: Cheryl Finley.

fig. 10.8. Courtesy of the artist and Jack Shainman Gallery.

fig. 10.9. Courtesy of the artist.

fig. 10.10. Yale University Art Gallery, Janet and Simeon Braguin Fund.

fig. 11.1. Photograph: Franklin Reyes, Associated Press.

fig. 11.2. Photograph: Cheryl Finley.

fig. 11.3. Photograph: Cheryl Finley.

fig. 11.4. Photograph: Cheryl Finley.

fig. 11.7. © Yinka Shonibare MBE. All Rights Reserved, DACS 2015. Image courtesy Stephen Friedman Gallery, London, and James Cohan Gallery, New York.

fig. A.1. Yale University Art Gallery. Gift of The Woodward Foundation.